# The Mexican Government Today

*William P. Tucker*

# THE
# MEXICAN
# GOVERNMENT
# TODAY

*UNIVERSITY OF MINNESOTA*
*PRESS, Minneapolis*

*To*

MY WIFE, MY PARENTS, AND MY CHILDREN
*who have been a source of help in more ways
than they know during the long months of research and writing*

# *Preface*

Mᴇxɪᴄᴏ is the second largest and the most populous Spanish-American country. It is one of the two Latin American countries of most importance commercially to the United States. In terms of the needs for friendly political relationships, many feel that Mexico ranks first among our Latin neighbors.

Yet, aside from superficial knowledge and contacts, Mexico still remains largely a *terra incognita* to the people of this country; and this is true about adequate knowledge of its government and political life, as it is of Mexican life and culture in general.

American scholars have published able general treatises on the government and politics of other Latin American countries; but none has published such a treatise on our nearest Latin American neighbor, though there are a number of able monographic and shorter studies on special aspects of Mexican government. And no adequate general treatise, in the North American sense of the word, has appeared in Spanish.

The aim of the writer has been to prepare such a treatise that will serve the needs of the college student and the intelligent layman interested in Latin American government. All the principal aspects of the national government's structure and functions are treated, but a paucity of suitable materials limited the adequacy of treatment of certain topics. This is true, for example, of public administration (as that discipline is known in this country), state government, and local government. Adequate treatment of some such topics must await the availability of more basic data and will require extended research in those specialties.

The study of Mexican government from published materials encounters certain difficulties. The first is the legalistic and exegetical approach of most Mexican social science materials. Study of actual governmental functioning is in its infancy. A second difficulty is the scattered character of published materials. (The helpfulness of librarians and booksellers cannot entirely make up for the gaps in their resources.) The differences between appearance and reality, between law and practice, are partly accounted for by the country's diversities and contradictions — in its history, geography, economy, and rapidly changing society. Political realities often diverge considerably from legal forms. Custom, tradition, and forms are strong forces in Mexican life. Personalism, as Professor Mecham and others have emphasized, has long been the determining factor in Mexican politics.

As Ernest Gruening noted in 1928, Mexico is a hard country "in which to reach the rock bottom of fact. . . . The reader will find numberless contradictions and inconsistencies. They are an integral part of the Mexican complex." Statistics, for example, are often a difficult problem; but their adequacy and reliability have been improving slowly.

For these and other reasons, historical background has been provided in connection with the topics treated; and extensive use was made of personal interviews with government officials, former officials, and informed professional people.

For most of the topics treated, many more sources could have been cited; but enough have been noted to give the flavor of Mexican and foreign findings on the matters treated.

Theses of the National University are in general of rather limited usefulness; still, quite a number of them provide some useful data. Those cited have been clearly labeled as theses, though bibliographies often leave the impression that such items are publications of the University.

The writer's interest and study of the Mexican government extends back over more than a decade and includes use of the significant materials in the libraries of both the United States and Mexico. His latest period of study in Mexico was a half year during 1953–54, which included travel to most parts of the country. Developments since then have been covered by published data, private communications, and personal contacts.

The author of a book is indebted to hundreds of people, directly or indirectly. The works cited in the bibliography and the courteous granters of countless interviews are examples. Numerous others inside and outside government service gave valuable assistance with that unfailing courtesy and friendliness that one learns to expect and prize in the Mexican people. Reluctantly, the author refrains from listing by name these dozens of helpful Mexicans. One reason is lack of space. Another is the desire to offend none – either by oversight or by inclusion of some who might be "politically sensitive."

Among North Americans, the author wishes to give special thanks to Professors J. Lloyd Mecham (University of Texas) and Asher N. Christensen (University of Minnesota), who read most of the book in manuscript form and offered most helpful suggestions. To the author's wife and to Jessica Fredricks go deep appreciation for much and varied assistance. Nor should the author forget the many kindnesses of numerous librarians and of the staff of the University of Minnesota Press.

William P. Tucker

University of Puerto Rico

# *Table of Contents*

## I. BACKGROUND

## II. ORGANIZATION AND STRUCTURE

## III. INTERNAL AND EXTERNAL RELATIONS

## IV. PUBLIC UTILITIES AND PUBLIC WORKS

# PART I

# Background

# 1

## Land, People, and Economy

Mexico is tritely but truly called a land of contrasts. Mountains, jungles, deserts, lakes, rivers, all combine to produce a variety of everything in the physical make-up of this horn-shaped land. "Lush, barren, cragged, flat, solemn, capricious, gnarled, slashed, smoothed, and painted, the landscape of Mexico unfolds like the shuffling of thousands of colored postcards, none the same, all extremes." [1]

The greater part of Mexico comprises a V-shaped plateau, broad at the north, narrowing and rising toward the south. To the east and the west, the heartland is flanked by the parallel ranges of the Sierra Madre. The southern edge of the plateau is walled in by an east-west mountain range, featuring the great snow-capped peaks — Orizaba, Popocatepetl, and Ixtacihuatl. The western border of this dissected highland plateau, the Sierra Madre Occidental, is the most forbidding barrier in a land of mountain barriers. A hundred miles and more in width, it rises to lofty peaks and drops precipitously to a narrow lowland along the Pacific Ocean. The Sierra Madre Oriental, less forbidding, allows somewhat easier access to the coastal plain on the Gulf of Mexico. Rail and highway routes penetrate the highland from Veracruz to the east, Monterrey to the north, and Texas and Arizona in the northwest.

Within this V-shaped plateau are numerous intermountain basins, from 6,000 to 8,000 feet above sea level in southern and central Mexico, separated by great expanses of mountain and semiarid plateau. Toward the north, the plateau is broader, the elevation is lower, and the climate is drier. Settlements have developed mainly in these interior basins, their economies based upon agriculture and mining. In the more arid north, population thins out and is based more on cattle raising and mining activities. South of the southern highland mountain barrier the

3

Isthmus of Tehuantepec is a transition zone, separating geologically true Mexico from the Central American mountain highlands of the State of Chiapas and Guatemala.

This crazy-quilt patterned terrain produces an equal diversity of climate, and of flora and fauna; and it has conditioned a diversity of racial and population patterns. The results are isolation and localism. "There is a note of tragedy in the Mexican landscape," says Moisés Sáenz. "The flat-topped, pyramidal hills seem to bear the weight of the skies. The mountains are bare and ragged, the highlands cut deep by gully and ravine. . . . Deep ravines and impassable canyons cut mercilessly into the broad and high central plateau where most of Mexico lives. Land on end, a tumbled down world, unfinished to look at and yet firmly set." [2] It is a land of great beauty and charm.

Mexico is a country that lives on the land, but topography and rainfall conspire against her. Therefore, only about one ninth of the land area is cultivated, much of it on erosion-prone slopes. Probably an equal area could be cropped if irrigation were provided. Pasture and forest lands together comprise nearly two thirds of the land area. Centuries of thoughtless exploitation of the land have left a heritage of serious erosion over much of Mexico's area.[3]

Much of agricultural Mexico lacks adequate rainfall. One estimate says that half the total area is deficient in moisture throughout the year, while another 36 per cent has a moisture deficiency in the winter months.[4] The areas having adequate moisture are in general tropical and more sparsely inhabited; but current governmental programs are emphasizing development of these regions. Considerable annual variation in rainfall in various regions adds to the problems of agriculture.

Aside from a few unhealthy lowland regions, climate is a favorable factor in Mexico; and climate varies chiefly with altitude, not latitude. In such a rugged land, contrasting nearby altitudes produce widely contrasting climates, vegetation, land use, and human culture patterns.

The lowest of these vertical climatic zones is the *tierra caliente* (the hot country) which extends upward to an elevation of 2,000 feet or more. Where rainfall is adequate, tropical and semitropical forests prevail; and the seasonal variations of temperature are slight. The *tierra templada* (temperate lands) extends upward to an elevation of some 6,000 feet. Oaks and other mid-latitude trees are characteristic of this altitude, and a somewhat lower temperature average is combined with a

4

larger daily and seasonal temperature range. Rainfall here is often less and more variable. The *tierra fría* (cool region) rises above 6,000 feet. Where rainfall is adequate, oaks and similar trees characterize the areas of forest coverage. Above 9,000 feet, the conifers are mixed with the oaks; and the evergreens predominate from about 11,000 to 13,000 feet, the approximate tree line. The *tierra fría* has a lower average temperature, with greater daily and seasonal changes, than the lower zones. These conditions prevail in central and southern Mexico. The northern arid and semiarid regions, of lower elevation than the central and southern highlands, approximate the climate of Texas and Arizona, with considerable extremes of temperature.

Mexico was once a country of extensive forests, but centuries of heedless exploitation have made it a land of forest famine throughout wide areas, a land deteriorated by extensive erosion. Conservation is only beginning, while population growth is pressing heavily on the means of subsistence.

*The people.* Mexico is still a country of rural people, geographically and culturally isolated, despite the recent rapid growth of the larger cities. There is little immigration, and the natural increase in population was slow until about 1930. During the last two decades it has spurted. The increase was more than 18 per cent between 1930 and 1940 and some 31 per cent between 1940 and 1950, bringing the 1950 figure to 25,791,017. The population density per square mile among the twenty-nine states and two territories ranges from .2 to 27.5, with a national average of 5.[5] The population is quite centralized, largely concentrated in the central highlands. This area is broken down into separate clusters of villages, each village the focus of a rural-urban community. The national life focuses on Mexico City, which, like other cities, is growing much faster in population than the rural areas.

A salient feature of Mexico is its heterogeneous population. Historical influences have shaped the social and cultural landscape to mold a new people, the mestizos, a European-native amalgam. One estimate is that some 90 per cent of the people are Indian or part Indian, with 60 per cent mestizos. Over the past century, the Indian portion and the whites have declined, with the white percentage losing most — by half. The "Indian world" is being slowly modernized, but several million live in relative cultural isolation, and about a million speak only an Indian language. Another two million speak little Spanish.

One grouping by "cultural divisions" puts the "Indian world" at 15 per cent of the people; the "transitional world" at 37 per cent; the "modern world" at 48 per cent. A very small well-to-do class heads the 48 per cent, and a small but growing middle class is developing in the fast-growing cities.[6] The culture of Mexico derives largely from Spain and France, but the influence of the United States is steadily growing. Withal, Mexico is still "many Mexicos," a land of local and regional cultures and patriotisms.

Official statistics commonly group the states and territories into five large regions.[7] The central region almost spans the country, from the Pacific to the Atlantic lowland, and comprises the bulk of the central highland plateau. It contains some 14 per cent of the country's area and about half of the population, which has been increasing there faster than in any other region. Here is the rapidly growing Federal District (similar to the District of Columbia), the focus of commercial, industrial, and political power. But here also is the focus of Mexico's twin problems — agriculture and industry. This core region has 15 per cent of the agricultural land but 45 per cent of the nation's farmers. Here were the core of early Spanish settlement, the densest Indian population, and the core of the Spanish mineral empire. The rural population is still predominantly Indian.

The Gulf Coast and Yucatan region comprises about 12 per cent of the country's area and has about 12 per cent of the population. Unlike most areas, it is well endowed with moisture and level farming lands, which admit of substantial further development. The port of Veracruz is of major importance, and plantation agriculture has long been developed. The nation's oil industry centers in this region, and Yucatan is the center of the country's henequen production.

The south Pacific region is comparable to the Gulf region in area and population, but its ruggedness is in contrast with the geography of the latter. The northern part is separated from the plateau by rugged terrain, while the highlands of Chiapas were long isolated by distance from the central region.

The north Pacific region borders on the United States, and includes 21 per cent of the country's area and some 6 per cent of the people, but the population is growing fast in some sections. It is largely desert and rugged mountains of the Sierra Madre Occidental, across which few travel routes have been developed. Scattered irrigated agriculture and mining characterize the region.

The northern region, like the north Pacific, is arid and relatively isolated from the central region. It has some 40 per cent of the area and 19 per cent of the population. Mining and cattle raising are important industries for its scattered population. The Laguna district and a few other areas have developed commercial agriculture of importance. To the east, Monterrey has developed into an industrial center second only to the nation's capital.

*The economy.** Is Mexico a rich land or a poor land? It was long regarded as a fabled cornucopia; and its mineral resources have given substance to that view. Its potential as a producer of meat and dairy products is good. Its southeastern lowlands give promise of substantial agricultural development, and irrigation can open up other interior lands. The potentialities of its tourist industry are excellent, and this industry already holds high rank as a national income producer. But, agriculturally speaking, Mexico is a poor country; and its potential in this direction is limited.

For about two decades Mexico has been in the throes of an industrial revolution.[8] In manufacturing and industry, expansion has been rapid, but it has been uneven from one industry to another. Some consumer-goods production has boomed while other more important lines of activity have lagged. The means of transport, especially roads, have increased, but they have not yet met the pressing demand. Agricultural output has long been a problem, but recently the picture has been improving slowly. Per-capita income and standards of living are still low compared with the more advanced industrialized countries.

The average annual rate of increase in industrial production compares very favorably with other countries. It was calculated at 4.4 per cent annually for 1929–39, 7 per cent for 1940–44, 3 per cent for 1945–49, 5 per cent for 1950–55 (including the two bad years of peso difficulties), and 8 per cent for 1955. (The annual increase is about 3 per cent for the United States.) Such progress is needed to bring a rise in living standards in the face of a high rate of population increase — some 3 per cent annually.[9]

In the "reluctant" capital market of Mexico, the government has played an important role in stimulating economic development — by en-

* Discussed at length in Chapters 15–21.

couraging private investment, by participating in development (through loans and through joint ownership in important firms with private capital), and through wholly government-financed investments. The climate for private investment is favorable because of relatively moderate taxes, important specific tax concessions, high rates of return on industrial capital, and absence of exchange controls. Capital originating in the United States is currently calculated at slightly over $1 billion. Of this total, $825 million is long-term capital which can be broken down as follows: $600 million, direct private investment; $120 million, Export-Import bank credits; $81 million, public debt; $24 million, obligations with commercial banks.[10] Direct public investment accounts for nearly 40 per cent of the total, but much of it is in those fields (like railways, highways, electric power, and irrigation) which are of aid to private investments. Import controls are also used to promote industrialization; there are restrictions on the importation of luxury goods and concessions are granted to machinery, machine tools, and other capital goods. Machinery imports, irrigation developments, crop insurance, and agricultural credit are government aids to agriculture.[11] Some able critics feel that the last administration overemphasized industrialization, thus creating an imbalance and leaving agriculture and the consumer behind in the march of progress. There are signs that the present administration is weighing these criticisms and is striving to produce a more well-balanced economy and to raise the low standard of living of the average consumer. Inflation, while much less than in some countries, has outdistanced average wage increases and thrown into bold relief the small profits of most small businesses and the substantial profits of most large industrial firms.[12]

The way ahead will not be easy. But the leadership of the present administration is honest, earnest, and competent. These qualities — too often lacking in the past — lend encouragement for the future.

### NOTES

[1] T. C. Call, *The Mexican Venture* (1953), pp. 26–27. See also Emilio Alanis Patino, "Zonas y Regiones Económicas de México," *Problemas Agrícolas . . .* (hereafter cited as *Prob. Agr.*) July–September 1946, pp. 90–104; F. A. Carlson, *Geography of Latin America* (1952), Chs. 27–28; H. F. Cline, *The United States and Mexico* (1953), Chs. 2, 6; Preston James, *Latin America* (1950), Ch. 20; Jorge Tamayo, *Geografía General de México* (1949); Jorge Vivó, *Geografía de México* (1948); Nathan Whetten, *Rural Mexico* (1948), Ch. 1. For uniformity of appearance, English rules of capitalization have been used throughout.

[2] Moisés Sáenz, in H. C. Herring and K. Terrill, eds., *The Genius of Mexico* (1931), pp. 5, 8, 13.

[3] William Vogt, *Road to Survival* (1948), p. 161.

[4] James, *op. cit.*, p. 614.

[5] Julio Durán Ochoa, *Población* (1955), *passim*; José Iturriaga, *La Estructura Social y Cultural de México* (1951), *passim*; Secretaría de Economía (hereafter cited as Sría. de Econ.), *Compendio Estadístico*, *passim*.

[6] Sría. de Econ., *op. cit.*; Cline, *op. cit.*, p. 67. For a good review of the field, see Gordon W. Hewes, "Mexicans in Search of the 'Mexican': Notes on Mexican National Character Studies," *American Journal of Economics and Sociology*, January 1954, pp. 209–23.

[7] Sría. de Econ., *op. cit.*; Cline, *op. cit.*, Ch. 6; James, *op. cit.*, Ch. 20; Whetten, *op. cit.*, Chs. 2, 3; U.S. Bureau of Foreign Commerce, *Investment in Mexico* (1956), Ch. 13.

[8] Cline, *op. cit.*, Chs. 16–17; Call, *op. cit.*; S. A. Mosk, *Industrial Revolution in Mexico* (1950); *El Mercado de Valores* (hereafter cited as *MV*), February 27, 1956, pp. 97–98; *Revista de Economía* (hereafter cited as *Rev. Ec.*), October 1955, pp. 343–47.

[9] *MV*, January 9, 1956, p. 14; *Hispanoamericano* (hereafter cited as *HA*), January 9, 1956, pp. 48–49, January 16, 1956, p. 5, and January 23, 1956, p. 39.

[10] *MV*, April 2, 1956, pp. 157–58. A useful study is U.S. Bureau of Foreign Commerce, *Investment in Mexico* (1956). It gives first a general economic survey, then an industry-by-industry report.

[11] *MV*, December 5, 1955, pp. 577–78; New York *Herald Tribune*, December 4, 1955, Sec. 10, pp. 1–14; *Fortune*, January 1956, pp. 103–12, 173–76; *Rev. Ec.*, October 1955, *passim*.

[12] *HA*, September 1, 1950, p. iv and March 13, 1953, pp. 3–7; Rodrigo García Treviño, *Precios, Salarios y Mordidas* (1953), Chs. 1, 4, 5.

9

# 2

## History

F ᴇᴡ countries have had a more colorful history than Mexico; and the sense of history is strong among her educated people.[1] Mexico's history can be approached in several ways. One meaningful approach is the division into four broad periods. The first is the precolonial era of native civilizations. Then come the three centuries of colonial rule. The third is the century of revolutions, painfully establishing a stable representative government. The fourth is the past quarter-century of peaceful national progress.

When the Spaniards came to Mexico, they found a wide range of native cultures. The central plateau, under the uneasy rule of the Aztecs, was already rather densely populated. These last of the aboriginal invaders, past the zenith of their rule, soon fell before the Castilian crusade for "gold, glory, and God." From the Valley of Mexico as a base, the Spanish pushed into the outlying areas at varying speeds – conquering, consolidating, and colonizing.

For nearly three centuries New Spain was ruled by a viceroy. He was assisted by an *audiencia* (administrative and judicial tribunal), which served as a judicial court of appeal and gave advice in administration. Subdivisions of the country were governed by *corregidores* (governors of geographical areas), or by *alcaldes mayores* (governors of municipal areas). The *ayuntamientos* (town councils) were the only democratic structural elements of government, but their power was small.[2] The prevailing unit of agricultural economy and rule was the *encomienda*, a device for Christianizing the natives, subjecting them to the Crown, and rewarding the conquistadors. One or more villages were given in trust to an individual, who had the right to collect tribute and exact labor from the inhabitants. Thus a feudal pattern of land tenure developed.[3]

Spain and the Spanish monopolized government offices, foreign trade, and ecclesiastical power. The establishment of manufactures was discouraged or prohibited. The abuse of power blighted the native culture. The building of roads and harbors, the encouragement of literature and art, the beautifying of cities, and the establishment of higher schools by a strong government — these virtues of paternal rule could not offset the growing demands for self-government.

The revolt against Spain came in 1810, led by the patriot-priest, Hidalgo. His defeat was followed by the unsuccessful revolt of another liberal priest, Morelos. Separatist and republican revolts beat against the capital, Mexico City, without success until the conservative elements of the country were convinced that their interests lay in separation from Spain. Their immediate answer was not a republic, but an independent Mexican monarchy under the older colonial groups. From 1810 to 1815, Hidalgo and Morelos had fought for expulsion of the governors from Spain, for racial equality, for abolition of military and clerical privileges, and for restoration of lands to the Indians. A new elite of creoles replaced the rule of the governors from Spain.[4]

The first independent government, a council of six with General Iturbide as president, was established in 1821. The next year the general was proclaimed emperor; but his rule was short, ending in 1823. A new congress assembled and adopted a federalist constitution in 1824, which was patterned after that of the United States. The country was divided into nineteen states and four territories, with the people of the states electing their legislatures and governors. The nation's president and vice-president were to be chosen by the state legislatures. The Church was to be deprived of its monopoly of education. The threefold separation of powers was set forth, with a two-house congress. Two senators were chosen by the legislature of each state for four-year staggered terms. The judiciary consisted of supreme, superior, and district courts, with the supreme court elected by the state legislatures. The supreme court judges were to have tenure. The "sovereignty" of the states was proclaimed, but it was limited. A weakness lay in placing the settlement of disputes between the states in the hands of the congress. The political immaturity of the people at that time foredoomed this constitution, but its idealism lived on in the charter of 1857.

# BACKGROUND

For a decade after 1824 governments rose and fell with the fortunes of military power. In 1836, with the centralists (conservatives) in power, a new constitution was installed, which ended the liberties of the states and established property qualifications for voting. Strong executive rule was in favor.[5]

The two decades following 1836 featured mainly the fortunes and misfortunes of war, highlighted by the disastrous war with the United States of 1846–47. For about a decade and a half after 1855, Mexico underwent a social revolution known as the *Reforma*. Influenced by French philosophy and mestizo (mixed Indian-Spanish) pressures, its protagonists sought to destroy feudalism, establish constitutional government, clip the powers of the clergy and the generals, and develop a nation of small property owners. Its aims were only partly successful, but it marked a turning point in Mexican history by bringing the mestizo to power.[6] The Juárez Law (1855) reorganized the system of justice, ending the military and ecclesiastical courts' jurisdiction over civil cases. The Lerdo Law (1856) ordered Church and other corporate bodies to dispose of their lands. The aim was to promote land ownership by small holders, but the unforeseen results were the opposite.

*The Constitution of 1857.* The high point of the *Reforma,* or Reform Era, was the new constitution.[7] The convention was a moderate group, influenced by the thinking of the French Revolution and the Constitution of the United States. Like the convention of 1823, its members were predominantly creole and mestizo intellectuals, most of them lawyers. The spirit of nineteenth-century individualism in the convention produced a federalist document, providing a detailed listing of civil and political rights, a tripartite separation of powers with a unicameral congress, and indirect election. The central authority was predominant, with the Congress empowered to impeach state governors and the federal Supreme Court charged with deciding disputed state elections. The presidency, despite seemingly narrow restrictions, could be made supreme, as Díaz was later to prove. "Once again Anglo-Saxon democracy was to be imposed upon a country of peonage and illiteracy." But within a year came the conservative overthrow.

The three-year civil war, the War of the Reform (1858–61), was a contest of the country and the towns against the City of Mexico. Juárez led the liberals. His decrees (later made constitutional amendments in the 1870s) disestablished and disendowed the Church and made its properties subject to nationalization. His short-lived triumph in 1861 made Juárez Mexico's first real civilian ruler.[8]

The defeated conservatives sought aid abroad, and Maximilian was installed as emperor under the sponsorship of French arms. The rule (1864–67) of this honest and democratically inclined romantic was doomed from the start, when he alienated conservative and papal support by trying to act like a liberal. The phantom empire was soon gone.

Juárez was re-elected to the presidency in 1867, but his term of office was obstructed by an irresponsible congressional opposition. Promotion of education and ending the power of the military were close to his heart, but the achievement of both was to be a slow process. His re-election in 1871 touched off revolt, and he died soon after peace was restored. "With Juárez was buried the last hope for at least half a century of combining peace with freedom." [9]

Four ineffectual years of Lerdo's presidency brought a successful revolt by Porfirio Díaz when Lerdo sought re-election. Thus began the thirty-four-year rule of Díaz — four of them served by a puppet president — which transformed the constitutional government into a personal dictatorship.[10]

Díaz rose to power on a military coup and a program of no re-election, but the last was soon forgotten. It is debatable how much his regime rested on bayonets and how much on ideals and a plan for national economic advancement. Foreign capital was invited; domestic capital was courted. Peace was maintained by judicious mixtures of political favors and force. Personal friendships and favors took the place of political parties of principle. Constitutional forms were maintained, but administrative rule replaced political and elective machinery; and the will of the government was the will of the president and his assistants. Foreign capital produced railroads and other needed improvements. Stability brought some administrative reforms, such as financial administrative improvement. A degree of security of tenure brought special abilities to the fore — the *científicos*. Science was to be applied to the work of government, and national economic greatness was to result. But the welfare of the vast majority of the people got short shrift; and Mexico was labeled "the mother of foreigners and the stepmother of Mexicans." [11]

Despite economic "prosperity" and the appearance of peace, the Díaz regime was weakening after 1900. The few ruled in their own interest, ignoring the well-being of the people. Hunger for lands, for bread, and for justice, says a well-known leader, were the main factors moving toward change.

After 1900, increasing numbers became dissatisfied with the dictatorship, though they disagreed much among themselves. So in this sense it cannot be said that the Revolution of 1910 which overthrew Díaz was a spontaneous popular uprising of the masses without intellectual leadership before the coming of Madero. The leaders of the movement were liberals of high ideals and considerable ability, working within the country and from exile.

*The Revolution of 1910.* A mistake of Díaz's touched off the fires of opposition. In an interview with the American journalist, James Creelman, the aged dictator welcomed the growth of an opposition political party. Ferment came into the open. Young lawyers and intellectuals openly demanded freedom and reform. Molina Enriquez, the agrarian authority, wrote *The Great National Problems*, a devastating analysis of Díaz's disastrous agrarian policy.

The year before (in 1908) Francisco Madero, a wealthy *hacendado* (landowner) of politically liberal sentiments, had written *The Presidential Succession in 1910.*[12] A work of no extraordinary merit, it proclaimed the need for political freedom, accepted the idea of re-electing Díaz, and urged freedom of popular choice for the vice-presidency. A mild book, Madero's volume ignored the more basic economic ills and needs of the country. But the time was ripe; the spark caught fire. The little volume was one of the chief contributory causes of the popular wave that swept Díaz from power.

As the election campaign of 1910 progressed, Madero's criticisms of the regime became more direct; and his meetings aroused more official repression. Madero was jailed for a short time, and dissension developed in the ranks of his party. In September, the Congress declared Díaz and Corral "elected" as president and vice-president; and Madero saw insurrection as the only way to free Mexico. In October, he fled to Texas, and the next month he issued his revolutionary declaration, the Plan of San Luis Potosí.[13] He declared the Díaz election void, called for insurrection, assumed the title of provisional president, and pledged an election when his forces regained the capital and half of the states. Upon the *de facto* assumption of power, there was to be a general revision of the laws along the lines of justice. Illegal acquisitions of land were to be reviewed, and officials were to be held responsible for their acts.

The revolutionary propaganda was having its effect. Uprisings developed in Veracruz, Puebla, Durango, Chihuahua, and other areas, as Madero crossed the border to head insurgent forces in the north. The inauguration of Díaz in December added fuel to the flames of discontent. Zapata, the peasant leader of Morelos, made war on the *hacendados*, adding a passionate agrarian flavor to the struggles. State capitals were seized by guerrilla leaders and mobs. The tide rolled on against the weak Díaz regime with its deceptive façade of strength. Efforts at compromise failed, and in May the agreement was signed. Díaz was to resign and de la Barra, Mexican ambassador in the U.S., was to be provisional president pending an election. Mob action in the capital forced Díaz's speedy departure for Europe. In October, Madero and Pino Suárez were chosen president and vice-president in the freest Mexican election yet held.

The people expected miracles, and disillusionment was swift. Madero's program was political, but the needs of the people were economic, and this he never fully understood. He thought the people wanted freedom and political democracy, when most of them were illiterate and wanted chiefly bread and land. Zapata took up arms again for the peasants in Morelos, and revolts spread when President Madero seemed unable to provide a program benefiting the masses. Madero's failure to please either radicals or reactionaries spelled doom for his temporizing program. The army became riddled with intrigue. February 1913 saw the series of machinations which caused Madero's death and placed the sinister Huerta in power.

From then until 1917, chaos was the rule. Carranza, governor of Coahuila, led the constitutionalist forces in a war to overthrow the usurper Huerta.[14] Obregón, Calles, Villa, and others from the north joined Carranza. U.S. intervention aided their side, and Carranza came to power in August 1914. Internecine strife continued. In 1915, in desperate need of support, Carranza issued the decree for agrarian reform, to restore to Indian villages lands previously taken from them. Also promised were strict enforcement of the Church's restrictive laws, civil and criminal code revision, effective suffrage legislation, and full enjoyment of all civil and political rights. Mecham, a prominent investigator in the field, regards these decrees as among the first constructive acts of the Revolution. Apparently to legalize his position, Carranza held elections for delegates to a constitutional convention to be held in the winter of 1916–17.

*The Constitutional Convention, 1916–17.* In the unsettled condition of the country, it was probably inevitable that the delegates were supporters of the Carranza regime. What was surprising was the high degree of independence the delegates showed in going beyond the President's desires by incorporating advanced social legislation in the basic document, when Carranza had called only for minor reforms to the Constitution of 1857. The machinery of government was left with few changes. Minor changes dealt with matters like no re-election for the president and a guarantee of freedom for the municipalities. The liberal and democratic character of the Constitution of 1857 remained.

The *basic* additions, however, made the new Constitution a revolutionary document. These additions included agrarian reform, a charter of labor protection, anti-imperialism, and an expanded anticlericalism. There is some evidence that much statutory-type detail was included in these additions, showing distrust of future legislative action or inaction.

Article 27 gave a new definition to property rights, attempting to return the alienated lands to the peasants and to assert national ownership of the subsoil wealth which had long been benefiting foreign investors. It denied the absolute right of private property and specifically provided for government regulation in behalf of the general welfare.

Article 123 sought to protect wage earners in all lines of work, and included the protections against exploitations discussed in the most advanced countries. These safeguards included the eight-hour day, a minimum wage, abolition of peonage and child labor, a compensation for accidents and improper dismissal, and the right to organize and strike.

The 1857 prohibition against clerical ownership of property, which Díaz had shelved, was renewed and extended to Church buildings. Priests were required to register with the civil authorities and were forbidden to take part in politics or to control primary schools.

In the present long, detailed Constitution one finds traces and influences from other charters — the earlier Mexican constitutions, that of the United States, and of the Spanish Constitution of 1812. The influences of Rousseau, Montesquieu, Marx, and colonial institutions rub shoulders with the hard-won tenets of the Mexican Revolution. Thus, it is little wonder that students find contradictions between the liberal individualism of yesterday and the labor and agrarian "guarantees" of the day. In structure and basic ideology, the document resembles the United States Constitution. But to this is added a considerable measure of the welfare state. Yet, in the opinion of Mecham, the resulting amalgam is in a real sense an indigenous document.[15] A developing welfare state requires increased powers and a more complex administrative apparatus; therefore we find an increased number of delegated powers granted to the central government and wider limitations placed upon the actions of the states. In a considerable measure, all Mexican constitutions have been statements of aspirations rather than of accomplished facts. But the current charter approaches reality more closely than its predecessors.

Carranza promulgated the Constitution, reluctantly, but he sabotaged its letter and spirit. The promise of land for the peasants remained largely unfulfilled; labor was dealt with drastically. Carranza attempted to impose a puppet at the next presidential election, but Obregón replied with rebellion, which met with speedy success.

In an important sense the revolutionary government of real achievements began with Obregón in 1920. He enacted agrarian laws and accelerated the distribution of land grants to the villages; but he was opposed to any drastic redistribution, regarding his program as a safety valve. Organized labor, which had fared poorly under Carranza, was now encouraged — but not to excess. As a counterbalance, the new strong man also swung support to agrarian groups. One of the most important advances of the Obregón regime was in the promotion of education. Unprecedented budgets were given to the newly organized Ministry of Education led by the able Vasconcelos, noted philosopher and man of letters.[16]

For some time Calles, Obregón's successor, tried to carry out the program of his predecessor. He promoted business, advanced the educational program, and built roads and irrigation projects. His most serious opposition came from the Church; whereupon he vigorously enforced the long-ignored anticlerical clauses of the Constitution.

When Portes Gil took office in 1928, after the assassination of president-elect Obregón, he began a succession of presidents under the influence of Calles. In the process, the *Callista* political machine changed from a group still somewhat interested in reform to one characterized by reaction. Portes Gil was still forward-looking, promoting the agrarian program and labor organization. One of his chief accomplishments was consolidating the hitherto temporary combinations into the National Revolutionary Party (PNR). Every important political group was incorporated, and the required contributions of public employees gave the new party an important semiofficial status.

Ortiz Rubio, who served as president from 1930 to 1932, was also controlled by boss Calles. The interests of both peasants and labor went by the board. The Revolution was buried — but not permanently.

During the next two years, in the administration of Rodríguez, younger men gained some influence in the official party. Education and land distribution received some impetus, and in 1934 an agrarian code was enacted. In the same year, Mexico's first Six-Year Plan was published by the official party.

*The Revolution revived.* It is said that party boss Calles gave his assent reluctantly to the nomination of Lázaro Cárdenas for president.[17] Soon his fears were verified, for Cárdenas would be no tool. He went to the grass roots throughout the country, even though his election was a foregone conclusion. Thus he built a powerful personal political machine. He vigorously championed the cause of organized labor and the peasantry; promoted education, sanitation, and good roads; reduced the power of the army; gave Mexico a greater degree of political stability and civil liberties; and sought to bring about national unity. He sought a return to the original goals of the Revolution: social, economic and political reform.

By 1934 Mexico had run through a conservative cycle under ex-revolutionists. Cárdenas brought a turn in the tide. In six years he distributed more land to the peasants than all previous governments together. In addition to allotting small parcels to the *ejidos* (cooperative or semi-cooperative farms), he organized large cooperative farms for producing commercial crops. Despite shortcomings, substantial strides forward were made.

Though his usual policy was close and friendly cooperation with organized labor, Cárdenas dealt firmly with the unions when he felt the national interest required it. When worker control fared poorly in the nationalized oil and railroad industries, he made administrative changes. Cárdenas was a strong advocate of education, for he recognized that a regime of political and economic democracy could not be built on the basis of an ignorant citizenry.

The world spotlight was on Mexico when the oil companies were expropriated, a move both economic and nationalistically political. The dispute arose from the companies' refusal of wage increases ordered by the courts, which Cárdenas regarded as a direct affront to Mexican sovereignty. Profits had been high and frictions many, though possibly the profits were less exorbitant than government economists maintained. The immediate economic effects involved a national hardship, but no previous event had produced such national solidarity.

The pillars on which the Cárdenas regime rested were the workers, the farmers, and the ranks of the army. He encouraged these people to organize as groups; then he made these groups integral parts of the official Party of the Mexican Revolution, as reorganized in 1938. Thus, the control of local politicos was weakened.

Cárdenas had collectivist tendencies, but he was not a doctrinaire socialist. He preferred socially responsible private ownership to expropriation; but he didn't hesitate to use this weapon when he felt it in the national interest. In the then current Mexican environment, the president could hardly have been other than a dictator; but he was a benevolent one. A vigorous, tireless, honest, shrewd man, and an able politician, Cárdenas has been variously evaluated as an administrator. He worked for closer cooperation between state and federal governments. He secured passage of a civil service law; established scientific research bureaus; and sought better fiscal organization and tax enforcement (though his friends were not all above suspicion). While his policies were not always considered economically sound, his integrity was unquestioned. The *Bankers Magazine* of New York declared, "It is the settled purpose of . . . Cardenas to substitute strong institutions for a strong man." [18]

*Middle-of-the-road.* When Cárdenas handed the reins of office to Manuel Ávila Camacho in December 1940, moderation was enthroned — or the Revolution died, depending on the point of view.[19] "Middle-of-the-road" is probably a better term. Pressing economic problems faced Mexico — in the nationalized railroads and oil, in communications, in agriculture, and in foreign trade. Ávila Camacho kept his promise to conduct a peaceful campaign. He promised to carry on and consolidate the program of the Revolution, with the emphasis on "consolidate"; and he drew much strength by declaring himself a practicing Catholic, in a land of official anticlericalism.

Some said the Revolution had died because the necessary crusading

BACKGROUND

had been done and peaceful fulfillment was needed; that the Party machine had become corrupt and required cleansing; and that Mexico was
becoming the prey of the struggle of Europe versus America in World
War II.

Ávila Camacho surprised friend and foe alike by being a skillful, if
unsensational, leader, ably steering the ship of state through domestic
shoals and showing leadership in the field of war-torn foreign policy.
Cárdenas's stands against fascist dictators found their counterpart in the
new president's staunch support of the Allied war effort. Cárdenas
joined the cabinet as Defense Minister, and the domestic semifascist,
religiously fanatical *Sinarquistas* and other subversive elements were
dealt with firmly. Machinery for price and other economic controls
was only partially successful in coping with inflation and other problems, while a new elite of wealth flowered on the wartime scene.

In its swing to the middle of the road, the Ávila Camacho administration gave the labor movement less support than the previous administration, shifted the agrarian emphasis toward small and medium-sized
individually owned farms, and gave a new emphasis to the growth of
native industry. The labor policy featured a moderate change of emphasis. The agrarian program began an emphasis on mechanization,
other technical improvements, and an expansion of irrigation projects
to improve the country's food production. High tariff walls and reduced imports produced a substantial growth of light and heavy industry; while direct and indirect capital investment reached sizable
proportions — possibly as a substitute for the Cárdenas agrarian program.

While frowning on the "socialist" education of his predecessor, Ávila
Camacho expanded support for schools, extended public health work,
and established a national system of social insurance. In administration
the President relied increasingly on nongovernmental advice in shaping
his program, appointing numerous advisory commissions during the
war years.

*Alemanismo.* Miguel Alemán, Mexico's first real nonmilitary president, took office in 1946 after a peaceful election.[20] His campaign for
office had featured a series of round-table conferences, in which there
was opportunity for numerous leaders of opinion to present their thinking about the nation's needs.

Alemán, who had held Ávila Camacho's chief cabinet post, presented a program similar to that of his predecessor. It was to build on and improve on the past. Relations with the United States remained favorable, and Mexico was an active member of the United Nations and other international organizations.

Agriculture was not forgotten, but the emphasis was placed more on developing irrigation projects and technical agricultural improvements. These included mechanization, technical education, developing improved strains of plants, and combating plant and animal diseases. Industrialization, however, received the greatest emphasis. To achieve this goal, Alemán gave many inducements to native and foreign capital. Many firms were given tax reductions or exemptions for a term of years. The government itself joined private enterprise in providing an increasing percentage of the total amount of risk capital. This was done largely through the Nacional Financiera, a government-owned bond and investment corporation somewhat similar to the RFC which extends industrial credit and acquires part ownership in basic industries. In addition, much government aid continued to come from other government credit institutions specializing in agricultural credit and foreign commerce. During these years, the Mexican economy benefited substantially from United States and other foreign loans for development of roads, railways, electric power, etc.

Alemán's government, like that of his predecessors, was a strong-man regime — the rule of a predominant political party under the dominance of its chief. The official party habitually has won the presidency, the Congress, and the state regimes because of the advantages it offers to a coalition of the principal sectors of the national life — organized agriculture, labor, small business, and public servants. Withal, an increasing degree of popular influence is being exerted on government policies and programs through the party's constituent sectors.

*Ruiz Cortines.* In July 1952, Mexico elected its second civilian president, Adolfo Ruiz Cortines.[21] According to custom, the presidential incumbent selected his successor. There is widespread belief that Alemán "selected" his Minister of Government as Calles "selected" Cárdenas — under some pressure from strong dissident elements in the party. Suspicion of widespread corruption and graft at high levels had grown rapidly, at times breaking into print.

Ruiz Cortines's extensive, if unspectacular, background of experience and integrity in public service made him a promising candidate.

He methodically discussed the real issues facing the country, and promised to carry forward the general program of his party. Upon being inaugurated president, he announced a vigorous program to moralize public life. People had heard that before, and shrugged their shoulders. But the new man meant it. He fired considerable numbers who didn't measure up to the new standards of honesty and financial integrity.

On assuming office the new president faced many pressing problems besides morality in public life. There is considerable feeling that Alemán overextended some of his public works programs; and many feel that the development of industry and agriculture have not been carried out as a balanced program of expansion, and that agriculture has suffered. There are indications that Ruiz Cortines agrees with these points and is seeking to bring them into balance. During the first part of his term of office, the president worked hard to curb price rises by stimulating production of the basic necessities, sought a more equitable distribution of the national income, and encouraged domestic and foreign capital investment.

*Perspective.* Lord Bryce has been quoted as saying that democracy had failed in Latin America for these lacks: racial unity, a middle class of small property owners, communication facilities, experience in self-government, and education. On all these points, Mexico has been making slow progress in recent years against great odds. The geographic environment and the physical resources have been far from the best. In this setting a semifeudal society has been slowly working its way toward political democracy and economic health, with many backsets and detours.

Three major events have largely determined the course of Mexico's history: the revolution for independence, the *Reforma* (the struggle for clerical reform and political democracy following 1855) and the Revolution (1910 to date). The Revolution has been a long-term process, guided in general in the interests of the public welfare. Despite the mistakes made and the excesses committed, there is a general feeling that a net positive balance remains — that progress has been made. This is the feeling of even such a staunch liberal and critic of the Ávila Camacho and Alemán regimes as Silva Herzog, who feels that the Revolution died in their era. Its end, he says, brought victory for a new middle class.

# HISTORY

## NOTES

[1] H. B. Parkes, *A History of Mexico* (1950); Hubert Herring, *A History of Latin America* (1955), Chs. 20-25; H. I. Priestley, *The Mexican Nation, a History* (1926); H. H. Bancroft, *History of Mexico* (1883-88); F. F. Palavicini, *México, Historia de su Evolución Constructiva* (1945); L. B. Simpson, *Many Mexicos* (1952).

[2] Julio Jiménez Rueda, *Historia de la Cultura, el Virreinato* (1950); Priestley, *op. cit.,* Ch. 7; Parkes, *op. cit.,* pp. 87-129.

[3] L. B. Simpson, *The Encomienda in New Spain* (1950), *passim.*

[4] Parkes, *op. cit.,* pp. 133-65; John C. Patterson, "José María Morelos" (Ph.D. thesis, Duke University, 1930).

[5] Parkes, *op. cit.,* pp. 206-10.

[6] *Ibid.,* pp. 233-50.

[7] W. H. Callcott, *Liberalism in Mexico, 1857-1929* (1931), Ch. 1; Priestley, *op. cit.,* Ch. 20; Herring, *op. cit.,* Ch. 20.

[8] Herring, *op. cit.,* Ch. 20; Ralph Roeder, *Juárez and His Mexico* (1947), *passim.*

[9] Parkes, *op. cit.,* p. 282.

[10] Herring, *op. cit.*

[11] Herring, *op. cit.,* Ch. 21. See also Carleton Beals, *Porfirio Díaz, Dictator of Mexico* (1932), *passim*; Parkes, *op. cit.,* pp. 277-322; and C. C. Cumberland, "Precursors of the Mexican Revolution of 1910," *Hispanic Amer. Hist. Rev.,* May 1942, pp. 344-56, for discussions of the political, social, and economic events leading up to the Revolution of 1910.

[12] Francisco Madero, *La Sucesión Presidencial en 1910* (1908-9). Further insight into the issues is offered by Andrés Molina Enríquez, *Los Grandes Problemas Nacionales* (1909); C. C. Cumberland, *Mexican Revolution, Genesis under Madero* (1952); Floyd Rittenhouse, "Emiliano Zapata and the Suriano Rebellion" (Ph.D. thesis, Ohio State University, 1948); and S. R. Ross, *Francisco I. Madero, Apostle of Mexican Democracy* (1955).

[13] Texts of the "Plans" of Madero, and of Zapata and Carranza, are found in Alberto Morales Jiménez, *Historia de la Revolución Mexicana* (1951), pp. 86-95, 126-34, 143-45.

[14] See Parkes, *op. cit.,* pp. 335-67; Nettie L. Benson, "The Preconstitutional Regime of Venustiano Carranza" (M.A. thesis, University of Texas, 1936); Audrey Hollenback, "The Carranza Regime" (M.A. thesis, University of California, Berkeley, 1924).

[15] Parkes, *op. cit.,* pp. 360-61; J. Lloyd Mecham, "An Appraisal of the Revolution in Mexico," in A. C. Wilgus, ed., *The Caribbean at Mid-Century* (1951), pp. 181-82; Herring, *op. cit.,* Ch. 22.

[16] Herring, *op. cit.,* Ch. 23; Donald Johnson, *Álvaro Obregón and the Mexican Revolution* (Ph.D. thesis, University of Southern California, 1946).

[17] See Herring, *op. cit.,* Ch. 24; Cline, *op. cit.,* Chs. 11, 12; William C. Townsend, *Lázaro Cárdenas, Mexican Democrat* (1952); and Nathaniel and Sylvia Weyl, *The Reconquest of Mexico* (1939).

[18] Betty Kirk, *Covering the Mexican Front* (1942), Ch. 2.

[19] Herring, *op. cit.,* Ch. 25; Eduardo Correa, *El Balance del Ávila Camacho* (1947); Sría. de Gobernación, *Seis Años de Gobierno . . . 1940-46* (1946); S. E. Stone, "The Mexican Presidential Election of 1940, As Seen through the Press of the Capital" (M.A. thesis, Columbia University, 1949); Cline, *op. cit.,* Chs. 13, 14.

[20] George S. Wise, *El México de Alemán* (1952); Mosk, *op. cit.*; Miguel Alemán, *Program of Government* (1946); Cline, *op. cit.,* Chs. 15-18; Mecham, *op. cit.*; Herring, *op. cit.,* pp. 387-90.

[21] Cline, *op. cit.,* pp. 328-32; Herring, *op. cit.,* pp. 390-93; Bernardo Ponce, *Adolfo Ruiz Cortines* (1952); New York *Herald Tribune,* December 4, 1955, Sec. 10, pp. 1-14.

# 3

## Church and State

The Catholic Church has played such a prominent role in Mexican history and public life that an understanding of the role of the Church is essential to an understanding of Mexican politics and government. In this overwhelmingly Catholic country, clericalism and anticlericalism have been powerful strands in the fabric of the nation's history. The close and vital relations of Church and state during the colonial regime are too well known to require retelling.

As Mecham has shown,[1] the country's first independent government was established "under clerical auspices," after the prelates of the Church had condemned earlier struggles for independence as heresy. The Church as a state church was a continuation of the colonial relationship. It was probably natural that the Church, as the pre-eminent institution in Mexican society, would also become the locus of great economic power. "Independence under creole leadership only served to aggrandize the Church in wealth and prestige. During the next thirty years its strength and riches continued to increase until it became the most powerful institutionalized force in the country."[2]

Castañeda,[3] a prominent Catholic historian, points out that the fact is often forgotten that "a large portion of the land estates [owned by the Church] were endowments held in mortmain for the maintenance of hospitals, charity institutions, schools, and scholarships for the training of young priests." Even so, he continues, "the fact remains that it constituted a considerable portion of the national wealth and gave great political power to those who held it."

For the first decade after the winning of independence, Church-state relations were generally close and secure. But anticlerical sentiment was gaining prominence. In 1833 some of the first serious attacks on the

Church came, under the leadership of Vice-president Gómez Farías. While there seems to have been no organized assault on religion as such, the efforts to secularize education, nationalize mission properties, and end legal enforcement for monastic vows, were premature and impractical at the time. A similar attack on military privileges united Church and army in removing the liberals and returning the conservative forces to power in 1834. From then until 1846, the Church enjoyed a generally favored position, while not achieving its aims in all matters.[4] However, it was of this period that an official Catholic Church history stated: ". . . Mexican history began to follow the familiar pattern in which clericals insist on their traditional privileges, while admitting no responsibility for abuses, whereas anticlericals rob the Church and the poor, while professing to defend liberty and democracy. Throughout the century the fortunes of the Church rose and fell with political tides."[5]

The wartime pressures for increased government revenue in 1846–47 again brought threats to Church properties in the form of a government effort to raise funds by mortgaging or selling certain ecclesiastical properties; but this was forestalled by clerical payment of a lesser sum than sale or mortgage would have brought. Again, the period 1847–54 was one of satisfactory relations for the Church. Especially during 1848–51, "the Church gained in wealth and influence. It became the dominant factor in Mexican politico-economic affairs."[6]

The mid-1850s were the start of two decades of seething turmoil and change, the first part of the period known as the *Reforma*. What started as a mere protest against the despotic President Santa Anna soon turned into a long conservative-liberal struggle for power. The former sought full restoration of clerical-military-landlord privileges and control. Liberals made the first serious effort in Mexico to establish democratic constitutional government. A revolutionary *junta* meeting in October 1855 chose Juan Álvarez provisional president, and included as cabinet members Benito Juárez and Miguel Lerdo de Tejada.[7]

*Rebirth and reaction.* One of the first fruits of the *Reforma* was the Juárez Law (1855), which eliminated all the special courts except those of the military and the Church; and it removed all civil jurisdiction from them. This uncompromising move brought strong opposition from the clergy. Armed revolts, financed by the clergy, broke out in some places and were put down.

The Lerdo Law (June 1856) produced even greater repercussions, some of them unforeseen and undesirable. Aimed at Church properties, it ordered corporate groups to dispose of their land-holdings. While the disamortization decree failed in its aim of channeling property into the hands of the middle and lower classes, the Church reacted with full vigor. Mecham finds that "the envenomed fierceness with which the clergy resisted provoked new reform measures, some of which really did assault the purely spiritual dominion of the Church. Decrees were issued allowing those who had taken religious vows to forswear them and once more the Jesuits . . . were expelled from the country." [8] Limits were placed on fees for the performance of religious ceremonies.

The Constitution of 1857 codified the religious policy of the liberals. Compulsory fulfillment of religious vows ended, which the clerics felt was a blow at the Church's foundations. The Juárez Law and the Lerdo Law were incorporated as Articles 13 and 27, the latter allowing religious groups to administer no real property except that used directly for worship. There was no mention of Catholicism as the state religion, nor was there any specific mention of religious liberty. However, freedom of speech, press, and education were guaranteed; and public education was to be free. [9]

Constitutional enactment was one thing, but enforcement was another. The clergy forbade officials to swear allegiance to the Constitution, and threatened offenders with deprivation of the sacraments and Christian burial. In December 1857, a clerical-military alliance announced the Plan of Tacubaya and came to power. The Plan called for restoration of Church properties and privileges, press censorship, Catholicism as the exclusive religion, and the establishment of a monarchy if possible. The liberals under Juárez established a counter-government in Veracruz. "The War of the Reform was essentially a religious conflict," Mecham finds, "and for that reason, perhaps, it was characterized by excessive plunder, rapine, brutal reprisals, and a general spirit of extermination. . . . The clergy made it a holy war." [10]

From Veracruz, the Juárez government issued numerous laws attacking even the spiritual basis of Church power. These included separation of Church and state, closing of convents and dispersing of religious congregations, nationalization of Church property, and freedom of conscience. Nationalization of Church property was held necessary to prevent Church resources from financing the war, since the clergy were in rebellion against the Juárez government. Many of these measures became effective only after the constitutionalists were installed in Mexico City in December 1860.[11]

Failing in domestic battle, the Church forces "turned to intrigue and worked for the founding of a monarchy under European protection . . . to save the Church from serious injury at the hands of the Liberal Reformers," Mecham found; "the clericals were willing, in 1861, to compromise the independence of their country." And, he says further, "the clergy were the real authors of the French intervention."[12]

Maximilian (1864–67), a moderately liberal man, sought to reconcile contending groups by putting into effect some of the Juárez program, which alienated both groups. When Juárez overthrew Maximilian, the Church was forced to obey the existing laws. Much Church property was liquidated, since the main purpose of the Reform was to destroy the economic power of the clergy; but much Church property was still held for it by proxies.[13]

In 1873, several important reform laws were incorporated in the Constitution, while the rest were codified in the following year. "The constitutionalizing of the Laws of the Reform marked the end of an epoch in the ecclesiastical history of Mexico. Henceforth, there was to be no open attempt of the clergy to dominate politics. Church and state were definitely separated. The Reform had been won at last, for notwithstanding its disregard during the subsequent Díaz period its existence as constitutional law was a constant deterrent to extravagant clerical pretensions. . . . They declared themselves as being eminently satisfied if accorded the guarantees of a free Church in a free State."[14]

Under Díaz, the religious laws fell into disuse without being repealed; and the resulting growth of Church influence provided fuel for the Revolution of 1910.[15] A Catholic historian reports that "Spiritually . . . the prolonged presidency of Díaz proved a great blessing to the Church." There were over 1,400 parishes and about 5,000 clergy "and the new fervor was revealed in the founding of several Mexican religious orders."[16] The Church again came to own buildings and other property, re-established schools and colleges, opened some seminaries, and operated convents and hospitals. Religious garb was worn openly on the streets and religious services were performed outside churches. By the 1890s, Díaz's policy of "conciliation" became obvious enough to be discussed in the press.[17]

27

# BACKGROUND

*Decades of turmoil.* The Revolution of 1910 was opposed by nearly all the clergy, and they attacked Madero's motives and policies, including agrarian reform. Possible agrarian and educational reforms were feared as threats to the Church's properties and schools, respectively. A National Catholic Party was active in the 1911 electoral campaign. While Madero began no anticlerical policies, the clergy hailed his overthrow by Huerta, an avowed supporter of the "Porfirian system." [18]

While Carranza's overthrow of Huerta performed an important and useful function, outrages against the clergy and the faithful were numerous and revolting. In 1914 and 1915, decrees legalized divorce and remarriage, and Carranza announced his intention to enforce the long-standing anticlerical laws.[19]

The 1916–17 Constitutional Convention (made up of supporters of the current regime) varied in religious matters mainly in the degrees of anticlericalism of its members. In several important respects the constitution produced by the Convention went beyond both previous legislation and the recommendations of Carranza.[20] One of the first and most discussed provisions was Article 3 on education. "Liberty of education" was provided, but all education was to be secular and not given by Church officials. Religious schools were to be abolished. The Church was still forbidden to own or administer real property not connected with religious worship; and the Convention added such a prohibition regarding all property. Forbidden also was participation in eleemosynary and charitable institutions.

Most of the constitutional innovations regarding religion were placed in Article 130. This article, in addition to continuing previous restrictions, included the following prohibitions: it recognized no legal personality in religious institutions; it allowed state legislatures to limit the number of practicing ministers; it allowed only native-born persons to serve as ministers; it classed ministers as members of a profession (thus subject to government regulation); it forbade ministerial voting, holding of office, criticizing of the basic laws, or inheriting of real property; it prohibited political group names from containing religious terminology; it allocated governmental supervisory authority to the three levels of government; and it forbade jury trials in cases involving infractions of the law. Thus, in seeking to remove the Church completely from politics, the Convention clearly transgressed religious freedom in important respects and gave the state domination over the Church.

Enforcement of these constitutional provisions has varied widely. They were largely ignored until 1923. This was especially true of Church elementary schools, religious orders, use of foreign clergy, and public ceremonies and demonstrations outside Church buildings. Church progress was substantial.

In January 1923, however, an especially well-publicized public Church celebration was held in Guanajuato; and President Obregón struck back at this constitutional violation by expelling the Apostolic Delegate, who was a prominent participant. This was followed by a spate of state laws (mostly of short duration) unreasonably restricting the number of priests allowed to practice; and an abortive effort was made to promote a schismatic "national" Catholic Church.

But drastic steps were not taken until February 1926, under President Calles. In a press interview, the Archbishop of Mexico criticized the religious articles of the Constitution and seemed to call on the faithful to disobey them. Promptly, the government nationalized all Church property not already in its control, deported foreign-born clericals, ordered all private schools to register with the authorities, and forbade their teaching religious subjects or having any Church connections. The states quickly passed laws placing oppressively small limits on the number of priests allowed to function.[21]

The answer of the Church came in the form of a nationwide economic boycott, organized by the National League for the Defense of Religious Liberty and endorsed by the Archbishop of Mexico. At the same time, the Church hierarchy ordered all priests to suspend religious services. Numerous Church and other groups abroad sought to have pressure brought on the government; but the government's material power was in no danger, with the support of both organized labor and the army. Despite its numerous restrictive measures, the government denied that it was infringing on religious liberty. Church petitions to the president and the Congress were turned down.[22]

When the boycott failed, some Catholic organizations and a few priests resorted to armed revolt—the "Cristero" revolt—which lasted in one area for nearly three years. The government response was to charge the clergy with responsibility for the rebellion and deport the Archbishop and five other prelates. It was not until June 1929, after the inauguration of President Portes Gil, that the executive and the Church leaders arrived at a verbal understanding and regular church services were resumed. Despite the law, the agreement amounted to virtual recognition of the Church's corporate rights in designating priestly personnel.[23]

An American Catholic study finds that "even at the time of the Calles persecution, [Church] schools continued. Although their existence was precarious and their work interrupted, they managed to carry on the task of imparting religious instruction. True enough, this had to be done . . . *sub rosa*." [24]

Regarding this period, Mecham finds that "although it is true that Calles acted with excessive severity, it is equally true, keeping in mind the intentions of the constitutional fathers, that his acts were violative neither of the letter nor the spirit of the constitutional mandate which required that the Catholic Church, the traditional enemy of liberalism and social revolution in Mexico, must be kept under the strictest governmental surveillance." [25]

During 1931 and 1932, several states and the Federal District resumed oppressive measures by unreasonably restricting the number of practicing priests and deporting the Apostolic Delegate as an "undesirable alien";[26] and by the end of 1934, at the low point in Church-state relations, less than five hundred priests were in practice.[27] However, an American Catholic investigator found that much depended on the state governors and local military commanders. Here and there, by 1931, schools, colleges, and hospitals were starting up.[28]

In November 1934, just prior to Cárdenas's inauguration, Article 3 of the Constitution was amended to require the schools to teach "socialism," combat "fanaticism and prejudice," "create . . . a rational concept of the world and social life," and remain free from any religious connections. This included theological seminaries. The Church regarded this as complete opposition to religion, not merely secularism. At first, its opposition had been to the constitutional prohibition of religious schools; to this was now added its vehement opposition to the content of the education provided.[29] During 1935 there were further restrictions. One decree barred the mails to religious publications. Another extended the threat of nationalization even to homes and rented buildings where religious services might be held in violation of the restriction of such services to churches exclusively.[30]

*Improved relations.* In 1936, however, the tide turned; and since then Church-state relations have continued to improve without substantial setbacks, though the legal provisions have not been changed. Cárdenas, never a rabid anticlerical, saw that continued bad relations would hinder his important social and agrarian programs.[31]

The first half of 1937 saw several steps toward improvement. Cárdenas intervened in one state against oppressive limitation of priests, and the Supreme Court did likewise in another state. The Church also took two important steps. The appointment of the present archbishop, Luis María Martínez, brought to the helm a native of Cárdenas's home state and a leader with considerable diplomatic skill. At the same time, a Papal Apostolic Letter declared that the Church must recognize the good features of the Revolution and not think that a return to the days of Don Porfirio Díaz would settle everything.[32] While relations steadily improved, nevertheless for over a decade most new priests had to be trained outside the country — mainly at Montezuma Seminary in New Mexico.[33]

Near the end of Cárdenas's term of office, presidential nominee Ávila Camacho declared himself "a believer"; and Archbishop Martínez said, "I feel certain that freedom of conscience and religious peace, which made great progress in the Cárdenas administration" would be still further improved during the next six years.[34] The one important legal change was the amendment of Article 3 to change the requirement of "socialistic" education to an emphasis on democracy, nationalism, and justice; and, as the *Catholic Encyclopedia Supplement* reported: "Ávila Camacho . . . did not enforce the antireligious laws and gave a 'social' interpretation to Article 3." Definite and important support which the Church hierarchy gave the government was its endorsement of Mexico's war effort, after the archbishop moved pro-Falangist priests from key posts. Similar Church support was given the Cárdenas government when oil was expropriated in 1938.[35]

At the mid-point (1944) of the Ávila Camacho administration, an American Catholic investigating committee found that "there is still much of the Cristero [revolt] mentality" as well as "a very strong *hacendado* mentality among many Catholics." But it felt that the bulk of lay and clerical thinking "accepts the suggestions of the Holy See on seeking to work out relations with the state." It even goes so far as to say, regarding the breaking up of large estates, that "responsible Catholic thinking along this line follows fairly closely the action of the government itself." But disagreements are noted over the execution of the program.[36]

This committee found that religious instruction in private schools formerly "had to be done and still has to be done somewhat *sub rosa*." This was done "at odd hours and under special conditions in order to comply with the regulations." "Formerly," the committee reported, "the presence of any religious subjects would have been tantamount to closure. Today, respect is still maintained for the appearances." But the religious dress and religious objects are not conspicuously in evidence. Moreover, "Catholic schools have sprung up like mushrooms." And "Mexican seminaries have slowly come back into existence. . . . Most of the dioceses now have their own seminary." Moreover, "Catholic influence in the [National] University is considerable. A large number of its faculty members are active Catholics." And the freedom of teaching is very broad. Also noted were the large number of official and unofficial Catholic journals being published. The general press also had broad freedom of expression.[37]

Church-state relations since 1946 have in general been uneventful and increasingly favorable to the Church. First should be mentioned the general attitude of the state toward the Church.

An increasing number of buildings have been turned over to the Church for church or school purposes; and it has been alleged that some of these were formerly used for public schools.[38]

There has been increasing tolerance of outdoor religious observances. One such celebration occurred in Guanajuato in 1955.[39] A similar celebration at the same place in 1923 brought the exile of the Apostolic Delegate.

The increasing social activity of the hierarchy is often noted. An American Catholic journal finds that the archbishop "takes an active part in social and civic affairs," and it comments on "his democratic spirit."[40]

The friendliness of Alemán toward the archbishop was well known; and *Time* states that the prelate visits Ruiz Cortines in the presidential offices without publicity almost monthly.[41]

The late Archbishop was recently quoted as saying, regarding the last three presidential administrations, that their regimes "have intelligently combined the interests of the State and of the Church to such an extent that relations between the two sectors could not be better," except for the Church's desire for amendment of Article 3 of the Constitution. But there seems little chance of this in the near future, despite continuing pressure from the Church and some of the minority political parties.[42] Anticlericalism is still an important factor; and, as one authority notes, many government leaders "are exceedingly sensitive to criticism and react impulsively to the slightest hint that they have relaxed their vigilance in regard to the violation of the anti-Church legislation."[43]

Viewed the other way around (the attitude of the Church toward the state), an American Catholic leader reported in 1947 that "Archbishop Martínez . . . within recent months, has ordered all pastors to obey the law and stop all demonstrations of public worship outside the church edifices."[44] Other evidences of Church cooperation have followed.

Church-state relations are of growing importance in the field of education. Authorities report that Catholic schools have increased greatly in numbers in recent years. Although the officials know it, "they assume an indifferent attitude as long as the outward formalities of the law are observed." "The curriculum does not include Christian doctrine, but this is taught at hours off the schedule." Teachers don't wear religious habits in school, and "Catholic books are not conspicuous, and every reasonable effort is made to avoid antagonizing the sensibilities of the government inspectors."[45] While clearly unconstitutional, government subsidies, Mexican Protestant leaders charge, were given to certain private schools until Ruiz Cortines assumed office.[46] As early as 1947, the Church reported that secondary schools had "assumed again an important position, to the point that various Catholic schools are affiliated with the National Autonomous University."[47]

Theological seminaries were clandestinely operated during the 1930s, and several hundred students were in training by 1950. In 1955 some 2,000 students were reported as attending thirty-four seminaries.[48]

Public education, even under current and recent moderate regimes, has often been condemned as Communist or Marxist; and the present administration has removed certain textbooks which drew fire from religious quarters.[49] Whetten and other investigators have felt that rural priests have often not supported the public school program.[50]

There seems to have been increased but uneven Church support for various government social-economic programs. Castañeda finds that "since the war, Catholics in Mexico have taken a greater interest in the basic problems of the Revolution," such as land distribution, labor, farm labor, education, and welfare work.[51] The *Catholic World* reported that Alemán gratefully incorporated the services of the rural priests into "his drives for improved agriculture, the success of the foot-and-mouth disease campaign, the acceleration of highway construction."[52] Possibly this trend is very recent. In 1947, Whetten found good cooperation only "among a few of the younger Mexican priests" in such social betterment programs of the government.[53] In earlier years, the clergy and the hierarchy had strongly condemned the government's land reform program.[54]

*Pro's and con's.* As for its own social program, the Mexican episcopate celebrated the sixtieth anniversary of the *Rerum novarum* encyclical in 1951 with the following declaration: "We have no hesitation in affirming with the Pope 'that it is your obligation to fight for a more equitable distribution of wealth.' This is and continues to be the heart of the Catholic social doctrine."[55] In 1953, the first national congress of Catholic leaders since the Revolution devoted much of its time to social and economic problems.[56]

Castañeda discusses four national Catholic congresses held between 1903 and 1909, which considered the problems of labor, agricultural labor, farm credit, and the Indians; while a 1913 congress offered a program "as advanced" as that in the 1917 Constitution. In 1936, he reports, the "position of the Church in social matters was repeated in clear and emphatic terms. It was affirmed that the Church stood for a just wage . . . the material welfare of the individual, the right of labor to organize, and for every principle of Christian democracy."[57] Gruening, however, reported in 1928 that the Church "has countered the development of labor unions by the formation of *Sindicatos Católicos* that reject the labor provisions of the constitution." He found that the "regular labor groups" strongly opposed these Church-sponsored unions, and that the "influence of the Catholic labor movement has been negligible."[58]

Whatever the details of its past social philosophy and practice, an investigator from the American Catholic clergy has stated that "the Church in Mexico must gird its loins for an intensive program of social welfare work among the masses." He feels that unless the traditional religion "is unmistakably linked with a clear understanding of the social gospel of Christ and with a practical growth in Christian ethics, it can fail in the development of a genuinely Christian society." [59] Both Church and non-Catholic reporters attest to progress in the growth of social welfare institutions." [60]

The question is often asked, "Where does the Mexican Church stand on political democracy?" In contrast with earlier periods, some favorable points of recent years can be presented. The moderately conservative unofficial Catholic party (the National Action Party — PAN) has functioned in the tradition of political democracy. It has criticized the operation of Mexican "federalism," centralization of power, and dominance of the executive. It has urged an independent judiciary and congress, effective suffrage, and greater freedom and power for local governments. The Church hierarchy itself has attacked Sinarchism, an extremist political movement formerly enjoying considerable Catholic support.[61]

On the other side are the comments of some prominent American investigators. As late as 1947, Whetten found that the "heroes of Mexican Independence and of the Revolution are frequently looked upon as villains. Church leaders often speak apologetically of the work of Father Hidalgo and of Benito Juárez, and they idealize such characters as Iturbide and Don Porfirio. They have tended automatically to brand most government-sponsored programs with the stigma of 'communism.'" [62] Stokes, a specialist in Latin American government, recently said of all Latin America, "The techniques and methods of Catholicism in Latin America do not instruct citizens in the meaning of the democratic process." He says further, "Review of outstanding Catholic periodicals published in Latin America reveals similar findings. There is a uniform lack of interest in democracy. In many instances one finds a hostility toward democracy." [63]

While the population is overwhelmingly Catholic, Protestants have been active since the mid-nineteenth century. They have made modest progress in recent years, operate a theological seminary, and reported 330,111 members in 1950. (The 1940 census figure was 177,954.) Actual outbreaks against Protestants have been few recently; and Protestant church leaders report fair treatment by the present administration.[64]

*Summary.* It should be recalled that some Church-state conflict was found even in colonial times; and it developed into vigorous conflict in the early decades of independence. According to Arciniegas, the "clash was less acute in the rest of America. The Church elsewhere did not take such a stubborn stand in the political struggle, nor was the State so uncompromising." [65] The bitter conflicts of the mid-nineteenth century were followed by a steady improvement of the Church's lot under Díaz — an obvious reason for the Church's support of his regime and opposition to the Revolution of 1910 and the Madero government.

The 1917 Constitution and its subsequent executives sought to remove the Church completely from politics and social influence, to confine it entirely to the field of religion. As Mecham has emphasized, in this effort "they contradicted the guarantee of religious freedom and, instead of separating Church and State, put the Church under the domination of the State." [66] At various times anticlericalism served as a demagogic cement to bind together the "revolutionary family." On occasion this device cloaked corruption and excesses within the ruling groups. And there were unconscionable excesses and ruthlessness on both sides at such times as the Cristero revolt period of 1927–28. [67]

There has been steady improvement in *de facto* Church-state relations since 1936, when Cárdenas recognized extreme anticlericalism as a deterrent to the government's program of social and economic progress. However, since nearly all the framework of Church legislation remains on the statute books and *could* be enforced, it is well to review these provisions. Whetten aptly classifies the constitutional provisions into five categories. [68]

1. Property-holding provisions prohibit churches from holding or administering real property or mortgages; nationalize all places of worship; require government permission for opening new churches; and prohibit ministers from inheriting real property from religious organizations.

2. Churches are forbidden to administer institutions for charitable or research purposes.

3. Ministers' freedom of expression is restricted by their being forbidden to criticize "the fundamental laws," authorities, or the government. Nor may they attend political meetings, vote, or hold office.

4. The number of priests may be restricted by state legislatures; [69] and only Mexicans by birth may serve as ministers.

5. General limitations on Church authority include: forbidding monastic orders; recognizing no legal personality for churches; regarding ministers as members of a profession which, like others, is subject to

regulation; holding marriage and related matters to be solely subject to the civil jurisdiction.

The Law on Nationalization of Properties, elaborating on constitutional Article 27, declares nationalized all temples, seminaries, asylums, convents, and other buildings used directly or indirectly for religious propaganda or teaching; and temples are regarded as all buildings open for public worship with authorization of the Ministry of Government and all other locations used for public worship.[70]

The temples and their appurtenances, as well as other religious controls, are under the principal jurisdiction of the Ministry of Government; but certain controls are shared with the Attorney General, the Ministry of Finance, the Ministry of National Properties, and the state and local governments.[71]

Most of the Ministry of Government's pertinent work is in charge of its General Bureau of Government, which is charged with administering most of the legal provisions regarding religion; controlling persons in charge of the temples; maintaining inventories and vigilance over investments and gifts; opening and closing temples; and maintaining registers of priests and pertinent statistics.[72]

Before giving authorization for the opening of a new place of worship, the Ministry of Government confers with the other interested agencies — the state government (which limits the number of priests), the Ministry of National Properties (which has general control over government properties), and the Attorney General (whose office handles expropriation proceedings). The Ministries of Finance and Education may also be involved under certain circumstances.[73]

For many years, the Catholic Church regarded the administration of the religious laws as highly discriminatory. Then, during the Alemán administration, Protestant groups felt that discrimination had turned against them — and in favor of the Catholics — in the granting of permission sought for opening new churches. It was alleged that hundreds of applications were unanswered, for formal rejection would have made possible appeal to the courts.[74]

It is virtually impossible to secure details on the actual procedure of administration in Church regulation. However, both Catholics and Protestants seem fairly well satisfied with the present *de facto* situation. Therefore, the near future will probably bring no substantial change in the *legal* status of religious groups.[75] In this way, Church-state relations remain reasonably satisfactory, while the revolutionary tradition of anticlericalism doesn't lose face.

In 1950, the Ministry of National Properties reported that only 2,500 of the country's 22,000 real properties of Church origin had been turned to non-Church use.[76]

NOTES

[1] J. Lloyd Mecham, *Church and State in Latin America* (1934), pp. 395–97. See also Ernest Gruening, *Mexico and Its Heritage* (1928), pp. 171–89.

[2] Mecham, *op. cit.*, p. 402. See also W. E. Shiels, "Church and State in the First Decade of Mexican Independence," *Catholic Historical Rev.*, July 1942, pp. 206–28.

[3] Carlos Castañeda, "Social Developments and Movements in Latin America," in J. N. Moody, ed., *Church and Society* (1953), p. 753.

[4] Mecham, *op. cit.*, pp. 402–22; Herring, *op. cit.*, pp. 313–16; W. H. Callcott, *Church and State in Mexico, 1822–1857* (1926), Chs. 3–4.

[5] Joseph McSorley, *Outline History of the Church by Centuries* (1954), p. 796.

[6] Mecham, *op. cit.*, pp. 422–26. See also McSorley, *op. cit.*, pp. 796, 829; and Callcott, *op. cit.*, Chs. 8, 9.

[7] Mecham, *op. cit.*, Ch. 15; Cline, *op. cit.*, pp. 44–51; Callcott, *op. cit.*, Ch. 10.

[8] Mecham, *op. cit.*, pp. 435–36. See also Herring, *op. cit.*, Ch. 20; Callcott, *op. cit.*, Ch. 10.

[9] Mecham, *op. cit.*, pp. 436–39; Parkes, *op. cit.*, pp. 233–50; Callcott, *op. cit.*, Ch. 11.

[10] Mecham, *op. cit.*, pp. 440–41.

[11] *Ibid.*, pp. 442–44; W. H. Callcott, *Liberalism in Mexico, 1857–1929* (1931), Ch. 2.

[12] Mecham, *op. cit.*, pp. 445–46. See also Callcott, *Liberalism in Mexico*, Ch. 3.

[13] Mecham, *op. cit.*, pp. 445–55.

[14] *Ibid.*, pp. 454–56. See also Frank Tannenbaum, *Mexico, the Struggle for Peace and Bread* (1950), pp. 130–31.

[15] Mecham, *op. cit.*, pp. 454–56; Tannenbaum, *op. cit.*, pp. 130–31; Callcott, *op. cit.*, Ch. 8.

[16] Castañeda, *op. cit.*, p. 756.

[17] Tannebaum, *op. cit.*, pp. 130–31; Mecham, *op. cit.*, pp. 456–60.

[18] Mecham, *op. cit.*, pp. 460–62.

[19] Mecham, *op. cit.*, pp. 462–67.

[20] On the constitutional convention, see E. V. Niemeyer, Jr., "Anticlericalism in the Mexican Constitutional Convention of 1916–1917," *Americas*, July 1954, pp. 31–49; Mecham, *op. cit.*, pp. 467–74.

[21] Mecham, *op. cit.*, pp. 478–87; Franklin S. González, "Church-State Controversy in Mexico Since 1929" (M.A. thesis, University of California at Los Angeles, 1948), pp. 12–21.

[22] Mecham, *op. cit.*, pp. 487–92; González, *op. cit.*, pp. 12–21; Gruening, *op. cit.*, pp. 275–88.

[23] Mecham, *op. cit.*, pp. 493–98; Emilio Portes Gil, *Quince Años de Política* (1941), pp. 297–318; Alfonso Toro, *La Iglesia y el Estado en México* (1927), pp. 399–484 (documents); Alphonse Lugan, "Church and State in Mexico," *Current History*, February 1931, pp. 672–76.

[24] Richard Pattee, *The Catholic Revival in Mexico* (1944), p. 21.

[25] Mecham, "An Appraisal of the Revolution in Mexico," in A. C. Wilgus, ed., *The Caribbean at Mid-Century* (1951), p. 185. See also González, *op. cit.*, Chs. 2–3.

[26] Mecham, *Church and State in Latin America*, pp. 499–501; *Commonweal*,

March 2, 1932, pp. 483–86; Portes Gil, *op. cit.*, pp. 481–93. Earle James, "Church and State in Mexico," *Foreign Policy Reports*, July 3, 1935, pp. 110–11.
[27] Charles Macfarland, *Chaos in Mexico* (1935), pp. 70–71; *New Republic*, March 13, 1935, pp. 123–25.
[28] Wilfrid Parsons, *Mexican Martyrdom* (1936), pp. 119–22, 138–40.
[29] González, *op. cit.*, Chs. 3–4; Mecham, "An Appraisal . . . ," p. 186.
[30] Macfarland, *op. cit.*, pp. 158–59; Parsons, *op. cit.*, pp. 264–66; Mecham, "Church vs. State in Mexico," *Southwest Rev.*, April 1938, p. 289.
[31] Mecham, "*An Appraisal* . . . ," p. 187; Tannenbaum, *op. cit.*, p. 135.
[32] Weyl, *op. cit.*, p. 168; Frank L. Kluckhohn, *The Mexican Challenge* (1939), pp. 270, 276; Castañeda, *op. cit.*, pp. 759–60.
[33] *America*, February 20, 1954, p. 525.
[34] *America*, December 14, 1940, p. 255.
[35] Kirk, *op. cit.*, pp. 124–26, 138.
[36] Pattee, *op. cit.*, pp. 15–17, 56–57. See also M. S. Bates, *Religious Liberty: An Inquiry* (1945), pp. 69–73.
[37] Pattee, *op. cit.*, pp. 21–22, 28–30; *Catholic World*, April 1952, p. 32; González, *op. cit.*, Ch. 5.
[38] *Christian Century* (hereafter cited as *Chris. Cent.*), June 21, 1950, p. 766.
[39] *Ibid.*, November 23, 1955, p. 1374.
[40] *Commonweal*, October 31, 1947, p. 63.
[41] *Chris. Cent.*, January 7, 1953, p. 27 and November 23, 1955, p. 1374; *Time*, May 9, 1955, p. 57; New York *Times*, February 20, 1952.
[42] *Chris. Cent.*, January 7, 1953, p. 27 and November 17, 1954, p. 1410. The late prelate's obituaries discuss his success as a moderate and able leader; *HA*, February 13, 1956, p. 11; New York *Times*, February 10, 1956.
[43] Castañeda, *op. cit.*, p. 760. See also New York *Times*, October 5, 1954.
[44] *Amer. Eccles. Rev.*, December 1947, pp. 427–28.
[45] Castañeda, *op. cit.*, p. 761. Also *Time*, May 9, 1955, p. 56.
[46] *Chris. Cent.*, July 29, 1953, p. 874.
[47] *Commonweal*, October 31, 1947, p. 64. See also *Amer. Eccles. Rev.*, December 1947, pp. 426–27.
[48] *America*, June 3, 1950, p. 267; *Time*, May 9, 1955, p. 56.
[49] *Hispanic American Report* (hereafter cited as *HAR*), March (April) 1953, p. 10.
[50] Whetten, *op. cit.*, p. 470; G. M. Foster, *Empire's Children*, quoted in Paul Blanshard, *American Freedom and Catholic Power* (1950), pp. 283–84.
[51] Castañeda, *op. cit.*, p. 768.
[52] *Catholic World*, April 1952, pp. 30–36.
[53] Whetten, *op. cit.*, pp. 470, 481–82.
[54] Gruening, *op. cit.*, p. 216.
[55] Germán, Arciniegas, *The State of Latin America* (1952), p. 326.
[56] *HAR*, January (February) 1953, pp. 11–12.
[57] Castañeda, *op. cit.*, pp. 756–59, 770–73.
[58] Gruening, *op. cit.*, pp. 221–22, 341. See also Marjorie Clark, *Organized Labor in Mexico* (1934), pp. 86–96; Joaquín Márquez Montiel, *La Iglesia y el Estado en México* (1950), pp. 26–31.
[59] *Amer. Eccles. Rev.*, December 1947, pp. 429–32.
[60] Erna Fergusson, *Mexico Revisited* (1955), p. 317; *Catholic Encyclopedia Supplement*.
[61] Partido de Acción Nacional, *Plataforma*; Ralph Eisenberg, "Presidential Election in Mexico: 1952" (M.A. thesis, University of Illinois, 1953), pp. 73–74; Cline, *op. cit.*, pp. 320, 329.
[62] Whetten, *op. cit.*, pp. 481–82.

# BACKGROUND

[63] William S. Stokes, "Catholicism and Democracy in Latin America," in Angel del Rio, ed., *Responsible Freedom in the Americas* (1955), pp. 361–65, 376.

[64] *Chris. Cent.*, September 2, 1953, p. 998 and February 3, 1954, p. 156. However, one recent historical sketch of Mexican Protestantism listed 76 acts of violence against Protestants from 1944 to 1951 (*HA*, February 8, 1952, pp. 49–53). The same journal reported a much larger number of such occurrences in the three years before 1946 (*HA*, August 9, 1946, pp. 6–7).

[65] Arciniegas, *op. cit.*, p. 325.

[66] Mecham, "An Appraisal . . . ," p. 180.

[67] Carleton Beals, *Mexican Maze* (1931), Ch. 18.

[68] Whetten, *op. cit.*, pp. 471–72; Constitution, Arts. 3, 5, 13, 27, 130.

[69] Granting the impropriety of the state's limiting the number of priests, the actual number functioning does not compare unfavorably with the other large Latin American countries. The ratio of priests to population is only a little more favorable to the Church in Argentina and much less favorable in Brazil — both of them countries where Church-State relations have usually been much smoother than in Mexico. (McSorley, *op. cit.*, p. 954.)

[70] Manuel Andrade, ed., *Constitución Política Mexicana . . . Anotadas y Concordadas . . .*, pp. 397–404.

[71] *Nueva Ley General de Bienes Nacionales* (hereafter referred to as *Nueva Ley*), in Andrade, *op. cit.*, p. 223.

[72] Secretaría de Bienes Nacionales, *Directorio del Gobierno Federal: Poderes Legislativo, Ejecutivo y Judicial* (1951) (hereafter referred to as Sría. de Bienes Nacionales, *Directorio . . .* (1)), p. 73.

[73] *Ibid.*; Sría. de Gobernación, *Informe . . .* (1948–49), pp. 12–13; *Nueva Ley*, Art. 33; Virginia Stullken, "Keystone of Mexican Government: Secretaría de Gobernación" (M.A. thesis, University of Texas, 1955), pp. 40–41, 82.

[74] *Chris. Cent.*, April 11, 1951, p. 472 and September 2, 1953, p. 998.

[75] *Ibid.*

[76] *HA*, May 26, 1950, p. ii.

# 4

## Parties and Politics

IN MEXICO, the land of contrasts, it is significant that the two most important forces in public life are nonofficial organizations — the Church and the "official" political party.* In the last chapter we saw what an important role the Church has played in Mexican history. The Church's frequent adversary, the government, has sometimes appeared hard to distinguish from the official political party, the machinery which puts the government in power and keeps it there. Mexican *government* has been, to a considerable degree, *party politics*. Therefore, Mexican government can be understood only after the role of the party has been examined.

*History.* During the first half-century of independence, Mexico's history was marked by the struggles of two main groups or parties, the Centralists and the Federalists. The Centralists were conservatives, representing the professional soldiers, the Church, large landowners, and wealth and power inherited from colonial days. The Federalists were liberals, representing the middle class, merchants, and anticlericals.

The liberals were behind the Reform Laws and the anticlerical regime of Benito Juárez of the mid-nineteenth century. Out of this period of liberal rule came the increasingly conservative Díaz dictatorship. Permanent political parties in the current sense of the term hardly existed until after 1900.

Soon after 1900, a few clubs were formed to voice mild protest against some aspects of the Díaz rule. After 1908, a few groups arose, like Madero's Liberal Opposition Party and the Constitutional Progres-

* The terms "Party" and "official party" refer to the present predominant political party — the Party of the Institutional Revolution (PRI) — and its predecessors, which have controlled the federal government for nearly three decades.

sive Party — none of them allowed by the Díaz dictatorship to become strong, well-knit parties in the modern sense of the term. Even the overturn of Díaz and its aftermath didn't produce such results. The next decade was a period of chaos, when party labels meant little and personalistic leadership held sway, usually based on armies.

Change came slowly in the 1920s. The Constitutional Liberal Party and the Mexican Labor Party were established to elect President Obregón, but no strong party survived his four-year personal rule. Calles's presidency (1924–28) was supported by shifting coalitions of labor leaders, agrarians, militarists, and others.[1]

The death of President-elect Obregón in 1928 led to a crucial step — the decision by strong-man Calles to perpetuate his control from behind the scenes and stabilize the machinery of political control. He sought to do this by binding the regional and state political machines and the major interest groups into a permanent official party, the National Revolutionary Party (PNR). Local clubs were formed; men from all walks of life saw the advantages of belonging to the official party which controlled the government; interest-group support was consolidated; and, with changes of name, the Party has held control of the government to date. Some thought the Party could minimize the need for charismatic qualities in the president, permit the choice of better administrators, and institutionalize the power and authority of the presidential office. An important achievement was the change of the basis of power from regionally based political-military chieftains to regular state party units and the main organized groups — labor, agrarian, and military. But until 1935 strong-man Calles held the substantial balance of control over these constituent elements of the Party, and, through it, the government.[2]

The unified Party included widely varying shades of opinion, excluding the Communists. After 1930, the Party's work was financed largely through deductions from government employees' salaries, part of which provided a substantial social-service program for public employees. As Calles became more conservative, tensions developed within the Party through increasing agrarian and labor demands for further reforms. The Party's 1933 convention showed dissension on several points; but it agreed sufficiently to produce a platform (the first Six-Year Plan) that included self-criticism of some past efforts and a broad-gauged program for the coming years. Apparently with some reluctance, Calles gave approval to the presidential nomination of Cárdenas, a loyal supporter of Calles thus far. The campaign set new marks in the intensity of activity by the candidate and the party leaders.[3]

If the first six years of the Party's life could be characterized by the word "personalism," the period from 1935 to the early forties could be called the period of "collectivism." Cárdenas, unlike puppet predecessors, was both president and the true head of the Party — a status likewise held by his successors. Moving steadily, but cautiously at first, he ensured the support of the army before he met the challenge thrown down by party boss Calles. The President then exiled Calles, replaced Calles's henchmen in government and Party offices, and proceeded to promote his advanced labor and agrarian program. One of his first moves was to begin an intensified program of organizing the peasants into national, state, and local groups to serve as one of the Party's bulwarks.[4]

Midway through the Cárdenas presidency (in 1938), the Party made certain changes and took a new name. The National Revolutionary Party (PNR) became the Party of the Mexican Revolution (PRM), and the organization was given a broader base. Theretofore, Party membership was effected through membership in constituent organizations of the military, agrarian, or labor sectors. Now a "popular" sector was added, in which membership was on an individual basis and open to all citizens not qualified for any of the other three sectors. In recent years this group has become the most influential within the Party. Army members were later encouraged to enter the popular sector, and about 150,000 federal civil servants and thousands of members of cooperative organizations were added to this group. In these ways, Cárdenas had first sought to build up the strength of the agrarian and labor sectors; then he sought a balance among all elements in the Party.[5]

In the absence of established procedures for promoting presidential aspirants, during 1938 and 1939 Cárdenas received suggestions on candidates from most major groups; and apparently the final decision was his. Prior to the official endorsement of the Party convention, an informal promotional group — the National Directive Committeee — set to work promoting Ávila Camacho's candidacy. According to the Mexican pattern, the convention approved the presidential candidate previously endorsed by its various sectors, and adopted its platform —

the second Six-Year Plan. The campaign was bitter and accompanied by some violence, with Almazan, a wealthy and popular revolutionary general, the chief opponent. He was supported by the National Action Party (PAN), a newly organized conservative party whose strength has grown slowly but steadily since that time. Both men were middle-of-the-road candidates; and, despite widespread claims of election frauds, probably a majority of the votes were cast for Ávila Camacho. Cárdenas, who had tossed out the cabinet named for him by Calles, provided the formula for the new president's official family. Suggestions were made by Party leaders, businessmen, and others; but the decision was to be made by the President himself.[6]

To quite an extent, "politics" was adjourned in wartime Mexico as in the United States. Former presidents gave public endorsement to the regime, and Cárdenas served as Minister of Defense. There were two Party developments of importance during the early part of the new regime. The military sector was eliminated, with encouragement to its former members to enter the popular sector. The latter, in turn, was strengthened and institutionalized by the establishment of a national organization — the National Confederation of Popular Organizations (CNOP) — discussed below (see pages 56–58). Separate subdivisions were provided for small merchants, small industrialists, small farmers, women's groups, youth groups, professionals and intellectuals, and others.[7]

The "collectivist" era of the Party certainly ended no later than the early part of the Ávila Camacho regime; and what one author calls the present era of "institutionalism" began about 1942 or 1943. Cárdenas's skill as a politician had won him and the Party greater power and public support than any of his predecessors had enjoyed. Then came the war era and the time of consolidation and conservatism. Being a comparative newcomer politically, Ávila Camacho was in need of the increasing support lent the Party by its rapidly growing popular sector, which won more seats in the Chamber of Deputies in 1943 than the labor and agrarian Sectors combined. This was in the face of increasing local support received by the conservative National Action Party (PAN) and the Popular Force Party of fanatically reactionary *Sinarquistas*.[8]

Alemán became the Party's 1946 presidential candidate in the approved manner — by choice of the incumbent president. The candidate was a civilian, the chief cabinet officer, and Ávila Camacho's 1939–40 campaign manager. Again on precedent, Alemán appointed a National Directive Committee to push his campaign before his formal nomination by the Party convention. At its convention in January 1946, the Party of the Mexican Revolution (PRM) became the Party of the Institutional Revolution (PRI), thus emphasizing its stable and increasingly conservative character. With a popular presidential candidate, election day was peaceful and the victory was unquestioned. However, PAN won four deputy seats and the Popular Force Party, one. Within the official Party, the popular sector again won the majority of the seats.[9] Stability and economic expansion were increasingly the watchwords, in contrast with the class struggles of the Cárdenas era.

The Alemán era was marked by important Party developments. The 1949 electoral law sought to purify the electoral process by providing for an electoral vigilance commission with opposition party representation. Intra-Party election procedures were made more flexible. However, Brandenburg, a recent American investigator, found an important element of retrogression: Alemán's numerous interferences in intra-Party contests. Increasing opposition to the President resulted from his dictating the choice of gubernatorial candidates. The absolute and relative strength of the popular sector continued to grow.[10]

The choice of the presidential candidate in 1951 seemed to bring internal Party dissensions to the fore. Alemán at first let it be said that he favored Casas Alemán, governor of the Federal District, as his successor. It is alleged that Cárdenas, Ávila Camacho, and other powerful leaders demanded that the candidate be some other man of real administrative ability and unquestioned honesty and integrity, such as Ruiz Cortines. He was the man finally announced as the President's choice.[11]

Close observers have differed on the amount of "unjustified enrichment" (graft) during Alemán's administration, as compared with that of his predecessors.[12] Whatever the degree, it seemed sufficient to cause considerable comment;* and, from the day of his inauguration, Ruiz Cortines has striven valiantly against corruption in public life.

The PRI candidate conducted the usual vigorous election campaign, receiving nearly 75 per cent of the vote cast; but the chief opposition candidates received a much larger vote than in any previous year. The

---

* One should probably guard against too broad a generalization. For example, the two top Alemán agency heads with whom the author is acquainted are widely known as men of outstanding ability and integrity.

Party's majority in the Congress remained almost as large as before. Subsequent Party developments have included increased political participation by women and increased democratic control within the Party.[13] Temporary internal rifts have been rumored (*Alemanistas* versus *Ruizcortinistas and Cardenistas*); but increased self-criticism and internal democracy would seem to preclude drastic changes.[14]

Thus, we have seen the rise of a strong official party from its roots in transitory and conflicting groups. The trend has been toward inclusion of broader population segments, increased internal popular control, and increased degrees of rational criticism and control, as will be indicated in the following sections on the organization and functioning of the PRI and its constituent sectors.[15]

## Party Structure

*National Assembly (convention).*[16] Ordinary assemblies (national conventions) of PRI are held every three years, with extra sessions held on call of the Central Executive Committee. Between 1929 and 1933, the Party rules provided for indirect representation on a territorial basis. *Municipios* elected delegates to the district convention, which in turn chose delegates to the National Assembly. A 1938 rule placed representation for all areas on a functional basis for each of the sectors. In 1946, the basis became territorial again, with 10 delegates chosen in each electoral district. Since 1950, representation has been functional through the three sectors. The number of delegates assigned to each sector is decided by the Central Executive Committee. An equal number has been assigned to each sector in each federal entity. In 1951, each sector was allotted 30 delegates for each state and 10 for each territory, or a total of 2,760 authorized delegates. Actually, more were elected and attended.

The order of business and procedure are rather similar to those of our own national party conventions. The Central Executive Committee makes its report to the Assembly, but there is little if any discussion of this report. Proposals for revision of the Party statutes also come from this Committee, not the Assembly. The proposals are considered in committees and are approved in the Assembly by acclamation. The committees are filled by sector nominations. Usually, the Assembly seems to be a formalizing organ for decisions that have been made beforehand, in the sectors, in Party committees, in formal and informal group meetings on the eve of the convention, etc. In terms of the total context of national political activity, Padgett finds the assemblies fulfilling the following functions: furthering understanding by bringing together outstanding leaders and vitalizing personal ties; providing the Party with a vehicle for producing understanding of and enthusiasm for the program, within the limits of carefully guided proceedings; and dramatizing Party solidarity, strength, and legal and moral correctness. The last has been done, for example, by seating on the platform the current and past presidents and other high officials and leaders. Much emphasis is placed on loyalty to the revolutionary heritage and fulfillment of social and economic goals.

Formal proposals (*ponencias*) are presented ahead of time by the various delegations and member organizations. These are often well publicized ahead of time, are submitted for committee discussion, and are then presented to the Central Executive Committee for its serious consideration. The *ponencia* brings credit to its authors with their own members, acquaints the whole Party with the desires and needs of the constituent parts, and shows the relationship between such fruitful ideas and the total program. The *ponencia* also gives indications of the degree of success of the total Party program and of its parts.

*The Grand Commission.*[17] This is a group of varying size. In 1946 the president of the Central Executive Committee was made president of the Grand Commission (then the National Council). The group's degree of influence has varied, but prestige of membership has been much more than actual power. It has always occupied a subordinate position, and its location in the hierarchy is between the Assembly and the Central Executive Committee. Its size has tended to be increased during the country's presidential succession period, thus providing broader sources of advice for the new administration. Conversely, at mid-term the membership has declined.

*The Central Executive Committee (CEC).*[18] This group of six to eight men has always been at the top of the Party's organizational structure and influence, often serving as arbiter of intra-Party problems and disputes. It has had broad power over Party financial and personnel matters, and its power over lower Party levels (in contrast with the United States) is great. The secretary-members in charge of important Party activities have played an important role, but the ultimate power has been located largely in the hands of the Committee's president.

47

The power of this official is probably attributable largely to his close relationship to the president of the republic. The former is in a real sense the right-hand man of the country's president. This status of confidence has usually developed through years of working his way up through the Party channels and a long-demonstrated relationship of confidence and trust with the chief executive.

The position seems to be at least as important as that of the chief cabinet officer; and it is politically sensitive. This official puts his stamp of approval on potential Party nominees for important elective offices, and their ability and reliability mean much to the success of the organization. He is often an arbiter for groups as well as areas, for normally group strength and significance in an area decide which sector will provide the Party nominee for a congressional seat in that locality. Moreover, the president of the CEC is expendable. If he loses the chief executive's confidence, he is out.

Second in rank on the CEC is the secretary general. He and his staff check on the activities of offices of the Party that are subordinate to the CEC. These offices have several hundred employees. One of the secretary general's most important links is with the Office of Legal Affairs, which in turn is a link with the presidents of the Party's Regional Committees in matters concerning the suitability of candidates.

Several secretary-members of the CEC are in charge of interest-group work of basic importance to the strength of the Party. These include the secretaries of Agrarian Action, Labor Action, Popular Action, Political Action, Feminine Action, and Youth Action. Thus, the CEC gives greater recognition to interest groups than does the national committee of a major U.S. political party.

The offices of the secretaries of Agrarian and Labor Action are the oldest of this group, dating from 1933. The first stimulated the political and economic organization of *ejidatarios* (members of the *ejidos*, cooperative farm communities), non-*ejido* peasants, and rural wage workers; intervenes on their behalf with governmental agencies when such action is needed; promotes appropriate legislation for the improvement of rural life; and stimulates the improvement of rural educational facilities. Naturally, this office works with the National Peasants Confederation.

Like the work of the secretary of Agrarian Action, the functions of the secretary of Labor Action have not changed greatly through the years. He lends support to legal measures for improvement of labor welfare; promotes the unionization of workers; promotes technical education for wage workers; and aids in achieving the labor-welfare objectives of the federal Constitution. He also promotes cooperation among labor organizations; tries to keep down interunion difficulties; and, above all, seeks to consolidate labor support for the Party through encouraging the rise of "reliable" men to union leadership posts. Whereas the secretary of Agrarian Action deals with one unified agrarian organization, Labor Action has to deal with several labor confederations. This sensitive job has been held in recent years by the head of the largest labor confederation, the Mexican Workers Confederation (CTM).

The post of secretary of Popular Action was established in 1938 to deal with the interests of the numerous and important groups outside the labor and agrarian sectors. These groups include professional people, small industrialists, small farmers, artisans, students, and civil servants. The farmers, industrialists, and merchants have been popular sector interests for some time, while the specific efforts in behalf of professionals and civil servants have been more recent. Concern with special programs of broad public concern has been placed here. Examples are matters of health, housing, and inflation. Liaison with the National Confederation of Popular Organizations (CNOP) is effected by having the Popular Action secretary and his deputies sit on the Central Committee of the CNOP.

The Political Action secretaries (a senator and a deputy) were first provided for in 1946. Obviously, their clientele is quite different from the preceding action secretaries. They serve as liaison between the CEC and their respective houses and coordinate Congress-Party plans and actions. Even though there is a predominance of President and Party in Mexican legislation, the executive and the Party have found it desirable to achieve the maximum feasible consensus; hence the value of such liaison.

Two other national Party administrative offices are of growing importance — those of Feminine Action and Youth Action. The Feminine Action Division is of growing importance because of the recent grant of woman suffrage in national elections; this office goes beyond the confines of strictly Party work to promote campaigns to raise the level of women's civic life. The active leaders, chiefly professional women, have come largely from the popular sector. The Youth Action Division has put increasing emphasis on work with young people, especially university students.

Studies and public discussions are promoted by the Institute of Political, Economic, and Social Studies. A related function is performed by the publicity division, which handles press work, publishes books and pamphlets, and issues the magazine *La República*.

*The Regional Executive Committee (CER).*[19] The topmost Party organ in each state and territory and the Federal District is the CER. In size, role, and personnel, it is similar to the national Central Executive Committee (CEC). Since 1946, the CEC has issued the calls (*convocatorias*) for the presidents of the Party's municipal committees of the state to assemble. This assembly elects the president and the secretary general of the Regional Executive Committee (CER). The sector organizations name their representatives on the Committee. The member who is Political Action secretary is chosen by the Party members in the state legislature. The CER appoints a Youth Action secretary and a Feminine Action secretary; meets as often as once a week; conciliates differences arising between leaders and groups; promotes the program of the national Party organization; and keeps its superior, the CEC, informed of state developments.

The Federal District has a CER as the states do. The nineteen federal deputy electoral districts have district committees and subcommittees, comparable to the municipal committees and subcommittees within a state. Since the Federal District is the most populous entity, its Regional Committee is quite important.

The Regional Committee's president holds an important Party office. While he is responsible to the CEC, he is an important member of the state governor's team; and he is usually the governor's choice. In essence, the president chooses the Committee's appointive personnel. He usually follows the governor's desires in promoting the nomination and election of state legislators and municipal officials; and the CEC normally allows them much leeway in such matters. As discussed elsewhere (see pp. 79–80), the governor is removed by the federal authorities only for great abuse of power or clear unreliability.

In recent years there has been a trend toward broadening the CER's scope of activities. In 1953, the first of a projected series of annual meetings of CER presidents urged their groups to emphasize such improvements as reforestation, combating increases in the cost of living, promoting the political competence of youth and women, combating illiteracy, and strengthening local government. This action seems to reflect a feeling that the Party's success will depend in considerable measure on its ability to improve the material welfare of the under-privileged. It may also reflect Ruiz Cortines's known interest in in-creasing both Party democracy and local self-government.

*The Municipal Committee.*[20] The building block of the Party struc-ture is the Municipal Committee, consisting of five members named by the CEC on proposal of the Regional Executive Committee. Normally, one member is a woman and each sector organized locally is repre-sented. They choose their own president, secretary-treasurer, and secre-taries of Organization, Propaganda and Civic Education, and Social Action.

The Social Action secretary serves as liaison with the local Board of Moral, Civic, and Material Improvement, a quasi-public citizen group to be described in Chapter 23. The Propaganda and Civic Edu-cation secretary promotes education, participation in cultural affairs, and women's participation in Party and civic affairs.

The more general functions of the Municipal Committee as a whole include reporting monthly to the Regional Executive Committee, ad-vising the latter on local Party and municipal elections, maintaining lists of members, and carrying out the Party program.

Some larger municipalities have subcommittees, which represent the federal election areas. These groups are proposed by the Municipal Committee and approved by the Regional Executive Committee. In the best-organized urban districts they are aided by ward and block leaders, who are charged with getting out the vote at election time.

The Party is also aided much locally by the community's agrarian and labor committees — where such groups are organized.

In the larger municipalities the local Party organization often has considerable influence. However, despite the importance of munic-ipal affairs, municipal committees exist in probably not more than two thirds of the municipalities; and in many of these, activity is found mainly around election time, which means they are losing important opportunities to expand the Party's influence through promoting pro-grams of economic and social betterment. The appeal of municipal af-fairs is *potentially* substantial because of the average Mexican's strong love for his local community, in contrast to the dim view he often holds of the larger community of state and nation. Such development of Party support would hasten the much-desired demise of the *cacique* (local boss), who still thrives in some communities through a combination of force, guile, public ignorance, and appeal to local pride against "outside" politicians and their "interference."

The mayor (municipal president) is the titular leader, and often the actual leader, locally. Where his influence is actual, candidates for other offices seek his blessing before the intra-Party election is held.

The maximum regular personnel working for the municipal committees and subcommittees is estimated by Brandenburg at about 6,500, with some 700 at the regional level and 400 at the national level. Civil servants' financial contributions on the national level provide an important source of income for the Party on that level, while state government employees afford their level of the Party important support. The local Party organizations, however, have few paid local government employees to depend upon, and other sources of Party funds are very limited. Success in developing direct individual Party memberships has been small outside the Federal District.

*The sector organizations in general.*[21] To a large extent the strength of the Party, in contrast with major U.S. parties, lies in the support of its directly affiliated sector organizations — agrarian, labor, and popular. This is true because the large confederations of economic interest groups have catered to the felt needs of the "little man" in agriculture, industry, public service, etc. Their horizontal and vertical organization pattern somewhat resembles that of the Party; and such a pattern has facilitated contacts of the sector groups with Party and government officials. Thus, these organizations have served as a means for rank-and-file participation in some significant decision-making, as proving grounds for potential leaders, and as channels of political action for important segments of Mexican society. One of the important virtues of the sector-Party arrangement is that it has replaced the control of government and political life by the regional military-political chieftains who played an important role until the Cárdenas era.

*Agrarian sector.*[22] In large measure, the driving force behind the Revolution in 1910 was the half-articulate demand of the rural people for land reform. Madero moved too slowly; Huerta made no real advance; and Carranza's moderate measures were not proclaimed until

1915. Progress was slow until the strong declarations of the 1917 Constitution; but these were little more than ideals for several years, despite the pressure from Zapata's forces, the first thoroughgoing fighters for real agrarian reform.

The slowness of results led to the forming of the National Agrarian Party in 1920. Obregón supported it, and vice versa; and the two were victorious in the 1920 election. However, Obregón and his successor refused to effect large-scale expropriations and extensive land distribution; dissensions arose, the party declined, and in the late twenties various agrarian leagues came to the fore.

One of the first leagues was started in Veracruz in 1923, supporting the revolutionary program of Zapata. In 1926, fifteen state leagues established the National Peasant League. In 1929 this League worked briefly with Communist groups against the Calles regime, which it considered reactionary. In 1930, it was again giving its support to the official Party; but for various reasons disintegration set in.

In anticipation of the 1933 nominating convention of the official Party, delegates from several state agrarian leagues formed the Mexican Peasant Confederation. The peasants were also organized in competing groups, and there was substantial dissension within the groups. However, Portes Gil feels that the result of this organized activity was a factor influencing boss Calles to support Cárdenas for the presidency.

For probably the first time, a Mexican president did more than was expected. Cárdenas carried through the country's most extensive land reform program, and he vigorously promoted the organization of the peasantry. He felt that the Party and the *ejido* farmers needed each other; and he thought that an organized peasantry would be needed to protect its gains under any possible future swing of the government toward conservatism.

The National Executive Committee of the Party was charged with organizing the *ejidos* for political action within the Party. In the interest of homogeneity and unity of purpose, small independent farmers and laborers were not included. First, local associations were organized; then state leagues were established in a half-dozen states during 1935. With opposition from local *caudillos* (leaders), it was 1938 before the rest of the states were organized and the National Peasant Confederation was established. Problems also arose over the jurisdiction of peasant organization versus labor organization, since some peasants had already been organized by labor unions. But Cárdenas was firmly behind peasant autonomy.

The National Peasant Confederation (CNC) was established in 1938 and given legal standing, in contrast with earlier groups. There are four levels within the organization. The basic unit is the *ejido*, which operates through two committees — a Commissariat and a Vigilance Committee. These are provided for both by federal law and the CNC statutes. The Commissariat is the executive body of the *ejido*, as well as the legal representative of the government. The Vigilance Committee keeps an eye on the Commissariat. Both groups are elected for two-year terms by the *ejido* members.

Every three years, two Commissariat members from each *ejido* in a given area meet to choose a five-member Regional Peasant Committee. There are over five hundred such committees in the country. These committees, in turn, meet every three years to choose a state League of Agrarian Communities and Peasant Unions. Like the Regional Peasant Committee, the League consists of a secretary general, a treasurer, a Youth Action director, a Feminine Action director, and a secretary of organization. The secretary general is the chief directing official of the group.

The real power of the CNC lies in its National Executive Committee — fourteen members chosen at the national convention, which, in turn, consists of the members of the thirty-two state Leagues of Agrarian Communities and Peasant Unions. It has been estimated that over 90 per cent of the million and a half *ejidatarios* belong to the CNC. The organization is supported by nominal individual membership dues plus some aid from the federal and state governments, as in the case of the Party itself.

Party liaison with the CNC is maintained through the former's secretary of Agrarian Action. On the different levels, the Party officials have important influence in CNC affairs, and CNC officials have influence in the Party. Likewise, in areas where the CNC is stronger than the other sectors, the CNC normally has a large or predominant say in Party nominations for government offices. In 1943, the agrarian sector elected 46 of the 147 federal deputies; in 1952, 36 of 161. This decline is relative to the increased strength of the popular sector, since there has been absolute growth in the CNC.

*Labor sector.*[23] Labor organization came late to industrially backward Mexico, and few permanent significant unions appeared before 1900. Madero was not unfriendly to labor, but unions played no prominent role until a pro-anarchist group (the *Casa del Obrero Mundial*) aided Carranza's army to re-establish peace. In 1918, capitalizing on the advanced labor philosophy embodied in the 1917 Constitution, the Regional Confederation of Mexican Workers (CROM) was organized as the first really national federation of craft unions. In 1919, Luis Morones and other CROM leaders established the Mexican Labor Party to elect Obregón president. The government-labor entente throve until Calles turned against labor in the mid-twenties; and in 1929–30 Portes Gil largely ended the power of what had become a corrupt CROM labor dictatorship under Morones.

In 1935, the interregnum of labor stagnation was ended. Numerous unions united to support Cárdenas in his showdown with Calles. Cárdenas, in return, aided labor to develop its powerful Mexican Confederation of Labor (CTM). For several years, Mexico's best-known leftist, Vicente Lombardo Toledano, headed the CTM; but since 1940 more moderate leadership has been in control. Likewise, since the strong prolabor Cárdenas era, organized labor has played a lesser — but still very important — role as one of the three functional sectors in the Party. In fact, even under Cárdenas, sector was balanced against sector in preventing any such overweening labor power in government as many people have assumed.

Organized labor chooses its representatives on the Party committees at all levels. On the national level and in most other cases, these representatives are from the CTM, since it is the largest labor organization. Some twenty national industrial unions comprise the CTM, with a National Executive Committee at the head. Subordinate are the federations of the state, region, and municipality. Maximum political participation is facilitated by the fact that CTM-geographical lines in general approximate Party electoral-geographical lines. Padgett finds there is considerable lethargy in the rank and file, and that the ranks have exerted only limited (but at times crucial) influence.

Rough approximations of union membership are as follows: CTM, a million plus; Civil Service Workers Union (a popular sector group), 250,000; Railway Workers Union, 100,000; Revolutionary Confederation of Workers and Peasants, 85,000; Miners' and Steel Workers' Union, 80,000; Regional Confederation of Mexican Labor (CROM),

35,000; and several other smaller groups. The total strength, aside from the civil servants, is over a million and a half.

The labor sector had thirty-five deputies in the Congress of 1952–55, of which nineteen were CTM men. Labor held only five seats in the Senate. This underrepresentation of the CTM within the labor group may be due in part to the effort made by the Party and the CTM to prevent labor jurisdictional disputes and to lessen the chance of the smaller groups being attracted by opposition parties.

The agrarian and labor sectors have shown a modest absolute growth in recent years; but their relative influence has declined somewhat, due to the rapid growth of the popular sector.

*Popular sector.*[24] The term "popular sector" refers to no specific class or group (such as the middle class). Rather, it was simply a convenient name to apply to the varied groups of potential Party supporters that could not be included in the agrarian, labor, or military sectors when Cárdenas was consolidating the Party. After the 1937 congressional elections showed the potential of such support, Cárdenas brought about the establishment of this sector, which was to serve in part as a balance against the other sectors. To prevent monopoly by the lawyers, Cárdenas gave great strength to the new group by bringing the federal civil servants' unions and the co-op organizations into its fold. The new sector differs from the others, in which membership was by groups, in that individuals could join its ranks. What Cárdenas did for the workers and agrarians, Ávila Camacho did for the populars. He added small farmers and the military officers (dropped as a separate sector), and in 1943 he encouraged the establishment of the powerful National Confederation of Popular Organizations (CNOP) to consolidate the strength of the disparate groups — small industrialists, small farmers, small merchants, artisans, cooperatives, youth, women. A hallmark of the sector's significance is the fact that it has won a majority of the seats in the Chamber of Deputies since 1943 and it spearheaded the nomination and election of both Alemán and Ruiz Cortines. While the other two sectors are first economic organizations, the popular sector is more definitely political.

The basic popular unit is the municipal union of people in the same field of work. Five or more municipal unions comprise a municipal league. The leagues, in turn, comprise a state federation. The Municipal League Committee consists of six members elected for three-year terms by the constituent unions. These officers consist of a secretary general and secretaries of economic and agricultural matters, Social Action, Feminine Action, Youth Action, and Organization. This group names the local-government candidates for offices which the Party awards the popular sector. The strongest Municipal League Committees are in the chief urban areas. Due to local conditions, these committees are still not found in the majority of communities.

The state machinery consists of a Federation of Popular Organizations, plus a ten-member Regional Council (representing the ten-member interest groups, called branches) and a seven-member Federation Committee (with offices similar to those of the Municipal League Committee). The latter holds the real power of the organization on the state level. A Regional Assembly, meeting triennially, adopts programs and elects members to the Council and the Committee.

The national machinery consists of a National Assembly, a National Council, a Consultative Technical Council, and a National Executive Committee. The National Assembly, meeting at six-year intervals, approves a program of action and chooses the members of the National Executive Committee and the Consultative Technical Council. The top legislative organ is really the National Council, which is the supreme body between the sexennial Assembly meetings. The Consultative Technical Council consists of two members from each of the ten functional branches; and it is chiefly concerned with problems affecting those branches. The National Executive Committee of twelve members is the top administrative organ of the CNOP. Its chief figure is the secretary general, and its membership includes functional and interest-group secretaries like those found on the lower levels of the CNOP.

The basis of the strength of the CNOP lies largely in its chief constituent organizations, with organizational memberships totaling well over a million. The three largest are the federal civil service unions and the National Cooperative Confederation (each with about 250,000 members) and the National Confederation of Small Agricultural Proprietors. The latter claims some 750,000 members, but at least half are said to be also either *ejidatarios* or large farmers.

Much smaller are the organizations of the artisans, the small merchants, the small industrialists, and the professionals-intellectuals. The some 75,000 artisans consist of workmen not fitting into any other category. In the National Confederation of Intellectual Workers, the lawyers are probably the most active of the some 25,000 members grouped in nineteen occupational classes. A large proportion of the prominent intellectuals are or have been prominent supporters of the Party.

The youth and feminine branches are the nonoccupational groups. The first comprises mainly college students. The feminine branch has been increasingly active in recent years and played a prominent role in the instituting of woman suffrage. Professionals and intellectuals have played the principal role thus far.

In terms of electoral victories, the popular sector holds a wide margin over the agrarian and labor sectors. Within the ranks of the populars, the civil servants have probably been most successful in terms of material gains. All in all — and despite incongruities and interest conflicts within the popular sector — the main outlines of the Party's broad support are likely to remain for some time to come.

*Non-Party interest groups.*[25] The Party and its related groups are the chief elements influencing Party and government decisions and actions. However, other groups have exercised varying degrees of negative and positive influence. These groups are military, religious, intellectual-professional, landowning, foreign investment, and big business and industrial elements.

The religious influence was discussed in the previous chapter. The military as a group still has importance, but much less than formerly. The bulk of the prominent intellectual leaders are within the Party or close to it; but there are some able and prominent intellectual leaders who are in agreement with the Party's main goals but remain aloof from it and are outspokenly and effectively critical.

The influence of foreign capital has varied significantly with the various governments, but its positive influence on Party programs and actions has been slight. Much the same might be said for the influence of the large landowners. Party programs continue avowedly agrarian in orientation, while the need for expanded food production has led the government in recent years to give some encouragement to large landowners to increase cultivated acreage and output.

Business and industrial groups are organized in economic groups under legal requirements; and the government consults with these groups regarding proposed legislative and administrative actions. Business men and firms often contribute substantially to the presidential campaign funds of the Party nominee (as well as to those of the more conservative parties), because in general such circles have been satisfied with the government's program as it touches business matters.

## Opposition Parties

The past few decades have seen many parties; but most of them have been short-lived, one-election, personal-leader oriented parties. This is a reflection of the relationship between the government and an official Party with its functionally organized power groups. The official Party's "revolutionary" tradition has also caused most of the opposition parties to be conservative. While the official Party seems firmly entrenched, there has been a noticeable increase in recent years in the fraction of the vote going to opposition party presidential candidates – about 7 per cent in 1940, 21 per cent in 1946, and 26 per cent in 1952. Of current and recent importance, certainly most worthy of mention, are the National Action Party (PAN), the Popular Party (PP), and the Communist Party (PC). More fleeting – but of recent significance – were the Federation of Parties of the Mexican People (FPPM) and the Sinarchists' Popular Force Party. All have a party machinery in general resembling that of the PRI.

*National Action Party (PAN).*[26] PAN is clearly the strongest among the permanent opposition parties. It is middle- and upper-class, conservative, and Church-oriented, with a minority inclined toward the position of the Sinarchists (discussed below pp. 61–62). Its leaders are largely business and professional men.

Since the Church hierarchy was opposed to having a Church party as such, PAN was established in 1939 by Manuel Gómez Morín, a prominent lawyer, and a group of young business and professional men. From the start, the party entered local, state, and federal elections; but it did not launch a presidential candidate until 1952.

In its early years, the party leaders were charged with being friendly to Franco and the program of *Hispanidad* * and with being opposed to "individualist democracy and the parliamentary system"; a writer for the Catholic journal *Commonweal* found the PAN's comments sometimes "hysterically anti-United States."

As a conservative, Church-oriented, largely middle-class party, PAN's increased support may be accounted for in part by increases in urbani-

* Passionate attachment to things Spanish.

zation, industrialization, and the middle classes. However, many Mexican intellectuals probably agree with the leading economist-historian Cosío Villegas that in part PAN's success is due to shortcomings of the program of the official Party and governmental regimes. Since 1946, PAN has usually had four or five members in the Chamber of Deputies, while claiming the actual election and non-seating of many more.

A principal plank in PAN's program has been the changing of Article 3 of the Constitution, which seeks to exclude religion from all elementary and secondary schools. The 1952 platform also, in addition to many broad goals similar to those of the PRI, urged less government participation in and control over the economy, denationalization of the *ejidos*, less centralized governmental power, strengthening of state and local governments, an independent Congress and judiciary, restrictions on union activities in elections, and exposure of alleged corruption in ruling circles.

Some 4,000 delegates attended the PAN national convention of 1951, according to press reports. Of these, half were said to represent farmers; 15 per cent, labor; 25 per cent, industry and business; and 10 per cent, students. During and since the 1952 campaign, PAN has received support from the National Sinarchist Union (UNS), discussed below. Needless to say, PAN's legislative proposals have not been adopted.

*Popular Party (PP).*[27] While PAN is conservative and the Popular Party is leftist, they agree in criticizing alleged corruption and lack of democracy in the PRI and the government, and they call for purified elections, increased respect for law, and strengthened local self-government. The PP calls for improved educational and social security services and extension of agrarian reform.

The PP was established in 1948 under the leadership of Vicente Lombardo Toledano and others who broke with Alemán and the PRI, unlike the leaders of PAN who were never important members of the official party. Lombardo Toledano, a former prominent union leader and university professor, is most generally regarded as a fellow-traveler for his own purposes, but not an actual Communist Party member. He received the support of the Communist Party in the 1952 election, but seems to have broken with them since then on tactical matters. His break with Alemán and the PRI was on the basis that the Party was corrupt and had sold out the Revolution. As the PAN extremists shade into Sinarchism, so the PP extreme shades into Communism.

The PP has claimed as many as 90,000, and in recent years it has had one deputy in the Congress. While PAN polled 178,952 votes in 1949 and 285,555 in 1952, the PP polled 38,712 and 72,482 in those years — or a combined total of about one tenth of the votes.

*Communist Party (PC).*[28] The Communist Party has always been weak in total membership in Mexico, although during the late thirties it gained strength in a few labor groups and one or two government agencies. The party was established in 1919, but it was split into rival groups during the twenties. At one time, several unions belonged to the Communist Federation of the Mexican Proletariat. After being virtually underground from 1929 to 1935, it made more progress in the late thirties. However, it was never admitted to the official party. During the forties, the party claimed some 25,000 members; but in 1952 there were not enough members to qualify for the ballot — probably about 10,000.

*Sinarchists.*[29] Two transient opposition parties of significance (neither having legal status) were the Popular Force Party (Sinarchists) and the Federation of Parties of the Mexican People (FPPM).

Sinarchism is the ultra-conservative, highly nationalistic, deeply religious, pro-*Hispanidad*, and anti-Communist movement that threatened during the forties to take Mexico to rightist isolationism. Sinarchism's rapid growth and potentialities as an opponent of the existing regime made this distinctive Mexican peasant movement highly controversial. While the Church always disavowed any formal alignment (and in recent years criticized the movement), Sinarchism seemed to meet with considerable support among the clergy. Even able and moderate Church leaders like Pattee found it to be a worthy "expression of Mexican traditionalism, enveloped in the modern garb of social justice and agrarian reform [which] merits the attention of Americans." From the opponents come charges of out-and-out pro-Axis totalitarianism during World War II.

What is the true picture? Scholarly, on-the-spot investigators like Whetten seem to present the most accurate analysis. He finds its origins much in dispute — whether it was founded by a group of young lawyers under their own inspiration in 1937 (the official version) or whether its actual inspiration came the previous year at the hands of a German professor at the University of Guanajuato.

In any case, the salient characteristics of the movement might be summarized as follows. It is a protest against certain excesses and short-comings of the Revolution. Areas of Sinarchist strength are, in general, those in which agrarian reform and rural welfare have made least progress. The movement is a strong protest against anticlerical or anti-Church legislation, including exclusion of religion from the schools. It is militantly opposed to Communism (which it has professed to see even in the Mexican government) and Anglo-American culture (which it regards as imperialistic, materialistic, and atheistic).

Making use of self-sacrifice, martyrdom, and a military-like training and discipline, the Sinarchist organization is definitely hierarchical, authoritarian, and totalitarian. Democracy is excluded from the organization and condemned on the outside, along wtih Communism and Nazism-Fascism. The call is for ending the *ejidos*, re-establishing private ownership of land, and restoring the Church's former power. The dangers in 1944 were well summarized by an investigator for the Catholic journal *Commonweal*: "If *Sinarquistas* succeed in growing considerably more in numbers, there is real danger of a bloody civil war. . . . Were they to win, we should once again have a dictatorial state adorned with Catholic symbols and forcibly repressing all opposition — until the whole kettle boils over once more, to the terrible detriment of the Church."

By the mid-forties, the organization claimed over 900,000 members and elected a member to the Congress, as well as succeeding in some local elections. The movement had split into two factions in 1944, one group eschewing politics and the other becoming the Popular Force Party. The ballot rights of the party were canceled in 1949, with the government statement that religious influence had become marked in the management of the party.

While the party is not on the ballot and the movement has been considerably weakened in recent years, much discontent may remain until substantial improvements are made in rural life. The party was reformed in 1951 under more moderate leadership.

*Federation of Parties of the Mexican People (FPPM).*[30] From 1951 to 1954 the FPPM was the second and most recent vigorous challenge to the present regime; and it also has been removed from the ballot for its political excesses. The party was formed in 1951 by dissidents from the PRI and other groups, to promote the presidential candidacy of

General Miguel Henríquez Guzmán, who had tried for the PRI nomination for the first time in 1945.

The FPPM seemed to lack a clear-cut ideology, seeking to capitalize on the discontent of various groups and appear as the true heir of the Revolution. Its platform (like those of PAN and PP) called for greater local and state self-government, agrarian reform, women's rights, and some means of coping with the rising cost of living. Henríquez's followers engaged in a violent campaign; and their total vote was a surprising 579,745. In the former Mexican tradition, Henríquez claimed victory after the election and refused to accept defeat, while his followers engaged in dark talk of revolution. Sporadic disturbances continued, culminating in February 1954 in pitched battles by his followers with the police. Promptly, the government canceled the party's registration.

*The 1952 election.*[31] The 1952 presidential election was noteworthy for being the first time that three well-organized opposition parties conducted a vigorous campaign against the incumbent regime. The PAN and the PP were important in opposition because of their age and their presentation of real issues; the FPPM, because of its fast growth and considerable support.

In traditional fashion, the support for the PRI candidate came in successive announcements. Before the Party convention, the CTM had first pledged its unions to support Ruiz Cortines. Then came pledges from other labor groups, agrarian groups, public officials, and others. The bandwagon was in motion. The first sector to pledge officially was the popular, followed soon after by the others. This is in contrast with group contests that are carried into a U.S. party convention.

In this campaign, as in the preceding one, the PRI program had points dealing with improving the lot of farmers, labor, the middle classes, and women; encouraging national economic development; and aiding youth and education, and local government.

All parties emphasized industrialization and economic progress, living costs, civil liberties, and women's rights. Two or more of the opposition parties emphasized honest elections, improved local government, and concentration of power in the executive branch. The PAN and the PP were strongly opposed on the issues of education, religion, and the government in business.

While there was some campaign violence, the election day was probably the first such event without bloodshed. All presidential candidates toured the country in person; and all parties (but especially PRI) made ample use of pamphlets, broadsides, rallies, and newspaper and magazine ads. Former presidents and other leaders made announcements of support for Ruiz Cortines, carefully timed to capitalize on the support of the personal following of each.

The 4,925,900 registered voters comprised at least 85 per cent of those eligible to register. The vote totaled 3,651,483, of which 74.3 per cent voted for the PRI candidate, 15.8 per cent for the FPPM, 7.9 per cent for the PAN, and 2 per cent for the PP. The total vote cast had risen more slowly than the population increase between 1929 and 1946. However, the total vote rose from 2,259,976 in 1946 to 3,651,483 in 1952 — representing in the later year a slightly higher percentage of the total population actually voting (about 13 per cent) than in 1946. The comparable figures for male voters in recent U.S. elections have ranged between 17 per cent and 20 per cent of the total population.

Tentative indications of a democratic trend are the increasing peacefulness of elections, the rise in the minority vote, and the conciliatory attitude of the current president. The relative calm of the last two presidential elections has been noted. The total recorded vote of minority parties, as a percentage of the total vote cast, has risen in round numbers from 7 per cent in 1940 to 21 per cent in 1946 to 25 per cent in 1952. Finally, after the 1952 elections, Ruiz Cortines made a definite effort to secure the cooperation and support of opposition groups.

*Elections.*[32] The federal government and the states have separate election laws dealing with the choice of their respective officials. The federal offices served by election are those of president, senator, and deputy. Their terms of office have varied throughout the years, at present standing at six, six, and three years, respectively, thus requiring elections at three-year intervals. The Constitution provides for direct election for all three offices, according to the terms of the electoral law.

Earlier constitutions placed restrictions on the suffrage, but the present document and its predecessor have provided for universal adult male suffrage, despite the demand of experts for a literacy requirement. The voting age is eighteen for married persons and twenty-one for the unmarried.

The demand for woman suffrage came mainly after 1918. The 1917 convention paid no great attention to the subject; but the wording of the document has led some, including some convention delegates, to claim in recent years (probably erroneously) that no discrimination was intended against woman suffrage. In 1940, the official party's second Six-Year Plan called for the national vote for women. The Alemán administration gave women the right to vote in municipal elections; and in 1954 their franchise was extended to the national level.

The federal electoral law, unlike that of the United States, deals in some detail with general elections and enjoins the parties to provide by rule for their primary elections or conventions; but the law doesn't provide machinery for governmental control of such primaries or conventions.

The basic electoral law was passed at the end of 1945 and sought to end the period of inadequate electoral control which allowed widespread perversion of the electoral process at the hands of local political bosses and others. At various times this had meant preventing opposition voters from casting their ballots, stuffing the ballot boxes, alleged perversion of the vote-counting process, and a resulting apathy of the electorate.

In addition to requiring the registration of political parties, the basic law as amended prescribes the federal electoral procedure and establishes agencies to administer the process. At the top is the Federal Electoral Commission headed by the Minister of Government and including a senator, a deputy, and three representatives from the political parties. Its functions are to divide the country into electoral districts, investigate complaints, and in general supervise the electoral process. Also at the capital is the National Registry of Voters which maintains lists of voters and election records. Each state is provided an electoral committee; and the state is divided into districts, each of which has a district electoral committee. The local (state) electoral committee consists of three members chosen by the Federal Electoral Commission. At meetings, each party may have a representative present to participate in discussion but not vote. The district electoral committee is named by the Federal Electoral Commission, on proposal of the local (state) electoral committee.

On April 30 in election years the Federal Electoral Commission and the local (state) and district electoral committees publish a notice that filings are open until May 15. Presidential candidates file with the Federal Electoral Commission, senatorial candidates with the local (state) committee, and candidates for deputy with the district committee. Before May 25, the federal government's *Diario Oficial* and two other papers publish the lists of candidates. On the first Sunday in June, the district electoral committee publishes in each municipality a preliminary notice of proposed polling places and personnel. Objections to this may be filed with the committee, which publishes the final listing on the third Sunday in June.

The election is held on the first Sunday in July, from 8 A.M. to 5 P.M., in the presence of watchers representing the parties and the candidates. Citizens, whose names have previously been entered on the list of voters, are given separate Australian-type ballots for each office to be voted on, which they are supposed to mark in private. Write-in candidates are allowed. Inebriates and armed persons are excluded. At the close of voting, the votes for deputy are counted and announced; the proceedings are attested by the election officials and the representatives of parties and candidates; and the ballots and records are sent to the district electoral committee.

On the third Sunday in July, the district electoral committee counts the votes in the presence of watchers, issues certificates of election to winners, and makes note of any claims of irregularity. The results of the vote for president and deputy are sent to the Chamber of Deputies, which verifies the vote for these officials. The votes for senator are sent to the local (state) electoral committee for counting. This group transmits the vote to the state legislature for verification. On the national level, the Federal Electoral Commission hears complaints and announces the winners. However, these electoral bodies do not have the final decision. That rests with the Congress, which announces the decisions on its own membership and officially announces the winner of the presidency.

The electoral process has been definitely improved in recent years, but there is still room for much improvement. Conditions for peaceful functioning of the polls are generally quite good, though scattered claims of intimidation are still heard. The Registry of Voters seems to work quite well, but corruption in the vote-counting is still possible. Violation of the electoral law and regulations is punishable and is under the jurisdiction of the federal courts. The Federal Electoral Commission of six member formerly had, in effect, five members for the government and one for opposition parties. Now, in effect, four of the six represent the government viewpoint and two represent opposition parties, with other minor parties allowed at sessions as observers. Thus, the government viewpoint is still in the majority on the top electoral body, as well as on the subordinate state and district bodies.

## NOTES

[1] Alberto Morales Jiménez, *Historia de la Revolución Mexicana* (1951); E. M. Braderman, "A Study of Political Parties and Politics in Mexico Since 1890" (Ph.D. thesis, University of Illinois, 1938); Felipe Celorio Celorio, *Los Partidos Políticos y el Sufragio en México, Inglaterra y Estados Unidos* (1949); Antonio Huitren Huitren, *Los Partidos Políticos* (1947); Alfonso Méndez Barraza, *Los Partidos Políticos en México* (1949); Frank R. Brandenburg, "Mexico: An Experiment in One-Party Democracy" (Ph.D. thesis, University of Pennsylvania, 1955), pp. 33–48; Robert E. Scott, "Some Aspects of Mexican Federalism" (Ph.D. thesis, University of Wisconsin, 1949), pp. 162–75; Marjorie Clark, *op. cit.*, pp. 97–131; H. B. Parkes, "Political Leadership in Mexico," *Annals of the American Academy of Political and Social Science* (hereafter cited as *Annals*), March 1940, pp. 16–17. There are only two thorough studies of the official party — Brandenburg's, cited above, and Leon V. Padgett's Ph.D. thesis, "Popular Participation in the Mexican 'One-Party' System" (Northwestern University, 1955). Both are detailed and able field studies of great usefulness to students of Mexico. Both are available on microfilm from University Microfilms, Ann Arbor, Michigan.

[2] Brandenburg, *op. cit.*, Ch. 2; Padgett, *op. cit.*, Ch. 2; Scott, *op. cit.*, pp. 162–75; Clark, *op. cit.*, pp. 132–47; Celorio, *op. cit.*, pp. 67–81; Parkes, *op. cit.*, pp. 16–17; Weyl, *op. cit.*, Ch. 4.

[3] See note 2. See also Partido Nacional Revolucionario, *Constitución del P.N.R.* (1929), *Plan Sexenal del Gobierno Mexicano* (1934); Weyl, *op. cit.*, Ch. 5; Portes Gil, *op. cit.*, pp. 461–68; Luis Cabrera, *Veinte Años Después* (1937), pp. 139–82.

[4] Brandenburg, *op. cit.*, pp. 76–85; Parkes, *op. cit.*, pp. 17–21; Cabrera, *op. cit.*, p. 203 *et seq.*; Portes Gil, *op. cit.*, pp. 497–509; Weyl, *op. cit.*, Ch. 13; Mecham, "Mexican Federalism — Fact or Fiction?" *Annals*, March 1940, pp. 34–37.

[5] Brandenburg, *op. cit.*, pp. 85–92; Parkes, *loc. cit.*; Weyl, *loc. cit.*; Mecham, *loc. cit.*; J. H. Plenn, *Mexico Marches* (1939), p. 297 *et seq.*; Hubert Herring, *History of Latin America* (1955), Ch. 24.

[6] Cline, *op. cit.*, pp. 262–65; Brandenburg, *op cit.*, pp. 92–97; Eduardo Correa, *El Balance del Cardenismo, passim*; Herring, *op. cit.*, Ch. 25.

[7] Padgett, *op. cit.*, pp. 248–54; Brandenburg, *op. cit.*, pp. 98–101.

[8] Brandenburg, *op. cit.*, pp. 98–107; Herring, *op. cit.*, Ch. 25; Correa, *El Balance del Ávila Camacho* (1947), *passim*.

[9] See note 8. See also Cline, *op. cit.*, pp. 307–12; Herbert Cerwin, *These Are the Mexicans* (1947), Ch. 23.

[10] Brandenburg, *op. cit.*, pp. 307–12; G. S. Wise, *El México de Alemán* (1952), Ch. 4.

[11] Cline, *op. cit.*, pp. 328–32; Eisenberg, *op. cit.*, pp. 46–53; Brandenburg, *op. cit.*, pp. 111–13; Bernardo Ponce, *Adolfo Ruiz Cortines, Ensayo para una Biografía Política* (1952).

[12] Cline, *op. cit.*, p. 322; Brandenburg, *op. cit.*, pp. 112–13; *HA*, July 27, 1953, p. 6.

[13] Eisenberg, *op. cit.*, pp. 53–64; Brandenburg, *op. cit.*, pp. 113–20; Cline, *op. cit.*, pp. 324–26; *Foreign Policy Bul.*, June 15, 1952; *La República* (PRI magazine).

[14] *HA*, December 5, 1955, pp. 5–6; *HAR*, July 1954, pp. 9–10.

[15] For names and data on Party leaders see: Brandenburg, *op. cit.*, Ch. 8; Padgett, *op. cit.*; PRI, *Asamblea Nacional Informe*; and various issues of *La República, El Nacional*, and *Hispanoamericano*.

[16] Partido Revolucionario Institucional (PRI), *Declaración de Principios, Programa de Acción, y Estatutos* (1953), *Asamblea Nacional Informe*; Celorio C., *op. cit.*, p. 83 *et seq.*; Brandenburg, *op. cit.*, pp. 135–36; Padgett, *op cit.*, Ch. 4; Eisenberg, *op. cit.*, pp. 46–50; PRI, *Instructivo para la Organización y Afiliación de los Miembros* . . . (1953).

[17] PRI, *Declaración*, especially pp. 28–29, 54–56; Padgett, *op. cit.*, Ch. 5; Brandenburg, *op. cit.*, pp. 136–38.

[18] PRI, *Declaración*, especially pp. 56–57, 60–70, 81–90; Brandenburg, *op. cit.*, pp. 138–46; Padgett, *op. cit.*, Ch. 6; Portes Gil, *op. cit.*, pp. 511–39. Padgett (pp. 120–24) gives a case study of the rise of a Central Executive Committee president.

[19] PRI, *Declaración*, especially pp. 69–74; Padgett, *op. cit.*, Ch. 7; Brandenburg, *op. cit.*, pp. 147–48; Padgett (pp. 151–68) gives an interesting picture of "Internal Elections at Puebla (State): A Case Study of Interaction Between Leaders and the Rank and File." He shows the constellation of forces at work which provide a significant limitation on the possible abuse of power.

[20] PRI, *Declaración*, especially pp. 75–76, and *Instructivo*; Brandenburg, *op. cit.*, pp. 148–55, 334–38, 362–66; Padgett, *op. cit.*, Ch. 8.

[21] Padgett, *op. cit.*, Ch. 9; Brandenburg, *op. cit.*, Ch. 4.

[22] Clark, *op. cit.*, pp. 153–60; Brandenburg, *op. cit.*, Ch. 4; Whetten, *op. cit.*, pp. 187–90; Cline, *op. cit.*, pp. 221–23; Padgett, *op. cit.*, Ch. 9; Portes Gil, *op. cit.*, pp. 405–9, 460–68; Cabrera, *op. cit.*, pp. 271–81; José Iturriaga, *La Estructura Social y Cultural de México* (1951), pp. 35–40; Confederación Nacional Campesina, *Declaración de Principios* . . . (1954). Padgett (pp. 207–16) gives a case study of the political process in an *ejido*.

[23] Alfonso López Aparicio, *El Movimiento Obrero en México* (1952), pp. 246–50 (labor history); Clark, *op. cit.*, Ch. 4 (labor history); Padgett, *op. cit.*, Ch. 10; Brandenburg, *op. cit.*, Ch. 5; Cline, *op. cit.*, pp. 221–23; Guadalupe Rivera Marín, *El Mercado de Trabajo* (1955), Ch. 3; Iturriaga, *op. cit.*, pp. 40–57; Mosk, *op. cit.*, Ch. 6; Padgett (Ch. 10) gives an interesting case study of the decision-making process in a union, showing the opportunity for popular participation.

[24] Brandenburg, *op. cit.*, Ch. 6; Padgett, *op. cit.*, Ch. 11; Confederación Nacional de Organizaciones Populares (CNOP), *Bases Constitutivas, Declaración de Principios y Estatutos* (1947); Rosendo Rojas Coria, *Tratado de Cooperativismo Mexicano* (1952), Pt. 2; Iturriaga, *op. cit.*, pp. 67–79. For an account of the first national women's congress, see *HA*, August 17, 1953, pp. 3–4.

[25] Brandenburg, *op. cit.*, Ch. 7; Rivera Marín, *op. cit.*, Ch. 4; Iturriaga, *op cit.*, pp. 79–89; Mosk, *op. cit.*, Ch. 2–3.

[26] Eisenberg, *op. cit.*, pp. 68–76; Cline, *op. cit.*, pp. 292–93, 320, 327, 329, 331; Manuel Gómez Marín, *Diez Años de México* (1950); Efraín González Luna, *Humanismo Político* (1955); Partido de Acción Nacional (PAN), *Estatutos* (1955), *Plataforma* (1951), *Programa Mínima* . . . (1952); Pattee. *op. cit.*, pp. 33–36; *La Nación* (weekly organ of PAN); Kirk, *op. cit.*, pp. 311–14; *HA*, June 11, 1956, p. 10.

[27] Eisenberg, *op. cit.*, pp. 76–85; Martin Ebon, *World Communism Today* (1948), pp. 299–303; Cline, *op. cit.*, pp. 321–22, 329, 331; Partido Popular, *Razón Histórica, Principios* . . . (1948); *El Popular* (daily organ).

[28] Ebon, *op. cit.*, pp. 299–303; Cline, *loc. cit.*; New York *Times*, October 17, 1954.

[29] Whetten, *op. cit.*, Ch. 20; Kirk, *op. cit.*, pp. 317–22; Cline, *op. cit.*, pp. 293–94, 318–20; L. B. Simpson, *Many Mexicos* (1952), pp. 299–303; Margaret Shedd,

"Thunder on the Right in Mexico . . . ," *Harpers*, April 1945, pp. 415–25; *HA*, February 4, 1949, pp. 3–4 and March 9, 1951, pp. 3–4; Pattee, *op. cit.*, pp. 36–43; *Commonweal*, June 9, 1944, p. 178.

[30] Eisenberg, *op. cit.*, pp. 85–89; Cline, *op. cit.*, pp. 328–31; *Time*, September 10, 1951, p. 44; *HAR*, February (March) 1954, p. 8; *HA*, March 8, 1954, pp. 5–6; Padgett, *op. cit.*, pp. 39–43.

[31] Cline, *op. cit.*, pp. 326–31; Cline, "Mexico, a Maturing Democracy," *Current History*, March 1953, p. 142; *Nation*, July 19, 1952, pp. 52–53; Eisenberg, *op. cit.*, Ch. 5–6; New York *Times*, July 7 and February 2, 1952; *HA*, May 16, pp. 4–9, and July 4, 1952, pp. 6–14.

[32] Eisenberg, *op. cit.*, Ch. 2; Padgett, *op. cit.*, Ch. 3; Clara Luna Morales, "El Sufragio Femenino en México" (thesis, Universidad Nacional Autónoma de México (hereafter cited as UNAM) (1947); María E. Manzanera Del Campo, *La Igualidad de Derecho Políticos* (thesis, UNAM, 1953); *Ley Electoral* (*Diario Oficial*, December 31, 1945); *Ley Electoral* (Sría. de Gobernación, 1951); *Decreto que Reforma . . . la Ley Electoral . . .* (*Diario Oficial*, January 7, 1954); Scott, *op. cit.*, pp. 157 *et seq.*, 234 *et seq.*; Medina and Ortiz, *op. cit.*, pp. 130–41; Cline, *U.S. and Mexico*, pp. 326–28; Whetten, *op. cit.*, pp. 556–58.

# PART II

# Organization and Structure

# 5

## The Constitutional System

THE Mexican government is said by one of its leading commentators to be a representative, democratic federal republic in which the people participate in the sovereignty only through elected officials. The Constitution is regarded as the supreme law of the land.[1] Its broad outlines are similar to those of the U.S. Constitution. Mexico regards her regime as constitutional because it operates under the detailed Constitution of 1917; as republican, since sovereignty is said to rest ultimately with the people; as representative, because popular control is indirect; as democratic, because of the role of the electorate; as federal, because of the constitutional allocation of powers to central and state governments; as presidential, because of the contrast with the parliamentary form of government and because of the concentration of power in the hands of the chief executive. Individual rights are discussed in the second part of this chapter.

Mexico belongs by tradition to the civil law system of Europe, rather than to the common law system; and her statute law is largely in the form of codes. Codes govern the Federal District and the territories, and they are widely copied in the states. The first truly Mexican Civil Code was issued in 1870, while the present basic code dates from 1932. The Penal Code and the Code of Commerce are other examples.

Most of Mexico's independent history has been under governmental regimes labeled federal, with three of her constitutions modeled more or less closely on that of the United States. Some writers feel that a limited federalism exists; but most writers agree that in practice the country has always had a centralist regime. One leading constitutional authority labels his country's federalism "precarious and fictitious."[2] Another authority says the political entities don't exist "in other than a purely formal sense" as states.[3] A general assumption about federalism is its original establishment by independent states; but the Mexican states were never independent. The country before independence was one governmental unit under a centralist regime; and the "states" were created by the Constitution of 1824, with a limited degree of self-rule.

Article 39 of the 1917 Constitution reads: "National sovereignty resides essentially and originally in the people. All public power emanates from the people and is instituted for their benefit. The people have at all times the inalienable right to alter or modify the form of their government."

Article 40 states: "It is the will of the Mexican people to constitute themselves into a representative, democratic, federal Republic composed of States that are free and sovereign in all that concerns their internal government, but united in a Federation established according to the principles of this fundamental law."

And Article 41 states: "The people exercise their sovereignty by means of the powers of the Union, in the matters pertaining thereto, and through those of the States in matters relating to their internal affairs, in the manner respectively established by the present federal Constitution and the individual ones of the States, which latter shall in no case contravene the stipulations of the federal pact."

Despite the language of Article 40, the states are not truly sovereign even in their internal or local affairs.[4] This is largely due to the constitutional grant of powers to the central government for intervention in the affairs of the states. Thus, in actual practice, the country is essentially a unitary republic, largely ruled from Mexico City. This practice has crystallized largely through the personal influence of the national executive, his control over military and administrative power, and his leadership of the dominant political party.

Federalism in Mexico has long had definite value as a symbol, as an embodiment of the desired "democracy" and "liberty." A less frequently noted fact has been the utilitarian value of "federalism" in reinforcing the existing power arrangements. Due to the realities of central power, shortcomings of state and local units in carrying out national policies can be focused on the lower levels; and thus popular dissatisfactions can be deflected downward. Conversely, the credit for success tends to be deflected upward, reinforcing the prestige of the central regime.[5]

Hierarchically, the principal legal norms are the federal Constitution, the laws and treaties issued under it, and the state constitutions and laws. The secondary norms are the executive and administrative rules and regulations and the decisions of the courts.

*Development of federalism.* Throughout the war for independence, the country adhered to the principles of centralism. The U.S. constitutional experience, in the opinion of Mecham, seems to have had limited influence on Mexican thought before 1820. In that year, the liberal Spanish Constitution was promulgated in Mexico, and its personal guarantees opened the way for much freedom of discussion. Federalist ideas were discussed rather widely. Santa Anna's revolt of 1822 produced the Plan of Veracruz, which implied that each province should assume provisional powers of government.[6]

The contest between centralists and federalists was strong in the Congress of 1823 and the Constitutional Convention of 1824. The reasons for adopting the federalist document and its separation of powers seem to have been varied. Mexican authorities differ in their estimate of the extent and depth of the delegates' understanding of the spirit and functioning of the U.S. Constitution, though the letter of the document was known.[7] The imitation of the American document is evident.

There was widespread feeling that federalism would safeguard democracy, while a unitary government would do the opposite. The liberal movement in Spain also had its influence. The local interests and leaders apparently lent their support to federalism for selfish reasons of maintaining their own autonomy.

According to the Constitution adopted in 1824, the central government was provided with a bicameral congress. The Senate was composed of an equal number of members from each state, chosen for four-year terms by state legislatures. The Chamber of Deputies had one member for each 80,000 people in the states, serving two-year terms. A three-man national executive was named by the Congress for a four-year term. The Constitution went into much detail on the government of the states and municipalities and closely circumscribed their powers. Federal justice was to be administered by a supreme court and district courts. In emergencies the Congress could confer "extraordinary powers" on the president.

Many feel that the adoption of federalism in 1824 was unfortunate, though understandable. Mexico had a unitary regime well suited to a then politically backward people, while a successful federal regime called for a politically sophisticated electorate, which was then non-existent. The result was a quarter-century of struggle for power between federalists and centralists.

Federalism was abandoned in 1835, and a highly centralized government was established in the Constitution of 1836, the *Siete Leyes*. This regime was inadequate and was followed by the even more centralistic Organic Bases of 1843. In 1847 the Congress decreed the re-adoption of the federalist Constitution of 1824.

*Liberalism enthroned.* The constituent convention of 1824 seemed free to choose between federalism and centralism; but this choice was no longer open by 1857. By that time the liberal tradition had been identified with the form of federalism, and the people were attached to this cause. And no serious effort has been made since then to return to the forms of centralism. Many of the features of the 1824 Constitution were carried over into the document of 1857, which in turn was incorporated in the document of 1917 — with a few minor changes, plus a few highly important additions.[8] The 1857 Constitution imitated the United States document more closely than its predecessors had.

*The charter of 1917.* "The year 1917," which produced the present Constitution, "is probably the most significant date in the whole panorama of Latin American constitutionalism," according to one leading authority on Latin American government.[9] The principles and provisions of the 1917 Constitution have been widely borrowed by subsequent Latin American constitutions. It retained the classic features of nineteenth-century constitutionalism — federalism, separation of powers, and a bill of rights.

The basic structure of the 1857 Constitution was retained; but a charter of social-economic rights was added, which strongly modified the individualist orientation of the former charter. Private property is held to have a social function, and individual rights must be subordinated to social welfare. Some of the most basic changes related to education, labor's rights, and land ownership and subsoil rights. Government was now to promote, rather than merely to conserve. To promote, departments were later added dealing with education, labor, agriculture, and public works. The power of the executive was greatly expanded. The role of the central government grew in relation to that of the states.

*Federalism and centralism.* As in other federal systems, the central government in Mexico has certain important powers, specified and implied; and certain restrictions on powers are indicated. These delegated powers are broader than those of the U.S. Constitution. In addition, the central government's role has been expanded by the institution of a strong executive as the leader of the dominant political party of the country. The states have reserved powers, but they also have numerous specified obligations and limitations on their powers. Thus, through broad specified and implied powers, stipulated limitations on the powers of the states, the legal and political power of a strong executive, and a consequent ease of amending the Constitution, a strong centralizing tendency has been at work in the Mexican government.

The central government has the powers usually granted by a federal constitution. In addition, it has several others of great importance. These include the power to function in the following fields: education, general public health matters, mineral industries, commerce in general, social security, regulation of religious activities, and labor relations.

While the field of education is a concurrent function of state and nation, the work of the latter has greatly expanded since the amending of the Constitution in 1934. The proportion of this service provided by the central government is high, but it varies considerably from state to state. The national jurisdiction pertaining to "the general health of the Republic" places most of the important public health work in the hands of the central government, leaving mainly lesser local matters strictly in the hands of the states and the municipalities. Legislation in the fields of labor relations and commerce is in the hands of the central government. The same is true with regard to regulation of the public exercise of religious practices, though the states may limit the number of priests in active service.

The states, as in our country, are conceded the reserved powers (those not expressly granted to the central government). But their role is restricted by concurrent powers exercised by the central government and by obligations, both positive and prohibitive.[10] Thus, there is recognized the essentially centralized character of "Mexican federalism."

Among the positive obligations, the states must have a representative, republican form of government; give their municipalities local self-government, under specified details as to structure and functioning; conform with certain requirements regarding the governorship and the state legislature (Art. 115). The prohibitive obligations, or limitations, are absolute and relative. Among the relative limitations, the state may not do such things, *without the consent of the Congress*, as establish taxes on imports or exports; maintain permanent troops; and make war except in case of invasion (Art. 118).* The absolute limitations, complete prohibitions, are mainly a limiting of functions (Art. 117) which other articles of the Constitution give exclusively to Congress. These include making treaties, coining money, and prohibiting or taxing the circulation of national or foreign merchandise.

In addition to the above-mentioned broad grant of powers to the central government and limitations on the states, the central government has expanded its power by other important means. These include the following: relative ease of constitutional amendment, with the president as leader of the dominant party; presidential persuasive influence over state governors and legislatures in legislative and administrative matters, and also through control of the dominant party; and replacement of state governors and legislatures, through persuasion or action by the federal Senate (Art. 76, V and VI), to be discussed later in this chapter.

*Centralization.* As mentioned above, additional powers are rather easily given to the central government through constitutional amendment. This requires only a two-thirds vote of a quorum in the Congress, followed by approval of a majority of the state legislatures. The Congress counts the votes of the legislatures and announces the approval of the amendment (Art. 135). Throughout Mexican constitutional history there has been frequent discussion of the scope of the power to revise or amend the Constitution. Some have felt that certain provisions are so basic as to be beyond the scope of the usual amending power. This is a minority view, and the practice has been clearly to the contrary.[11]

The central government is charged by the Constitution with ensuring democratic governments in the states, seeing that the Constitution and federal laws are enforced by the states, guaranteeing individual liberties, and maintaining peace within the states. If a state or federal constitutional provision is infringed by a state, there may be a political or a judicial recourse. If an offense by state authorities is subject to judicial

* Articles cited will be from the Constitution unless another document is specified.

78

decision, a writ of *amparo* \* can bring it before the federal judiciary (Art. 105). However, most of the constitutional intervention by the federation in the affairs of the states has been political. This involves Article 76, which provides for the overturning of the incumbent state regimes by Senate action, or the threat of such ultimate action. Electoral fraud has often been alleged by defeated candidates and parties, which implies violation of popular sovereignty and the republican principle of government.[12]

Presidents have secured state compliance with central desires through means ranging from suggestion and mild influence to military occupation. Unconstitutional or undesired state laws may be removed through presidential pressure or by federal Senate action. Presidential intervention in states following elections, which was most frequent between the mid-twenties and the mid-thirties, was usually based on charges of electoral fraud.[13] At other times illegal state administrative actions were charged. These are considered disputes of a political, rather than of a justiciable, nature. Therefore, the Supreme Court has for long refused to consider such matters.

In dealing with the states, the President makes use of his foremost ministry, the Ministry of Government. Most of its differences with states are settled amicably. If not, at the direction of the President the findings and recommendations are turned over to the Senate by the ministry. The Senate is empowered (Art. 76, V) to make a finding that "all the constitutional powers" of a state have disappeared and "that the occasion has arisen to appoint a provisional governor, who shall call for elections to be held in conformity with the constitutional laws of the same State." The Senate by a two-thirds vote appoints the provisional governor from a list of names presented by the President. The Permanent Committee of the Congress performs this function when the Senate is not in session. Senate action has become more and more a *final* disciplinary action. For a period, such action was taken despite the sentence (Art. 76, V) that says, "This provision shall govern provided that the constitutions of the States do not provide for such a case." Federal intervention on request of the state authorities (Art. 122) has not functioned. Mecham and others have found that political expedi-

---

\* A writ mainly for protection of individual rights; broader than our writ of *habeas corpus*. It is discussed in the chapter on the judiciary.

ency has often determined the exercise or non-exercise of the interventionist powers.[14]

Much of the basis for national governmental predominance lies in the national economic predominance. Administrative powers have developed alongside of constitutional powers because of the economic advantages of cooperation between the state and national governments. The states are largely nourished through financial grants-in-aid, shared taxes, cooperative provision of services, etc.

Should Mexico abandon the federal form of organization to conform with the centralist realities? Such proposals have been heard in recent years; but they seem largely academic. The attachment to federalist forms is too long-standing and too strong. The concept "democracy" has become too widely and popularly linked with the concept "federalism."

*Separation of powers, and checks and balances.* The Mexican Constitution, like the U.S. document, provides for a separation of powers among the legislative, executive, and judicial branches (Art. 49). And subsequent articles deal with the legislature (Arts. 50–79), the executive (Arts. 80–93), and the judiciary (Arts. 94–107).

Mexican constitutionalists, however, have long recognized the practical impossibility of an absolute separation of powers. Therefore, the President has powers commonly found in republican constitutions, such as those of naming executive officers, vetoing legislation, and granting pardons. He also exercises considerable rule-making power.

The text of the 1857 Constitution allowed legislative supremacy, though the practice became otherwise. The 1917 Constitution in effect changed this to executive supremacy through its numerous grants of power to the President. The extent of this concentration of authority is such as to cause both Mexican and foreign commentators to regard the presidency as almost a temporary (six-year) dictatorship, now usually of a benevolent type.[15]

One of the most potent of the executive powers is the one whereby emergency *extraordinary powers* in legislative matters are granted by the Congress to the President, a procedure of no great difficulty since the Congress and the judiciary support the President. In addition, Article 29 provides for the President's suspending "throughout the country or in any part specified, the guarantees that might be an obstacle to a rapid and easy adjustment of the situation" involving invasion, "serious disturbance of the peace, or any other emergency that may place the people in great danger or conflict." This first step in meeting an "emergency" involves three governmental organs and actions: the President proposes the suspension; the cabinet agrees to the proposal; and the Congress issues the law decreeing the suspension of the individual guarantees in question. During a congressional recess, the Permanent Committee of the Congress gives the approval. Such a suspension should be for a limited time and involve general prohibitions, not restrictions aimed at a single individual. The breadth and flexibility of the provision is obvious.[16]

The second step in meeting an "emergency" is for the Congress to "grant the powers deemed necessary so that the Executive may meet the situation." These powers are those of an extraordinary nature, otherwise exercised only by the Congress (Art. 49). As in the case of suspension of guarantees, these powers must be enumerated and have a time limit. If the Congress has not first granted the suspension of guarantees, technically its grant of extraordinary powers to legislate is improper. Commonly, the President formerly asked for the grant of powers near the end of the congressional session; Congress has granted the powers for a broad field or a specific task and has placed a time limit on the grant (usually the beginning of the next congressional session); and, after presidential use of the powers, the executive decrees that have been issued are approved by an act of Congress. The Supreme Court has always upheld such decrees.

The use of the *extraordinary powers* has been extensive until recent years. The procedure was well established when the 1917 Constitution was adopted. Carranza promptly made use of such powers, and most of the important legislation between 1920 and 1938 was thus enacted by executive decrees. This was often done even though there existed no true emergency and there was no prior suspension of the individual guarantees. Most important of the measures thus enacted were the financial decrees; but other important legislation has dealt with labor conciliation, creation of some government agencies, and codes dealing with crime, penal procedure, commerce, agriculture, and health. There has been no extraordinary grant of powers in peacetime since 1938, when Cárdenas secured an amendment to Article 49, adding a final sentence to restrict its use. During the war years, 1942 to 1945, Ávila Camacho used such powers to establish emergency agencies, control prices and production, and effect other controls. His use of the powers was judicious.[17]

*Checks on the executive.* The possible dangers inherent in the concentration of power are obvious; but in the Mexican past the only alternative seemed to be the absence of adequate governmental power. Only minor attention was paid to the question in the 1917 Constitutional Convention.

Devices which the Congress could use as checks on presidential action include those of approving or refusing presidential nominees; refusing to approve taxes and loans; refusing to approve budgets; changing or abolishing offices; and impeaching and removing officials, including the president (Arts. 73–76, 108). With strong party government under presidential leadership, these checks seem largely theoretical. The implied power of Congress to conduct investigations has had little effective use.

Mexican legal theory includes the doctrine of judicial review, but its influence has been small regarding unconstitutional developments. The relations of the President and the courts have been close, with the judges nominated by the President and subject to possible impeachment by a cooperative Congress. Therefore, we find that the Supreme Court has not invalidated any policy of an incumbent President nor curtailed any important executive powers. The Court has held to a restricted jurisdiction, giving a broad interpretation to the non-justiciability of political questions.[18]

In the final analysis, the more effective checks have been political, not legal. The realities of power have minimized the possibility of the executive's being checked by the Congress, the courts, or the states. However, the realities of politics tend to soften the use of executive power. The President's program, to be successful, needs maximum support from the Congress and the states; hence, the realities of presidential consultation with geographical and interest groups (within and without the Party), as discussed earlier (see pp. 58–59).

## Individual Rights and Citizenship

The "Bill of Rights" of the Mexican Constitution is contained essentially in the first twenty-nine articles, although others may be involved through interpretation of the "due process" section (Art. 14). Like the rest of the Constitution, these twenty-nine articles are much more detailed than their counterpart in the United States Constitution. In addition to rights dealt with by their North American counterparts, the Mexican articles deal with education, freedom of occupation, work without compensation, travel, retroactive laws, imprisonment for debt, and prohibition of most monopolies.[19]

Articles 1 and 2 are a sort of preamble and anti-slavery guarantee, respectively. (Slavery was abolished in 1837.) Article 3 seeks to make education free, obligatory in the primary years, democratic, scientific, and separated from religious control. Related provisions are found in Articles 73 (Sec. 25) and 123 (Sec. 12). The subject will be treated more fully later in the chapter on education as a government service; but here mention should be made of the secular and "socialistic" provisions. There has always been opposition to prescription of a completely secular public education, and various subterfuges have been tried. Article 3 still prevents religious organizations and ministers from having any control over primary, secondary, and normal school education. Under Cárdenas the article provided that "the education imparted by the state shall be socialistic. It shall exclude all religious doctrine, and shall combat fanaticism and prejudice. . . ." The religious opposition varied with the degree of strictness of enforcement. Under Ávila Camacho this item was removed, but aloofness from religious doctrine and control is still prescribed.[20]

Article 4 guarantees the right of a person to engage in lawful occupations, subject to professional licensing laws which the states and the nation may pass. Recently, the Supreme Court invalidated an article of the Law of Professions for being in conflict with the Constitution's Article 4. The offending item had attempted to prevent *all* foreigners from practicing scientific and technical professions, while Article 4 does not restrict its protection to citizens.

Freedom from compulsory labor is provided by Article 5. Excepted are military and jury duty and penal servitude. Work as a means of regeneration is declared to be the aim of the penal establishments (Art. 18). Related constitutional provisions require citizens to have an honest means of livelihood (Art. 34) and establish a charter of labor rights and obligations (Art. 123). The Penal Code proscribes vagrancy and other offenses.[21]

Freedom of expression and of the press are established, within the limits of morality, public order, and the rights of other persons (Arts.

6, 7). The Law of the Press deals with the rights of publishing, while the Penal Code punishes obscene publications (Art. 200).[22] Freedom of the press currently measures up well among the Latin American countries.

The right to petition public officials and receive a reply is established (Art. 8), but in political matters it is restricted to citizens. The right of "meeting peacefully for any lawful purpose" is protected, but not for aliens in political matters (Art. 9). The Civil Code (Arts. 2670 *et seq.*) details the rights of associations. The right to possess and carry arms is granted with restrictions (Art. 10). Freedom to travel and change residence is established by Article 11. Related provisions are found in the Civil Code, the Law of Extradition, the Law of Population, and the Law of Colonization.[23] Titles of nobility are not recognized (Art. 12).

The principle of the equality of citizens before the law is contained in Article 13. "No person may be judged by private laws or special tribunals." This is interpreted as not being an interdict, however, against the use of specialized occupational tribunals, such as those for the military and for labor relations, which are established features of the Mexican system.[24]

Equally important guarantees are found in Article 14, which provides that the laws shall have no injurious retroactive effect on persons. It also provides that no person may be deprived of life, liberty, property, possessions, or rights "except by means of a direct judgment before previously established tribunals, in which the essential formalities of procedure are complied with, and in conformity with laws enacted previous to the commission of the act." This guarantee of a proper "audience" extends to proceedings before administrative bodies as well as the judiciary.[25] The Civil, Penal, and Procedural Codes elaborate these protections. One of the most important means of protecting these and other constitutional rights is by means of the writ of *amparo.* This has been defined by a leading jurist as "a constitutional suit of a summary nature, the object of which is to protect, in a special case and at the request of an injured party, private persons whose individual rights . . . have been violated through laws or acts of the authorities." In some respects it can be compared with our remedies of habeas corpus, injunction, and writ of error.

Persons are protected against molestation of their persons, homes, and possessions except by established legal proceedings; and arrests and detention are to be only by judicial warrant, except in cases in *flagrante delicto* (Art. 16). Imprisonment for civil debt is prohibited (Art. 17). Precautionary custody is limited to offenses carrying corporal punishment. Detention, arrest, and the use of warrants are regulated by Article 19, while Article 20 details the guarantees in a criminal suit.[26] The imposition of true penalties is restricted to the judiciary, while the prosecution of crimes is in the hands of the Public Ministry (Art. 21). Cruel and excessive punishments and double jeopardy are forbidden (Arts. 22, 23).

When it comes to religious rights, we should note first the tradition of anticlericalism. It has long characterized Mexican public life, as a reaction against earlier political and economic excesses of ecclesiastical authorities. The guarantee of the right of religious belief and practice is tempered by important restrictions (Art. 24). The section on religion restricts practice to homes and recognized places of worship. The churches "shall always be under the supervision of the authorities." Article 130 declares marriage a civil contract and places religious supervision in the hands of the central government; in it ministers are labeled members of a profession and subject to regulation as a profession; it prohibits ministers and religious groups from participating in politics and from inheriting real property; and it empowers the states to limit the number of ministers within their borders. Article 3 has already been mentioned as eliminating religious influence and controls from elementary and secondary education. The tense relations between the Church and the government have greatly improved since the mid-thirties, and religion is again having a greater influence on public life than it had from 1910 to 1940. The antireligious laws on the books are to a considerable extent not applied.[27]

The sanctity of the mails and prohibition against quartering of troops in private homes in peacetime are set forth in Articles 25 and 26.

Article 27 is largely a "social" guarantee, rather than an individual right. It is one of the most important in the Constitution. It sought to define the nature of private property, to limit and regulate its ownership and use, and to provide a formula for solving the agrarian problem. The original ownership of lands and waters was said to rest in the nation, but it could be transmitted to individuals. The nation was also declared the owner of the waters and the subsoil, but it could grant certain rights of exploitation. Surface land granted as private property could be subjected to limitations. Private property could be expropriated for a public purpose, subject to payment of indemnity. Aliens could own land if they renounced the protection of their governments with reference to it; but they could not own land near the frontiers. Religious institutions could not own property; commercial stock companies could not hold rural property; banks were restricted in their possible ownership; and communal land rights were legalized.[28] The agrarian aspects of the article will be discussed in a later chapter.

The attempt to outlaw monopolies (Art. 28) is another important "social guarantee." Exempt from the rule were the various monopoly services of government, cooperatives, workers' associations, and the works of authors and inventors. Combinations tending to restrain free competition and trade were denounced, especially those tending to raise the cost of the prime necessities of living. Monopolies have been known in Mexico since colonial times, and the subject received considerable debate in the constitutional conventions of 1857 and 1917. Antimonopoly legislation was passed in 1926, 1931, 1934, 1941, and later years; but concentrations widely regarded as monopolies exist, or have existed until recently, in sugar, salt, *masa* (dough), meat, and other commodities. In recent years, federal agencies have administered price controls, direct distribution of basic foods, and other measures to combat monopolies — but with only moderate success.[29]

One of the most important of the "social guarantees" is contained in Article 123, which deals with labor protections. This constitutional provision was the world's most advanced at the time of its establishment in 1917. Implementation came slowly, but it has been important since 1935, as discussed in later chapters.

Suspension of the individual guarantees (Art. 29) was discussed earlier in this chapter. Its last important use was during World War II from 1942 to 1945, when the following were suspended: Articles 4 (occupational freedom), 5, I (forced personal service), 6 (speech), 7 (censorship), 10 (arms), 11 (travel), 14 (due process), 19 (detention), 20–21 (prosecution), and 25 (the mails).[30]

If the preceding discussion has dealt only with the legal provisions, this is because of the shortage of factual data on actual administration. However, a few tentative observations can be made.

Universal and obligatory public education is far from a reality — despite the great efforts made – for financial reasons. With regard to the role of religion and of the Church in education, I have shown in an earlier chapter that the *de facto* situation is in general satisfactory. The people, aside from the clergy, enjoy a very real freedom of speech and assembly. This is observed by careful investigators like Whetten, who remarks, "The personal freedom enjoyed by the general population is probably the greatest achievement of the Mexican Revolution. In the long run, this may . . . counterbalance whatever mistakes have been made." [31] Not so much can be said for the press. There is some criticism of governmental policies and actions, but it almost always stops short of the presidency itself.

Administration of justice through the courts seems in general to be satisfactory, but departures from judicial rectitude are probably more frequent than in the older democratic countries. One sign of striving toward improvement is the drive toward the "moralizing" of the judiciary, which has led to the removal of some judges since 1952. To an unknown (but probably significant) degree, social and economic factors prevent individuals from asserting their constitutional rights.

Suspension of the individual guarantees of the Constitution – a frequent occurrence in many Latin American countries – has not been used in Mexico since the emergency days of World War II.

*Citizenship.*[32] Mexican nationality is acquired by birth or by naturalization. Persons born in Mexico, regardless of the nationality of their parents, are considered Mexicans by birth. The same is true of those born on Mexican ships, of those born abroad of Mexican parents, and of those born abroad of a Mexican father or of a Mexican mother and an unknown father (Art. 30). An alien acquires nationality by obtaining a letter of naturalization from the Ministry of Foreign Relations. His application to that office includes certifications of legal immigration, age, and good health. Completion of the process involves a court procedure to verify minimum residence of five years, a means of livelihood, good conduct, and ability to speak Spanish. Then come publication of intention, petition to the Ministry of Foreign Relations, and receipt of the final certificate. A shortened period of naturalization procedure is available to some persons. These include a foreigner who marries a Mexican, a businessman, a parent of Mexican-born children, and one who has lost his Mexican nationality. Duties of Mexican nationals include sending their children to school, paying taxes, and being subject to military service (Art. 31). Mexicans have preference over aliens for concessions and government positions; no alien may serve in the army or the public safety forces during peace (Art. 32).

A distinction is made between nationality and full citizenship. Citizens are those nationals who have attained the age of eighteen if married and twenty-one if not. Citizens have the rights of voting, holding public office, assembling for political purposes, petitioning public officers, and serving in the armed forces; they have the duties of registering for voting and tax purposes, voting, and performing electoral and jury services (Arts. 34–36).

Mexican nationality is lost by voluntary acquisition of a foreign nationality; accepting or using titles of nobility that imply submission to another country; living continuously for five years in the country of one's birth after being naturalized; or representing oneself as an alien "in any public instrument" or using a foreign passport. Mexican citizenship is lost by accepting titles of nobility; voluntarily and officially serving a foreign country without permission of Congress; accepting foreign decorations, titles, or offices without permission of Congress; or aiding a foreigner or foreign government in a diplomatic claim against Mexico (Art. 37).

The rights or privileges of Mexican citizens may be suspended for the reasons listed in the above paragraph, and also for being subjected to criminal prosecution for an offense punishable by imprisonment; during a term of imprisonment; for vagrancy or habitual intoxication; for being a fugitive from justice; and for other reasons established by law (Art. 38).

Aliens, obviously, are those who do not have the qualifications of nationals. They have the guarantees contained in the first twenty-nine articles of the Constitution, but they may not take part in politics. The President has the unrestricted authority to banish, without judicial process, any alien deemed undesirable (Art. 33). Aliens must obey the laws and pay taxes, as citizens do. They must secure the permission of the Ministry of Foreign Relations before doing business with a government agency, and agree not to invoke the protection of their governments in that connection.

### NOTES

[1] Miguel Lanz Duret, *Derecho Constitucional Mexicano* (1947), p. 3; Felipe Tena Ramírez, *Derecho Constitucional Mexicano* (1949), p. 51.

[2] Tena Ramírez, *op. cit.*, p. 114.

[3] J. Lloyd Mecham, "Federal Intervention in Mexico," in A. C. Wilgus, ed., *Hispanic-American Essays* (1942), pp. 256–57.

[4] Tena Ramírez, *op. cit.*, pp. 51, 101–2; Lanz Duret, *op. cit.*, p. 4; Emilio Rabasa, *El Artículo 14, Estudio Constitucional* (1906), pp. 127–28.

[5] Padgett, *op. cit.*, pp. 7–8.

[6] J. Lloyd Mecham, "Origins of Federalism in Mexico," in Conyers Read, ed., *The Constitution Reconsidered* (1938), p. 349 *et seq.*

[7] Carlos Sánchez Mejorada, "The Evolution of Federal Institutions in Mexico," *Journal of D. C. Bar Association*, April 1944, pp. 169–74; Emilio Rabasa, *El Judicio Constitucional* (1919), pp. 158–59. For subsequent constitutional history, see also Tena Ramírez, *op. cit.*, pp. 7–42; Lanz Duret, *op. cit.*, pp. 69–86; A. C. Matulewicz, "The Mexican Constitution of 1824" (thesis, Mexico City College [hereafter cited as MCC], 1952).

[8] *Annals* supplement, May 1917.

[9] R. H. Fitzgibbon, "Constitutional Development in Latin America: A Synthesis," in A. N. Christensen, ed., *The Evolution of Latin American Government* (1951), p. 219.

[10] Tena Ramírez, *op. cit.*, Ch. 6.

[11] *Ibid.*, Ch. 2.

[12] Mecham, "Federal Intervention in Mexico," pp. 256–57.

[13] S. S. Goodspeed, "Mexico: President and Constitution," *Mid-America*, April 1954, pp. 111–15.

[14] Mecham, "Federal Intervention in Mexico," pp. 256–57. For an account of proceedings in such a case, see *El Nacional*, May 22, 1954.

[15] Mecham, "Mexican Federalism — Fact or Fiction?" *Annals*, March 1940, pp. 32–34.

[16] *Ibid.*; Rafael Matos Escobedo, *La Crisis Política y Jurídica del Federalismo* (1944).

[17] Goodspeed, "The Development and Use of *Facultades Extraordinarias* in Mexico," *Southwestern Social Science Quarterly*, December 1953, pp. 17–33; Procuraduría General, *Breve Reseña de la Legislación de Emergencia Expedida en los Estados Unidos Mexicanos* (1944).

[18] Tena Ramírez, *op. cit.*, Ch. 22.

[19] Alberto Trueba Urbina, *¿Qué es una Constitución Político-Social?* (1951); Hernan C. Medina and Manuel Ortiz C., *Las Instituciones Jurídico-Políticas de México* (1953), Chs. 13–14.

[20] Celia Alarcón García, *Estudio y Crítica del Artículo Tercero Constitucional* (1947).

[21] Luis Muñoz, *Comentarios a la Constitución Política* (1947), pp. 50–54.

[22] *Ibid.*, pp. 54–56.

[23] *Ibid.*, pp. 56–60.

[24] *Ibid.*, pp. 60–62; Ernestina Ortega Deciga, *Interpretación del Artículo 13 Constitucional* (1941).

[25] Gabino Fraga, *Derecho Administrativo* (1952), pp. 170–76; Mario Villarreal Carrillo, *La Garantía de Audiencia en Materia Administrativa* (1948); Muñoz, *op. cit.*, pp. 62–103.

[26] Muñoz, *op. cit.*, pp. 104–7; Suprema Corte de Justicia, *Jurisprudencia Definida* (*1917-1948*) (1949), pp. 1216, 1347.

[27] See notes to Chapter 3, especially notes 66–73.

[28] Muñoz, *op. cit.*, pp. 115-61; Whetten, *op. cit.*, pp. 116-23.

[29] *Ley Orgánica del Artículo 28* . . . , in Manuel Andrade, ed., *Constitución Política Mexicana* (1953), pp. 192 *et seq.*; *Ley de Monopolios*, in Andrade, *op. cit.*, pp. 187-91; Muñoz, *op. cit.*, pp. 161-65.

[30] Ignacio Burgoa, *Las Garantías Individuales* (1944); Mariano Cantoral Hernández, *La Suspensión de Garantías* . . . (1942).

[31] Whetten, *op. cit.*, pp. 571-72.

[32] *Ley de Nacionalidad* . . . and *Ley General de Población*, in Manuel Andrade, ed., *Constitución Política* . . . (1953), pp. 199-212 and 423-36; Muñoz, *op. cit.*, pp. 168-78; Medina and Ortiz, *op. cit.*, Ch. 10.

# 6

## *The Congress*

T HE Mexican Congress[1] is similar in structure to that of the United States, and its constitutional position is also similar — but much less strong. The strength of the Congress is limited by the constitutional power of the President and by the very great political power of that office.

The official name of the legislative body has varied, but it has always included the word *congress* in its title. The Constitution of 1824 provided for a two-house body, a Chamber of Deputies and a Chamber of Senators. The Constitution of 1857 established a unicameral body, a Chamber of Deputies, which was replaced by a bicameral Congress in 1873. This arrangement has continued until the present (Art. 50). Since 1824, the Chamber of Deputies has been regarded as representing the people and the Senate as representing the states. The imitation of the United States Constitution was clear.

The members of both houses are chosen by direct popular vote. The 161 deputies are elected for three-year terms on the basis of one member for each 170,000 people in the state or territory, with no state having less than two members and no territory less than one. The people of each state and of the Federal District elect two senators for six-year terms, and there is a complete turnover every six years. The member of Congress must be a natural-born citizen in good standing and of minimum age — twenty-five for deputies and thirty-five for senators. He must be a native of the state or territory or a resident of more than six months at the time of election. Excluded are those who *within ninety days* before the election have served in the federal army or had a command in the local police force, served as a federal supreme court judge or ministry secretary or subsecretary, or served as a state government department head or as a state or federal judge in the district in question. No member may be a minister of any church. A substitute is elected for each deputy and each senator. The position of substitute is of Spanish origin and is found in all the Mexican constitutions since 1824. With the ease of holding elections, the need for the job has been questioned. Senators and deputies cannot be re-elected for the immediately succeeding term as members or as substitutes; but substitutes may be elected for the succeeding term as members, if they did not exercise that status in the preceding period (Arts. 51–59).

The Congress meets in annual sessions. The 1857 Constitution provided for two meetings a year — fall and spring. The current document establishes one regular annual session, beginning on September 1 and ending before January 1. The President prorogues the session in case of disagreement between the two houses on adjournment time. One or both houses may be called into extraordinary session by the Permanent Committee (discussed below, pp. 98–99), with deliberations limited to matters named in the call. Neither house may recess for more than three days nor move its meeting place without the consent of the other. The President must attend the opening of the regular session and present a written message on the state of the union (Arts. 66–69).

The organization and general conduct of the Congress are also subject to more detailed prescription in the Mexican Constitution than in our own. Each house is the final judge of the election of its own members, with preliminary post-election qualification of senators done by the state legislature (Arts. 56, 60). The credentials of members are approved at a preliminary meeting of each house before the opening session. In the past, approval was often "politically" determined. That is, the majority party tended to declare its own candidates elected, regardless of the actual ballot results.

Members "are inviolable for opinions that they express in the discharge of their duty and they shall never be called to account for them" (Art. 61). However, the rules of the Congress allow a slandered citizen to protest to the house concerned and to seek a retraction of the offending statement. Members may not, without permission of their house, hold any other federal or state-paid position (Arts. 62, 108–9).

A quorum is two-thirds of the senators and more than half of the deputies. A lesser number opening the session may seek to compel the appearance of the absentees; and after thirty days they may have the substitutes fill the positions of the absentees. After this period, unexcused absences of ten days will likewise lead to replacement by substitutes (Art. 63). Unexcused absences mean a loss of per diem pay (Art. 64).

*Legislative structure and procedure.* Bills may be introduced in the Congress by the President, members, and the state legislatures (Art. 71). Individual members, however, seldom introduce bills of importance; the bulk of legislation is introduced by the executive. Individual citizens and groups may petition either house and have their proposals considered, according to the *reglamento* (by-laws) of the Congress. Preference is automatically given to bills introduced by the President, the state legislatures, and deputations of members. These are sent directly to a committee; bills of individual members are handled under other rules.

The houses work through standing and special committees, of which each has between sixty and seventy. Of this number, about a dozen are first, second, and third committees dealing with the same subject. Most committees have four members, but there are a few that consist of nearly two dozen members apiece. The most important of these few is the Committee on Legislative Studies — one in each house — which often meets during the recesses of the Congress to study legislative proposals. Among the more important standing committees are those on agriculture, social security, education, *ejidos*, labor, and legislative studies. Most standing committees are appointed for the three-year term corresponding with the electoral period, but a few are renewed annually. There is no formal seniority in committee membership.

Each chamber chooses its president and vice-president for a month's tenure. Short tenure does not conduce to making the position of presiding officer a strong one. He declares the meetings opened and closed, presents matters for discussion, recognizes members alternately for and against an issue, calls for and announces the votes, and performs other functions common to presiding officers. A strong position is that of majority party leader in each house.

Each house names its other officers, appoints its employees, and arranges its other internal matters. As early as 1924 the Congress published and considered a proposal for a civil service law covering legislative employees, but without producing results.

The Great Committee (*Gran Comisión*), composed of one member from each state, is important in the overhead organization of each house. It proposes the names of members for the permanent and special committees and makes recommendations on the naming and removal of employees. The Committee on Administration presents monthly the internal budget for the house and reviews its accounts. The Inspection Committee of the Auditing Office watches over that office, which in turn, as a dependency of the Chamber of Deputies, checks on the federal Treasury Department. The Committee on the Budget considers the budgets and tax proposals for the federal, Federal District, and territorial governments. The Library of Congress is a dependency of the Chamber of Deputies.

When a bill is introduced in either house it is normally sent to a committee. From then on, the procedure is similar to that in other legislative bodies. The committee must report every measure back to the house, where it is placed on a calendar in the order of receipt. Later, Party leaders give priority to certain measures on the calendar. Normally in debate at least three speakers are allowed on each side of discussion on a bill. Measures may be introduced in either house, except for bills dealing with loans, duties, taxes, or recruitment of troops. These must originate in the lower house. If a bill has been introduced in one house and no committee report results within a month, then the other house may introduce and discuss the measure (Arts. 72, Secs. 8–9). The final vote is taken by roll call (Art. 72, Sec. 3). A favorable majority vote of the quorum is necessary for passage. The bill is then passed by the second house and sent to the president, who signs it and has it published in the *Diario Oficial*. (The journal of proceedings for each house is published in full.) Unless otherwise provided, the laws become effective three days after publication (Art. 72, Sec. 1).

A bill may encounter various obstacles in enactment. First, it may fail to pass the first house; if rejected, it cannot be reintroduced during that session. Second, it may pass the first house but be rejected in whole or in part in the second house. Then it returns to the first house. A bill totally rejected in the second house returns to the second house after being repassed by an absolute majority of a quorum in the first house. If, on its second appearance, the bill is passed by the same majority in the second house, then it goes to the President for his signature. If defeated in the second house, it may not come up again that session. Third, a bill may be changed in part by the second house. Then only the changed part is considered again by the first house. A majority vote of approval sends the measure to the President; a vote of disapproval sends the bill back to the second house. If the second house then again rejects the part it originally objected to, the parts approved by both houses go to the President (Art. 72). Any bill not returned by the President within ten working days to the chamber of its introduction is considered approved, if the Congress is still in session.

The President may veto a measure in whole or in part, sending it with his objections to the chamber of origin. A two-thirds vote in both houses sends the bill back to the President for its promulgation. There has been some discussion of the power of the President to refuse to publish and put into effect a law passed over his veto. But under the existing strong presidential regime this, like the possibility of passing a bill over a veto, is largely an academic question.

The sessions held by the Congress are ordinary and special, and either kind may be public or secret. Secret sessions are not infrequent. They may deal with accusations against congressmen and high officials, questions of foreign relations, and other matters.

*Powers and duties of Congress.* The actions that the two houses of Congress take are in the main very clearly *powers*. They are stated as such in the constitutional articles 73–77. Others are powers that are stated as duties. Two of these dealing with the procedure in enactment of a law have been discussed (Arts. 71–72). Article 65 lists three other duties. First, the Congress *shall* meet on September 1 to audit the accounts of the previous year. This is done by the Chamber of Deputies. Secret items in the budget are limited. Secondly, the Congress provides the budget and enacts the necessary taxes. Finally, it shall "study, debate, and vote on the bills" presented for consideration. To provide data for such study, cabinet members may be called before committees to give information regarding measures, but they seldom have been.

The general powers of the Congress and of the separate houses might be classified as legislative and nonlegislative; the nonlegislative are those that are executive, judicial, or electoral in character.

The general legislative powers of the whole Congress are listed in Article 73. These are the powers to legislate regarding important economic matters — mining, petroleum, commerce, labor, electrical energy, the central bank, other credit institutions, and games of chance; on admiralty matters; regarding nationality, citizenship, colonization, im-

95

migration and emigration, and "general public health" matters; on communications; on federal waters; on money, weights, and measures; on unoccupied lands; on federal crimes; on the foreign service; on education; on the office of the Auditor General; and on all matters relating to the Federal District and the territories. Finally, the Congress is empowered to "enact all laws that may be necessary to carry into effect the foregoing powers and all others granted by this Constitution to the branches of the Union." The importance of this elastic provision is diminished by the ease and frequency of constitutional amendment, as compared with the United States. The above-mentioned powers are the truly legislative powers according to one outstanding Mexican constitutional authority, Lanz Duret. The other principal authority, Tena Ramírez, would also regard the following as legislative rather than administrative functions: levying taxes; approving loans; forbidding states to place restrictions on interstate commerce; creating and abolishing public offices and providing for their remuneration; providing for and regulating the armed forces; and granting amnesties for federal offenses.

Lanz Duret discusses the following as powers of an executive type: admitting new states; levying taxes; creating offices and providing for compensating employees; maintaining armed forces; providing for loans; and declaring war. Tena Ramírez regards the following as executive functions: admitting new states; compensating public employees; approving loans; and declaring war. In addition, he adds the following: requiring the attendance of members and punishing their improper acts; examining the annual accounts of the executive branch; and dealing with a temporary absence of the President or a vacancy in the office.

Lanz Duret recognizes a category of electoral powers: making substitute, interim, or provisional appointments to the presidency; the confirmation that one house gives to certain presidential appointees; and the confirmation that the other house gives to other appointees. The same authority regards the following as functions of a judicial type: granting amnesties; taking cognizance of accusations against public officials for official offenses.

Some of the most important powers of the Congress deal with the government of the Federal District and the territories, taxation and the budget, commerce, education, public health, and defense. These topics will be treated in Chapters 11, 14, 15, 16, 23, 24, and 27.

The result of an act of legislation is called a law or a decree. Technical distinctions have been made between the terms, but in actual practice the terms are interchangeable. Laws can be classified as ordinary, organic, and regulatory. The first is the result of an activity authorized by the Constitution. The second regulates the structure or functioning of organs of the government, e.g., the judiciary and the departments. The regulatory law develops in some detail a basic provision in the Constitution, e.g., the Regulatory Law for Article 27 of the Constitution. But specific enactments don't always follow the theoretical principle.

The legislative branch has declined in importance compared with the executive, due both to the growing complexity of life and the problems faced and to Mexico's own national tradition and history. These factors and the code-law character of the Mexican system are reflected in the legislative output. A recent twenty-year study shows ordinary laws and *reglamentos* (important executive rules) in approximately equal numbers, with about ten times as many circulars, *acuerdos* (decisions), and similar detailed executive rules of a lesser nature.[2] Legislation and administrative rules of the various kinds are published in the *Diario Oficial*. The important items, as well as important state legislation and the Supreme Court's decisions, are indexed in the *Revista de la Escuela de Jurisprudencia* of the National University.

*Powers of each chamber.* Each house has several important exclusive powers. The Chamber of Deputies verifies the electoral returns in the presidential race. It appoints the officials and employees of the Auditor General's office, approves the proposed annual budget, and discusses the taxes needed to cover it. It takes cognizance of accusations made against officials for official offenses, and institutes impeachment before the Senate. It approves presidential appointments to the territorial courts and the Federal District's superior court; and, along with the Senate, it approves presidential requests for the removal of any federal judges (Art. 74, III). In theory, the Chamber of Deputies might exercise great power over the executive through its functions of verifying the presidential electoral returns, passing the budget, and being the first body to consider tax bills. These fade, however, before the realities of the strong presidential system.

The Senate has several important exclusive powers. Among these are the powers to approve treaties; ratify most of the high civilian and military appointments; authorize the President to make certain extraordinary uses of the military forces; and approve dismissals and resignations of high officials and their requests for leaves of absence. The Senate has two other very important powers. The first is "to declare, when all the constitutional powers of any State may have disappeared, that the occasion has arisen to appoint a provisional governor" and to make such appointment. The extensive use of this provision was discussed in Chapter 5. The second and similar power is that of deciding "political questions arising between the powers of a state whenever one of them appeals to the Senate for the purpose, or whenever a conflict of arms has arisen to disturb constitutional order" (Art. 76).[3] This provision has not been used so extensively. In case of rebellion, the President may use the armed forces to maintain peace (Art. 89, VI). Nonpolitical peaceful controversies are supposed to be settled by the Supreme Court.

It will be noted that most of these exclusive powers of the two houses might be called executive in character.

Each of the houses may by itself handle such internal matters as organizing its internal administration, appointing its employees, handling its financial affairs, communicating with the executive and the other house, and issuing calls for special elections to fill vacancies among its members (Art. 77).

The two houses meet in joint session for the opening meeting of ordinary sessions, to witness the oath of office of an incoming President, and to designate an interim or provisional President in the absence of such an elected and qualified official (Arts. 69, 84, 85, 87).

*The Permanent Committee.* The Permanent Committee is a distinctive feature of the Mexican Congress. This group of fifteen deputies and fourteen senators is appointed at the end of the regular session, to serve during the recess of the two houses. Such a committee is thought to have originated in Spain in the thirteenth century, and has been used at various times since then in that country. A number of Latin American countries have used this device, but its current use is restricted to five countries.

Article 79 commits six duties to the Committee. It approves presidential use of a state's contingent of the national guard outside its borders; administers the oath of office, when necessary, to the President and federal judges; passes judgment on matters left undecided by the

Congress; calls special sessions of one or both houses of Congress by a two-thirds vote, either on its own initiative or on request of the President; approves the appointment of federal judges; and may grant a thirty-day leave of absence to the President.

Other articles prescribe additional functions during the recess of the Congress. These include approving the presidential suspension of guarantees in time of emergency (Art. 29); depriving persons of citizenship for certain unauthorized relations with foreign governments (Art. 37, Sec. 2); appointing a provisional President and calling the Congress into session to take permanent action, in case of a vacancy in that office (Arts. 84, 85); witnessing the oath of office of the President (Art. 87); approving the appointment of substitutes for absent Supreme Court judges (Art. 98); approving acceptance of the resignations of such judges as well as their leaves of absence (Arts. 99, 100); witnessing the oath of office of such judges (Art. 97).[4]

Mexican constitutional authorities quite generally disapprove of the Permanent Committee, although a few think it might serve as a check on undue power in presidential hands. It is criticized on the practical grounds that it is in general unnecessary, that it operates without fixed rules, that it has no minority members, that its only power not possessed by the Congress — calling special sessions — could be exercised as well by the President; and that it might become dominant over the Congress.[5] However, there seems to be no strong move to eliminate the Committee.

*General remarks.* The constitutional provisions dealing with the Congress, as with other matters, are probably excessively detailed; and they are not entirely free from occasional ambiguities or contradictions. The constitutional leadership in the two houses suffers from lack of experience due to the short tenure of the position; but this is partly offset by the leadership of the predominant official party. The annual changes in committee membership are a weakening factor. Low pay is probably one deterrent to the recruitment of congressional candidates in many cases; however, the current quality of members seems definitely higher than in the past. Committee investigations of administrative agencies have never been frequent and seldom important. However, during the current administration, formalized meetings of committees with individual agency heads have been developing. Legislative sessions have often been slow in getting under way (often meeting only two or three times weekly) and subject to various organizational shortcomings, which is, of course, true in the United States and elsewhere. There seems to be little real need for the Permanent Committee.

Since the President is still clearly predominant in actual lawmaking, the functioning role of the Congress in Mexican government has received little systematic study. Therefore, we can in the main hazard only generalized statements and tentative conclusions about this body, which one Mexican leader has labeled the "silent, *potential* censor" of the executive.[6] Despite the preponderant role of the President, a few investigators have noted the significance of the Congress' informal, institutional role in the decision-making process. The members are groups of economically like-minded persons who have been chosen usually because of their abilities as leaders of locally important groups. Within the over-all support of the Party's program, the member tends to represent first the interests of his local economic group; second, the interests of such groups nationally — a pattern not too unlike that of U.S. congressmen. Conflict tends to be minimized by the institutionalized place of the organized sectors within the Party machinery (as discussed in Chapter 4). Senators tend to represent the over-all interests of a state more than deputies do. Therefore, a senator can serve as one liaison between the state's governor and the central power, the Party leadership and the president. This two-way process is facilitated by each house having a representative on the Party's Central Executive Committee. As in any legislative body, the complexities of interpersonal relations often modify original views; and at times the thinking of the legislative interest groups and the crystallized feelings of the whole body are a significant influence on decisions of the President.

Before the President submits highly controversial proposals to the Congress, he has usually consulted formally or informally with congressmen, Party leaders, governors, and affected interest groups, in order to ensure maximum support for — or at least to minimize disaffection from — the final legislative approval. The business groups consult with the President through their chambers of commerce and industry, which are given legal standing.

The interest-group strength in the Chamber of Deputies for 1952–55, as discussed in Chapter 4, was as follows: agrarian sector, 36; labor sector, 35; popular sector, more than half the Chamber's membership. The multi-interest popular sector has been increasing in strength, both relatively and absolutely. Looked at in another way (largely a breakdown of the popular sector), the 1949 Chamber of Deputies had 55 lawyers, 7 engineers, 6 military men, 5 physicians, 7 professors, and 67 unspecified.

## NOTES

[1] Lanz Duret, *op. cit.*, pp. 127-227; Tena Ramírez, *op. cit.*, Chs. 10-18; Fraga, *op. cit.*, pp. 39-50; Muñoz, *op. cit.*, pp. 187-219; Andrade, ed., *Constitución Política Mexicana*, Arts. 50-79; Mario F. González Reyes, *El Órgano Legislativo y su Función en el Derecho Mexicano* (1950); Marino Reyes Morales, *El Senado Mexicano* (1939); A. F. Macdonald, *Latin American Politics and Government* (1954), pp. 269-73; Sría. de Bienes Nacionales, *Directorio* . . . (1), pp. 1-46; José María Oceguera Ochoa, "La Presidencia de la Cámara" (UNAM thesis, 1945).

[2] Pedro R. Suinaga Lujan, *Veinte Años de Legislación Mexicana, 1931-50* (1951), Vol. I, p. xi; Enriqueta Laguna Arcos, "El Ejecutivo y la Promulgación de las Leyes" (UNAM thesis, 1950).

[3] Emma Loredo Castaneda, "El Senado en la Teoría Jurídica del Estado Federal" (UNAM thesis, 1950).

[4] Guillermo Ducker Calo, "La Comisión Permanente" (UNAM thesis, 1947).

[5] Lanz Duret, *op. cit.*, pp. 213-17; Tena Ramírez, *op. cit.*, Ch. 18; Ducker Calo, *op. cit.*

[6] Padgett, *op. cit.*, pp. 25-32, 140-42; *HAR*, September 1949, p. 6; José María Súarez Tellez, *¿Quiere Usted ser Diputado?* (1946).

# 7

# The Presidency

The real concentration of power and influence in Mexico is in the office of the President. Tannenbaum, a close observer of long standing, goes so far as to say, "The President is the government, and all discussion of Mexican politics must assume that fact." He feels that the tripartite division of powers is still much more form than substantial reality, that "the alternative to highly centralized power is anarchy." [1] There is some difference of opinion among investigators on the relative balance of authority between President and Congress in the text of the Constitution; but there is little disagreement about the actual concentration of power in practice. This has been achieved at different times and in varying degrees by such devices as the following: strong leadership of the predominant party; a broad power of appointment and removal; control of finance; and control of the army.

Before discussing the dynamics of presidential leadership, I shall consider the constitutional basis of the presidency — the legal-personal requisites, the "no re-election" principle, and the functions, powers, and duties of the office.

*Requisites of the office.* The President is elected by direct popular vote "in the manner that the electoral law provides" (Arts. 80–81). He must be a native-born citizen, the son of Mexicans by birth (Art. 82). The requirement of Mexican parents was added in 1917 as a result of the prevailing spirit of militant nationalism. The minimum age is put at thirty-five but, unlike the prescription for Supreme Court judges, no maximum age is set. This anomaly has been properly criticized by Mexican jurists. The advanced age of Díaz might have been expected to lead to such a provision, as it did in the case of the "no re-election" provision. A full year's residence is required prior to election day, a provision stemming from the Constitution of 1857. It was aimed against repetitions of Santa Anna's return from abroad *after* his election, a situation presumably featuring foreign influence in the presidency.[2]

In contrast with the United States, several occupational disqualifications are then set forth (Arts. 82–83). The President may not be a minister or have ecclesiastical status nor have been in active military service for six months prior to election day. These provisions reflect the prevailing anticlerical spirit and apprehension about the political power of the military. The latter provision has apparently had no great effect on army influence. The six-months rule is also applied to holders of the civil offices of cabinet members and their chief assistants, the attorney general, and state and territorial governors.

The "no re-election" principle was a slogan of Madero's revolution against the long tenure of Díaz. The 1917 Constitution prohibited re-election for the elected President but allowed re-election after an intervening term for the substitute or interim President. After changes in 1927, 1928, and 1933, the present absolute prohibition was adopted. Any person who has served as President, through election or otherwise, may never again hold the office (Art. 83). A similar provision applies to elected state governors (Art. 115). Members of Congress and elected municipal officials may not be chosen for the immediately succeeding term (Arts. 59, 115). The presidential provision has been successful for over a quarter of a century. Mexican jurists decry the undemocratic nature of the provision, but they feel it has been necessary to protect Mexico's developing democracy.[3]

The President serves a six-year term; the term was four years until 1928. His tenure begins on December 1, a time not auspicious for the first year's executive-congressional relationship since the Congress must adjourn on December 31.

*Presidential succession.* In the absence of the popularly elected President, the office is filled in one of three ways. Since there is no vice-president, an interim President is appointed by the Congress when a vacancy occurs during the first two years of the term or when the person elected fails to qualify. Then the Congress calls elections to choose a President. The same procedure is provided for a person chosen by the Congress to fill the office during the temporary absence of the President. A substitute President is chosen by the Congress when the office falls vacant in the last four years of the term, and this official fills out the term. A provisional President is named by the Permanent Committee when the vacancy occurs at any time during the recess of the Congress (Arts. 84–85).[4] The absence of provision for a vice-president or similar successor, combined with these procedures, has produced criticism. The result is at least a partial exception to the basic constitutional principle of direct choice by the nationwide electorate.

The vice-presidency had been a feature of the Mexican system, but intrigue by the heir-apparent to the presidency in the nineteenth century led to its being discredited. The 1824 Constitution had such an office, filled by the runner-up in votes for the presidency; but the documents of 1836 and 1843 made no provision for the office. The 1857 document provided for succession by the chief justice of the Supreme Court, which produced similar undesired results. An amendment of 1904 re-established the vice-presidency, and he was to preside over the Senate without a vote except in case of tie. He was to be followed in the presidential succession by the Minister of Foreign Relations.[5]

*Presidential functions.*[6] The President's powers are broader and more extensive than those of the President of the U.S. His powers or functions are in varying degrees executive, legislative, and judicial in character. The more important among them deal with initiating, securing the passage of, and vetoing bills; promulgating and executing the laws; issuing regulations; appointing and removing high officials; and using the pardoning power.[7]

An important executive type of power the President has is that of naming and removing high officials. He has complete freedom in such matters regarding heads of departments, the federal attorney general, the governor of the Federal District and territorial governors, the attorney general of the Federal District, and all other officials whose appointments or dismissals are not otherwise provided for by the Constitution or by law. He also has the power to remove freely the diplomatic agents and the higher treasury officials (Art. 89).

The Senate approves presidential appointments of consuls, diplomatic officials, and colonels and higher officers of the armed forces. Removals are at the discretion of the President. He appoints judges of the superior court, subject to approval of the Chamber of Deputies, or of the Permanent Committee in the recess of the Chamber. The Senate approves the appointment of Supreme Court judges, as well as their leaves of absence and resignations. The Permanent Committee performs these functions during a recess of the Senate. Interim appointments are valid (Art. 89).[8]

Under rules set by statute, the President appoints members of the civil service and lower personnel of the armed forces. He does not have a free hand in promoting or removing such personnel. A civil service law was proposed in the Congress as early as 1911, but it didn't become a reality until the thirties.

A very effective and frequently used power of the President is that of replacing state administrations of which he disapproves, as outlined in Chapter 5 (see pages 79–80). It is related to the appointment and removal powers discussed above and the military powers discussed below. If persuasion doesn't get the desired results, the President, through the Ministry of Government, gets the Senate to declare that the constitutional powers of the state have disappeared and to appoint a provisional governor suggested by the President, pending new state elections. This power is less frequently used than formerly.

The President's military powers are extensive, and at times they have been "stretched." In addition to his powers of appointment mentioned above, the chief executive has the power "to dispose of the permanent armed land, sea, and air forces for the internal security and external defense of the Federation." The use of such forces for "internal security" has been much the more extensive. They have often been used for suppressing open rebellion in a state, and at times, as just mentioned, they have been used to settle electoral questions in the state governments. With the consent of the Senate, the President makes similar use of the national guard units outside their own states or territories. The Congress has the power "to raise and maintain" the armed forces and "to regulate their organization and service" (Art. 73). The President has the power to declare war in the name of the country after passage of a favorable resolution by the Congress. With the consent of the Senate, the President may send Mexican troops abroad and permit the passage of foreign troops through Mexican territory (Art. 76). A declaration of war, as in 1942, is normally followed by suspension by the President of some of the constitutional guarantees and granting of power by the Congress to the President for legislating by decree.

The President's power in the conduct of foreign affairs is extensive. The Foreign Minister is freely appointed and removed by the executive, while diplomatic and consular officers are subject to Senate approval. Aside from a required Senate approval for treaties, the executive's other powers over foreign affairs are quite complete. (Although Article 89, X still speaks of treaty ratification by the Congress, it is actually done by the Senate (Art. 76, I). The anachronism stems from the days of the unicameral Congress under the Constitution of 1857.) The range of presidential power includes the whole list of actions involved in diplomatic negotiation, as well as the recognition of governments and receiving of their diplomatic representatives (Art. 89). In addition, in time of war the President has the exclusive power to make pacts of a military nature for such purposes as the exchange of prisoners, making armistices, resuming hostilities, and negotiating for peace.[9] The following question has often been asked: Can valid treaties effect any infringement on the Constitution? Jurists say no, for Article 133 declares the Constitution to be the supreme law of the land, with statutes and treaties emanating from it. A more specific provision (Art. 15) forbids treaties for the extradition of political offenders and treaties seeking to alter the constitutional rights of the individual. A person feeling deprived of some such right may seek redress through a writ of *amparo*.[10]

The domestic effect of treaties varies. Like statutes, they are part of the supreme law of the land. Some treaties require no complementary legislation to give them full domestic effect, while others do require it. An example is a claims treaty which requires an appropriation to be fully effective. Naturally, the Congress may later pass legislation affecting or terminating a treaty, just as the Senate's power of treaty approval includes the power of changing its terms before approval.

Those of the President's powers described above may be regarded as executive or administrative in character. The same is true of the following powers: to aid the judiciary in carrying out its functions; to carry out maritime functions; to grant exclusive privileges under law to inventors; and to request the removal of judges for misbehavior. Calling Congress into special session with the approval of the Permanent Committee is likewise an administrative act; it is also a political act since it involves a fundamental relationship between the two branches of government (Art. 89).[11]

Many of the President's actions in connection with the laws, prior to their execution, may be regarded as legislative in character. As mentioned above, the introduction of bills is done by the President, as well as by congressmen and by state legislatures. This act is legislative in character, as is the effort made to secure passage of a bill. The President is the source of most of the important legislation, and his efforts in securing passage of measures — even though they be informal efforts — are actions of a legislative type. The same is obviously true of the use of the veto.

After the legislature's task is finished, presidential actions of great importance must still be taken to give full effect to legislation. These acts are promulgation of the law, its publication, its execution, and presidential use of the *reglamento* (rule or regulation).

Promulgation is the act by which the President authenticates the existence and regularity of a law which has been signed by him or passed over his veto by the Congress. He seems legally required to perform this act, but there is no constitutional means to force such action. Before doing so, the President is likely to consult with the *Secretaría de Gobernación* (often called the Ministry of the Interior, or of Government), the agency through which legislative proposals are channeled to the Congress. *Gobernación*, in turn, is likely to consult with any ministries affected by the act before the President promulgates the measure. Some jurists consider promulgation a legislative type of action, while others consider it executive.[12] Only the President can promulgate a law. Publication, effected by *Gobernación* in the *Diario Oficial*, is an executive or administrative act.

The character of the President's use of the *reglamento* has been much discussed. It is the basic form of what might be called sublegislation or rule-making, whereby only the President may lay down basic rules giving effect to a more general provision of a statute. The *reglamento* cannot change any parts of the law; and some subjects — like individual guarantees, taxes, and punishments — can usually be treated only by statute.

All the constitutions prior to 1857 expressly provided for the *reglamento*. Since then, there has been no express constitutional provision, which seems to have been an oversight by the constitutional conventions. Governmental necessities have caused the continued use of such an instrument to be based on an implied power, jurisprudence of the Supreme Court (*jurisprudencia*), and custom. The implied power is based on the constitutional provision that the President has the obligation "to promulgate and execute the laws that the Congress of the Union enacts, providing within the administrative sphere for their exact observance" (Art. 89, I). The *reglamento* is referred to, without elaboration, in Article 92: "All regulations, decrees, and orders of the President shall be signed by the Secretary of the Cabinet to whose department the matter pertains, and they shall not have force without this requisite." The countersignature referred to is the so-called *refrendo*. The *reglamento* cannot be based on or "regulate" constitutional provisions — only Congress can regulate constitutional provisions — but only statutes. Nor can the President use it independently of a statute. This measure, like the statute, must be published in the *Diario Oficial*.[13]

The valid *reglamento* has the same force as law that the statute has. But the opinions have been varied on its exact legal character. One leading authority, Fraga, considers it in form an administrative act; but materially, in substance, he calls it legislative — of general applicability. Tena Ramírez disagrees.[14] In any event, this device is the form in which much valid "law" is found.

The President's legislative-type powers have not been limited to rule-making and securing congressional enactments; until recent years he frequently took over the principal legislative function by enacting legislation by means of the decree power (as discussed in Chapter 5, pp. 80–82). While constitutionally intended as a true emergency power, before 1940 the presidents frequently got the Congress to grant them this virtually complete legislative power — the extraordinary powers; and much of the country's important legislation was enacted in this way. Its last use was during the World War II emergency, when Ávila Camacho received from Congress the power to suspend the individual guarantees and enact laws by executive decree.

The judicial-type powers of the President are few. They might be regarded as direct and indirect. The indirect, which is more executive in character, consists of appointing judges and seeking their removal at the hands of the Congress. The direct type consists of granting pardons, a function which is regulated by law. This law, the Penal Code (Arts. 96–97), calls for the pardon when innocence is shown or where the prisoner has rendered important services to the nation. It is granted by the President only after an irrevocable sentence has been given. It affects only the execution of the sentence. Its use in cases of political offenders is at the discretion of the executive.[15]

# THE PRESIDENCY

The ceremonial and quasi-public functions of the President are numerous. He dedicates new highways and public buildings, receives visiting dignitaries, congratulates scientists and other public benefactors, speaks to conventions of farmers and workers and professional people, and performs a myriad other civic and social duties. These duties, together with his constitutional and political functions, combine to make the days of the Mexican President as full as those of any president. For he is, to a considerable degree, the government.

*The presidency. Operations.* I have discussed the President's extensive powers, legislative and executive in character. He is expected to make wide use of them, and most presidents have done so. The strong concentration of power in the hands of the executive is recognized by Mexican and foreign experts alike. While the general nature of Mexican presidential power and its exercises are known, published material on operating details is extremely limited — unlike the data on the U.S. presidency. Therefore, to a considerable degree, knowledge of operating details must await the availability of published materials and the results of specialized field studies.

The army, a diminishing source of presidential support, was formerly a mainstay. The same has been true for the support of important independent factions and leaders. For the past quarter-century, the dominant political party has been the backbone of presidential support. Its dominance has been due largely to an effective amalgam of the chief interest groups — labor, farmers, civil servants, and lower middle-class professional people. Some have felt that the President's control over the party has been almost absolute.

The personal, individual nature of presidential politics resembles that of the United States — after the nominating convention. The North American voter regards the President as the repository of responsibility and power, as the Mexican voter does — but in a different degree. As the symbol of the family is strong in Mexico, so is the half-conscious concept of the President as the father of the national family. He epitomizes "The Revolution," despite its many changes in content.

Slowly, however, political loyalties are being institutionalized; representative institutions and party programs are coming to play a larger part in the voter's picture of "government" as issues become more pressing and education slowly lays a better basis for intelligent citizen action. Meanwhile, as the nation's chief legislator and undisputed mas-

# ORGANIZATION AND STRUCTURE

ter of the administrative apparatus, the President is still in a real sense of the word "the government."

NOTES

[1] Tannebaum, *op. cit.*, p. 84.
[2] Tena Ramírez, *op. cit.*, p. 345.
[3] *Ibid.*, p. 348; Lanz Duret, *op. cit.*, p. 232.
[4] Tena Ramírez, *op. cit.*, pp. 353–54.
[5] *Ibid.*, pp. 349–52; Lanz Duret, *op. cit.*, pp. 237–44.
[6] Goodspeed, "Mexico: President and Constitution," *Mid-America*, April 1954, pp. 111–15; Goodspeed, "The Development and Use of *Facultades Extraordinarias* . . . ;" W. G. Schaeffer, "National Administration in Mexico . . ." (Ph.D. thesis, University of California, 1950).
[7] Lanz Duret, *op. cit.*, pp. 229–79; Tena Ramírez, *op. cit.*, Chs. 19–20; Fraga, *op. cit.*, *passim*; Salvador Urbina, "Organización Ejecutiva," *Rev. de la Escuela Nacional de Jurisprudencia*, April–June 1940, pp. 139–46; Laguna Arcos, *op. cit.*, *passim*; Muñoz, *op. cit.*, pp. 220–28.
[8] Lanz Duret, *op. cit.*, pp. 249–54; Tena Ramírez, *op. cit.*, pp. 370–72.
[9] Lanz Duret, *op. cit.*, pp. 257–58.
[10] *Ibid.*, pp. 259–62.
[11] Fraga, *op. cit.*, pp. 88–89.
[12] Tena Ramírez, *op. cit.*, pp. 361–63; Laguna Arcos, *op. cit.*, *passim*.
[13] Tena Ramírez, *op. cit.*, pp. 364–70; Flavio Ruiz Esparza y Yarza, "La Reglamentación de las Leyes por el Ejecutivo" (UNAM thesis, 1942).
[14] Fraga, *op. cit.*, pp. 125–30; Tena Ramírez, *op. cit.*, pp. 366–69.
[15] Lanz Duret, *op. cit.*, pp. 263–64; Tena Ramírez, *op. cit.*, pp. 372–74.

# 8

# The Judiciary

Under the separation of powers principle, the judiciary[1] has been a separate branch of government since the country won its independence. The colonial courts had been a maze of separate tribunals. The structural appearance of the court system reflects some American influence, as does procedure; but in general the Spanish influence has been predominant. A debate (mainly academic) has existed over whether or not the judiciary comprises a third "power" comparable to the legislative and executive powers; but the reality until recently has been one of executive predominance over the other two powers.[2]

During the Cárdenas era, the Supreme Court judges' terms were made to coincide with that of the President. Since the early 1940s, they have had constitutionally designated tenure during good behavior, which has been carried out in practice. The President may remove a judge for misbehavior, with the support of a majority in both houses of Congress. Since 1952 a few district judges guilty of corruption or improprieties have been removed as a result of Ruiz Cortines' "moralization" campaign.

Mexico, like many federal states, has two full sets of courts — federal and state. The regular federal court system has three levels of courts — Supreme Court, circuit courts, and district courts. The Constitution provides for no "special tribunals" except the military courts; but specialized tribunals regarded as consonant with this provision have been provided by statute in the last two decades. These include the Fiscal Tribunal and the Boards of Conciliation and Arbitration.

*Jurisdiction.* Jurisdiction of the federal courts can be classed as ordinary and extraordinary. The "extraordinary" jurisdiction, which includes most of the cases, is exercised by means of the writ of *amparo.*

These cases are controversies arising "1st. Out of laws or acts of the authorities that violate individual guarantees; 2nd. Because of laws or acts of the federal authority restricting or encroaching on the sovereignty of the States; 3rd. Because of laws or acts of State authorities that invade the sphere of federal authority" (Art. 103).

The "ordinary" jurisdiction of the federal tribunals includes the following: all civil and criminal cases involving federal law and treaties (with some exceptions for state courts); admiralty law cases; cases to which the federation is a party; cases involving a state and the federation or two or more states; cases involving a state and residents of another state; and cases involving members of the diplomatic or consular corps (Art. 104).[3]

Disputes over jurisdiction are settled by the Supreme Court, whether they arise between federal courts, between federal and state courts, or between the courts of two states (Art. 106).

*Supreme Court.* The Supreme Court of Justice of the Nation was set up in 1824, replacing the former *Audiencia* as the supreme judicial body. Its members were to be chosen for life by the state legislatures. The 1824 Constitution also provided for circuit and district courts, which at various times were later reorganized, abolished, and reestablished. The 1857 Constitution continued the main outlines of the judicial system, similar to that of the United States. The Supreme Court was divided into three *salas*, or chambers; and the judges served six-year terms.[4]

The Supreme Court under the present Constitution has increased from eleven members in three divisions to twenty-one members in four divisions, plus an auxiliary division to cope with the backlog of cases.

The qualifications for judges (ministers) are: citizenship by birth; a minimum age of thirty-five and a maximum of sixty-five; five years of law practice; a good citizenship record (Art. 95). The maximum age applies to no other high official. Appointments to the Court are made by the President, with approval of the Senate. Interim appointments are possible (but never necessary) if the Senate should turn down two successive nominations to a post (Art. 96). Judges' salaries may not be reduced during their tenure (Art. 94). Leaves of absence are granted by the Court if they are for less than a month; longer leaves are granted by the President, with Senate approval. Resignations are accepted by the President and approved by the Senate (Arts. 99,

100). Retirement with pay is voluntary after fifteen years' service or after ten years' service and attainment of the age of sixty.[5]

The Supreme Court's work consists largely of appellate cases from the lower courts, mentioned above under ordinary and extraordinary jurisdiction. The exclusive jurisdiction of the Court covers all controversies between states, "between the branches of the same State regarding the constitutionality of its acts, and conflicts between the Federation and one or more States, and in all cases in which the Federation may be a party" (Art. 105). It also reconciles questions of court jurisdiction on the federal, federal-state, and interstate levels (Art. 106). In addition it has investigatory (but not punitive) power to consider "any act or acts constituting a violation of any individual guarantee or abuse of the public vote, or any other offense punishable by the federal law." This action is mandatory when requested by the President, a house of Congress, or a state governor (Art. 97). The Court's actions have been taken on request.[6]

The sessions of the Court are held as a single group (in *pleno*) and in the four separate regular divisions (*salas*). The Court has two periods of sessions — January 2 to May 15 and June 1 to December 15 — and its meetings are public, unless it feels that the public interest demands closed meetings. Meetings in *pleno* are held at least once a week, and decisions are taken by majority vote of a quorum — a quorum being fifteen. Such sessions have jurisdiction over such matters as annual election of the Court's president; naming the judges to the divisions; matters of internal administration; naming, allocating, and providing for supervision of lower court judges; controversies between states or powers of a state, the federation and a state, two federal courts, two state courts, or a federal and a state court; questions of jurisdiction between two of the Court's divisions (*salas*); and other matters not granted to the divisions by law.[7]

The Constitutional Convention of 1917 discussed at some length whether or not to organize the Supreme Court into divisions; but this device has been necessary to handle the large volume of cases. In 1934, a labor division was added to the existing three — penal, civil, and administrative — to handle appeals under the labor code. The division elects its own president annually; holds daily meetings, which are public unless otherwise ordered; and transacts its business by majority vote of a quorum, which is four members.[8]

The penal division hears appeals from the district courts on penal writs of *amparo*; some direct penal *amparos* from the collegial circuit courts; some direct (first instance) penal *amparos*; and penal cases in controversy between two district courts or two circuit courts (Art. 24).

The administrative division hears *amparo* appeals from district courts; some first instance *amparos*; and controversies between circuit courts (Art. 25). The civil division hears *amparos* appealed from the district courts and from the collegial circuit courts, as well as *amparos* brought directly before the Supreme Court. The auxiliary division hears civil *amparos* from the backlog of such cases before the court (Art. 26). The labor division hears *amparos* appealed on the basis of decisions of the federal and local councils of conciliation and arbitration for labor matters, appeals from the district courts, and appeals from the collegial circuit courts (Art. 27).

*Amparos* constitute the bulk of the appeals taken to the Supreme Court; and a large percentage of the cases are appealed to that Court, producing a congestion of the docket that has grown through the years and was regarded as serious by legal authorities as early as 1906.[9]

One of the great underpinnings of Anglo-American law is the doctrine of *stare decisis*. Mexico gives much less weight to precedent, while considerable weight is given to *doctrina*, or learned opinion. However, some importance is attached to a sort of limited *stare decisis* known as *jurisprudencia* (or ruling body of court decisions). This is the doctrine on a point of interpretation which results from five consecutive decisions, without an intervening contrary decision, made by the Supreme Court or one of its divisions. The vote in the division must be concurred in by four of the five judges. The resulting ruling is binding on all the lower courts of the nation, the Federal District and territories, and the states, as well as the Supreme Court itself. The Court, however, may overrule its *jurisprudencia*. Like the United States Supreme Court, its Mexican counterpart is usually slow to reverse itself. Therefore, many effective precedents result. The Mexican Court's ruling only suspends the effectiveness of a law or administrative rule or action in the instant case, without nullifying the law as such; so its effect is less complete than a similar Supreme Court decision in the United States.[10] The *jurisprudencia* is reported in the *Semanario Judicial*, the law journals, and the leading newspapers.

*Circuit courts (single judge).*[11] Before the recent establishment of the collegial circuit courts, the six unitary circuit courts comprised the only intermediate-level courts. To qualify for a unitary judgeship, a man must be a native-born citizen at least thirty years of age; be a lawyer; and have had five years of professional experience. Circuit and district judges are appointed by the Supreme Court for an initial four-year term. Reappointment brings them tenure during good behavior (Art. 97). They are subject to placement, transfer, and supervision by the Supreme Court.

These judges hear appeals from the district courts except in *amparo* cases; review denials of appeals; decide whether to excuse or disqualify a judge in a specific case except in *amparo*; and settle disputes in jurisdiction between district judges, except in *amparo*.

*Collegial circuit courts.* These are three-judge courts, which annually name their own presidents. Their decisions are by majority vote. There are five such circuit courts. Their jurisdiction covers appeals on *amparos* against civil and penal sentences and decisions in labor matters.[12]

*District courts.*[13] The forty-six district judges comprise the basic level of the federal court system. The Federal District has six judges, while the states and territories have from one to three each. They handle civil, penal, administrative, and labor cases; and most of the *amparo* cases originate in these courts. In districts having two or more judges, these magistrates specialize as to type of case handled. The judges must be native-born citizens, twenty-five years of age, lawyers, and have had three years of professional experience.

An additional responsibility of each district court is that of combating juvenile delinquency by promoting the establishment in each state capital and at the seat of each district court of a juvenile court. It consists of the district judge, as president, the local representative of the federal health service, and the local representative of the federal Education Ministry. The district judge sponsors a Council of Vigilance, parallel to the juvenile court, to combat delinquency. The Council and the juvenile court are also supervised by the Ministry of Government.

*The Federal District's courts.*[14] The Federal District has its separate system of courts. The highest court (*Tribunal Superior*) is appointed by the President, and they appoint the lower court judges. The *Tribunal* has eight sections of three judges each, which hear appeals from the lower civil and criminal courts. Appeals on constitutional violations can be taken from it to the Supreme Court of the nation. Below the *Tribunal* are separate criminal and civil courts. Next below these are the minor courts. At the lowest level are the Courts of Peace, which try only cases with small sums in controversy. Procedure is summary. Violations of constitutional rights may be appealed on *amparo*.

The juvenile court organization was mentioned above. In Mexico City there are two such courts. Their jurisdiction covers youths under the age of eighteen. Other agencies have been established to aid the court; these include observational centers, detention homes, and correctional schools. The Department of Social Welfare of the Ministry of Government has control of such institutions and of the juvenile courts in the Federal District and the territories. Important proposals along this line date from 1902. The present basic law dates from 1941. The first juvenile court was established in the Federal District in 1927.

*Other tribunals.* The most important tribunal outside the regular court system is the Tax Court (Fiscal Tribunal), to be described in chapter 11. The chief quasi-judicial bodies are the federal and local Boards of Conciliation, to be discussed in the chapter on labor relations (pp. 324–26).

*Public Ministry.*[15] The Constitution (Art. 102) and the law provide for the Public Ministry as an agency for the administration of justice which is closely related to the federal courts. It is headed by the attorney general (*procurador general*), whose agents are attached to the federal circuit and district courts. The officials of this office are appointed and removed at will by the President. The attorney general has the same qualifications as a judge of the Supreme Court.

The attorney general is the legal counselor of the government. He intervenes "in all matters to which the Federation may be a party; in cases affecting ministers, diplomats, and consuls general, in those that arise between two or more States of the Union, between a State and the Federation, or between branches of the same State" (Art. 102).

This office prosecutes all federal offenses before the federal tribunals; and it maintains a criminal investigation laboratory and other facilities for the work of investigation and prosecution. The federal judicial police collaborate with the attorney general's office in this work. An antecedent office extends back to the early years of independence, but the first law of the Public Ministry dates from 1903. The present office, in substantially its present form, dates from 1919.

A similar attorney general's office serves the Federal District and the federal territories.

*Court procedure.*[16] Mexican court procedure is similar to that of the United States. Testimony and cross-examination of witnesses are used regularly. But judges have greater power to guide the conduct of the trial than United States judges. They are much more than umpires enforcing the rules of the game.

In a criminal court case, the procedure has four stages. First comes the investigation by the officials prior to submitting the case to the court; this is done by the office of the prosecuting attorney and the judicial police. Next comes the preliminary examination; this includes actions taken by the court to determine the circumstances and responsibilities connected with the crime and the one accused. The third stage is the court trial, with the prosecuting attorney representing the government in its charge. A public defender is available to serve defendants unable to pay for counsel. The fourth stage is the passing of sentence and its execution.

The Latin American countries have never used the jury as much as the United States; the Constitution (Art. 20, VI) provides for its use in two types of situations. Offenses committed by means of the press "against public order or the external or internal security of the Nation shall in every case be tried by a jury." Other crimes "shall be tried at a public hearing by a judge *or* jury of citizens able to read and write and who are residents of the place and district in which the offense has been committed, provided the offense is punishable by a penalty greater than one year in prison." Most cases are tried without a jury. The various constitutional safeguards for fair treatment and a just trial have already been discussed (see Chapter 5, pages 83–87).

The popular jury consists of seven members drawn by lot from lists drawn up throughout the country every two years. Members must be citizens in good standing, residents of the district, and able to read and write. In addition to certain criminal cases and press cases, the jury handles cases of gross wrongdoing brought against public officials.

*Amparo.*[17] Judicial protection through the writ of *amparo* is generally regarded as Mexico's most important contribution to jurisprudence. It had its origin in the Yucatan State Constitution in the 1840s, and was incorporated in the Mexican Constitution of 1857. The present Constitution and subsequent laws have continued and rationalized its use.

*Amparo* means protection and combines features of such American writs as habeas corpus, mandamus, and certiorari. This exclusively federal writ has for its object constitutional protection in controversies arising from laws or acts of authorities violating individual guarantees; laws or acts of the federal authorities that injure or restrict the sovereignty of the states; and laws or acts of the state authorities that invade the federal sphere of action (Art. 103). Most cases have dealt with the violation of individual guarantees contained in the first twenty-nine articles of the Constitution, but other articles at times have an indirect effect. The writ may be sought only by or for the individual plaintiff whose right is affected; and the court's decision is binding only in the instant case. The successful action does not repeal the law itself. The Constitution (Art. 107) and the Organic Law make detailed provision for the procedure; and hundreds of books and monographs have dealt with its nature and functioning.

The law distinguishes direct *amparos*, when application is made to the Supreme Court in certain types of cases, and indirect *amparos*, which are filed in the district court. Most of the cases are indirect; and most of these are appealed to the Supreme Court. Naturally, this places a heavy burden of cases on the Supreme Court.

The district court's procedure in indirect *amparo* cases involves the following procedure: the plaintiff files his complaint; if the complaint is admissible, the court serves copies on all parties; the responsible authorities reply; the attorney general's office files its reply; the hearing is held; and the decision is handed down. Court action is limited to dealing with the case at hand and does not effect a repeal of any offending law. Thus the *amparo* proceeding subordinates the safeguarding of the Constitution as such to the protection of the affected individual. Only action taken under the law is dealt with.

In one sense, the system of *amparo* has been successful — in the sense of being solidly established as a basic feature of the Mexican legal system. However, abuse of the use of the writ has often brought great delays in justice. Therefore many authorities have recommended basic reforms in the system.[18]

*Administrative justice.* Mexico, like the United States, has no special administrative court system. A measure of opportunity for appeal to the courts is provided through *amparo*, when an administrative official or tribunal violates an individual guarantee protected by the Constitution.

A century ago, Mexican law made specific provision for separating control over the administration from jurisdiction by the courts. But this was fleeting; and the present Constitution makes no such provision. As in the United States, there has been much controversy over the desirability of establishing tribunals for separate functions of administration. The Fiscal Tribunal was established as a full-scale court in 1937. The same year saw the establishment of the labor Boards for Conciliation and Arbitration and the Tribunal of Arbitration for civil service employees. *Amparos* in all three areas can be carried to the Supreme Court.[19]

Full constitutional recognition was given to such administrative tribunals in 1946 (Art. 104). Supreme Court review in such matters through *amparo* is not considered by authorities as a fully adequate device for judicial control.[20]

### NOTES

[1] Ignacio Burgoa, "La Supremacía Jurídica del Poder Judicial de la Federación en México," *Anales de Jurisprudencia*, February 15, 1941, pp. 469–547; Paul B. Comstock, "Federal and State Jurisdiction in Mexico" (M.A. thesis, Columbia University, 1950); Lanz Duret, *op. cit.*, pp. 281–376; Tena Ramírez, *op. cit.*, Chs. 21–22; Helen L. Clagett, *The Administration of Justice in Latin America* (1952); *Ley Orgánica del Poder Judicial de la Federación*, in Andrade, *op. cit.*, p. 362 bis 9a–30a; *Directorio* . . . (1), pp. 567–99.

[2] Tena Ramírez, *op. cit.*, pp. 375–78.

[3] Lanz Duret, *op. cit.*, pp. 322–27.

[4] J. T. Vance and H. L. Clagett, *A Guide to the Law and Legal Literature of Mexico* (1945), pp. 105–6.

[5] Lanz Duret, *op. cit.*, pp. 289–96; *Diario Oficial*, February 19, 1951; *Directorio* . . . (1), pp. 567–84.

[6] Lanz Duret, *op. cit.*, pp. 305–40.

[7] *Ley Orgánica* . . . , Arts. 2–12.

[8] *Ibid.*, Arts. 15–19.

[9] Emilio Rabasa, *El Artículo 14*, *Estudio Constitucional* (1906), p. ii; Suprema Corte, *Informe* (1953).

[10] Clagett, *op. cit.*, pp. 123–26; Tena Ramírez, *op. cit.*, pp. 425–26.

[11] *Ley Orgánica* . . . , Arts. 31, 36; Comstock, *op. cit.*, pp. 45–48.

[12] *Ley Orgánica* . . . , Ch. 3 bis.

[13] *Ibid.*, Chs. 4, 6; *Directorio* . . . (1), pp. 591–99.

[14] *Ley Orgánica de los Tribunales del Fuero Común*; José Almaraz, "Law and Justice," *Annals*, March 1940, pp. 39–47; Salvador Mendoza, "Recent Tendencies in Mexican Criminal Procedure," *Pan American Union Bulletin*, May 1930, pp. 433–39.

[15] *Ley Orgánica del Ministerio Público Federal* (*Diario Oficial*, January 13, 1942); José Aguilar y Maya, *El Ministerio Público Federal en el Nuevo Régimen* (1942); *Directorio* . . . (1), pp. 535–47.

[16] *Ley Orgánica del Poder Judicial* . . . , Ch. 5; Almaraz, *op. cit.*, pp. 43–44; Clagett, *op. cit.*, p. 120.

[17] *Nueva Ley de Amparo*, in Andrade, ed., *op. cit.*, pp. 315 *et seq.*; Muñoz, *op. cit.*, pp. 238–42; Ignacio Burgoa, *El Juicio de Amparo* (1946); Tena Ramírez, *op. cit.*, Ch. 23; Clagett, *op. cit.*, pp. 136–37; Carlos Sánchez Majorada, "The Writ of Amparo," *Annals*, January 1946, pp. 107–11.

[18] Tena Ramírez, *op. cit.*, pp. 379–80.

[19] *Directorio* . . . (1), pp. 549–62; Clagett, *op. cit.*, pp. 61 *et seq.*

[20] Antonio Carrillo Flores, *La Defensa Jurídica de los Particulares Frente a la Administración en México* (1939), Chs. 15–16.

# 9

## Public Administration

As MODERN life becomes more complex, more problems must be solved by organized effort. Government is called upon to meet much of this challenge; and the administrative aspect of government work becomes increasingly important. The following chapter will first consider the administrative organization, then the civil service.

### Administrative Organization

Basic political and governmental institutions have changed slowly in Mexico. Even the 1917 Revolution did not lead to many basic constitutional structural replacements. When the Castilians reached New Spain, they found an advanced aboriginal civilization in the Valley of Mexico. An Indian king was head of the public administration, aided by a numerous nobility, clergy, and military. The military organization of the Aztecs included the machinery for the administration of justice, diplomacy, and espionage. The regular machinery of justice included special tribunals of various kinds. Other personnel were in charge of planning and executing important public works — roads, aqueducts, public buildings, and religious monuments. Taxes were levied and tributes were exacted from surrounding subject peoples, with effective tax-collection machinery. Welfare assistance was provided for the people in time of adversity from stocks of stored commodities. And officials were subject to stern punishments for wrongful acts.[1]

During the colonial days, the important parts of the administrative apparatus included the king, the Council of the Indies, the *audiencia* (the territory, with its judicial-administrative tribunal), the viceroy (the king's representative in the territory), governors, *adelantados* (royal judicial officials), *corregidores* (executive officers in a smaller area), and *ayuntamientos* (municipal councils).

The ultimate power and authority resided in the king. The Council of the Indies was a tribunal with legislative, administrative, and judicial powers. It reviewed actions taken by the viceroy and the *audiencias* and took part in ecclesiastical affairs. The *audiencias* were appellate tribunals to review the acts of the viceroy and the governors. Under the viceroy were various governors. The viceroy was president of the *Audiencia* of Mexico. On the local level were the *ayuntamientos*. Their powers of local self-government were quite variable, and they were subject to supervision from higher authorities. The administrations of the government and of the Church were closely linked.[2]

Colonial administration carried out important public services. Defense was in the hands of a standing army which was reported to be some 10,000 strong by 1804. Provincial militias were a reserve force, totaling about twice that number. The viceroy was commander-in-chief.[3]

The administration of justice was in the hands of a hierarchy of tribunals of considerable variety. Municipal *alcaldes* (judges) tried minor cases, while *tribunales ordinarios* handled more important cases not committed to a specialized body. Separate specialized tribunals existed for the Indians, the treasury, the Church, commerce, mining, irrigation, the military, and other matters.[4]

Important public services rendered by one or another level of government included education and important public works such as roads, public buildings, gardens, water supply, and lighting.[5]

*Independence: the nineteenth century.* With the coming of independence, administration became a clearly separate function under the executive. It was no longer performed by the same officials who exercised legislative and judicial powers — the viceroy, the *audiencia*, intendants, etc. The states were given local administrative authority. In the early constitutions, an executive council was provided to assist the President with administration.[6]

By mid-nineteenth century, the emphasis of government was largely negative. It was no longer the sustainer of religion, and the Díaz era, which was to promote foreign investments in Mexico, was yet in the future. The services were largely limited to foreign relations, maintenance of peace, judicial administration, and the raising of revenue. Strife between army factions promoted personalism and spoils politics in administration, with shifts of power bringing mass shifts of personnel and disorganization.[7]

The present basic type of administrative organization was adopted with the winning of independence. The short-lived empire established in 1822 had four ministries (*secretarías*): those of State and Foreign Relations, Justice and Ecclesiastical Affairs, Treasury, and Army and Navy. The first included post offices and roads. A Ministry of Development and one of the Interior were established in 1835 and 1837, respectively. In 1861, the ministries were reduced to four: those of Foreign Relations and Gobernación; Justice, Development, and Education; Treasury and Public Credit; and Army and Navy. Gobernación, the foremost ministry under the present Constitution, first appeared at that time. In 1891, the Ministry of Communications and Public Works was added, and it included the work of development, formerly linked with justice and education.[8]

In 1917, the Organic Law of the Public Administration was issued. It established nine agencies — six ministries and three departments. The ministries were those of Foreign Relations and Gobernación, Finance and Public Credit, War and Navy, Communications, Development, and Industry and Commerce. The departments were those of Justice, University and Fine Arts, and Public Health. Education was not included, being left to the states. Since the time of their establishment, the ministries still existing have in general had the same types of functions.[9]

Later in 1917, changes were made among the nine agencies, including establishment of Gobernación as a separate ministry. The Ministry of Education was established in 1921, with divisions of University and Fine Arts. In 1934, the ministries totaled eight — those of Gobernación, Foreign Relations, Finance and Public Credit, Army and Navy, Economy, Communications and Public Works, Agriculture and Development, and Public Education. The five departments were the Agrarian and those of Labor, Public Health, Manufacturing and Military Provisions, and the Federal District. The other two agencies were those of Attorney General for the nation and Attorney General for the Federal District and the territories.[10]

*Present organization.*[11] By 1947, Army and Navy comprised two ministries, Hydraulic Resources (formerly a commission) was a ministry, and minor shifts had been made. Since that date the ministries have been those of Foreign Relations, Finance and Public Credit, National Defense, Navy, Agriculture and Stockraising, Communications and Public Works, Economy, Public Education, Health and Assistance, Labor, Hydraulic Resources, and National Property and Administrative Inspection. The departments are the Agrarian and that of the Federal District. The national Attorney General is on a par with the ministries.

The New Law of the Ministries and Departments of State provides for the general structure of the ministries. Each ministry (*secretaría*) is headed by a minister (*secretario*), a *subsecretario* (under-secretary), and an *oficial mayor*. The *oficial mayor* corresponds roughly to a chief clerk or general manager of the detail work of the agency. The department (*departamento*) is headed by a chief (*jefe*), a general secretary, and an *oficial mayor*. The law may designate more than one subsecretary for a large ministry. The *secretarías* are organized into *departamentos*, which in turn are often divided into the *dirección general* (bureau) and the *departamento*. Other subdivisions, used without any uniformity or standardization, include the *oficina*, the *división*, and the *instituto* (Art. 23).

The President sets forth in detail the functions of each *secretaría* and *departamento* by means of *reglamentos* (Art. 18). Such a document for an agency designates the line of succession to the headship in the absence of the head, and determines the functions of the offices and the principal officials (Art. 26). Sometimes the understanding is labeled *acuerdo* or *decreto*.

The heads of the *secretarías* and *departamentos* exercise their functions in and through agreements with the President (Art. 21), and meetings of a single agency head with the President are apt to be frequent. Announcements of new policies and arrangements are often made at the conclusion of such meetings. Ministry and department heads may delegate the various functions among their subordinates. However, if a ministry has more than one *subsecretario*, the President designates which is second in command and will be in charge in the absence of the chief (Arts. 23, 24).

The ministries are declared by law to be equal in rank (Art. 20); but there are certain qualifications to this statement. In case of a dispute among agencies over the jurisdiction in a matter, the question is decided by the President, acting through Gobernación (Art. 28). This ministry has a *de facto* pre-eminence through serving as the presidential channel for relations with the Congress, the state governments, etc. Two other limitations on ministries should be mentioned. Each agency is free to maintain its own statistical service, but it does so under norms established by the Ministry of Economy. Each agency is expected to cooperate with the others by providing data that may be needed. The Finance Ministry works with other agencies when they organize or deal with specialized institutions of public credit (Arts. 22, 29).

Each ministry or independent department drafts for the President proposed laws, *reglamentos*, decrees, etc., dealing with matters of its concern which it wishes to see put into effect (Art. 19). Promulgation of such items of "law" involves use of the ministerial *refrendo*, discussed earlier in Chapter 7 (pages 108–9). Thus Article 25 provides that "the laws, decrees, *acuerdos* (decisions), and orders issued by the President, shall, for their validity and constitutional observance, be signed by the Minister or Chief of the Department" concerned. When a matter concerns two or more such agencies, the heads of all concerned shall countersign the document. There has been some speculation about the power of an agency head to refuse his signature; but this question is largely academic, for the President has complete freedom in appointing and removing such officials.[12]

From time to time, the President assigns new duties to various offices and officials. Every President has intervened more or less frequently in the functioning of the various agencies. Much of such supervision is done through the office of his personal secretary.[13]

Data on the details of administrative policy formulation and execution are scant compared with such data for United States government agencies. This is in part due to the high degree of centralization of authority in the hands of the chief executive.

The heads of agencies are required by the Constitution (Art. 93) to make annual reports to the Congress at its opening session, a provision extending back to 1827. The requirement is not always fulfilled. However, the President's annual message at the opening session serves to some extent as a summary of agency reports. The same constitutional article allows either house of the Congress to summon an agency head to testify, but this has not been a frequent practice. Occasionally the agency heads have appeared at their own request to testify on a pending bill.[14]

There has often been a substantial carry-over of upper-level personnel from one presidential administration to the next, often with some cabinet officers serving successive administrations in a number of different posts. Often these men have had experience as governors or as congressmen.* Methods of selection are not always clear, but important factors are personal, political, and family ties. Contributions of money or service to the official party have naturally had their reward. The "inner circle" of ministries — those of Defense, Finance, and Gobernación — has tended to contribute both influence and presidents to the country.[15]

The constitutional equality among ministries has been mentioned above. In actual practice, departments have the same status as ministries. The Constitution assumes the existence of departments, but it makes no clear distinction between them and ministries. Discussion in the 1917 Convention foresaw the department as an agency that would have purely administrative duties; the ministry's duties were to include participation in policy determination, including use of the *refrendo*. But in the absence of a clear constitutional provision, the two types of agencies have been treated as equals.[16] In addition to these two types of agencies, there are "independent" agencies, whose growing importance will be discussed in a later chapter (see pages 206–19).

*The Cabinet.* The President is assisted by an advisory group which is commonly called the Cabinet, but its constitutional basis is somewhat ambiguous. Article 29 refers to the Council of Ministers as the group whose approval the President must get before suspending the constitutional guarantees in a time of emergency. The New Law of the Ministries and Departments of State says the group includes the ministers, the department heads, and the federal attorney general, and that the President presides over its meetings (Art. 27). The group could be enlarged by the Congress, which creates new agencies. In recent years, the President's personal secretary has been included in the meetings.[17]

Only the President can call Cabinet meetings; and the meetings have

---

* As mentioned above, most of the present ministers have had considerable governmental experience. Of the eighteen top men installed by Ruiz Cortines in December 1952, the following occupational backgrounds are noted: law, 13; university teaching, 5; engineering, 2; military, 2; economist, 2; architect, 1. A number had had more than one occupation. Three had held posts abroad, and three had been leaders in the Party. Eleven had held posts in other departments, and five had been state governors. Six had authored books. The ten known ages ranged from 38 to 61, with seven older than age 50.

not been frequent, since most presidents have chosen to meet with the ministers singly or in small groups. A quorum of the Cabinet is two thirds of the members, with agreements being reached by majority vote. The decisions reached at the meetings are usually secret, and the law gives no force to such decisions. Therefore, they are advisory.[18]

## Public Administration and the Civil Service

*The field — study and practice.* The term "public administration" has generally been understood in Mexico to mean the structure and functioning of the executive branch of government. Only recently has the North American viewpoint begun to make headway — the idea that administration is concerned with the problems of top management, its hierarchical relationships, and the staff-and-line relationships at all levels. The old viewpoint, which still dominates, can be accounted for by the fact that political science is not yet a well-recognized discipline in Latin America. The study of law still dominates the social science field, and it is predominant in the training of the middle and higher civil servants. As in much of Europe, its principal emphases pertaining to government have been on constitutional law and — more recently — on administrative law. The emphasis has been on legal structure rather than on political and administrative processes and problems.

The recent rapid growth of business, industry, and cities in Mexico has multiplied government's problems of promotion and control. This, in turn, has brought increased interest in the study and practice of administration. Two decades ago, the interest of law students produced the first administrative law text, written by the distinguished jurist Gabino Fraga. It has gone through six editions, and administrative law still represents the chief approach to administration.

The first general text on public administration appeared in 1942 from the pen of Lucio Mendieta y Núñez, an outstanding sociologist, jurist, and authority on agrarian law. His broad treatment included the nature of the field and its history in Mexico, the national administrative structure, the civil service, the responsibilities of officials, and a sociological examination of the bureaucracy. He has done much to awaken interest in a realistic appraisal of the work of government.

During much of this time, economics was a rising discipline that attracted more attention than public administration, because it seemed to offer quicker solutions to pressing problems. Under the prompting of

Jesús Silva Herzog, then dean of the National School of Economics and a distinguished civil servant, courses in public administration were started at that school in 1946. He and a few other perceptive leaders had a few trainees sent each year for study and field work in the United States. The returned trainees took positions and spread their influence in the various agencies, including the Bureau of Administrative Inspection of the new Ministry of National Properties. Álvaro Rodríguez Reyes, an able former trainee in the United States, headed the program of studies in administration. But progress was slow in the face of low government salaries for graduates and the frequent preoccupation of officials with trying to solve pressing problems piecemeal, and the training program was recently suspended, at least temporarily.[19]

*The civil service.* The importance of the civil service is well known, but until recent years little was done in a systematic way to study the problems and meet the long-term needs. Under the Spanish regime, a sizable bureaucracy grew up; and a government position was one of the main occupational opportunities of the middle class. To a lesser extent, this remains true even today.

After the revolutionary period of 1910–17, there was increasing concern over the mass changes of personnel that came with the changes of governmental regime. In 1911 and later years, the Congress considered enacting a general merit system law, and in 1924 it discussed such a law for congressional employees. But it was not until 1934 that President Rodríguez issued an *acuerdo* (decision) putting into effect the first such general plan, effective at the end of his term of office on November 30. This measure was transitory in character and had the disadvantage, among others, of being an executive concession rather than a measure with rights and obligations of employees firmly grounded in statute.[20] It set forth norms for naming employees; designated their rights and obligations; and said that no covered employee would be removed without just cause proved before Civil Service Committees. It was a step in the right direction, although not always adequately enforced.

The present basic civil service law was enacted in 1938 and amended in 1941. This basic statute recognizes that one of the most fundamental problems is that of defining the relations between the employee and the government. In earlier years, the assumption was held that the rights of public and private employees were nearly identical and that the constitutional charter for labor (Art. 123) covered both. The present civil

service statute and its predecessors have (in effect) modified the constitutional article in important respects, but the statute is unusual in
granting specifically a limited right of strike to most civil service employees. Successive sections of the law deal with rights and obligations
of employees; hours of work and rest periods; compensations; obligations of the government as employer; obligations of the employees;
suspension and termination of employment by the government; unionization; conditions of work; strikes; strike procedure and arbitration;
illness and sick leaves; the Tribunals of Arbitration; and penalties for
infractions of the law.[21]

The present statute covers the regular employees of the federal government — those in the legislative, executive, and judicial branches, the
Federal District, and the territories (Art. 1). Employees are divided
into two groups, "base workers" and "confidence workers." "Confidence workers" are appointed by the President. In general, they correspond to the administrative class in other countries. These include the
positions of the minister, his chief assistants and the private secretaries,
the *oficial mayor*, chiefs and subchiefs of bureaus and offices, certain
specialized personnel, and corresponding positions in nonministerial
agencies (Art. 4). Those not enumerated in the law are considered
"base workers," whose positions are classified into several categories
ranging from unskilled to specialized personnel. The detailed protections of the statute protect the base workers rather than the confidence
group. One of the chief reasons for establishing the latter classification
was to deny certain workers the right to unionize and strike under certain conditions.[22] The Ávila Camacho law of 1941 marked a retreat
from the Cárdenas statute by broadening the classifications comprising
confidence workers, thus withdrawing the unionization privilege from
a considerable number. Only citizens may fill positions so long as qualified Mexicans are available (Art. 6).

The basic statute enumerates the general conditions of work. These
protections include maximum hours, minimum salaries, special protection for women and child workers, paid leave before and after childbirth, the six-day work week, and two ten-day vacation periods per
year to employees of six months' standing (Arts. 11–27).

Salaries are uniform within a category, with bonus adjustments for
employees in high-cost-of-living areas; and discrimination is forbidden
on the basis of age, sex, or nationality. Pay is to equal or exceed the

minimum fixed for the same job in private enterprise. Double pay is provided for overtime work. Proposed pay cuts and lay-offs are to be discussed with the union beforehand. (Arts. 31–40.) Salary rates are set forth in the annual budget of the government.

Compensation is one of the most pressing problems of the civil service. Employees have had several increases in the last few years, but the cost of living has risen even faster. And salaries have always been very modest, except for department heads and other top personnel who receive special allowances. The salaries of such professional men as lawyers and doctors range between $75 and $125 (U.S. money) per month, which makes it necessary for many to hold two jobs. Another factor partially compensating for low salaries is the provision by the government of medical, educational, recreational, social security, and other services free or at nominal cost. Recently, low-rent housing has been provided for many. But in terms of the total budget, the percentage allotted for salaries has been modest — and it is slowly decreasing.[23]

The total regular personnel of the federal government has doubled since about 1938 and now approximates 200,000. The ratio of government employees to total population is about 1:160, compared with a U.S. federal government employee-population ratio of about 1:65. One tabulation of positions places 34 per cent of them in education and 29 per cent in defense work. About two thirds of the total number are in the "base worker" classification.[24]

Placement of personnel prior to the passage of the statute was largely on the basis of spoils politics. Family and military relationships and the leadership of the official party were the principal controls over personnel placement. These factors have been much diminished in base worker placements, but they have retained considerable influence in the higher categories. Original and promotional examinations and placements are administered by each principal agency for its own personnel, and their quality varies considerably. There is no uniformity in the structural location of this function; sometimes it is handled by a separate personnel office, while other agencies combine personnel administration with budgeting and other staff services in a general bureau of administration.[25] Job tenure for a base worker is attained after a six-month probation period; and after six months of service a person may become eligible for a promotional examination (Art. 41).

In original and promotional examinations, first consideration is given to competence and seniority. Then consideration is given to union membership and veteran's status. Promotions are decided by the agency's Promotions Committee, which is composed of two agency members, two union members, and a fifth member chosen by these four. A base worker's status is in suspension when he serves in a "confidence" post. Temporary vacancies in base positions may be filled for six-month periods without examination. Proficiency tests are required each two years, and low scorers enroll in the agency's in-service training courses. Practitioners of a profession requiring a registered title receive their placements on the basis of recommendation by their professional schools and passing a problem-test dealing with the work of the agency. The chief of the department chooses the successful contestants. (Art. 41.)

*In-service training.* The basic statute provides that the government shall establish in-service training programs for employees who feel the need of such preparation as the basis for promotion and to maintain occupational skills (Art. 41, VIII). Some of the larger agencies have developed such programs, with varying degrees of success. The program of the Ministry of Finance is one example.[26] Another is the police training school of the Federal District. The federal highway police agency established a program in 1953 for giving its personnel instruction in highway vigilance, tourism, first aid, legal elements, and self-defense. The federal tourist bureau has found training beneficial in promoting an industry of vital importance to the economic life of the country. The need in this field is recognized, but progress has not kept pace with the need.

*Retirement.* Provision of pensions is both an old and a new service in Mexico. The first law was passed in 1761, with limited coverage. After independence, the piecemeal approach slowly extended inadequate coverage to several categories of employees. The General Law of Civil Pensions was enacted in 1925 to give coverage to all public employees of the federal government. It was followed by the laws of 1946 and 1947, the latter being currently in force.[27]

The program is one of joint contribution by employer and employee: the employee's contribution has been 5.5 per cent of his salary; the government contributes a similar amount and guarantees the solvency of the funds. Retirement because of age is allowed at fifty-five, after fifteen years of contribution to the fund. The retirement allowance is 100 per cent of the salary figure after thirty years of work. Retirement is also allowed for incapacity, and pensions are given to the family in case of the employee's death while in service. Medical and other auxiliary services are still restricted largely to the Federal District. Funds are used for mortgage and other loans to employees and for construction and operation of low-rent housing projects in the Federal District and elsewhere.[28]

The General Bureau of Civil Pensions is headed by a board of directors of six persons. Three are named by the President through the Ministry of Finance, and three are named by the Federation of Unions of Government Employees. The Director of Pensions functions as the executive officer of the board.[29]

*Employee responsibilities.* Two other aspects of public employment are of great significance: the legal responsibilities of officials and employees, and the role of unions in the public service. One of Mexico's oldest problems is that of honesty in public life. Corruption and graft on a sizable scale developed in the colonial period, and the situation has improved substantially only since 1953. Obviously, corruption is a serious problem in even the most advanced countries; but its prevalence in Mexico has been doubly serious, since the country has sought so hard to enhance its economic welfare through productive effort.

The Law of Responsibilities for Officials and Employees became effective in February 1940 under President Cárdenas. It is complementary to the constitutional provisions for impeachment of high officials by the Congress (Arts. 108–11). The President is subject to trial during his term of office only for treason and grave offenses; but other officials and employees may be tried for more than seventy listed offenses, for which punishments are listed in detail. Articles 103–11 seek to curb graft by civil servants: they are required to declare their assets to the Attorney General upon entering office; and provision is made for investigation and prosecution of those who give evidence of sudden and apparently inexplicable personal enrichment. This may take place during their terms of office or at the conclusion of such terms. The administration of the law was not strict until 1953, and circumvention of its provisions was aided by the provision that proceedings against malefactors were limited to the duration of the office and one year thereafter. These limited results paralleled those obtaining under previous Mexican constitutions, dating from the early years of the republic.[30]

One authority – Mendieta y Núñez – found corruption and graft

132

widespread during the early nineteen forties, while wartime economic developments seemed to intensify the problem. President Alemán promised to "moralize" government, but charges of considerable corruption in some offices persisted. One able economist testifies to the frequent occurrence of the *mordida* (graft) in the various levels of employment in 1952.[31]

A real change accompanied the inauguration of President Ruiz Cortines. He speedily secured amendments putting teeth into the Law of Responsibilities and dismissed hundreds of offending employees. Officials and employees are required to inventory their wealth upon entering and leaving office, and prosecutions for illicit gains can be made more easily. The legacy of the past cannot be changed overnight, but competent observers within the government report very substantial progress toward rooting out the long-standing evil. The incidence of graft in higher levels is now said to be small, but its removal on the lowest levels takes longer. Salary increases, enabling employees to live within their legitimate incomes, are essential; and some steps have been taken in this direction.

*Unionization.* The extensive social guarantees granted to labor have long been considered one of the highlights of the 1917 Constitution (Art. 123); and the government since then has usually been solicitous of the workers' rights, in private employment, to organize, bargain collectively, and strike. Naturally, the demand for these rights carried over into public employment; and the civil service law contains a rather extended statement of such matters.

The law has encouraged base workers to unionize to promote their interests, since the statute gives union members preferential treatment. Joining a union is voluntary for an employee, but maintenance of membership is obligatory after joining. However, an employee may be expelled by majority vote of the membership. Only one union functions in each agency, and the successful one is determined by majority vote. (Arts. 45–47, 52.)

Important obligations of government employee unions include the following: to register with the Tribunal of Arbitration; to prohibit re-election to union offices; to represent their members before the authorities; to make reports to the Tribunal of Arbitration. The unions are specifically prohibited from using force to secure members and from affiliating with a nongovernmental federation of unions. Unions may be dissolved for reasons specified in the statute. Interunion disputes are settled by the Tribunal of Arbitration (Arts. 53–61). Other rights and duties pertain to the strike situation.

Conditions of work are fixed at regular intervals by the head of the agency, after consultation with the union representatives. If the union objects to matters that have been established, it may appeal to the Tribunal of Arbitration for a final decision. (Arts. 63, 65.) If the normal procedures of negotiation fail, the union may consider strike action. The strike, a "temporary suspension of work," can come only as the result of a favorable vote by a majority of all the workers in the agency, with the vote taken according to the procedure established in the law. The strike may be taken only for repeated violations of the statute, denial of the services of the Tribunal, or disobedience of its decisions. This pertains to the "partial strike," a strike against one agency. The "general strike" is one taken against all the agencies of the government for failure to pay the salaries for a month or more, denial of basic rights under the law, ignoring or impeding the work and decisions of the Tribunal, or using pressure to prevent a "partial strike." (Arts. 66–73.)

Before suspending work, the employees must comply with the following requirements: present their written decision to the Tribunal; allow the Tribunal seventy-two hours for deciding whether the above-mentioned requirements for a legal strike have been fulfilled; allow a period of ten days for efforts at conciliation by the Tribunal. Upon the strike's being declared legal, the Tribunal will fix the number of workers that must remain at their posts if the public welfare or safety are at stake. (Arts. 74–76, 83.) Strikes are limited to the suspension of work, and acts of violence are subject to penalty (Art. 72). If the strikers have failed to comply with all the listed requirements, the Tribunal will declare the strike illegal or nonexistent, according to the facts involved; and penalties are prescribed (Arts. 77–82). There have been few strikes of government workers, and almost none in recent years.

The Tribunal of Arbitration has three members: one member designated by the government, one by the federation of unions, and one named jointly by the first two members (Art. 92). The jurisdiction of the Tribunal includes individual and union conflicts with the agencies, interunion conflicts, and registering and canceling the registration of unions. The procedure in a case consists of the Tribunal's receiving a complaint from a union, receiving a reply from the other party within three days, and holding a hearing. The Tribunal uses informal procedures and sets forth in its decision the bases on which it was made. Its decisions are not subject to ordinary appeal, but a writ of *amparo* may be sought in the Supreme Court when infringement of an individual guarantee is claimed. Infractions of the statute or failure to obey the decisions of the Tribunal are punished by fines and other means. (Arts. 99–115.)

The organized public employees have registered a number of important gains under the statute. They have received medical and social security protection. Many have been provided low-rent housing or loans for purchase of individual homes. Salary increases and equalizations and a pension plan have been achieved. The bureaucracy has been organized into administrative careers, and a start has been made in the field of in-service training. And an increasing measure of protection is being given to the individual in fair recruitment, tenure, and promotion procedures.[32]

On the other hand, various studies of the public service have pointed out shortcomings, especially in connection with unionization. One student feels that unionization has brought few gains that would not have come anyway, in the Mexican pro-labor environment.[33] Many feel that the union maintenance-of-membership requirement and the union's power to expel members put undue power in the hands of union leaders, even though the complete closed shop does not exist.[34] One authority — Mendieta y Núñez — recognizes important gains but feels that the statute and its functioning are open to considerable criticism, especially in granting the "right" to strike. He considers such action inappropriate for public employees, and he feels that union leaders have developed too much power over their members.[35]

Another study concludes that a rational personnel system has not yet been developed because of such factors as the prevalent labor ideology, undue addiction to established detailed routines, red tape which impedes personnel transfers across agency lines, lack of uniformity in job classifications — which are done by each agency, opposition by those with vested interests against change, and low pay scales.[36] However, various bonus and other incentive features have been adopted for employees of the Federal District, and other agencies are considering their adoption.

An American observer, Ebenstein, feels that the more rapid development of an adequate career merit system is impeded by Mexico's following the European system of leaving personnel administration up to the individual departments, rather than establishing a national civil service commission.[37] Such an agency could tackle all the problems of the civil service — job classification, standards for entry and promotion, salaries, transfers, etc.

### NOTES

[1] Lucio Mendieta y Núñez, *La Administración Pública en México* (1942), pp. 21–26.

[2] *Ibid.*, pp. 26–45.

[3] *Ibid.*, pp. 46–49.

[4] *Ibid.*, pp. 49–55.

[5] *Ibid.*, pp. 60–65.

[6] Schaeffer, *op. cit.*, pp. 41–42 (also in *Prob. Agr.*, January–March 1955, pp. 209–314).

[7] *Ibid.*, pp. 45–49.

[8] Mendieta y Núñez, *op. cit.*, pp. 68–71.

[9] *Ibid.*, and José Mijares Palencia, *El Gobierno Mexicano, su Organización y Funcionamiento* (1936), pp. 15–18.

[10] Mijares Palencia, *loc. cit.*; Mendieta y Núñez, op. cit., pp. 71–73.

[11] *Nueva Ley de Secretarías* . . . , in Andrade, ed., *op. cit.*, pp. 363–96; Tena Ramírez, *op cit.*, pp. 355–59; Fraga, *op cit.*, pp. 322–43; Mendieta y Núñez, *op. cit.*, pp. 79–126.

[12] Fraga, *op. cit.*, pp. 326–28; Felipe Hernández Rodríguez, "El Refrendo en el Derecho Mexicano" (UNAM thesis, 1944).

[13] Goodspeed, *op. cit.*, pp. 405–7.

[14] *Ibid.*

[15] Schaeffer, *op. cit.*, pp. 183–87; Mendieta y Núñez, *op. cit.*, pp. 299–302.

[16] Tena Ramírez, *op. cit.*, pp. 355–59.

[17] Goodspeed, *op. cit.*, pp. 397 *et seq.*

[18] Mendieta y Nuñez, *op. cit.*, pp. 120–21.

[19] Alexander Cloner, "The Cultural Setting of Mexican Public Administration" (manuscript, 1952); *Rev. Ec.*, 1947. No. 1, pp 34–40; William Ebenstein, "Public Administration in Mexico," *Public Administration Review*, Spring 1945, pp. 102–12; Mendieta y Núñez, *op cit.*; Álvaro Rodríguez Reyes, "La Economía y la Administración," *Rev. Ec.*, November 1951, pp. 335–39.

[20] Mendieta y Núñez, *op. cit.*, pp. 150–51.

[21] *Estatuto de los Trabajadores al Servicio de los Poderes de la Unión*, in Alberto Trueba Urbina, ed., *Ley Federal del Trabajo Reformada* . . . (1953); Mendieta y Núñez, *op cit.*, Chs. 5–6; Fraga, *op. cit.*, pp. 255–92.

[22] Ernesto Lobato, "La Burocracia Mexicana," *Rev. Ec.*, October 1951, pp. 307–12.

[23] *Ibid.*; Lobato, "Situación Económica de la Burocracia Mexicana," *Rev. Ec.*, December 1952, pp. 380–88; Cloner, *op. cit.*

[24] See note 22.

[25] Sría. de Bienes Nacionales, *Directorio* . . . (1), *passim*.

[26] *Hacienda y Finanzas*, April 1946, pp. 9–10.

[27] Fraga, *op. cit.*, pp. 378–80.

[28] *Ley de Pensiones Civiles* (1948); Fraga, *op. cit.*, pp. 279–86.

[29] Sría. de Bienes Nacionales, *Directorio del Gobierno* . . . : *Organismos Decentralizados* . . . (1951), pp. 116–19. (Hereafter referred to as *Directorio* . . . (2).)

[30] *Ley de Responsabilidades* . . . (1953); Mendieta y Núñez, *op. cit.*, Chs. 7–8.

[31] See note 23; Ebenstein, *op. cit.*, pp. 110–11.

[32] Cloner, *op. cit.*; Mendieta y Núñez, *op. cit.*, pp. 199–200.

[33] Schaeffer, *op. cit.*, p. 177.

[34] Ebenstein, *op. cit.*, p. 108; Schaeffer, *op. cit.*, p. 170.

[35] Mendieta y Núñez, *op. cit.*, Chs. 5–6.

[36] Schaeffer, *op. cit.*, pp. 189–202.

[37] Ebenstein, *op. cit.*, pp. 109–10.

# 10

## Administration and Its Improvement

In CONSIDERING the President as the head of the administration, I must repeat the fact that in considerable measure he is still the government, supported by the dominant official party with its principal constituent interest groups. This is still true, even though the movement toward institutionalizing governmental power has been slowly developing since the days of President Cárdenas.

*Executive leadership.* Cárdenas developed the power and functions of the executive office as no President had since 1917, while trying to institutionalize governmental power. New departments, nationalized industries, and growing budgets were included in the extensive reforms of the first Six-Year Plan. To handle the increased burdens, Cárdenas turned much far-reaching detail over to the office of his personal secretary, who became involved in planning, legislative drafting, and some measure of coordination of the administrative agencies.[1] Cárdenas' administrative qualities have been debated by competent observers. He failed to develop a sizable body of able administrators to continue in office; but so have his presidential successors. Many feel he spent too much time in the field at non-presidential detail to supervise his immediate subordinates effectively. Others regard his record as that of an able organizer and administrator.[2]

President Ávila Camacho was not regarded as a man of great administrative talent; but he surrounded himself with a number of good administrators. His handling of the war effort was able. He made considerable use of his personal secretary's office for administrative work; and he used a number of advisory committees — of official and nonofficial members — in the making of decisions.[3]

Alemán's regime was an all-out drive for industrialization, characterized by capable political leadership, large-scale achievements, and moderate (or large-scale — depending upon one's sources of information) corruption and graft. Several of Alemán's ministers were men of great ability, but his own administrative ability seems not to have been outstanding.

President Ruiz Cortines may be more of a presidential surprise than Ávila Camacho. Both had been relatively obscure officials, working outside the political limelight; but Ruiz Cortines' varied practical experience in government exceeds that of any of his predecessors. He has thus far produced no brilliant administrative reforms; but his rigorous campaign for efficiency, official honesty, and a balanced governmental program give promise of better days for Mexico.[4]

*The Cabinet.* In Chapter 9, I referred to the scant constitutional provision for the Cabinet as a group, and noted that it meets only at the call of the President for purposes of giving advice and receiving presidential instructions. There is no legal pre-eminence for any ministry; but practice gives primacy to Gobernación, since it is the presidential channel for communicating with Congress and the states and for determining the jurisdiction of an agency when that is in question.[5]

Use of the Cabinet as a group for administrative coordination is greatly limited by the infrequency of its meetings. Some presidents have held several meetings in a year, but they are usually held less frequently. Presidents have often felt too busy with other matters to institutionalize the coordination of ministerial work. Therefore, two other devices have been used: inter-ministry coordinating committees and the office of the President's personal secretary.

Such coordinating committees have been used for well over a decade to seek agreement on specific tasks. But their use, like other devices, has depended mainly on the personality of the President; and results have been limited, due to the absence of any full-time machinery for seeing to the initiation and follow-through in such matters. The committees have often lacked speed and flexibility through being composed of subalterns whose decisions are subject to higher approval. A full-time agency would seem essential for dealing with projects requiring the combined efforts of two or more agencies.[6]

*The President's secretary.* Routine communications between ministries and between the President and ministers are expedited by the President's personal secretary. The secretariat of this office might be considered as the nucleus of an auxiliary staff unit for planning, coordination, and supervision; but it has not been organized or staffed for such work. However, some presidential private secretaries have become almost ministers without portfolio. Still, there is much duplication and uncoordinated activity within the administration.[7]

*Presidential supervision.* The President does not have the time to supervise effectively the work of all the ministries; still, the chief executive does a lot by direct contact. He has private telephone lines to the offices of the agency heads, and he uses them frequently. The head of one of the most important agencies told the author that President Ruiz Cortines confers with him by phone almost daily, evidencing a detailed interest in the work of the agency. This is a good illustration of the highly centralized character of Mexican public administration.

While Ruiz Cortines has held few full cabinet meetings, he often meets with small groups of agency heads dealing with a specific problem.

*Administrative planning.* Of the two main types of planning – program and administrative (or management) – considerable effort has been put into program planning, as will be discussed later (Chapter 15 et seq.), although it has not been too well systematized or institutionalized. But little has been done in administrative, or management, planning – the process of planning dealing with improvement in administrative organization, staffing, direction, and coordination of operations.

In the first place, the demands of substantive programs facing the Mexican government have seemed to require all its attention, leaving little time for anything else. Mexico is a country "in a hurry" to advance its material welfare. Public administration has been regarded almost solely as the carrying out of substantive programs. This conception has been enhanced by the legal tradition in which government developed in Mexico. The study of government was until the last two decades the study of constitutional law. Slowly the study of administrative law gained a foothold in the National University, branching out into the study of the law of program fields such as labor and agriculture. So, administration has become largely a preserve of the lawyers; and writers have not shed much light on the true nature of the administrative process.

In the last few years, there has developed some recognition of the need for administrative planning. In Chapter 9, I mentioned the internship training of small numbers of Mexicans in North American administrative centers, their return as "staff" employees in various agencies, and the establishment of public administration courses in the University's School of Economics. Conferences on methods of administration have been held; and the functional and analytical approaches to administration have made slow headway, without wholehearted government support. And research in the problems of administration is only beginning. Thus, little attention has been given to planning as a management tool which could do much to facilitate the pressing substantive programs which the government has under way.[8] And progress is also slow in the teaching of public administration, through lack of adequate governmental support for the program.

*The ministries.* As discussed in Chapter 9, the ministry is established according to constitutional mandate (Arts. 89–93) and the Law of the Ministries. The top officials are the secretary (minister), subsecretaries, and *oficial mayor.* The agency subdivisions are by subsecretaries, departments, bureaus, offices, divisions, etc., without complete uniformity in designation. The minister is under the unqualified control of the President, and the President issues the *reglamento* which governs the organization and functioning of the agency. In the colonial regime there was considerable dispersion of authority. Under the present Constitution there is much dispersion of functions among agencies, but authority and power are highly centralized through the prevailing presidential-ministerial relationship.

Within the agency we find the same extensive centralization of authority in the minister. Naturally, this produces a high degree of routinizing of operations, both important and unimportant decision-making concentrating on the minister's desk. The result is a slowing down of operations, both at the capitol and in the field service.[9]

An important element in efficient administration is the span of control of top personnel. This is sometimes excessive. Among sixteen principal agencies, it ranges from six to twenty-two offices supervised by a superior, with a median of nine. The role of the *oficial mayor* varies considerably from that of manager of housekeeping functions to that of supervisor of all agency units. In one agency he seems to supervise no line units; in two he supervises some; in six, many or most units; in seven, all units. The housekeeping functions under him may be concentrated in one over-all unit, or they may be found in two or more.[10]

Numerous operating inefficiencies, due both to structure and procedures, are pointed out by both Mexican and foreign students of the problem.

*Decentralized agencies.* Mexico, like the United States, has for a number of reasons carried on much of its credit and developmental work through channels outside the regular ministries. A recent tabulation includes eighty-five decentralized agencies, owned entirely or in considerable measure by the government. Eight of these agencies are banking and general financial institutions; five deal with pensions, social security, and insurance; and fifteen deal with banking, subsidies, and agricultural promotion work. The largest group, thirty-four, deals with industrial development. (Of this number, five are promotional-developmental, eleven deal with basic industry, five with the cinema industry, and three with construction.) Another group of five deals with transportation; four are for commerce; seven are hospitals; and seven are miscellaneous — including two multiple-purpose, TVA-type valley authorities.[11]

The reasons for establishing the decentralized, wholly government-owned agencies included greater adaptability for commercial operations than regular departments; escape from the routines of such departments (where procedural etiquette and administrative formalities are often excessive); freedom from circumscription by the vested interests characterizing long-established agencies; and freedom to pay more attractive salaries than the ministries, through remaining outside the control of the regular budget. This separate status obviously has raised unsolved problems of importance in the realms of budgeting, planning, coordination, and control. Only now are serious efforts being made to cope with these problems.

Government participation as a stockholder in private companies is obviously an important flexible means of aiding economic development through private enterprise. In an underdeveloped country like Mexico where risk capital has been scarce and reluctant, the advantages of this device are felt to outweigh by far any possible disadvantages of government influence on the private sector.

*Reorganizations effected.* Administrative reorganization has been for many years a pressing problem even in the United States; and serious students of the problem in Mexico have long felt the need for a thoroughgoing program. Government agencies have been added from time to time without integration with existing agencies. And established agencies have been slow to modernize their structures and practices. Occasionally, a bureau has been shifted from one ministry to another, but this has not been frequent in peacetime. During World War II, agencies in the field of price control were shifted to improve enforcement.[12]

There have been several laws since 1917 providing for major reorganizations in the administrative branch of the government; and from time to time other laws have established new ministries, provided for new functions, or redistributed existing functions. But, as in the United States, important changes have usually come slowly.[13]

The Mexican literature on administrative organization in government is still very scant, though a few good works dealing with business organization and administration have appeared.[14] Also scant is the published literature on administrative reorganizations; and the tendency has been to report the few studies made only after their recommendations have been at least partly put into effect. Such actions are usually reported only in the most general terms.

The first serious study on reorganization was published in 1918. The financial organization of the country was studied with the aid of American experts, and recommendations were made to secure more effective financial control. A new accounting system was installed, better business methods were suggested, and improvements were suggested in the revenue system. The financial system of the Federal District was also studied, and changes were suggested.[15] Improvements came slowly.

Another reorganization study dealt with the Finance Ministry in 1927–28.[16] Improper allocation of functions and duplication of functions among the ministry's offices were pointed out; and recommendations dealt with better control and use of stenographic personnel through the establishment of a centralized office of correspondence; concentration of the planning function in the administrative office; standardization of statistics; centralization and improvement of archival work; development of an adequate financial library; establishment of a central office to direct the agency's numerous tax offices in the field; and development of an adequate system of examinations for selection of personnel. Progress was made on most of these points; but there is still room for much improvement.

Data are scarce on subsequent attempts at reorganization; but scattered examples are found during the next two decades. Some attempts were made toward improvement in the Cárdenas administration. Modest improvements were made in record-keeping, and shifts of certain offices effected financial savings. Important events were the establishment of several major agencies. The labor and agrarian departments were established as autonomous departments in 1932 and 1934, respectively, and Cárdenas gave their work major emphasis. The railroads and oil were nationalized and became important government agencies; and the Ministry of Public Health and the Federal Electricity Commission were established in 1937.[17]

The wartime administration of Ávila Camacho established several emergency agencies, and effected some minor reorganizations in ministries for greater economy and efficiency. Health and Welfare, Labor, and the Navy were raised to the status of ministries.[18]

Two ministries were added under Alemán in 1946 — that of Hydraulic Resources, which replaced the National Irrigation Commission, and that of National Properties and Administrative Inspection.

The potentially important administrative role of National Properties has been ably analyzed by Alexander Cloner, a government consultant trained in American public administration.[19] This Ministry is an operating and control agency as well as a staff department. It plans and directs the construction of public buildings; maintains an inventory of federal holdings; regulates public works contracts; supervises federal purchases; and makes administrative improvement studies.[20]

The over-all achievements of the Ministry are significant, including substantial savings through contract and purchasing controls. It is a department of increasing importance which also oversees the activities of the Federal Committees for Material Improvement, groups which function in the various municipalities. "Participations" from customs receipts and other federal subsidies provide them with resources for local public works and other programs of community betterment.

Its staff advisory services include the making of economic and administrative analysis studies; but this aspect of the Ministry's work, potentially one of its most useful, has made comparatively little headway. Some agencies have achieved substantial savings and increased efficiency through adopting the Ministry's recommendations for standardization and simplification of forms and reporting techniques. But, lacking compulsory powers in such matters, the Ministry can make studies and recommendations for other agencies only upon request.

Reorganizations of lesser importance have taken place in recent years in the Treasury, the tax offices and the archives of the Ministry of Finance, purchasing agencies, and the Ministry of Communications and Public Works.

One Mexican authority,[21] writing in 1942, felt that the reorganization efforts had been sporadic and yielded slim results; that they had slighted the details of agency functioning; and that they had sought "economies" more than efficiency. He urged a permanent agency for making studies and supervising the adoption of the resulting findings. The picture seems brighter now than as he viewed things then; but there is still much room for improvement. His picture in 1942 was one of servile conformity to mechanical rules of procedure; widespread corruption and inefficiency; poor personnel procedures; inertia; both overstaffing and understaffing in the same agency; and unplanned growth.[22] Despite many improvements, an informed journalistic observer in 1953 pointed to considerable disregard for good administrative practices, as evidenced by the continued failure to adhere to the hierarchical principle; undue centralization of the power of decision; inadequate coordination of work; and slowness in execution of work.[23]

*Coordination.* I have already discussed inter-agency coordination through the President, his personal secretary, and the Cabinet, as well as limited coordination through the Ministries of Finance and National Properties in matters of the budget, purchasing, contracts, and property management. Here I should mention more specific arrangements for coordination.

First, I should mention certain general provisions of the Law of the Ministries and Departments of State. The Ministry of Economy sets general standards to which the various agencies' statistical offices conform (Art. 22). The Ministry of Gobernación is the President's channel for resolving jurisdictional questions among agencies (Art. 28). Agencies are charged with cooperation through providing each other with needed information. And the Ministry of Finance participates in actions of the agencies dealing with the administration of credit. (Art. 29.)

An example of a permanent coordination device established in the thirties was the Permanent Fiscal Committee, a group to aid the Finance

Minister by studying revenue resources and making proposals for tax changes.

The war era produced a number of examples of coordinative machinery. A Supreme Defense Council was established in 1942, composed of representatives of the executive, the Congress, the judiciary, agriculture, commerce, industry, labor, the professions, etc. Upon the declaration of war, the President set up an Emergency Economic Planning Board in July 1942, to provide data on industrial necessities and production. A War Production Board was set up in October of 1942 to secure coordination over production of war materials. In 1943, a consortium of agencies dealing with price control and agricultural and industrial production was established. The Emergency Economic Committee was established in the same year (1943) as an interministerial group. In 1949, the Consultative Council on Economic and Fiscal Policy was established, with membership from the executive branch, the Bank of Mexico, commerce, and industry.[24]

In general, the interministry committee has often failed to achieve its full objective because its members have been subordinates whose decisions have had to await ministerial ratification.[25]

*Decentralized agencies.* In an earlier section of this chapter I listed the large number and variety of decentralized agencies that have been established in Mexico, especially in the last two decades. These agencies outside the regular ministries have varying degrees of autonomy, but in the last analysis they are under the President's control. The Constitution did not foresee their growth; but their legal basis is codified in the Law for the Control of the Decentralized Organizations, effective in 1948. It covers organizations in which the federal government participates, wholly or in part, through providing capital, properties, concessions, budget, subsidies, or a specific tax yield. Technical or specialized public services are the functions of such agencies.

With few exceptions, the President exercises close control through appointment of board members, the manager, and sometimes other personnel. For some agencies, the President directly or indirectly appoints all board members, while in other cases some members are appointed by interested unions or other groups. This last is the case for the pension, railroad, and petroleum agencies. In some cases the President's appointments are made on nomination by one or more ministries with related functions, especially by the Finance Ministry. This Minister is chairman of the board of one agency (the railroads) and has a general veto over its actions.[26]

The budgets of autonomous agencies are separate from the general government budget; and part or all of the operating funds may come from the government. The Finance Ministry supervises these agencies through reviewing their financial reports; reviewing and modifying their budgets; exercising controls over their annual programs of operations; auditing their accounts; giving prior approval to expenditures; and promoting innovations in their organization and functioning. The Ministry of National Properties participates in approval of contracts.[27]

The government authorities are conversant with the advantages, disadvantages, and desirable criteria of decentralized agencies. As in the United States, however, there is far from being a consensus in terms of practice; and a number of practices are debatable. One local commentator feels that in practice the President does not have adequate control over the agencies, and that supervisory powers delegated to the ministries are being used inadequately and without uniformity. Some agencies are held rather closely under ministry control, while others of importance are not controlled closely enough. Some duplications of function are found here as among the ministries; and a need has been felt for a strong coordinating office in the Finance Ministry, with its personnel specialized as to type of agency "coordinated." [28] One step was taken in this direction in 1953 with the establishment of an inter-ministry committee to plan a six-year investment program.

A limited use has been made of citizen advisory committees in recent years. Examples are those which counsel the head of the Federal District government and advise the Finance Minister on tax problems. Informal counseling with citizen groups has also increased recently.

*General observations.* The rapid economic and social changes of recent years have produced heavy demands on government, especially regarding government's role in the economy. The administration enjoys a large measure of autonomous power in Mexico, since the Congress, dominated by the official party, has placed few obstacles in the executive's path. The same is true of the courts.

Recent years have seen increased attention paid to problems of personnel, budgeting, taxation, and program planning — but little attention to true management planning — and an atmosphere of business-like procedure is slowly developing. The personnel problem is still acute, with "real wages" still very low and no increase in the total proportion of the budget going to salaries. The personal element is still strong in government, as it has been throughout Mexican history. So the need is still great to delegate increased responsibility, thus freeing agency heads from details to provide more time for true administrative work. The work of some ministries needs to be coordinated more closely with that of related decentralized agencies. And there is considerable functional overlapping between agencies.

The movement for administrative rationalization might well be advanced at the present rate of the campaign for honesty in government. Here, as in other aspects of administration, more precise and detailed evaluation must await the availability of more suitable data.

### NOTES

[1] S. S. Goodspeed, "The Role of the Chief Executive in Mexico . . ." (Ph.D. thesis, University of California, 1947), pp. 306 et seq.

[2] Ebenstein, op. cit., pp. 107-8.

[3] Goodspeed, op. cit., p. 358; Ebenstein, op. cit., pp. 111-12.

[4] Time, September 14, 1953, pp. 40-48.

[5] Nueva Ley de Secretarías . . . , in Andrade, ed., op. cit., pp. 363-96.

[6] Mendieta y Núñez, op. cit., pp. 118-21; Rev. Ec., February 28, 1947, p. 6.

[7] See note 6; Schaeffer, op. cit., pp. 89-90.

[8] Rev. Ec., January 31, 1947; Schaeffer, op. cit., pp. 212, 236-43; Ebenstein, op. cit., pp. 105-6.

[9] Rodríguez Reyes, op. cit., pp. 335-39.

[10] Sría. de Bienes Nacionales, Directorio . . . (1), passim.

[11] Sría. de Bienes Nacionales, Directorio . . . (2), passim.

[12] Goodspeed, op. cit., pp. 341 et seq.

[13] Sría. de Bienes Nacionales, Directorio . . . (1), passim.

[14] Ángel Caso, Principios de Organización (1948).

[15] Comisión de Reorganización Administrativa y Financiera, Finances of the Federal District of Mexico (1918).

[16] Sría. de Hacienda y Crédito Público Comisión Reorganizadora, Informe de sus Labores (1928).

[17] Goodspeed, op. cit., pp. 307-8, 359; Sría. de Bienes Nacionales, Directorio . . . (1), passim.

[18] See note 17.

[19] Cloner, op. cit.

[20] Sría. de Bienes Nacionales, Informe (1952); Directorio . . . (1), pp. 443-64.

[21] Mendieta y Núñez, op. cit., pp. 203 et seq.

[22] Ibid., Ch. 9.

[23] El Universal, September 17, 1953.

[24] Presidente, La Hacienda Pública de México a través de los Informes Presidenciales . . . (1951), pp. 664-88, 714; Goodspeed, op. cit., pp. 337 et seq.

[25] Mendieta y Núñez, op. cit., pp. 119 et seq.; Schaeffer, op. cit., pp. 109-10.

[26] Ley para el Control de los Organismos Decentralizados . . . (1948); Fraga, op. cit., pp. 370-85.

[27] Fraga, op. cit., pp. 370-78; Schaeffer, op. cit., pp. 101-2.

[28] Fraga, op. cit., pp. 367 et seq.; Excelsior, November 17, 1953.

# 11

## Public Finance

THE problems of public finance comprise a most important part of government. This is especially true of a country like Mexico, in which the government plays such an important and growing role in the economy. Mexican public finance will be considered first in terms of expenditures and then in terms of revenue.

### Expenditures

Government expenditures (in pesos) increased some nineteen-fold between 1928 and 1955. In recent years nearly nine tenths of all public spending has been by the central government; and about 40 per cent of all capital investment, public and private, is by government.[1]

*General considerations.* While it is difficult to consider budgetary administration apart from revenues, the latter will be deferred to the second part of this chapter. Budgeting, as "the heart of management," is a fiscal blueprint of projected government activities, involving the stages of planning, enactment, administration, and control of government spending.

The first stage, planning, is covered by the Organic Law of the Budget. Enactment is covered by the Constitution and the law. Administration, including internal controls, is covered by the law. Post-audit controls are provided by the Constitution.

The conception of financial management as the focus of good administration is comparatively new in Mexico, despite the fact that Mexico has long had an executive budget. The basic constitutional provisions regarding budgetary introduction, enactment, and post-audit have remained much the same under the present Constitution as in its predecessor. However, the first three presidents under the present Constitution adopted budgets by decree. Cárdenas put through a budget law in 1935 that was technically adequate. While budgetary administration improved under him and his successors, true budgetary planning and control were not achieved until about 1949. Structurally, the budget document is broken down into fixed expenditures (salaries, etc.), materials, construction, acquisitions, investments, debts, and special expenditures.[2]

Several agencies participate in the financial process, but the Ministry of Finance has full control under the President in the budget preparation process. And it shares few, and less important, functions with other agencies in budgetary administration. The Ministry's budgetary function is performed by the General Bureau of Expenditures, which has four main subdivisions.[3]

The Department of the Budget has general charge of the preparation of the budget for submission to the Chamber of Deputies. Other functions include making studies and recommendations on budgetary work in general, position and staff additions, and reductions. The Department of Control of the Budget handles the budgetary administration. The work of accounting is done here. The Office of the Registry of Federal Personnel keeps certain personnel files and records. The Office of Contracts, Compatibilities, and Exemptions reviews contracts and certifies regarding the compatibility of employments in case of question.[4]

Final accounting and the administrative audit is done in the Federal Accounting Office, another Finance Ministry dependency, which prepares the annual account for submission to the Chamber of Deputies for the legislative audit.

*Composition of the budget.* The Organic Law of the Budget defines the budget as the combination of documents prepared by the executive branch to present its program of activities before the Chamber of Deputies. These documents include the President's report on the economic situation of the government; the estimate of income for the next year; the estimate of expenses for each agency; past, current, and estimated future income and expenditures; and any other data the President desires to submit. (Arts. 15, 16.)

It is helpful to consider the Mexican budget in connection with certain well-known budgetary criteria: comprehensiveness and unity of treatment, intelligibility, classification of expenditures, types of appropriations, and flexibility of enforcement. Like most national budgets, Mexico's does not meet the ideal of complete comprehensiveness and simultaneous treatment. Improvements have been made and others are being considered, but the decentralized organizations and those in which the government participates with private business are still outside the main budget.[5] The goal of comprehensiveness is also thwarted by the fact that the law and the practice sanction "reforms of the budget," whereby the President (and later the Congress) approves expenditures beyond those originally approved. (Arts. 29–31.) This practice also affects the budget's "intelligibility."

In its final form, the budget document itself contains only expenditures; revenue figures are included in the supplementary data. The breakdown of the budget is by each of the three branches of government into the following categories: debt, direct and indirect investments, and subsidies. Within each branch and agency, there are breakdowns by personnel, and character and object of expenditure (Art. 18). There is considerable itemization except for the "secret" category granted to the President (Art. 65). Budgetary flexibility is provided by the Organic Law and its *reglamento*, which govern transfers between budgetary items, as well as by the "reforms of the budget" mentioned above.[6] And revolving funds are granted to some agencies.

The federal government grants various subsidies to the state and local governments, in addition to loans which have often been canceled at a later date when repayment was difficult or impossible. In other cases, a direct service is provided by the federal government for local areas. Matching grants have been used, as well as centrally collected, locally shared taxes. In addition, subsidies have been granted for a number of years to agencies engaged in distributing basic food necessities at low controlled prices. The general protective tariff system constitutes an indirect subsidy for manufactures, while specific tariff provisions encourage such imports as machinery. Tax concessions to new and essential industries are another indirect subsidy.[7]

Capital investments are an important budgetary problem that is covered only in part by the regular budget. One official study indicates that the various units of government allocated from 31 per cent to 38 per cent of their expenditures in 1946–49 to gross capital investments, and these investments represented from 29 per cent to 36 per cent of the country's gross capital formation. A large portion of the private segment went into residential construction. In highly important fields such as transportation, communications, and electric power, the government has invested two to three times as much as private enterprise. Somewhat more than half the government investment is by decentralized organizations and governmentally aided companies, which are outside the general budget.

The reasons for government's extensive economic role are numerous. Among them are the social security program, the agrarian reform and the agricultural credit programs, nationalization of the oil and railroad industries, and the extensive industrialization program.[8]

The need is being recognized for preparing investment programs on a long-term basis, so that projects and programs can be coordinated with each other and investments can be accelerated or decelerated to meet changing conditions. And the need is recognized to bring all programs into a consolidated budget. During Alemán's regime, the Law for the Control of Decentralized Organizations was passed, granting special powers to the Ministry of Finance to coordinate the activities of these organizations. But only now is a consolidated budget being seriously considered.[9]

In 1953, the President and the ministers of Finance and Economy announced the establishment of a coordinated investment program for the years 1953–58. An investments committee of four members was established, representing the Ministries of Finance and Economy, the Bank of Mexico, and the chief government lending agency, Nacional Financiera. The Committee is charged with the responsibility of making studies that will enable it to determine the desirable level and distribution of public investments, correlating them with available private investments. The Committee's favorable status in the governmental hierarchy seems to lend promise to this first full-scale coordinated attempt at programming of public investments in Mexico.[10]

*Preparation of the budget.* The preparation of the budget follows a detailed calendar or schedule set forth in the Organic Law of the Budget and its *reglamento.* The Law provides that the agencies shall send their preliminary requests to the Bureau of Expenditures, Finance Ministry, before July 31 of each year (Art. 5). The Bureau studies these, and by September 1 it sends budgetary instructions to the agencies, giving tentative allotments and breakdowns (Art. 6).

By October 1, the Bureau has notified the agencies of the amount that is to be recommended by the President for their next budget and has made a preliminary distribution of the amount. During the first half of October, the agencies continue studying their proposals. During the second half of the month, the Bureau calls together the representatives designated by the agencies and gives them instructions on preparing their proposed budget in its final form. These representatives constitute the Permanent Committee on the Budget, under the chairmanship of the director of the Bureau of Expenditures. The Committee's role is advisory, and it seeks to coordinate the requests of the various agencies. The Committee works in part through subcommittees. (Arts. 5–8.)

By November 1, the agencies send their revised estimates to the Bureau, together with justifications and other supporting data. November is a month of conferences and adjustments, with the Bureau studying the documents submitted and seeking to prevent duplications. A two-week period after December 1 is allowed for the Bureau to present the final budget document to the President for his approval and for his conferences with agency heads on policy matters before his transmitting of the budget to the Chamber of Deputies. (Arts. 9–13.) [11]

*Enacting the budget.* The present Constitution, unlike its predecessor, does not provide for the President to initiate the budget; but the Organic Law (Art. 21) and the practical situation require it. Thus the President is to present the proposed budget to the Chamber of Deputies not later than December 15.[12]

The Chamber alone enacts the budget, which the Senate may consider but not change. Upon receiving the document, the Chamber immediately passes and sends to the Senate a tax bill to cover the proposed budget. Then it turns its attention to the budget. Members having proposals regarding the budget can send them to the Chamber's various committees for study, but any proposal for adding to the proposed budget must be accompanied by a proposal for raising the necessary revenue. The Chamber and its Committee on the Budget may call in the Finance Minister for information and assistance, since the committees do not have expert staff personnel to help them with their work. No agency may counsel the Chamber to change the President's proposed budget. (Arts. 21–26.) If the Chamber fails to make provision for an office, the funds for it remain at the same figure as for the previous year.[13] The President has the item veto power, but the realities of Mexican politics make its use unnecessary.

The Chamber's attention to the budget must of necessity be perfunctory. At best it has less than two weeks for the task, and often the late arrival of the document further reduces the time available. One Mexican fiscal authority reports that the budget is often presented without adequate explanation. The few changes that the Chamber makes in the proposal are upward revisions, not cuts. The inadequate time available for the budget bill is matched by similar limitations on time available for the Chamber's consideration of the tax bill, since it must send this measure to the Senate before it can give adequate consideration to the budget proposal. The congressional shortcomings in fiscal matters have often been pointed out by Mexican experts — including the placing of budget enactment entirely in the hands of the Chamber. However, any later authorization for spending must be enacted by both houses.[14]

*Execution of the budget.* Budgetary execution in Mexico involves a rather complicated set of procedures and a number of control agencies to serve as checks on the legality and adequacy of procedures. These are followed by the post-audit under the direction of the Chamber of Deputies.[15] In general, the Ministry of Finance — the principal agency concerned with budget execution — intervenes to a greater degree in the work of the agencies than the budgetary control agencies do in the United States.

The process begins with the fixing of allotments for the spending of funds by each agency, as a curb against an improper distribution of spending throughout the year. Agencies are required to submit a suggested allotment plan for spending, which is approved and enforced by the Bureau of Expenditures.[16]

The spending process begins with the authorized functionary in an agency making an official request for an expenditure to be charged against a budget item. The request is approved by an authorization for payment being issued in accord with the rules of the Bureau (Art. 35). Payment is effected when the paymaster of the Treasury, stationed in the agency, orders payment by the Bank of Mexico, which manages the funds of the government.[17] When a purchase order or a contract is involved in payment, the Ministry of National Properties and Administrative Inspection also intervenes in the process. That agency does not intervene, however, in purchases on contracts of less than 1,000 pesos. (Arts. 172–87.) Despite the rather complicated process involved, procedural delays are not usually considered excessive.

Just as the Bureau of Expenditures' Technical Department of the Budget handles budget preparation, its Department of Control and Vigilance of the Budget handles the administration of expenditures. This includes budgetary accounting and keeping the registers of certain personnel. The Office of the Registry of Federal Personnel maintains personnel files on federal employees, except those of the Defense Ministry, with the object of ensuring conformity with the civil service statute and other measures. The personnel officers in the agencies are charged with cooperating with the central Office of the Registry, and the Office provides them with a copy of the registry of their employees. Employees in the professional categories are also registered in the Bureau's Office of Contracts. (Arts. 97–99.) Details on payment of salaries and related expenses and on the compatibility of employments are covered by the *reglamento* (Title 2, Chs. 5–8; Title 3, Ch. 3).

Budgetary flexibility is provided by transfers of funds and the power to "reform" the budget. The Organic Law and the *reglamento* seek to limit closely the transfer of budgetary fund items. "Reform" of the budget is effected by an agency petitioning the Finance Ministry. The Ministry prepares initiatives of reform in the same form and terms as in the regular budget, with the President's approval. The expenditures are made and listed in provisional form until approved by the next session of Congress. (Arts. 29–31.) [18]

It is a function of the Congress to authorize the President to secure loans, to approve such loans, and to provide for payment of the debt. Aside from those made by the President during an emergency or to deal with monetary regulation, loans may be contracted only for "the execution of works that may directly produce an increase in public revenues" — mainly public works (Art. 73). The Organic law provides for relating the public debt to the budget (Arts. 47–53), and the item for debt payment is running about one seventh of the budget total.

The administrative audit is done by the Federal Accounting Office (Contaduría de la Federación) in the Finance Ministry. It receives the income and expenditure accounts of the agencies; reviews them to discover any irregularities which may produce administrative, civil, or penal actions; and prepares the annual accounts for approval by the Finance Ministry and transmission to the Chamber of Deputies for its post-audit action. [19]

*The post-audit.* This is a responsibility of the Congress. The President is required to present the post-audit document to the Chamber of Deputies within the first ten days of the session (Arts. 65, 73). To aid it in this technical field, the Congress has created a staff arm in the General Auditing Office, a dependency of the Chamber of Deputies. The report is approved successively by the Chamber and the Senate.[20]

*Size of the budget.*[21] One measure of budgetary significance is the magnitude of the budget. As various tabulations indicate, it has increased steadily in recent years and in 1956 it stood at 6,696,000,000 pesos (12½ pesos = $1). The accompanying list shows a breakdown

| | | | |
|---|---|---|---|
| Communications | 16.70% | Interior | .73% |
| Education | 12.53 | Military industry | .69 |
| Public debt | 14.07 | Economy | .66 |
| Hydraulic resources | 8.61 | Legislative | .54 |
| Investments | 11.82 | Judicial | .52 |
| Defense | 7.95 | Agrarian Bureau | .45 |
| Health | 4.08 | Labor | .30 |
| Navy | 3.98 | National Properties | .17 |
| Treasury | 3.82 | Attorney General | .15 |
| Agriculture | 2.04 | Presidency | .14 |
| Foreign relations | 1.46 | Other expenses | 8.59 |

of this total. With the exception of one small item, these all represent absolute increases over the previous year, with an over-all increase of 17.86 per cent. Some of the percentage increases over 1955 indicate program emphases (in round numbers): hydraulic resources, 70 per cent; labor, 31 per cent; health, 22 per cent; agriculture, 21 per cent; navy, 20 per cent; investments, 20 per cent; Attorney General, 19 per cent; education, 18 per cent; communications, 14 per cent.

A functional breakdown of the 1956 budget gives the percentages shown in the accompanying tabulation. Obviously, the main emphasis

| | | |
|---|---|---|
| Economic development | | 49.10% |
| Transport and communications | 25.13% | |
| Forestry and agriculture | 16.14 | |
| Commerce and industry | 7.83 | |
| Social and related services | | 22.35 |
| Education and culture | 12.42 | |
| Health, hospitals, and assistance | 5.37 | |
| Social security and welfare | 4.56 | |
| Defense services | | 9.44 |
| General administration | | 6.60 |
| Public debt | | 12.51 |

is on the various aspects of national economic development. This would be even more obvious if the government's decentralized agencies were also brought into the budget picture.

*Final remarks.* The size of the budget, its steady growth, and the dominant role of government in the economy, all emphasize the importance of an efficient budget system as a key tool in effective public management. Certain improvements could be suggested, however.

Students of the problem feel that the control machinery in budgetary preparation and execution is reasonably adequate. Until recently, the budget has been largely a device to classify and account for the expenditure of funds. Often budget preparation has been a repetition of previous figures. Recently some attention has been paid to the budget as a tool for planning and control, which the government's economic role demands. Apparently, the President still needs to be better supplied with data on the agencies' operations, which he can check against their budget requests. On a smaller scale, the same is probably true for the heads of ministries.

The frequent use of budget "reforms" has pointed up substantial differences between budgeted funds and actual expenditures.[22] This emphasizes needed improvements in fiscal statistics. Recently the Subsecretary of Finance announced the establishment of the Public Finance Commission, an interagency group to provide more complete and useful fiscal statistics for economic analysis. One achievement has been a new classification of receipts and expenditures. One goal is a consolidated budget, including the independent agencies. Another is an adequate economic classification of capital expenditures and a better performance budget system.[23] Achievement of these aims will make possible better evaluation of the progress of government programs.

Certain personnel problems such as low pay and overstaffing are interrelated and are very important to budgeting. Overstaffing is obvious in many offices, while the salary index has fallen much behind that of the cost of living.[24] But the present administration is trying to improve the situation.

Purchasing and inventory procedures have often been subject to criticism; but the last few years have seen the establishment and successful development of the Ministry of National Properties as a central agency for control of purchasing and contracts, among other duties. Its over-all accomplishments on purchases and contracts have been quite successful, according to Alexander Cloner, an able student of public administration who has had valuable experience as a consultant in the government.[25] Substantial savings have been effected through contract readjustments and purchasing controls. The Ministry also directs the construction of federal buildings, supervises the use of furniture and equipment, and maintains a catalogue and inventory of federal holdings.[26]

The legislative post-audit of the administration's accounts, like its examination of the budget proposal, is of necessity somewhat superficial. In both cases, the limited time precludes more adequate consideration. One suggested change is to have a second regular legislative session for such work.[27]

## Revenue

The problem of revenues (mainly taxation) is especially important in Mexico, because of the pre-eminent role the government plays in the economic life of the country. To fulfill its fiscal and nonfiscal functions, the government has taken about one tenth of the gross national product in taxes since 1939; and the prospects are for an increase in this figure. Less important revenue sources have included loans, income from government-owned enterprises, fines, fees, etc.

The valid tax burden must in general be established by statute and must be proportional and equitable, which is held to mean "fair" or "just." Virtually complete latitude is allowed the Congress in determining taxes, since the constitutional rule against confiscation of property (Art. 22) does not apply even to the most rigorous tax.[28]

Taxes can be considered first from the standpoint of their purposes. Obviously, most taxes are solely for revenue of the levying unit of government. Other taxes are solely for raising revenue, but the yield is devoted in whole or in part to some purpose other than use of the general funds of the levying unit of government. In general, application of revenues to a specific purpose is prohibited. But the Fiscal Code (Art. 6) makes such exceptions as grants-in-aid to lower levels of government, payment of loans, subsidies to public or semipublic agencies, and disaster-relief aid. A third type is the tax that serves both fiscal and nonfiscal purposes. Examples are the upper brackets of the income and inheritance taxes which seek in part to redistribute wealth. Finally, some levies are made for strictly nonfiscal purposes, such as tariffs with such high rates as virtually to exclude some kind of import.[29] Despite the constitutional prohibition against "exemption from taxes" (Art. 28), interpretation has sanctioned partial exemptions, such as those for new industries (to be discussed later in this chapter).[30]

As in most countries, certain personal characteristics are considered in determining tax liability — such as sex, age, marital status, occupation, and domicile. Wives are given tax concessions in inheritance. Young persons are affected favorably by certain tax exemptions. Occupations affect the tax burden, since Mexico's income tax is schedular. As elsewhere, domicile is a basis for many taxes.[31]

*The taxing power.* The taxing power in Mexico is concurrent for the central government and the states, with the specified powers going to the nation and the significant body of such authority strongly oriented in that direction.

There are three forms in which the federation is conceded such exclusive powers. The Constitution specifies the powers to tax foreign commerce, the use and exploitation of certain natural resources, credit institutions and insurance companies, electrical energy, petroleum products, matches, *aguamiel* (an intoxicant), forest products, and beer. Through the sole power to legislate on such matters, the federation has the exclusive taxing power over petroleum, mining, the cinema industry, commerce, games of chance, credit institutions, and labor legislation. The states are prohibited from issuing stamps; thus they cannot levy stamp taxes. (Arts. 73, 117.) [32]

There are also three sources of the states' taxing powers. First, the states levy certain duties on tobacco (Art. 117). They can make levies on imports or exports only with the consent of Congress (Art. 118). But the chief source is Article 124, which reserves to the states the powers not expressly granted to the central government.[33]

The legislative process for tax measures is similar to that for the budget. The President has no specific charge to introduce tax bills (as he did under the 1857 Constitution), having only the general power to introduce bills. The realities of political practice, however, place this function almost entirely in his hands. As with the budget, tax bills are introduced in the lower house; and the timetable of budget enactment causes tax measures also to be given brief and inadequate consideration at the very end of the legislative session. Occasionally, they have been issued a few days after the start of the new fiscal year. In addition to his other sublegislative powers, the President may, on proposal of the Tariff Committee, raise and lower tariffs; and he may restrict or prohibit imports or exports that may be unfavorable to the economy.[34]

Revenue legislation is of three kinds. The first, the Revenue Law is the annual measure that enumerates the separate taxes to be collected during the next year. The authorization of these taxes is found in separate basic laws (e.g., the Law of the Tax on Sugar), plus the related *reglamentos*, circulars, etc. Finally, many of the most basic norms of the fiscal regime are found in the Fiscal Code. Its seven Titles deal with definitions, tax obligations, administrative agencies, the work of the Fiscal Tribunal, violations and penalties, fiscal offenses, and fiscal investigations.[35]

*Characteristics of the fiscal system.* Important characteristics of the Mexican fiscal system include those of overlapping taxes and jurisdictions between levels of government, the *alcabala* levies (excises) which impede interstate trade, the regressive character of much of the tax system, and the concentration of tax power in the central government's hands — with the trend still in that direction.

Overlapping of taxes and multiple taxation have long been a pressing problem, with more than a hundred different taxes being levied in Mexico in a recent year. Organized efforts have been made to improve the situation, with only moderate success, as will be discussed later in this chapter.[36] As is true with most other countries, a recent study finds the Mexican system still quite regressive, except for the very high incomes. Most of the state and local taxes are very regressive,[37] with much emphasis on taxes on consumption.

Centralization of tax power has been growing steadily through the years, mainly through specific reforms to the Constitution. Appropriation of important tax fields by the central government has often been accompanied by granting the states "participations" in the yield; but the result has been a decrease in state and local autonomy.[38] It is virtually impossible to state any precise delimitation of the state-federal tax field. Therefore, some of the specific aspects of the problem are discussed in the following section and in the last section of this chapter.

*The tax burden.* Mexico is one of the least heavily taxed countries in Latin America, as ex-President Alemán has acknowledged. From 1939 to 1951, the percentage of the national income going to the federal government increased only from 7.8 per cent to 11.1 per cent, with the total for all units of government going from 11.5 per cent to 13.7 per cent. State-local revenues dropped from 3.7 per cent to 2.6 per cent. In recent years, increased economic activity and improved methods of collection have tended to bring tax receipts somewhat above estimates.[39]

The Revenue Law for 1953 lists nineteen types of federal taxes. These might be grouped into four categories: taxes on income; taxes on foreign trade; taxes on production, consumption, and domestic trade; and taxes on gratuitous transfers of property (gift and inheritance taxes), stamp taxes, etc. Another tabulation for a recent year divides the total tax yield as follows: foreign commerce, 36.1 per cent; internal commerce, 10.0 per cent; income, 23.7 per cent; production, 12.9 per cent; others, 17.3 per cent.[40] The income tax percentage has been still higher in 1954 and 1955.

In comparison, the average annual state revenue sources (1939–49) were: federal aids, 23.3 per cent; real property, 18 per cent; industries, 15.8 per cent; commerce, 6.8 per cent; services, 6.5 per cent; agriculture, 5.7 per cent; and lesser amounts from miscellaneous sources.[41]

A similar breakdown of municipal income (1939–48) shows the following: contributed services, 35 per cent; state and federal aids, 14 per cent; surtaxes on federal tax rates, 11 per cent; exploitation taxes, 10.1 per cent; commerce, 9.7 per cent; industries, 8 per cent; real property, 4.8 per cent; and miscellaneous sources.[42]

In general, federal income and other direct taxes increased in importance between 1939 and 1950, while the importance of indirect taxes declined in the same period. Revenues from direct taxes on personal income and profits (excess profits, import, export, surtaxes, and mineral production taxes) rose from 28.5 per cent to 47 per cent of net federal income between 1939 and 1950. Income tax receipts accounted for most of this increase, rising from 7.5 per cent of the total to 24 per cent in that period. The yield from this tax increased at a greater rate than the national income. But despite the increase in direct taxes, approximately half of the public revenue still comes from indirect taxes.[43] The rates on income and profits taxes are still moderate compared with those in the United States.

*The income tax.*[44] The income tax was adopted on a temporary basis in 1921 and was made permanent in 1924, with important reforms being made in 1925, 1939, and 1942. The 1924 law was part of a broader program aimed at gaining increased revenue and reducing overlapping federal-state taxation. The law has been schedular from the start, with the equivalent of three schedules in 1924; and the highest rate of 6 per cent was levied against interest income. The 1925 law established seven schedules: commerce, industry, agriculture, investments, concessions, salaries and wages, and professions. Since 1942, the first three have been combined in a single schedule.

Some feel that the thinking of the Revolution influenced the use of separate tax schedules, for the rates on salaries and wages are lower than those on interest from capital; and the differences between the rates of the earned income schedules and the others have tended to increase the discrepancies. Schedule 1 covers incomes from a combination of capital and personal effort in commerce, industry, or agriculture; it produces the most revenue. Schedule 2 covers income from capital alone, including certain rents, interest, dividends, etc.; and the rates have run from 10 per cent to 36 per cent. This schedule is next in importance to Schedule 1. Schedule 3 covers income from capital in government concessions such as mining and forestry. The rates have run from 18.7 per cent to 41.2 per cent. Schedule 4, covering salaries and wages, is the only one covered by collections at the source rather than declarations. Employers withhold the tax for the government at rates ranging upward from 1.4 per cent for the lowest taxed wages, the smallest incomes being exempt from tax. There is no provision for deductions for dependents, etc. Schedule 5, professional incomes, has rates ranging from 1.4 per cent to 33 per cent.

Corporate income may be taxed by one or more of the first three schedules. Higher incomes may be subject also to an excess profits tax, the rates of which are progressive, applying to profits exceeding 15 per cent return on the capital. Tax rates are much lower than in the more developed countries, and high tariff protections are another factor of encouragement to business. As in the United States law, most public service agencies and welfare and educational organizations are exempt from the tax.

The use of the income tax is denied to the state governments. The Fiscal Code (Art. 30) limits the state and municipal government exemptions to their regular governmental functions; their proprietary functions are taxed like private businesses.

Trends regarding the income tax have included the following: a general increase in the absolute rates and the progressivity of the taxes; an increase in the upper limit of the progressive rate; a steady increase in the yield and relative importance of the tax; and some decline in the considerable evasion which has long characterized Mexican tax collection. The 1953 revision of the tax law aims at a better distribution of the burden, with some shifts from various production and export taxes to income taxes. A 10 per cent transaction tax has been levied on real estate to divert investments from real estate speculation (a long-standing problem) to productive enterprise.

One criticism of the law is the non-allowance of various deductions. Another is that if the tax were on the person rather than on the income sources, the yield would increase and evasion would be more difficult.

*Tariffs.* Import and export duties, once a mainstay of the Mexican tax system, have been slowly giving way to other levies. They declined from 34.5 per cent of the total in 1939 to 30 per cent in 1951, while the proportion for the income tax was increasing. Nevertheless Mexico is definitely a high-tariff, protectionist country.

The tariff is a single-column schedule, not affording preference among the various countries. It applies to both imports and exports, and both specific and ad valorem duties are applied. The nonfiscal aim of the import tariff is to encourage the entrance of certain raw materials and capital goods which promote industrialization and to discourage luxuries and imports competing with domestic industry. The Mexican-American reciprocal trade agreement of 1942 was ended in 1950; but trade relations have been satisfactorily continued, with Mexico substituting higher import duties in cases where it had formerly prohibited imports.[45]

*Other taxes.* Mexico has long used a variety of other taxes. I have already mentioned the inheritance tax, which is a concurrent power of state and nation; and efforts have been made since 1933 to bring about some degree of uniformity in federal and state laws. State and nation participate in the proceeds of the national tax. The rates are progressive by rate and by distance of kinship. Successful evasion is extensive, and the tax produces only about 1 per cent of the total tax yield. The gift tax applies similar rates.[46]

There is no general tax on capital, but there are such special taxes, besides those on gifts and inheritances, as those on lotteries and games of chance. One student of taxes feels that the substantial secular rise in capital assets values presents a good source of revenue for a capital gains tax. He feels that the present levy on income derived from government concessions points the way.[47]

Both federal and state governments have levied various taxes on commerce and industry, which have been used both to produce revenue and to encourage or discourage certain forms of consumption. The principal special taxes of the federal government have been those on production and consumption of electrical energy, gasoline, railway income, sugar, matches, tobaccos, alcohols, forest exploitation, radio broadcasting, migration, and the stamp tax.[48] A tax on commercial incomes was established in 1948 to replace the stamp tax, which was not a single levy but a series of different taxes. Their only common element was that they were paid in stamps. These were taxes on rents, purchases and sales, legal documents, etc.

The tax on commercial incomes made possible the suppression of a number of similar state taxes by giving the states nearly half (1.2 per cent) of its 3 per cent yield. This system of "participations" provides such a share in the federal tax for those state governments abolishing such local taxes and accepting the new arrangements. Participations have also been used in connection with the taxes on electrical energy, matches, tobaccos, beer, shops selling alcoholic drinks, inheritances, and mining. In some taxes (such as those on matches and liquor stores) both states and municipalities share.[49]

The participations are paid automatically to the states and municipalities benefited, the only requirement being abstention from collecting such local taxes. Payments are not usually earmarked for specific uses. States have been able to borrow from the federal government against anticipated allotments, and they have often gone far into debt, as have the municipalities. Then they request, and often receive, cancellation of the debt. A number of state administrations have criticized this approach toward tax improvement, and some legal and tax authorities have questioned its constitutionality; but it is making progress.[50] In a real sense, participations are forms of subsidy.

A substantial use has been made of subsidies since about 1897, especially in the last decade or two. These include various subsidies to agriculture — land, credit, irrigation, etc.; to the export trade — mainly agricultural products; to certain agricultural imports; to cooperative societies; to manufactures — such as cotton goods, alcohol, and sugar.[51] Closely related to subsidies as such are tax exemptions. Since 1941, and especially under the law of 1946, important tax concessions have been made to important new and "necessary" industries by the federal government. In addition, a number of state governments have also embarked on such programs of inducement to industrialization.[52] Tax exemptions and subsidies will be considered further in connection with the economic development programs (see Chapter 15).

*Administrative machinery.*[53] There is no one central unit in the Finance Ministry charged with revenue matters. Instead, there are four bureaus dealing with different kinds of taxes and three auxiliary agencies. The Bureau of Financial Studies plans financial policy on both the income and expenditure sides. This includes making studies on tariffs, subsidies, commercial agreements, etc. The Undersecretary of Finance in charge of taxation is also advised by the Executive Committee of the National Tax Plan. The Executive Committee's ten members comprise five representatives of the states, two for the municipalities, two from taxpayers' organizations, and one from the federal government.

The Income Tax Bureau examines and passes on the returns made by taxpayers. Different schedules of the income tax are administered in separate offices of the Bureau. The Bureau of Mercantile Income administers that tax. The Customs Bureau administers import and export duties and makes studies on which to base legislative and administrative changes. The Bureau of Internal Taxes administers the various lesser revenue fields not covered by the three preceding bureaus. Under it come the hundred or more federal tax offices throughout the country. The various collecting offices deposit their receipts in the Treasury.[54]

Tax collection enforcement in cases of dispute is done through a quasi-judicial process within the Ministry of Finance. Enforcement decisions may be reversed by the Fiscal Tribunal for such reasons as incompetence of the deciding functionary, noncompliance with prescribed legal formalities, or violation of the law in issuance of the decision. Certain individual constitutional guarantees are especially applicable in tax matters. "No person may be deprived of the product of his labor except by judicial determination" (Art. 4). Protections are extended against any "private" laws and "special" tribunals; and the person is protected against retroactive laws and improper deprivation of life, liberty, or property (Arts. 13, 14). Security is offered to the home, papers, and possessions (Art. 16). Article 27 deals with the expropriation of land for a public purpose.[55]

The law office of the agency furnishes legal advice and defends the Ministry in appeals by writs of *amparo* which are appealed from the agency's administrative decisions to the Fiscal Tribunal. The law office imposes the fines for infractions of the fiscal laws. Its Department of Legislation drafts proposed fiscal laws, *reglamentos*, etc.; interprets fiscal legislation; and compiles the legal dispositions, including the *jurisprudencia* (body of ruling decisions) of the Fiscal Tribunal.

*The tax court.* The Fiscal Tribunal is one of the most highly developed tribunals of its kind in Latin America. It is divided, like the Supreme Court, into chambers to hear tax litigation and other cases involving relationships of the individual to financial legislation. The Tribunal has seven chambers of three judges each. Annually, the members choose their own president; and they meet in plenary sessions for establishing their *jurisprudencia* and for certain other functions. The Tribunal was established in 1937. During its first years, its powers were somewhat limited; but its usefulness in recent years seems attested by the substantial proportion of cases which it decides against the Finance Ministry. The Supreme Court will hear appeals by *amparo* when individual constitutional rights seem to be violated.[56]

*Problems of taxation.* Tax evasion has long been an important problem in Mexico, and only the last few years have seen much headway being made toward improvement. Legal evasion may occur when the person or object taxed is shifted to another jurisdiction where the tax is less; and it occurs within the same governmental unit by the shifting of capital from more to less heavily taxed investments. Solution may be sought in a better integration of the tax system in terms of the entire country and in terms of the things taxed. Some progress is being made in both ways, as will be discussed later in this chapter.[57]

Illegal evasion, or tax fraud, may occur through ignorance, through taxpayers' deliberate wrongdoing, and through inadequate or corrupt administration. Such actions by taxpayers and collectors are often linked. Means of improvement include better and faster methods of tax collection and investigation; more effective penal action; and better personnel administration. The last includes a thorough campaign of "moralization" of the public service (now being seriously undertaken) and raising the pay of public employees to the level of a full-time living wage (on which slow progress is being made).[58]

Double or multiple taxation has long been a pressing problem in Mexico, with the exception of a few exclusively federal levies such as those on customs and incomes. Double taxation on the same governmental level is found in many countries; but the pressing problem in Mexico has been levies on the same thing for two or three levels of government.

Solutions have been sought along several lines for this and related problems — by unilateral federal action and by various approaches to cooperative federal-state action. One approach — tried between 1824 and 1867 — was that of seeking to delimit or allocate fields of taxation by various statutes. The second approach was that of constitutional reform, enumerating the exclusively federal taxes (Art. 73). A third was the holding of conventions of federal and state representatives to seek agreements on allocation of fields of taxation. Such efforts were made by the First, Second, and Third National Fiscal Conventions, of 1925, 1933, and 1947, respectively. Their antecedents were conventions in 1851 and 1883. A fourth approach involved agreements with the states to improve their tax systems, with the federal government conceding reductions in certain federal taxes. Finally, as has been mentioned before, the federal government has granted the states and municipalities "participations" in the yield of certain federal taxes if the states eliminate such taxes of their own.[59]

Each of the three national fiscal conventions studying these plans stated its conclusions as a "National Tax Plan"; suggested constitutional amendments to effectuate its recommendations; and set up an executive committee to counsel with the federal tax authorities.

The first two conventions emphasized delimitation of the fields of tax authority by levels of government, as a means of providing adequate and stable incomes for the states and municipalities. The third convention didn't do so. Experience showed the inadequacy of certain taxes previously suggested for the states, and there has been a shift of taxable values to other forms of wealth. One or more of the conventions also emphasized the following needs: providing more adequate local tax sources; bringing fiscal independence to the municipalities — heretofore under state dominance; unifying state tax systems and coordinating them with the federal; uniform inheritance and retail sales tax laws and taxes on commerce and industry; abolition of the stamp tax; and equitable distribution of the fiscal burden among all elements in society. Federal subsidies, formerly opposed by the states, were urged by the third convention in the form of more "participations."[60]

Recommendations of the conventions that have been established at least in part by the federal government include consultation with taxpayer groups on fiscal proposals; elimination of taxes on certain items of basic necessity; elimination of the federal real property tax; repeal of the stamp tax on commercial activities; establishment of the Executive Committee of the National Tax Plan as a group to advise the Finance Ministry; and extension of the system of participations for states and municipalities. The national tax system is being increasingly centralized, but it is still much lacking in coordination. And the tax resources of the states and municipalities are quite inadequate for their needs. Some authorities feel that the most effective solution would be central collection of all taxes and distribution of a fair share of the proceeds to the state and municipal governments on the basis of a study of state and local needs.[61]

## NOTES

[1] Robert E. Scott, "Budget Making in Mexico," *Inter-American Economic Affairs*, Autumn 1955, pp. 3–4; International Bank, *The Economic Development of Mexico* (1953), pp. 144–45.

[2] Gustavo Aguilar, *Los Presupuestos Mexicanos, desde los Tiempos de la Colonia hasta Nuestros Días* (1947); Fraga, *op. cit.*, pp. 457–66; Scott, *op. cit.*, pp. 4–5, 10–11.

[3] Sría. de Bienes Nacionales, *Directorio* . . . (1), pp. 157–58.

[4] *Ley Orgánica del Presupuesto de la Federación y su Reglamento* (1948).

[5] Henry Laufenberger, *Finanzas Comparadas* (1951), pp. 96–99.

[6] *Ibid.*, pp. 103–4; Fraga, *op. cit.*, pp. 461–66.

[7] Laufenberger, *op. cit.*, pp. 68–69; Gustavo Romero Kolbeck and Victor Urquidi, *La Exención Fiscal en el Distrito Federal* . . . (1952), *passim*.

[8] Rafael Mancera Ortiz, *The Budget as Stabilizer of Economic Growth* (1953), *passim*; Mosk, *op. cit.*, *passim*.

[9] Mancera Ortiz, *op. cit.*, pp. 6–7, 13.

[10] Mancera Ortiz, *Mexico's Attitude Towards Development Programs* (1953), pp. 9–16; Schaeffer, *op. cit.*, pp. 126 *et seq.*; Leopoldo Monzón A., "El Control de Presupuestos en Materia de Egresos," *Rev. Ec.*, June 1947, pp. 28–31; Scott, *op. cit.*, pp. 9–10.

[11] Laufenberger, *op. cit.*, pp. 28–30; Schaeffer, *op. cit.*, pp. 127 *et seq.*; Scott, *op. cit.*, pp. 9–10.

[12] Tena Ramírez, *op. cit.*, pp. 274–75.

[13] Scott, *op. cit.*, pp. 13–15.

[14] Tena Ramírez, *op. cit.*, Ch. 13; Scott, *op. cit.*, pp. 15–16.

[15] Fraga, *op. cit.*, pp. 472–76.

[16] Monzón A., *op. cit.*, p. 29.

[17] Laufenberger, *op. cit.*, pp. 319–20.

[18] Laufenberger, *op. cit.*, p. 104.

[19] Sría. de Bienes Nacionales, *Directorio* . . . (1), pp. 159–60.

[20] Fraga, *op. cit.*, pp. 474–76.

[21] *MV*, December 19, 1955, pp. 201–11; *HA*, December 26, 1955, pp. 6–7; J. G. Maddox (unpublished study).

[22] Schaeffer, *op. cit.*, p. 130.
[23] U.N. Economic Commission for Latin America, *Gastos de Capital del Gobierno Federal* (1953), p. 2.
[24] Lobato, "Situación Económica . . . ," *op. cit.*, p. 387.
[25] Cloner, *op. cit.*, pp. 11–12.
[26] Sría. de Bienes Nacionales, *Informe* . . . (1952); Sría de Bienes Nacionales, *Directorio* . . . (1), pp. 443–64.
[27] Laufenberger, *op. cit.*, pp. 53–54.
[28] Fraga, *op. cit.*, pp. 441–51; Ernesto Flores Zavala, *Elementos de Finanzas Públicas Mexicanas* (1951), pp. 199–204.
[29] Flores Zavala, *op. cit.*, pp. 263–66.
[30] Fraga, *op. cit.*, pp. 449–52.
[31] Flores Zavala, *op. cit.*, pp. 79–90.
[32] *Ibid.*, pp. 220–40; Ramiro González Casales, "Nuestra Organización Tributaria Constitucional y el Centralismo Económico . . . ," (UNAM thesis, 1952), *passim*.
[33] Flores Zavala, *op. cit.*, pp. 220–40, 348 *et seq.*
[34] *Ibid.*, pp. 216, 235, *et seq.*
[35] *Ibid.*, pp. 241 *et seq.*; *Código Fiscal de la Federación* (1949).
[36] Fraga, *op. cit.*, pp. 454–55.
[37] John V. Deaver, "The Mexican Income Tax and Some Related Problems" (M.A. thesis, Mexico City College, 1949), pp. 136–37.
[38] Octavio Senties G., "Federalismo Constitucional y Centralismo Económico" (UNAM thesis, 1942), pp. 67–68.
[39] R. G. Stone, *Economic and Commercial Conditions in Mexico* (1953), pp. 11–12.
[40] *Mexican American Review*, August 1953, p. 20; H. F. Cline, *op. cit.*, p. 420.
[41] *México en Cifras.*
[42] *Ibid.*
[43] International Bank, *op. cit.*, p. 105.
[44] Stone, *op. cit.*, pp. 20–21; Deaver, *op. cit.*, *passim*; Flores Zavala, *Panorama de la Tributación en México* . . . (1948), pp. 47–50; Laufenberger, *op. cit.*, pp. 187–91, 225–28; Flores Zavala, *Elementos* . . . , pp. 126–30; *Mexican American Review*, August 1953, pp. 20, 28. In 1954 there were again seven schedules in the income tax law. U.S. Bureau of Foreign Commerce, *op. cit.*, pp. 151–57.
[45] Stone, *op. cit.*, pp. 33–35.
[46] Laufenberger, *op. cit.*, pp. 241–43; Flores Zavala, *Panorama* . . . , pp. 110–12.
[47] Deaver, *op. cit.*, pp. 79, 85.
[48] Flores Zavala, *op. cit.*, pp. 96–116; Laufenberger, *op. cit.*, pp. 259–60.
[49] See note 48.
[50] Senties, *op. cit.*, pp. 41–52; Darío Córdoba Ladrón, *Breves Consideraciones sobre el Estado Federal Mexicano* (1948), pp. 124 *et seq.*
[51] Carmen Galán Balboa, "Subsidios en México" (UNAM thesis, 1945), *passim*; Gonzalo Mora Ortiz, *El Banco Nacional de Comercio Exterior* (1950), *passim*.
[52] Mosk, *op. cit.*; International Bank, *op. cit.*; Romero Kolbeck and Urquidi, *op. cit.*
[53] Sría. de Bienes Nacionales, *Directorio* . . . (1), pp. 145–75.
[54] Fraga, *op. cit.*, pp. 467–72.
[55] Flores Zavala, *Elementos* . . . , pp. 156–94.
[56] *Ibid.*, pp. 208–12; Sría. de Bienes Nacionales, *Directorio* . . . (1), pp. 549–56.
[57] Flores Zavala, *Elementos* . . . , pp. 280 *et seq.*
[58] See notes 56 and 57; Deaver, *op. cit.*, pp. 87, 139.
[59] Flores Zavala, *Panorama* . . . , pp. 25–29.
[60] Flores Zavala, *Elementos* . . . , pp. 365 *et seq.*; Flores Zavala, *Panorama* . . . , pp. 27 *et seq.*; *Mexican American Review*, August 1953, pp. 20–21; *Rev. Ec.*, June 15, 1950 and May 1950.
[61] See note 60.

# PART III

# Internal and External Relations

# 12

## The Ministry of Government

THE possibility of grouping together the Ministries of Government, Foreign Affairs, Defense, and Marine is reasonable for study, despite a possible first impression that the fields of work are unrelated. The Ministry of Government is the foremost cabinet post; and it has important relationships with the other agencies, though most of its work deals with domestic affairs. The Ministries of Defense and Marine perform important functions in the field of domestic affairs. The Ministry of Foreign Affairs obviously has a field of work almost exclusively "foreign"; but its work has an important impact on that of the other ministries, especially the ones grouped here.

*The field of Gobernación.*[1] As the chief cabinet office, with many duties closely related to the work of the other agencies, the Secretaría de Gobernación is one of the oldest of the ministries. It was provided for under the first independent governmental establishment of 1821, in the Ministry of Foreign Relations; likewise, in the Constitution of 1843. The decree of April 1853 established the Ministry of Interior Relations, Justice, Ecclesiastical Affairs, and Public Instruction; then the decree of May 1853 established separately the Ministry of Gobernación. It has held that status and designation since that date. As the chief cabinet office, Gobernación has served as a stepping stone to the presidency.

Gobernación serves as the right hand of the President. Its minister is the channel for convoking cabinet meetings, on call of the President, as well as meetings of the state governors and other officials. He prepares agenda of cabinet meetings for the President; keeps records pertaining to the meetings; and checks on the execution of matters decided. He processes the President's appointments to the headship of the many agencies within the sphere of presidential appointment; and he is the channel for many presidential contacts with agency heads, the courts, the Congress, and governors of the states and territories. He is also the channel for processing resignations. His Ministry gathers and coordinates much information for the President. It advises him on needed legislation, drafts bills for him to submit to the Congress, and makes recommendations before he signs them. Another important duty is assembling material from the reports of the ministries for the President's annual message (*informe*) to the opening session of the Congress, which message is published by Gobernación. Another way in which Gobernación aids the President is by its minister's serving as chairman of various interministerial committees for administrative coordination. The administration of the federal territories, which are dependencies of the executive, comes under Gobernación.

Of great importance is Gobernación's role as liaison between the administration and the Congress. Its formulation of bills, decrees, and proposed constitutional amendments has been mentioned; in addition, it publishes such measures when enacted. The Ministry takes some of its problems with the states before the Congress for action, as discussed later in this chapter.

Gobernación is the liaison between Congress and the states, as well as between the President and the states. It keeps a file of state legislation, decrees, etc., examining them for their constitutionality. When they are found to be in conflict with federal jurisdiction, the Ministry procures their repeal by the state or nullification by federal action. It is the channel for settling conflicts between the branches of government within a state, as discussed in Chapter 5. If negotiation fails, Gobernación gets the Senate to declare that the state's constitutional powers have disappeared, and, in behalf of the President, presents to the Senate names of candidates for the post of provisional governor.

One of the important noncoercive services that Gobernación performs for the state and local governments is that of supervising the work of the more than three thousand local Boards of Moral, Civic, and Material Welfare. These boards, a special interest of President Ruiz Cortines, use funds from the federal and local governments and civic-minded organizations to establish or improve a variety of municipal public services. Many public works have been constructed, such as schools, street paving, markets, parks, playgrounds, waterworks, and electric service. Other services include literacy campaigns and medical service.[2]

Gobernación's relation to political parties and elections has been discussed earlier (see Chapter 4, pages 65–66). It registers political parties and certifies them for the ballot when it has determined that they meet the legal requirements; and it is the channel for revoking registrations. It checks on the work of the electoral commissions in federal elections, and in state elections as to the fulfillment of constitutional requirements.

A protective function is that of seeking removal by the Congress of an erring judicial official. This request is made by the President through Gobernación. A related protective function is that of seeing to the maintenance of individual guarantees and the rights of citizens. A similar function is in the field of internal security. The Ministry does investigative work in connection with naturalization, election frauds, espionage, and matters pertaining to social order.

*Penal jurisdiction.* Federal crime prevention and punishment is one of the most important functions of Gobernación. It is charged with both the preventive and the punitive aspects of the delinquency problem. It sponsors studies regarding delinquency and its prevention, and uses propaganda and other means for combating juvenile delinquency, vagrancy, drug addiction, and alcoholism. On the punitive or correctional side, the Ministry administers the federal and territorial prisons, reformatories, correctional schools, and related institutions.

Mexico has made only moderate progress in the field of delinquency studies, most of which have been journalistic or purely legalistic. However, advanced thinking was incorporated in the new federal penal system that was established in 1929. It abolished the death penalty and the jury in penal cases, substituting a council of experts for the latter. The 1929 code replaced the idea of vengeance with the philosophy of individual rehabilitation through re-educative work and other means.[3]

Punishment for adult offenders includes pecuniary penalties (fine plus reparation of damages) and imprisonment, which varies from three days to thirty years. Imprisonment brings suspension of political and various other rights. The trial judge is enjoined to consider, in passing judgment on the case, the nature of the offense, the age and background of the individual, and pertinent special circumstances. The attempt is made to organize the prisons on the basis of work as a means of regeneration, with emphasis on individualized treatment. Prisoners receive compensation for their work, and this is divided among payment for their food and care, aid to the prisoners' families, and payment toward damages involved in the crime committed. Release prior to the term of the sentence may be effected by parole, commutation of sentence, or pardon.[4]

The important problem of sex in prison has been faced in one way by the practice of the "conjugal visit," when the spouse may come for weekly sojourns. Another innovation is that of keeping the family unit as much intact as feasible by letting the mother keep her small children with her in the prison.[5]

Juvenile delinquency is an important and growing problem in Mexico, as in other countries; and the government, as mentioned earlier (see Chapter 6, pages 115–16), has established juvenile courts and other specialized institutions to deal with it. The first juvenile court was established in the Federal District in 1927–28. Today, two such courts function in the capital and others are located in the federal judicial districts, as mentioned in Chapter 6.[6]

The juvenile court has three judges: a lawyer, a physician, and a teacher. Auxiliary agencies are centers for observation and investigation of offenders; various schools, reformatories, foster homes, etc.; and a special police group. The proceedings are individualized. The minor is sent first to the observation center, which studies his case and makes a recommendation to the court. The court's decision may be to send him to a foster home, trade school, reform school, or other agency. Specialized treatment is provided for alcoholics, drug addicts, and others in need of such atypical care. In general, the social welfare approach is the one used; and the aim is to help juvenile delinquents to become socially useful citizens by providing proper education and environment.[7]

Despite the numerous obstacles and shortcomings of the system, an American student of world penal systems concludes "that the Mexican prison system is at least unique. It has wrestled with many conventional problems found in prisons all over the world and has had courage enough to experiment boldly with radically new ideas." [8]

*Population problems.*[9] The Ministry's Department of Migration administers the General Law of Population which deals with the whole range of demographic matters. In performing these functions, the Department makes use of the Consultative Council on Population. The

Council's members represent the ministries most concerned with population matters — these of Economy, Foreign Relations, Agriculture, Education, Health, Labor, and the Agrarian Department — with Gobernación's member as chairman. Gobernación deals with problems of population increase, its rational distribution throughout the country, immigration and emigration, protection of the rights of Mexicans and foreigners, repatriation of Mexicans abroad, and colonization of surplus populations on new lands. It advises the states on population matters, coordinates their efforts, and has the last word in such matters. (Arts. 1–15.)

The work of population redistribution and colonization is a problem of the most pressing importance, due to the rapid population increase and the country's limited resources; and it is a field in which only slow progress has been made. The present administration is intensifying its efforts in this direction. But there has been little done in the way of birth control.

Permanent immigrants have not formed a large percentage of the population; but some two dozen nationalities are represented. The 1950 census lists 182,707 persons as foreign born. Of these, 105,666 were born in America (83,391 in the U.S.); 37,540 in Spain; 15,015 in Asia; and less than 10,000 in each of the other large areas of the world. The total with foreign citizenship was 106,315. Of these, 47,271 are from America (U.S., 30,454); 26,876 from Spain; and 11,437 from Asia.[10]

The law regulates immigration matters in some detail; and Gobernación has broad powers to limit and restrict immigration. The spirit of nationalism is thought to be a considerable factor behind the long-standing restrictions on the employment of foreigners. The labor law limits foreign employees to 10 per cent of a firm's total, exempting indispensable supervisory personnel. But the firm is expected to train Mexican personnel as rapidly as possible for higher positions held by foreigners. Mexicans complain that there is widespread evasion of this and other features of the law. Whatever the facts, public opinion apparently puts considerable pressure on Gobernación in such matters.

The actual process of naturalization (already discussed in Chapter 5, pages 87–88) is directed by the Ministry of Foreign Relations; but Gobernación's control over foreigners entering and remaining in the country gives it an important part in the total picture. Gobernación registers the certificates of naturalization issued by Foreign Relations.

*Tourism.* The tourist business is of the greatest importance to Mexico, because it is the third or fourth largest industry in terms of income. Therefore, promoting and regulating this field of activity is one of Gobernación's most important functions.

The more than 400,000 tourists (mostly American) that go to Mexico each year have a great influence on both the governmental and the nongovernmental sectors of the economy. The influence of such a large industry on the nongovernmental sector is obvious. Its direct influence on the governmental sector is reflected in payments made for visas and tourist permits, taxes on various forms of transportation, and taxes on goods purchased. Indirect benefits to the government include increased taxes which come from businesses benefited by tourism and the foreign good will which tourists generate. Such increased governmental income has aided industrialization and other governmental programs.[11]

The establishment of the tourist industry really came in the Cárdenas administration, with the opening of the Pan-American Highway from Texas to Mexico City and the establishment of the official tourist bureau. In recent years, Gobernación's Tourist Bureau has increased its expenditures for tourist promotion in the United States; but the amount spent is small compared with those of other countries and compared with the profitable possibilities. Much aid in tourist promotion comes from Petróleos Mexicanos (Pemex), the government oil industry. In 1954 significant contributions came from American business circles in Mexico.[12]

The Federal Tourist Law [13] provides that the Tourist Bureau shall maintain tourist promotional offices in Mexico and abroad; maintain a registry of hotels, restaurants, and other establishments catering to tourists; regulate such establishments; stimulate the development of private tourist promotional organizations; promote the establishment of hotels and other facilities in locations of interest to tourists; regulate prices and conditions of service in tourist-serving establishments; and license tourist guides (Art. 2).

The head of the Tourist Bureau is secretary of the National Tourist Council: a body composed of the ministers of the leading government agencies, the Bank of Mexico, the National Railways, Pemex, and the Mexican Tourist Association. The Council's functions are advisory. (Arts. 5–11.)

The recent trend has been toward a correlated program of promotion, including public and private travel interests, aid from other government agencies, road-building, new airline routes, etc. A significant amount of the recent road-building has been tourist-oriented. Many fiestas are arranged for the tourist trade, and ancient rites of the native peoples are re-enacted. One of the newer projects is the Gulf Circuit Tourist Project, inaugurated in 1953, which is planned to link the United States, Cuba, and Mexico through a combined land, sea, and air transport system.[14]

The first National Tourism Congress was held in 1953, representing all groups interested in tourist promotion. Among the principal proposals discussed were the following: a request for governmental aid in training hotel employees; a better check by the Ministry of Health on restaurants and markets; construction of more hotels and motor courts; and greater protection for tourists against unscrupulous merchants.[15]

*Miscellaneous.* Gobernación also has a miscellaneous group of functions, including a general information program, promotion of the motion-picture industry, maintenance and publication of the nation's archives and the official periodical, and regulation of Church matters.

The general informational services include promoting good relations with the press and the radio; publication of the *Diario Oficial*, the official journal containing all laws, decrees, and regulations of a general nature; publication of important archival materials; sponsorship of the National Hour and other radio programs of national interest; and preparation for the President of a daily bulletin of data and commentary from the Mexican and foreign press.

Mexico holds high rank among Latin American countries in regard to freedom of the press; but critical analysis of government agencies and their functioning is not yet as extensive as it is in the United States. And the President himself is seldom subjected to journalistic criticism. With the current President's emphasis on honesty in government and freedom of expression, it is felt that there has been a considerable decline in the former practice of some officials "buying off" certain journalists to secure favorable publicity.[16] Such freedom of political discussion and criticism has only recently been extended to the radio.

The *Diario Oficial* is the only regularly issued official channel for the government's information program. Its rather small circulation has led civic organizations to urge the publication of all laws and important rules by the leading metropolitan dailies. Possibly the nearest present approach to such a general source of government news is *El Nacional*, the organ of the official party. Gobernación maintains the National Archives and publishes significant materials from its files. The radio National Hour, which the Ministry sponsors, includes considerable material of a general cultural interest, as well as government information.[17]

Business and industrial promotion, aside from tourism, includes sponsorship of trade fairs and the film industry. A national fair has been held to promote Mexican-German relations; and such a fair to promote Mexican-American trade has been discussed. The Bureau of Cinematography is the government's channel for promoting motion pictures for educational and entertainment purposes. It cooperates with the Ministry of Public Education in promoting film use for educational purposes. The government's extensive financial and other aid to the film industry is managed by Gobernación with the assistance of two groups — the National Cinema Bank, largely government owned, and the National Council of Cinematographic Art, a consultative group which includes the Bank, the more important ministries, and the associations of film producers, distributors, exhibitors, and the unions. In 1954, the government formed a company, Cimex, to handle the work of foreign distribution of Mexican films.[18]

A final function — Church regulation — was discussed in Chapter 3 (see pages 36–38).

As with certain other aspects of Mexican government, available data on the actual process of administration are quite limited and are restricted mainly to published material that is lacking in much significant detail.

## NOTES

[1] Sría. de Bienes Nacionales, *Directorio* . . . (1), pp. 47–52, 67–96; Sría. de Gobernación, *Informe* . . . (various years); Virginia P. Stullken, "Keystone of Mexican Government: Secretaría de Gobernación" (M.A. thesis, University of Texas, 1955); José Mijares Palencia, *El Gobierno Mexicano* (1936), Ch. 2.

[2] *El Nacional*, June 14, 1954; *News* (Mexico City), September 30, 1953.

[3] Salvador Mendoza, "El Nuevo Código Penal de México," *Hispanic American Historical Review*, August 1930, pp. 299–312; N. S. Hayner, "Criminogenic Zones in Mexico City," *American Sociological Review*, August 1946, pp. 428–31.

[4] *Código Penal para el Distrito y Territorios* . . . (1953), Arts. 25–98.

[5] N. K. Teeters, *World Penal Systems* . . . (1944), pp. 172–73. For an article on the women's prison, see *HA*, August 23, 1954, pp. 8–12.

[6] María Lavalle Urbina, *La Delincuencia Infantil* (1948); Mendoza, "Recent tendencies . . . ," *op. cit.*, pp. 435–36; José A. Ceniceros, *La Delincuencia Infantil en México* (1948).

[7] *Ley Orgánica y Normas de Procedimiento de los Tribunales para Menores* (1953).

[8] Teeters, *op. cit.*, pp. 175–76.

[9] *Ley General de Población*, in Andrade, ed., *op. cit.*, pp. 423–36.

[10] Sría. de Econ., *Séptimo Censo . . . , Resumen General* (1953), pp. 163, 197.

[11] J. R. Reese, "The Effects of Foreign Tourist Trade on Mexico's Balance of Payments" (M.A. thesis, Mexico City College, 1952), *passim*.

[12] *MV*, June 28, 1954.

[13] *Ley Federal de Turismo . . . ,* in Andrade, ed., *op. cit.*, pp. 476 *bis* 9a *et seq.*

[14] J. A. McKeever, "A History of the Tourist Trade in Mexico . . ." (M.A. thesis, Mexico City College, 1951), *passim*; *News*, July 16, 1953.

[15] *News*, July 15, 1953.

[16] New York *Times*, January 9, 1953.

[17] *News*, November 5, 1953; Marvin Alisky, "Radio's Role in Mexico . . . ," *Journalism Quarterly*, Winter 1954, pp. 66–72.

[18] New York *Times*, July 5, 1954; *Directorio . . .* (1), pp. 81–84; *HA*, March 19, 1956, pp. 8–12.

# 13

## Foreign Relations

THE Ministry of Foreign Relations deals mainly with foreign affairs, although some of its functions — like naturalization and alien property ownership — are mainly domestic in character. Its principal "action" organizations are the diplomatic and the consular services.[1] Naturally, the Ministry was among the first agencies established by the first independent government in 1821, when the functions of Foreign Relations and Interior were combined in the same ministry. It has been a separate ministry since 1836. Its organization and functions are similar to those of the U.S. Department of State.

The Bureau of Diplomatic Service deals with political, cultural, and other matters abroad, including the participation in the work of the international organizations. It deals with the placement of diplomatic personnel, international conferences, and the making of treaties and other agreements. Of the Bureau's two subdivisions, the Department of Political Affairs operates the diplomatic service through geographic sections. The sections are the United States and Canada; Latin America; and Europe and Asia. The Department of the Chancellery has sections dealing with personnel, treaties, cultural relations, control of correspondence, and archives. In 1951 the country's foreign representatives consisted of twenty-five ambassadors and seventeen ministers.

The Bureau of Consular Service provides, through its foreign representatives, the usual services of a consular organization: promotion of commerce, protection of the interests of Mexicans abroad, passports, and migratory workers' permits. For supervising this work the Bureau is divided into the Departments of Consular Personnel, Migration, Protection, and Consular Information. Its other subdivisions are the Office of Passports and the Office of Mexican Agricultural Workers. The latter implements the Mexican-American agreement of 1949 regarding agricultural labor for American farms.

The Ministry's third "action" organization is the Bureau of International Organizations. Its separate sections deal with the principal organizations to which Mexico belongs: the United Nations, the International Labor Organization, the International Court and the Universal Postal Union, UNESCO and international conferences and congresses, the Food and Agricultural Organization, and the World Health Organization. Permanent representation is maintained at the seats of the United Nations, UNESCO, the Organization of American States, the Inter-American Economic and Social Council, the Inter-American Juridical Committee, and the International Civil Aviation Organization.

A listing of the thirty-one international organizations to which Mexico belongs is one indication of the active interest which the government has maintained in international affairs. By subject field, these are as follows:

1. Agriculture: Food and Agricultural Organization; Inter-American Institute of Agricultural Sciences; Central American-Mexican Coffee Federation.

2. Economics: Inter-American Economic and Social Council; Inter-American Institute of Statistics; International Bank; International Monetary Fund; International Office for the Publication of Tariffs; International Union for the Protection of Industrial Property; International Office of Weights and Measures.

3. Educational, Scientific, Cultural: International Meteorological Organization; Pan-American Institute of Geography and History; UNESCO; Inter-American Cultural Council.

4. Political and Legal: United Nations; Organization of American States; International Court of Justice; Permanent Court of Arbitration; Inter-American Juridical Committee.

5. Welfare: International Women's Commission; International Institute for Protection of Chidren; Inter-American Indian Institute; World Health Organization; International Labor Organization; Pan-American Sanitary Organization; International Committee for Military Pharmacy and Medicine.

6. Communications: International Civil Aviation Organization; Universal Postal Union; Postal Union of the Americas and Spain; International Telecommunications Union; Inter-American Radio Office.

Two of these — the Pan-American Institute of Geography and History and the Inter-American Indian Institute — have their headquarters in Mexico City.

Several subdivisions of the Ministry perform "housekeeping" functions, or otherwise carry out their work, in Mexico City. The Ceremonial Bureau deals with recognizing the credentials of diplomats accredited to Mexico; their reception by the Minister and by the President; according diplomatic privileges to such representatives; management of receptions and other affairs held by the Minister and the President; and entertaining distinguished citizens of other countries.

The Legal Bureau applies the law of nationality and handles the naturalization of foreigners, as well as extradition and related matters. It also applies the legal and constitutional provisions dealing with alien land ownership.

The Department of External Information is the channel for carrying Mexico's message to people in other countries. It publishes the *Boletín del Servicio Informativo Mexicano* and *Información Consular* to aid its foreign representatives in this task. The Department is charged with collaborating with other ministries in the organization of cultural and other expositions abroad; and it promotes the interchange of publications with other countries.

The International Commission on Boundaries and Waters has two sections. One deals with such boundary problems between Mexico and the United States, while the other deals with such problems connected with the Mexican-Guatemalan border.

The Superior Council on Foreign Commerce is an inter-ministry coordinating group formed in 1941 and composed of representatives from the Ministries of Economy, Finance, Agriculture, Communications, Marine, and Foreign Relations, under the chairmanship of the latter. Its role is that of coordinating the actions of the various agencies in matters relating to foreign commerce and coordinating the private and governmental sectors in such matters.

*The foreign policy process.** As in other republics, the foreign policy process is divided between the executive and the legislative branches. But in Mexico, under the system of strong presidential leadership, the role of the Congress is usually a minor one.

* As in a number of other aspects of Mexican government, almost no useful data are available on the actual process of foreign-policy formation; so the student is largely restricted to the legal-constitutional side of the problem.

The President appoints and removes freely the Minister of Foreign Relations, as is true with other cabinet members. He appoints "ministers, diplomatic agents, and consuls general with the approval of the Senate." But he removes diplomatic agents without the consent of the Senate. The President has full power "to direct diplomatic negotiations and to negotiate treaties," which function, of course, is performed through the machinery of the Ministry in most cases. Treaties, once negotiated, must meet the approval of the Senate. Certain important powers related to the foreign policy process — like levying taxes and authorizing foreign loans — require approval of both houses of Congress. Certain functions connected with defense and war require the approval of one house; others, of both houses. (Arts. 73, 76, 89.) The President usually plays a strong role in the conduct of foreign affairs.

*Development of Mexican foreign relations.*[2] During the century and a third of its independent history, Mexico has played an active role in foreign affairs — and an important role, in proportion to its size.

The winning of independence by Mexico and other Latin American countries brought Britain and the United States into considerable rivalry over that area. Britain, having traded illegally with the Spanish colonies, soon signed treaties of commerce and friendship with these countries; and Mexico floated two loans — at unfavorable rates for Mexico — on the London stock exchange. Trade followed loans, and England soon acquired a large part of Mexican foreign commerce. German capital came to Mexico, and France got a considerable share of Mexican commerce.

United States trade with Mexico increased more slowly, because border problems and U.S. hunger for southwestern lands brought violent suspicion from the southern republic. This suspicion was encouraged by the British and by the inept intervention in Mexican politics of the first U.S. minister to Mexico, who was accused of trying to promote a civil war as a cover for seizure of Texas. Failure of the two countries to agree on a treaty before 1826 increased the difficulties; and only in that year was a treaty of friendship and trade signed, without settlement of the border question.

Mexican-American relations deteriorated throughout the 1820s; and the movement of U.S. citizens into Texas, which at first was encouraged by Mexico, soon brought bitter relations. Contributing causes were some improprieties by U.S. agents and aggressive expressions from the press and platform. Mexican efforts to stop further immigration, abolish slavery, and secure predominance of Mexican nationals in Texas made the Texas revolution a foregone conclusion. The United States' refusal at first to annex Texas was not final; and European interference in Texas finally brought annexation – something which most Mexicans believed was planned all along. Subsequent U.S. efforts to effect a settlement, with compensation to Mexico, failed; and war came in 1846.

Through the treaty of 1848, Mexico lost about half her territory – including New Mexico, Arizona, and California – and the boundary between the two countries was settled. This line was modified somewhat in 1853 by the Gadsden Purchase.

Mexican relations with the rest of the world were shaky during the 1850s, with threats of foreign intervention. Guerrilla actions threatened the property and sometimes the persons of British, French, Spanish, and U.S. citizens. The European countries recognized Miramón as president of Mexico, while the United States preferred to support Juárez – the while debating whether to intervene in Mexico to prevent European intervention. A U.S. treaty for a trade route across the Isthmus of Tehuantepec was denounced in both countries as a sacrifice of Mexican sovereignty and was never ratified; and the U.S. Civil War and its preliminaries occupied northern attention for the next several years. The French intervention and the empire of Maximilian coincided with the northern Civil War. In 1867, Juárez came to power; and the revived republic received U.S. support.

During the long reign of Díaz – from 1876 to 1911 – Mexican policy was strongly oriented toward favoring national development by foreign capital. But after 1900, popular resentment against the excesses of foreign enterprises became vocal. European capital was important in Mexico, but U.S. capital came to predominate. Foreign interests owned more than three fourths of the mines and half the oil fields, plus cattle ranches and plantations of cotton, coffee, and maguey. This billion-dollar investment was more than the Mexicans owned themselves. The English were prominent in oil, mining, public utilities, coffee, and sugar. The French were investors in textile mills.

Mexican reaction to foreign influence was intense and was an important influence in the successful Revolution of 1910. The spirit of nationalism was reflected in the 1917 Constitution, producing the articles requiring Mexican birth for important officeholders; declaration of

national ownership of subsoil wealth; restrictions on alien land owner-
ship; and giving advanced status to labor — since large employers were
mainly foreigners. This sentiment had been reinforced after 1910 by the
U.S. ambassador's role in Madero's fall; by the U.S. occupation of
Veracruz and the threat of intervention by other countries; and by the
U.S. expedition against Villa.

At one time, President Wilson was on the verge of war with the
Carranza government. But the United States was preoccupied with the
World War, so better counsels prevailed and Mexico's relations with
America and Europe improved slowly during the 1920s, though the
Obregón government was not recognized by the United States during
its first three years.[3] The interpretation of the constitutional article on
subsoil ownership as being nonretroactive was viewed favorably abroad.
A foreign debt settlement was negotiated, and Mexico undertook to
resume interest payments to foreign bondholders. And trade increased
with the United States.

Tense times came in 1925–27 when Calles sought to enforce anti-alien
ownership clauses affecting oil lands, and ordered owners to exchange
their titles for leases they considered less favorable and contrary to
previous understandings. Catholic Church leaders charged the government with religious persecution and talk of American intervention
increased. But again wiser counsels prevailed; a new U.S. ambassador
(Morrow) won much respect and friendship by treating Mexicans with
respect and understanding; and oil questions were settled temporarily.

The Cárdenas administration of 1934–40 brought a new era in both
domestic and foreign policy. Foreign affairs were conducted with both
new vigor and considerable consistency. Mexico joined the League of
Nations and condemned German rearmament as a violation of the Ver-
sailles Treaty. In 1936, she urged sanctions against Italy in the Ethiopian
War. When the sanctions failed to get support, the Mexican delegate
foretold the inevitable consequences, and refused to be a party to the
failure — withdrawing from the League assembly. From the start of
the Spanish Civil War, Mexico insisted on adherence to the international law principle that distinguishes between a *de jure* government
and a rebellious faction and allows the purchase of munitions by the
former. In 1937 and 1938, Mexico's voice was raised against the inva-
sions of Austria and China, and it demanded concrete measures against
Japan.[4]

In this same period, Mexico's foreign economic relations were seriously strained by her oil expropriations and her labor program. The expropriation was the result of the spirit of nationalism; adherence to the Mexican legal doctrine of original government ownership of the subsoil wealth; apparent intransigence of the oil companies; and adherence to the government's pro-labor program. International pressures were strong, but the government successfully maintained its position. This was largely due to the basic friendship of the Roosevelt administration and its foreign policy of seeking hemispheric unity against a possible Axis aggression. Thus, an important task of the Foreign Ministry in that era was explaining to the world Mexico's determination to bring about economic reform.[5]

Another era in foreign relations was introduced in 1941 by President Ávila Camacho. It was a period of conservative consolidation. Agreements were reached with the United States for settlement of oil and agrarian expropriation claims, a trade treaty, monetary stabilization, and close collaboration in the war effort. The Mexican-American Commission for Economic Cooperation brought broad financial and technical aid for Mexican industrial and transportation development.[6]

In the postwar era, Mexico has played a consistent role of strong support for the United Nations, its related organizations, and other international agencies. It was host to the Inter-American Conference on Problems of War and Peace in 1945, which laid a basis for the establishment of the United Nations in San Francisco. It has contributed able leaders to the United Nations system — among them being Luis Padilla Nervo (as president of the UN General Assembly) and Jaime Torres Bodet (as head of UNESCO).

Mexico has been a supporter of the international economic organizations; and it has benefited greatly by substantial financial and other aid from them and from the U.S. Export-Import Bank. In the last few years, American technical assistance programs have aided Mexico in several fields. Two of such greatly different aids are in the fields of railroad development and public health service. To this should be added such important nongovernmental programs as that of the Rockefeller Foundation, which has given technical assistance to the Ministry of Agriculture.

*Cultural relations.* The government's work in the cultural relations field dates from the establishment of the Mexican Commission on Intellectual Cooperation in 1931. In 1936, the Mexican government was the first in America to send an exhibition of its national art on a tour of the United States. Established in cooperation with the League of Nations' Commission on Intellectual Cooperation, the Mexican body functions in the Ministry of Public Education. In recent years, cultural exhibits have toured many countries of the western hemisphere. Artists and other intellectuals have accompanied such groups. In the field of formal education, the summer school of the National University was established in 1920 to enable foreigners to study the history, language, art, and society of Mexico. Some provincial universities have established similar schools. Foreign students from other Latin American countries have been granted numerous scholarships for Mexican study.[7]

Several foreign governments and civic groups sponsor institutions which provide important educational and cultural relations services. The Mexican-American Institute for Cultural Relations is an important example. The American government also sponsors the Benjamin Franklin Library, the only large circulating public library in the country. Unfortunately, its usefulness has recently been reduced in Mexican eyes by fund restrictions and U.S. congressional "book purges."[8]

*Foreign policy principles.* Since the Carranza administration, Mexico has adhered consistently to several important foreign policy principles. From the first, these included the propositions that all countries have equality under international law; that outside intervention in a country's internal affairs is intolerable; that foreign residents can expect only equality of treatment with citizens under the law; that diplomatic recognition does not depend on moral approval of the recognized regime by the recognizing country. In addition, the following principles are held to: no secret agreements; opposition to aggressors; opposition to a unilateral interpretation of the Monroe Doctrine; arbitration of disputes; and the right of asylum. There have since been added the need for collective security machinery and recognition of political democracy and a healthy economy as protection against totalitarianism.

Mexico's policy against outside intervention worked both ways, in 1954, regarding the same country — Guatemala. While opposing Communism, Mexico was very chary about recognizing any right of collective intervention in any country except under extrahemispheric attack conditions. It refused to sign the Caracas Declaration; and Mexican sentiment was strongly expressed against alleged plots to invade Guatemala. The other side of Mexican restraint was shown by not aiding the Arbenz regime when its overthrow was launched openly by Guatemalans based on Honduran soil.[9]

The Mexican recognition policy was stated by a former Foreign Ministry head as that of "establishing, maintaining, or suspending diplomatic relations with other states in accordance with the circumstances, but without qualifying the legitimacy or the stability" of such governments. But governments imposed from abroad are another matter. ". . . Mexico has not recognized the territorial conquests of Ethiopia, Czechoslovakia, and Poland."[10]

Opposition to aggression has been shown also through urging sanctions against Italy in Ethiopia; calling for aid to the legal government of Spain at the time of the Civil War; sending medicines and food to Korea; and restricting shipment of possible strategic materials to Communist countries during the Korean war.

Mexico had always opposed interventionism and unilateral application of the Monroe Doctrine. Finally, at the Pan-American Conference of 1936, the Latin American opinion bore weight, when it was agreed that any threats to the peace in the Americas would bring consultation among the governments before action. A related matter is Mexico's insistence on a "Calvo Clause" in concessions, grants, or contracts involving foreigners, placing the latter on the same plane as nationals in such a question.[11]

Mexico's historic policy has been one of firm support for the right of asylum for political offenders. The latest application of this principle came with the Mexican Embassy's granting asylum in Guatemala to leaders of the overthrown Arbenz regime.[12]

*Mexican-American problems.* Despite the fact that Mexican-American relations have been good for many years, some cooling was noted in Mexico's attitude for a period in 1953–54. In general, this seemed to involve economic problems. Mexico's dissatisfaction was evident over the continuing and crucial difficulty of the "wet-back" migrant labor problem; the alleged poaching of American shrimp fishermen in Mexican waters; the alleged non-reciprocity for Mexican airline flights in the United States; threats in the American Congress to raise tariffs against Mexico's lead and zinc exports; and even some popular allegations that the difficulties attendant on peso devaluation could be traced to alleged American reprisals against Mexico's independent position at the Caracas Conference.[13] But the heads of both governments seem determined to keep relations on a high and favorable level. This was shown by Ruiz Cortines' statement after his March 1956 meeting with Eisenhower. He announced a meeting of minds on migrant labor, commercial fishing, and continued economic aid matters.[14]

The problem of widespread popular attitudes (often erroneous) in both the United States and Mexico remains to be reckoned with. One of Mexico's leading philosophers states some of these attitudes as follows. Too many in the U.S. still picture Mexicans as semi-savages, lacking intellectual capacity and engaged in endless revolt, living under despotic governments. Mexicans admire the U.S. for the libertarian and humanitarian traditions of Lincoln and Franklin D. Roosevelt and for the philosophy of the "good neighbor" policy. But they dislike or suspect what many regard as U.S. characteristics — undue pursuit of investments and profits, "imperialism," "interventionism," materialism, lack of religion, and lack of true culture.[15]

### NOTES

[1] Sría. de Bienes Nacionales, *Directorio* . . . (1), pp. 97-114; Mijares Palencia, *op. cit.*, Ch. 3.

[2] Presidente, *Un Siglo de Relaciones Internacionales de México* . . . (1935); Alberto Carreño, *La Diplomacia Extraordinaria entre México y Estados Unidos, 1789-1947* (1951); Jesús Guzmán y Raz Guzmán, ed., *Las Relaciones Diplomáticas de México con Sud-América; Colección de Documentos* . . . (1925); J. Fred Rippy, *The United States and Mexico* (1931); J. M. Callahan, *American Foreign Policy in Mexican Relations* (1932).

[3] John M. Wilson, "The Relations Between the United States and Mexico, 1917-1935" (M.A. thesis, University of Southern California, 1936).

[4] Roy Caldwell, "Our Recent Relations with Mexico" (M.A. thesis, Southern Methodist University, 1941).

[5] Ramón Beteta, "Mexico's Foreign Relations," *Annals*, March 1940, pp. 170-80.

[6] Presidente, *México Coopera con los Naciones Aliadas* . . . (1944); V. R. Stevens, "United States-Mexican Relations During World War II" (M.A. thesis, University of Southern California, 1948); *Cuadernos Americanos*, November-December 1947, pp. 8-27; *Pan American Union Bulletin*, January 1942, pp. 47 *et seq.*

[7] Ruth McMurry and Muna Lee, *The Cultural Approach* (1947), pp. 201-6.

[8] *Christian Science Monitor* (hereafter cited as *CSM*), November 23, 1951.

[9] *El Nacional*, March 14, 1954; New York *Times*, March 25 and June 14, 1954; *Excelsior*, June 21, 1954.

[10] Beteta, *op. cit.*, p. 174.

[11] *Ibid.*, pp. 175-80.

[12] New York *Times*, July 7-14, 1954.

[13] *El Universal*, November 27, 1953; *News*, May 14 and November 27, 1953; New York *Times*, May 10, 17, 22, and June 9, 1954.

[14] New York *Times*, March 30, 1956.

[15] Leopoldo Zea, *América como Conciencia* (1953), Ch. 9.

# 14

## Defense

The role of the military in Mexican public life has always been important, and until recent years usually preponderant.[1] For long the army was in a real sense the government; and the foremost military leader became President. Recent years have seen the steady withdrawal of the military from the affairs of civil government. Today, the role of the army includes much work of a welfare or public service character, such as flood control work, road-building, disaster relief, reforestation, etc.

Constitutionally, the President is the commander-in-chief of the armed forces. He appoints and removes the War and Marine ministers; appoints the colonels and higher officers of the army, navy, and air force; and appoints the other officers of the armed forces according to the terms of the law. Approval of the Congress is necessary for his declaration of war; while the Senate is the body that approves the President's sending troops outside the country, the passage of foreign troops through Mexican territory, and the use of the national guard outside the home states of such units. (Art. 76.)

### The Army

Certainly, the army itself is the oldest organ of the independent Mexican government. The constitutional decree of 1821 established the Ministry of War and Navy, which retained the combined status until the law of 1939 constituted the two as separate ministries. The fortunes of the army fluctuated through the years, but it usually fared better in the national budget than the other agencies.

In the last years of Díaz, the army had steadily weakened; and at the end of his regime it had only 18,000 men, who were "unwilling conscripts badly equipped by grafting war department officials." No true single army existed in the early years of the revolutionary regime — rather, there was a series of motley bands under separate strong men. After Carranza came to power, Obregón began to reorganize the army. A general staff school was founded in 1917, which became the War College in 1920. In 1925, Mexico started sending military missions for study in Europe and the United States. In 1932, the Higher School of War was established. In 1938, the office of the Minister of Defense became more administrative in nature; and the following year the navy was established as a separate ministry. Despite the administrative character of these ministries, the top positions are always held by a general and an admiral, respectively.

*The army in politics.* Until recent years, the army played an important political role. It was often the machinery for establishing regimes and keeping them in power. No regime has been established by military revolt since 1920, however; and the serious attempts have been few. The last two real revolts were those of Escobar in 1929 and Cedillo in 1938. And the failure of these two showed questionable officers that it paid to remain loyal to the incumbent regime.

The army, under the President's Defense Minister, is deployed in thirty-three military zones, with the zone headquarters and barracks usually located in a state capital. In the past, zone commanders were influential in politics and often overshadowed the state governors in influence. They served as powerful agents of the central government in asserting its will against a recalcitrant or rebellious governor.[2] The army has always been used at election time to "preserve order," and until recent years that term was often true in the manipulative sense.

Under Ávila Camacho, the army officers lost their direct representation as a group in the official party and the influence of the military in the civil government has been steadily declining since that time. Today, only seven of the twenty-nine state governors are military men. In the President's cabinet, only the Navy and Defense posts are held by military men. Their numbers have likewise been declining in the Congress.

On occasion, the army has been used to remove a rebellious or "unconstitutional" state regime, after the Senate has declared the erring regime at an end. This process was discussed in Chapter 5 (pages 79–80).

*Army structure.* The army and the air force have shown much progress since 1940. The present preparedness program can be traced to the conscription law prepared under Cárdenas and put into effect under Ávila Camacho in 1941. The law provides for military training for men of eighteen, the obligatory training being done mainly on weekends. Most of the standing army forces are volunteers.[3]

To a large extent, the Mexican army follows the pattern of the U.S. Army, with which there has been effective cooperation since 1941. The basic school for military education is the War College. Service schools are provided for engineering, military medicine, signal work, cavalry, noncommissioned officers, and male and female nurses. The Higher School of War provides the highest level of studies for the army.

The regular army includes these units: 1 infantry division, 1 mechanized brigade, 1 mechanized cavalry regiment, 1 mixed brigade of presidential guards, 51 infantry battalions, 20 cavalry regiments, 2 artillery regiments, 3 independent artillery companies, 1 coast artillery battery, 2 combat engineer battalions, 1 radar observation company, 1 signal battalion, and 1 quartermaster battalion.

The corps of engineers divides the country into eight engineer districts. The regular army and air corps include some 3,500 officers and 55,000 men. For army purposes, the country is divided into ten regions (each under a lieutenant general) and subdivided into thirty-three zones (usually under a major general).

*Defense Ministry structure.*[4] Directly responsible to the Defense Minister is the subsecretary, through whom the Ministry functions. Three other important parts of the structure are directly responsible to the Minister. These deal with the administration of military justice – the Supreme Military Tribunal, the Attorney General for Military Justice, and the Corps of Official Defenders. The Tribunal is an appellate body which hears appeals from decisions of the military judges in the military zones of the country. It also hears requests for pardons, commutations, and reduction of penalties. The Attorney General gathers evidence through the military police and prosecutes cases. The Official Defenders, headed by a brigadier general, provide free defense to defendants.

The *oficial mayor* is the immediate subordinate of the Subsecretary. He handles matters brought to the Ministry by the civil authorities and the general public, and he has under his control the Central Recruiting Office.

The General Staff Office has technical direction of the rest of the agency's machinery and is the technical adviser on such matters to the Minister. A dozen offices are directly subordinate to it. Of first importance are the military schools mentioned above. Then come the legal office, the Commission on Rules, and the Military Cartography Commission. The other offices are those of the general administration of the army (housekeeping functions, supplies, equipment, transportation), military regions, command of garrisons, general inspectorate of the army, the air force, and the General Bureau of Personnel.

The other seven subdivisions come under the General Bureau of Personnel, which deals with personnel services for the entire army — active, inactive, and retired. It has offices of administration, recruitment, arms, and services. The seven subdivisions are the Bureaus of Engineers, Military Sanitation, Military Archives, Social Services, and Reserves, the services of armament and munitions control, and the Office of Communications.

The Bureau of Military Sanitation looks after the army's health needs and administers its medical school and hospitals. The work of the Bureau of Social Services includes development of agricultural colonies for military personnel and administration of commissaries, cemeteries, and life insurance.

The foregoing description applied to the Ministry's organization in 1951. In 1954, a reorganization created a Bureau of Military Education; re-established the Department of the Arms (headed by the chiefs of infantry, cavalry, and artillery); created a Department of Justice; and transformed the Bureau of Reserves into the Bureau of Rural Defenses.[5]

The army has achieved a fair degree of mechanization in recent years. The reserves of several hundred thousand are provided by those who are or have been under the compulsory training program. The potential armed force strength in an all-out emergency would probably total some two million, including the National Guard (a home defense force).[6] In peacetime, the army does much constructive work, such as work on hoof-and-mouth disease and black fly control, narcotics control, reforestation, public health work, disaster relief, and literacy. The Defense Ministry's budget has usually ranked fourth among the agencies in recent years (7.5 per cent of the budget for 1956), being outranked by those of Education, Communications, and Hydraulic Resources. If the navy budget were added, however, Defense would vie with Education for second place.

## The Air Force

The air force is a division of the Defense Ministry, located under the army staff. It is small, consisting of four groups, plus a training group, ten separate squadrons, and a paratroop battalion. Schools include a military flying school, a meteorology school, an aviation mechanics school, and a parachutist school company. But, despite its modest size, the air force has a proud tradition. Mexican pilots were the first in the world to drop aerial bombs on warships, during the Revolution in 1913. A fighter squadron served in the Pacific area during World War II.

The overhead organization of the air force has two subdivisions: the administrative and the operative (including schools). The first includes offices dealing with shops, storage, armament and munitions, and aerial photography. The second has units dealing with strategy and tactics, aerial troops, logistics, and training. The air force strength is about 3,500 men.

## The Ministry of Marine

The Ministry of Marine includes the Bureaus of Merchant Marine, Maritime Works, Dredging, Lighthouses, Naval Construction, Fishing, and the Navy. The navy is small, consisting of 14 frigates, 3 gunboat-transports, 1 transport, 21 coast patrol craft, 4 auxiliary coast patrol craft, and 2 auxiliary ships. The navy has about 8,000 men.

Mexico's maritime area is divided into eight naval zones — four on each of the two coasts. There is a marine battalion, as well as marine detachments, in each naval zone.

The principal schools are the Naval Military School and the Naval War College. There is a naval aviation school at Veracruz and a school for sailors at Mazatlán. A nautical school for the merchant marine is also located at Veracruz.

The Ministry builds lighthouses, dry docks, port works, etc., as well as promoting the fishing industry and seeing to the conservation of fishery resources. The present administration's "march to the sea" program of development for ports and coastal lands brings added responsibilities to this agency.

Under the Minister comes the subsecretary, who has as direct dependencies the Marine Inspection Commission, a Commission on Public Relations, and a Commission for Development of Rural Fisheries. The latter seeks to promote fishing as a means of bringing to the populace a more protein-rich diet. Like several other agencies, it has benefited by the services of technicians from the Rockefeller Foundation. Under the subsecretary comes the *oficial mayor*, who has as dependencies these operating Bureaus: Maritime Works, Dredging, Fishing and Related Industries, Naval Construction, Merchant Marine, and the Fleet. Housekeeping units are the Bureau of Accounts and Administration, the Legal Department, and the Medical Department.

## NOTES

[1] General references on the Mexican defense system are Sría. de Bienes Nacionales, *Directorio* . . . (1), pp. 177–201; Tena Ramírez, *op. cit.*, Ch. 15; Mijares Palencia, *op. cit.*, Ch. 5; Virginia Prewett, "The Mexican Army," *Foreign Affairs*, April 1941, pp. 609–20; Carlos R. Berzunza, "National Defense," *Encyclopedia Americana* (1954), v. 18, pp. 779–80; *Statesman's Year-Book*.

[2] Mecham, "Mexican Federalism — Fact or Fiction?" *op. cit.*, p. 34. Brandenburg (*op. cit.*, pp. 324–26) gives an eye-witness account of the removal of one recalcitrant state administration.

[3] Parkes, *A History of Mexico*, p. 320.

[4] *Mexican American Review*, October 1952, p. 11.

[5] *HA*, July 12, 1954, pp. 3–4.

[6] Call, *Mexican Venture*, pp. 250–51.

# 15

## Government's Positive Economic Role

THE broad role of all government is advancement of human welfare; and in Mexico the avowed special aim is raising the standard of living of the masses of the people, a goal slowly being attained. It is a difficult task for an underdeveloped country with modest resources to effect a rapid industrialization through domestic capital accumulation and simultaneously raise consumption standards; and the second gives ground to the first.

In this forced march of progress, government plays an important role, both negative and positive. Private property, says the Constitution (Art. 27), is a thing that society creates; so the government has the right to regulate or take property for a public purpose. A strong nationalistic spirit underlay the drafting of the Constitution and still underlies the negative and positive approaches the government takes toward property.

The government's relationship to the economy is eclectic rather than dogmatic. It intervenes little or much, as it feels the situation demands. The present Minister of Economy says that "Mexico lives in an economic regime of private initiative and public responsibility. This means that the state should not intervene in the economic life in every case or at every moment, but only in the cases in which the social or national interest makes it necessary . . ." [1] Mexico has a directed economy rather than a socialist economy, as its spokesmen and their actions indicate. [2]

The principal device used to advance the national welfare has been the drive to industrialize, since this is regarded as the means of escape from a "colonial," raw-material-exporting economy. The tempo has intensified, but the effort dates back over a century, when the first bureau for industry was established. The movement really started about the turn of the century; stagnated in the early revolutionary era; and revived after the mid-thirties. For the past decade and a half, the federal government has largely determined the direction and rate of economic development through its policies and investments.[3] The striking thing is that there has been little true planning, though the government has been providing nearly 40 per cent of the total capital investment for increased production.

The constitutional basis for the government's active economic role is found in the provisions that subordinate the individual's rights to those of society (Art. 4); provide for regulation of property and for its expropriation for a public purpose (Art. 27); forbid private monopolies (Art. 28); and empower Congress to legislate in economic matters (Art. 73). Effective control over commerce had been secured by federal law by 1884; and many statutes in recent years have established the legal basis for federal power over the economy. One of the most important is the law of 1950 (Law on Powers of the Executive in the Economic Field).[4] It gives the President regulatory powers over production and distribution in commerce and industry of foods, clothing, and raw materials, thus providing an important control over the economy by laying the basis for price and allocation controls. On the positive side, the preponderant role that the government plays in new investments will be discussed below.

*Some indices.* Mexico has been fighting a battle of production the past two decades, and many of the achievements are impressive. The net domestic product more than doubled between 1939 and 1950; and the average annual increase exceeded 7 per cent, with increases in almost all sectors of the economy. Only mining suffered a decline. A substantial shift of employment from the extractive to the manufacturing and processing industries was noted.[5]

The main emphasis has been placed on capital formation, while wages and social service expenditures have lagged behind. From 1939 to 1946, the fraction of the net product going to profits climbed from 26 per cent to 45 per cent, while the portion for wages and salaries declined from 31 per cent to 22 per cent. There was some narrowing of this discrepancy by 1950. This meant that per-capita consumption increased very little because of population increase. The increase in per-capita industrial production was quite different. It was 195 for 1954 (1929 =

100), while the average for western European countries in 1954 was 153 and of the United States, 152.[6]

The government's aim has been to promote the production of basic materials used by secondary industries, thus reducing the country's dependence on imports. In the pursuit of this goal, nearly 40 per cent of the public expenditures went into direct and indirect public investments; and almost 40 per cent of all investments from 1939-50 was public investment. These expenditures went into a host of "productive" investments, as well as into auxiliary investments such as roads and irrigation projects.[7] Such government investments covering a wide range of projects increased some six-fold in pesos from 1939 to 1949, leaving an impressive picture even after adjustment for peso devaluation. The investments in schools and industry increased ten- and twenty-fold, respectively; while the factors for municipal works, communications and transport, and irrigation were five, six, and eight. The greatest increase of all was for electrification. Agriculture and conservation fared poorly.[8]

To enhance purchasing power, the government has used price controls and direct sale of corn products at controlled prices. Such sales have been used with varying degrees of effectiveness, with considerable success since 1953. Some precedents go back as far as 1901. Price controls have been used at various times and with varying degrees of success (usually modest) since 1931.[9]

The economic program of the government has enjoyed substantial support. The New Group of industrialists has enjoyed the protections of high tariffs, low taxes, and much government credit. Organized labor has enjoyed the various social measures and government protection for collective bargaining.

*The program develops.* The program of President Cárdenas was one of raising the living standard of the people through agrarian and social reform, diversifying production, and escaping from "colonialism" through reducing foreign control. First came the strengthening of agriculture through an extensive redistribution of lands, with related programs of agricultural credit, irrigation, education, sanitation, etc. Collectivized farming was also tried in certain localities, with varying degress of success. Cárdenas' program was epitomized in the first Six-Year Plan, an elaborate campaign platform of the official party, which revived and extended the salient thinking of the era of the Revolution and the Constitutional Convention of 1917.[10]

The text of the Six-Year Plan covered agriculture, labor, the national economy, communications, and public works, health, education, and other matters. Much of it dealt in generalities, but some fields were provided with annual schedule goals; and Cárdenas strove hard for their implementation. Substantial achievements were made in land distribution, education, irrigation, and roads.

The Cárdenas program had little place for large-scale industrialization. He favored the development of industries in the smaller communities rather than in the large cities. While Cárdenas looked with suspicion on many foreign companies, there is evidence that his aim was fairness to all fairly operated foreign enterprises.[11] His program of industrial management seemed to come through necessity rather than long-range plan. The railroads and the oil industry were nationalized; and their early difficulties were due in part to the heritage of the past and pressures from abroad. The highway and electrification programs, of great future importance, were started under Cárdenas. The tourist "industry" (now one of the three or four most important) got its first impetus under his administration.

There seemed more change than continuity between the agrarian and social reform program of Cárdenas and the conservative industrialization program of Ávila Camacho. However, the expanding public works program under Cárdenas laid the basis for its extension under his successor; and the construction industries, supplying materials for public works, received a stimulus that was passed on to other industries. Ávila Camacho seems to have entered office without any consistent economic program; and some investigators feel that he adopted a pro-industrialization program as a substitute for the Cárdenas small farms program, of which he disapproved. In any case, he soon enacted the law of manufacturing industries; supported tariffs to protect industries; extended tax exemptions to encourage the same groups; and otherwise gave strong encouragement to industry.[12]

The increased emphasis on industrialization both aided and was aided by the demands of a war economy. Various successive agencies were established for economic "planning," coordination, development, and control over wartime production, distribution, allocations, price control, etc. Their effectiveness varied greatly, but they represented a governmental awakening to the imperatives of a complex economy.[13]

Mexico's war economy was greatly aided by loans from the U.S.

Export-Import Bank. A related success was the work of the joint Mexican-American Commission for Economic Cooperation, whose task was to promote the industrialization program as an aid to the war effort. This included substantial American expenditures in developing the steel, cement, textile, chemical, and paper industries. By the end of Ávila Camacho's administration in 1946, industrialization had become the heart of the government's program.[14]

The Alemán administration concentrated even more completely on industrialization than its predecessor — too much so, according to some competent economists. Industrialization was viewed as *the* way to economic salvation. The upward trend was aided by increased tariffs, tax exemptions, foreign loans, foreign investments in Mexico, currency devaluation, and import restrictions.

Because of his determination to advance industrialization, Alemán gave much more encouragement to foreign capital — private as well as public — than had his predecessors. Development loans from the United States government were a substantial aid to his program. While welcoming foreign investors and businessmen, he warned them against expecting exorbitant profits or special privileges.[15]

While concentrating on industry, Alemán's administration continued a substantial program of development in the fields of irrigation, electrification, and highway construction.

The feeling had been growing that Mexico's headlong industrialization drive had gone too fast; that a period of consolidation was needed; that agriculture and other aspects of the economy should be brought into line with industry. Economic experts had been making such suggestions, and Ruiz Cortines seems to agree. In his inaugural address in December 1952, the new President pledged that his government would consolidate the gains of his predecessor and spare no effort to increase agricultural production, promote a balanced industrialization, and bring down basic food prices.[16] The 1954, 1955, and 1956 budgets put greater emphasis on aid to agriculture and rural projects — secondary roads, irrigation, electricity, etc. The Papaloapán Valley's TVA-type project is being pushed, as an aid to the people of that area and as a colonization area for overpopulated and unproductive areas.[17]

Industrialization is being continued at a substantial rate, but the establishment of new industries of doubtful economic worth and the earning of excessive profits are being questioned. Public works contracts are being combed for possible graft; and increased government expenses are being met by improved tax collection procedures. Financial difficulties in 1954 brought a devaluation of the peso, which it was hoped would bring additional investments, stimulation to the tourist industry, etc. This was accompanied by increased tariffs on luxury imports and reduced export duties to encourage many exports. Economic recovery following devaluation has been most encouraging.[18]

The present administration is less spectacular than its predecessor, but it seems to be more down-to-earth regarding the country's needs.

*The agrarian program.* In discussions of the modernization of Mexico, the fact is often forgotten that Mexico is still an agricultural country, with the great majority of the people dependent on the land. Despite great urban-industrial progress, the strength of the country still depends largely on the strength of its rural economy — a subject considered in detail in Chapters 20 and 21.

The basis of the Revolution of 1910 was largely the cry of the rural landless for land, a demand that the various forward-looking developments of the nineteenth century had failed to meet. In 1915, to strengthen support for his regime, Carranza issued a law which made a start toward restitution of village lands alienated illegally under earlier regimes. The Constitution of 1917 sought to broaden and expand this program as the most basic of the government's programs. But progress was slow and halting for many years; and the program came to life only during the Cárdenas administration, when more land was distributed to more farmers than in all the rest of Mexican history.[19]

For reasons discussed later (see pages 269–94), the agrarian problem is still one of Mexico's most pressing. The Ministry of Agriculture, the Agrarian Department, the Agricultural Bank, the Ejidal Bank, the Irrigation Commission, the Ministry of Hydraulic Resources, and various decentralized agencies have played prominent roles. But making Mexico's agricultural basis healthy remains a task to be done.

*Tariff policy.*[20] Among the important government aids to the industrialization program are favorable credit, tax exemption, and tariff policies. Of the Latin American countries desiring to industrialize, Mexico has the longest and most consistent record of protectionist tariffs. Once revenue was the principal aim, but the protectionist element has been present for many decades; and it has been growing steadily. Since the early forties, the tariff has been used increasingly as an aid to industrial development; and, in general, it has been used to bolster most industries that want to produce things formerly imported.

In general, the highest duties are found on agricultural and food products competing with domestic production; next come manufactures produced in Mexico, and luxuries. Moderate duties are found on raw materials and equipment needed in manufacturing plants; while free entry is often granted to prime necessities and some equipment.

While trade is important to Mexico, industrialization has had clearcut priority over efforts to promote freer world trade. This is true because local industry is based on internal consumption rather than on export. The end of the recent war left Mexico in a weak trade position; so, in 1947 she modified her trade treaty with the United States in the direction of greater restrictions, and she let it lapse at the end of 1950. But trade relations between the two countries have been moderately satisfactory since then.

It is difficult to determine the role of the tariff in aiding industrial development, since its considerable aid has benefited industries unevenly, not being applied as a planned instrument of industrialization. Protection has had widespread support from both industry and labor, but it has been applied and increased without real studies of the industries concerned. An advisory tariff commission with representation from various industries has functioned since 1927. The dangers of improper application of tariffs have been emphasized by both Mexican and foreign investigators. These include application as the result of pressures rather than the needs of a balanced economy, and penalizing the consumers with support for uneconomic industries selling products at excessive prices.

*Tax concessions.*[21] I have mentioned earlier that Mexico has a very moderate tax burden, even compared with other Latin American countries. An added inducement to industry is a system of partial and total tax exemptions. This, added to various import and export tariff concessions, makes a very attractive climate for industrial enterprise.

The first limited program of tax exemptions was enacted in 1926. Its importance was enhanced by broader concessions in the laws of 1932 and 1939. The first two laws were limited to small firms, and their use was not extensive. Under the more pro-industry Ávila Camacho administration, the 1941 Law of Manufacturing Industries gave five-year tax concessions to new industries and to industries considered necessary for the development of manufacturing. The Minister of Economy approved the applications and determined the degree of tax exemption for each case. This law was revised in 1946, classifying firms into three groups and granting exemptions for periods of five, seven, and ten years. The program of tax exemptions became an important part of the government's industrial policy after 1941. The four industries most aided by tax exemptions have been metal manufacturing, chemical products, electrical apparatus, and machinery. Naturally, all federal government undertakings as well as true public enterprises of the states and municipalities are tax exempt.

It is doubtful whether the concessions have had the desired effect, for beneficiaries have done more expanding of existing industries than establishing of new industries; and exemptions have been on the increase in recent years.

A number of the states have followed the lead of the federal government since 1940 in establishing similar exemptions from state taxes. The State of Mexico, bordering the Federal District, has been generous in such matters; while Nuevo Leon, with its industrial center of Monterrey, gives 75 per cent reductions for from five to twenty years for new industries. Here, likewise, the results are questionable.

Credit.[22] More important than most tariffs and tax reductions has been the problem of credit for industrialization. This means foreign investment capital and loans, as well as domestic credit. The government has aided along both lines, especially since 1940; and today it plays the dominant financial role, in recent years furnishing as much as 45 per cent of the gross investment.

Direct investments by foreigners have played an important role in the economy for over a century. Before the 1870s, such investments were mainly by venturesome individuals; but corporate investments became substantial during the Díaz regime, with foreign-owned enterprises probably controlling the major part of capital investments by the time of the Revolution. The revolutionary period discouraged investments, but the influx in recent years reached sizable proportions. However, domestic private and public investments grew rapidly enough so that the relative importance of foreign funds declined after 1939, being about 7 per cent of the total industrial investment in 1946–49. The United States leads among the foreign investors, with England still holding an important place.

Foreign investments require the permission of the government; and the law requires 51 per cent ownership by Mexicans, but legal and administrative discretion has prevented its severe application. Recent administrations have been increasingly friendly to foreign investments; freedom from expropriation is substantial; and freedom to transfer profits abroad is virtually complete.

Foreign borrowing by the government began in 1824, and was marked by numerous defaults prior to the Díaz regime in the 1880s. That regime's credit standing made possible heavy borrowing from private sources abroad. Default characterized most of the period from 1914 to 1940. The debt service has been continued since that period, partly aided by the International Bank, the International Monetary Fund, and the Export-Import Bank. By 1950, the latter's outstanding Mexican loans totaled more than $36 million for roads, $40 million for railways, and $20 million for electrical development. By January 1, 1955, Export-Import Bank loans outstanding were some $120 million. Other industries to which the government channeled such loans include steel, oil, sugar, and meat packing. It is recognized that less foreign aid and government credit would be needed if less native capital were invested in speculative undertakings.

Mexico's postwar levels of savings and investment have been high for a country with such a per capita income, with investment reaching about 14 per cent of the gross national product for 1947–50. Transport and communications were first among the investments, with industry and construction second and third. Some 84 per cent of the investment came from domestic savings in the period 1939–45, and 91 per cent in 1946–50.

Private banking is a comparatively recent development in Mexico, with much of it done in the nineteenth century by foreign-owned institutions. The first general banking laws were not passed until 1897. Banking pretty much came to a standstill during the Revolution, and development afterward was slow. Some changes in the system were made in 1921, but the present system really dates from the establishment of the Bank of Mexico as the central bank in 1925. It did not receive its full powers until 1931.

*Banking system.*[23] Over the whole banking system, private and public, is the Ministry of Finance. Then come the National Banking Commission, the Bank of Mexico, the system of specialized credit institutions, and the private banks. Advisory and inspectional services are provided for the banking system by the National Banking Commission, a body with six members named by the Ministry of Finance and three from the institutions of credit. The Commission's functions include inspecting the institutions of credit; participating with the central bank in issuance of paper money, bonds, etc.; reporting on credit operations; deciding on the solvency of banks; and advising the Ministry of Finance.

*Bank of Mexico.* The cornerstone of the banking system is the Bank of Mexico, the country's central bank. For several years after its founding in 1925, the Bank carried on some commercial banking activities, as well as issuing money, regulating interest rates, and stabilizing the rate of exchange. Through the reforms of 1931 and 1932, the Bank withdrew from the commercial banking field; received the power to rediscount the paper of other banks; required private banks to maintain reserves in the central bank; and regulated the circulation of money.

At present, the Bank of Mexico has these important characteristics. It is the sole bank of issue; coins money; guards the country's foreign exchange reserves; regulates credit and monetary circulation throughout the country; rediscounts commercial paper; serves as the clearinghouse for other banks; serves as treasurer, financial adviser, and representative of the government; guards the cash reserves of the other banks; and regulates the maximum interest and discount rates.[24]

The Bank of Mexico, as the government's chief financial institution, can play an important role in the country's economic life. During inflationary periods, it has been moderately successful in controlling the price spiral. It uses its authority to expand or contract money circulation through discounts and loans to governmental and private institutions, as well as using its power over bank reserve requirements as a credit control measure.

The Bank has collaborated extensively with the government in the financing of public works and other industrial developments; but it is felt that the policy has not been conceived or applied well enough to prevent considerable unevenness of industrial development. Nor has it influenced the savings and investment habits of the public as well as some have desired. At times the Bank has been used to finance the government's deficits and in other ways has contributed to inflation, though other policies have been anti-inflationary.

*Other government banks.*[25] The Mexican government's banking system has adopted the principle of specialized credit institutions. The foremost of these official investment banks is the Nacional Financiera, which specializes in industrial development and is often called the Mexican RFC. It will be discussed at the end of this section.

Two banks have been established to provide credit for agriculture. The National Bank for Agricultural Credit was established in 1926 to aid small farmers, *ejido* farmers as well as others. The Cárdenas administration's emphasis on aid to the small farmers and the rural proletariat led to emphasizing the work of the Agrarian Department and establishing the National Bank for Ejido Credit. The success of these banks has been limited, due to inadequate financing and other factors, as will be discussed in Chapter 21.

The National Urban Mortgage and Public Works Bank, dating from 1933, promotes and directs investments in public works, the public services, and certain low-rent housing. The government holds about three fourths of its stock, while most of the rest is held by the Bank of Mexico, Nacional Financiera, and other decentralized agencies.

Two banks serve the field of commerce, of which the National Foreign Trade Bank is the more important. It was established in 1937 to finance the export of Mexican products. Exports it has aided include henequen, coffee, bananas, cotton, chicle, and rice. More than 80 per cent of its capital has come from the government, with some 10 per cent from the Bank of Mexico. The Small Business Bank began operations in 1943, to provide credit at moderate interest rates for small business undertakings in the Federal District. Most of its capital comes from the government, but about one fifth comes from the associations of small businessmen served by the bank.

Three banks operate in the field of industry. The National Cinema Bank, formed in 1941, serves the movie industry. Most of its capital comes from Nacional Financiera, with substantial amounts from the government and the Bank of Mexico. The National Bank for Cooperative Development aids cooperatives through loans and through serving as an agency for purchases and for sale of their products. The present organization dates from 1941, its predecessor from 1937. Nearly all its capital comes from the government. Nacional Financiera, discussed below, is the third.

The National Bank of the Army and Navy, started in 1947, serves the needs of the army and the navy, including certain agricultural and other undertakings of those organizations. Nearly all its capital comes from the government.

Some other decentralized organizations finance important development projects with their own funds. These include Petróleos Mexicanos (Pemex), the Bureau of Pensions, and the Social Security Institute. The last two have financed considerable housing for low-income persons.

Nacional Financiera is the most important public institution directly concerned with providing funds for industrial development.[26] Its importance has increased greatly in recent years, because the government has increasingly emphasized industrial development. Its complex, many-sided operations make use of large sums of public money and increasing amounts of private funds, with which it assumes a dominant position in guiding the country's industrial development. Its functions might be compared with those of the RFC, the Securities and Exchange Commission, and a government-sponsored investment trust in the United States. In addition, government bonds are floated through this agency, which also intervenes in the securities market to support stocks and bonds.

Most of the stock is owned by the government; and because of its financial relationships with the Bank of Mexico, Financiera performs the functions of an investment banking department for the Bank.

Financiera was established in 1933 with the functions of supervising and regulating the securities market; promoting investments in industrial enterprises; supervising stock exchanges; acting as a savings bank and an investment company; and advising the government in financial transactions. Growth was slow during the first years. In 1937, attention was turned to the stock market and the agency issued its first bonds.

The second stage in Financiera's development started about 1941, after the Ávila Camacho administration shifted the government's emphasis to industrialization. Industrial promotion was given a substantial start in the war years, with loans from the Export-Import Bank and other sources channeled into the steel industry and other basic industries. After the end of the war, important investments went into railways, oil, and sugar mills.

The current stage dates from 1947, when the capitalization of the agency was greatly increased and it was made the channel for negotiating and administering loans obtained from abroad. The program has steadily expanded and in recent years the agency's functions have included regulating the stock market and long-term credit operations; acting as agent and adviser to the government in bond sales; serving as the channel for official loans from abroad; promoting industrial and other investments which fit into the government's development program; serving in a fiduciary capacity for the government; acting as a financing and investment society.

The direct investment role of Financiera has in general been limited to helping start or expand important enterprises that are not attractive to private capital because of the need for large sums or the anticipation of slow returns on investment. A suitable climate for private investment has been the main objective, with government money being limited to fields of crucial importance. Government funds thus invested in some two dozen or more basic industries may be found alongside private capital and money originally from the Export-Import Bank. The aim is to shift government funds to new concerns as those aided earlier get well on their feet. The major projects to be aided are selected with the counsel of experts, including those from the United States or from other foreign agencies involved in making the loans.

As I have indicated, Financiera's funds come from several sources, including the government, the Bank of Mexico, the Export-Import Bank, the International Bank, and the floating of its own security issues. One of the chief sources has been its certificates of participation, each issue of which is backed by definite securities in its portfolio of investments. This type of investment, which is very attractive to investors, bears a fixed and substantial rate of interest.

Another means of stimulating industry is the making of secured loans to private *financieras*. These are financial institutions which organize and promote business enterprises; hold shares of stock in such firms; float securities issues for businesses; and make intermediate and long-term loans. The growth of these firms has been rapid since 1940. In this way, Nacional Financiera serves as a central bank in the field of investment banking.

An official of Financiera has summarized its industrial role as follows. First, it aims to direct its resources toward strengthening the economy through using insufficiently exploited natural resources; developing the most important branches of industry; and improving the balance of payments through making possible reduction of certain imports or developing industries that bring in foreign exchange. Second, it tries to operate within the limits of an anti-inflationary policy. Third, it seeks to elicit maximum participation by private investment in the enterprises it aids. Fourth, it purchases private securities under certain circumstances. Fifth, it handles the negotiation and administration of credits obtained from abroad.

Between 1942 and 1952, the ranking of the more important industries receiving Financiera credits was as follows: transport and communication, electrification, irrigation, steel, and oil refining. The first two were far in the lead. Financiera's share in the total capital investment has been modest, but its achievements have been substantial through the placing of its investments at strategic points.

One criticism of Financiera has been that it has given little aid to the small manufacturer, although small industry is often better adapted to the current Mexican scene than is large industry.

*The National Securities Commission.* This is an independent, quasi-judicial agency of significance in the field of investment. Created in 1946, its chief purpose is similar to that of the United States Securities and Exchange Commission, since its role is that of building a stronger securities market freed of malpractices. Its directors come from the government's financial institutions and the field of private banking.[27]

*Planning.* There has been an abundance of "planning" in Mexico; but there has been little true planning in the sense of coordinated formulation of broad goals, elaboration of detailed programs, and integrated supervision and execution, which in turn would be the basis for subsequent programming and execution.

Some form of planning is as old as the conquest, when the Council of the Indies served as the embryo of a planning agency. The Díaz rule, with its emphasis on railroad construction and foreign investment, was a form of planning. The same has been true, on a much larger scale, of the important governmental programs since 1934.

But the true planning concept is not yet widely appreciated in Mexico. It is commonly regarded as a political or an operational, not a broad administrative, process. Production necessities have seemed pressing; and plans formulated have tended to be *ad hoc* undertakings, without adequate continuity, systematic follow-up, and revision in the light of changing needs and conditions. The inadequate conception or appreciation of planning is related, as both cause and effect, to the lack of adequate central planning machinery. Numerous offices in the various agencies make valuable contributions in the form of economic, fiscal, engineering, and other studies; but integration and central direction have been lacking. Coordinative efforts were mentioned in Chapters 9 and 10; but Mexican political realities have made the office of the President the only effective center for such work, and that office has not been fully equipped for the task.[28]

The Great Depression brought new problems and an increased role for government. One answer was the adoption of the first Six-Year Plan, drafted in 1933–34 by the official political party. In the main, it was stated in very general terms and was something more than an ordinary party platform, but it was much less than a full plan in the true sense of the word. It was the beginning of a program of increasing participation of government in the economy, especially in agriculture and public works, but also in industry. An early institutional arrangement for planning was made by Cárdenas when he constituted the heads of agencies and the government banks as an advisory committee for that purpose in 1935. This arrangement proved unsatisfactory, and in 1938 the President replaced it with a special division for planning in the Ministry of Government. This division worked with the official party in drafting the second Six-Year Plan. Nationalization of oil and the railways, foreign affairs, and many weighty problems faced the Cárdenas administration; but planning was insufficiently developed to make much of a contribution to their solution.[29]

The Ávila Camacho administration was definitely oriented toward industrialization; but the frequent talk of a plan of industrialization in reality meant simply increased government encouragement toward building new plants, with such inducements as tax exemptions and government credit. Usually, it meant the government's aiding industrialists to carry out decisions made entirely on their own. Little broad-scale planning was attempted. But important long-range plans were carried out in important sectors of the economy such as the programs of the Federal Electricity Commission and the National Irrigation Commission.[30]

The 1941 Law for Manufacturing Industries gave a boost to industrial development by providing tax exemptions for new or expanded industries. The same year saw the establishment of the first of a series of committees or commissions aimed at promoting and coordinating economic development. The National Economic Council was established in 1941, with its members drawn from various agencies as well as from certain private and semipublic organizations with functions in the economic field. It was replaced in 1942 by the Federal Economic Planning Commission, which, in turn, was replaced in 1944 by the Federal Industrial Development Commission. This body was intended to be both a planning and a functioning organization, charged with planning, organizing, and financing concerns needed for Mexico's well-rounded economic development but which private investors shunned. It gave promise of effectively guiding the developing economy through making needed studies, filling gaps in the industrial structure, avoiding needless duplication, and providing necessary capital. Despite the temporary character of its ownership role, business circles feared a broad-scale development of government ownership; and the work of the Commission ended with few accomplishments.[31]

Several emergency agencies of significance for planning were established to cope with wartime problems. The most important of these was the Mexican-American Commission for Economic Cooperation, established by the two governments in 1943. Through this channel, the United States gave Mexico substantial aid in the development of nearly two dozen projects in important industries. Other emergency agencies dealt with price controls, regulation of commodity markets, and other forms of governmental intervention. One of the few successful undertakings was the National Distributing and Regulating Agency, which had some success in preventing excessive price increases for basic food items. It was succeeded in 1949 by CEIMSA (Mexican Exporting and Importing Company), which has been very active under Ruiz Cortines in holding down certain basic food prices.[32]

In recent years, several committees have been established to plan and coordinate certain segments of the government's program. A Committee on Imports and Exports was established in 1950. In 1953, an Investments Committee was created to prepare and coordinate the government's long-range program of investments. It represented the chief economic and financial agencies — the Ministries of Finance and Economy, the Bank of Mexico, and Nacional Financiera — replacing a similar agency of the preceding administration which had been unsuccessful.[33]

In recent years, individual studies of importance for planning have been made by such Mexican and American groups as the Bank of

Mexico, Nacional Financiera, the National Bank of Foreign Commerce, the National Bank of Mexico, the Armour Research Foundation, Higgins Industries, and Bacon and Davis.

As the previous discussion indicates, the Mexican government is playing an important and positive role in the economy; but it has no single over-all plan or planning agency to guide the total program. Industrialization is the general goal, but often pressing problems seem to demand immediate solution and unforeseen results occur later in related fields.

Planning responsibilities are scattered among a number of loosely coordinated agencies concerned with particular aspects of economic development. Prominent among these are the Ministries of Finance, Economy, National Properties, Communications, and Hydraulic Resources, the Bank of Mexico, and Nacional Financiera. Some have considered the Department of Economic Studies of the Bank of Mexico one of the most important of such agencies.

There have been few substantial efforts at local planning except for the vicinity of the Federal District, where there has been little attempt at coordination for an area until recently. The Regional Planning Commission of the Valley of Mexico was established to coordinate the efforts of local commissions for Mexico City, the Federal District, and the parts of surrounding states within the Valley.[34] Planning in the Federal District got its start in 1930s.

Authorities agree on the need for adequate systematic planning machinery. The time has come, it is felt, when a comprehensive approach should replace the project-to-project approach to economic development. A central agency should be given this function. The resulting plan should not be rigid, but sufficiently flexible to meet changing needs. The aim should not be a rigorously controlled economy but a moderately directed economy, ranking the goal priorities in both the public and the private sectors and using devices of both encouragement and discouragement — for which the government has many tools.[35]

Certain goals are of recognized importance. But there are large questions. One question is whether manufacturing capacity has nearly outrun current purchasing power and whether the rate of industrial development should be reduced until agriculture and other aspects of the economy catch up. A question about agriculture is whether emphasis should be shifted from export crops to cutting down on foodstuff imports. There is considerable agreement, however, on acceleration in the fields of electric power, natural gas, oil, and road building. In any event, Mexico needs to make effective use of her rather modest physical resources.[36]

Present resources may be augmented by atomic energy. There seem to be substantial sources of the raw material; and the government has established a monopoly on such resources and has created an atomic energy commission to guide the development.[37] Whatever the specific lines of development may be, the government seems destined to continue playing a very active role. Increased rates in higher-bracket taxation should be considered as an aid to financing the government's economic program, for these rates have been very "favorable" to the taxpayer thus far.

### Government's Regulatory Role in the Economy

In the preceding section government's principal economic role was discussed — the role of initiator and stimulator of economic development. Tariffs, tax concessions, favorable credit, and other devices have been used to stimulate the industrial development that was government's principal goal. Government's economic role has been chiefly that of stimulating and assisting private enterprise (aside from nationalized oil and railways), with intervention by government only where the general welfare dictates.

Even the numerous government aids to the economy can have their negative or control aspects. These effects can be achieved through determining the time and rate of assistance; the geographic areas to be aided; the industries — or firms within an industry — to be aided. Some or many of such effects can be achieved through direct government investments, credit, tariff policy, monetary policy, tax concessions, and banking policy. Withholding action, or its selective application, in these lines of activity can produce important effects on the economy. An example is the 1954 peso devaluation, which was aimed at reducing nonessential imports, stimulating exports, promoting domestic investments, and expanding the tourist industry. The effects on the economy have been important, varying from sector to sector.

In addition to these direct aids, with their indirect control effects, the government has taken various regulatory actions of importance to the economy. The constitutional basis of the government's power in economic matters is found mainly in four articles, Arts. 4, 27, 28, and 73, as discussed on pages 83, 85, 86, 95–97.[38]

Besides these governmental powers, the economic regulatory powers of the President have also become extensive. His powers of appointment and other powers give him control over the nationalized industries. There are extensive presidential powers for encouraging or discouraging enterprises or industries. He may do so by placing controls on equipment and other items, tariffs on imports and exports, bank credit, tax exemptions, and closing "saturated" industries to the establishment of new firms.

*Financial controls.* Numerous governmental and nongovernmental financial institutions, directly or indirectly under the control or influence of the Ministry of Finance, have the power to exercise important financial controls over business and industry. A number of these were discussed in the first part of this chapter.

The Bank of Mexico, ultimately answerable to the President through the Finance Minister, may regulate credit and the circulation of money; sets the rediscount rate for commercial paper; and regulates maximum interest rates. It makes loans, underwrites the loans of other credit institutions, and regulates commercial bank reserve requirements.

Other government banks exercise financial power through granting or withholding credit in their respective spheres: industrial finance (Nacional Financiera), agriculture, the *ejidos*, urban mortgages and public works, foreign commerce, small business, and cooperatives.

The National Banking Commission has both advisory and inspectional relations to the country's general banking system. A majority of its board members are named by the Minister of Finance, to whom the Commission has an advisory relationship. It inspects institutions of credit and decides on the solvency of banks.

The field of investment control is served by the National Securities Commission, which is similar to the U.S. Securities and Exchange Commission. Its work is that of regulating the securities market.

*Price control.* Scattered price control precedents date back before 1910; but systematic efforts to control the prices of basic food items in behalf of low income consumers date from 1931, when ceilings were placed on bread and tortillas. The law of 1934 allowed such action against any industry adjudged as seeking monopoly control in the market. A decree of June 25, 1937, empowered the Minister of Finance to control the production, distribution, and prices of certain agricultural and industrial products. But enforcement proved difficult, and several agencies were tried in this field through the war period.[39]

Two agencies were established in 1951 to combat speculation in the items of basic necessity: the Bureau of Prices in the Ministry of Economy and the National Price Commission, an advisory body appointed by the Ministry. The Bureau controls the prices of articles of basic necessity, and has the power to establish priorities in the use of scarce commodities. The Commission is headed by the Minister of Economy and includes representatives from other agencies and from civic organizations.[40]

Another approach to control of prices of basic necessities is that of CEIMSA (Mexican Exporting and Importing Company), which seeks to maintain sufficient supplies and reasonable prices for basic food items by means of export, import, and direct sale of commodities. This agency has been very active during the present administration in reduced-price, direct-service sales to the lowest income groups of bread, rolls, reliquidized milk, eggs, and corn meal for tortillas. A considerable measure of success was achieved in lowering such food prices, despite opposition from certain segments of the business community. CEIMSA replaced a similar agency (the National Distributing and Regulating Agency), which functioned from 1941 to 1949.[41] The predecessor of both was the Comité Reguladora del Mercado de la Subsistencias (Committee to Regulate the Market in Necessities of Life), formed in 1938.

*Various business controls.* One of the broadest bases for executive regulation of the economy is contained, as I have already mentioned, in the Law on Powers of the Executive in the Economic Field, passed in 1950,[42] which gives the President broad regulatory powers over production and commerce in the field of foods, clothing, and raw materials. President Alemán's "Exposition of Reasons" in sponsoring the measure included the following objectives: to prevent excessive price rises; to prevent scarcities of industrial raw materials and of articles of general consumption; and to prevent developments prejudicial to the populace and to important branches of the economy.

More specifically, the law applies to firms engaged in the production and distribution of basic food and clothing items; essential industrial raw materials; products of basic industries; and the products of important branches of industry. The President has the power to impose maximum wholesale or retail prices based on a reasonable profit. When goods are in short supply, he may establish rules for distribution and impose rationing and priorities. He may determine which articles will be produced; restrict imports and exports; and require satisfaction of domestic needs before allowing exports. The Ministry of Economy administers the law.[43]

Mexico, like the United States, has been concerned with the problem of monopolies since colonial days. The 1857 Constitution (Art. 28) forbade monopolies except for the postal service, coinage of money, and the rights of inventors. The 1917 Constitution listed other government services as exceptions; and it prescribed penalties for any cornering of the market on necessities, stifling of free competition, or other seeking of advantages to raise prices unduly (Art. 28). The various regulatory laws passed since 1931 have already been mentioned. However, as in the United States, enforcement in a rapidly industrializing society has been very difficult; and the main efforts have been against undue price rises. A study made in 1949 treats the following fields as examples of virtual monopolies in recent years: sugar, salt, *masa* (corn meal dough), meat and fish in the Federal District, and transport in the District.[44]

An important channel for aid, coordination, and possible control of the private sector of the economy is the system of chambers of commerce and industry. All firms are legally required to belong to the chamber in their particular lines of endeavor. The Ministry of Economy approves each chamber as the agency in its field for consultation by the government. The Minister may even appoint a delegate to sit as a nonvoting member of the chamber's directive council. The Ministry's Bureau of Manufacturing Industries applies the law in this field, and thus far the restrictions have not been onerous. Mexican legislation has regulated such chambers of commerce and industry in the laws of 1908, 1936, and 1941; but only the current statute is very specific in constituting them as semipublic bodies under substantial potential or actual government influence. Criteria are set forth for a chamber to meet in order to be registered by the Ministry; provision is made for recognizing confederations of chambers; and the Ministry has certain powers of dissolution.[45]

Lobbying as it is known in the United States hardly exists. The organized business interests, as described above, consult with the ministries concerned and with the President. But they do not normally extend their efforts to the Congress. A United States business journal describes the process as it involves the association of automobile producers and the auto dealers' association. Since the government puts annual quotas on auto production, the two associations meet together to agree on a total to recommend to the Ministry of Economy. A compromise is arrived at between the free-market desires of the producers and the quota desired by the dealers. The compromise agreed upon goes to the Ministry, which tends to make some reduction before sending the figure to the President for approval, where many such decisions are finally made. Both dealers and producers seek to argue their respective cases before both the Ministry and the chief executive. When his decision is made, the case is closed.[46]

A power, potentially great, over economic life is the law of 1936 enabling the President to declare a particular industry "saturated" and not subject to the entry of additional firms or the expansion of existing firms. The President may do so whenever he feels that an industry has reached a state of development beyond which additional expansion would be harmful for labor, management, or the general public. The theory is that the government has an obligation to maintain an equitable relationship among prices, wages, and profits. Only five industries have been declared "saturated": silk and rayon, matches, flour milling, rubber, and cigarettes. These actions occurred between 1937 and 1944. Only the rubber industry has since been removed from the list.[47]

*Control agencies.*[48] I have mentioned important financial, monetary, credit, association, and "saturated industry" controls, exercised by the Ministry of Finance, the official banking agencies, CEIMSA, and the Ministry of Economy. I will now consider a number of more specific controls, exercised mainly by the Ministry of Economy. The fields controlled include foreign commerce, domestic commerce, mining, petroleum, silk, wheat milling, chicle, pineapples, bananas, cocoa, sugar, electric energy, and iron and steel.

The Ministry's Bureau of Manufacturing Industries administers the law dealing with chambers of commerce and industry; passes on requests for tax exemption; is empowered to enforce minimum standards of quality on such firms (which has not been much enforced); maintains a register of industries; recommends tariffs and tariff changes and the free importation of certain materials and equipment; exercises controls over the silk and wheat milling industries; fixes chicle export quotas; and exercises controls dealing with foreign technicians and Mexican apprentices. Nonregulative functions include compilation of data of aid to industry; sponsorship of industrial fairs and expositions; and general promotion of industry.

The Bureau of Commerce applies the law regarding chambers of commerce; incorporates firms; supervises companies producing and exporting pineapples and bananas; controls the sale and distribution of cacao; and exercises vigilance over the sale of automobiles. It exercises controls over certain imports and exports, issuing permits for the importation of necessary raw materials and articles necessary to the economy; and it exercises controls over basic items of consumption.

The Bureau of Mines and Petroleum regulates the rights to explore and exploit crude oil and other minerals, maintaining mining and petroleum field offices in pertinent areas. A related development was the creation in 1954 of a Coordinating Committee on the Steel Industry, which is mainly promotional and coordinating in character but which also incidentally has control potentials. It contains representation from the Ministry of Economy, the Bank of Mexico, Nacional Financiera, and private industry. A similar group is planned for the chemical industry.

The Bureau of the Sugar Industry exercises various important promotional and control functions, such as stimulation of better manufacturing and market-control of sugar standards, and promoting increased consumption.

The Bureau of Electricity regulates the generation, transmission, sale, and use of electricity. It administers the Law of the Electric Industry, the National Electric Code, and the relations between companies and consumers. A related agency is the Commission on Electric and Gas Rates, which was a dependency of the Ministry of Economy until 1949. Their relations are still close. The Commission approves rate schedules and the issuance of company securities.

A broad-scale approach to economic development is that represented by the Council for Development and Coordination of Production, created in 1954. It is divided into agricultural and industrial divisions, and its role is more advisory than regulatory.

The Ministry's Bureau of Cooperative Development promotes, inspects, and secures credit for producers' and consumers' cooperatives.

The Bureau of Industrial Property grants patents, trademarks, and commercial names, and cancels them when they are abused. The Department of Social Security has important relations with the Mexican Institute of Social Security — establishing bases for determining social security coverage; interpreting the law and rules; and punishing their violation. The Bureau of Economic Studies and the Bureau of Standards carry out self-explanatory research and advisory functions. The former publishes a journal of economic statistics, *Trimestre de Barómetros Económicos.*

A most important nonregulatory function — carrying out the census — is performed by the Bureau of Statistics. This important and ably performed service is similar to that of the U.S. Bureau of the Census.

Other regulatory functions are performed by the Ministry of National Properties, the Ministry of Agriculture, and the Agrarian Department. The first combs possible graft out of public works contracts. The other two agencies have both regulatory and promotional functions in the field of agriculture. The Ministry of Agriculture has relations with local, regional, and national associations of agriculturalists similar to those which the Ministry of Economy has with the chambers of commerce and industry.

### NOTES

[1] *HA,* February 8, 1954, p. 5.

[2] Antonio Carrillo Flores, *La Economía y los Derechos del Hombre . . .* (1952), pp. 34–35.

[3] International Bank, *op. cit.,* p. 148; *Mexican Life,* October 1953, pp. 15–16.

[4] G. N. Sarames, "Third System in Latin America: Mexico," *Inter-American Economic Affairs,* Spring 1952, pp. 61–69; *Ley sobre Atribuciones del Ejecutivo Federal en Materia Económica (Diario Oficial,* December 30, 1950); Tena Ramírez, *op. cit.,* Ch. 14.

[5] Sría. de Hacienda, *Tres Años (1947–49) de Política Hacendaria . . .* (1951), pp. 19–33; International Bank, *op. cit.,* p. 3. See also Antonio Carrillo Flores, "Industrial Mexico," *Americas,* June 1956, pp. 3–7; George Wythe, *Industry in Latin America* (1949), pp. 274–324.

[6] International Bank, *op. cit.,* pp. 7–17; *MV,* February 27, 1956, pp. 97–98; *Rev. Ec.,* October 1955, pp. 343–47.

[7] Laufenberger, *op. cit.,* pp. 142–45; International Bank, *op. cit.,* p. 110.

[8] Sría. de Hacienda, *Tres Años (1947–49) de Política Hacendaria . . .* (1951).

[9] Carrillo Flores, "La Constitución y la Acción Económica del Estado," *Investigación Económica* (hereafter cited as *Inv. Ec.*), No. 3 (1941), pp. 292 *et seq.*

[10] Mosk, *op. cit.,* pp. 53–57; *Foreign Policy Reports,* August 1 and 15, 1937.

[11] Josephus Daniels, *Shirt-sleeve Diplomat* (1947), pp. 70–71.

[12] Mosk, *op. cit.,* pp. 53, 58–61; R. W. Holman, "Planning in the Mexican Federal District . . ." (M.A. thesis, Mexico City College, 1950), pp. 10–11.

[13] D. I. Patch, "The International Bank . . ." (M.A. thesis, Mexico City College, 1950), p. 26 *et seq.*

[14] Mosk, *op. cit.*, Chs. 4–5.

[15] Universidad Nacional . . . , Escuela Nacional de Economía, *La Intervención del Estado en la Economía* (1955), pp. 55–99. See also U.S. Bureau of Foreign Commerce, *op. cit.*, Ch. 3.

[16] *Rev. Ec.*, September 1953, pp. 261–62; *MV*, September 11, 1950, p. 4.

[17] *World*, June 1954, pp. 18–21; *CSM*, July 27, 1953.

[18] *MV*, May 31, 1954; *Rev. Ec.*, September 1953, p. 264 *et seq.*

[19] Whetten, *Rural Mexico*, *passim*; and see later chapters on agriculture.

[20] Mosk, *op. cit.*, pp. 67 *et seq.*; International Bank, *op. cit.*, pp. 79–80; Tannenbaum, *Mexico* . . . , pp. 197 *et seq.*; Frank De Luna, "The Reciprocal Trade Agreements Act . . ." (M.A. thesis, Mexico City College, 1951), pp. 59–77.

[21] Mosk, *op. cit.*, pp. 63 *et seq.*, pp. 190 *et seq.*; Romero Kolbeck and Urquidi, *op. cit.*, pp. 23–24; Flores Zavala, *Elementos* . . . , pp. 67–68; International Bank, *op. cit.*, pp. 80–81.

[22] U.N. Econ. Comm. for Latin America, *Legal and Economic Status of Foreign Investments* . . . *in Mexico* (1950), pp. 4–5, 11–15; International Bank, *op. cit.*, pp. 11, 15, 81–82; Wise, *op. cit.*, pp. 217–21; Sría. de Gobernación, *Seis Años de Gobierno* . . . *1940–46* (1946), Ch. 11; Carrillo Flores, "Financiamiento del Desarrollo Económico de México," *Prob. Agr.*, January–March 1950, pp. 9–47.

[23] Sría. de Bienes Nacionales, *Directorio* . . . (2), *passim*.

[24] Banco de México, *Asamblea General* . . . (various years); R. S. Mora, "The Capital Market in Mexico . . ." (M.A. thesis, Mexico City College, 1952), pp. 43–45, 92–93.

[25] See note 23 above; Gonzalo Mora Ortiz, *El Banco Nacional de Comercio Exterior* (1950).

[26] See note 23; Nacional Financiera, *Informe* (annual); *MV* (weekly), and its *Quince Años de Vida* (1949); Mosk, *op. cit.*, pp. 236–49; International Bank, *op. cit.*, pp. 62 *et seq.*

[27] See note 23.

[28] Holman, *op. cit.*, *passim*; Ebenstein, *op. cit.*, pp. 106–7.

[29] Bosques, *op. cit.*, *passim*.

[30] Mosk, *op. cit.*, pp. 307–8.

[31] Patch, *op. cit.*, pp. 26–27; Mosk, *op. cit.*, pp. 94 *et seq.*

[32] Sría. de Gobernación, *op. cit.*, Chs. 4–5; Mosk, *op. cit.*, pp. 91 *et seq.*; see note 22.

[33] Mancera Ortiz, *Mexico's Attitude Towards Development Programs* (1953), *passim*.

[34] Holman, *op. cit.*, pp. 25 *et seq.*

[35] International Bank, *op. cit.*, pp. vii and 151–52; Mosk, *op. cit.*, pp. 44, 307.

[36] Mosk, *op. cit.*, p. 222, pp. 309 *et seq.*

[37] *HA*, August 15, 1955, pp. 40–44; *HA*, October 31, 1955, pp. 3–4; *HA*, December 12, 1955, pp. 6–7.

[38] Fraga, *op. cit.*, pp. 513–31.

[39] *Ley de Monopolios*, in Andrade, ed., *op. cit.*, pp. 187 *et seq.*; *Foreign Agriculture*, November 1947, pp. 164–65.

[40] Sría. de Bienes Nacionales, *Directorio* . . . (1), pp. 280 *et seq.*

[41] *Ley de Monopolios*, *op. cit.*; *CSM*, August 17, 1953; *HA*, March 13, 1953, pp. 3–7; *Humanismo*, January 1954, pp. 91–92.

[42] Tena Ramírez, *op. cit.*, Ch. 14; *Ley sobre Atribuciones del Ejecutivo Federal en Materia Económica* (*Diario Oficial*, December 30, 1950).

[43] *MV*, December 25, 1950.

[44] Filiberto Ney Morales, "Los Monopolios en México" (UNAM thesis, 1949) See also Rodrigo García Treviño, *Precios, Salarios y Mordidas* (1953), Ch. 1.

[45] Fraga, *op. cit.*, pp. 387–91.

[46] *Fortune*, January 1956, p. 107.

[47] Mosk, *op. cit.*, pp. 97–98.

[48] Sría. de Bienes Nacionales, *Directorio* . . . (1), pp. 267–79; Sría. de Economía, *Memoria* (various years) and its *Resumen de Labores, 1947–1952* (1952); Mosk, *op. cit.*, pp. 64–65; *MV*, March 29, April 19, and July 5, 1954; Sría. de Bienes Nacionales, *Directorio* . . . (2), pp. 337–44; Fraga, *op. cit.*, pp. 391–92.

PART IV

# Public Utilities and Public Works

# 16

## Communications

THE means of transportation and communication are of the foremost importance to a country — for both its government and its economy. Efficient modern government of a country is necessarily based on its transport-communications network. Such a network is necessary for a government to maintain its rule. The economic necessity for such a network is too obvious to require comment. And government's role in transportation-communication is basic — as promoter, proprietor, or both.

### Railroads

A country's size, topography, products, population density and distribution, and economic development influence and are influenced by its means of transportation. These elements have conspired against Mexico in the development of its transport. The size of the country is substantial. Its topography is hostile to road building, being elaborately dissected by lofty longitudinal and transverse mountain ranges. The central plateau has the most important population centers, with the rest of the populace widely scattered. And the economic resources for railway building came late to Mexico. So the problem of railway expansion and improvement is still one of the country's most important. Railways and main highways each total about 15,000 miles today, with the latter being extended steadily and the former growing but slowly.

*Development.* The government's role in the railway field has been important for many decades, but at first it was one of nonintervention. The first construction concession was granted in 1837, but the first eight miles were not finished until 1850. The line from Veracruz to the capital was not opened until 1873. The civil war (*Reforma*), French intervention, anarchy, and scarcity of capital combined to hinder progress. For many years, there was much opposition to allowing American capital to build lines from Mexico to the United States; and only a few short interior lines were constructed.[1]

The Díaz regime gave many inducements to foreign capital to build lines that would encourage the export of raw materials and the importation of foreign goods. Concessions were given in 1880 for the construction of two lines from the capital to the United States – to El Paso and to Laredo. Important inducements granted the companies were rights of land expropriation; land grants; free importation of materials and equipment; tax exemptions; and substantial financial subsidies by the government. This produced extravagance and a heavy drain on the Treasury. In 1898, the Treasury adopted a national railroad plan which would accomplish the following: check excessive government generosity; have the government acquire a principal interest in the chief rail lines; avoid bankruptcies among ailing lines; and form the nucleus of a nationwide railway system. Under this plan, before 1910 several lines were built, consolidations were effected, and the government acquired a 51 per cent interest in the principal lines.[2]

The revolutionary era put an end to railway progress, and the chaos of the times brought general stagnation and disintegration. Carranza's government took over the principal lines in 1914; and since then the railroads of Mexico – like those of many other countries – have been one of the country's most important unsolved problems. Efforts were made to reorganize the lines and consolidate their debt in 1922, 1926, and 1930; but little progress was made, and only one line of importance was built between 1911 and 1930.[3]

During the early 1930s the financial condition of the railways became even more precarious, and the workers demanded increased wages. Finally, in 1937, Cárdenas expropriated the lines of the National Railways, which represented more than half of the existing mileage; and the government promised eventual payment to the bondholders. This was the first large-scale application of the expropriation law of 1935, which authorized the government to expropriate private property when it is in the public interest to do so.

The principal object of nationalization seems to have been to apply new methods to the country's railway development in order to get better service for the public, improved conditions for the railway workers, and ultimate achievement of a single nationally owned railway system. Two lines of action seemed open under a nationalized regime. The first was operation directly by the government. The second was to place the administration in the hands of the workers. The second alternative was chosen, and the law of 1938 turned the operations over to an autonomous organization managed by the railway workers' syndicate. This was ended by the law of December 24, 1940.[4]

The results were not satisfactory because of inefficient management and the poor physical condition of the enterprise when the workers assumed control. Cárdenas, though a close friend of labor, arranged for a change when the poor results were evident. The law of December 24, 1940, transferred control to a self-governing corporation, headed by a board of seven members — four to be appointed by the government and three by the union. The general manager was named by the President. The union soon considered its situation ambiguous and untenable, for its board members were expected to be both its employers and its defenders; and the union members withdrew from the board in March 1941. The concern has remained under a decentralized administration since 1941.[5]

The organization has been modified somewhat by legislation in 1944 and subsequent years, but its essential character has remained much the same since 1941. The administration of the National Railways of Mexico is in the hands of a board of eight members. One is named by the Minister of Finance, who serves as president; one each by the Ministers of Communications, Agriculture, and Economy; one by the federation of chambers of commerce and industry; one by the federation of industrial chambers; and two by the railway union. The government keeps an important direct power over the agency, since the Minister of Finance has the power of suspensive veto over actions of the board. The "non-confidence" personnel of the agency organize and bargain collectively under the federal labor law as employees of private firms do.[6]

But the National Railways is not the sole government agency for railway administration. In the last few years, the government has acquired almost all the remaining privately owned commercial firms. There have been official dissatisfactions with the functioning of the National Railways; and lines acquired in recent years have been placed under the Ministry of Communications and Public Works. This agency has separate bureaus handling the work of construction and of operations. The Department of Railway Operations plans new railways and handles repairs as part of the task of operations. New construction of lines is handled by the Bureau of Railway Construction.[7]

*Modernization.* As part of the wartime American assistance program, in 1943 the United States sent a railway mission to Mexico to aid in rehabilitating the railway system, which by then was suffering from antiquated and insufficient equipment, labor troubles, and a high accident rate. The first mission failed to cope with the labor problem; President Ávila Camacho instituted changes; and a second Mexican-American team was called in. When the mission's work was finished in 1946, both governments felt that substantial progress had been made. Better operating and maintenance conditions had been gained for Mexico, with a plan for continuing modernization. The program had provided the United States with means of securing vitally needed materials in wartime; and it showed the mutual advantages of a technical assistance program. For the four-year period of the program's existence, the United States had spent nearly $7,000,000 and Mexico some $40,000,000.[8]

This was only a good beginning, however. There was still need for extensive rehabilitation and modernization, as well as construction of new lines to meet the needs of Mexico's expanding economy. Railways were a bottleneck. So new administrative provisions were made for the National Railways in 1948. The present eight-member council was placed at the head of the agency, and a five-year plan was formulated for the period 1948–52. New financing was needed, so Nacional Financiera secured a loan from the Export-Import Bank; and both rehabilitation and rail line extension have gone forward. For the first time, the capital has been linked by rail with the far reaches of the country. Yucatan and the southwest have rail connection with Lower California. Narrow-gauge lines have been turned into standard-gauge lines; and these lines have been modernized by replacing lighter rails with heavier rails to cope with heavy traffic loads. Obsolete equipment has in part been replaced with Diesel engines and new freight cars, while tourist travel has been promoted by "luxury trains." By 1953, about a billion pesos had been spent in railway rehabilitation, half of it from foreign loans.[9]

The International Bank's survey of Mexico, published in 1953, finds the country's railroads still in need of much expansion, modernization, and improved administrative practices. The industry is still a bottleneck in the national economic development, and the need is one which highway transport cannot fill in terms of volume or comparable cost per ton-mile. Emphasis is placed on both financing and better administrative and operating procedures.[10]

Railway expansion and improvement have been handicapped by low operating income, limited government funds for investment, the high cost of renting freight cars from the United States, and a high employee ratio. The problem of overstaffing is still considered serious by some; but its solution would be strongly opposed by the railway union. However, savings on better overtime and vacation procedures were inaugurated in 1953. Other operating improvements promised to bring the National Railways out of the red in 1954. This was partly due to the greater amount invested in railways in 1953 than in previous years.[11]

Some experts feel that important developments have been carried out for uneconomic reasons. Cases cited include building too many highways parallel to railroads, when the railroad could fill the needs; constructing some lines with small prospect of their being economically feasible; and replacing some narrow-gauge lines with standard-gauge ones when the volume of business did not warrant it.

The government-operated railways of Mexico have faced many problems common to railways elsewhere — and still unsolved elsewhere. Many feel that the railroads should not be judged solely on their being financially remunerative; that they should also be judged in terms of the stimulus they give to national economic development.

## Highways

*Developing a road system.*[12] The same physical conditions that faced the railroads also challenged the builders of a system of roads. A principal difference is that the challenge goes back to the conquest; for roads were virtually the only means of transport and communication until comparatively recent years. And even the well-traveled road from Mexico City to Veracruz was an ordeal for the voyager of a century ago.

And today, with some 15,000 miles of surfaced highways and an intensified building program under way, most of Mexico is still geographically and culturally quite isolated from the general life of the nation. A program of village-to-market roads is still in its infancy; and in many areas important markets are so poorly linked with their hinterlands as to prevent the marketing of perishables. And most rural people are still dependent upon the burro and their own backs for the transport of goods. This physical isolation brings cultural isolation—a dual challenge to the road builders.

The first beasts of burden were the horses of Cortez's soldiers; and the first wheeled vehicles were the conquerors' gun carriages. But true roads were slow in coming. The period of instability that followed the war for independence produced few roads. These were so poor that transport of goods was largely by pack animals rather than carriages and wagons for many years. Funds for road building and maintenance were secured through taxes levied on those who used the roads, assessed on goods, beasts of burden, and travelers. No public transportation service appeared until about 1850, when one Manuel Escandón established the first line of stagecoaches between the capital and Puebla — a distance of about ninety miles. His successor extended similar coach lines to other centers of population.

After mid-century, the period of peace and development under Díaz made road building more feasible. But by then the age of the railroad had arrived throughout the world, and the main lines of communication no longer had to be highways. The available governmental resources and foreign capital for transportation were channeled into railroad building; the principal highways fell into disuse; and only local roads were maintained, with their termini at railway lines. The revolutionary decade of 1910–20 was concerned with the consolidation of governmental authority and there was little time or money spent on road building. This was left for the next decade, a period of relative stability.

The modern period of highway development dates from 1925, when the National Road Commission was established as an independent agency charged with developing a full-scale highway building program. This predominant role of the federal government is in contrast with the U.S. Impatience produced some ill-considered projects and waste of effort, but the important start was made. The first auto assembly plant was established in 1925; and the increasing number of machines gave impetus to the construction program, which has been financed largely by a gasoline tax since that date.

In 1929, the Commission was abolished and the work of road construction and maintenance was placed under the Ministry of Communications and Public Works, where it is still administered along with the other transportation and communication services. Within the next decade, most of the important centers of population were linked by road with the capital. The opening of the Pan-American Highway from Laredo to Mexico City during the Cárdenas administration gave an impetus to commerce and marked the start of the tourist industry, one of the country's most important sources of income. Until 1932, the program was one of building main highways that were complementary to the railway system. In that year the program was broadened to include secondary road development, when a law was passed allowing the federal government to contribute half the cost of state road construction, the roads to become part of the national highway system. States were also given a share of the gasoline tax for road purposes.

In the past two decades, considerable highway construction has paralleled existing railroads. This has brought the criticism that the result is often a situation in which neither means of transport is a paying proposition. Others have maintained that even parallel lines have proved feasible through stimulating an economic development in areas previously backward economically. The early years were marked by low highway traffic loads and seemed to give little support to the road advocates in their arguments with the railroad supporters; but the economic development of recent years has brought substantially increased traffic for both roads and rails.

It was discovered long ago that railroads could not cover all the country's transportation and communication needs, since many areas were too remote, isolated, rugged, or thinly populated to make railway building feasible. Without question, highways were the answer for these areas.

The Alemán administration added some 5,000 miles to the country's roads between 1946 and 1951. About 1948, the administration started its program of emphasizing secondary road construction. First, the main roads were constructed; then came the plan to build a network of country feeder roads, ranging from fifteen to a hundred kilometers in length, paid for jointly by federal, state, and private funds. Much of the federal money has come from the issuance of bonds, which are retired with proceeds from the federal gasoline tax. Other loans have come from foreign sources. The promotion of the lesser roads has been coordinated by the National Committee for Rural Roads, which has representation from the federal and state governments and from the business community. In 1953, this body was reported to have invested some $14 million in construction since 1949 and to be spending currently at the rate of $8 million a year. It reported 120 roads under construction and 500 more being planned. The goal has been 60,000 miles of feeder roads, or an average of some five miles of secondary roads for each mile of present all-weather trunk highway. This goal would bring the thousands of small, isolated Mexican communities into the national market and the country's social life. The importance of such a program was emphasized recently by the International Bank's survey of Mexico.

*The current program.*[13] The present administration has increased its expenditures for roads; put increased emphasis on rural roads; and sought to coordinate the development of the various means of transportation. The importance of the rural road program was attested by the holding in 1954 of the first national convention on rural roads. There the interested groups announced plans for the expanded program, as well as funds being secured from auto assembly plants, tire manufacturers, and other private sources. The previous year, Mexico's current program received high praise by a representative of the International Road Federation. Since the completion of the Mexico City–Juárez highway, Mexican highway engineers have become well recognized for their mountain-road building skills.

During the last few years, the following important highways have been constructed: Pan-American Highway to the Guatemala border; Guadalajara to Nogales, Arizona; Mexico City to Acapulco; the trans-isthmian highway; Jiquilpan to Manzanillo; and several shorter but important routes.

Mexico's longest highway was completed in 1950, when the Christopher Columbus Highway was opened between Juárez and Ciudad Cuauhtemoc on the Guatemala border, a distance of nearly 2,200 miles. This extensive route, inaugurated by the first Pan-American auto race, opened up the north-central part of the country from Texas to Mexico City, as well as the country south of Oaxaca. The next longest road was opened in 1954 — the western highway from Nogales, Arizona, to Guadalajara, some 1,070 miles. This route opens up the northwest section of Mexico, a thinly settled but rapidly developing area comprising the states of Nayarit, Sinaloa, Chihuahua, Durango, and Sonora. This road skirts the Pacific Ocean for some distance and links up new farming areas with growing modern cities and bustling ports, benefiting under the administration's program of maritime development. This highway, costing $50 million and twenty years in the making, traverses Mexico's principal wheat-growing area. Extensive irrigation projects are also being developed in the region.

A short but important highway now links the Atlantic and Pacific coasts across the Isthmus of Tehuantepec. This three-hour drive is the first paved coast-to-coast highway north of Panama and south of Texas. It is the basis for a developing network of roads to open up the southern area.

An important area isolated from the rest of the country is the Yucatan Peninsula, until recently without even rail connection with the rest of Mexico. A highway program is being pushed in this area, partly to develop the economy of the region and partly to link the area with the rest of the country for promotion of tourism.

In the metropolitan area of the capital, the new four-lane express toll highway from Mexico City to Cuernavaca is an important indication of traffic development. This ten-million-dollar, forty-five-mile mountain road of 4 per cent grade is the first link in a developing super highway to cut in half the driving time between Mexico City and the Pacific resort of Acapulco.

The government has been considering construction of a network of highways around the capital to provide by-passes for the principal highways and keep the fast-growing through truck traffic out of the already heavily congested city. This is in addition to the highways being built within the city proper to encircle the metropolis.

Mexico's highway program has not been confined to promotion within the country. The tourist advertising campaign abroad was discussed in Chapter 12 (pages 178–79). Mexico has also been active in the International Road Federation and the Pan-American Highway Congress, as well as regional meetings of the Caribbean area countries. It is seeking to develop a land-sea-air tourist circuit via Florida–Cuba–Yucatan–the Mexican mainland–Texas. And it has encouraged the completion of missing links in the Pan-American Highway through Central America, especially in Guatemala.

*Traffic.*[14] In 1940, one authority reported that the Mexican highways were used mainly for passenger traffic, with the railways continuing to be the prevailing system of transportation. Recent years have seen a relative increase in transport by truck. Between 1944 and 1950, truck and bus registrations were up 77 per cent, with much increase in the areas of expanding agricultural production. One tabulation shows the number of trucking companies operating between Mexico City and Laredo as two and a half times the 1938 figure by 1950, while the number of truck units operated was six and a half times the 1938 figure. One estimate of truck-hauled tonnage places it almost on a par with railroad tonnage.

Much of the increase in trucking since 1940 has been attributed to the shortcomings of the railroads. The heaviest cargoes are carried more cheaply by rail, but the faster and safer journey by truck route often wins the argument with shippers. In 1949, there were 106,321 cargo trucks and 16,169 buses registered in the country. This represented a 97 per cent increase in trucks and a 30 per cent increase in buses since 1943. There is a considerable concentration of motor traffic in the Federal District, which in 1949 had 12 per cent of the country's registered trucks, 26 per cent of the buses, and 33 per cent of the passenger cars.

Despite substantial progress, a recent study by the National Bank of Mexico expresses the feeling that truck transport has not expanded as rapidly as the increased road construction, "whereas the two should operate as complementary elements." Lack of up-to-date data on the needs of various regions is cited as a big obstacle to such development. There was said to be a need for information to indicate the potential cargo traffic on each route, as well as seasonal variations and long-term prospects. Often lack of statistical data was said to result in setting freight rates too high, thus discouraging optimum development of the trucking industry.

Buses are the chief means of passenger transportation in Mexico. A 1948 study showed intercity buses carrying 55 per cent of all passengers. There are first- and second-class buses, and the fares are reasonable. It is estimated that private automobiles in the United States handle about 85 per cent of the passenger traffic; but in Mexico the figure is about 10 per cent.

Gasoline sales increased ten times between 1925 and 1948, while vehicle registrations rose from 40,000 to 250,000.

*Highway administration.*[15] The administration of highways is entrusted to the Ministry of Communications and Public Works, where separate bureaus deal with the different means of transportation and communication.

The National Bureau of Roads, the Ministry's division concerned with roads, has the function of planning, constructing, and handling the upkeep of the federal roads; and it cooperates with the state road agencies in their construction work. The Bureau is divided into the following eight departments.

1. The Department of Plans and Technical Studies lays out the routes of federal highways and plans their execution, in conformity with the basic decisions of higher authorities.

2. The Department of Bridges handles the planning, construction, and repair of bridges built on federal roads, and it cooperates in the construction of bridges on local roads.

3. The Department of Construction cooperates with the Department of Plans in elaborating the plans for roads; and it organizes, directs, and inspects federal road construction. In highway construction, standard specifications are followed, as in the United States. Road design is being improved, with first-class highways being built with a maximum grade of 4 per cent instead of the former steep grades commonly used. Construction work is done by private firms, while maintenance work is done by the Bureau of Roads. The country is divided into maintenance areas and subdivided into superintendencies for each section. Hand labor is being displaced by maintenance machinery.

4. The Department of Conservation sees to the conservation or repair of completed roads. Road conservation is facilitated by the establishment of truck load-limits, which are checked by strategically located weighing stations.

5. The Department of Machinery procures and controls the use of the Bureau's machinery and equipment.

6. The Department of Accounting is a housekeeping office.

7. The Department of Cooperation with the States makes studies of local road programs, lays plans, and sees to the execution of such programs involving the cooperative efforts of the federation, the states, and private initiative.

8. The Department of Planning and Development of Local Roads performs related functions.

The Technical Advisory Committee on General Ways of Communication is a top-level group that advises the Minister of Communications regarding all types of communication and transportation, of which the above-mentioned functions make up an important segment. The committee has one member each from the Ministries of Marine and Economy and the "action" subdivisions of the Ministry of Communications.

The Department of Tariffs applies the Law of the General Ways of Communications in the matter of rate-making for all kinds of transport and communication. The Department has offices of rate-making and inspection.

The Advisory Committee on Tariffs advises the Minister on rate matters. It has representatives, from this Ministry and from each other interested ministry, of the regulated activities, of the unions concerned, of the confederations of commerce and industry, and of other sectors of the economy.

There are two other important Ministry-wide subdivisions: the Department of Research and Laboratories and the Central Planning Bureau. The first seeks to improve the quality and improve construction practices in the various fields of communications and transport.

The Central Planning Bureau was established in 1952. It is linked with other government agencies and commercial organizations. It has five subdivisions to effect better coordination of the Ministry's work — the international, national, regional, Valley of Mexico, and urban. The regional group makes studies of the economy of communities, as a service of general usefulness as well as for communications development.

The highway police provide an important service. Their patrol cars are equipped with radio communication apparatus. In addition to the usual patrol duties, they have conducted highway-user destination surveys to use as one basis for road improvements and developments.

The highway agencies and functions discussed above account for over half of the Ministry's budget. Mexico's highways are new enough so that the problem of upkeep has not become so pressing as it has in other countries. But steadily increasing road use points to the time in the not too distant future when the financing of upkeep will be a major problem. The financing of transport activities in the Federal District has been aided by a special bank, the National Transport Bank.

## Civil Aviation

Civil aviation has made considerable progress in Mexico, without a great deal of government assistance (in contrast to the U.S. government's extensive aid to U.S. civil aviation). This development has been a response to the physical characteristics of the country, the distribution of population, and the economic service needed. As in other mountainous Latin American countries, communication by means of highway and railroad has been difficult; and the airplane has often been the most feasible means of transport and communication. Often high-value commodities have been most suitably transported by air, so air express is a growing service.

The location of Mexico between the United States and the other American republics makes her an increasingly important link in the chain of western hemisphere air routes. The tourist industry provides the airlines with a considerable share of their patronage.

A capsule picture of the growth of Mexican civil aviation is provided in the following tabulation.[16]

|  | 1940 | 1946 | 1952 |
|---|---|---|---|
| Miles flown | 4,897,400 | 20,224,803 | 28,736,826 |
| Passengers transported | 89,242 | 528,098 | 1,088,591 |
| Federal airports in use | 1 | 2 | 13 |
| Aviation company airports in use | 0 | 8 | 50 |

Domestic air transport developed quite differently in the United States and in Mexico. In the former, this growth coincided with a great deal of governmental interest and support. Not so in the earlier years in Mexico. Legislation providing pay for air-mail transport was not passed until 1928. The carrier had to do the pioneering work. While certain concessions are made, there is still no system of subsidies for Mexican civil aviation.

Air communication and transport in Mexico are regulated by the Law of General Lines of Communication of 1940, the act governing communication and transportation in general. This law was revised and supplemented by the Law of Civil Aviation of December 1949. This latter statute deals with the obligation of government to assure security for air navigation; the principle of reciprocity in international matters; responsibility for damages by companies; standards regarding investigation of accidents; promotion of safety measures through obligatory use of aeronautic communication services, radio aids, etc.

The Bureau of Civil Aviation in the Ministry of Communications is the agency charged with administering civil aviation. It is divided into three departments, which in turn are subdivided into offices. The Department of Aerial Navigation has Offices of Airports, Schools, Studies and Plans, and Inspection (of planes and personnel). The Department of Air Transport has Offices of Aeronautic Registry and International Affairs and the Commission for Investigation of Accidents. The third division is the Department of Administration, with Offices of Budget, Statistics, and Personnel.

The Bureau regulates aviation, ultimately, through its licensing of airlines and operating personnel and the revocation of licenses. The permits for airlines have been of two types, temporary and permanent. The first one secured is the temporary. Upon its expiration, the airline may apply for the permanent concession if it wishes to continue serving the area. The Bureau issues these permits upon determining that the contemplated service will be in the public interest. The permit is both a restriction and a protection for the carrier. To achieve a sound climate for the industry's growth, protection is given against inauguration of competing services that would be uneconomic.

The Bureau is also the agency that approves the companies' schedules of fares, though the agency does not propose the fares. It also approves schedule changes, unlike the Civil Aeronautics Board in the United States. In addition to the controls mentioned above, the Bureau regulates technical schools of aeronautics, airports, and agricultural aviation (planting and plague combat from the air).

Mexico has good air service for a country of its size. A 1950 tabulation shows 44 companies maintaining scheduled service over 40,467 miles of routes. Each of the larger states has a local airline that links it with the more important airports. These, in turn, provide service to the United States and other countries. In 1950 there were 36 main airports and 210 auxiliary airports. The quality of service is good in most cases, and fares are reasonable.

As in other fields, the government has wanted more Mexican capital to invest in aviation; but American capital has played a major role in the more important airlines. The general rule (subject to relaxation) has been that 51 per cent of the stock should be owned by Mexican citizens. However, only the numerous smaller lines have majority ownership by Mexicans; and they do less than a tenth of the airline business. American Airlines leads all the other firms in the international traffic. One of the large gains in the past few years has been in air express service.

As mentioned above, the government has been rather slow in aiding the airline business; and, unlike the United States, it gives the lines no direct subsidy. However, the government makes payments for the carrying of air mail on an economic basis; and at one time discounts were given on aviation gasoline. Exemptions are granted from paying import duties on certain items used by the airlines.

The principal government aid in recent years has been an expanded program of building and maintaining airports. Until recent years, the operator had to build his own airports and buildings. When the federal government or the cities entered the picture, they usually provided only part of the cost. Nor did the government do much in the way of providing radio and other aids to aerial navigation. In 1947 the government began a program of airport construction and improvement, to ensure a more balanced development of air traffic throughout the country and to improve the financial position of the domestic concerns. Increased regulatory activity has come with this program.

In 1951, Guadalajara's airport was considered the best in Mexico. Its field had two main landing strips, each some 7,000 feet in length. Since then airport construction has increased steadily. Mexico City's new five-million-dollar terminal building was opened in 1953, and it was said to rank in size and facilities with that of any capital in the world.

The government's current aviation policy is a progressive one, and the prospects for continued development are bright.

## Postal Service and Telecommunications

*Postal service.*[17] The postal service is one of the oldest of Mexican governmental functions. At first it was a monopoly sold to individuals by the colonial government, but the government took over the work in 1766. The transportation of letters and packages is done by rail, highway, and plane. In 1878, Mexico joined the Universal Postal Union. The parcel post and domestic money order services were begun in 1895; and the international money order service to the United States was started in 1900.

The Post Office Bureau is in the Ministry of Communications and Public Works. The services provided are those common to postal systems in other countries. They include parcel post, regular mail, air mail, registered mail, money orders, insured service, postal savings accounts, etc. For administrative purposes, regional offices are maintained in each of the states and territories. The service employs more than 16,000 persons in more than 4,300 local post offices.

*Telegraph service.*[18] The first concession to build a telegraph service was granted in 1849. Since 1865 the service has been a government monopoly, with permission given for exceptions for separate operations by public services. These separate services include aeronautical services, Petróleos Mexicanos, the railways, the highways, etc. Telegraph connections have been maintained with the United States since 1873. For about a decade after 1933 the postal and the telegraph services were combined under a single administration. Since then they have been separate bureaus in the Ministry of Communications and Public Works.

Until 1947 the nation's telecommunications services did not make much progress. Since then considerable extension and improvement of services has taken place. The telegraph services have been modernized and make use of such facilities as radio relay stations, multiplex transmission and printing, and simultaneous transmission of several messages on the same line.

*Telephone service.* Telephone service is supplied in Mexico by private companies and by the government, but mainly by the companies under government regulation. The companies have installed services in communities where profitable operations can be carried on, while the Ministry of Communications has established and operated facilities in places not feasible for private operations. While most international telephone service is handled by private concerns, the government has handled telephone service to some Latin American countries through its radio installations. Until a few years ago Mexico City was served by competing telephone companies.

*Radio and television.*[19] Radio broadcasting got an early start in Mexico. The Constitution makes provision for "radio telegraphic" services (Art. 28); and the first broadcasting station was started in 1923. Stations increased steadily in numbers, and the first basic law governing communications (including radio) was passed in 1931 and has been revised at various times. One provision has sought to require "at least 25% of typically Mexican music" on each program over commercial and other stations. Regulations have also sought to limit the proportion of advertising on programs.

Educational or cultural broadcasting had an early start in Mexico, with the Ministry of Education starting the broadcasting of weekly extension course lectures for teachers in 1926. A study in 1936 includes in the Education Ministry's Office of Educational Extension by Radio the following kinds of programs: gymnastics, other school subjects, home medical advice, child culture, home economics, concerts, and varied lectures. Similar programs are still being given.

For some time the government's Press and Publicity Department operated an official station, offering varied programs. The government's general radio broadcasting now, however, is carried on the weekly National Hour over all the country's radio stations. The programs are of a varied character and have maintained a generally high level of quality.

The radio industry is regulated by the Communications Ministry's Bureau of Telecommunications. A recent tabulation lists 1,276 radio stations of the following types: 215 commercial, 636 private, 338 experimental and amateur, 30 boat, 54 aircraft, 3 cultural.

Television got a later start than in the United States, but its technical production is of good quality.

## NOTES

[1] Javier Sánchez Mejorada, "Communications and Transportation," *Annals*, March 1940, pp. 83–85.

[2] *Ibid.*, Tannenbaum, *op. cit.*, pp. 210–11; *Encyclopedia Americana* (1954), v. 18, pp. 771–73.

[3] Sánchez Mejorada, *op. cit.*; Tannebaum, *op. cit.*

[4] D. W. Beck, "The Railroad and its Economic Significance in Mexico" (M.A. thesis, Mexico City College, 1952), pp. 15–16; A. W. Macmahon, "The Mexican Railways under Workers' Administration," *Public Administration Review*, Autumn 1941, pp. 458–71.

[5] Beck, *op. cit.*, p. 57; Sánchez Mejorada, *op. cit.*, p. 85; *Mexican Life*, May 1952, p. 22.

[6] Sría. de Bienes Nacionales, *Directorio* . . . (2), pp. 539–50; Fraga, *op. cit.*, pp. 382 *et seq.*

[7] Sría. de Bienes Nacionales, *Directorio* . . . (1), pp. 250, 256; Sría. de Comunicaciones . . . , *Memoria*.

[8] Beck, *op. cit.*, pp. 37–52.

[9] Nacional Financiera, *Informe* (annual); Cline, *op. cit.*, pp. 346–47.

[10] International Bank, *op. cit.*, pp. 44–45, 89–93.

[11] *News*, August 12, November 8, December 30, 1953; U.S. Bureau of Foreign Commerce, *op. cit.*, pp. 65–68.

[12] Sánchez Mejorada, *op. cit.*, pp. 78–93; *Civil Engineering*, November 1949, pp. 22–23; *CSM*, May 22, 1953; International Bank, *op. cit.*, pp. 94–95; files of McGraw-Hill Company's *World News Service* (Mexico City).

[13] *Mexican Life*, April 1954, pp. 15–16; *HA*, June 28, 1954, pp. 10–11 and June 6, 1955, pp. 6–9; *MV*, June 21, 1954; *News*, August 31, 1953; *Engineering News Record*, October 9, 1952, p. 55, December 18, 1952, p. 66, April 16, 1953, p. 77; *CSM*, July 20, 1954; *El Nacional*, July 16, 1954; *News*, September 20 and October 25, 1953; McGraw-Hill Company, *op. cit.*; U.S. Bureau of Foreign Commerce, *op. cit.*, pp. 68–71.

[14] Sánchez Mejorada, *op. cit.*, pp. 82-83; *Civil Engineering*, November 1949, pp. 22-23; *News*, January 13, 1954.

[15] Sría. de Bienes Nacionales, *Directorio* . . . (1), pp. 239-62; *MV*, June 29, 1953; *News*, August 15 and November 8, 1953; McGraw-Hill Company, *op. cit.*

[16] J. W. Goldsberry, "The Airlines of Mexico . . ." (M.A. thesis, Mexico City College, 1951), especially pp. 36-37, 73-75; Sría. de Comunicaciones . . . , *Memoria* (1952-53); *Mexican Life*, August 1952, pp. 14-16, September 1951, p. 25, July 1952, p. 103; *Aviation Week*, July 2, 1951, pp. 52-53, March 2, 1953, pp. 269-70; International Bank, *op. cit.*, pp. 86, 96.

[17] Sría. de Comunicaciones . . . , *Memoria* (1952-53); *Directorio* . . . (1), pp. 248-49; Mijares Palencia, *op. cit.*, Ch. 8.

[18] For information on telegraph and telephone systems, see Sánchez Mejorada, *op. cit.*, pp. 90-93; Mijares Palencia, *op. cit.*, Ch. 8; *Encyclopedia Americana* (1954), v. 18, pp. 771-73.

[19] P. L. Barbour, "Commercial and Cultural Broadcasting in Mexico," *Annals*, March 1940, pp. 94-102; Sría. de Comunicaciones . . . , *Memoria* (1952-53).

# 17

## *Electrification*

ONE of the government's most important roles in the field of public utilities is in electrification, because the country's advancement — both industrially and agriculturally — rests largely on the basis of electric power. Mexico's coal reserves are not too favorable for metallurgy because of their distance from the iron ores. And coal's relative contribution to mechanical energy has declined in the past two decades, while that of electrical energy has been increasing.

Mexico's hydroelectric potential is important — an estimated seven million horsepower; and only about 8 per cent of the estimated potential has been harnessed. But developing this potential will call for very large investments because of such limiting factors as irregular rainfall, fast runoff due to deforestation and porous soil, silting of power-plant dams, and distance from markets. Slow amortization of investments adds to the problem. The population is thinly and unevenly spread, which adds to the difficulties of providing a profitable service. Therefore, it is small wonder that less than 2 per cent of all the communities have electric service, and even in the Federal District only 37 out of 260 communities were serviced in a recent year.[1]

*History*.[2] Electric power development had its origins in the late nineteenth century, but government's deep interest in the field came much later. A law of 1910 charged the Ministry of Development with promoting such work, consulting with the Ministry of Communications and Public Works on projects affecting the navigable rivers. The *reglamento* of this law provided for the establishment of the Hydraulic Service in the Ministry of Development, which was charged with developing a national policy for the use of the hydraulic resources both for irrigation and for industry.

Progress was slow during the next two decades of revolution and gradual revival; and hydraulic functions were placed under various agencies, the names of which changed from time to time. Most of the laws regarding the electrical industry in this period dealt with establishing the supremacy of the federation over the states in jurisdiction over the field — and without full success.

In 1932, the National Power Commission was established as the first independent agency for the serious regulation of the electrical industry. It was to cooperate with the Ministries of Agriculture and Industry, to see to the conservation and development of electric power resources, and to regulate the private power concerns. The same year a tax was levied on the production of electrical energy. In 1934 electrical matters came under the control of the new Ministry of Economy.

The Cárdenas administration was faced with such pressing problems as land reform, irrigation, and road building, so the expanded hydro-electric program was not started until 1937. The apparent slowness of power expansion by private industry and the critical attitude toward foreign-owned companies were elements in deciding Cárdenas to take action. In February 1937, the Ministry of Economy was assigned the task of studying and reporting on a proposed program of government operation. On August 14, 1937, the law was approved creating the Federal Electricity Commission, the first important government venture into public utility ownership outside of the railroad field.

The Federal Electricity Commission has been headed by an administrative council of five members: the Minister of Economy (chairman); three members named by the President on the proposal of the Ministers of Finance, Hydraulic Resources, and Economy, respectively; and the head of Nacional Financiera. The role assigned the Commission by the law is "to organize and direct a national system of generation, transmission, and distribution of electric power, based upon technical and economic principles, non-profit, and with the aim of obtaining, at minimum cost, maximum benefits for the nation."

The role of the Commission has been that of exercising preferential rights in acquiring and using water power sites; building and operating systems of power generation and distribution; and providing aid to the private power concerns. Its dam-building activities have often been co-ordinated with the government's irrigation program.

The first budgets of the Commission proved totally inadequate to launch a program, so in 1939 a 10 per cent tax was levied on all electric power consumed, the proceeds going to the Commission. These resources have since been supplemented by funds contributed by the government, the sale of bonds, and loans from abroad. Before the program of the Commission got well under way the war brought difficulties in obtaining generating equipment; so no substantial investments were made by the agency before 1944. During the next few years, about two thirds of the power investments were made by the Commission and the New Chapala Company, a government corporation. About a third of the amount invested by the private companies came from loans by government agencies and by government-guaranteed loans from the International Bank.

In 1943, only 7 per cent of installed generating capacity of electric utilities was in the hands of the two chief government agencies, while 86 per cent was in the hands of the two largest private utilities. By 1950, the proportions had changed to 28 per cent and 60 per cent respectively. However, the major portion of the power produced by the Commission is distributed by the private companies; and they have made most of the investments in distribution facilities. The Commission's investments in 1939 totaled only 4 million pesos; but by 1949 the sum had jumped to 168 million pesos, and in 1952 to 1,396 million pesos. In 1952 its units were located in twenty-four of the states.

*The Commission: organization and functioning.*[3] The composition of of the five-man Commission was mentioned above. Detailed policy-making and the work of administration are under the direction of the Commission's Council of Administration. The operating staff is headed by a director-general, a deputy director-general, and an *oficial mayor*. These officials are appointed with the approval of the President. Operating subdivisions of the Commission include departments of engineering and operations. Auxiliary subdivisions include departments of planning, imports, purchases, administration, accounting, and legal counsel.

The annual budget of expenditures is approved by the Council of Administration and then submitted to the President through the Minister of Economy; and the annual administrative audit is submitted through the same channels. The Commission's operations are also subjected to the scrutiny of the National Committee on Investments.

An advisory council aids the Commission. It includes a representative from the Ministry of Agriculture, one from each of the state governments, three from the consumers, and one from the power companies.

The functions of the Commission have already been stated in general terms: to develop and direct a national system of electric power at minimum cost. In more detail, its work has included carrying out any type of electrical energy operation; planning a national system of electrical service; carrying out works related to power generation, transmission, and distribution; acquiring existing power installations; organizing operating companies; building and operating power systems, especially in underserved areas; doing part of its own construction work (the rest being done by contract); organizing firms for the making of electrical apparatus. In addition to these direct operating functions, the Commission aids operating companies, citizens, and others in the following ways: selling current to companies for distribution; making loans to companies and municipalities for power development; aiding in the establishment of undertakings; aiding organizations of consumers. It has used these various powers and functions to group the country's electric plants into five regional systems and to strengthen them by new construction.

The Commission's planning in the field of electrical energy has developed further than that of almost any other sector of the economy. Two of its important goals are the provision of energy where needed for industrial development and the provision of service to unserved areas. Even the second promotes economic development in the field of agriculture. Thus, the work of the Commission includes both direct operations and varying degrees of assistance to the private electric industry. Its goal in both cases is seeing that the country has a cheap and abundant supply of electric power for both home and industrial use, in the city and on the farm. The direct regulatory work in the electrical field is done in the Ministry of Economy, as discussed below.

*Related agencies.*[4] Agencies with a significant relation to the work of the Federal Electricity Commission are those with which the Commission has cooperative operational relations (like the Ministry of Hydraulic Resources) and the Ministry of Economy, which controls an entire segment of electrical matters — rate-making.

The construction and operation of irrigation works is in the hands of the Ministry of Hydraulic Resources. Cooperative relations often result when the latter uses water from a dam operated by the Commission. When the alternatives of irrigation or power production arise, irrigation is supposed to have priority, according to an agreement between the two agencies. Another example of cooperation is the agreement between the Federal Electricity Commission and the Commission of the Tepalcatepec (a valley authority), whereby the two cooperate in the production of electricity in that area.

Under the second type of relationship — functional division of the field of work — the Ministry of Economy does the regulatory work in the electrical field. Its Bureau of Electricity is charged with granting concessions for the operation of private firms; regulating the generation, transmission, sale, and use of electrical energy; promoting and coordinating the development of the electrical industry (an apparent overlap with the work of the Commission); enforcing the Law of the Electric Industry, the National Electrical Code, and related regulations; and setting rates and regulating services. For carrying out these functions, the Bureau has offices of concessions, plants, rates and contracts, special services, inspection, studies and reports, and infractions.

Thus, electricity is one of the most closely regulated industries, with the regulatory agency intervening in the important actions extending from the granting of the concession or franchise until the dissolution of the firm or the transfer of its concession. Rates are supposed to be set on the basis of a fair return on invested capital in proportion to the risks of similar undertakings in other fields. Among the other powers exercised are those of approving the issuance of securities and requiring the interconnection of plants and systems when in the public interest.

The private concerns maintain that the rate structure does not provide sufficient profit for needed expansion, even though the profit margin allowed the principal firm has been between 8 per cent and 10 per cent in recent years. Hence, important government and international loans have been provided. There is a general feeling in the business community that under the present administration private power will fare better in comparison with public power than in earlier years.

*Progress.*[5] Production of electrical energy approximately doubled from 1941 to date and trebled between 1933 and 1950. Hydroelectric's share of mechanical energy has been increasing, but it has not yet taken the lead over steam plants. During the six years of the Alemán administration, about $115 million was invested in electric power developments; and the present administration is increasing the rate of such investments. The Federal Electricity Commission planned a 1954 investment budget of 445 million pesos, compared with 360 million pesos for 1953. About half of the consumption of energy is by industry.

Past progress and programs under way owe much to loans obtained from the Export-Import Bank and the International Bank. A recent estimate puts the total of such loans to the government and large private undertakings at about $100 million over the twelve years ending in 1954. By 1955, nearly half of the country's electric generating capacity had been financed in this way.

The program of the current administration is ambitious but fully needed. The schedule calls for an aggregate capacity of two million kilowatts by 1958, putting Mexico well in the lead among Latin American countries. Government plants will still lead in the generation of power, but private plants will probably still lead in its distribution.

Power development is now recognized as a prerequisite for industrial development and of much agricultural improvement, whatever may be the decisions about the optimum rate of industrial and agricultural development. The UN Economic Commission for Latin America recently stated that on the basis of consumption trends, a considerable increase in electrical output is necessary if Mexico is to continue its present rate of economic development; and, therefore, a large fraction of the next five years' investment will need to be in the power industry.

The Federal Electricity Commission reports that only 45 per cent of the people live in communities where electricity is available.

### NOTES

[1] Tannenbaum, *op. cit.*, pp. 216–17; Mosk, *op. cit.*, p. 305.

[2] On the history of electrical development and the Federal Electricity Commission, see Carlos Reyes Valenzuela, "Carácter Jurídico de la Comisión Federal de Electricidad" (UNAM thesis, 1950), pp. 39–40; Jorge Martínez y Martínez, "Nacionalización de la Industria Eléctrica" (UNAM thesis, 1949), pp. 43–48; H. A. Watson, "Electrification in the Industrialization of Mexico . . ." (M.A. thesis, Mexico City College, 1952), *passim*; International Bank, *op. cit.*, pp. 55 *et seq.*; Americas, January 1953, pp. 3–5; Cristóbal Lara Beautell, *La Industria de Energía Eléctrica* (1953), *passim*; *Rev. Ec.*, October 1955, pp. 253–56.

[3] Sría. de Bienes Nacionales, *Directorio* . . . (2), pp. 345–53; U.N., *Economic Development in Selected Countries* (1947), v. I, pp. 10 *et seq.*

[4] Sría. de Economía, *Resumen de Labores* . . . ; Fraga, *op. cit.*, pp. 399–435; McGraw-Hill Company, *op. cit.*; *El Universal*, December 18, 1953.

[5] See note 1. See also *HA*, July 19, 1954, p. 33; *CSM*, January 14, 1952, and July 25, 1953; *El Nacional*, June 25, 1954; *News*, April 14 and December 30, 1953; *Rev. Ec.*, October 1955, pp. 253–56; *MV*, March 19, 1956, pp. 133–34; New York *Herald Tribune*, December 4, 1955, Sec. 10; U.S. Bureau of Foreign Commerce, *op. cit.*, pp. 56–59.

# 18

## *Oil*

The petroleum industry is a key element in the Mexican governmental picture. It is the second largest of the nationalized industries, and by far the most profitable to the government. It provides about a tenth of the government's total tax yield, which is more than half of all mineral taxes. Oil is the basis of transportation, and the output of natural gas is of growing importance to industry.

*History*.[1] Petroleum was used for medicinal and specialized purposes by the Aztecs. Minor efforts were made at oil drilling and exploitation between 1876 and 1900, but with scant results. British and American enterprisers secured concessions and began drilling in 1900. The payoff came in 1910 when the British company El Águila drilled a gusher that spurted 150,000 barrels a day. Other British and American enterprises were no less spectacular, and by 1921 Mexico was second only to the United States (but considerably below it) in oil production.

Production declined after 1921, reaching a low point in 1932; no substantial and continuous increases occurred then until after 1945. The appearance of competition from Venezuela and other quarters was an important factor in the decline; but Mexican governmental policy was at least as important a factor in discouraging expansion by foreign firms.

The legal basis for governmental policy was laid in the Constitution of 1917 (Art. 27), which provided that land ownership "is vested originally in the Nation," which may transmit it to individuals as private property. The government may impose limitations on private property in behalf of the public interest and may expropriate it with compensation for the same reasons. Under foreign pressure, President Carranza continued the existing relationships with the foreign companies; and likewise the Obregón regime held the Constitution to be nonretroactive regarding oil rights acquired previously.

Foreign forebodings were again aroused when a Calles law of 1925 converted the preconstitutional titles into fifty-year concessions; but this action was reversed in 1927 when confirmatory concessions were given to those with preconstitutional property rights. No drastic change was to come for a decade, but lesser steps were taken toward increasing government's role in the oil industry. The National Petroleum Administration was established in 1925 with wide powers over oil reserves and concessions. Petro-Mex (Sociedad Petróleos de México) was established as a mixed company to secure private capital under government control for petroleum exploitation in 1933. It was replaced in January 1937 by the Administración General del Petrolero Nacional, with operational rather than regulatory functions. This agency never handled more than 3 per cent of Mexican production.

By 1935, the scene was unwittingly being laid for a showdown between the government and the oil companies. Labor charged the companies with failing to grant equal pay for equal work and with various abuses, and the government's friendly Labor Department got the unions to form a single organization. In 1936, the new union demanded an industry-wide contract with large wage increases and more social services. The companies refused; the union decided on a strike; and Cárdenas stepped in, providing for a series of conferences. By May 1937, with no agreement reached, a strike was launched and then called off in favor of arbitration, at the President's insistence. A committee of experts reported to the government in August, giving a critical analysis of company profits; and in December the labor board awarded the workers pay increases of 26,329,393 pesos, plus retroactive pay and a restriction on the number of "confidential employees." The Supreme Court upheld the award on March 1, 1938. By then the companies had agreed to the wage increases but had reservations about the other issues. Negotiations were held with the President, but the likelihood of agreement was lost when the companies seemed to challenge the integrity of the chief executive. On March 18, the President ordered expropriation of most of the companies. The Supreme Court upheld the action as a lawful expropriation; and popular support was overwhelming.

The sudden action of expropriation was apparently unpremeditated, and the government had to provide administrative machinery for the new undertaking. A new agency, the Petroleum Administrative Council, was established, with the Ministers of Finance and Economy first and second in command. The law of June 1938 created Petróleos Mexicanos (Pemex) to operate the industry. It was headed by a board of five government representatives and four from the union. In June 1938, Distribuidora de Petróleos Mexicanos was established as the government's sales agency for oil. In 1940, Pemex, Distribuidora, and Administración General del Petróleo Nacional, were merged as Pemex. It was authorized to carry on any kind of operation dealing with the oil industry. The governing board contained five appointees of the President and four of the union.[2]

The government recognized from the start its obligation to make compensation to the former owners. Since the government stood by its contention of ownership to the subsoil wealth, the question boiled down to agreement on the value of above-ground properties. The United States suggested determination of a figure by arbitration. With the general support of Latin America, Mexico declined on the basis that the domestic legal resources for settlement had not been exhausted. In November 1941, the Mexican and United States governments announced agreement on the claims of oil companies and agrarian lands, on a reciprocal trade treaty, and on extension of certain credits to Mexico for highway construction. The general and agrarian claims were settled for $40,000,000. The value of the oil properties was set at $23,995,991. The figure finally agreed upon for the expropriated English firms was $81,250,000, to be paid over a fifteen-year period.[3]

For several years after expropriation, the oil industry faced many pressing problems. These included labor problems, production costs, foreign marketing difficulties, and shortage of capital for expansion. Personnel and wage problems soon faced Pemex. The number of its personnel swelled, nepotism developed, and salary rates went much higher than those of other comparable government positions. President Cárdenas, following recommendations of a committee of experts and the Conciliation and Arbitration Board, reduced numerous salaries and total personnel.

The difficulties that foreign companies and some governments placed in the way of Mexico's efforts at marketing abroad have been labeled by careful students with terms ranging from "boycott" to "economic warfare." Foreign oil companies switched their oil purchases elsewhere.

British, American, and French markets were largely closed to Mexican oil; so Mexico reluctantly turned to those countries that were politically anathema to her — Germany, Italy, and Japan. Reduced markets brought less money for industry expansion, which was also hindered by pressures applied on equipment manufacturers not to sell to Mexico. Tankers were largely controlled by the expropriated interests. Tetra-ethyl lead, a monopoly of Standard Oil, was denied Mexico. As a result, production fell greatly. The agreement on compensation for expropriation and the closing of Axis-country markets by the war brought a resumption of relations with the United States; but real expansion of the industry did not come until after the war.

Since 1945, there has been slow expansion in oil explorations, drillings, exports, and refinery construction. Production has about doubled since 1945. An estimate of oil reserves in 1946 placed their life at a hundred years, at the then current rate of production. The increasing economic importance of oil is indicated by the UN Economic Commission for Latin America, which reported that in 1930, 64 per cent of Mexico's mechanical energy was derived from oil and related products, while in 1950 the figure was 75 per cent.

Most of the well-drilling in recent years has been in proven or known fields; and Pemex has not been able to drill new wells fast enough to expand its production as rapidly as desired. However, the number of drillings in 1951 was 268, compared with 64 in 1947.

One or two important new fields have been discovered in the last few years, but most of the announced "new" areas are considered by some authorities as being really the edges of existing fields. Thus far, the Poza Rica field has shown the largest reserves and the largest production — about 60 per cent of the total output of the country. Natural gas production from this field has been expanding, and an important gas line from there to Mexico City was completed in 1948. Another potential for gas and oil fields is the continental shelf, over which Mexico, the U.S., and other countries had asserted jurisdiction by 1947.

Refineries have been one of the industry's principal needs. The country had only five in 1941. Four were built between 1948 and 1953.

Mexico has been a small to moderate exporter of oil since 1948. For this and other transport needs, it has its own fleet of tankers for ocean transport. Pemex is working on a shipyard, the first major yard to be built in Mexico. It will be used to build and maintain oil tankers.

*Organization of Pemex.*[4] Pemex is a decentralized public corporation with its own resources. The Council of Administration is composed of ten members, of which four are named by the oil workers union. Of the six appointed by the President, two each are proposed by the Ministers of Finance and Economy, and one each by the Ministers of National Properties and Foreign Relations. The Council approves the annual program, the budget, contracts, and the annual audit. The President appoints the director general of Pemex and his three chief assistants; and the chief executive approves the annual budget.

The director general of Pemex heads the General Bureau, which has general administrative direction of the organization's work. Under it come the three sub-bureaus — those of Production, Marketing, and Administrative and Legal Affairs. The General Bureau has also an important staff service — the Office of Coordination and Economic Studies. It makes studies and recommendations about problems dealing with exploration, exploitation, drilling, transportation, etc. It studies production costs, recommends work programs, and exercises certain control functions, such as controls over purchasing. The Office's Department of Control and Statistics has sectors dealing with coordination, consumption, prices, statistics, sales, taxes, production, refining, and personnel.

The Sub-bureau of Production has charge of exploration, drilling, extraction, transportation, storage, and refining, which functions are committed to corresponding subdivisions of the Sub-bureau. The Management of Exploration does exploratory work, makes geological studies, and collaborates in the original development of fields. The Management of Exploitation handles the drilling, pumping, and transporting of the oil to the refinery. The Management of Refineries handles the distribution of petroleum derivatives, as well as general refinery operations. The Department of Materials handles the acquisition, control, and use of machinery and equipment. The role of the Department of Civil Engineering and Architecture can be inferred from its title.

The Sub-bureau of Marketing has seven subdivisions. The Management of Domestic Sales handles the transport, distribution, and sales of petroleum derivatives within the country, while the Management of Exports handles exports. The Department of Inspection and Shipments also deals with the delivery of commodities. The Marine Department handles the Pemex tanker fleet. The Management of Finances handles accounting, auditing, and credit management. The Department of Insurance and Bonds protects the organization in that field. The New York Office represents Pemex in relations with the United States government, American purchasers, and American material and equipment supply firms.

Staff and auxiliary functions are under the Sub-bureau of Administrative and Legal Affairs. Its Administrative Department represents the agency before the other government agencies, railroads, commercial concerns, and foreign consulates. It negotiates contracts, controls properties, deals with central office personnel, and handles correspondence. The Department of Personnel handles the agency's labor relations, since the workers function under a collective contract as in private business. The role of the Legal Department is obvious, as is that of the advisory Commission on Rents, Gifts, and Exemptions. The Department of Medical Services and Social Welfare, in addition to providing medical services, supports a number of elementary schools, provides scholarships for special training, promotes safety measures, and sponsors credit unions and consumers' cooperatives.

*Policies.*[5] The oil industry has long been a very substantial taxpayer. The highest tax paid under private ownership was some 86,000,000 pesos, in 1922. Later, it stood at 54,521,509 in 1938; 190,968,832 in 1946; 335,524,605 in 1949. Taxes, including petroleum consumption taxes, represented 27.6 per cent of gross receipts for the years 1938–50.

In addition to taxes, Pemex has paid substantial sums into the national treasury. In 1950, taxes and subsidies to special consumers totaled 33 per cent of Pemex's gross income. The provision of some schools in the oil-producing areas has been mentioned. In a recent year – 1950 – it gave $50 million of profit to the Treasury. Tourist promotion is an important subsidy.

The industry's investments have been determined by the pressing needs of the expanding domestic market and by its own limited financial resources. Most of the investments have gone into refineries, expansion of transport facilities for oil, and increasing the production of existing oil fields. Investment in drilling lagged seriously until 1948 and is still below the desired level. Efforts have been made to interest foreign capital in exploration and drilling, but without much success. Mexico has made it clear that it does not intend to alter its nationalization policy. During the recent war, the Export-Import Bank loaned Pemex $10 million for expanding refinery equipment; but the industry's investments have come mainly from its own profits. For the period 1938–50, 87 per cent of the investments were financed in that way.

Pemex's labor policy has been liberal. The wages in the industry are among the highest in the country, while the price policy keeps costs to consumers at levels below those in the United States.

Thus, Pemex has several policies that are at least partially incompatible. These include high wages and workers' social benefits, payment of substantial taxes, provision of various subsidies, providing the expanding economy with cheap and plentiful products, and finding the means of financing much-needed expansion. Because of trying to meet all these goals, the achievement of expansion has been difficult.

One of the important factors in Pemex's success in recent years has been the business ability of its director general, Antonio Bermúdez. His successful career in the business world preceded his entry into political life as the reform mayor of the border city of Juárez. Then came his election as a senator; and finally Alemán chose him to head the ailing oil industry in 1946. His success in putting the ailing industry on its feet was such that for a time he was talked of as a successor of Alemán; and today he is one of the most influential leaders in the country.

*Related agencies.*[6] Pemex has important relationships with other agencies. One way of coordinating the work of the oil industry with other agencies is by means of their representation on Pemex's Council of Administration. There we find the Ministries of Finance, Economy, National Properties, and Foreign Relations represented, since the oil industry touches their spheres of work in important ways. The relationship of the Ministry of Economy to Pemex is especially important. The Ministry's Bureau of Mines and Petroleum deals with the granting of permits for exploration, exploitation, refining, and sale of petroleum and other minerals. This offers no impediment to the work of Pemex, but the Bureau regulates retail concessions for the marketing of petroleum products.

### NOTES

[1] A. W. Macmahon and W. R. Dittmar, "The Mexican Oil Industry Since Expropriation," *Political Science Quarterly*, March and June 1942, pp. 28–50, 161–88; Jesús Silva Herzog, *Petróleo Mexicano, Historia de un Problema* (1941); Weyl, *op. cit.*, Ch. 11; H. G. Hambleton, "The Petroleum Industry in Latin America" (M.A. thesis, Mexico City College, 1949); *Excelsior*, March 25, 1938.

Certain points discussed in this chapter are treated in detail in J. Richard Powell's *The Mexican Petroleum Industry, 1938–1950* (University of California

Press, 1956), an important study that was published after this chapter was written. Mr. Powell discusses the serious difficulties faced after expropriation and seeks to assess the degrees of achievement of short-run and long-run objectives, both political and economic. He feels that closer regulation would have been a feasible alternative to government operation, and one that would have been better for Mexico economically. But, he concludes (p. 197), "it is unlikely that such measures would have satisfied the basic political and social aspirations of the people." Hostility to the foreign companies and the revolutionary tradition "were too deeply imbedded in Mexican consciousness to stop short of expropriation."

[2] For selections from the extensive literature on the period since expropriation see J. H. Plenn, *Mexico Marches* (1939), Ch. 2; *U.S. Law Review*, June 1938, pp. 322–36; J. L. Kunz, *The Mexican Expropriations* (1940); José D. Lavín, *Petróleo* . . . (1950); *International Conciliation*, December 1938, pp. 511–20; *Mexico and the United States*, Southern Methodist University, 1938, pp. 45–66; *Inter-American Economic Affairs*, Summer 1951, pp. 52–70, and Winter 1952, pp. 14–31; McGraw-Hill Company, *op. cit.*

[3] *Journal of Business*, October 1952, pp. 246–47.

[4] Sría. de Bienes Nacionales, *Directorio* . . . (2), pp. 383–99; Fraga, *op. cit.*, pp. 384–85.

[5] International Bank, *op. cit.*, pp. 48 *et seq.*; Cline, *op. cit.*, pp. 251–60; *18 de Marzo* (Pemex house-organ); *HA*, March 26, 1956, pp. 7–10; *Humanismo*, April-June 1955, pp. 258–73; U.S. Bureau of Foreign Commerce, *op. cit.*, pp. 51–56.

[6] Sría. de Bienes Nacionales, *Directorio* . . . (1), pp. 270–72; *Nueva Ley Reglamentaria del Art. 27* . . . , in Andrade, ed., *op. cit.*, pp. 312.1 *et seq.*

# 19

## Public Works and the Public Utility Program

IN EARLIER chapters I have considered the separate programs dealing with railways, highways, civil aviation, postal and telecommunications services, electrification, and oil. In a later chapter irrigation works will be discussed in connection with agricultural development. In this chapter I will consider the broad outlines of the public works program and important aspects of the program, such as maritime works, the valley authorities, housing, and miscellaneous construction.

*General features.*[1] The Alemán administration spent nearly $400 million on public works in its six-year term, and it left unfinished a program of nearly half that amount. Thus, most of the first year's construction budget of the present administration was taken up with completion of the previous program; and this administration's expanded public works program is scheduled to take more than a third of the federal budget.

The International Bank's study of the period 1939–50 found public investments for public facilities accounting for an over-all average of 36 per cent of the total investment. These facilities included highways, railways, electric power, large-scale irrigation projects, and community works. A relatively small amount was invested in housing and public buildings during that period. The investments for petroleum, electric power, communications, and transportation have been rising since 1947; and the relative importance of public investment in the total investment picture has been rising. It accounted for only 38 per cent of the total in 1939. In 1950 it reached 45 per cent of the total. Capital investments for welfare-type services lagged, however. Such investments for construction in the fields of public health and welfare, and of education for the twelve-year period averaged only about 12 per cent of the total public investment.

Each year since 1952, the present administration's budget has shown an increase over that of the preceding year. These increases include the ministries of Hydraulic Resources, Communications, and Marine.

The growth of highways was shown in the increasing proportion of the transportation investment going for roads. This proportion grew from 43 per cent to 52 per cent in the period 1945-50. The same period saw the railways' proportion falling from 46 per cent to 37 per cent. These facts, plus increasing competition from road traffic, caused the railroads' conditions to deteriorate. And they are just beginning to improve under the government's recent rehabilitation efforts. The development of highways has been the chief transportation development of the last two decades. But there has not been much coordination among the various agencies involved in developing and operating the different transportation facilities. As a result, there have been cases of unnecessary duplication of railroads, highways, and oil pipelines along the same routes. A much-needed over-all policy is just appearing.

Of the federal public investment in 1955, the following agencies accounted for the highest percentages of the total: Communications, 17.7 per cent; Hydraulic Resources, 16.1 per cent; Pemex, 12.7 per cent; Federal Electricity Commission, 9.3 per cent; National Railways, 7.8 per cent; Pacific Railway, 5.9 per cent.[2]

*The maritime program.*[3] Under the slogan "march to the sea," the Ruiz Cortines administration has launched one of its most popular programs. The goal of development for the coastal and lowland areas includes the related projects of intra-region and inter-region highways, improved port facilities, development of the fishing industry, expansion of the merchant marine, agricultural development, and development of integrated multipurpose river valley projects. This long-term program started with monthly investments of about $1½ million in 1954.

Under the leadership of the Ministry of Marine, the principal ministries participating through an interagency committee are the Ministries of Communications, Economy, Finance, Agriculture, National Properties, and Labor. Geared in with the program are the local Boards of Material Welfare, discussed in Chapter 26 (see pages 399-400). They are to work in cooperation with the pertinent ministries — with Education in building schools, with Communications in road building, etc. The decentralized agencies such as Pemex and the National Railways are also participating in the program.

These varied developments in the maritime areas are intended to develop the economies of these regions for their present inhabitants; provide homes for surplus populations of other areas — which now often provide much migrant agricultural labor for the United States; link these economies better with the rest of the country; and make better provision for maritime commercial development.

The plan for developing or rehabilitating some seventy ports calls for contributions from the budgets of the participating agencies totaling over $50 million a year in the future. The President's annual report in 1953 indicated that port development would include installation and maintenance of shipyards and plants for the construction and repair of naval vessels. The ports initially selected on the Gulf coast included Veracruz, Tampico, Tuxpan, Alvarado, Coatzacoalcos, Frontera, and Progreso. The first chosen on the Pacific coast were Salina Cruz, Puerto Ángel, Chacahua, Acapulco, Zihuatanejo, Manzanillo, Mazatlán, Guaymas, and Ensenada. Work on the port of Veracruz was one of the first projects completed. A shipyard for the repair of the Pemex merchant fleet will be built there.

One source listed thirty-nine ports as being active in 1953, with Veracruz and Tampico the most important. Shipping under the Mexican flag in 1951 included 9 steamers of 16,362 tons, as well as numerous small craft of 12,000 net tons. In addition, the oil fleet comprised 19 tankers and 200 vessels totaling 230,000 dead-weight tons.

*Valley authorities.*[4] The valley authority approach to regional multipurpose development has seized the imagination of Mexico. The first such TVA-type authority to be established was the one covering the watershed of the Papaloapán River and its tributaries, which was placed under the jurisdiction of the Papaloapán Commission in 1947. This area, about twice the size of the state of New Jersey, was to have its principal problems treated in an integrated manner.

The chief problems of areas like this one were planning and construction of river control against floods, power development, sanitary developments, transportation projects (air, rail, and road), agricultural development through drainage and irrigation, and balanced industrial development. The aim is to expand the opportunities for improved living for the present inhabitants and for colonists from more populous areas.

Frequent devastating floods had long made life difficult and unsanitary for the population of the Papaloapán valley. Therefore, one of the prime objectives was flood control and sanitary engineering. The dams and straightening of the river are the principal physical developments to this end. Power development is planned from a group of four dams. The first of these, the Alemán Dam, has been put into use; it is comparable in size to the Bonneville Dam in the United States and is probably the largest in Latin America. While principally for flood control and power development, the dam will irrigate an area of 420,000 acres.

Agriculture is being developed by means of both drainage and irrigation, as well as by the application of sanitary measures and provision of transportation for agricultural commodities.

The development of the economy is sought through building a series of planned communities as the centers of economic subregions, the hinterlands of which grow both subsistence and commercial crops — sugar cane, cotton, bananas, pineapples, etc. An aluminum plant and a paper factory were among the first light industrial developments, and the presence of iron and coal in the area makes possible the development of some heavy industry. At the center of the area is the first planned city, Ciudad Alemán, intended as the hub of the developing area. Road building is being pushed rapidly.

The magnitude of the project is of obvious importance, but more significant is the application of the scientific approach to the rounded development of this virgin territory. In all the aspects of development mentioned, the program had to start from scratch. The area was backward and handicapped in every way — except in having potentials. Social scientists, scientists, engineers, and officials have worked together in the planning of the area's development and the execution of the plans. Anthropologists, historians, sanitarians, economists, and other specialists cooperate to preserve the best of the past and build for the future. The aim is to interweave the desirable aspects of rural and urban life in the economy of the new region.

This first valley authority, under the direction of the Papaloapán Commission, is a decentralized agency under the sponsorship of the Ministry of Hydraulic Resources. The Minister is the chairman of the Commission. Of the other two members appointed by the President, one represents the Ministries of National Properties and Finance. He is the active executive of the organization. Monthly reports are provided the two interested ministries.

Important top-level subdivisions of the agency are the Bureau of Planning and the Technical Advisor's Office. The first studies all matters dealing with the planning of works to be constructed, seeking a balanced development of the program and conservation of the valley's resources. It maintains liaison with the other interested federal agencies. The Technical Advisor's Office studies special problems arising in connection with the works being carried out. Its work is coordinated with that of the different ministries that are involved in various phases of the program.

The Commission's Bureau of Social Studies studies the social, economic, and sociocultural problems of the area. It has sections dealing with education, economics, anthropology, sociology, and urban problems. The action division of the Commission is the Bureau of Engineering. It has Departments of Surveying, Hydraulic Measurements, Geology, and Sanitary Engineering. The Commission's divisions dealing with housekeeping functions are the Medical-Sanitary Bureau and the Administrative Bureau. The latter has Departments of Audit and Accounts, Personnel, Warehouses, and Purchasing.

The watershed of the Tepalcatepec Basin is the location of Mexico's next most important valley authority project. It is located on the opposite side of the country from the Papaloapán, on the Pacific slope. The two are about equal in size — 27,000 square miles. The Tepalcatepec program was also started in 1947; and it seeks to improve the economic, material, and social life of this large and potentially rich area extending from western Michoacán to the Pacific coast.[5]

The government's expenditures on this project have been much less than on the Papaloapán project; but its possibilities are substantial. The first developments call for small irrigation works, railroads, and roads, to be followed by larger works. The first stage of the project produced some 90,000 acres of irrigated land, while the completed project calls for several times that amount. A substantial amount of electric power is generated at the dams. Here, as with the Papaloapán, a balanced agricultural-industrial development is the goal.

The organization of the Tepalcatepec Commission is similar to that of the Papaloapán Commission. The chairman of the three-man Commission is the Minister of Hydraulic Resources, while a second member — former President Cárdenas — is the active director of the program.

The agency is divided into three bureaus — Hydraulic Resources,

Communications and Plans, and Agriculture and Stockraising. The first has charge of the study and control of the rivers, canals, hydraulic works, and sanitary engineering. The second formulates the plans for construction, including roads, railroads, and telephone lines. The third, in cooperation with the two agricultural banks, promotes agriculture, stockraising, and soil and forest conservation.

The success of the Papaloapán and Tepalcatepec projects has led to the starting of two other basin development programs. That of the Río Fuerte, in the northwest Pacific area, was started in 1951. That of the Grijalva River, in the far southern states of Chiapas and Tabasco, was started in 1952. The latter project will include the reclamation of 1,200,000 acres of Chiapas jungle for agricultural development, including a dam on the Grijalva River for the generation of electricity for industrial development.

The presidential message to the Congress in 1953 announced that the following sums were being spent currently on the river basin projects: Papaloapán, 76 million pesos; Río Fuerte, 30 million; Tepalcatepec, 12 million; Grijalva, 2 million.[6]

*Housing.* Adequate housing is a pressing problem in Mexico; and little has been done along this line by the government, in comparison with other aspects of its investment program. However, in recent years funds of the Bureau of Civil Pensions and the Social Security Institute have provided for housing construction to serve low-income families. This work has taken the form of constructing large apartment houses and making loans to individual government employees for the purchase of individual houses. This field of government activity will be discussed in Chapter 23.[7]

*Other construction.* Other construction of importance has been carried out in a number of fields. Hydraulic projects have been of importance from the standpoints of both irrigation and electrification. The country's high birth rate has made the provision of school buildings a crucial problem. The same is true of hospital construction. Only the largest cities have drinking water and sewage systems that approach adequacy; thus a large backlog of needed construction exists in this field. In addition, the capital is faced with a pressing problem in the sinking of the subsoil on which the city is built, and the solution can only be accomplished at great cost. These various needs will be discussed in later chapters.

### NOTES

[1] International Bank, *op. cit.*, pp. 13, 17, 84–99; Antonio Manero, "Public Works in Mexico," *Social Sciences in Mexico*, May 1947, pp. 51–55; D. W. Beck, *op. cit.*, *passim*; Tannenbaum, *Mexico* . . . , pp. 209–16; *Mexican American Review*, July 1953, pp. 24–25; *MV*, December 21, 1953; New York *Times*, January 6, 1954.

[2] Banco de México, *Asamblea General* . . . , 1956, p. 68; *HA*, March 28, 1955, pp. 11–12.

[3] *News*, April 14 and 23, July 15, August 15 and 17, September 30, October 1, December 11, 1953, and January 13, 1954; *El Universal*, September 2, 1953; *MV*, April 13, 1953; *Statesman's Year-book*; *HA*, July 20, 1953, pp. 3–7.

[4] Guillermo Armas Arias, "Planificación Económica Regional . . ." (UNAM thesis, 1950, pp. 130 *et seq.*); Sría. de Bienes Nacionales, *Directorio* . . . (2), pp. 615–21; José Attolini, *Economía de la Cuenca del Papaloapán* . . . (1949); Wise, *op. cit.*, pp. 95–96; Cline, *op. cit.*, pp. 374–75, 382–85; *Reader's Digest*, August 1951, pp. 129–32.

[5] Sría. de Bienes Nacionales, *Directorio* . . . (2), pp. 623–27.

[6] *El Universal*, September 2, 1953.

[7] *HA*, September 9, 1949, pp. xxx–xxxvi.

# PART V

# Agriculture

# 20

*Agricultural History and Problems*

M EXICO is a rural country, only recently beginning to industrialize. Some of her most serious problems stem from the physical environment, for Mexico is not a rich country and her physical resources are not well distributed. Therefore, economic, political, and military struggles have usually been closely related to the problem of land, its distribution and use. The lives of most of the people have been bound to the land; so the rural problem is an important and complex one for government.

*History to 1910.*[1] Current land legislation and administration can be properly understood only with its antecedents in mind. Mexico's agrarian history has rather largely revolved around the struggle between the land-holding village and the semifeudal estate, the *hacienda*. Until 1910, the struggle went steadily in favor of the latter. Only recent years have seen a serious effort to reverse the trend and solve the problem.

In the important agricultural areas of Mexico before the conquest, a village pattern of land tenure existed which has exerted important influence on land-tenure patterns and legislation to the present day. The economic, social, and land-use unit was the village, whose lands included tillable areas, timberlands, and hunting grounds. Water rights for irrigation were clearly defined. The village's tillable lands were distributed as plots among the heads of families, who could pass them down from father to son. While the land-holding village was the dominant agrarian unit, certain precedents had been established for the later growth of the large estates. Thus we find here the seeds of both the *hacienda* and the present *ejido* systems.

In spite of some changes, the land-holding village continued in the colonial era as a basic type of land tenure, for the conquerors were well acquainted in Spain with both land-holding village and individual estate.

The crown established rules for protection of the villages and tried to assure adequate lands for their support. An agricultural area included the town site and its lands for agriculture, timber, and grazing.

Despite this support for the agrarian village system, the *encomienda* * developed as a powerful means for achieving the subjection of the natives. This device to Christianize the Indians, subject them to the crown, and reward the *conquistadores* achieved mainly the third goal. One or more villages were allotted in trust to an individual, who was empowered to collect from them taxes and personal services. A feudalistic system of land tenure resulted, with the Indians in the role of serfs. A royal edict "abolished" the system in 1720, but by other measures the great landowners retained much of their original sway. By the end of the colonial period, large numbers of natives were landless and destitute.

Reaction to this maldistribution of the land was a major factor in the success of the war for independence. But the gaining of independence was largely a political conquest, without immediate economic results in favor of the landless rural populace. With the problem unsettled, the pressure for improvement continued; and the landless continued to fill the ranks of countless successive revolutionary movements, which seldom gave any lasting substance to the amorphous yearnings for change.

The early decades of independence saw little effort to produce better land distribution in the settled areas. Instead, efforts were made to promote settlement of newer lands by both Mexicans and foreigners. A series of colonization laws began in 1833, seeking to achieve that goal. But they largely failed to achieve their objectives because revolutionary agitations discouraged immigration; they were not widely accepted by the Indians they were supposed to benefit; and there was no adequate machinery for their efficient administration. Subsequent efforts to promote colonization were also of limited effectiveness.

Another approach — well-intended, but disastrous in effect — was taken. The Law of Desamortización (Law against Entails) was promulgated in 1856, to force the Church to sell its vast land holdings in small parcels. This effort to aid the landless masses was largely thwarted by ecclesiastical threats of excommunication against purchasers. However, many already prosperous persons thought more of earthly rewards and took advantage of another provision of the law. This provision allowed

* The semifeudal holdings of a large landlord, including control of the natives on the land.

any person to denounce tenants who had not availed themselves of purchase rights within three months, such action rewarding the denouncers with an eighth of the property's value. Another serious mistake of the law was to cover civil as well as religious corporations, and Indian villages were civil corporations. These lands, divided among family heads, were easily dissipated by their impecunious owners. Public lands also gravitated to the hands of the powerful few in the 1880s and 1890s through edicts which forced villages to sell their lands and allowed "surveying companies" to gobble up vast tracts of vacant public lands by sharp practices. Soon a small number of these new owners held a fifth of the national territory, thus preventing numbers of landless from securing needed lands. Thus the monopoly of the land by great *haciendas* grew, and with it grew the pressure that gave steam to the explosion – the Revolution of 1910.

*The revolutionary period.*[2] The revolution that started in 1910 is referred to in Mexico as "The Revolution"; and it is often called an agrarian revolution. The first point is well taken. The term distinguishes this event from the less thoroughgoing changes of the reform period of the 1850s; and it distinguishes this more thoroughgoing change from the numerous previous changes of minor significance. The causes of the Revolution were numerous and complex. There is no doubt that the people's desires for freedom, land, bread, and justice were important elements in the picture. But only in the broader sense of the word was this event in its origin an "agrarian revolution," because the landless peasants were not prepared to stage a revolution. They lacked leaders, finances, organization, and plans. The leadership came from middle-class and upper-class circles.

But the conditions had been laid for agrarian support for a revolution. Mexicans had worked in the United States, returning with ideas on what their standard of living should be. The peasants saw the urban workers getting somewhat better incomes in the rising industries. While urban wages rose somewhat in the years before the Revolution, the wages of rural workers remained almost the same between 1900 and 1920. And price rises outran wage increases in that period, adding to the misery of the peasants. While the agrarians could not be expected to carry through an "agrarian" revolution, they were ready to give vital support to a revolution started and led by others.

The first leader of the Revolution was a well-to-do *hacendado* (large landowner), Madero; and the intellectual leaders of the movement were upper- and middle-class people who had not found a place for themselves in the Díaz bureaucracy or the rising industrial society. In the beginning, the Revolution had no firm organization or positive ideology. Economic problems were minimized, and the goals were mainly those of political democracy. Nevertheless, despite the inadequate emphasis on agrarian matters, there was at least some verbal recognition of these problems. Madero's revolutionary proclamation had a plank that declared:

In abuse of the law on public lands numerous proprietors of small holdings, in their greater part Indians, have been dispossessed of their lands by rulings of the department of public development . . . or by decisions of the tribunals of the Republic. As it is just to restore to their former owners the lands of which they were dispossessed in such an arbitrary manner, such rulings and decisions are declared subject to revision, and those who have acquired them in such an immoral manner, or their heirs, will be required to restore them to their former owners, to whom they shall also pay an indemnity for the damages suffered.[3]

Soon afterward, Juan Saravia and Antonio Díaz Soto y Gama proposed a law giving villages again the right to have *ejidos* * and setting a limit on the amount of property an individual could own. The first strong presentation of the agrarian cause within the government was Luis Cabrera's speech to the Chamber of Deputies in October 1912. He criticized the ineffectiveness of Madero's Minister of Public Development and urged restoring the *ejidos* to the villages as the only effective way to benefit large numbers of landless. He felt that slow halfway measures would be useless, that the *ejidos* should be re-established by expropriation under broad powers for such seizure of needed properties placed in the hands of the President. Madero, in the grip of his enemies, opposed the proposal as dangerous and did nothing.

Madero's disillusioned agrarian supporters fell away, and action was left for others (see Chapter 2). An independent peasant leader who was soon in opposition to the government's inaction was Emiliano Zapata. His one burning ambition was to return the land to the landless. Strong peasant support soon enabled him to control the states of Morelos, Jalisco, Guerrero, and Puebla. His Plan of Ayala, one of the Revolution's most famous documents, was more a battle cry than a plan

* Villages practicing cooperative or semicooperative land ownership and use, as discussed in Chapter 21.

for agrarian reform. His uncompromising devotion to his cause finally, through other hands, brought enactment of the government's agrarian reform measures. One leading authority regards him as "the most powerful single influence in the shaping of the agrarian program of the revolution." [4]

Madero's inaction and bad judgment brought about his downfall, the bloody interval of Huerta, and the accession of Carranza in 1914. In a crisis and in need of popular support, Carranza followed Cabrera's suggestions and issued his Plan of Veracruz, the first specific program for social and economic reform. In the following month, January 1915, he issued the agrarian decree, which was later partly incorporated in the agrarian article of the 1917 Constitution.

Despite its advance over past inaction, the decree of 1915 left much to be desired. Its one approach was that of giving land to villages, and the emphasis was the negative one of restoring to villages the lands wrongly taken in the past. The outright grant of lands otherwise was intended to have very limited application. In other words, it was a negative program for righting past wrongs and not a positive program to solve the land program as a whole.

The decree was to benefit only one kind of village, the village that had political status. Those eligible were specifically limited to *pueblos*, *rancherías*, *congregaciones*, and *comunidades*.* This alone was quite limiting, since many states had few villages bearing these designations; and all states faced great unsolved land problems. Moreover, the emphasis in the decree was not on the village or the former *ejido* as a communal unit; it was placed on the individual. The proprietorship of the land was not to be placed in the corporate body but in the hands of the separate inhabitants, safeguarded only by limitations to prevent speculators from monopolizing property. Furthermore, the decree placed the initiative on the village, not the government. The village needing land had to petition the government, with supporting proof of necessity. This requirement opened the doors to many abuses and inaction due to adverse local factors — ignorance of the peasants, intimidation from affected landholders, and the like.

Some authorities have considered one of the worst features of the

* These terms have little more than historical significance. The settlements average between 100 and 1,000 population, with the *pueblos* (the largest of the four) near the upper average figure.

273

decree its provision allowing landowners to appeal to the regular courts against actions taken by the government. In many cases this meant that the purposes of the reform were defeated, and in nearly all cases it meant the annoyance and delay of long drawn-out legal battles.

The decree strengthened Carranza's power, but its aid to the landless was modest and its incitement to disorder was great. Military leaders were accorded the right to dispose of land with great freedom, which many did with bribery and fraud. Disillusioned peons seized lands without too much adherence to the law; and *hacendados* defended their lands with guns and court proceedings.

*The Constitution and land reform.*[5] Carranza's next bid for popular support was his calling of the Constitutional Convention of 1916–17. All the evidence indicates that the President desired only relatively minor political changes in the existing Constitution; he had no desire for including in the document any fundamental social and economic changes. But Carranza was surprised by the convention he thought would be tractable.

The convention included a radical group with surprising strength, which succeeded in securing inclusion of the two important new provisions — protections for agriculture (Art. 27) and labor (Art. 123). The leaders of the successful group were the powerful Generals Obregón and Múgica, followers of the intellectual father of Mexican agrarian reform, Andrés Molina Enríquez.

In general, Article 27 sought to do three things: define and limit property; decide what natural and legal persons may hold property; and set forth principles and some procedures for solving the agrarian problem. The following is a topical, rather than a sequential, analysis of the Article.

1. The nature of property: Private property in lands and waters is not "original" but is the result of an act of the nation. Such title "is vested originally in the Nation, which has had, and has, the right to transmit title thereof to private persons. . . ." The nation retains the right to impose limitations on property in the public interest, including regulation of the development of natural resources. Provision is made for dividing great landed estates, developing small holdings, establishing new population centers, and encouraging agriculture. Expropriation may be used "for reasons of public utility and by means of indemnification." Payment could be before the act, simultaneously, or afterward.

The government has chosen the last. Payment is to be based on the declared value of the land plus 10 per cent, with only the value of improvements subject to judicial determination. The nation's ownership of water and minerals is declared inalienable, with only the right of exploitation that may be conceded to private parties.

2. The right to hold property: This right is not universal, but may be limited or prohibited. Mexican citizens and companies may own lands, waters, or mineral concessions. Foreigners may be given these rights when they renounce the right of protection in such matters from their governments. Foreign ownership is forbidden near the coasts and frontiers. Religious institutions may not hold or administer real property. Commercial stock companies cannot "acquire, hold or administer rural properties." Nor may banks, in general, own such properties. "Properties held in common by co-owners, settlements, towns, congregations, tribes and other bodies of population, which . . . conserve their communal character shall have legal capacity to enjoy in common the waters, woods and lands belonging to them, or which may have been or shall be restored to them according to the law of January 6, 1915, until such time as the manner of making the division of the lands shall be determined by law."

3. Principles for solving agrarian problems: Four principal approaches are provided for solving the agrarian problem. First, lands are restored to villages formerly possessing them, when deprivation was improper. This principle is spelled out with reference to certain laws of the past. Second, communities lacking sufficient lands and waters for their needs "shall have the right to be provided with them from the adjacent properties, always having due regard for small landed holdings." Transactions under the law of 1915 are validated. Third, the government is expected to recover the public lands and waters improperly alienated under the Díaz regime. Fourth, provision is made for the enactment of federal and state laws to break up the great estates. The nation and the states, within their respective jurisdictions, shall set the maximum size of private holdings and "measures governing the division of excess lands, in accordance with the following bases": maximum individual areas are to be set by law; the excess areas are to be subdivided and sold by the owner or, failing this, be subdivided by the government; landowners are obliged to accept agrarian bonds as payment.

Thus, Article 27 is seen to be a substantial advance over the law of

1915, in the matter of land reform. First, creation of *ejidos* by grant is on a par with land restoration. Second, lands for *ejidos* no longer have to be immediately adjoining to be subject to expropriation. Third, *ejidos* are clearly defined in the text of the Article. Article 27 grants to the nation wide powers over private property, but it does not establish socialism. The thinking in the Constitutional Convention varied widely on this matter. Some wanted to socialize all land; others wanted to do very little in this direction. The result was a compromise on granting wide powers of regulation and of expropriating the bulk of a large individual holding. And various forms of land-holding are recognized, of which the *ejido* is one. The *ejido* was looked upon, at least by many, as a transitional form of property on the way to widespread individual ownership. But regarding waters and subsoil wealth, complete socialization was established, at least in theory.[6]

*Slow progress.*[7] The constitutional foundation was laid for far-reaching agrarian reform, but progress was slow for many years. However, the next decade and a half did not lack for laws, decrees, and other legal enactments. About a hundred of this bewildering array dealt with the distribution of lands and waters, and almost an equal number dealt with related aspects of the agrarian reform — irrigation, credit, markets, agricultural education, etc.

Action came more slowly. Carranza reduced the effectiveness of his 1915 agrarian decree by various means and did little to carry out the program of Article 27. He distributed only about 445,000 acres of land to 190 villages between 1915 and the end of his rule in 1920. The strength of Zapata's rebel movement was an index of the agrarian opposition to inaction; and in 1920 the successful revolt of Obregón was due to his pledge to carry out the true objectives of the Revolution.

After Obregón came to power, serious but intermittent efforts were made by his and succeeding regimes to carry out the constitutional mandate. The execution of the laws varied considerably from one administration to another; but the *ejido* program slowly emerged as a basic objective of the Revolution. The total number of acres distributed and the number of persons benefited rose rather slowly but steadily between 1920 and 1929, except for two years — 1922 and 1928.

One of Obegón's first acts as President was to secure enactment of the Law of Ejidos. It was a confused, complicated piece of legislation which was difficult to administer; but at least it indicated that the administration was determined to take some action. This law of 1920 was repealed the following year; and in 1922 the Agrarian Regulatory Law was passed. This measure introduced for the first time some order into the agrarian program; and the spirit of land reform began to change from one of restoration to one of solving the social-economic-technical problem of how best to distribute the country's agricultural resources.

The act of 1922 made several improvements, including the following: adding to the list of types of communities that were eligible to receive lands; clarifying the amounts of land to be given to villages, to provide each family with from three to eight hectares (7.4 to 19.8 acres) — depending on the type of land; and providing agencies for the distribution of the land. A petition for land (by restitution or dotation) went first to the State Agrarian Commission, which made recommendations to the governor. The governor's favorable decision was approved by the National Agrarian Commission; and the village's Executive Committee was given provisional possession of the land. Prior to final decision by the President, on recommendation of the National Agrarian Commission, owners of affected properties could be heard in opposition. This measure, with its reforms, functioned until 1927.

Three other measures were passed under Obregón. The Idle Lands Law (1920) was an emergency measure of an interim nature to allow anyone to cultivate for a year any privately owned land not planted by a certain date. A homestead-type decree of 1923 allowed any adult Mexican to secure title to land by occupying and tilling it for two years. A decree of January 10, 1920, authorized the issuance of federal bonds to indemnify expropriated owners.

Obregón distributed much more land than Carranza had. But, despite this and the legal advances made, Obregón was too cautious in the opinion of later authorities. Simpson feels that his "failure to take the quickest and least complicated route" (confiscation of the large estates) lost the best chance for an effective solution, leaving much of the area still in large holdings.[8]

Calles (1924–28) distributed much more land than did Obregón. Under Calles, the emphasis was even more on individual ownership. The *ejido* was regarded as a step toward creating a large body of individual small owners, necessary because of the backward character of much of the rural populace. In 1925 he promulgated the Regulatory Law on Division of Ejido Land, the first legal attempt to regulate the internal functioning of the villages. This measure sought to divide the *ejido*'s crop lands into parcels, the titles of which were vested in both the village and the individuals concerned. The aim was to limit the power of the village authorities and take a step toward making the village members individual property owners.

Criticism of the land program grew with the years — by those who opposed it entirely and by those who wished to improve it. After considerable study, Calles sought to make a new start with a new Law of Dotation and Restitution of Lands and Waters, passed in 1927. It clarified the principles contained in the previous Law of Dotation and Restitution. First, it reduced injustices by extending eligibility to most populated places, excluding mainly the smallest villages and resident laborers on exploited lands. This measure also clarified the functions of agrarian authorities; subordinated the state commissions to the National Commission; simplified petition procedures; in general, took the proceedings out of the reach of court action; and gave the landlords certain protections. Finally, the new law exempted 370 acres of a property from expropriation; and it set rules for petitions seeking expansion of *ejido* areas.

Numerous other enactments occurred in the Calles administration, of which the most important were those establishing the National Bank of Agricultural Credit and *ejido* banks, the Law of Irrigation with Federal Waters, the National Irrigation Commission, and the Law of Colonization. The Bank was established in 1926 to provide credit for small farmers. The National Irrigation Commission was established in the same year to recommend irrigation developments and to carry them out in certain areas. The Law of Colonization of 1926 was the first effort to modernize the colonization principle, much abused before 1910.

During the Calles years, real progress was made — in recovery of national lands from large owners, in distribution of lands, in settlement on homesteads, in providing agricultural credit, and in starting agricultural education. Three times as much land was distributed as in the entire period before 1925. Still, there was considerable lack of agreement on the exact future course of the agrarian program and how best to get there. These uncertainties involved the method of land-holding (private or collective); the size of the holdings; and ownership of the land (private or public).

The presidency of Portes Gil (1929) saw the high point of land distribution; and important clarifications were made in the laws. Evasions by large owners were reduced, and provisions were made to speed up the action of state agrarian authorities in handling petitions. The National Waters Law was passed in 1929.

Ortiz Rubio's administration (February 1930–September 1932) was a rather thoroughgoing return to conservatism in agrarian matters. Restrictive reforms were added to the Law of Dotation and Restitution, including the requirement of previous payment before expropriation to add to the lands of a village. In addition, "stop" laws were enacted by the state and national governments, attempting to bring an end to expropriations in about a dozen states. Naturally, the result was a drastic reduction in land distribution in 1930–33. However, advances were made in this period. The law of December 23, 1931, ended the availability of court review for expropriated owners. In August of 1931, the first general law was passed to regulate the labor provision of the Constitution (Art. 123). It contained important provisions for agricultural labor. These included the minimum wage, payments in legal tender, the eight-hour day, the right to unionize, and protections for accidents and illness.

When Rodríguez (September 1932–December 1934) took over from Ortiz Rubio, the administration turned again to a program of promoting agrarian reform. Land distribution was not increased immediately, the increase coming in 1934. But important legislation was enacted. One of the most important items was the decree of July 14, 1933, which put an end to the "stop" laws of the previous administration and reestablished the State Agrarian Commissions. The most important of the other laws was the Agrarian Code of 1934, a full revision of existing laws relating to land distribution and the organization and functioning of *ejidos*.

*The Cárdenas era.*[9] Other presidents had supported the agrarian program, but none before or since has given it such passionate devotion as Cárdenas. While Ortiz Rubio was leading the agrarian reform in the direction of conservatism, a struggle was going on within the official party over its program. The "veterans" wanted a retreat from the *ejido* program. The "agrarians," a younger and more radical group, wanted to push the *ejido* program. Both agreed that something had to be done. The agrarians and army leaders threw their support to Cárdenas in the race for the Party's nomination; and Party boss Calles, leader of agrarian conservatism, felt it necessary to support him for President.

The official party's support of Cárdenas would have won him the election in a silent race; but General Cárdenas' unprecedentedly thorough campaign, which took him to every corner of the republic, gave valuable popular support to his future agrarian program.

In Cárdenas' first year in office, he distributed a fourth of all the land that had been granted up to that time; and by the end of his term in 1940, he had distributed more than twice as much as all previous governments put together. Even so, the problem had been so great that over half of all the land was still in the hands of some 10,000 *hacendados*.

Prior to Cárdenas, the *ejido* had usually been regarded as a transitional device to provide a system of subsistence agriculture, but not a vital element in the economy of the country. This was no longer the policy. In addition to the ordinary *ejido*, large cooperative commercial farms were promoted. The Laguna cotton-growing area was an important example. Other important examples among some five hundred such cooperative farms were the sugar-producing regions in Sinaloa and Tamaulipas; the wheat and rice areas of the Yaqui Valley in Sonora; the wheat and cotton area of Mexicali; and the henequen region in Yucatan. On the whole, Cárdenas seemed to prefer a cooperative system of agriculture, something between the *ejido* and the collective type of farm. This was hindered by the peasant's preference for his own plot of land; by local *caciques* (leaders), sometimes as bad as the former *hacendado*; and by a shortage of machinery, credit, and technical skills.

Under Cárdenas, the agrarian law was changed to allow expropriation of most of the area of a large plantation. The Agrarian Department, especially devoted to *ejido* development, had been established in 1934; and the Ejido Bank was founded in 1936 to deal with the credit needs of these organizations. Colonization of new lands received increased emphasis in this period.

*Post-Cárdenas era.*[10] The Cárdenas administration had not produced a complete agrarian revolution by universal nationalization of lands — a course recommended by some experts; but it had moved rapidly enough to produce much dissension. Ávila Camacho faced this problem in a war period, and did a better job than many expected. He slowed down the rate of land distribution; gave assurance of "no nationalization" to most remaining large landholders; gave *ejidatarios* the option of deciding on whether to till their land communally or individually; and placed more emphasis on technical and auxiliary aids to agriculture. In the latter field, he increased irrigation, sought to bring increased mechanization to agriculture, promoted conservation, and made a start in the establishment of experiment stations. Mexican–United States cooperation in agriculture, as elsewhere, characterized the war period.

The Alemán era was one of continued de-emphasis on land distribution and substantial growth in other aspects of the agricultural program. Large irrigation projects were pushed, and the river basin development programs were inaugurated. Electrification was brought to many small communities, though this represented only a beginning. The production of fertilizers was increased. Campaigns against animal and crop diseases were featured. Mechanization of agriculture was promoted, as one aspect of development of commercial farming. Crop improvements paid big dividends in increased output, a program aided by cooperative projects such as that with the Rockefeller Foundation.

Despite progress made, the feeling grew that the Alemán emphasis on industrialization had produced an imbalance in the economy, that a greater emphasis was needed on agriculture. The Ruiz Cortines administration seems to recognize this problem clearly. This fact is reflected in the budget figures since 1952. The budgets for the Ministries of Agriculture and Hydraulic Resources and the Agrarian Department changed little from 1952 to 1953; but all three showed substantial increases for 1954, especially the Ministry of Agriculture. At the same time, the capital of the two agricultural banks has been substantially increased to provide expanded credit for the rural economy.

## Challenge and Problems

A century ago, Alexander von Humboldt spread the notion that Mexico was the treasure chest of the earth, and periodically the idea has been revived. This picture is dispelled by the long, hard governmental struggle for agrarian reform discussed in the preceding section. The present section seeks to clarify the manifold aspects of the agrarian problem which government has faced and sought to solve: the organization and functioning of *ejidos*, colonization, irrigation, conservation, and the application of technology to agriculture.

Two thirds of the Mexican people live on the land, a none too hospitable land that has been deteriorating for centuries. An eighth of the land is potentially arable, compared with a fifth in the United States; but two thirds of the people live from the land, compared with a fifth or less in the United States. Only a third of the land is level enough to be more or less suitable for crops, and most of the country is deficient in rainfall.

Thus, it is not surprising that Mexico was the first country in the world to attempt basic agrarian reform of considerable scope. As shown earlier, this reform has been prosecuted with much irregularity. The main systems of land-holding today are the *ejidos*, small and medium-sized private properties (with a few remaining large properties), and colonies.

*The ejidos.*[11] The term covers agrarian communities that have received and use land at least in part cooperatively. The collective *ejido* is worked jointly by its members and will be discussed later. The overwhelming majority of the *ejidos* are of the individual type, in which crop lands are worked individually and pastures and woodlands are used collectively. Thus, the bulk of the farming operations are individual in character. At present, the *ejidatarios* comprise about half of the agricultural population, have about half of all crop land, and use about one fourth of all agricultural land.

The *ejido* comprises at least twenty eligible persons, and the average community comprises from a hundred to a hundred and fifty farmers. For purposes of self-government, the administration of the *ejido* is done through a general assembly, an executive committee (*comisariado*), and a vigilance committee.

The general assembly, composed of all the members of an *ejido*, is the highest local authority. It usually meets monthly and a quorum of a simple majority of members transacts business. Failing a quorum in attendance on the first call to a meeting, those present at a second called meeting transact any business necessary. The assembly's main functions are to elect and remove the members of the executive committee; to approve or modify that committee's decisions, reports, and accounts; to rule on the use of the *ejido*'s common lands; to request that the agrarian authorities intervene in any matters involving penalties against individuals.

The executive committee consists of three members — a chairman, a secretary, and a treasurer. They have the following functions: representing the *ejido* before higher authorities; administering the collective property; supervising the division of collective land into plots; calling meetings of the general assembly monthly or on request of the vigilance committee, the Agrarian Department, the Agriculture Ministry, or the Ejido Bank; rendering accounts and making recommendations to the general assembly; and carrying out the assembly's decisions. The committee members are elected by a majority vote of the assembly and serve a term of three years. They may be removed for specified reasons of misfeasance, malfeasance, and nonfeasance.

The vigilance committee is elected by those general assembly members who were in the minority in the vote on the executive committee. Its three members see that the actions of the executive committee conform to the Agrarian Code and the decisions of the general assembly. They may be removed before the end of their three-year terms by a two-thirds vote of the assembly. In addition to other powers, they may report on pertinent matters to higher agrarian authorities and request the executive committee to call a meeting of the general assembly.

The local *ejido* is under some supervision and control from the Ministry of Agriculture, the Agrarian Department, and the Ejido Bank, all of which will be discussed in the next chapter (see pages 295–302). Such ministries as Education, Hydraulic Resources, and Public Health also have functional contacts with the *ejido*. The procedure involved in land distribution is discussed in the following chapter in connection with the Agrarian Department.

The rules under which *ejidos* use their lands include the following. Pasture and wood lands are used collectively, unless divided up as plots to cultivate. The same communal use is true of water rights. Each family may own a house lot on the town site. Cultivated lands may be tilled individually or collectively. Loss of land or crop rights results from certain specified actions. The average of an *ejidatario*'s allotment is about 45 acres, of which between 10 and 12 acres is crop land.

Only a small proportion of the *ejidos* are true collective farms in the sense of producing crops collectively as well as using other lands jointly. These collective *ejidos* are mainly concentrated in commercial farming areas and usually make extensive use of irrigation. The first to be established, and the largest, is the one in the Laguna region, which produces cotton and wheat. Other important ones are located in Sonora, Sinaloa,

Michoacán, and Chiapas. The Laguna project has served as a pattern for the others.

The Laguna project is equalitarian in structure, but it provides higher compensation for skilled and more efficient workers. One of the three members of the *ejido* executive committee is chosen to be the executive officer to handle certain matters. The vigilance committee sees that the land and investments are properly used. The general assembly elects a foreman, his assistants, a warehouseman, a herdsman, a cooperative store manager, and other officers. The foreman meets weekly with the two committees and a representative of the Ejido Bank to set a work program. The bank works through the local *ejido*'s credit society. Each member of the project carries a work card, which indicates at the end of the week his accomplishments and his compensation. More than one method of compensation is used; skill and piece rates are paid currently. At the end of the season, part of the net proceeds is divided among the members. This is done after payments are made on loans contracted with the Ejido Bank and other expenses. The Bank provides marketing and other services, as well as loans.

The *ejido* program is obviously and closely tied in with the country's political life, as discussed in Chapter 4 (see pages 52–54). First came the Cárdenas-sponsored organization of the National Peasant Confederation (1938), which was given legal status and became virtually the agrarian sector of the official party, with representation on the Party's Central Executive Committee. There is similar Confederation and Party agrarian sector organization on the state and local levels. Finally, the local *ejido*'s commissariat is both its executive committee and the government's legal representative.

*Non-ejido agriculture.* While the *ejido* has been the chief article of faith in the agrarian revolutionary movement, it is by no means predominant in agricultural production. In 1950 about half the cultivated land was held by *ejidos*. However, Whetten found that "agricultural production appears to be lower on the *ejidos* than on the private holdings," the vast majority of the former being operated on a small-unit, subsistence basis.[12] In recent years, the government has been giving more encouragement than formerly to owners of private holdings, both small and large. In the case of the large landowners, government encouragement has brought back into production some lands that had long been left idle because their owners felt uncertain about the possibility of their being expropriated.

Some progress has been made in resettlement of people from overcrowded areas through colonization. The Ruiz Cortines administration's "march to the sea" developmental program in the coastal areas promises to expand the colonization approach in such areas.

Financial and other aids furnished to *ejido* and non-*ejido* agriculture are discussed in the next chapter.

*Irrigation.*[13] A recent Minister of Hydraulic Resources has stated that Mexico is one of the least well endowed of all countries as to soils and water. In 93 per cent of Mexico's area irrigation is necessary for dependable agricultural production; and in much of the rest of the territory rainfall is sufficient, but costly drainage and sanitation works are necessary. One acre of Mexican irrigated land yields on the average three times as much as an acre of seasonal land. With the country's difficulty in feeding its rapidly growing population, the importance of irrigation is obvious. The great need for hydroelectric power causes the construction of dual-purpose dams whenever feasible.

The Indians had some small irrigation works before the Spaniards arrived. After the colonial plantations were developed, they were served by private irrigation systems. By 1910, there were some 700,000 acres under irrigation. Irrigation under the present regime started under Obregón, when an irrigation office was established in 1921. But it was five years later before a program really got under way. The laws of December 1925 and January 1926 established the National Irrigation Commission and provided for its use of federal, state, and local funds in its work. In the first period of its work, 1926–28, the Commission worked under the handicap of small budgets and the lack of complete engineering studies; but it was able to get seven large projects under way. The depression years of 1929–34 brought budget reductions; but the first projects were continued, five new ones were started, and colonization and agricultural production were started on the projects completed. The Commission's budgets were raised substantially between 1935 and 1940 under Cárdenas, and its work was given a more important status in the government's total program. During those early years, the Commission did more than build dams and irrigation works; it also promoted better agricultural practices by introducing improved strains of seeds and better breeds of livestock, promoted soil conservation practices, developed experimental farms, and did road building and drainage work.

The increased interest of the Ávila Camacho administration in irrigation was partially shown in the budget increases (in millions of pesos): 55 in 1941, 65 in 1942, 85 in 1943, 107 in 1944, 155 in 1945, and 189 in 1946. The figure for 1946 was 15 per cent of the total federal budget. The seven projects with which the Commission began its work in 1926 had increased by 1946 to fifty-four large projects and sixty small ones.

In December 1946, the Alemán administration gave irrigation increased importance by replacing the Commission with the Ministry of Hydraulic Resources. During this administration's six-year term, about 10 per cent of the federal budget was devoted to irrigation. With the year 1947 as a base, the index rose steadily to the figure of 279 per cent in 1952. During these first six years of the Ministry's existence, almost as much land was placed under irrigation as had been in the preceding twenty-one years under the Commission. It was said that only India, Russia, and the United States had opened comparable or greater areas through irrigation during that six-year period.

The program of the Ministry of Hydraulic Resources is a multiple-purpose program. It includes preparing an inventory of the country's hydraulic resources, both surface and subsoil; making an inventory of the country's soil; utilizing water for irrigation, municipal water supplies, and electric power generation; drainage of lands; flood control; and promotion of such multiple-purpose agencies as the river valley authorities. The Ministry's work has not ended with construction of irrigation works; it has also included administration of the completed projects under cultivation. This has involved the selection of settlers, promoting the better distribution of rural population, helping to organize agricultural production, and assisting in the securing of credit.

The Ministry's predecessor, the Commission, opened contracts for the purchase of irrigated lands in 1930. Regulations were tightened in 1932 to combat abuses like these: owners renting their lands and turning others into tenants; resale at speculative prices; and the enlarging of uneconomic holdings. The operation of the completed projects was under the Commission until 1935, when this function was turned over to the Agricultural Bank. By 1937 the Commission was again operating some districts where *ejidos* predominated; and in 1944 it resumed operation in all districts. In 1946, the law charged the Ministry of Agriculture with the operations. The plan calls for gradually turning over the districts to the organized users, except for important plants such as dams and some main canals, since the government has found its operation of many small districts to be uneconomic. Charges for water have gradually been raised to make the service self-supporting; and in recent years administrative councils of the users have been organized to aid in the administration of the local districts. In 1953 there were nineteen major projects under various stages of construction. It was estimated that on completion they would provide new or improved irrigation to 1,250,000 acres more than were being served in 1952.

Irrigation is still the most important function of the Ministry of Hydraulic Resources. This work is done through the Bureaus of Hydrology, Studies and Plans, Construction, Small Irrigation Works, Hydraulic Developments, and Federal Hydraulic Police. In 1951, the Ministry of Hydraulic Resources again took over from the Ministry of Agriculture the operation of the irrigation districts.

Despite commendable progress in irrigation developments, several critical points are made by the International Bank's study of Mexico. Irrigation accounted for nearly 60 per cent of the total investment in agriculture from 1939 to 1945 and 40 per cent between 1946 and 1950. But not more than 30 per cent of the agricultural production increase in recent years can be traced to irrigation. The gross irrigation investments rose from an annual average of 49 million pesos in 1939–42 to 278 million pesos in 1947–50. Production results have been slow in appearing because of the high proportion of investments going into large-scale projects, which show results more slowly. The lag has been prolonged by the spreading of funds over a large number of projects, delays in completion of auxiliary works, and some slowness to improve farming methods in the new areas. A substantial part of irrigation money has gone into the large river basin projects, which are not yet substantial producing enterprises. Small irrigation works investments declined from 12 per cent of irrigation investments in 1941–46 to 7.5 per cent in 1947–50, but in the latter period they accounted for 27 per cent of the increased irrigated areas.[14]

*Soil conservation.*[15] Acres added through irrigation and reclamation are much needed by Mexico's fast-growing population. At the same time, much more land is being lost through soil erosion and depletion — a centuries-old problem that is growing worse. One conservation authority, William Vogt, estimates that "the greater part of Mexico will be a desert within one hundred years," unless great improvements are made in land utilization.[16] Even if this estimate errs on the side of pessimism, other specialists say that 12 per cent of the plains and 30 per cent of the slope lands are now totally unproductive, while much more land has been seriously injured by erosion — one estimate says 50 per cent.

While erosion is one of the country's most serious problems, the awakening is coming late; and land hunger has brought overuse and improper use of soil resources by millions of small farmers ignorant of the ultimate costs.

The soil conservation movement did not really get under way until 1940, although Cárdenas and some others had preached its importance. In that year, a group of agronomists and others in the National Irrigation Commission began propagandizing; and in 1942 a Department of Conservation of Soils was established in the Commission. The Second Mexican Congress on the Social Sciences in 1945 dealt with conservation of resources; and later that year the Law on Soil and Water Conservation was enacted, establishing the Bureau of Soil Conservation in the National Irrigation Commission. This bureau was transferred to the Ministry of Agriculture in 1947. The organization was inspired by the Soil Conservation Service of the United States.

The Bureau, which has not been adequately financed, has been largely promotional in character, and its regulatory powers have been small. Its program in recent years has included research on erosion conditions; establishment of soil and water conservation districts where demonstrations are conducted; establishment of experiment stations; organization of farmers into local soil and water conservation boards; cooperation with the local *ejido* committees in the establishment of good practices; training of technicians; and conservation education work. Through cooperation with the Ministry of Education, conservation education courses have been developed in the public schools and in the higher normal school in Mexico City.

The Bureau functions throughout the country through soil and water conservation districts, motorized missions, and agreements with state governments and private persons. The structure of the Bureau includes three divisions: the Division of Field Operations formulates the program of action for the country; the Division of Inspections does its work in the various districts; and the Internal Management Division performs housekeeping functions.

The needs in this field are tremendous, for, as one authority says, "Mexico must prevent erosion or face disaster." A good start has been made, but budgets are still small.

*Forest conservation.*[17] About a fifth of the area of Mexico is labeled as forested, with possibly half of that area in true timber. The country has timbered areas of considerable size in some of the jungle lowlands and in higher reaches of the mountains. Unfortunately, a serious condition of deforestation has existed for some time in the heavily populated areas; and the volume of timber products harvested almost doubled in the decade following 1941.

Forest destruction has proceeded apace. With the wanton destruction of the forest protective cover, soils have eroded extensively; crop and pasture lands have suffered; irrigation systems have suffered from extensive silting; ground water levels have dropped; lakes and wells have shrunk; and the whole nation has suffered extensively. A country once heavily timbered in large areas has slipped into a forest famine.

Some farsighted Mexicans voiced a warning long ago, but they were few and not influential. A Mexican Forestry Society was organized in 1921. The first issue of its journal in 1923 contained a proposed forestry law, but public sentiment was slow in developing. President Cárdenas sounded an alarm and discouragingly reported that "The task of replacing the trees is difficult. In fact, the total work of reforestation . . . doesn't amount to 12,000 acres."

Adequate forest practices legislation was not passed until 1944, giving adequate conservation authority to the federal government. The Ministry of Agriculture was empowered to create forest reserves, protection zones, and parks, as well as to regulate cutting and grazing practices and conduct conservation campaigns. The law of 1948 strengthened the earlier statute, providing for restrictions on cutting practices and requiring replanting on both public and private lands. Since then, campaigns have been launched for reforestation, and the government is seeking forest protection through gradual prohibition of the use of charcoal for fuel. Timber-cutting concessions have been canceled and total cutting prohibitions have been decreed for several states. The present administration seems to be doing more in this direction.

But the mere passage of laws does not protect forests. For a long time, extensive illegal cutting continued, often through the use of graft. This was true even in the two million acres of the forty-three national parks, where extensive cutting, charcoal burning, and overgrazing have occurred. Funds have not been adequate to provide sufficient well-trained personnel for the adequate administration of the program. The low salaries paid personnel have not attracted enough good forestry students.

The present administration is making a real effort to protect the forest resources. The chief of the forest service has been made an assistant secretary of agriculture, and technical assistance has been provided by the UN Food and Agricultural Organization. Nurseries have been expanded to provide seedlings for planting. The nurseries have been established in various districts throughout the country.

The Agriculture Ministry's Forestry Bureau includes subdivisions devoted to technical inspection, control of exploitation, hunting, forest police, and representations in the various states. A liaison organ is the National Forest Council, of which the Minister of Agriculture is chairman. Other ministries represented are Economy, Hydraulic Resources, Communications, Education, and Finance.

*Conservation in general.*[18] One difficulty under which Mexican conservation work has labored has been the lack of a comprehensive, coordinated program of land management. The failure to recognize the interdependence of the renewable resources has produced programs that have at times been isolated, uncoordinated, and even contradictory. Improved agricultural practices have been sought without planning to meet erosion from cut-over mountain slopes. Irrigation works are subject to silting from waters off naked mountains. Hydroelectric and irrigation programs may be uncoordinated. A comprehensive program covering the various resources fields is required for the best administration; but there is no single agency concerned with producing such a unified program and seeing to its execution. Only a beginning has been made with liaison committees like the National Forest Council. Much the same comment could be made, of course, about the more advanced countries.

*Agricultural education and research.*[19] Mexico has agricultural schools that provide education on three levels — advanced, practical and special, and elementary. Three institutions correspond roughly to American agricultural colleges. The largest and most important of the three is the National School of Agriculture at Chapingo, near Mexico City. The enrollment is about four hundred, all students are supported by scholarships, and the school is under the Ministry of Agriculture. The curriculum covers seven years. The first three years include general courses, while the last four provide some specialization – in irrigation, forestry, parasitology, and agricultural industries. The degree of Agricultural Engineer is awarded. Graduates find jobs easily (mainly with the government), since there is a shortage of trained personnel. The faculty members are largely government workers who teach only part time, which has both its advantages and its disadvantages. The other two institutions are located at Juárez and Saltillo. They are smaller and less adequately supported.

The elementary course is given in rural communities, and its program of study is supposed to be adapted to the needs of the locality. The intermediate type of agricultural training is provided in some fourteen vocational schools, of which the first was opened in 1927. Each school of two hundred students or fewer has a three-year course, with each day's work divided between classroom studies and practical work in the fields, in the shops, and with livestock. The aim is to equip students to operate their own farms efficiently. The more able and ambitious students can compete for scholarships to the National School of Agriculture. The agricultural schools below the level of the National School are under the Ministry of Education.

Agricultural research is carried on at about a dozen experiment stations, where the most-publicized work has dealt with developing of improved strains of corn. Other work has dealt with beans, chile, sesame, rice, sugar cane, rubber, and various other plants.

Cooperative work was started in 1944, when the Mexican–United States Agricultural Commission started a program of research, exchange of technical experts, and promotion of increased production. But the most fruitful work has been promoted by the Rockefeller Foundation.[20] Its program began in 1941 when the Foundation, at the request of the Mexican government, sent three specialists who visited half the states of Mexico in a preliminary survey. Their report was favorable, and the Office of Special Studies was established as a semiofficial agency related to the Ministry of Agriculture in 1943. The Foundation has provided assistance in financing, direction, and operation of the program, which has been devoted largely to fundamental research into the methods and means best suited to increase the country's basic food crops. A secondary aim has been to provide a training program for selected scientists who will carry on the program in the future. The headquarters has been at the National School of Agriculture.

The work on improving strains of corn was started in 1944. By the end of 1947, the work was well enough advanced for the President to establish the Corn Commission. Taking high-yield seed which had been developed, the Commission placed such seed with selected farmers and purchased back part of their crop to be used in turn for seed. By 1950, enough seed was available to provide for about 8 per cent of the national production; and the Commission's experts estimated there would be a crop increase of about 20 per cent compared with former corn yields. Now the country is virtually self-sufficient in corn production.

Similar effective improvement work has been done on wheat, beans, and other crops. Whereas formerly wheat-growing had not been successful, today the Yaqui River area of Sonora is becoming known as the nation's breadbasket. Potato and bean production have been expanded substantially, and sorghum and soy beans are being produced commercially for the first time in Mexico. Other experiments have been made with soil management, insecticides and fungicides, fertilizers, irrigation, and labor-saving machinery.

The initial staff of the Office of Special Studies included one or two American scientists, but by 1950, the staff numbered eleven Americans and more than sixty Mexican associates. In addition to research, much valuable training has been done. Mexican trainees have been joined by agricultural workers from other Latin American countries. By the end of its first decade, the Foundation had invested more than two and a quarter million dollars in the program.

The program has involved interagency cooperation with the National School of Agriculture, the Institute of Agricultural Investigations, the Bureau of Agriculture, the Office of Agricultural Defense, the Bureau of Soil Conservation, the Bureau of Stockraising, the Wheat Commission, and the Health Ministry's Department of Nutrition.

A related program of importance has been the campaign against plant and animal diseases, carried on by the Agriculture Ministry's Bureaus of Agricultural Defense and Livestock Investigation. The joint Mexican-American battle against hoof-and-mouth disease is the best-known.

*Production.* The activities in the fields of irrigation, colonization, plant improvement, etc. have had modest but important results. The average annual rate of increase in agricultural production from 1940 to 1949 was 4.7 per cent; but better farming methods were only a minor factor. The increased yields per acre were due mainly to cultivation of better new lands and irrigation of old lands, rather than to improvements in agricultural methods. Citrus fruits and vegetables provide a growing export trade. The increases in corn and wheat production have been mentioned. The three years from 1953 to 1955 saw an unusual increase in agricultural output (nearly 50 per cent), which was due partly to adequate rains and increased irrigation and partly to a large increase in fertilizer output.[21]

### NOTES

[1] Andrés Molina Enríquez, *Los Grandes Problemas Nacionales* (1909); Whetten, *op. cit.*, Chs. 4–5; E. N. Simpson, *The Ejido, Mexico's Way Out* (1937), Chs. 1–3; Frank Tannenbaum, *The Mexican Agrarian Revolution* (1929); G. M. McBride, *The Land Systems of Mexico* (1923); Lucio Mendieta y Núñez, *El Problema Agrario de México* (1946), and "The Balance of Agrarian Reform," *Annals*, March 1940, pp. 121–31; Helen Phipps, *Some Aspects of the Agrarian Question in Mexico . . .* (1925).

[2] Simpson, *op. cit.*, Chs. 4–5; Whetten, *op. cit.*, Ch. 6; Mendieta y Núñez, "The Balance of Agrarian Reform . . . ," *loc. cit.*; Phipps, *op. cit.*, Ch. 8; Tannenbaum, *op. cit.*, *passim.*

[3] Simpson, *op. cit.*, p. 48.

[4] Tannenbaum, *op. cit.*, p. 161.

[5] See also Molina Enríquez, "El Artículo 27 . . . ," *Boletín de la Sría. de Gobernación*, September 1922, pp. 2–32; F. F. Palavicini, *Historia de la Constitución de 1917 . . .* (1938).

[6] Simpson, *op. cit.*, pp. 72–74.

[7] Simpson, *op. cit.*, Chs. 6–8; Whetten, *op. cit.*, Ch. 7; Mendieta y Núñez, *El Sistema Agrario Constitucional . . .* (1940).

[8] Simpson, *op. cit.*, p. 88.

[9] Tannenbaum, *Mexico . . .* (1), pp. 148–53; Weyl, *op. cit.*, Chs. 4–8; W. C. Townsend, *Lázaro Cárdenas . . .* (1952), Ch. 16; Mendieta y Núñez, "The Balance of Agrarian Reform," *op. cit.*, pp. 127–31.

[10] Mosk, *op. cit.*, Ch. 11; Cline, *op. cit.*, pp. 371–82; Wise, *op. cit.*, Ch. 5; U.S. Bureau of Foreign Commerce, *Investment in Mexico* (1956), Ch. 4; *Rev. Ec.*, October 1955, pp. 248–52.

[11] Simpson, *op. cit.*, *passim*; Tannenbaum, *Mexico . . .*, pp. 182–92; Whetten, *op. cit.*, Chs. 9–11; *Código Agrario . . .* (1953); W. J. Foreman, "Changing Land Tenure Patterns in Mexico," *Land Economics*, February 1950, pp. 65–77; Ana M. Gómez, "The Mexican Agrarian Program Since 1940" (M.A. thesis, Columbia University, 1948); Departamento Agrario, *Informe*; Enrique Munguia, *The Agrarian Problem in Mexico* (1937).

[12] Whetten, *op. cit.*, pp. 252, 566.

[13] Sría. de Gobernación, *Seis Años de Gobierno . . .*, 1940–46, Ch. 14; *Prob. Agr.*, April 1950, pp. 49–168; F. J. Albarelli, "The Importance of Irrigation in the

Economic Development of Mexico" (M.A. thesis, Mexico City College, 1953); Comisión Nacional de Irrigación, *La Obra de la Comisión . . . , 1934-1940* (1940); *Rev. Ec.*, September 1951, pp. 276-79; Adolfo Oriva Alba, *Política de Irrigación en México* (1945); *Hacienda y Finanzas*, April 1951, pp. 18-22; *Foreign Agriculture*, October 1946, pp. 138-46; *HA*, November 21, 1952, pp. 39-44, September 28, 1953, pp. 8-12.

[14] International Bank, *op. cit.*, pp. 23-27.

[15] Enrique Beltrán, *La Protección de la Naturaleza . . .* (1949); Beltrán, *Los Recursos Naturales . . .* (1946); *Boletín de la Sociedad Mexicana de Geografía y Estadística*, July-October 1949; Jorge Tamayo, *Geografía General de México* (1949), Ch. 25; William Vogt, *Road to Survival* (1948), pp. 168-77; Whetten, *op. cit.*, pp. 274-79; *HA*, May 23, 1955, pp. 34-36.

[16] Vogt, *op. cit.*, p. 152.

[17] Tom Gill, *Land Hunger in Mexico* (1951), pp. 43-50; Sría. de Bienes Nacionales, *Directorio . . .* (1), pp. 215-17; Whetten, *op. cit.*, pp. 276-79; M. S. Cave, *Forest Legislation in Mexico* (1945); *Rev. Ec.*, March 1952, pp. 88-91; *Mexican American Review*, June 1952, pp. 26-27; *Mexican Life*, June 1953, p. 19.

[18] Gill, *op. cit.*, pp. 6, 70-72; Tannenbaum, *op. cit.*, pp. 185-86. A 1955 law created a Council on Non-Renewable Natural Resources (*HA*, January 2, 1956, pp. 7-8).

[19] Whetten, *op. cit.*, pp. 428-29; Gonzalo Blanco, *Agriculture in Mexico* (1950), pp. 17-18; Rockefeller Foundation, *Annual Report*, 1952, pp. 172-73; *Mexican American Review*, February 1951, pp. 12, 26; *Mexican Life*, May 1953, pp. 62-63; *HA*, February 22, 1954, pp. 33-37.

[20] Blanco, *op. cit.*, pp. 19-20; R. B. Fosdick, *Story of the Rockefeller Foundation* (1952), pp. 185-88; Rockefeller Foundation, *op. cit.*, p. 167 *et seq.*, and its *Programa Agrícola Mexicano* (1950); *MV*, May 15, 1950; *Mexican American Review*, November 1947, p. 11, September 1949, p. 18, February 1951, p. 27.

[21] International Bank, *op. cit.*, pp. 27-35; *MV*, March 5, 1956, pp. 109-10.

# 21

## Government in Agriculture

As INDICATED earlier, agricultural matters are the concern of a number of different agencies, as is also the case in the United States. The principal ones are the Ministry of Agriculture and Stockraising, the Agrarian Department, the Ministry of Hydraulic Resources, the National Agricultural Credit Bank, and the National Ejido Credit Bank. Three decentralized commodity agencies are of importance: the National Commission on Coffee, the National Commission on Corn, and the National Commission on Olives. The regional commissions on the Papaloapán and the Tepalcatepec have been discussed, as has the work of the National Colonization Commission. The work of the National Commission for Struggle against Hoof-and-Mouth Disease is self-evident. The work of two agencies in the field of commerce that perform services related to the field of agriculture was discussed in an earlier chapter (see pages 213, 217) — the National Foreign Commerce Bank (which aids in the marketing of export crops) and CEIMSA (which does importing and distribution of basic foods to maintain reasonable prices at retail).

*The Ministry of Agriculture and Stockraising.*[1] The work of this Ministry dates from the law of 1853, which established the Ministry of Development, Colonization, Industry, and Commerce. After intermediate changes of name, it became the Ministry of Agriculture and Development in 1917, and the law of 1946 gave the agency its present name. The work of the Ministry is allocated to three subsecretaries, dealing with agriculture, forestry, and stockraising — in approximately that order of importance.

The Division of Agricultural Affairs is by far the largest of the three, comprising twelve bureaus, an institute, and a school. The Bureau of

Agriculture has an Office of Agricultural Development and an Office of Agronomy. The first office seeks to promote agriculture through making studies of the different agricultural areas; promotes the use of agricultural machinery; formulates plans for rural construction work and social services; does agricultural extension work; and distributes literature. Its field representatives are located in the principal agricultural centers. The Office of Agronomy watches over commerce, including seed imports; regulates the trade in fertilizers; studies fruit culture; maintains nurseries for propagation of fruit trees; and controls the export of plants.

The Bureau of Ejidal Agricultural Promotion provides the *ejidos* with weather data, soil studies, and studies of fertilizers. It provides information on drainage, irrigation, improved agricultural methods, use of machinery, livestock improvement, prevention of animal diseases, and the improvement of rural life. The Bureau of Small Property sees to the legal protection of such holdings.

The Institute of Agricultural Investigations includes the Office of Experimental Farms and the Office of Plans and Special Studies; and its work includes both experimental developments and the diffusion of findings.

The Bureau of Agricultural Defense is concerned with entomology, plant pathology, insecticides, and other means of combating plant diseases. Campaigns of importance which are being carried out include those against locusts, black flies, and rats, as well as those against diseases affecting cotton, cereals, cacao, rice, and sugar.

The Bureau of Rural Economy makes studies and recommendations on production of animal and vegetable products, including credit and marketing problems. It also makes studies of rural social problems.

The Bureau of Soil and Water Conservation performs functions dealing with prevention of erosion and efficient use of waters. The Bureau of Geography and Meteorology deals with surveying and map-making, meteorological investigations, and meteorological operations. The work of the Bureau of Planning in National Irrigation Districts is self-evident.

The second main division of the Ministry is that dealing with forest resources, which is divided into three bureaus. The Bureau for Development of Desert Zones deals with the exploration, propagation, and control of plants of economic importance that are suitable for growing in such areas. Two bureaus deal with forestry matters. The Bureau of

Conservation of Trees and Reforestation deals with forestry investigations, prevention of forest diseases, experimental work, and growing trees for planting in reforestation work. The Bureau of Forestry and Hunting also deals with conservation and protection of forests; its Department of Control deals with authorizations for forest exploitation, while the Federal Forest Police checks on enforcement. Field offices are maintained in the states, and a special office deals with forestry and hunting in the Valley of Mexico.

The third division of the Ministry deals with livestock matters. The Bureau of Livestock has departments dealing with animal production, animal health, livestock planning, and regional veterinary doctors. The Bureau of Livestock Investigations has laboratories for animal pathology, production of vaccines, control of biological products, parasitology, bromatology, artificial insemination, and diagnosis.

Certain observations on the organization and functions of the Ministry are pertinent. There are obviously problems of functional delimitation both among subdivisions of the Ministry and between the Ministry and other agencies involved in agricultural work. There is some overlapping of functions between Ministry bureaus that could well be reduced. Problems of delimitation and coordination occur with the Agrarian Department, which handles most *ejido* work, although the Ministry still maintains a Bureau of Ejidal Agricultural Promotion. The latter bureau does some work in the field of irrigation, although most of it comes under the Ministry of Hydraulic Resources.

An obvious problem is involved in relations between the Ministry and the three decentralized commodity commissions — those on corn, coffee, and olives. One suggestion is that the latter should be restricted to promotional work, leaving to the Ministry the field of scientific investigation on the commodities in question. Decentralization is said to have been effected in order to give needed emphasis, flexibility, and efficiency to the work involved.

Other functional overlapping seems to occur between the Bureau of Geography and Meteorology in the Ministry of Agriculture and the Commission on Military Cartography of the Defense Ministry. Agricultural extension and promotion work is done in several bureaus of the Agriculture Ministry, as well as in the three decentralized commissions and in the cultural missions and the practical schools of agriculture under the Ministry of Public Education.

Similar problems of overlapping and coordination, of course, are found in all countries.

*The Agrarian Department.*[2] The principal agency for administering the law regarding the creation, expansion, development, and promotion of the *ejidos* is the Agrarian Department. The importance of the work is attested by the fact that about half the cultivated land is farmed by members of ejidal communities. In 1910, an Agrarian Bureau was established as a division of the Ministry of Agriculture. In 1917, the Agrarian Bureau was merged with the National Agrarian Commission. In 1934, the National Agrarian Commission was replaced with the present Agrarian Department. The chief of the Department is named by the President and is directly responsible to him.

The Agrarian Department applies the provisions of the constitutional Article 27 and the agrarian laws regarding the dotation and restitution of lands and waters to the eligible rural population groups; participates in the subdivision of *ejidos*; creates new centers of agrarian population; makes censuses of ejidal properties, in cooperation with the Ministry of Agriculture; and deals with questions of *ejido* boundaries and land titles.

Three types of land grants are provided for by the Agrarian Code — restitution, dotation, and amplification. The first restores to a community lands formerly belonging to it. The second is an outright grant, without reference to any prior ownership. The third is a form of the second and applies when a previous grant has proved insufficient for a community's needs. Dotation has for some time been the most important of the three and has been responsible for at least three fourths of the land granted.

Under the Code, the agrarian community needing land may seek it in parcels no more than seven kilometers (four and a third miles) from the center of the community. At first acreage allocations were too low under the grants. In 1947, individual grant limits were set at 24.7 acres of humid or irrigated land and 49.4 acres of land dependent upon seasonal rainfall; but the actual grants are often much less and are thus still inadequate. In the taking of large estates for such purposes, certain minimum areas are exempt (*inafectabilidad*), ranging from 247 acres of irrigated land to several thousand acres of land that is arid or is used for the cultivation of certain favored crops.

The process of land acquisition starts when the representatives of the local community send their request for the grant to the governor of the state. His favorable decision puts the community in temporary possession of the land and sends the application to the Agrarian Department, which in turn makes its recommendation to the Agrarian Advisory Board. Affected landowners may present their complaints before the Agrarian Department before the Board issues its opinion. The Board in turn makes a recommendation to the President, who makes the final decision. The Board also advises the Agrarian Department on carrying out awards that have been made. Thus, the Board is advisory to the executive as the mixed agrarian commissions are advisory bodies to aid the state governors in their preliminary decisions.

The Agrarian Department has nine subdivisions. The Bureau of Agrarian Rights formulates the decrees and decisions for presidential approval; provides for their execution; and issues and records the land titles. The Bureau of Lands and Waters makes the land grants; sees to changes in the ejidal regime; sees to the division of ejidal lands; and creates new centers of population. The Bureau of Agrarian Ejidal Organization intervenes in the election and changes of status of ejidal authorities and sees to their compliance with the law and regulations. The Bureau of Agrarian Exemption deals with proposed exemptions from expropriation actions. Subdivisions performing staff or auxiliary functions are the Department of Planning, the Bureau of Administration, the Legal Department, the Department of Inspection, Promotion, and Complaints, and the Office of Control and Efficiency. The agrarian delegations, or field agents, are located in the principal areas of the country.

At times, there has been considerable complaint about the functioning of the Agrarian Department. These points have included such matters as speed of proceedings and coordination of actions with those of other agencies dealing with irrigation, education, etc.

*Agricultural credit: history.*[3] One of Mexican agriculture's greatest needs has always been adequate credit – plus technical assistance. A small beginning was made in 1908, when an Office of Loans was organized. By 1914 it was bankrupt, the victim of official corruption. A similar experience resulted from such an effort made in 1916. In 1922–23, the Bureau of Agricultural Cooperation of the Ministry of Agriculture organized several cooperative societies to which it extended credits in the form of machinery, implements, and cash. Small amounts of credit were extended by the National Agrarian Commission after

1923, when the Bureau of Agricultural Cooperation was merged with it.

In 1926, the National Agricultural Credit Bank was established to make loans to individuals, issue bonds, guarantee securities issued by agricultural credit institutions, and otherwise aid small farmers and *ejidatarios* through promoting cooperative credit institutions. In the same year, the Law of Ejido Banks established a group of *ejido* banks, separate from the above-named bank, which could operate only with their associated cooperative societies. From the start, these two systems of credit had only limited success. The National Bank's work was limited by its small capital; and its aid went more to private individuals than to *ejidatarios* and other small farmers organized in societies. "Political" loans and poor lending judgment were further limitations on the bank's success. Similar shortcomings — especially small funds — attended the program of the Ejido Banks.

The Law of Agricultural Credit of 1931 eliminated the Ejido Banks; reorganized and sought to strengthen the National Agricultural Credit Bank; and provided for the establishment of regional banks to do business only with bona fide local credit societies. By 1933, seven regional banks and a system of agricultural credit warehouses were operating. Shortage of capital remained a big difficulty.

The Law of Agricultural Credit of 1934 was intended to help mainly the *ejidatarios,* but it opened the door to limited loans to individual farmers. Success up to that time was very limited. Despite much talk about the importance of agricultural credit, less than forty thousand *ejidatarios* out of a million or more in the country were beneficiaries of such credit.

The National Bank of Ejido Credit was established in 1936 to supply credit to *ejidatarios*; and the National Agricultural Bank was to restrict its loans thereafter to non-*ejido* agriculture. The potential role of the Ejido Bank is important, because *ejido* lands cannot be mortgaged; therefore, this agency is almost the only source of credit for such farmers. Despite improvements in recent years, the Ejido Bank does not deal with more than about half of the organized *ejidos*, while the National Agricultural Bank serves only a minority of the independent farmers. Much of the credit obtained by independent farmers comes from individual moneylenders charging exorbitant rates of interest.

The amount of crop loans granted annually by the two agricultural banks plus the National Foreign Trade Bank rose from 58 million pesos in 1939 to 338 million pesos in 1950; but this remained at only about 5 per cent of the value of the production during that period. The most important loan development has been in the field of medium-term investment loans by the public banks. The annual average of these loans rose from 10 to 20 million pesos in 1939–46 to 195 million pesos in 1950. This increase had an important effect on production because it was largely concentrated on irrigation, land-clearing, and farm machinery. The two agricultural banks account for over 90 per cent of the credit granted by the three banks. The loans of the Ejido Bank (in millions of pesos) rose from 52.6 in 1939 to 228.6 in 1950. The loans of the National Agricultural Bank rose from 5.1 to 90 millions. The provision of credit is still small compared with the needs, but the government provided substantial expansion of agricultural credit in 1954.

*The Ejido Bank.*[4] The Bank is under the direction of a board of nine members and six alternates, appointed for four-year terms. The board members are related to the three kinds of stock comprising the Bank's capital. Series A stock, comprising the great bulk, is held by the government. Series B may be subscribed by the states, and Series C by ejidal credit societies. The heads of the Ministry of Agriculture and the Agrarian Department are among the government members of the board by virtue of their positions. For administration in the field, the Bank has an average of one branch per state; and the area served by each branch office is divided into several zones.

The Bank is much more than a moneylending institution. It also stores and sells the peasants' crops; maintains irrigation canals; builds power plants; buys machinery and gives instruction in its use; experiments with soils, animals, and crops; combats plant and animal diseases; promotes cooperatives; helps plan production on collective *ejidos*; and does other things to promote the *ejido* program.

To do these things, the Bank is divided into ten departments and other offices, under the general manager and the assistant general manager. The Department of Credit makes studies of the various areas, in the process of administering the Bank's credit operations. The Technical Department makes the plans for construction and conservation of buildings and other installations, as well as establishing small irrigation works. The Trust Department handles such matters for both the government and the Societies of Ejidal Credit. The Agricultural Services Department has charge of the centers for maintenance of machinery and equipment used on *ejidos*. The Forestry Office is concerned with the considerable amount of *ejido* property that is timberland. Other divisions are the Treasury, the Accounting Office, the Legal Department, and the Administrative Department. One or more field offices are located in each state.

Loans are of the seasonal, intermediate-term, and long-term types. The seasonal loans comprise the bulk of all credit, lasting up to eighteen months and serving to aid in the planting, care, and harvest of the crop. Intermediate-term loans are for the purchase of livestock, equipment, and certain slow-maturing crops. Long-term loans (up to thirty years) are for making permanent improvements. In the earlier years, delinquencies were high, but collections have been much better in recent years.

Loans have been distributed unevenly, both as to area and type of *ejido*. The northern part of the country and the larger collective *ejidos* have benefited most, on the whole, and the highest ranking crops in terms of areas benefited have been corn, wheat, cotton, and beans. The Bank deals with the associations of *ejidatarios* rather than with individuals. Such a society is limited to the local *ejido*, and the *ejido* usually initiates its organization. Each local society must have as members a majority of the local *ejidatarios*, with a minimum of fifteen members. The society's organization and functioning parallel those of the *ejido* organization, often using the same officers.

*The National Agricultural Credit Bank.*[5] The origin and development of the National Agricultural Credit Bank have been described above. Originally, it was intended to serve both *ejidatarios* and individual farmers. But since the establishment of the Ejido Bank, the older institution has dealt with individual farmers and non-*ejido* credit societies, with the bulk of its loans being made to societies. Like the Ejido Bank, it grants loans of the following types: short-term; production (up to eighteen months); land and equipment (up to eight years); and land purchases and improvements (up to thirty years). In recent years, the Bank has had a policy of encouraging loans for purchase of machinery and livestock and for land improvements, feeling that other sources of credit are least adequate in this field. The crop receiving the greatest amount in loans from the Bank has been cotton, followed by corn, wheat, and rice.

The clients of the Bank in recent years have been as follows: 1,125 local credit societies with 34,691 members in 1946, and 1,500 societies with 46,683 members in 1951. In the earlier year, most of the societies and members were "in liquidation" or "in suspension" rather than in "operation."

The administrative organization is similar to that of the Ejidal Bank, headed by a Council of Administration representing the three types of stockholders. The National Agricultural Credit Bank, however, is more minutely subdivided for administrative purposes. The principal divisions are the Bureaus of Accounting, Credit, and Law, and the Departments of Commercial Banking and Administration. As in the case of the Ejido Bank, the stock is in Series A, B, and C, with the government providing more than nine tenths of the money (Series A).

*A balance sheet.* Despite recent crop increases and planned agricultural expansion, agriculture is still one of the government's chief unsolved problems. The most basic problem is shortage of good land. Less than half of the families desiring land have been able to get it; and the average allotment has been too small to provide the farmer with an adequate living.

One attempted solution has been through guiding the economy toward full-scale industrialization, thus indirectly aiding agriculture through raising the level of the whole economy. The present administration seems to have recognized the unwisdom of a one-sided industrialization, and moved toward a middle course. The desirability of a balanced development is emphasized by Mosk.[6] The opposite goal is apparently favored by those like Tannenbaum who see the solution in a relatively self-sufficient agrarian economy, with industry only a supplement to the economy.[7]

Viewing the agrarian part of the economy by itself, a few would like to see a return of the old *hacienda* system. Some others, like Eyler Simpson, feel that the government should have socialized all the lands; have all the agricultural lands exploited cooperatively by the farming communities; and have thoroughgoing national planning and effective centralized control of agriculture.[8] The Cárdenas administration moved in that direction; but the next two administrations reversed the trend and "retreated" toward industrialization.

Since 1952, a sporadic debate about the *ejidos* has erupted. Some of the old-time agrarian leaders have recently proclaimed the failure of the *ejido* program and urged a general transfer of such holdings to individual small holders. Soto y Gama, a pioneer agrarian leader, is a prominent proponent of the change; while ex-President Portes Gil as strongly defends the *ejido* system. *Ejido* supporters tend to feel that shortcomings would be corrected through the provision of adequate education, credit, technical services, and resettlement programs.[9]

Whatever the philosophy of the ultimate goal, most observers recognize both strengths and weaknesses in the agrarian regime today. The democratic, social values achieved in some of the cooperative agrarian communities are recognized; but the shortcomings are numerous. The small size and poverty of a large proportion of the farm units have been mentioned. Charges of inefficiency and other shortcomings have been more frequent since 1952. Cases of corruption and bureaucratic ineptitude have been noted by Mexican and foreign authorities.[10]

Despite inadequate funds and other shortcomings, the two banks (and especially the Ejido Bank) have tried to promote better farming practices and responsibility on the part of the farmers. The nonbanking activities of the Ejido Bank have caused it to be condemned by some writers for "welfare" activities and criticized by others for not doing more along that line. Loans have tended to concentrate in the larger and richer farm units, where some say private credit could be obtained. And a frequent criticism is the dual organization of farm credit work in the two banks.[11]

One of the country's great needs is an adequate agricultural extension service. Some of this type of work has been done by the Ejido Bank, the Education Ministry's Cultural Missions, and other agencies; but a single adequate program is needed.[12]

Minimum price supports by the government have been of aid to the farmer recently; and increased capital has recently been provided for the two banks. A joint program of crop insurance is being started by private enterprise and government.[13] In addition, an improved development program is being sought by the present administration through improved coordination of the various agencies' programs by establishment of the Council on Development and Coordination of National Production, an advisory body, and by other measures.

NOTES

[1] Sría. de Bienes Nacionales, *Directorio* . . . (1), pp. 203–37; Ramón Fernández y Fernández, "La Secretaría de Agricultura y Ganadería," *Rev. Ec.*, October 1951, pp. 297 *et seq.*; Sría. de Agricultura . . . , *Plan de Movilización Agrícola* . . . (1945); Sría. de Agricultura . . . , *Resumen de Informe* . . . , *1951–52* (1952).

[2] *Código Agrario*; Mendieta y Núñez, *El Sistema Agrario* . . . (1940), Chs. 11, 17; Mijares Palencio, *op. cit.*, Ch. 11; Sría. de Bienes Nacionales, *Directorio* . . . (1), pp. 465–78; Departamento Agrario, *Informe*; Foreman, *op. cit.*; Gómez, *op. cit.*, pp. 18–25; Mendieta y Núñez, *El Problema Agrario* . . . (1946); Gontrán Noble, *La Reforma Agraria en México* (1949).

[3] Simpson, *op. cit.*, Chs. 21–22; Tannenbaum, *Mexico* . . . , pp. 188–89; *Prob. Agr.*, July–September 1952, pp. 303–16; Raul Lemus García, *El Crédito Agrícola* . . . (1949); Mendieta y Núñez, *El Crédito Agrario en México* (1933); Noble, *Crédito Agrícola en México* (1949); International Bank, *op. cit.*, pp. 20–22, 214.

[4] Simpson, *op. cit.*, Chs. 21–22; Whetten, *op. cit.*, pp. 191–202; Weyl, *op. cit.*, pp. 192–97; Sría. de Bienes Nacionales, *Directorio* . . . (2), pp. 181–93; Banco Nacional de Crédito Ejidal, *Informe*; Noble, *Crédito Agrícola* . . . ; *Mexican Life*, August 1950, pp. 58 *et seq.*

[5] *Directorio* . . . (2), pp. 165–80; Banco Nacional de Crédito Agrícola, *Informe*; Gómez, *op. cit.*, pp. 49–52; Noble, *op. cit.*; Sría. de Agricultura, *Resumen de Informe* . . . ; *Foreign Agriculture*, February 1943, pp. 27–38.

[6] Mosk, *op. cit.*, p. 307.

[7] Tannenbaum, *op. cit.*, Chs. 11–13. For the opposite viewpoint see Manuel Germán Parra, *La Industrialización de México* (1954).

[8] Simpson, *op. cit.*, Ch. 27.

[9] New York *Times*, March 10, 1954; *HA*, February 22, 1954, p. 4, March 8, 1954, p. 9; *HAR*, February (March) 1953, p. 9, and February (March) 1954, p. 10. For a recent *ejido* study, see H. F. Infield and K. Freier, *People in Ejidos* (1954). In 1948, Whetten (*op. cit.*, pp. 144–51) designated nine shortcomings in the program. García Treviño, *op. cit.*, Ch. 6, gives a detailed and highly critical evaluation.

[10] Mendieta y Núñez, "The Balance of Agrarian Reform," *Annals*, March 1940, pp. 128–29; *CSM*, February 1, 1953.

[11] Lemus García, *op. cit.*; *Rev. Ec.*, November 1943, pp. 29–31.

[12] Whetten, *op. cit.*, pp. 280–81.

[13] *HA*, January 2, 1956, p. 39; *HAR*, August (September) 1955, p. 354.

# PART VI

# Social Services

# 22

## Government and Labor

L_ABOR relations are important in the Mexican governmental scene because of the extensive protection the law gives to labor and the active and influential role that organized labor has played in Mexican political life (see Chapter 4). From a status of repression before the Revolution of 1910, labor soon rose to a position of privilege and protection. In general, governments have supported labor, and labor has been a pillar of support for governments.

*Early years.*[1] Mexico's backward industrial development in the nineteenth century gave little incentive to the development of an organized labor movement. One of the few unions of that period was the Grand Circle of Workers, founded in 1876, a period of considerable labor unrest and several strikes. Labor activity increased until 1884, when it entered a period of suppression corresponding roughly with the reign of Díaz. The Penal Code punished organization, strikes, and even petitions.

In 1906, the Circle of Free Workers was formed; and this organization promoted textile strikes for the eight-hour day and minimum wages, but these strikes were put down harshly. Between 1907 and 1910, other unions appeared, notably the linotypists. A number of them gave effective support to Madero in his overthrow of the Díaz regime, though Madero's ideas on labor matters were very mild by subsequent standards. The atmosphere of the new regime was favorable to labor organization, and the anarcho-syndicalist doctrine had much support in labor circles. The Madero government established a Department of Labor; and its settlement of a textile dispute in 1912 included provisions that foreshadowed parts of the 1917 Constitution's Article 123 (labor's Magna Charta). At the time of its overthrow, the Madero government was formulating substantial proposals for legislation.

The next important step came in 1915. The Carranza forces had their backs to the wall and sought support from labor and farmers. The agrarian decree was issued to gain the peasants' support, while Obregón got government support from the workers in return for a decree supporting labor. He formed a personal alliance with the leaders of the Casa del Obrero Mundial (House of the Workers of the World), then the country's strongest union group, in return for a promise of government support in unionization and in labor disputes. Six labor battalions were provided for Carranza's army, and the Casa organized branches in various parts of the country. This labor support may well have been what kept the government in power.

When the 1916–17 Constitutional Convention met to frame a new fundamental charter, the labor-political alliance paid off, despite Carranza's growing hostility to organized labor. The convention's "radical" forces, led by Generals Obregón and Múgica, gave both peasants and workers their "bills of rights" — Articles 27 and 123. Even though Mexico had only about 30,000 unionized workers, they were given privileged legal status. Though it was the world's most advanced charter of labor rights at the time, its provisions were not self-executing; and enforceable labor legislation was slow in coming.

In 1918, dissident elements of the Casa del Obrero Mundial founded the first really national federation of unions — the Regional Confederation of Mexican Workers, or CROM — under the leadership of Luis Morones. The new organization abandoned syndicalism and espoused craft unionism of the A.F.L. type, while accepting the doctrines of class conflict, ultimate abolition of private property, and use of both economic and political action. Morones soon became the czar of organized labor, and in 1919 the leadership organized the Mexican Labor Party to promote Obregón's candidacy for the presidency.

*Recent decades.* During the administration of Obregón and the first part of Calles' regime — from about 1920 to 1926 — labor made considerable progress in terms of some legislation, rapidly growing membership, and political power. Its strength rose from seven thousand to a claimed membership of over two million in 1927. Preferred status for labor came with Morones in the Calles cabinet, but "leaderism" produced an iron domination over union members and many excesses. Independent unions were smashed, and a labor dictatorship ruled most of the field.

The rapid rise of the CROM was matched by its speedy disintegration. About 1926, Calles cooled toward labor, and Morones was out of the cabinet. President Portes Gil crushed the Morones-CROM labor dictatorship, favoring the independent and Communist unions in order to gain that end. As President, however, he did seek fuller enforcement of the provisions of Article 123 by getting the first full-scale labor code enacted in 1931. The present labor code is an expanded and revised version of that document.

As the depression deepened and left-wing pressure grew, anti-Morones forces under the leadership of Lombardo Toledano organized the General Confederation of Workers and Peasants (CGOC) in 1932, which united most of the former CROM unions, certain other established groups, and a number of new unions. It sought revision of the labor laws, opposed compulsory arbitration of disputes, and demanded respect for the right to strike.

The power and influence of labor mushroomed under President Cárdenas, because he had a strong belief in the justice of labor's cause and because he regarded a strong labor movement as one essential support for a progressive government. "The various selfish groups in the country," he said, "will offer resistance to radical legislation . . . and only when organized are the workers in a position to force me, or any other citizen who is in power, to satisfy the needs of the people."[2] Not regarding the state as a balance wheel between conflicting classes, he regarded himself in a sense as an organizer of labor and farmer groups. While repudiating the soviet system, Cárdenas' program looked toward eventual worker control of the important industries. He at times intervened directly to bring together contending union groups. In one such move, his support helped bring about the establishment of the Confederation of Mexican Workers (the CTM).

Lombardo Toledano, the organizer of the CTM, had served his apprenticeship in the CROM and then in the CGOC. With the support of the government, the CTM grew rapidly, having over a million members by 1940. The new organization abandoned craft unionism for industrial organization, with its principal centers of strength located in the railroad, mining, electrical, and petroleum unions. It was composed of national industrial unions and local federations of unions, and it maintained working relations with important non-member unions. Both the political and the economic power of the organization increased with its membership; and for some time its class-struggle philosophy was directed by pro-Communist leadership. Lombardo Toledano, the CTM's leading light, also organized and headed the Confederation of Latin American Workers. In Mexico, the CTM profited by native collectivist trends, as well as by a widespread nationalism directed against foreign firms in Mexico.

Government support for labor decreased greatly when the Ávila Camacho administration swung the pendulum at least as far back as the center. This fact and the pro-Communist policies of the leadership brought large drops in membership by 1942. Later, under more conservative leadership, the CTM regained some of its strength; and today it probably speaks for a majority of the organized workers in a non-agricultural labor force of more than three million. The Alemán and Ruiz Cortines administrations have continued a friendly but moderate relationship with organized labor, without giving preponderant support to any one group.

The role of labor unions in the field of government employment was discussed in Chapter 9. Such unions have a separate federation of their own, being forbidden to join a general labor federation.

*Laws before 1917.*[3] Labor legislation, aside from the repressive variety, was of little significance before the Revolution, although some statutes dealt with labor matters as early as the 1860s. In 1904, the state of Mexico passed a law dealing with occupational risks, and Nuevo León did likewise in 1906. Madero established a Department of Labor, but its powers and budget were very limited. It could act in a labor dispute if requested to do so by both parties to the dispute. In 1912 the Department succeeded in establishing a ten-hour day, wage increases, and improved working conditions in the textile industry; but later it served mainly as a statistical office. Between 1914 and 1916, labor laws were passed in four states: Jalisco, Veracruz, Yucatán, and Coahuila. Carranza's labor decree of 1915 has been mentioned above.

Carranza made promises to labor in consolidating his power; but he feared the growing power of labor and actually did little to improve the lot of the workers. Carranza wanted to give the federal government exclusive power over labor matters; but labor, fearful of hostile treatment, wanted the power delegated to the states at first.

Labor as such had little strength in the Constitutional Convention, and it was not favored in the Carranza draft for the new document; but favorable forces were at work in the Convention. Generals Obregón and Múgica were sympathetic. Little is known in detail of committee deliberations on Article 123 except that they were not lengthy; nor were the discussions of the final proposal on the floor of the convention very long. But the support of the two generals and their followers was sufficient to ensure success for the most advanced labor text then in existence. It is likely that Article 123 was in considerable degree an "anti-foreign" measure, since most of the large employers were foreign owners.

*Article 123.*[4] Just as Article 27 elaborated a Mexican charter on property rights, so Article 123 established a far-ranging charter of rights for labor. It included advanced provisions about working hours, wages, working conditions, health and accident matters, collective bargaining, and provisions about related social services. Though only half as long as Article 27, Article 123 went into considerable detail about protections for labor, since its authors seemed to fear leaving anything except details to the hands of future (and possibly hostile) legislative bodies.

The numerous provisions of Article 123's thirty-one main subdivisions can be considered under about a dozen larger categories. Many of these points remained for years as goals rather than achievements, since the constitutional provisions are not self-executing and the first general labor code to enforce them was not put into effect until 1931.

The Congress is charged with legislating regarding urban labor of all kinds engaged in the important fields of activity; and the states are charged with aiding the federal government by enforcement of federal laws within their areas.

The article made the following principal provisions.

1. Hours of work: The maximum work day was set at eight hours, while night work was limited to seven hours. Six hours was to be the work day for persons from ages twelve to sixteen. Women and persons under sixteen were not to do overtime work, and for others it was to be limited to three hours daily. One day of rest was to follow the six-day work week.

2. Conditions of work: Unhealthful and dangerous work were forbidden to women and persons under sixteen, as was industrial night work and work in commercial establishments after 10 P.M. Children under twelve were not allowed to work.

3. General protections: The following conditions are not valid in a labor contract: an excessive day's work; substandard wages; wage payments less frequent than weekly; payments involving obligation to buy at company stores; renunciation of occupational accident or illness indemnities; and renunciation of any other labor right.

4. Compensation: Minimum compensation is what is regarded as sufficient in a particular region to satisfy the normal needs of life, education, and "honest pleasures" of a family. Profit-sharing is also envisaged. Equal pay is decreed for equal work, without regard to sex or nationality. Minimum wages are to be set in each community by a local committee, subordinate to the board of conciliation and arbitration located in each state. Overtime work shall be granted double pay. Working women are to receive full rest with pay for a month following childbirth.

5. Protections for compensation: The minimum wage is exempt from attachment or discount. Wages must be paid in legal tender, not by promissory notes, merchandise, or other means. Wages are a first charge against the assets of a firm that ceases to function. Only the worker, not members of his family, is responsible for obligations contracted. Wages may not be withheld in payment of fines. And employment placement services, whether public or private, shall be free.

6. Employers' obligations: Employers are granted the right to organize associations in behalf of their own interests; but the specification of their obligations is quite detailed. These points are in addition to the items mentioned above. Under certain circumstances, employers are required to furnish housing, schools, hospitals, and other services. They are responsible for compensation in cases of industrial accidents and diseases which are work-connected; and they are responsible for maintaining safe and hygienic conditions of work. Lockouts are forbidden except when necessitated by excessive production and approved by the conciliation and arbitration board. An employer's refusal to submit a labor-management dispute to arbitration or to abide by an arbitration board's decision brings a penalty of three months' wages to the employees involved. A similar penalty results from unjustified dismissal of an employee.

7. Employees' rights: In addition to obligations of employers and rights of workers mentioned above, employees have the rights of vocational organization, resort to the strike, and use of the conciliation and

arbitration machinery for settlement of disputes. Workers may form unions and make proper use of the strike. Such proper use is in seeking to attain an "equilibrium among the various factors of production, harmonizing the rights of labor with those of capital." Ten days' strike notice is required in the public services. Strikes are illegal only when the majority of the strikers engage in violence against persons or property. Refusal of workers to submit to arbitration or to carrying out an arbitral decision will result in termination of the labor contract.

8. Machinery: Boards of conciliation and arbitration are provided for settlement of disputes between capital and labor. The boards are composed of an equal number of members representing workers, employers, and government.

*Regulatory legislation.*[5] For some time, the federal government failed to offer much leadership in labor legislation, although many of the most important industries were under its jurisdiction. No general federal labor law was enacted until the Code of 1931. All the states had set up some kind of labor board, but there was little uniformity among these bodies as to their powers and functions. Until the mid-twenties the Supreme Court held that the labor boards were not true courts and therefore had no power to enforce their decisions. Thereafter, the boards were regarded as having powers of final decision and as having jurisdiction over both individual and collective contracts of labor and over both terminated and operating contracts. However, other weakness prevented their functioning adequately in that period. By 1929, two thirds of the states had passed comprehensive labor laws; but they differed widely from state to state, varying with the attitudes of state officials and the political power wielded by labor. The demand for change was so strong that in 1929 Article 123 was amended to give the federal government the exclusive power to legislate in labor matters. This amendment sought to unify the country's labor legislation and to eliminate the confusion that had often prevailed in the past between the legal dispositions and administrative practices of different states.

Mexico's Federal Law of Labor was enacted in 1931; and, with subsequent amendments, it is the code still in force. Its principal features deal with aspects of the labor contract, unions, occupational risks, the labor authorities of government, and the rights and duties of labor and management in collective bargaining.

Mexican legislation requires employers to employ at least 90 per cent

Mexicans in each class of skilled and unskilled labor. The population law of 1936 strictly limits the practice of the liberal professions by aliens. And the restrictions on employment of foreigners in higher and confidential positions have varied, but in general they have been rather rigorous.

In 1951 and 1952 an important change in the law was urged by a group of labor congressmen. The proposal would allow the workmen to participate in the company's profits. It was strongly opposed by the employers' organizations and made little headway.

## The Federal Labor Law

Since the government has favored labor with extensive protective measures, the organized workers have usually been strong supporters of the regime in power. And since the employing groups have often regarded the law and its administration as being partial to labor, the employers have often been dissatisfied with the regime of labor-management relations. However, management is given certain important protections; and more than two decades of experience have produced a fairly stable system of worker-employer relations.

*General provisions.* Employer-employee relations are governed by the Federal Labor Law of 1931 as amended, which is based on constitutional Article 123. The Ministry of Labor and its subordinate boards administer the law regarding lines of work more suitable to national than to state control — mining, oil, transportation, textiles, electricity, fishing, merchant marine, etc. — as well as disputes involving workers in more than one state. The states apply the federal law to lesser and local employments.

The law deals with labor matters in general, and also contains sections that deal with such specific sectors of the economy as agriculture, domestic work, maritime work, and railroads. (Government workers come under a separate law, discussed on pp. 128–31.) Special sections deal with unions and employer organizations, labor contracts, occupational risks, strikes, collective bargaining, and the labor agencies of government.[6]

Title 1 of the law deals with definitions and other general dispositions. Title 2 deals in great detail with the labor contract, which may be an individual contract (Ch. 1) or a collective one (Ch. 2).[7] The individual contract may be written or verbal, and its existence is presumed between the one providing his service and the one receiving it. Persons sixteen years of age and older may be parties to a labor contract, while those between twelve and sixteen may be parties through their parents or legal representatives. A number of bad labor conditions which do not obligate the worker are listed (Art. 22), and these protections reiterate those of Article 123 of the Constitution. These include excessive hours of work, dangerous and unhealthful conditions, renunciation of a worker's rights, unequal pay for equal work, substandard wages, and bad working conditions for women and children.

The individual written contract includes the name, nationality, sex, age, and domicile of the worker; specification of the service to be rendered; duration of the contract; working hours; compensation; etc. Certain specified lines of work may be covered by a verbal contract. The absence of a written contract when specified by law, or of any of its required features, does not deprive the worker of any rights, since the fault is imputed to the employer. The labor contract may be in force for a fixed period, for an indefinite time, or until a task is completed. Labor contracts of workers in agriculture, domestic service, railways, maritime pursuits, and small industries are governed both by the general provisions of the law and by special sections devoted to those fields, as will be discussed below.

The collective contract of labor is an agreement between one or more unions and one or more employers. Every employer who hires workmen belonging to a union is required, on their request, to negotiate a collective contract. If there is more than one union represented among the same kind of employees, the employer must sign with the one representing the greatest number of workers; and the conditions in the contract cannot be less favorable than those contained in contracts then in force with the firm. When unions representing several different occupations have employees working for a firm, the collective contract may cover all or separate contracts may cover each group, whichever is mutually agreeable.

The collective contract is signed in triplicate, with a copy going to each of the parties and a copy to the appropriate Board of Conciliation and Arbitration. In the contract are fixed the wage rates, hours of work, the intensity and quality of the work, rest periods and vacations, and other appropriate matters. The conditions of the contract extend even to non-union members employed by the firm, except for confidential and similar employees. Contracts may, and usually do, include a clause whereby the employer must hire only union members. But this or any other clause favoring union members may not work to the disadvantage of other workers already employed at the time of signing the contract.

The contract may be for a fixed period, for an indefinite time, or for the duration of a task. In any case, it is reviewable every two years at the request of either party, made at least sixty days before completion of the contract term. If agreement is not reached within this period, the matter is submitted to the proper Board of Conciliation and Arbitration. During its review, the contract remains in force. The contract may be terminated in several ways: by mutual consent of the parties; for reasons stipulated in the contract; by judicial liquidation, under some circumstances; by completion of the work called for; by total closing of the enterprise; and by other factors making fulfillment impossible.

The collective contract is obligatory in certain circumstances. When two thirds of the employers and unionized workers in a branch of industry in a certain region desire it, the President may make the terms of the contract obligatory for all. Such a solicitude for an obligatory collective contract is taken to the Minister of Labor, who publishes it in the *Diario Oficial*. Fifteen days are allowed for complaints by any interested parties before the decree is made final, to be in force for not more than two years.

*The contract: hours and wages.* As in Article 123, hours of work are set at the regular maximum of eight for daytime and seven for night work, with exceptions made for hotels, hospitals, and some other establishments. Overtime work is allowed, but not exceeding three hours. The six-hour day is established for persons aged twelve to sixteen. Overtime, night work, and dangerous and unhealthful work are forbidden for women and persons under sixteen. Rest days are covered in the law. One day of rest for each six of work is prescribed; and four rest holidays are spread throughout the year. Annual vacations are also prescribed, as follows: at least four working days the first year and at least six working days after two years. The exact amount is fixed in the contract.

Wages are fixed by the contract, but must be at least up to the minimum fixed for each area according to law; and there shall be equal pay for equal work. Wage payments are made at least weekly in legal tender. Overtime work receives double pay. The minimum wage is the amount considered sufficient in each region to satisfy the normal necessities of life for the worker and his family, including education and recreation. Minimum wages are set for agricultural work as well as urban.

A special chapter on women and young workers forbids work for the latter in liquor establishments and in dangerous and unhealthful occupations. The same is forbidden for women, and dangerous and unhealthful jobs are enumerated. Heavy work is forbidden for women for three months before childbirth, and leave with pay is granted for eight days before the event and one month afterward. Establishments employing more than fifty women are to maintain nurseries.

*The contract: regulations and obligations.* The Internal Work Rules are an elaboration on the provisions of the contract. Among other matters, these rules cover working hours, rest periods, safety and first-aid rules, dangerous and unhealthful work forbidden for women and young people, medical examinations, and disciplinary matters. The employer files a copy of the document with the proper Board of Conciliation and Arbitration.

The employer's obligations are stated in some detail (Internal Work Rules, Ch. 8). Among other things, he must give employment preference to Mexicans, to capable former employees, and to union members; make prompt payment of wages; provide housing under certain circumstances; maintain suitable places of work and equipment; maintain good safety standards and pay indemnities for injuries and occupational ills; maintain schools, when such are not otherwise available; deduct union dues from wages; and provide first-aid services. Employers are forbidden to require workers to purchase from a company store; to use persuasion against union membership or the use of the vote; to carry on political or religious propaganda within the establishment; to appear at work under the influence of alcohol or drugs; and to use a "black list" against employees.

The obligations of the workers include (Ch. 9) doing their work properly under legitimate orders of the employer; observing the Internal Work Rules; submitting disputes to the proper machinery for settlement; guarding the firm's business secrets; and complying with the other obligations imposed by the law and the contract. They are also forbidden to appear at work under the influence of alcohol or drugs or to carry on any propaganda during working hours.

*Changing and terminating contracts (Chs. 10–13).* The bases of the labor contract (either individual or collective) may be changed on petition of either party, pursuant to proceedings established by law.

The employer may effect a temporary suspension of the work contract for various reasons, including lack of raw materials, lack of funds, a true excess of production in relation to the market, notorious unprofitability, irresistible force, workers' illnesses, incapacity of the employer, and lack of fulfillment of the contract by the workers. In many of these cases, the employer must get the approval of the Board of Conciliation and Arbritration before suspending the contract. The suspension is temporary and does not mean termination of the contract.

The employer may rescind the contract when the worker cheats and uses dishonesty; is guilty of violence and injury to persons and property on the job; does such after hours to the employer or his property; is guilty of numerous unjustified absences from work; disobeys orders without cause; appears at work drunk. The worker may likewise rescind his contract by reason of the employer's getting the contract by deception; using acts of violence; placing the worker's health and security in danger; reducing the worker's wages.

A labor contract may be terminated in one of several ways: by mutual consent of the parties; for causes stipulated in the contract; by completion of the specified work; by death of the worker; by recision of the contract by means mentioned above; by judicial liquidation; by closing of the enterprise; by incapacity of either party; and by resolution of a Board of Conciliation and Arbitration according to law.

*The contract in certain occupations (Chs. 14–18).* Special chapters in the labor law deal with the contract in domestic, maritime, railroad, agricultural, and small industry occupations. The details vary in many cases from the provisions discussed above, but the basic principles are the same. In agriculture, for example, the employer is expected to provide suitable free housing and certain other facilities, including medical aid. Small industry firms are those which employ up to ten persons if machinery is used and up to twenty if not. Small industries have the same general obligations as employers in larger firms, except that the Board of Conciliation and Arbitration fixes the amount of indemnity in injury cases in line with the financial ability of the small firm. And small firms are not required to provide paid vacations. Family shops are not subject to the labor law except in matters of health standards and minimum wages. Labor inspectors check on these firms as they do the larger ones.

*Apprenticeship.* Title 3 provides for apprenticeship contracts, which are arranged in a manner similar to that for the individual labor contract. Pay, training, and other matters are specified. Employers are expected to admit apprentices to the extent of 5 per cent of their labor force; and apprentices have the rights and obligations that a workman has. Preference is given in recruitment to the sons of union members.

*Employers' organizations.* The Federal Labor Law recognizes the right of employers as well as employees to organize in behalf of their own interests. The Employers' Confederation (Confederación Patronal de la República Mexicana) is their organization. They have not organized separate industrial bodies for labor relations purposes, and each employer joins the Confederation directly. Indirectly, it might be said that the chambers of commerce, the chambers of industry, and their national confederations serve such purposes, inasmuch as they are concerned with the whole range of interests of their members.[8]

*Unions.* Title 4 of the law deals with unions, and defines them as associations of those same or related occupations which organize for the study, improvement, and defense of their common interests. The law recognizes four types of unions: craft; industrial; plant, with several occupations under the same employer; and miscellaneous, in smaller places where there are fewer than twenty members engaged in a single occupation.

Workers and employers have freedom to form their own organizations, but they must register with the government. No one may be obliged to join or not join such an organization. Unions have the right to seek and obtain from the employer the dismissal of those who renounce or are dropped from membership, when the collective contract includes such an "exclusion clause."

A union must have at least twenty members. Young workers may be members, but they may participate in union affairs only when sixteen years of age. To be recognized, a union must register with the appropriate Board of Conciliation and Arbitration. And a union doing work within the area of federal regulation must also register with the Ministry of Labor. No union may be denied registration if it meets the few requirements set by the law. The union's registration may be canceled if the union is dissolved or ceases to meet the requisites set by the law;

this is a quasi-judicial type of action taken through the Board of Conciliation and Arbitration.

The regulations (*estatutos*) of the union provide for its name, domicile, and objectives; obligations and rights of the members; the manner of naming the officials; the conditions for admitting, disciplining, and expelling members (expulsion by a two-thirds vote of the members); meetings; administration of its financial affairs; and the manner of its liquidation.

Unions are obligated to provide the authorities with information about the organization and its affairs; and the union officials are obliged to give a financial accounting at least twice a year to their general assembly. Unions are forbidden to participate in religious affairs; to carry on business activities for gain; to use force to gain members; or to commit illegal acts against persons or property. Unions may form federations, which must also register with the Ministry of Labor and provide that agency with reports.

A union may be dissolved through completion of the life span fixed in its rules; through achievement of its objectives; or through a two-thirds vote of its members.

*Strikes and lockouts.* Title 5 deals with strikes and lockouts. The strike is defined as the temporary legal suspension of work by a union. Thus, the legal strike only suspends temporarily the labor contract, without terminating or extinguishing any of the union's rights and obligations. The strike may have any of four objectives: to secure an equilibrium between labor and capital, harmonizing the rights of the two; to secure from an employer the signing or fulfillment of a contract; to require the revision of a contract, during the final weeks of its life; or to aid a strike that seeks legal objectives. The strike must be limited to suspension of work; acts of force are punishable by law.

A legal strike must meet several requirements. It must have for its exclusive object one or more of the four objectives named above, and it must be approved by a majority vote of the workers involved. Before being effected, the strike must meet the following procedural prerequisites. First, the union gives the employer written notice of the proposed strike action at least six days before it is to take place. Ten days is required in the public services — services of transport, communications, light, gas, water, hospitals, health, etc. The Board of Conciliation and Arbitration is also notified, and the Board notifies the employer, who has forty-eight hours in which to reply to the union statement. The Board attempts to achieve agreement between the parties. If this fails, the Board declares the strike legal and the walkout takes place. The striking union is obliged to provide a skeleton crew to prevent grave injury to the struck property; and the employer cannot operate his concern with other personnel during the strike. During such a legal strike, the employer must pay wages to the strikers.

The strike may be ended by agreement between the employer and the union; by the decision of an arbitral body chosen by the parties; or by a decision of a Board of Conciliation and Arbitration. On resuming partial or total operations, the employer must return the workmen to their jobs.

A strike is illegal when a majority of the strikers commit acts of violence against persons or properties and, in time of war, when the workers have been in government agencies or establishments. If the Board declares a strike illegal, it declares the labor contracts terminated; and the employer is free to sign new labor contracts. Less drastic action is taken by the Board if it finds that the strike was called by less than a majority of the workers; if the union did not fulfill the procedural requisites named above; if the strike contravened agreements in the collective contract; or if the strike was not taken for one of the legally allowed reasons. In such a case, the Board declares that no strike exists and gives the strikers twenty-four hours to return to work. Those who do not return lose their contracts.

A lockout by an employer is legal only when a Board of Conciliation agrees that it is necessitated by a true excess of production, which seldom happens.

Labor law authorities differ on whether or not a sympathetic strike is constitutional. In addition to strike settlement methods mentioned above, the President has on occasion stepped in and ended a strike or strike threat. To secure compliance, he could threaten management with expropriation and labor with the use of troops.

*Occupational risks.* Title 6 deals with occupational risks, whether from accident or illness (mental or physical). Employer responsibilities are interpreted broadly, and the Supreme Court has held that it is not necessary to prove an immediate and direct causal relationship with employment. Such liabilities include death; total permanent incapacity; permanent partial incapacity; and temporary incapacity.

The employee who suffers as the result of an occupational risk has a right to medical service, drugs and other curative agents, and compensation as fixed in the law. When death results from an occupational risk, compensation includes a month's pay as funeral expenses and 612 days' pay to the worker's dependents. A total permanent incapacity brings the workman 918 days' pay. Compensation for permanent partial incapacity is calculated from tables included in the law. Temporary incapacity pays 75 per cent of the wage from the first day of incapacity. Employers may, and many do, cover their possible liabilities by means of insurance.

Each employer is required to provide first-aid treatment facilities, while larger establishments are required to provide varying amounts of hospital and surgical service.

The employer is not responsible for injuries when the worker incurs them while under the influence of drugs or drink or when he deliberately courts injury. But the employer is not freed from his obligation merely because the worker has sought to assume the risks or because the accident results from negligence. Employers are required to re-employ former workers who have suffered injuries, to the extent of the capacity of the workers.

*Labor authorities.* Title 8 covers the various labor authorities provided for by the labor law. These consist of the municipal conciliation boards; the central boards of conciliation and arbitration; the federal boards of conciliation; the Federal Board of Conciliation and Arbitration; the labor inspectors; the special commissions on minimum salary; and the Ministry of Public Education.

The municipal conciliation boards handle conciliation cases within their areas, which are not within the jurisdiction of the federal boards. They also keep the state's Central Board of Conciliation and Arbitration informed on matters exclusively within its competence, as well as on conflicts the municipal board has been unable to settle; and they ratify the agreements that the parties make before them.

The municipal boards are composed of a governmental representative appointed by the municipal council, one by labor, and one by the employer concerned. They are usually *ad hoc* bodies, established for a case whenever necessary. The board's president is the governmental representative, and he may not be a local government employee or official. He must have no relationship to the parties to the case; hold no ecclesiastical position; not belong to the labor or employer group; not be a stockholder in firms in the board's jurisdiction; not be economically dependent on labor or employer.

The central boards of conciliation and arbitration function permanently in the capitals of the states, in the Federal District, and in the federal territories. Governors of the more industrialized states may provide for more than one central board. Such boards are composed of a president, who is appointed by the governor, and a worker and an employer representing each industry or group of industries. If the conflict in question involves two or more industries, the board will be composed of worker and employer representatives of those industries. If the governor of the state feels it unnecessary to have each industry represented, he may have up to three members each to represent the general interests of labor and management, respectively. The functions of the central boards include conciliation; arbitration; deciding on the legality of work stoppages; deciding on questions of jurisdiction of the Municipal Boards and different groups in the central board; supervising the municipal boards; approving the Internal Work Rules of the employer-employee bargaining units; and setting minimum salaries.

The central board may be subdivided into special boards. The functions of these groups are: conciliation of cases arising in the municipality where the group is located; arbitration of such cases, when conciliation has failed; and handling the conflicts sent them by the municipal boards.

The Federal Board of Conciliation and Arbitration is a body located in the capital of Mexico to handle disputes involving firms that operate in federal zones or under a concession granted by the federal government. By virtue of subjects reserved to the federal government, this board has jurisdiction over cases involving the fields of transportation and communication, mineral exploitation, electrical energy, and any conflict involving the interests of two or more states.

The Federal Board includes one representative each from labor and employers for each industry or group of related industries, and the chairman, who represents the Ministry of Labor. The Board functions *en pleno* and in subdivisions. The functions of the Board as a whole include conciliation, arbitration, conciliation and arbitration involving the "obligatory contracts" discussed earlier, supervision of the federal conciliation boards, decisions about the competence of the federal conciliation boards. The board's subdivisions deal with cases involving a single industry.

The federal conciliation boards have the same jurisdiction as the Federal Board of Conciliation and Arbitration, except that their work is limited to conciliation. These boards are usually *ad hoc* bodies, composed as the municipal conciliation boards are, with a labor inspector designated by the Ministry of Labor serving as chairman.

The other "labor authorities" provided for by the law are the labor inspectors, the special commissions on the minimum wage, and the Ministry of Public Education. The labor inspectors are state and federal officials. The former are appointed by the governors and the latter by the Ministry of Labor. The inspectors see that firms observe the provisions of the law in labor matters, with special attention to the rights and obligations of workers and employers, safety and health measures, and the prohibition of night work for women and young workers. The Office of the Labor Defender provides free legal aid to workers in need of such service in labor relations matters. The special commissions on the minimum wage are established in each locality, and are composed of an equal number of representatives of workers and employers. They are subordinate to the state's Central Board of Conciliation and Arbitration. The Ministry of Public Education sees to the fulfillment of the employers' obligations to provide school services, an obligation existing in certain circumstances.

The procedure to be followed by the various boards is specified in great detail in Title 9 of the law; however, the actual operations are said to be characterized by informality rather than the opposite.

*General observations.* In addition to the regular legal machinery of labor relations discussed above, some companies and unions have developed quite workable voluntary mediation machinery to settle disputes before they reach the various boards.

While the labor code doesn't itself enact the closed shop, the collective contracts in most of the important industries contain such a virtual closed shop clause.[9]

The boards, as was seen above, are at the very heart of Mexican labor relations. Since the votes of the labor and employer representatives tend to cancel each other out, the decisions tend to reflect government policy toward labor — which has usually been very friendly. Otherwise, the decisions have been greatly lacking in uniformity and continuity.[10]

Board decisions may be reviewed by the ordinary courts only if they infringe constitutional rights. The chairmen of the central and the federal boards must be lawyers or specialists in industrial law, as must the board secretaries.

The law makes it difficult for an employer to dismiss a worker, a condition disliked by the employers. Promotion on the job usually is done by strict seniority. When a labor contract is about due for revision, the union often files notice of intention to strike, a device to be used partly as a bargaining weapon. One study shows strikes to be about as frequent as in the United States. By and large, the newer firms have maintained better relations with the unions than have the older ones.[11]

The labor code has, in general, been better enforced in the larger firms and industries than in the smaller ones and those located in the remoter parts of the country.[12]

*The Ministry of Labor and Social Welfare.*[13] The Ministry of Labor is charged in general with seeing to the observance of the Federal Labor Law and its *reglamentos*, which means the Ministry has varying degrees of relationship to and control over the labor functions discussed above. The Ministry's antecedents are traced to the law of 1911, which established the Labor Office in the Ministry of Development, Colonization, and Industry. This subordinate status continued until the law of 1933 established the Department of Labor as an autonomous agency. In December 1940, it became a ministry under its present name.

Like other ministries, Labor is headed by a minister, an undersecretary, and an *oficial mayor*. The Ministry has about a dozen subdivisions, in most cases labeled "departments." The Administrative Department handles the personnel, accounting, purchasing, and other staff functions of the Ministry. The Legal Department formulates proposed laws and regulations, renders legal advice, and represents the Ministry in any court cases. The Office of the Federal Attorney for Defense of Labor provides similar aid to workers or unions that request such assistance.

The Inspection Department sees to the fulfillment of the labor law, its *reglamentos*, and labor contracts. Under it come the federal boards of conciliation and about two dozen federal labor offices throughout the country. The Department of Registry of Associations handles the registrations of workers' and employers' organizations.

The Bureau of Social Welfare has several subdivisions. Its Department of General Protection does some inspection work, makes various studies, and sees to the enforcement of minimum wages. The Medical Consulting Department and the Labor Hygiene Department perform services related to industrial hygiene. The Social Insurance Department studies the problems of insurance dealing with unemployment, illness, and accidents. Separate offices deal with protection of women and young workers and promotion of cooperatives among working people.

The functioning of the Federal Board of Conciliation and Arbitration and the federal boards of conciliation come within the purview of the Ministry, since it names their chairmen and works closely with them.

The Department of Social Information and Statistics is a statistical and informational agency. It publishes the monthly *Revista Mexicana del Trabajo*, the annual *Memoria*, and other publications.

## NOTES

[1] Marjorie Clark, *Organized Labor in Mexico* (1934), *passim*; Vicente Lombardo Toledano, "The Labor Movement," *Annals*, March 1940, pp. 48–54; Alfonso López Aparicio, *El Movimiento Obrero en México* . . . (1952), *passim*; Weyl, *op. cit.*, Chs. 5, 9, 10; Call, *op. cit.*, pp. 164–75; Victor Alba, "Significado del Movimiento Obrero Latinoamericano," *Humanismo*, October 1952 to December 1953 (8 installments).

[2] Weyl, *op. cit.*, p. 127.

[3] José J. Castorena, *Manual de Derecho Obrero* (1949), pp. 27–35; Mario de la Cueva, *Derecho Mexicano de Trabajo* (1949), Ch. 5.

[4] Castorena, *op. cit.*; Cueva, *op. cit.*; Pastor Rouaix, *Génesis de los Artículos 27 y 123* . . . (1945); Alberto Trueba Urbina, *El Artículo 123* (1943).

[5] Tannenbaum, *Peace by Revolution* . . . (1933), Chs. 19–23; Cueva, *op. cit.*, Ch. 5; *Ley Federal del Trabajo Reformada* . . . (1953); Castorena, *op. cit.*; Guadalupe Rivera Marín, *El Mercado de Trabajo* (1955), Chs. 1–2, 6.

[6] *Ley Federal del Trabajo Reformada* . . . Analyses of the Law: Castorena, *op. cit.*; Cueva, *op. cit.*; J. M. Cormack and F. M. Barker, "The Mexican Labor Law," *Southern California Law Review*, March 1934, pp. 251–94; Cormack, "Operation of the Mexican Labor Law," *Southwestern Law Journal*, Summer 1953, pp. 301–26 and Fall 1953, pp. 464–95; Alberto Trueba Urbina, *Derecho Procesal del Trabajo* (1943-44), 4 v.; Mary Jo Banks, "A Study of the Federal Labor Code of Mexico" (M.A. thesis, Columbia University, 1948).

[7] Castorena, *op. cit.*, Chs. 4–5; Luis Muñoz, *Comentarios a la Ley Federal del Trabajo* . . . (1948); *Anales de Jurisprudencia*, April–June 1951, pp. 293–487.

[8] Guadalupe Rivera Marín, *El Mercado de Trabajo* . . . (1955), Ch. 4; R. G. Stone, *Economic and Commercial Conditions in Mexico* (1952), pp. 61 *et seq.*

[9] Banks, *op. cit.*, pp. 23–24.

[10] *Ibid.*, pp. 58 *et seq.*

[11] Mosk, *op. cit.*, p. 27; Cormack, "Operation . . . ," *op. cit.*, p. 464.

[12] Banks, *op. cit.*, pp. 68–69.

[13] Cueva, *op. cit.*, Ch. 75; *Reglamento Interior de la Sría. del Trabajo* . . . , in *Ley Federal del Trabajo* . . . , Alberto Trueba Urbina, ed., (1953), pp. 335–61; Muñoz, *op. cit.*; *Directorio* . . . (1), pp. 399–412; Sría. del Trabajo . . . , *Memoria* . . . , *1952–53* (1953); *Revista Mexicana del Trabajo* (organ of the Ministry).

# 23

## Social Security, Health, and Welfare

I N A country like Mexico, with a rapidly growing population and a relatively low per-capita income, the need for a broad program of welfare, health, and social security coverage is obvious. The program that Mexico has been developing ranks high among those of Latin America, providing protection against work-connected accidents and illnesses, nonoccupational ills, maternity needs, some other direct health services, and insurance and assistance protections against invalidity, death, and old-age retirement.[1]

### Social Security

*History.* The need for social insurance became evident as industrialization developed after 1910. This sentiment was reflected in Article 123 of the 1917 Constitution, which declared that the passage of a social security law "shall be considered of public interest and it shall include security against disability, of life, from involuntary stoppage of work, against sickness and accidents, and others with analogous purposes."

Actions were slow to match ideals, and it was not until 1921 that the first proposed social security law was drafted. In 1925, a law was proposed which would have required employers to guarantee medical attention to injured employees and the payment of indemnities for accidents and illnesses. In 1925, the pension law for federal employees was enacted, lending impetus to the general movement. In 1938, President Cárdenas sent a bill to the Chamber of Deputies to cover the risks of occupational accidents and illnesses, nonoccupational ills, maternity, old age, invalidity, and unemployment; but the proposal was not acted upon.[2]

In 1941, President Ávila Camacho set up a committee to study the social security needs of the country and draft a proposed bill. Two consultants from the International Labor Office worked with the committee on the project; and the law establishing a social security program was enacted in January 1943. This measure, as amended in 1947 and 1949, remains in force.

*The Social Security Law.* The law declares social insurance to be a national public service of compulsory character, although the program has not yet been extended to all parts of the country. As mentioned above, the program grants protection against risks of sickness, accidents, invalidity, maternity, old age, and death. Aid is in the forms of medical services and cash; and coverage, for the areas served, is for employed persons and their dependents. The administering agency is the Mexican Institute of Social Security.

Contributions by employers and employees toward financing the program are based on the amount of the employee's total income, with furnished food or lodging each to be considered the equivalent of one fourth of income. For the purpose of calculating contributions and benefits, daily wages are divided into eleven groups. Unpaid apprentices' contributions are paid by the employer. Employers remit the contributions to the Institute.

1. Occupational accidents and illnesses: Occupational illnesses covered are elaborated under some forty different categories in the Federal Law of Labor. In case of occupational illness or accident, the following aids are provided: medical, surgical, pharmaceutical, and related aids are available to all; and during the period of incapacitation, a money subsidy is paid the individual in an amount approximating two thirds of his daily wage. Calculations are based on the mid-point figure of the eleven wage ranges mentioned above. The limit to these grants is supposed to be fifty-two weeks.

When the incapacity is declared total and permanent, an approximately equivalent monthly pension is calculated from a similar wage-benefit table. A partial permanent disability is calculated from a similar table in the Federal Labor Law. Such "total" or "partial" cases are first granted the pension provisionally for two years; and the incapacitated persons are required to submit to medical examinations and treatments prescribed as a result thereof.

Workmen who are injured or become ill while under the influence of drink or drugs do not qualify for personal benefits.

Chapter 3 of the law also provides for benefits resulting from death in such cases. A month's salary is paid as a funeral benefit. The widow of the insured person then receives a pension equivalent to 36 per cent of the amount the insured had been receiving, while another 20 per cent goes to support orphaned children under age sixteen. Such aid to children is carried beyond age sixteen when they are infirm or are continuing in school. The widow's benefit may go to a common-law wife, if she is the only one who has lived as such with the deceased for the preceding five years. The total of all such aids will not exceed what the totally incapacitated workman would have received. If the widow or common-law wife contracts matrimony, she receives a final grant of three annual pension allotments.

The contributions that the employers remit to the Institute are in proportion to the salary paid and the risks inherent in the employment in question. A special *reglamento* classifies the firms by degree of risk of employment.

2. Nonoccupational ills and maternity: Chapter 4 of the law provides for two types of nonoccupational illness aids. The first provides medical, surgical, pharmaceutical, and hospital services for a maximum period of thirty-nine weeks for the same illness. The second is a money grant during incapacity, starting with the fourth day and lasting a maximum of thirty-nine weeks. The money subsidy approximates two fifths of the worker's wage. Incapacity lasting beyond thirteen weeks is increased by 10 per cent, and by another 10 per cent beyond twenty-six weeks. The family dependents of the insured also have a right to the first type of aid.

The insured woman receives, during pregnancy, childbirth, and for a period thereafter, such aids as necessary obstetrical assistance, a money subsidy, nursing aid, and an infant's wardrobe. Qualification for these aids is based on at least thirty weeks of insurance contributions in the previous ten months.

Nonoccupational illnesses and maternity benefits are financed jointly by workers, employers, and government.

3. Invalidity, old age, and death: Chapter 5 provides for an invalid's pension to such a person who has contributed for one hundred and fifty weeks. The worker becomes eligible for an old-age pension at

age sixty-five, after having contributed for five hundred weeks. At age sixty, if deprived of work, he may receive a reduced pension, after five hundred weeks' contributions. Invalidity and old age pensions provide for a basic pension, plus increased amounts based on contributions beyond the first hundred and fifty weeks, with 10 per cent added for each minor child.

Upon the death of the pensioner, the wife receives 40 per cent of the weekly pension the husband formerly received, provided a minimum time has elapsed since the marriage of the couple. Children under age sixteen continue to receive aid, and the age limit may be extended to twenty-five if illness prevents the person from earning a living or if he is attending school. The orphan's pension is 20 per cent of the parent's pension. The total of grants to widow and children will not exceed the amount of the insured parent's pension. The worker and the government each contribute half as much as the employer toward financing this program.

*The Social Security Institute.* The Mexican Institute of Social Security is the agency that administers the social security program. It administers all aspects of the program; collects the employer and employee contributions; makes the benefit payments provided for by the law; invests the funds of the Institute; acquires the property appropriate to the program; carries on social welfare propaganda; and formulates its own operating rules and regulations.

Chapter 7 of the law also provides that the Institute's resources include the employer and employee contributions collected; interest, rentals, profits, and other similar income; donations, legacies, inheritances, and subsidies; and other sources of income as provided by law.

The Institute's organs, as specified in the law, are the General Assembly, the Technical Council, the Vigilance Committee, and the director general.

The supreme authority of the Institute is the General Assembly, composed of ten members designated by the President, ten by the employers' organizations, and ten by the workers' organizations. They hold office for six years and may be re-elected. The director general and two administrative groups — the Technical Council and the Vigilance Committee — come under the General Assembly.

The Technical Council, the administrative body, is composed of the director general and nine members, with the former as chairman. The director general is named by the President. The nine members are chosen by the General Assembly to give equal representation to labor, management, and government, being selected from names presented by these three groups. They remain three years in their posts and may be re-elected. The Vigilance Committee has three members, representing the three sectors and serving six-year terms. They are chosen by the General Assembly, and may not be re-elected. The General Assembly, in addition to naming the Technical Council and the Vigilance Committee, discusses and approves the income and expenditure program; and it approves the Institute's annual report, the plan of operations, and the report of the Vigilance Committee. Every three years the General Assembly examines the actuarial status of the program and approves any changes.

The Technical Council is the legal and administrative agency of the Institute. It has supervisory power over the work of the Institute, except what is reserved to the General Assembly and the Vigilance Committee. It formulates the annual report, the statement of accounts, the plan of operations, and the proposed budget. It designates the credit institutions where funds will be deposited; formulates a program for investment of the reserve funds; establishes and closes local and regional offices; makes recommendations to the President on extending the service to new areas; and calls the General Assembly into session.

The Vigilance Committee watches over the investment of funds; has audits made; suggests to the Assembly and the Technical Council measures for improvement; and, in emergencies, convenes the General Assembly in extraordinary sessions. The Committee's reports are made to the Assembly.

The active administrative head of the Institute is the director general. He presides over the sessions of the Technical Council and the General Assembly; carries out the decisions of the Council; provides annual and other reports to the Council; represents the Institute before other governmental agencies with the powers delegated by the Council; and names and removes the Institute's employees, as well as supervising their work. He also has a suspensive veto in certain cases over the decisions of the Council, which is resolved by the General Assembly. Under the General Bureau, which the director general heads, come five sub-bureaus: Technical, Medical, Administrative, the General Secretary, and Servicios Foráneos (services outside the capital region).

The last-named sub-bureau administers the program of the regional offices in the areas served by the Institute. The Medical Sub-bureau has subdivisions dealing with medical services in the Federal District, laboratories and diagnostic services, occupational risks, and health education and labor welfare. The Administrative Sub-bureau has subdivisions dealing with personnel, budget, correspondence, warehousing, and transport. The offices in the Technical Sub-bureau handle accounting, actuarial work, applications, statistics, and machines. (The operations of the head office are highly mechanized.) The subdivisions under the General Secretary include those of legal and economic studies, purchases, collections, press and publicity, inspection and complaints, a pharmaceutical production laboratory, and the department serving the State of Mexico.

*The functioning program.* At the start of the program, many workers as well as employers doubted that it would work. But employers found the scheme better than expected because costs were systematized and propaganda reduced accidents; and the workers approve because the system works well.[3]

By July 1943 the Institute began enrollments in the Federal District; and by the end of the year, 185,000 workers of 20,300 employers were registered. The figures have risen steadily in the Federal District and in the regions later given coverage. In 1945 and 1946, coverage was effected in the Puebla, Monterrey, and Guadalajara districts, with coverage of between 22,000 and 32,000 employees in each area. By that time, most workers were covered in the Federal District except those in government, farm, domestic, and part-time employment. At first, the Institute had to do much of its work through contract with clinics and hospitals; but by 1947 the Institute's facilities in the Federal District had risen to twenty clinics, six general hospitals, and two maternity hospitals.[4]

By the end of 1947, about 265,000 workers were covered, about two thirds of them in the Federal District. In the beginning, the benefits were limited to workmen's compensation, health, and maternity insurance. In recent years, coverage has been extended to the risks of old age, permanent disability, death (survivor's benefits), and unemployment at an advanced age. By 1953, there were nearly half a million insured workers under the program, with nearly three quarters of a million dependents having coverage. Coverage has been extended to other populous areas in the last few years; and in 1954 plans were announced for the early extension of coverage to rural groups.[5]

In 1953, the Institute completed a new $4 million hospital group of buildings embodying many of the latest features in hospital design.

*Housing.* One of Mexico's greatest needs — and one of the Institute's important services — is provision of low-rent housing. Other important housing developments have been sponsored by the Bureau of Civil Pensions and the official banks.

The first public housing projects were sponsored by the Cárdenas administration, but the units came to serve middle- and upper-income persons rather than those most in need. Only toward the end of the Ávila Camacho administration did a successful program get under way. A law of 1946 allowed credit institutions to finance low-rent projects, and another law created a housing bank. Both the Bureau of Pensions and the Institute helped finance the bank. The first large project completed was the Centro Urbano Presidente Alemán, finished in 1950. It provided model facilities for some 1,100 families of government workers. The second large project, the Centro Urbano Presidente Juárez, completed in 1952, is almost as large. Included in the project are such facilities as a kindergarten, a school, a playground, and stores. Similar projects have been planned for other large cities.[6]

*Related agencies.* A number of other agencies perform related work, and the Institute of Social Security has cooperative relations with such agencies. The more important are the Ministries of Health and Assistance, Public Education, Labor, and Economy, and the Federal District.

The logical relationship between the Institute's program and that of the Ministry of Health is obvious, since the programs of the two are similar in many ways. Since 1946, the responsibility for construction of hospitals has been transferred from the Ministry of Health to the Institute. The opportunities for cooperation between the Institute and the Ministry of Labor are also obvious, since both agencies work with the employers and the employees as organized groups in a labor-welfare situation. The Ministry of Public Education does health education work of significance to the Institute's program. Relations with the Department of the Federal District are important since that area formed the nucleus of the Institute's program.

The link with the Ministry of Economy is important since the law charges the latter with the responsibility of "intervening in all matters related to social security." The Ministry's Department of Social Security is charged with the study of the legal, economic, and practical aspects of the problem; making recommendations for its improvement; imposing fines for violations of the Social Security Law and its *reglamentos;* and helping to determine the workers' and employers' organizations that participate in electing members to the Institute's General Assembly.[7]

## Health

*Background data.* Of all Mexico's pressing problems, one of the most urgent is that of improving the nation's health.[8] Much has been done, but budgets have been small and much more still remains to be done. As one outstanding study reports, "The death rate in Mexico has been one of the highest in the Western Hemisphere, although it is now slowly and steadily declining. This is also true of infant mortality. Routine preventive measures, such as vaccination against smallpox and inoculations against outbreaks of epidemics, are now widespread; but anything approaching adequate medical care is still confined to the large cities and to a few favored localities in the rural districts."[9] Due to the prevailing economic conditions, an adequate health service will mean in a large degree a government health service.

In the United States, the most important diseases include those related to old age, heart ailments, cancer, etc. In Mexico, the leading contenders, by a large margin, are diarrhea-enteritis, pneumonia, and malaria. Mortality rates have been declining steadily with the application of medical and sanitary knowledge; and the decline has been substantial since 1945. The rate had been 25.3 per thousand in 1922, and it declined to 20.6 by 1944, but it was still nearly twice the rate in the United States. Life expectancy was 36.3 years in 1930 and 39 years in 1940. Life expectancy in the United States was 63.8 years in 1940.[10]

Smallpox and typhus fever were formerly serious problems, but they have been controlled very largely by vaccination, popular health education, and greater cleanliness. Cholera, yellow fever, and plague have long been virtually eliminated.

Some of the causes of serious illness and death come within the scope of direct public health work; others pertain to medical care; still others — of great importance — depend on sanitation, housing, nutrition, and the general cultural level. These latter depend in turn largely on the general economic condition of the country. A large proportion of the people suffer from dietary deficiencies, which have a direct influence on health. Housing is also an important health factor, with the census showing more than four out of ten persons living in huts and hovels. Geographical factors also play an important role, and there are considerable differences in health conditions in various parts of the country. Geography also adds to the difficulties of meeting health needs, with isolation contributing to the fact that about a tenth of the people live in regions where only Indian languages are spoken and health education is more difficult.[11]

The health function has long been recognized in Mexican government, though the present Ministry of Health and Welfare is comparatively new. The Faculty of Medicine, established in 1820, had the power to prepare a health code. The Superior Council of Health was established in 1841. The 1917 Constitution converted the Board of Health of Mexico City into the federal Department of Public Health, with enlarged powers over all matters pertaining to transmissible diseases. It also gave the federal government control over the general health of the republic, leaving to the states only problems of local significance. This obviously is in contrast with the decentralization of health work which is found in the United States. In interpreting the constitutional provision, the Supreme Court has naturally leaned toward the central government; and it has held that each case is a question of fact for the courts to decide. Thus, the federal health agency becomes the supreme authority in sanitation, health, and hygiene matters affecting the "general health of the republic." The principal subjects left within the state and municipal jurisdictions are local sanitary engineering, and food and beverage inspection. The states and the municipalities are also required to help the central authorities to prevent and control communicable diseases.[12]

The year 1922 saw the establishment of a section on health education and propaganda in the federal Department of Health, but for long the work was intensive only near the capital. In 1926 and 1927, federal health offices were opened in all the states. In 1943, the Department was merged with the Ministry of Public Welfare to form the Ministry of Health and Welfare.[13]

The present Sanitary Code provides for a federal representative in each state and agreements for cooperative programs between federation and state. The state health officer is appointed through agreement between the state government and the federal agency. Thus, the Ministry coordinates health work and requires the development of a national health program.[14]

For its own employees, each federal agency has its own medical office and program of medical service, thus in effect adding to the otherwise very modest real income of the government employees.

*Sanitary Code.* Federal government health matters are governed by the Sanitary Code.[15] The authorities dealing specifically with health are the President, the General Health Council, and the Ministry of Health and Welfare. The Ministry is the administrative agency charged with federal health work; and temporarily it may take charge of local sanitary services "in those states where, due to special circumstances, such states are unable to undertake same." (Sanitary Code, Arts. 3, 5.)

The General Health Council is a policy-making body in the field of health whose function is to issue health regulations of a general character for the whole republic and to see to their fulfillment. The Council is "directly subordinate to the President of the Republic, without the interposition of any Ministry of State, and its general orders are obligatory throughout the country" (Constitution, Art. 73, XVI). The Council is composed of "a President, a Secretary, nine members of the Council, and such number of auxiliary members as the Council may decide on." All of them are appointed by the President of the country and are directly responsible to him (Sanitary Code, Art. 7).

The Minister of Health and Welfare is appointed by the President and has administrative control of the federal government's health work. His orders, and those of the Council, are followed by the other administrative authorities of the country. In the case of a serious general epidemic or the threat of invasion by foreign diseases, the Ministry has the responsibility of ordering the preventive measures immediately necessary, subject to the approval of the President. (Constitution, Art. 73, XVI.)

In more detail, the *reglamento* of the Law of the Ministries of State spells out the health functions of the Ministry. These include the following: organizing and administering general health services throughout the country; administering hospitals; sanitary policing work, especially at the ports, coasts, and frontiers; inspection and control of the preparation and use of foods and drinks; veterinary hygiene as it relates to human health; control of biological products, except for veterinary use; control over nonveterinary drugs and medicinal products; measures against transmissible diseases; industrial and social hygiene, except that covered by the Labor Ministry; maintenance of schools of health and other means of extending health knowledge and practice; coordination of federal and state health services; and giving effect to the other aspects of the Sanitary Code.[16]

The Sanitary Code deals in detail with the various aspects of the Ministry's work. Significantly, diffusion of health information is one of the first topics treated (Sanitary Code, Arts. 25–35). The Ministry is charged with nationwide diffusion of "the methods and practices of social and individual hygiene relating to foods, living quarters, sanitary methods, and training of the public to combat epidemics and endemic diseases." A related function is prevention of the circulation of advertising seeking to deceive the public about the qualities of foods, beverages, medicines, and medical and health apparatus and equipment. Approval is required for commercial propaganda for medical or health purposes. A special prohibition is extended against publicity for distilled drinks via radio, television, and moving pictures.

Special sections deal with sanitation measures related to maritime, air, and land transportation. Vessels entering Mexican ports are required to have the necessary papers and are subject to inspection by quarantine officials. (Sanitary Code, Arts. 36–67.) All airports open to international traffic are required to maintain a medical service; and a doctor of the health service is stationed at each such airport (Arts. 68–74). Health and sanitation requirements in connection with immigration, air, land, and water traffic are specified in some detail (Arts. 75–135).

Among the Code's provisions on sanitary engineering (Arts. 153–75) is one dealing with pure water supplies. Discharge of nonpurified water into rivers, lakes, and other sources of water for drinking and bathing is forbidden. Another provision empowers the Ministry to inspect and require the vacating of buildings deemed unsuitable.

Other sections of the Code deal with sanitary policing in connection with foods and beverages (Arts. 185–205); animals, dairies, drug firms, etc. (Arts. 206–61); narcotics, alcohols, and alcoholism (Arts. 262–97); and the practice of medicine and allied activities (Arts. 301–6).

Needless to add, the Code constitutes a good basic law; but restricted budgets and other limiting factors have often caused performance to fall far short of declared policy and goals.

*Hospital service.*[17] Mexico has always had a great shortage of hospital facilities, a condition the present administration is striving to improve. For a long time, the hospitals were more religious institutions than curative centers. At best, they were a mixture of convent and hospital. The buildings used for the care of the sick were usually not well suited to their purpose, to say nothing of their often lacking elementary hygienic facilities. Thus, the Juárez hospital in the capital is installed in an old convent, and the hospital of Puebla is located in an old temple.

The hospitals of the country can be classified into three groups: those operated by the Ministry for various states, with joint federal-state support; those operated by the states, assisted by federal financial aid; and independent institutions. To these should be added strictly federal government hospitals, such as those in the new medical center in Mexico City.

A recent study tabulates the following eight hospital institutions in the capital: two central general hospitals; one children's hospital; one heart disease hospital; one hospital for nutritional diseases; one maternity hospital; one neuropsychiatry institute; and one hospital for chronic cases. These institutions reported a total of 6,830 beds. Some of the hospitals receive assistance from private sources, but most of the support comes from the federal government. The same study listed the following hospitals in the various states of the republic: nine central general hospitals; twenty-six regional hospitals; ninety-six coordinated (joint federal-state) hospitals; twenty-one hospitals serving specialized "campaigns" (tuberculosis, venereal diseases, leprosy, tropical diseases, women and children, etc.); seventeen rural hospitals; and one institution for mental cases.

Of special importance is the developing medical center in Mexico City, composed of specialized hospitals, institutes, and research centers. Such agencies include the Institute of Health and Tropical Diseases, the Institute of Nutrition, and the Children's Hospital. The latter institution is the largest children's hospital in Latin America and one of the best in the world. It is part of the growing medical center (which is scheduled for early completion); and it has beds for some six hundred children, plus facilities for handling several thousand outpatients. The hospital is financed by government funds, gifts, and endowments.[18]

The present administration has announced an expanded program of hospital construction; but it will probably be many years before the needs are fully met. An illustration of the need is afforded by the capital — one of the best-served areas in the country. In terms of general hospital beds, one estimate of need calls for doubling the present capacity. This is based on the very modest ratio of 2½ beds per 1,000 population of the city.

Currently there are 186 hospitals reported under the partial or total control of the Ministry of Health, with a total of 16,426 beds. Of these, 67 are coordinated services (operated by the Ministry with joint federal-state support); 48 are state hospitals, subsidized by the federal government; and 71 are decentralized or regional hospitals. In 1954, 20 more hospitals were reported under construction in various parts of the country. Among these, 1 is for tubercular cases, 2 are for children, and 1 is for women and children.[19]

*Doctors.*[20] The scarcity of doctors in Mexico makes it possible for them to choose their locations; and, as in other countries, most of them choose the cities, where medical facilities, professional contacts, and professional incomes are best. Thus, the rural area has nearly two thirds of the nation's population but less than a tenth of the physicians. Whetten finds the doctor-population ratio to be 1 to 948 in the cities and 1 to 18,435 in the rural areas. Dentists are even more concentrated in the cities with a ratio of 1 to 4,132, compared with 1 to 140,137 in the country area. It was reported in 1936 that 2,000 of the country's 4,520 physicians were located in the capital; 1,500 were in seventy larger urban communities; and only 610 were in small towns.

One approach to solving the problem of maldistribution of medical service was to require the medical school students who had finished their courses to provide a five-month period of service in some unserved community before receiving their degrees. This program was started in 1936 through a cooperative arrangement between the National University's School of Medicine and the Ministry of Health and Welfare. The aims have been to provide the communities with some service and the young doctors with valuable experience, and to induce young doctors to settle permanently in the rural areas. The first two aims have been realized much more often than the third.

The Health Ministry provides the medical school with a listing and description of the communities needing service. After the student has chosen his post, he is provided with living and office facilities by the community and with a small stipend by the school and the Ministry. While at his post, the doctor carries on health education work, preventive medicine, curative medicine, and rudimentary scientific investigation. In health education work, he cooperates with the schools. In the preventive field, he sees to protecting the community's supply of drinking water and procures vaccines and other materials from the Ministry. In the curative field, he is supposed to keep in consultation with the medical school and make use of its laboratory facilities for analysis and diagnosis. His investigation consists of making a study of the community, with emphasis on its economy and its health needs. Before receiving his degree, the doctor writes up and usually publishes his findings as a thesis. About half of the 3,000 students taking such practice have later settled in the communities they had served.

Another medical training program of the federal government is that of the National Polytechnic Institute's Advanced School of Rural Medicine, founded in 1938 to provide a type of training allegedly not given by the traditional course of the University's medical school. Many members of the medical profession have opposed the program, alleging inefficiency and promotion of "socialized medicine."

*Other specialists.* Training for the other health service professions is not yet well advanced in Mexico. A good start has been made in the training of nurses; and plans have been laid for its expansion in connection with the program of the new medical center in Mexico City. The Health Ministry's School of Health and Hygiene, affiliated with the National University, gives training in sanitary engineering, some phases of nursing, extension courses, etc. Its functions include technical education for personnel in the Ministry and scientific investigation and experimentation.[21]

*Special service arrangements: Rockefeller Foundation.* The Rockefeller Foundation has cooperated effectively with the Mexican government in health work over a period of years. An outbreak of yellow fever in 1918 was the occasion for the start of this work, and since then cooperative work has included hookworm, malaria, and rural sanitation control. Since 1921, the Foundation has sent several dozen students to receive public health training in the United States. Most of them have returned to serve the Ministry or related organizations. Recent years have seen interest centered on training of personnel, since this is one of the greatest needs.[22]

*Rural cooperative service.* An important approach to rural health improvement was made in 1936 with the establishment of what is now the Ministry's Bureau of Cooperative Rural Medical Services. It was designed as a cooperative arrangement with the *ejidos*, which were expected to share an increasing part of its cost.

An elementary form of the service is financed by the Bureau at first. It consists of a doctor, a nurse, a midwife, a pharmacist, and a sanitary officer, located in a central village and serving small surrounding population centers. Many of these groups are found in primitive areas, where they concentrate largely on prevention and control of contagious diseases. A second, more elaborate, service is provided where the local community can share part of the cost. Its personnel includes medical specialists, and more attention is given to the individual needs of residents. A third type of service is provided some collective *ejidos* in commercialized farming areas, with *ejido* and Bureau sharing the costs about equally. Here hospitals are found, with such specialists as a surgeon, a dentist, and an obstetrician. Regional sub-units each have a doctor, a nurse, and a pharmacist. An increasing share of the total cost has been borne by the groups served, which has resulted in the concentration of services in the minority of communities that are able to finance such work.[23]

*Mexican-American cooperation.*[24] One of the most effective aspects of Mexican-American cooperation is found in the program of the Inter-American Cooperative Public Health Service. This joint service of the two governments operates as a bureau of the Health Ministry, with Mexican and American health personnel under an American chief. Its personnel includes doctors, engineers, nurses, and technicians. The bureau coordinates its activities with the rest of the Ministry of Health in matters of medical assistance, preventive medicine, environmental sanitation, health centers, malaria control, and nursing. In the construction of water and sewage systems, installation of chlorinators, and sanitary engineering matters, the bureau cooperates closely with the Ministry of Hydraulic Resources.

By 1947, three years after the start of the program, three large health centers had been built — at Boca del Río, Ciudad Juárez, and Xochimilco, near Mexico City. In addition to operating these demonstration health centers, the Bureau has performed other important services. It has developed a health program along the United States–Mexican border, with special reference to venereal diseases. The campaign to control malaria, a great tropical problem, has been of continuing importance. It has likewise done important work in the antituberculosis campaign, in research on *mal de pinto* (a skin disease), on oncocercosis (which causes blindness), and other diseases. More prosaic are the important construction projects that had by 1951 provided Mexican towns with forty-eight drinking-water systems and twenty-two sewage systems. Their significance healthwise has been great.

The bureau (also known as a *servicio*), though a part of the Health Ministry, is a complete operating unit. Its autonomy within the Ministry has contributed much to its successful operation, making possible the selection and retention of competent personnel without unfavorable influence from extraneous factors. The organization and program are flexible and adaptable to the local needs.

The bureau has three main parts. The medical section has charge of such projects as malaria control, health center operation, nursing activities, and training of nurses. The engineering section has charge of construction of health centers and of water supply and sewage disposal projects, as well as giving technical assistance in environmental sanitation work. The administrative section is a staff group that handles accounting, purchasing, warehousing, and personnel matters. The majority of the personnel are Mexicans.

The American basis of the bureau is found in the Institute of Inter-American Affairs, a U.S. government corporation attached to the Department of State (and thereby the U.S. Embassy). The bureau had its origin as a cooperative device in 1942, when the United States and its allies sought to strengthen themselves for the war effort. The agreement providing for the Mexican bureau was signed by the two governments in July 1943.

## Welfare

Public welfare work can be traced back nearly a century to its origins in public charity services; but even today, the nonmedical, nonhospital welfare function is the lesser half of the work of the Ministry of Health and Welfare.[25]

# SOCIAL SECURITY, HEALTH, AND WELFARE

A decree of February 28, 1861, created the Bureau of Charity Funds and provided that all the hospitals, poorhouses, and correctional and charity institutions in the Federal District would be under the protection of the federal government. The next year, the Bureau of Public Charity was created and put in charge of the charity establishments in the capital. Minor changes were made by the laws of 1877 and 1924. The law of December 31, 1937, created the Ministry of Public Welfare; and on October 15, 1943, it was merged with the Department of Public Health to form the present Ministry.

The *reglamento* of the Law of Ministries of State charged the Ministry with the welfare functions of organizing public assistance in the Federal District and the territories; creating and administering establishments of public assistance anywhere in the country; providing cooperative public welfare services jointly with the states in their areas; managing the national lottery and administering and using its resources; supervising private charity institutions; providing assistance to needy mothers and children.

Most of the government welfare service (of a nonmedical, non-hospital type) is concentrated in the Federal District; and the principal agency charged with such work is the Bureau of Social Welfare. The Bureau's Office of Social Work seeks to effect a coordination of such work in the Federal District. Its work is subdivided along the lines of the *delegaciones* (administrative areas) into which the Federal District is divided. Social work as a profession has been slow in winning recognition, and training programs have made a real start only in recent years.

The Bureau's Department of Mother and Child Welfare has offices of home schools for abandoned children, foster homes, and mothers' clubs. The first type of institution had its origins in private charitable institutions before 1900. The foster home has developed in Mexico only in the last decade and a half, but its use is already widespread. The mothers' clubs seek, through small groups, to better fit women of the poorer classes for meeting family and other problems.

The Department of Educational Action serves disadvantaged children between ages six and fifteen. Normal children receive the same education as students in the regular public schools. Those who are blind, deaf, dumb, or mentally deficient receive the required specialized training in institutions devoted to such work.

The Department of Miscellaneous Welfare Services provides various services to needy young people. One aspect of its work is the maintenance of dining rooms for university students.

The Department of Legal Assistance provides a free legal aid service for needy persons in the defense of their rights in civil or criminal cases. Its work has been expanded in recent years.

Two other agencies outside the Bureau of Social Welfare are of importance. The Bureau of Inheritances for Public Beneficence administers properties acquired through donation and bequest for welfare purposes. The Board of Private Welfare is the official agency that exercises vigilance over private welfare institutions. Of its six members, the chairman and three others are named by the Minister of Health and Welfare.

*Organization of the Ministry of Health and Welfare.* The work of the Bureau of Social Welfare has been discussed above, as has that of the Bureau of Inter-American Public Health Cooperation and the Bureau of Rural Cooperative Medical Services. The other bureaus and institutes will be discussed below.[26]

Aside from the Bureau of Coordinated Health and Welfare Services, the three largest budgets among the functional bureaus go to those serving the Federal District — the Bureaus of Health, Medical Welfare, and Social Welfare.

The Bureau of Health in the Federal District deals with the sanitation of foods and drinks; contagious diseases; the sanitation of such public places as baths, barber shops, and beauty salons; and antituberculosis campaigns.

The Bureau of Medical Welfare has three departments. The Medical Department has supervision of the government hospitals and clinics in the District. The General Hospital handles general illnesses, surgery, maternity cases, and specialties. The Juárez Hospital specializes in nervous and mental illnesses. There are two tuberculosis hospitals, one for curable cases and one for incurables. The Children's Hospital has the reputation of being one of the finest of its kind in the world. A number of clinics handle lesser cases. The Department of Neuropsychiatry plans and supervises that type of service in the various institutions. The Department of Investigation, Planning, and Administration of Welfare Works is the Bureau's physical planning division. The Bureau of Medical Welfare has the largest budget within the Ministry.

The Health Education, Statistics, and Legal Departments perform obvious services. The work of the Health Education Department is of great importance, but its budget, like that of many others, is very small.

The Bureau of Hygiene, one of the most important in the Ministry, serves the entire country. Its departments include those of Epidemiology, Sanitary Engineering, Industrial Hygiene, Control of Medicines, and Control of Foods and Beverages. Of equal importance are the national campaigns (departments) against venereal diseases, leprosy, oncocercosis, tuberculosis, and malaria.

Some of the most important medical work in Mexico is being done by four scientific institutes. The oldest is the Institute of Hygiene, which since 1914 has been an important producer of vaccines and serums. Of similar importance is the work of the Institute of Nutrition. The Institute of Health and Tropical Diseases, opened in 1939, makes studies of typhus, *pinta*, and other important diseases, opening its doors to foreign as well as Mexican students. The Institute of Cardiology, opened in 1944, is considered one of the best heart research institutions in the world. This autonomous institution is the best financed of the institutes, getting most of its budget from the government but also receiving fees for services rendered. The charges to patients are nominal.[27]

The work of the Bureau of Cooperative Rural Medical Services has been discussed above.

Finally, the agency of probably greatest day-to-day functional importance is the Bureau of Coordinated Services of Health and Welfare, providing a jointly financed, federally furnished service in the states and territories. The coordinated service was first provided for entire states in 1933, when coverage was given to Veracruz, Guanajuato, and Querétaro. The following year the coordinated service was extended to five other states; and now nearly all states are in the joint program. The program in an area is the result of a signed agreement between the state and central governments, whereby the terms of the service and the financing are specified. The federal government has tended to provide from two thirds to three fourths of the money. The result is a much more adequate service than any state alone could provide, for the poverty of some states would condemn them to the most inadequate health protection.

*Summary.* While Mexico's unfilled health needs are still vast, much progress has been made in recent years – in certain fields of research and training, in control of epidemics, in environmental sanitation, and in provision of health services to special groups such as women and children.

The government began to reorganize its services for children in 1920, and attention was also given to the health of mothers. A Child Welfare Bureau was established in 1937, to have general jurisdiction over matters dealing with children's and mothers' health. Today in the capital, health services for mothers and children include preventive care through health centers; medical care (hospital and outpatient care); social assistance, through children's breakfasts, day care, foster homes, nursery schools, etc.; and health education, through doctors, nurses, social workers, and teachers.[28]

Important progress has been made in providing pure drinking water and sewage systems to the cities, though about half the people still live in houses without water near at hand and the great majority still have no sewage disposal facilities.[29] Progress has also been made in health education and in the anti-alcoholism campaigns.

The Ministry of Health and Welfare has developed cooperative relations with such other agencies as the Ministries of Labor, Education, and Hydraulic Resources, and the Social Security Institute. Hydraulic Resources has constructed numerous sanitary engineering works. Important relations have been cultivated with such foreign and international organizations as the Rockefeller Foundation, the United Nations, the World Health Organization, the Pan-American Sanitary Bureau, and United States government agencies, several of which have given Mexico outstanding aid in her fight against sickness.

### NOTES

[1] *Código de Seguridad Social, sus Reglamentos* . . . (1953). For analyses see Alfredo Chavero, "Social Insurance Reform in Mexico," *Bulletin of the International Social Security Association*, July 1949, pp. 11–18; *International Labor Review*, March 1942, pp. 345–48; Belina Escobeda Tarango, "Observaciones sobre la Ley Mexicana del Seguro Social" (UNAM thesis, 1952); Miguel García Cruz, *La Seguridad Social* (1951); Instituto Mexicano del Seguro Social, *Memorias* . . . , *1951–52* (1953); Instituto Mexicano del Seguro Social, *México y la Seguridad Social* (1952), 3 vols.; Instituto Mexicano del Seguro Social, *El Seguro Social Mexicano* . . . (1952); Instituto Mexicano del Seguro Social, *La Extensión del Seguro Social al Campo* (1952).

[2] Instituto Mexicano del Seguro Social, *México y la Seguridad Social*, Ch. 20; *Directorio* . . . (2), pp. 144–45.

[3] *Directorio* . . . (1), pp. 273–74.

⁴ Cline, *op. cit.*, p. 303.

⁵ *Pan American Union Bulletin*, August 1948, pp. 938–42; *Mex. Amer. Rev.*, December 1945, p. 50; *Mexican Life*, September 1948, pp. 25–26.

⁶ *Mex. Amer. Rev.*, August 1953, p. 32; *MV*, June 21, 1954.

⁷ *Directorio* . . . (2), pp. 121–22; *American City*, November 1950, pp. 104–5; *Pan American Union Bulletin*, June 1946, pp. 354–55; *Mex. Amer. Rev.*, December 1948, pp. 27–28; Wise, *op. cit.*, pp. 153–58.

⁸ Call, *Mexican Venture*, pp. 154–64; Ernest Gruening, *Mexico and its Heritage* (1928), pp. 533–53; Tena Ramírez, *op. cit.*, Ch. 16; Alfonso and Gilberto Fábila, *México* . . . (1951), Ch. 11; *Directorio* . . . (1), pp. 335–77; Gustavo Argil, *Asistencia Hospitalaria en México* (1951); Miguel Bustamante, "Local Public Health Work in Mexico," *American Journal of Public Health*, July 1931, pp. 725–36, "Public Health and Medical Care," *Annals*, March 1940, pp. 153–61; *American Journal of Public Health*, October 1930, pp. 1125–28, April 1943, pp. 353–56; Sría. de Salubridad . . . , *Memoria, 1947–1950* (1951); Norberto Treviño, *Estudio sobre los Problemas de Salubridad y Asistencia en Tamaulipas* (1952); Wise, *op. cit.*, pp. 173–80; Whetten, *op. cit.*, Chs. 12–14.

⁹ Whetten, *op. cit.*, p. 570.

¹⁰ *Ibid.*, Ch. 14.

¹¹ *Ibid.*, Chs. 12–14; Bustamante, "Public Health . . . ," *op. cit.*

¹² See note 11; Robert E. Scott, "Some Aspects of Mexican Federalism, 1917–1948" (Ph.D. thesis, University of Wisconsin, 1949), pp. 443 *et seq.*

¹³ *Directorio* . . . (1), pp. 370–71; *American Journal of Public Health*, October 1930, pp. 1125–28.

¹⁴ *American Journal of Public Health*, April 1943, pp. 353–56.

¹⁵ *Código Sanitario Federal* (*Diario Oficial*, January 25, 1950).

¹⁶ *Directorio* . . . (1), pp. 371–75.

¹⁷ *Ibid.*, pp. 368–75; Sría. de Salubridad . . . , *Memoria* . . . (1951); *HA*, July 12, 1954, pp. 5 *et seq.*

¹⁸ *American City*, January 1944, p. 36.

¹⁹ *HA*, July 12, 1954, pp. 5 *et seq.*

²⁰ Weyl, *op. cit.*, Ch. 12; Whetten, *op. cit.*, pp. 344–54; *Directorio* . . . (1), pp. 357–58; Sría. de Salubridad . . . , *Memoria* . . . (1951), pp. 87–105; *HA*, July 12, 1954, pp. 5 *et seq.*

²¹ Sría. de Salubridad . . . , *Memoria* . . . (1951), pp. 259–68; see note 19.

²² Whetten, *op. cit.*, p. 354; Rockefeller Foundation, *Annual Report*, 1952; Fosdick, *op. cit.*, pp. 65–77.

²³ Whetten, *op. cit.*, pp. 349–54.

²⁴ Sría. de Salubridad . . . , *Memoria* . . . (1951), pp. 107–16; K. R. Iverson, "The 'Servicio' in Theory and Practice," *Public Administration Review*, Autumn 1951, pp. 223–28; *Mexican American Review*, December 1947, pp. 30–31, September 1950, p. 21, August 1951, pp. 22–23.

²⁵ *Directorio* . . . (1) pp. 363 *et seq.*; Mary M. Engle, "The History of Public Welfare in Mexico, 1920–1940" (M.A. thesis, Duke University, 1940); Sría. de Salubridad . . . , *Memoria* . . . (1951), and *Memoria de la Primera Reunión Nacional de Asistencia Social* . . . (1952); Josefina Gaona, *Introducción al Estudio del Trabajo Social* (1951).

²⁶ *Directorio* . . . (1), pp. 335–77; Sría. de Salubridad . . . , *Memoria* . . . (1951).

²⁷ See note 26; Charles M. Wilson, *Ambassadors in White* . . . (1942), *pp.* 34–35; *Mexican American Review*, June 1951, pp. 15–16; *Time*, May 3, 1954, p. 71.

²⁸ *The Child*, October 1950, pp. 42–43; *Pan American Union Bulletin*, September 1937, p. 729.

²⁹ Whetten, *op. cit.*, pp. 292–97.

# 24

Education

IT IS hard to rank in importance the many pressing problems of Mexico I have discussed to this point — health, agricultural reform and improvement, industrialization, transportation, and so on. But one of the most basic long-term problems is education,[1] for education can furnish the fundamental knowledge and skills for improving the other aspects of national life. This was recognized by the abler leaders of the Revolution who produced such slogans as "Land and Liberty," "Land and Books," "To Educate is to Redeem," "To Educate is to Govern." The first part of this chapter traces the main patterns of progress; the second part discusses specific institutions and services.

## Past and Present

Only minor efforts were made to promote education before 1910, and illiteracy stood at about 78 per cent of the population. The efforts of the last three decades have reduced the figure to about 50 per cent, working against the handicaps of limited resources, a high birth rate, rural lethargy, and the complex linguistic and culture patterns of much of rural Mexico. The illiteracy rate varied widely from region to region in 1940, ranging from 38.8 per cent in the North Pacific region to 73.8 per cent in the South Pacific — and from less than 10 per cent in a few cities to more than 80 per cent in the rural population of some states.[2]

Though the Constitution, laws, and budgets give a prominent place to education on both state and federal levels, the magnitude of the problem has been such that thousands of communities still have no schools, thousands of others offer no more than one or two grades, and the majority of elementary school students are enrolled in the first two grades.

# EDUCATION

The government's role in education can be appreciated only against a historical background of the present service.

*The early years.*[3] The Spanish conquerors found a fairly well-organized system of native education in New Spain. Mayan education and science were the charge of the priests, who registered high achievements in astronomy, mathematics, architecture, and art. Among the Aztecs there were three types of schools. The *calmecac*, attached to the temple, taught children of both sexes of the noble, priestly, military, and merchant classes. The training was for public office, the priesthood, and the army. The *telpochcalli* was an academy for the sons of artisans and farmers, oriented toward making good soldiers. The *cuicalco* was a general school for all other young people, which concentrated on the learning of songs, dances, and religious rites. In brief, the warlike virtues were exalted.

The conquerors were at first determined to destroy the cultural institutions of the natives, probably as a means of maintaining Spanish dominance. The various religious orders that came to the colony established schools and quite thoroughly monopolized education during the colonial period. Some of the leaders showed great talent in sensing the problems and needs of education in the New World, adapting their techniques to the practical needs of the natives. Fray Pedro de Gante established the first school in the New World (in 1523) — a "school of action." Other "activity schools" based on current life needs were established hundreds of years before Froebel and John Dewey. This responsiveness of the early priest-educators to the needs of an agrarian folk culture laid a foundation on which the schools of the Revolution built after 1910.

From the early years, Indians, mestizos, and Spanish children were educated in separate schools. The economic program and conditions of the times soon pushed the education of Indians and mestizos into the background, though an occasional school or leader persisted in the valuable tradition of practical education. Schools for Spanish children tried to establish the curriculum and standards of European schools.

The first half-century of the colony also saw the foundations laid in Mexican higher education. In 1551 the emperor ordered the foundation of the Royal and Pontifical University of Mexico, and its doors were opened in 1553. The same period saw the establishment of San Nicolás College in Morelia, and the two institutions share with the University of San Marcos in Peru the honor of being the oldest institutions of higher learning in the Americas. By 1775, the University had conferred more than a thousand doctor's degrees and twenty-five thousand bachelor's degrees.

*The nineteenth century*.[4] In general, education declined from its earlier favorable status during this period. As the Church gained wealth and became involved in politics, the educational program suffered. For some time before and after the achieving of independence in 1821, little change occurred in education. But finally criticism brought a challenge to the clerical monopoly of education and the attendant backward methods. In 1829 a statute was passed that secularized education (on paper). But until the liberal triumph in 1867, education and other matters were a field of conflict between conservatives (supporters of the Catholic Church and its secular power) and liberals (proponents of church-state separation and education under government auspices).

After the triumph of Juárez in 1867, education was reorganized on a secular basis. The National University was closed until 1910, being regarded as a center of reactionary influence; and higher education was established in separate professional schools, for which the National Preparatory School prepared students. The latter, founded in 1867, reflected the positivist philosophy of Comte, eliminated religion from the curriculum, and emphasized the teaching of science. Under the 1857 Constitution, elementary schooling was to be free and compulsory; but economic difficulties largely prevented achieving this ideal.

Some normal schools date from the last third of the nineteenth century, and were founded to end the educational influence of the clergy by providing trained lay personnel for the schools. Berreda, Rebsamen, Carrillo, Laubscher, and Justo Sierra were leaders in the movement to modernize Mexican education. Laubscher founded the country's first kindergarten in 1883, while Sierra was in charge of education during the last years of the Díaz regime and reopened the National University in 1910.

Despite the work of these leaders, at the end of the Díaz regime rural schools were almost nonexistent; and illiteracy had reached a peak, estimated as high as 85 per cent.

*The revolutionary era*. Madero had a real interest in promoting education, but little was accomplished during the near-anarchy that reigned during his administration. In 1911, the Congress passed a law whereby the central government for the first time accepted the responsibility for supporting education throughout the country; but the difficult times defeated the good intentions. And from 1914 to 1921, there was no federal ministry of education, such work being left to the states.

Chaos reigned during the decade in terms of educational service; but Article 3 of the 1917 Constitution represented a landmark in terms of declared educational policy. Its twelve brief paragraphs or provisions comprise a revolutionary pronunciamento embodying the convention's ideas on education, one of the prime concerns of the group — along with labor, agrarian reform, and control of subsoil wealth.

Education is "to develop harmoniously all the faculties of the human being and shall develop in him, at the same time, a love of the Fatherland and a consciousness of international solidarity, independence, and justice." Freedom of belief is to be maintained in education by the exclusion of all religious doctrine and by basing teaching "on the results of scientific progress." Education shall promote democracy as a way of life, as well as in the political sense. "It shall be national . . . without hostility or exclusivism." "It shall contribute to better human cooperation," promote "esteem for the dignity of the person," and produce an appreciation of "the general interest of society." At the same time, it shall avoid "privileges of race, sects, groups, sexes, and individuals." Private schools are allowed, but their authorization may be refused or revoked without appeal. Their programs must be adjusted to comply with official plans and programs. Ministers and religious bodies may not participate in educational work. Primary schooling is to be obligatory; and government schools are to operate without charge to the students.

Possibly due to a belief in states' rights, the Constitutional Convention gave the federal government no specific active role in education. Article 3 charged the Congress with "coordinating education in all of the Republic" through enacting "the necessary laws intended to distribute the educative social function among the Federation, the States, and the municipalities." This was not done for the federal government until 1921, when the Ministry of Education was created.

*The twenties.*[5] In 1921, the Constitution was amended to provide for federal authority in the field of education, and the Ministry of Public Education and Fine Arts was established. The states and municipalities were to continue their existing schools, while the work of the federal Ministry was to be an additional service; and schooling was to be compulsory for children of ages six through fourteen. As the program has developed since 1921, the federal government has come to play the principal role in education – in contrast with the situation in the U.S.

The new approach to education began with the appointment of the noted philosopher José Vasconcelos as the first Minister of Education; and the basic aims established then have, in the main, been continued with greater or lesser fidelity. These aims have included the spreading of elementary schools throughout the country; the extension of elementary schooling to the adults in need of it; the elimination of illiteracy; teacher training; the cooperation of school and family; and federal-state-local school coordination.

The philosopher-minister was a strong stimulus to the education movement. He denied that the Indians were an inferior group, and he put much emphasis on their cultural development. In fact, he went to the extreme of providing the rural masses with cheap editions of the classics before they were able to profit by such "alien" materials.

Under the Carranza administration, education had about 1 per cent of the federal budget. By 1923, Vasconcelos' new Ministry had some 15 per cent of the budget. Traveling teachers were sent to the rural areas to promote a desire for schools and help the people achieve their desires. These "missionaries" had little money and worked with the scant resources at hand. A teacher-training program was started, and the first normal school under the new regime was opened in 1922. By 1924, more than a thousand rural schools had been started.

Vasconcelos' successors in the Ministry continued his program, with modifications. These men were José Manuel Puig Casauranc (1924–28), Moisés Sáenz (1928), Ezequiel Padilla (1928–30), and Narcisso Bassols (1931–34).

It is in the field of rural education that Mexico has made the greatest contribution to educational theory and practice. One authority, Sánchez,[6] feels this is best illustrated in four fields that got their real start in the 1920s: the rural school, the Indian school, the cultural mission, and the rural normal school.

The rural school is typically a humble building, constructed from the community's resources and having little equipment. The teacher generally has more zeal than training. The school serves both children and adult students, and the teacher is supposed to be a leader in community improvement projects.

## EDUCATION

The Indian schools are elementary coeducational boarding institutions. The students do the work of school maintenance and operation of the attached farm. The teacher is paid by the federal government. The Indian school also serves the community, seeking to raise the standard of living in the area.

The cultural mission is one of Mexico's chief contributions to community improvement and teacher training.[7] It is the outgrowth of the initial steps taken in the field of rural education, when the "missionaries" were sent out as individuals in 1921 to establish the first schools in unserved regions. By 1923, the work of founding schools, choosing teachers, supervising them, and promoting the movement became too much for one person; so the cultural mission was organized to serve as a sort of traveling normal school, established temporarily in a community to improve rural teaching and aid the local community in a program of self-improvement.

The mission's personnel typically has consisted of a nurse, an educator, an agricultural worker, a music teacher, a manual arts teacher, a recreation director, and a welfare worker. These workers seek to link the school with the important problems of the community. Guidance is given in such matters as health, housing, farming, and cooperative marketing. In this work, the teachers in the nearby areas serve as understudies to the "missionaries."

Within a year of starting the cultural mission program, six were in operation; and in 1926 a missions department was established in the Education Ministry. In 1935 the country was divided into eighteen areas, each with a mission. In that year, seventy-five training institutes were held in the various centers, attended by some 4,500 rural teachers from twenty states.

After 1933, the missions came under increasing criticism, with charges that they engaged in political activities and did not stay in each locality long enough to produce lasting benefits. Between 1938 and 1942 they were closed, thereafter being reorganized with their emphasis shifted to adult education and community improvement.

In recent years, some forty mission teams have been functioning, living, and working in central villages for as much as from one to three years and serving nearby villages. The mission, newly arrived in an area, makes a study of the needs and establishes a program to fit the local requirements. A community organization, called an Economic and

355

Cultural Action Committee, is formed, plus subcommittees to deal with specific phases of the program. Such groups work with the mission and continue to serve the community after the mission leaves. Despite their shortcomings, the missions have served an important function as community organizers and teacher-training groups, especially before the provision of a training service from a nearby normal school.

The first post-Revolution rural normal school was established in 1922, the movement stemming from the work of the cultural missions. The program of these schools will be discussed in a later section.

The latter nineteen-twenties saw a decline in the tempo of educational development, and nothing spectacular happened until the Cárdenas regime.

*The "socialist" era.*[8] The Cárdenas era was a period of much constructive educational progress, as well as being the controversial period of "socialist" education. The first Six-Year Plan focused on the importance of schooling, calling for 2,000 new schools a year and substantially increased appropriations. These goals were not attained, but the achievements were substantial. An anti-illiteracy campaign brought substantial results. The number of federal rural primary schools more than doubled between 1934 and 1938, while the number of regional agricultural schools rose from 17 to 33. Increased literacy was reflected in the considerable increase in the number and circulation of weekly newspapers.

For some time past, the economic limitations of the state and local governments had brought increasing control of education into the hands of the central government. This process was intensified in the thirties, resulting in a rather high degree of central control. Before 1934, financial aid was given to the states for schools in proportion to population. Afterward, the federal assistance was given on the basis of cooperative agreements signed by the two levels of government. By 1940 some ten states had entered into such agreements, each being varied to meet the local needs.

Previous administrations had been embroiled in controversies with the Church. Under Cárdenas, dissension continued over the specific question of "socialism" in education. Between 1935 and 1939, nearly 300 rural teachers were said to have been killed by fanatical peasants and the armed employees of the *hacendados* in opposition to the program fought by the Church. The immediate legal basis of the contest was the 1934 amendment to constitutional Article 3, which required the teaching of "socialism" and the combating of "fanaticism" in the schools. For a period, some left-wing evangelists carried their campaign to extremes in the schools, seeking to impose doctrines of atheism and Marxian socialism. But, as the basic success of the first Six-Year Plan became assured, the required "socialist" teaching came to be generally interpreted as a left-wing democratic counterpart to the American New Deal.

The Cárdenas era in education was summarized by a prominent American educator, after recognizing shortcomings, who said, "Education in Mexico is outstanding in the world today for its effort to improve the conditions of health, housing, work and recreation in rural communities." "The stubborn facts of the situation have modified the methods of the early planners, but have not turned education aside from its excellent objectives." [9]

*Since 1940.*[10] The administrations since 1940 have followed a middle-of-the-road policy in education. Gross expenditures for education have increased; but the proportion of the budget going to schools has declined, due to the rapid tempo of the industrialization and public works programs. The budget increases for education under the Ruiz Cortines administration seem to give promise of more favorable days for the schools.

The Ávila Camacho administration sought improvements at both ends of the educational ladder. The anti-illiteracy campaign started in 1944 produced good results, but it failed to be the effective continuing instrument that was hoped for. Development of the National Polytechnic Institute, started under Cárdenas, was a valuable contribution to the Mexican economy. A good index of the tone of the administration was the rewording of the constitutional Article 3, eliminating the injunction to make education socialistic and calling for emphasis on democracy, humanism, and nationalism.

While the Alemán administration increased total peso expenditures for education, much of it went into construction of the elaborate new National University plant. Whatever the value of the latter, the potential amount available for mass education was reduced thereby.

A shortcoming of some recent administrations has been noted by various critics — the periodic shifting of Education ministers and thereby of policies. Three ministers served under Ávila Camacho, all holding quite different philosophies of education. And in a number of cases, the minister's background has been rather far afield from education.

*Data on progress.*[11] An important achievement of Mexican education has been that of federal participation in the development of rural schools. Rural schools were almost nonexistent in 1920; but today about 80 per cent of the elementary schools (with about half the elementary enrollment) are rural schools. Of these rural institutions, about 70 per cent are federal, 24 per cent state and municipal, and 8 per cent private or mixed.

Enrollments have grown steadily. In 1949 there were 837 kindergartens, 2,887 teachers, and 98,155 pupils; 24,493 primary schools, 66,937 teachers, 2,880,527 pupils; 440 secondary schools, 7,168 teachers, 72,773 pupils; 17 high schools, 1,873 teachers, 8,074 pupils; 57 teacher-training institutions, 2,788 teachers, 16,890 students; 43 technical schools, 2,556 teachers, 16,556 students; and about two dozen universities and higher technical institutions. The National Polytechnic Institute has over 15,000 students and the National University nearly twice as many as this.

Educational expenditures accounted for about 15 per cent of the total federal budget in 1943 and 20 per cent by 1949. Unfortunately, the proportion has declined in recent years. While the peso totals have increased with the years, the rapidly increasing population has prevented absolute national progress in this field. Facility shortages cause many schools to be run on a two-shift basis, and the school-age children out of school are probably almost as numerous as those in school.

## Educational Institutions

*General characteristics.* The federal educational system is governed mainly by the New Organic Law on Public Education.[12] The Law is nationwide in its scope, but does not apply to the National University or to the states' higher institutions, which are under their own laws. The powers and obligations of the federal government are listed as those of maintaining general, rural, agricultural, and technical schools. The federal government is also charged with promoting scientific investigation and the arts; granting and withdrawing the right for private schools to operate, and supervising their operations; carrying on anti-illiteracy campaigns; and granting scholarships for the education of poor students. (New Organic Law, Chs. 1, 2, 4.) This centralization is in contrast with the decentralization in the United States. Every municipality is obligated to provide primary education. Primary, secondary, normal, and special school education are to be free to the students. Schools must abstain from matters of religious doctrine. (Ch. 4.)

The national system of education includes preschool institutions (kindergartens and nurseries), primary schools, secondary schools, normal schools, vocational and preparatory institutions, higher professional and technical schools, laboratories and institutes, extension work, and specialized schools (including those for the mentally and physically abnormal) (Ch. 3).

Viewed from the standpoint of clientele, there are rural schools, serving peasant communities; semirural schools, in various towns; *escuelas tipos*, standard and model schools, in the more important population centers; and frontier schools, similar to the last, along the country's borders. From the standpoint of sponsorship, there are local, state, federal, and federalized schools — the last-named jointly supported by state and federal governments. In addition, there are private schools. Above the elementary level, the types of schools are the secondary (grades seven through nine), the technical secondary schools, the normals (offering a four-year course above the secondary level), the preparatory (offering a two-year pre-university training above the secondary level), and the various university-level institutions — the national and state universities, the National Polytechnic Institute, the Higher Normal School, etc. It is the obligation of the Ministry of Education to aid and coordinate the work of these institutions, except for the National University and the state universities. The Ministry prescribes curriculums and important administrative procedures, as well as providing varying proportions of the total state-local educational budget. However, the states and localities retain considerable autonomy within the general prescriptions laid down by the Ministry. This is in contrast with the high degree of state and local control of schools found in the United States.[13]

Because of the variety of schools, the educational picture may appear rather complex. In the cities there are kindergartens, primary schools, secondary schools, technical institutions, normals, and higher institutions. Support may come from the local, state, or federal governments, or a combination thereof. Private schools play a prominent role in the cities, despite the legal rules that govern their operation. These institutions are supposedly supervised by the Ministry, which checks on their curricular and pedagogical adequacy, their nonreligious character, and hygienic conditions.[14]

The Mexican preparatory school graduate is expected to have accomplished more than the average American high school graduate, therefore the Mexican schools are more subject-centered than ours. Extracurricular activities play a smaller part in the life of the southern student. Instruction is usually more didactic, in part because the shortage of books puts emphasis on the lecture method and note-taking. Thus, despite much progressive educational thinking (and practice in some places), the Ministry's aim of the child-centered school makes slow progress against traditional practices.[15]

One important factor in Mexican educational progress is the parent-teacher association. These groups are provided for in the Law and are grouped into local and national federations. The parent-teacher group has the usual functions associated with such groups. It may complain to higher authorities about educational administration, but it cannot interfere in the school's operations. These groups, combined with the teachers' union, form a strong pressure group in behalf of educational advancement.[16]

*The kindergarten.*[17] Nursery schools and kindergartens are given much importance in Mexican education. The former are under the Child Welfare Bureau of the Ministry of Health and Welfare, which also directed the kindergartens from 1937 to 1942. Kindergarten objectives and supervision are provided by the Education Ministry, as in the case of higher levels of education; but the local units enjoy a high degree of autonomy.

Urban children attend the kindergarten between the ages of four and six, whereas rural children's kindergartens provide only a one-year course. The kindergartens are of two types. The "complete" type has several hundred pupils and is a unit unto itself. The "annex" type is located in a primary school, where one or more rooms are reserved for its use. Kindergarten education is not compulsory, but it is considered a privilege and is eagerly sought.

*Elementary education.*[18] The six-year period of elementary schooling is divided into three cycles of two years each, with the students' ages normally running from six through fourteen. The public education law (Ch. 8) states the objective of elementary education as being the total, well-rounded educational development of the student — physically, intellectually, and ethically. Education is nominally obligatory through age fifteen, but shortages of personnel and facilities have left this as a goal for the future. Usually grades three through six are operated on a unisexual basis, but in the main the same courses are pursued by both boys and girls.

The basic outline of the curriculum is set forth for the schools by the Ministry, and the students are promoted on the basis of government-prepared examinations. But the teacher has considerable leeway in arranging the material and adapting the subject-content to the local conditions. This is in contrast with the greater number of elective studies pursued by American elementary school students. Due to the economic realities of the day, the elementary training is more terminal than specifically preparatory to advanced studies. The elementary schools have been criticized for their emphasis on manual arts and crafts, but these simple skills are basic to the country's needs and this seems to justify such a procedure. Many teachers use progressive teaching methods, but overcrowded classrooms and a shortage of books are an inducement to the use of traditional methods.

Several types of rural elementary schools have been mentioned in this and earlier chapters – cultural missions, Indian schools, and the practical schools of agriculture. To these should be added the schools for the children of the army. These institutions were founded to give schooling to children of army personnel whose work often keeps them moving and away from accessibility to other schools.

About three fourths of the public elementary schools are federal, and most of the rest are state- and municipality-supported. Also, about three fourths of the public elementary schools are rural; and they have about half the elementary enrollment.

*Current demonstration programs.* Two important demonstration programs in elementary education and community betterment are currently being sponsored by UNESCO and the Mexican government, the pilot projects at Lake Pátzcuaro and at the Santiago Valley in the state of Nayarit.

In 1947, the Mexican delegation to the second UNESCO conference proposed the joint sponsorship of a regional demonstration program in basic education. Since establishment of the program in 1948, the project has drawn the attention of educators and others in many countries. Progress has been substantial. In the formerly backward area, illiteracy has been greatly reduced, health services have been provided, roads have been built, farming practices have been improved, and handicraft industries have been promoted.[19]

At Lake Pátzcuaro, UNESCO and the Mexican government established the first of six projected Regional Fundamental Education Centers. Here the program concentrates on improving the economy and health, and providing for the other needs of a group of villages dependent on agriculture and fishing. Conservation work in its various forms is an important part of the program. Started in 1951, the project serves as a training-demonstration program for several dozen fellowship holders from other Latin American countries. The faculty of specialists in health, agriculture, audio-visual education, manual arts, home economics, and cooperatives has used the surrounding villages as laboratories for the foreign students, who return home to apply their knowledge after an eighteen-month training period. First on the program came reduction of illiteracy, with the resulting literacy being used as a functional tool for community life improvement. Then came the reduction of typhoid, the promotion of better agricultural practices, and the development of conservation work. The program has made mistakes, but its over-all success has been marked.[20]

*Secondary education.*[21] After six years of elementary schooling, the student may choose one of four main types of secondary training: general, pre-university, prevocational, or normal.

From the United States' viewpoint, secondary education could be considered as a five-year continuation; but in Mexico the term refers to the first three of these years, while the last two years comprise the work of the *preparatorias*. These are really lower colleges for the professional schools of the university or the higher technical institutions. The purpose of the secondary school, as stated in the law, is to expand and raise the general level of culture imparted by the elementary school, seeking to prepare the student to fulfill his civic and social duties in a democracy.

For long, secondary education was regarded as part of the college preparatory cycle, rather than as an entity in itself. Only in recent years have the two been separated. Secondary schools were long under the aristocratic influence of the university, with their curriculums minutely regulated by the latter. Only in 1926 was the supervision of these schools placed under the Ministry of Education, when there were four such institutions with a total enrollment of 3,860. By 1951, the schools had increased in number to 454, with 61,629 students enrolled.

*Vocational schools.*[22] Occupational training extends upward from grade seven through the National Polytechnic Institute or the university. The purpose of the first three years (the secondary period) is both terminal and preparatory for higher schools. This period is similar to that of the regular secondary school, except for shop courses taking the place of some minor subjects of the general curriculum. Some thirty of these prevocational schools serve the country, with about two thirds of them giving industrial or commercial training.

Agricultural schools have been discussed in Chapter 20. The first such institutions were started in 1925 under the Ministry of Agriculture, with the aim of providing at least one school for each of the types of agricultural regions. The present agricultural school is a combination rural secondary and vocational school, with a combined course averaging four years.

*Preparatory school.* Since Mexican education follows the European system, there is no real American equivalent of the preparatory school. A partial parallel might be drawn with the American junior college, to the extent that the latter may provide all college-level prevocational training prior to entry into certain professional schools.

The prototype of these institutions is the National Preparatory School in the capital, founded in 1867 under the influence of the positivist philosophy of Comte. Its relationship to the National University has been close, with what many regard as an undue dominance by the latter. The graduate of its two-year course receives the *Título Bachiller* in Sciences or in Humanities, which, of course, is not the equivalent of an American bachelor's degree. Its relationship to the National University, rather than to the Education Ministry, has ensured that the teaching at the School on the whole is traditional rather than progressive or experimental.[23]

*Teacher education.*[24] Institutions for teacher education got a feeble start in the Díaz era, but the chaos of the revolutionary decade left little work being done in this field. For a period following 1923, the rural cultural missions did work of the normal school training type. During the middle and late twenties, a number of rural normal schools were established, while the Ministry of Agriculture was establishing agricultural schools in various areas. During the early thirties, the Education

Ministry combined some agricultural schools and the rural normals. The number of these schools has varied since then, totaling thirty-three in 1951 — eighteen rural and fifteen urban. In addition, there were the Higher Normal School and several agencies for part-time and in-service teacher training.

The normal schools are of five types. Some are administered by the Ministry; others by the states. The rural normal starts with the seventh year of school and provides a course at least four years in length, with the effort being made to expand the work to six years. The first three years' work corresponds to that of the urban normal. The six-year course of the latter has the same prerequisite as the rural normal — the six-year elementary course. The specialized normal schools train for the teaching of physical education, manual training, primary education for adults, and the teaching of the physically and mentally defective. The prerequisites to entrance are regular normal graduation and two years of teaching experience. The course is two years. The normal school for preschool work provides a three-year course for women, after completion of the first three years of the regular normal course or a secondary school.

The Higher Normal School in Mexico City trains teachers for secondary, preparatory, industrial arts, and normal school teaching. The prerequisites are normal graduation and four years of teaching experience. The course covers at least four years, and the degrees conferred are those of Master and Doctor in Pedagogy. It was established in 1936.

Thus, the first three years of the six-year normal course is a kind of specialized secondary education. Since rural schools often do not provide more than four years of elementary schooling, the rural normal schools offer a two-year preparatory course, which precedes their regular four-year course. The urban and the rural normals emphasize the training of teachers for their respective types of communities. The rural normal also carries on a "social action" program to improve the economic and social conditions of the peasants in the area. This is a sort of extension program for training the students in leadership.

A systematic program of in-service training for active teachers began in 1945 with the opening of the Federal Institute of Teacher Training. The importance of such work is emphasized by the fact that a large proportion of Mexico's teachers have not yet had normal school training.

The normal schools are not yet adequately financed, and their equipment is still inadequate on the whole. The distribution of the schools is also unfortunately uneven, with two thirds of them located in one third of the states near the Federal District.

There are a few special schools such as those for the blind, the deaf and dumb, and the feeble-minded. These serve as practice schools for the students of the Normal School for Special Education.

The universities also give professional education courses.

*The universities.*[25] The universities have long been the culmination of the Mexican educational system, a position only recently subject to challenge by the new higher technical institutions. A recent tabulation shows fourteen universities with sixty-three faculties which enjoy considerable autonomy.

The most important of these is the National University, with a history going back to the establishment of the Royal and Pontifical University in 1551. During its four hundred years its inspiration has come from Europe; and its aristocratic and conservative outlook has conduced more to learning for its own sake than to research and preparation for practical living. The University was closed during the later nineteenth century, reopened in 1910, and granted full autonomy in 1929. Its thirty faculties, composed mainly of part-time instructors from the professional community, enroll nearly 30,000 students. Entrance is granted to graduates of the preparatory school; and the courses are rather rigidly prescribed in its professional schools, where the degrees require from four to seven years of work.

The present Organic Law of the National Autonomous University of Mexico dates from 1945. The University's internal organization and management are determined by its own authorities — the governing board, the University council, the *patronato* (finance committee), the rector, and the directors and technical councils of the faculties, schools, and institutes.

The governing board of fifteen is chosen by the University council, one member being chosen each year. Members must hold degrees and be distinguished in their respective occupations. The board's functions are to name and remove the rector, directors of schools and faculties, and members of the *patronato*; decide the question when the rector vetoes a decision of the University council; resolve conflicts between

University authorities; and issue and enforce the University's *reglamento*. (Organic Law, Arts. 3–6.)*

The council establishes teaching and administrative standards. It is composed of the rector; the directors of the faculties, schools, and institutes; and representatives of the faculties, the students, and the employees. (Arts. 7–8.)

The rector is the official representative of the University and chairman of the council, holding office for a four-year term with one possible re-election. He executes the decisions of the board and the council and exercises a conditional veto over actions of the council. (Art. 9.)

The three-member *patronato* administers the University's funds and resources; formulates the budget (to be approved by the council); reports to the council; and names the treasurer, the auditor, and their assistants. The members are experienced in finance and hold office for indefinite terms. (Art. 10.)

The directors of the faculties and schools and institutes are named by the governing board from lists of names presented by the rector, after approval by the technical councils of the respective faculties (Art. 11). The technical councils are advisory bodies for the faculties, schools, and institutes. The members of a council include one professor from each subject field and two representatives from the student body. (Art. 12.)

The faculty consists of full-time (career) professors, teachers, and investigators, and part-time personnel. Thus far most teaching personnel have been part-time; but since 1953 the effort has been made to develop a career service. The law forbids the use of ideological criteria in making appointments or removals; and a high degree of freedom of expression prevails. (Art. 14.) Likewise, the student organizations are free from control by the University authorities (Art. 18), which has both advantages and difficulties. Student strikes have been numerous and have often strongly affected University policies and actions.

The extreme classical bias of university education has been a factor in the tendency to teach codified knowledge and minimize the growth of creative research. A shortage of laboratory facilities, inadequate plant, a poorly paid faculty, and inadequate library facilities have been factors limiting the effectiveness of university education. The establishment of the National University in its commodious new campus is a

* In the following discussion, all Articles cited are from the Organic Law.

move to provide adequate facilities; but the problem of finance is still pressing, though the government provides a subsidy.

The state universities vary considerably in quality of work performed. They are patterned in general after the National University, and like the latter, they receive very modest subsidies from the federal government. The Women's University at the capital provides higher education for a student body of about a thousand women.

*Higher technical education.* At the top of the technical-vocational education pyramid is the National Polytechnic Institute, with more than 15,000 students in its eight professional schools of university rank. The Institute, administered by the Ministry of Education, seeks to do what the National University had failed to do in the field of scientific education.[26]

The Institute was founded under Cárdenas, but progress has come mainly since the middle forties. The top professional schools are the Advanced Schools of Mechanical and Electrical Engineering, Engineering and Architecture, Biological Science, Rural Medicine, Homeopathic Medicine, Textile Engineering, and the Federal School of Textile Industries. On a lower level, there are related to the Institute four vocational schools, five technical schools, and a number of shops and laboratories for scientific research.

Also of importance is the Technological Institute of Monterrey, founded in the northern industrial city in 1942. It is supported in large part by the business community of Monterrey and is modeled on the pattern of the Massachusetts Institute of Technology. It aids northern industrial development by turning out capable graduates and by providing a consultant service for manufacturers.[27]

The National School of Agriculture was discussed in Chapter 20, and the work of the medical research institutes was considered in Chapter 23 (see pages 290–91 and 340–41). These latter agencies have done important work in the fields of scientific-technical advancement.

*Other institutions.* Among other official scientific and cultural institutions, mention should first be made of the National Institute of Anthropology and History, which comes under the direction of the Education Ministry. The scientific side of its work includes historical, archaeological, and anthropological studies, and publication of its findings. Its subdivisions are the Bureau of Pre-Hispanic Monuments, the Bureau of Colonial Monuments, the National Museum of Anthropology, the National Museum of History, the Museum of Religious Art, the Bureau of Publications, and the National School of Anthrolopogy. The museums perform an educational service, and the School of Anthropology has done very important work in that field.

The National Institute of Fine Arts, also a dependency of the Education Ministry, is another important cultural institution, which is dedicated to promoting all branches of the fine arts. Both schools and artistic production are included in the programs of the Departments of Plastic Arts, Music, Theater and Literature, and the Dance. Also of importance is the Department of Theatrical Production.[28]

An important service to agriculture and aviation is provided by the Meteorological Service, which maintains two dozen or more weather stations throughout the country. It has received important cooperation and aid from the U.S. Weather Bureau.[29]

Science as applied to industry is represented by the Bureau of Standards in the Ministry of Economy, which establishes standards of quality for the products of Mexican industries. Attached to it are the National Laboratories for Industrial Development, which operate under a board having representatives from the banks, business, and industry.[30]

An important educational and cultural institution (though not a Mexican government program) is the Mexican–North American Institute for Cultural Relations, partially financed by the U.S. State Department. As one phase of its program, the Institute offers classes attended by several thousand Mexican youth and adults.[31] Similar institutes promote cultural relations with some other countries.

Libraries provide a service that is really just starting in Mexico. The Department of Libraries of the Education Ministry has made an earnest beginning in this field, including a school for the training of librarians; but small budgets have enabled the agency to make only a start in providing this important educational service. The existing scholarly libraries operated by the government leave much to be desired in both organization and resources. However, an important scientific and technical documentation center was opened in 1951. This UNESCO agency center provides scientific and technical workers, laboratories, and industries with up-to-date published information.

*Ministry of Public Education.*[32] Since the work of the Ministry is so varied and extends throughout the country, its budget has ranked second or third among those of all the government ministries. Operating through some fifteen general bureaus and several departments and other units, the Ministry determines educational policy and supervises its execution in varying degrees throughout the country except in university education. Thus, its administrative powers and functions are quite different from those of the federal educational agency in the United States.

Administration of education below the secondary level is handled by several offices — the Bureaus of Preschool Education, Elementary Education in the Federal District, Elementary Education and Supervision in the States and Territories, and Elementary Boarding Schools, and the Department of Cultural Missions. Kindergarten service is receiving increasing attention, and there are more than 1,300 such school units in the country — under federal, state, and private operation.

The Bureau of Elementary Education in the Federal District has charge of such instruction for both children and adults. There are offices of pedagogical studies, private schools, inspection, buildings, technique of adult teaching, and day and evening schools. Sixth-year examinations are administered and certificates of elementary school completion are granted. The Bureau of Elementary Education and Supervision in the States and Territories performs similar functions outside the Federal District.

The work of the Bureau of Elementary Boarding Schools and the Department of Cultural Missions has been discussed earlier.

The Bureau of Secondary Education has Departments of Day Schools in the Federal District, Night School in the Federal District, Secondary Education for the rest of the country, Special Schools, and Private Secondary Schools.

A division with a number of important units is the Bureau of Higher Education and Scientific Investigation. Its Department of University Studies keeps in touch with the curriculums of Mexican and foreign universities and promotes student exchanges. The Department of Intellectual Cooperation maintains relations with UNESCO and the United Nations, and administers scholarship grants for foreign study. The work of the Department of Libraries has been mentioned. The Institute of Pedagogy conducts a variety of educational studies. Of the other four units of importance, three are teaching institutions. The Preparatory School of Ciudad Juárez is under the Bureau. The Normal School for Special Education trains teachers for dealing with the mentally ill, the blind, and deaf-mutes. The work of the Higher Normal School has been discussed. The Institute of Astrophysics is also under the Bureau.

Six other bureaus deal with specialized functions.

The Bureau of Physical Education administers obvious and important functions. The Bureau of Agricultural Education administers the practical schools of agriculture which operate on the elementary-secondary level. From these schools students pass on to the National School of Agriculture. The Bureau of Normal Education administers the rural and urban normal schools and supervises the work of a number of privately incorporated normal schools. The Bureau of Social Action is an organ of consultation and aid for the other agencies of the Ministry in welfare matters as they affect education. The Department of Educational Hygiene performs obvious functions. Finally, the Bureau of Literacy and Out-of-School Education has the Departments of Literacy, Cultural Missions, and Radio Education. Important work has been done in all these fields. A specialized unit is the Institute of Literacy for Monolingual Indians.

A separate bureau serves as liaison with the UNESCO demonstration project in Nayarit. The Institutes of Anthropology and History, and of Fine Arts have been discussed.

A unit of interest to all the teachers is the National Teachers' Roster, which handles teacher promotions. It is composed of two representatives of the teachers' union, two of the Ministry, and a chairman chosen by the four.

Three other special groups are served by the Ministry of Education: Indians, the professions, and authors and inventors. The Bureau of Indian Affairs, established in 1937 as a department, has charge of schooling for the indigenous groups as well as other services. It has units dealing with education, agriculture, practical schools of agriculture for Indians, and legal protection for the native peoples. An important related agency is the National Indian Institute, established in 1948. It conducts important investigations dealing with Indian affairs and carries out programs for native improvement in cooperation with other agencies, especially the Bureau of Indian Affairs. On its governing council are representatives of the Ministries of Education, Health, Gobernación, Agriculture, Hydraulic Resources, and Communications, the Agrarian Department, the Ejidal Bank, the Institute of Anthropology, the University, the

Polytechnic Institute, and other agencies. Also of importance is the Inter-American Indian Institute with headquarters in Mexico, an agency in which that country has played a leading role.[33]

The Bureau of Professions is the link between the government and the members of the professions and their associations. It grants and cancels for cause the titles for professional practice achieved by graduates of the various professional courses. Of the 98,620 registered professional persons active in 1952, the leading professions and their members were as follows: teachers, 19,858; physicians, 12,980; lawyers, 6,769; engineers, 6,681; chemists, 2,919; midwives, 2,107; nurses, 1,640; dentists, 1,568; public accountants, 1,013. These are followed by lesser numbers of social workers, economists, veterinary doctors, metallurgists, notaries public, pilots, and architects.[34] There are also considerable numbers of "unregistered" personnel.

The Law on the Professions[35] charges the Bureau with issuing the rules governing professional licensing, after a hearing open to the professional associations; and the law and regulations are in force in the Federal District, the territories, and throughout the country in federal matters. The Bureau has the power to recognize the degree-granting institutions in the District, the states, and foreign lands. (Law on the Professions, Ch. 3.) The Law provides that there may be from one to five professional associations recognized in each field, with a minimum of a hundred members each; and that each must register with the Bureau (Ch. 6). A technical advisory committee for each profession aids the Bureau. It consists of one member each from the Bureau, the University or the Polytechnic Institute, and the profession. (Ch. 4.)

The Department of Authors' Rights in the Bureau of Legal Affairs handles the registry of literary and intellectual property.

*Summary*. It is often felt — and probably correctly — that one of the Revolution's greatest successes has been in the field of education. Mexico has a long way to go before achieving adequate educational coverage; but, despite the failures and partial successes, a great deal has been done with the meager funds available.

The rural nature of Mexican society, with its great needs, has meant that the basic educational need has been that of improving rural life and the agricultural economy. This has been the challenge faced by the different administrations with varying degrees of success since 1921, in response to which most of them have stressed the development of realistic rural education through elementary schools, normal schools, agricultural schools, and cultural missions. The earlier vision and programs won applause from John Dewey and other world leaders in education. And outstanding educational leadership has come through such men as Jaime Torres Bodet, former Education Minister and UNESCO head.

But the difficulties have been numerous and the shortcomings important. An important anti-illiteracy campaign was started in 1944 by Ávila Camacho, and from a quarter- to a half-million illiterates have been taught each year; but from 1945 through 1952 the numbers taught declined each year but one, while the population has been rapidly increasing.[36] An important related problem has been that of integrating the backward monolingual native peoples into the national society. Government policies have fluctuated much, and integration has made slow progress.[37]

Though the bulk of the education budget goes for elementary education, the population increases so rapidly that only about half of the children in the elementary age group are provided with schools. In the larger cities, an important beginning has been made in the use of radio and television for education. An important beginning has also been made in another field, conservation education, but there is a need for much greater emphasis.[38] The present administration has called for increased emphasis on the rural normal school, as a means of raising the educational and social level of the countryside.

In addition to the needs of elementary education, the need is great for providing technical and leadership training through expanded secondary and higher education with a realistic emphasis. Provision of educational plants, adequate teachers' salaries, and other elementary school needs are as pressing in the secondary and higher fields. The financial support for higher education has been disappointingly small, aside from construction of the new plant for the National University. The various state universities are receiving increased subsidies from the central government, but the support of most such institutions is still precarious. One reason for such federal support is to check the tide of provincial students that has threatened to swamp the National University.

Outside the field of formal schooling, an important cultural service has been provided by prominent publishing houses like the Fondo de Cultura Económica, which with government encouragement has become one of the foremost producers of published works in Latin America.

While important progress is being made in the field of education, the needs are still more pressing. One leading authority in the field, Sánchez, feels that the revolutionary (i.e., constructive) period of Mexican education ended in 1940.[39] He feels that the "middle-of-the-road" educational policies of the next two administrations were really reactionary and "dealt a serious blow to educational progress." He further believes that this is reflected in the lack of adequate financial support and the revival, during those administrations, of unisexual schools as "a response to reactionary norms." Traditionally, Mexican education adhered to the classical pattern of European schooling. This meant exalting literary and some professional pursuits and deprecating technical and "practical" training. Slow but substantial progress has been made since the 1920s in changing this traditional pattern.

The present administration has presented no radical departures in educational theory or practice, but its increased financial support for education seems to foretell some needed improvement.

## NOTES

[1] Francisco Larroyo, *Historia Comparada de la Educación en México* (1952) and "Breve Historia de la Educación en México," in Sría. de Educación, *Anuario de Estadística Educativa*, 1947, pp. 13–70; G. F. Kneller, *The Education of the Mexican Nation* (1951).

[2] Whetten, *op. cit.*, p. 418.

[3] Larroyo, "Breve Historia de la Educación . . . ," *op. cit.*, pp. 13–46 and *Historia Comparada de la Educación* . . . , Pts. 1–5; Virgil Logan, "Speech Education in Mexico" (Ph.D. thesis, University of Wisconsin, 1951), Chs. 2–4.

[4] Larroyo, *Historia Comparada* . . . , Pts. 3–5; Kneller, *op. cit.*, pp. 36–40.

[5] Larroyo, *Historia Comparada* . . . , Pt. 6; Logan, *op. cit.*, Ch. 5; Kneller, *op. cit.*, pp. 47–51; Simpson, *op. cit.*, Chs. 14–16.

[6] G. I. Sánchez, "Education," *Annals*, March 1940, pp. 149–52.

[7] Whetten, *op. cit.*, Ch. 18; Guillermo Bonilla y Segura, *Report on the Cultural Missions of Mexico* (1945); *Americas*, March 1954, pp. 19–20, 44–46.

[8] Larroyo, *Historia Comparada* . . . , Pt. 6; Kneller, *op. cit.*, pp. 52 et seq.; Goodwin Watson, *Education and Social Welfare in Mexico* (1940); G. I. Sánchez, *A Revolution by Education* (1936); G. C. Booth, *Mexico's School-Made Society* (1941).

[9] Watson, *op. cit.*, pp. 45–46.

[10] Larroyo, *Historia Comparada* . . . , Pt. 7; Logan, *op. cit.*, Ch. 5; Cline, *op. cit.*, pp. 299–302; Call, *op. cit.*, pp. 145–53.

[11] Iturriaga, *op. cit.*, pp. 154–87; Watson, *op. cit.*; International Bank, *op. cit.*, pp. 10, 100; *Mañana*, May 12, 1951, pp. 133–41; *HA*, February 28, 1955, pp. 5–8.

[12] *Nueva Ley Orgánica de la Educación Pública*, in Andrade, ed., *op. cit.*, pp. 157 et seq.

[13] Kneller, *op. cit.*, Chs. 3, 5–7; Scott, *op. cit.*, pp. 438 *et seq.*

[14] *Nueva Ley* . . . , Ch. 6.

[15] Kneller, *op. cit.*, Ch. 5.

[16] *Nueva Ley* . . . , Ch. 17; Scott, *op. cit.*, pp. 428 *et seq.*

[17] *Nueva Ley* . . . , Ch. 7; Kneller, *op. cit.*, pp. 92–93; Logan, "Mexico's Unified School System," *Journal of Educational Research*, October 1953, p. 119.

[18] Larroyo, *Historia Comparada* . . . , Pt. 7; Logan, *op. cit.*, pp. 117–26; Logan, "Speech Education . . . ," Ch. 6; Kneller, *op. cit.*, Ch. 4; Whetten, *op. cit.*, pp. 410–24, 429–32.

[19] Glen H. Fisher, "Directed Culture Change in Latin America . . ." (Ph.D. thesis, University of North Carolina, 1953), *passim*; *Mexican American Review*, February 1950, p. 16.

[20] *U.N. World*, December 1952, pp. 47–50; Cline, *op. cit.*, pp. 403–4; Kathleen Laughlin, *New Life in Old Lands* (1954), pp. 62–86.

[21] *Nueva Ley* . . . , Ch. 10; Larroyo, *Historia Comparada* . . . , Pt. 7; Kneller, *op. cit.*, pp. 112 *et seq.*

[22] *Nueva Ley* . . . , Ch. 12; Kneller, *op. cit.*, pp. 137–38, 141 *et seq.*; Whetten, *op. cit.*, pp. 424–26.

[23] Kneller, *op. cit.*, Ch. 5; Logan, "Mexico's Unified School System," *op. cit.*, pp. 117–26.

[24] Larroyo, *Historia Comparada* . . . , Pt. 7; Logan, "Speech Education . . . ," Ch. 6; Sánchez, *A Revolution by Education* (1936), Ch. 7; *Nueva Ley* . . . , Ch. 11; Whetten, *op. cit.*, pp. 407–10; Kneller, *op. cit.*, pp. 146–47, 152–58.

[25] *Ley Orgánica de la Universidad Nacional Autónoma de México*, in Andrade, ed., *op. cit.*, Appendix 3; Kneller, *op. cit.*, Ch. 7; *CSM*, April 30, 1953; *HA*, March 12, 1956, pp. 3–8; Portes Gil, *op. cit.*, pp. 319–38.

[26] *Nueva Ley* . . . , Ch. 13; Kneller, *op. cit.*, pp. 191 *et seq.*

[27] Kneller, *op. cit.*, Ch. 7; Mosk, *op. cit.*, p. 269; *Américas*, May 1955, pp. 16–19.

[28] *Directorio* . . . (1), pp. 311–13.

[29] *Mexican American Review*, December 1949, pp. 80 *et seq.*

[30] *Ibid.*, May 1950, pp. 12–13.

[31] *CSM*, March 26, 1952.

[32] *Directorio* . . . (1), pp. 285–331; Sría. de Educación Pública, *Memoria, 1951–52* (1952), and *La Educación Pública en México, 1934 a . . . 1940* (1941).

[33] *Américas*, March 1954, pp. 19–20, 44–46; *Directorio* . . . (2), pp. 635–43; International Labor Organization, *Indigenous Peoples* (1954), *passim*; *International Labor Review*, December 1955, pp. 514–20; *HA*, May 28, 1956, pp. 6–13.

[34] Sría. de Educación Pública, *Memoria, 1951–52*, pp. 415–34.

[35] Andrade, ed., *op. cit.*, pp. 172.45 *et seq.*

[36] *News*, August 21, 1953.

[37] *Annals*, March 1940, pp. 132–43.

[38] *El Nacional*, March 30, 1954.

[39] A. H. Moehlman and J. S. Roucek, eds., *Comparative Education* (1952), pp. 106–7.

# PART VII

# Governmental Subdivisions

# 25

## *State Government*

THE Mexican federal republic is divided into twenty-nine states, two territories, and the Federal District. The organization of the majority of the states dates from the early years of independence; but the newest state, Baja California, was admitted in 1952–53. As indicated earlier, the forms of state government and the relationships of the central government to the state governments are similar to those in the United States; but the powers of the Mexican states are much weaker.

The Mexican states present a picture of great and numerous differences, which produce great differences in the scope and effectiveness of their governments.[1]

The state areas range from 1,554 square miles to 94,806, with an arithmetical average of less than 25,000 — or about two fifths the size of the "average" state in the United States. The larger states are found in the more sparsely settled semiarid northern area, with only three states having an area of more than 50,000 square miles and four others having an area greater than 30,000 square miles.

Population ranges from 112,321 (Colima) to 2,040,231 (Veracruz), with seven states having more than a million people — five of them in the "core" region of the country. While the average population density in the United States is about 51 per square mile, the Mexican average is about 35 — the figure for the United States in 1920. The density per square mile by geographic areas ranges from 12.4 to 105.3 and for states from 6.2 to 182.1. Six states have over 100 people per square mile and four others over 60 — all ten in the "core" area.

The states also vary widely in other respects, such as urbanization. While the country is still overwhelmingly rural, urbanization is showing a larger proportional increase than the population in general for

377

the whole country, although this is not true for a number of states. In 1940, the rural population (communities of less than 2,500 people) varied by states from 85.4 per cent to 42.6 per cent and by regions from 83.8 per cent to 58 per cent with a national average of 64.9 per cent. Another index is the percentage of the working population engaged in agriculture, which ranged from 41 per cent to 80.8 per cent, with an average of 58.3 per cent.

A further indication of the problems facing state and local governments is the fact that the vast majority of the people live in isolated rural communities, cut off from neighboring communities by rugged mountains, lack of roads, and scarcity of other means of communication which would link local communities with the main stream of national life. One result of such isolation is that in 1940 there were 1,237,018 people (7.4 per cent of the population) who could speak only an Indian dialect, while another 7.4 per cent spoke little Spanish. In 1950, the number of people who could speak only an Indian dialect had decreased to 795,069.

In view of these facts, it is understandable that absolute and per capita expenditures for providing state and local government services vary widely.

*Constitutional position of states.* Despite frequent verbalisms about states' rights, the Mexican states have considerable autonomy but have never had sovereignty. It is recognized that the present federal regime is not the result of a compact between previously existing states; rather, the states have been created by the government of the whole country. Hence, states have no right of secession, which has been tried without success (e.g., in 1915 and 1920). As in the United States, the Mexican states are on a basis of legal equality with each other.[2]

Congress admits new states and territories into the Union; converts territories into states "when they have a population of 80,000 inhabitants and the means necessary to provide for their political existence"; and forms new states "within the boundaries of those already existing," when certain requirements are met. These requirements are as follows: at least 120,000 population in the proposed new state; proof to Congress "that the section has sufficient means to provide for its political existence"; provision of a hearing for the affected states; a report from the President; approval by a two-thirds vote of those present in each house of Congress; and ratification by a majority of the state legislatures. If not approved by the legislatures of the affected states, the ratification must be by two thirds of all the other legislatures. Adding to the members of the Union involves a constitutional amendment (Art. 73), since all members are listed in Article 43.[3]

Of the first nineteen state constitutions, one was adopted in 1824, thirteen in 1825, three in 1826, and two in 1827.

The states have the power to fix their boundaries by agreement among the affected members, but the agreements must be approved by the Congress (Art. 116). The Congress may adjust the states' boundaries in question, "unless these differences have a justiciable nature" (Art. 73, IV). In the latter case, the Supreme Court decides, since it has "exclusive jurisdiction in all controversies that arise between two or more states, between the branches of the same state regarding the constitutionality of its acts, and conflicts between the federation and one or more states, and in all cases in which the federation may be a party" (Art. 105).[4]

The Mexican Constitution, like that of the United States, conceded the reserved powers to the states; but the role of the states is restricted by concurrent powers exercised by the central government and by positive and negative obligations that the Constitution imposes on the states.[5]

Positive obligations require the states to have a government which is "popular, representative, [and] republican" in form and which provides the "free municipality" as the form of local government, under specified details of organization and functioning. Certain requirements are set forth regarding the governorship and the state legislature. (Art. 115.) Negative or prohibitive obligations are absolute and relative. Among the relative limitations, the state cannot without the consent of Congress, do such things as levy import or export duties; maintain permanent troops; make war except in case of invasion or its imminence (Art. 118). The absolute prohibitions are mainly a listing of functions that other constitutional articles give exclusively to the Congress. These include prohibitions against making treaties; issuing money and stamps; taxing the transit of persons or goods; negotiating loans which are not for revenue-producing purposes (Art. 117). Other absolute obligations are those of rendition of criminals wanted in another state or country; publishing and enforcing federal laws; and granting full faith and credit to the "public acts, registries, and judicial proceedings" of the other states (Arts. 119–21). The guarantees of civil rights found in the first twenty-nine articles are limitations on the states and municipalities as well as on the federal government and individuals.

Contrary to the usual doctrine of delegated and reserved powers, the states are also granted specific powers. The states are empowered to grant professional licenses (Art. 4); acquire and use real property for public purposes (Art. 27); expropriate agrarian properties within their areas (Art. 27); settle their boundary questions (Art. 116); initiate legislation in the federal Congress (Art. 71).

Few protections are given to the state governments as such. They are protected against invasion or internal uprising or disturbance, the latter on request of the governor or the legislature (Art. 122). Unfortunately, the frequent imitation of the United States Constitution was not extended here to protect the "form of government." The federal authorities have often intervened under Article 76, V and otherwise, without the federal courts' affording the states any protection.

*State constitutions.*[6] The state constitutions are like the federal document in being long, detailed, and rather frequently amended. The detail obviously necessitates ease and frequency of amendment. This is done by a two-thirds or a three-fourths vote in the legislature which is approved by a majority or two thirds of the state's *municipios.* An example of frequent constitutional change is the state of Mexico. The state adopted its fourth constitution in 1917, and it was amended one hundred thirty-nine times in the thirty years between 1921 and 1951.

Being modeled after the federal document, the state constitutions all make provision for protecting the "rights of man." Often these provisions are numerous. The "Rights of Man" title of the Nuevo León constitution, for example, has twenty-four articles. These specify no slavery; freedom in education; freedom of commerce and occupation; no forced labor; freedom of expression, press, petition, and assembly; the rights of travel and bearing arms; no private laws; no unlawful detention or imprisonment for debt; court trial rights; no double jeopardy or cruel and unusual punishments; indemnification for expropriated property; no monopolies.

Often, the state constitution — like that of the State of Mexico — has a substantial section dealing with the "conditions of persons," which is concerned successively with the rights and the obligations of persons and of citizens. In the cited document, state citizenship is provided for by birth or by six months' residence. Citizens by birth have preference in public employment. Obligations are taxpaying, voting, and military service. Political rights are specified as voting, election to office, and service in the national guard — which are also labeled in the next article as obligations. Provision is made for suspension and loss of citizenship rights.

Preambles are not common, but one of the state constitutions has, in its first sections, the most general provisions. In this document, the state is declared subordinate to the federal Constitution; the rhetoric makes the state "free, sovereign, and independent in its internal regime"; sovereignty is located in the people, exercised through their representatives; a republican form of government and the "free municipality" are provided for; and revenue and judicial districts are provided for. The constitution of Querétaro much more briefly states the principle of "internal sovereignty" and lists the municipalities.

The constitutions provide specifically for the separation of powers into legislative, executive, and judicial branches.

*State legislatures.* The section dealing with the legislature is usually the longest of all, with several subdivisions. The Querétaro constitution, for example, has subdivisions dealing with the legislative power in general, the body's installation and periods of sessions, the initiating and passage of laws, powers and obligations of the body, the permanent committee, and extraordinary sessions. In addition, the unicameral legislature (often called "Congress") is regulated by Article 115 of the federal Constitution, which deals with the election, terms, and numbers of legislators. Elections are direct and in accordance with the state electoral law. The number of representatives is in proportion to population but not less than seven, nine, and eleven in states of respective population size groups. Incumbent deputies may not be immediately re-elected or elected as substitutes; but substitutes may be next elected as deputies.

The provisions of the State of Mexico's document contain some three dozen articles (it is not the most voluminous of the constitutions) and are more or less typical. The legislature is unicameral and the members are called deputies, with one deputy and one substitute elected for each 100,000 of the state's 1,383,640 people. (Querétaro has one deputy for each thirty thousand of its 282,608 people.) Deputies are elected by districts for three-year terms (Querétaro, four years), fully renewed each three years. (Querétaro specifies the maximum size of the body and maximum pay.) Deputies must be at least twenty-five years old and Mexican by birth. Ineligible persons are ministers of the gospel, military personnel in service, and executive and judicial employees.

One ordinary session of the legislature is held annually, lasting from September 5 to not later than December 31. This contrasts with the U.S. state pattern of biennial sessions. (Querétaro and Baja California, the newest state, have two annual sessions, autumn and spring. The autumn session is devoted primarily to budget and tax matters.) Extraordinary sessions may be called by the governor or the permanent committee. Some states restrict special session business to the items named in the call. (Querétaro allows consideration of other matters by a two-thirds vote.)

Some states like the State of Mexico imitate the federal Congress in having an organizational session about a week before the legislature regularly convenes. At this presession, credentials are approved and legislative officers are chosen. Most of the rules of organization and procedure are provided in the *reglamento* adopted by the body. As in the federal government, the governor opens the legislative sessions with a reading of his annual report, and the presiding officer of the legislature gives a formal reply. In some states, the members of the state supreme court are in attendance. A quorum varies from a simple majority to two thirds of those elected in the various states. The session may compel the attendance of absent members.

Bills may be introduced by legislators, the governor, the state supreme court (judicial matters), and the municipalities (municipal matters). Bills are studied in the usual legislative committees. The executive may participate in debate on the floor, without vote, as may representatives of the court and the municipalities in matters concerning them. The rules may be suspended by a two-thirds vote in order that extraordinary action may be taken. The final action on a bill is a record vote. Legislative immunity is provided for expressions during sessions.

The governor has the usual executive veto power, which action may be overridden by a two-thirds vote in the legislature. The veto is not effective when the legislature is sitting as an electoral body or as a jury trying an official for an important offense.

A typical statement of the legislature's powers and duties is that of the State of Mexico, which provides that the body shall create the *municipios* and establish their limits and provide annually for their financing; promote education and public health; provide for elections; create and abolish state positions; provide the tax and budget laws for the same; name and remove the employees of the general auditing office; authorize and provide for the payment of debts; approve the governor's nominees to judgeships; legislate on state and municipal matters, within the limits set by the federal Constitution; initiate bills before the federal Congress; meet extraordinary conditions by the temporary delegation of certain legislative powers to the governor, through a two-thirds vote of the legislature.

The permanent committee is another legislative device in imitation of the federal Congress. It usually consists of three or more members and their substitutes, chosen at the last legislative session to function during the annual recess. It scrutinizes the observance of the laws; calls special legislative sessions; chooses an interim or provisional governor, in the absence of a governor; and performs lesser tasks enjoined by the legislature.

Despite the federal government's extensive ultimate power over the states, the states have a broad field of private law and considerable public law within their jurisdiction. These fields include the laws of crime, status of persons, domestic relations, torts, damages, real and personal property, inheritance, mortgages, suretyship, intrastate public utilities, nonfederal taxes, etc. State law also covers contracts, agency, and partnership, except where the federal commercial code applies.

Typical state laws are the civil code, code of civil proceedings, penal code, and code of penal proceedings. Other important laws are those of the treasury, judicial power, attorney general, elections, municipalities, public education, agriculture, and stockraising. Other typical laws, found in the State of Durango, include those dealing with drinking water, alcoholic beverages, arms, charity and welfare, roads, libraries, commerce, hunting, electricity, expropriation, entertainments, forestry, inheritance, markets, mining, planning and zoning, police, professions, public registry of property, health, civil service, insurance, labor.[7]

*The governor.* The principal concentration of state power and influence is in the hands of the governor, just as the federal power center is the presidency. But the governor must maintain substantially satisfactory relations with the federal regime or suffer removal, as discussed in Chapter 5.

The gubernatorial term of office has varied in the different states from four to six years, with a six-year maximum allowed by the federal Constitution. Governors holding office by popular election may never again perform the duties of that office. Substitute, provisional, or interim occupants of the office cannot be re-elected for the immediately following term. Governors must be Mexicans by birth, as well as natives of their states or residents for five years preceding election. (Art. 115.) A common age requirement is thirty years. Disqualifications are ecclesiastical status or military command within ninety days before the election. In the absence of an incumbent, the legislature names an interim governor. Commonly, the constitutions provide for new elections for a permanent governor only when the vacancy occurs in the first half of the regular term of office.

The governor introduces bills in the legislature and exercises the veto, as well as calling special legislative sessions through the permanent committee. In a typical state like Mexico, he names and removes such top officials as the secretary of the government, *oficial mayor*, director of finance, and chiefs of departments not otherwise detailed in the law. He has the power of granting pardons and commutations of sentence. In addition, the governor's responsibilities include preparing the budget of income and expenditures for the state; doing the same for the municipalities; handling urgent public health measures; promoting an education program; nominating judges; and in general seeing to the execution of the laws.

The more detailed provisions of the Querétaro constitution also specify the following duties for the governor: seeing to the collection and investment of public funds; supervising the municipal governments; advising the permanent committee and the legislature; commanding the national guard in the state; seeing to the execution of court decisions; presenting the real property census and tax list to the legislature. The governor is specifically forbidden, among other things, to interfere with the electoral process or judicial matters; take personal command of troops without legislative approval; take private property unless expressly provided by law.

*Executive officers and agencies.* The secretary of government is the governor's chief cabinet officer (somewhat similar to the federal Minister of Gobernación), through whom the governor carries out his program. The *oficial mayor* aids the secretary of government. Other agencies found in most or all states are bureaus or departments of finance, communications and public works, health and welfare, education, registry of property, agriculture, and justice. Among the other agencies found in some states are those of labor, statistics, and municipal coordination.

In the State of Mexico, the Department of Gobernación administers jails, state police, the juvenile court, sanitary and public assistance services, and the attorney general's office.[8] The sanitary and welfare services in this and many other states are provided mainly by the federal government. However, the State of Mexico was the first state to enact a code for the protection of children and to establish an agency for this function (in 1954).[9]

In the same state, the Department of Communications and Public Works includes supervision or regulation of telephones, public works, roads, irrigation works, electric services, and planning and zoning. (The Planning and Zoning Law dates from 1944.)

The importance of education is recognized by the states to the extent that the expenditures in that field rank first or second among the budget items in most states. In some states the education item has equaled as much as a third of the budget. The superior resources of the federal government have placed it in the lead in financing education, but from 1939 to 1950 the states have spent from two fifths to one third as much as the Ministry of Education – the states' proportion slowly declining.[10]

Despite the importance of public health improvement, the states have spent only one ninth as much since 1939 on health as on education. In the same period, the states have spent from a sixth to an eighth as much as the federal Ministry of Health.[11]

Since two or all of the three levels of government (federal, state, and local) perform or participate in financing a number of the services, there is no set way of determining which will do what and by what method of financing. There are many special arrangements among the three levels for certain services in particular states and localities. The answer in any particular locality is apt to be the result of the federal government's interest and ability and the state and local governments' financial inability.

*Expenditures.* The most obvious fact about expenditures is the preponderance of the federal portion. This was some 73 per cent of total government expenditures in 1939 and 72 per cent in 1951. However, the true federal figure in 1951 is about 81 per cent, including expenditures by autonomous federal agencies which were insignificant in 1939. The expenditures of the Federal District government remained at about 6 per cent of the total from 1939 to 1951, while the municipal fraction of the total government expenditure declined from 4 per cent to 3 per cent. The state and territorial expenditures declined from 17 per cent to 10 per cent, but much of the gap was filled by increased direct federal service expenditures in the states and territories.[12]

Per-capita expenditures have varied tremendously, often out of all proportion to relative per-capita wealth and income, though the wealthier states usually provide the larger budgets. Per-capita budgets for 1945 ranged from 5.87 pesos in Oaxaca to 179.45 pesos in Baja California Norte; in 1947, from 17.91 pesos in Querétaro to 420.07 pesos in Baja California Norte. The general proportions are considered similar today. Highest per-capita income is usually found in industrialized states, so one would expect to find higher per-capita taxes there; but that is not always the case. In 1940, the per-capita expenditures for the states were 16.33 pesos in the North Pacific Zone, 11.46 pesos in the Central Zone, 8.62 pesos in the Gulf Zone, 7.85 pesos in the North Zone, and 3.17 pesos in the South Pacific Zone. The national average was 9.56 pesos. The relative proportions for the different zones showed little change between 1946 and 1950.[13]

A breakdown by services for 1939–49 shows that an average of 22.9 per cent of the total went to public works, 15.7 per cent to education, 10.2 per cent to other items labeled "public services." Less than 2.5 per cent each went to the judiciary, administration of justice, the chief executive, welfare, public health, and the legislature.[14]

*Revenue.* Since the adoption of the present federal fiscal code in 1938, an effort has been made to work out a system of priorities and tax allocations among governmental levels; but even now the complex overlapping of direct and indirect taxes challenges good administration. Even within one state large differences are found at times, because taxes tend to be regressive and municipalities sometimes lack uniform legislation. The federal Constitution, as in the United States, establishes no allocation of taxes, so there has been a gradual encroachment by the federal government on the potential state tax resources — with little state opposition. Thus, though state and local government incomes rise slowly, they fail to keep pace with the income and expenditures of the national government. The state tax resources are small; the municipalities' resources are much smaller; and only increasing federal subsidies keep the present system of public services functioning at current levels.[15]

The heterogeneous nature of state taxes has been mentioned, with each of the states taxing its principal agricultural and industrial products. Prominent among these are cattle, agricultural products, alcohol, beer, mineral waters, sugar, and nonmetallic minerals. But the real property tax still leads all others, with a general mercantile tax becoming prominent recently. Between 1939 and 1949, the state governments on the average received 23.3 per cent of their income from federal aids; 18 per cent from real property; 15.8 per cent from taxes on industries; 6.8 per cent from commerce; 6.5 per cent from services; 5.7 per cent from agriculture; and lesser fractions from natural resources and miscellaneous sources.[16]

The great range and variation in the use of various taxes is shown by a study in 1948 which found these then current percentages of total income figures for the states — averages and ranges: real property, 17.2, 3.1 to 25.3; commerce and industry 26.4, 14.1 to 52.1; exploitations 21.6, 8.6 to 34.1; agriculture and stockraising 4.2, 0 to 40.2; services 8.3, .8 to 15.8; federal aids 22.3, 5.5 to 59.2.

The real property tax — one of the two most important levies — is based in some states on the usual valuation approach and in others on the rental income. The rate is more than four times as much in some states as in others. States also levy a transfer tax on the sale of real estate.[17]

There are many forms of taxes on business and industry, among them levies on textile factories, liquor sales, tobacco, excess profits, business transfers, and general and specific sales taxes. The various bases of assessment are volume of operations, capital, assets, and value of operations. Most states have used taxes on capital invested in businesses and industries, some being in lieu of sales taxes and others being in addition thereto.[18] Other levies are made on salaries, inheritances, etc.

In 1950, one study listed twenty-five state and local taxes in the state of Nuevo León. Fourteen of these were for the state government, the others for the municipalities. Of the total state-local yield, 80 per cent went to the state level of government. Many taxes in the Mexican system are of questionable wisdom, and some, like the sales tax, have long been a strong hindrance to the interstate commerce of certain commodities. Known as *alcabalas*, these taxes on sales were supposedly abolished in 1886, but taxes with substantially the same effects have frequently been revived, with more or less undesirable effects.[19]

*The courts.* The states vary in the composition and selection of their courts. The judges of the supreme court (*tribunal superior*) in some states are chosen by the governor, in others by popular vote, and in others by the legislature. The high court members serve four- or six-year terms, and the court functions in *pleno* and in *salas* (divisions). As with the federal Supreme Court, there are also supernumerary members. Common requisites for judgeships are a minimum age of thirty, being a licensed attorney, and five years of law practice.

The jurisdiction of the superior tribunal is both original and appellate. The Querétaro constitution, for example, includes the following in its original jurisdiction: initiating bills in the legislature; trying cases involving official offenses; naming the judges of first instance, the juvenile judges, and the municipal judges; settling controversies between municipalities and a branch of the state government or between branches of the state government, when not within the jurisdiction of the federal Supreme Court. The federal Constitution (Art. 104) provides for a sort of concurrent federal-state jurisdiction in civil and criminal cases involving federal laws and treaties, when such cases "affect only the interests of private parties."

The lower court judges may be elected or appointed by the superior tribunal, and their tenure may be for a fixed term or during good behavior. Lawyers are commonly required for these positions, and the minimum age may be as low as twenty-one. The attorney general is the chief legal advisor and prosecuting attorney for the executive branch, being appointed by the governor. The judicial police, functioning under the attorney general, see to enforcement of the laws and aid in the work of prosecuting offenders. The jury system is used in some states in criminal cases.

*The functioning organization.* In the state as in the nation, the real substance of power lies in the executive and the Party organization. The governor becomes governor because he is largely an embodiment of the Party's program in that state.

The Regional Executive Committee (CER) — chiefly its president — is the important link upward to the national Party and the President of the republic. The CER president is also normally one of the most important members of the governor's team. Officially and unofficially, the former is an important liaison for the governor to the legislature and to the municipal Party and government officials.

The governor may be separated from office by seeking permission from the legislature to step down, by an impeachment-like process, or by removal by the central government (as discussed in Chapter 5). The third procedure has been the more usual one. It is a potent lever, but recent studies seem to show that it has not been used capriciously in recent years. It has been a last-resort device to deal with flagrant political recalcitrance or abuse of power. Actual autonomy of state administrations has often seemed to vary with the state's size and importance and its distance from the national capital.[20]

Like the federal Congress, the state legislature plays a limited but useful role. Outside the formal lawmaking process, the legislator serves as an important link between the governor and important groups in the local district. With the legislator, as with other officials, official role and Party role intertwine. He may represent the Party and the governor by presiding over local Party meetings, conciliate varying viewpoints, and help achieve Party-determined objectives.[21]

In the past, political instability led to concentration of power in the central government; and the location of fiscal resources largely in central hands has reinforced that concentration of power. In recent years, there have been indications of a slow growth in political autonomy. But the achievement of state financial autonomy does not seem promising. Much the same might be said of state-municipal relations. Despite federal and state constitutional "guarantees" for the "free municipality," state governments have usually exercised close control — and often blighting control — over the municipalities.

### NOTES

[1] On the area, population, degree of urbanization, etc. of the states, see Cline, *op. cit.*, Appendix; Whetten, *op. cit.*, Chs. 1–3, Appendixes; Sría. de Economía, *Compendio Estadístico* (annual), *México en Cifras* (1952), *Séptimo Censo . . . , 1950, Resumen General* (1953); Brandenburg, *op. cit.*, Ch. 8; Medina and Ortiz, *op. cit.*, Ch. 9; *HA* carries governors' messages, giving varied data on state progress.

[2] Lanz Duret, *op. cit.*, pp. 377–78.

[3] Tena Ramírez, *op. cit.*, pp. 168 *et seq.*

[4] *Ibid.*, pp. 156–59. For a boundary dispute, see *HA*, December 27, 1954, p. 10, January 3, 1955, pp. 9–10.

[5] Tena Ramírez, op. cit., Ch. 6; Lanz Duret, op. cit., pp. 386–91; Comstock, op. cit., passim.

[6] Agustín Farrera, ed., Constituciones de los Estados . . . Concordadas (1949), and constitutions of individual states.

[7] Pedro Suinaga Luján, Veinte Años de Legislación . . . (1951), v. 3, pp. 1594–1603.

[8] Alfonso and Gilberto Fábila. México . . . (1951), v. 2, pp. 277 et seq.

[9] HA, June 27, 1955, pp. 9–13.

[10] International Bank, op. cit., p. 326.

[11] Ibid., p 326; Sría. de Economía, México en Cifras.

[12] International Bank, op. cit., p. 344.

[13] Eduardo Bustamante, "Los Sistemas Tributarios de los Estados," Rev. Ec., April 1950, pp. 124–27, May 1950, pp. 151–53; Sría. de Economía, México en Cifras; Compendio . . . (1953), p. 558.

[14] Sría. de Economía, México en Cifras.

[15] Scott, op. cit., pp. 298–312; Bustamante, op. cit.

[16] Sría. de Economía, México en Cifras.

[17] Flores Zavala, Panorama . . . , pp. 115–16; Laufenberger, op. cit., pp. 234–38.

[18] See note 17; Flores Zavala, Elementos . . . , pp. 221 et seq., Panorama . . . , Ch. 4.

[19] Flores Zavala, Elementos . . . , pp. 225–40; Revista Fiscal y Financiera, December 1948, pp. 60–71.

[20] Padgett, op. cit., pp. 144–47; Brandenburg, op. cit., pp. 315–26; HAR, July (August) 1953, p. 11.

[21] Padgett, op. cit., pp. 30–32. The same investigator presents a case study of the Party's internal elections in Puebla State, showing how interaction between leaders and rank and file tends to minimize possible abuse of power (pp. 151–68).

# 26

## Local Government

URBAN communities have played an important role in Mexican history, a role greatly out of proportion to their share of the country's population. The current process of rapid industrialization and urbanization underlines the growing importance of the cities. Despite their inherent importance in Mexican life, cities have been the stepchildren in the governmental scene — usually underprivileged and ignored.

*Environment.* Despite the importance of cities and other truly urban communities, their numbers are not large. This fact is indicated by the figures for the first three types of community listed in the accompanying table. The other seven types give a picture of rural Mexico.[1]

The 1950 census lists 99,028 localities, showing the preponderance of small communities in number of units and the tendency of population to concentrate in small to medium-size communities. In 1950, the 66.5 per cent of the localities with 1 to 100 people had 7 per cent of the population; the 25.1 per cent of the units of 101 to 500 had 22.7 per cent; the 7.4 per cent of the units of 501 to 2,500 had 28 per cent; and the 1 per cent of the units with over 2,501 had 42.3 per cent.[2] These figures represent a small ten-year decrease in population for places under 2,500 population and an increase for larger communities.

The city (*ciudad*) is usually a center of considerable importance but of no specified size (other than the minimum size for *municipios* (municipalities), which varies from 1,500 to 5,000 or more in the different states).[3] The approximately 2,400 *municipios* are rural-urban subdivisions of the states, resembling in varying degrees the U.S. county, township, and New England town.

The *villa* has lost its original meaning and merely indicates an urban center smaller than most cities. The same is true of the *pueblo*, which is the unit of next lower rank. The *congregación* also has uncertain characteristics aside from size. The *ejido*, a communal or semicommunal farming unit, has been discussed earlier. The *hacienda* is a large landed estate having a community of resident workers. The *rancho* is usually a small edition of the *hacienda*, while *ranchería* indicates an agricultural unit, but has a variety of meanings.[4]

Distribution of Population among Various Types of Mexican Communities

| Type of Community | Number | % of Total Communities | Population * | % of Total Population | Average Number of Inhabitants per Community |
|---|---|---|---|---|---|
| Urban | | | | | |
| Ciudades ......... | 310 | .3 | 5,150,317 | 26.2 | 16,614 |
| Villas ........... | 531 | .5 | 1,268,759 | 6.5 | 2,389 |
| Pueblos .......... | 5,377 | 5.1 | 4,631,313 | 23.6 | 861 |
| Rural | | | | | |
| Unidades industriales. | 113 | .1 | 40,223 | .2 | 356 |
| Congregaciones .... | 3,744 | 3.6 | 1,106,433 | 5.6 | 296 |
| Ejidos ........... | 4,029 | 3.8 | 881,218 | 4.5 | 219 |
| Haciendas ........ | 5,069 | 4.8 | 811,168 | 4.1 | 160 |
| Rancherías ....... | 11,711 | 11.1 | 1,539,358 | 7.8 | 131 |
| Ranchos .......... | 67,646 | 64.4 | 3,026,327 | 15.4 | 45 |
| Others ........... | 6,655 | 6.3 | 1,198,436 | 6.1 | 180 |
| Total .......... | 105,185 | 100.0 | 19,653,552 | 100.0 | |

* 1940 census.

The *municipio* is the only true governmental unit for local administrative purposes. There is no uniformity in area or population for these units, but the average *municipio* is largely rural, since the great majority have no urban centers of 2,500 people or more. The *municipio* may contain more than one community. State laws set minimum sizes for establishment at between 1,500 and 5,000 or more; but the actual 1940 populations ranged from 528 to 236,557. The national average was 8,453 people. The average by states ranged from 2,085 to 30,801. Similar differences are found in the average areas of the *municipios*. The national average was 326.2 square miles, with state averages ranging from 40 to 9,217 square miles—the latter in the semiarid north. The number of *municipios* per state ranged from 3 in Baja California Norte to 572 in Oaxaca. The median for the states and territories was 44.[5]

*History of the municipio.*[6] A considerable literature has developed about the *municipio,* one of the oldest of Mexican political institutions. The prototype of the present system was transplanted from Spain by Cortes and his followers. The Spanish *ayuntamiento* (municipal government or council) was the successor to a measure of free government granted to the peninsular cities and towns in the eleventh and twelfth centuries. But the New World copies lacked the extent of power enjoyed by their Spanish predecessors.

The first Mexican *municipio* was established in Veracruz by Cortes in 1519, while the first municipal council was formed in Mexico City in 1524. During the colonial epoch, the *ayuntamientos* were humble bodies and their *municipios* enjoyed little autonomy. They were charged only with the most pressing necessities in the way of public works and services, such as construction and care of streets and sidewalks, waterworks, markets, and police. The officials were unpaid, but they received certain emoluments when they carried out special commissions. By the last part of the sixteenth century, some two hundred municipalities — *ciudades, pueblos,* and *villas* — functioned in the Spanish colonies.

After the winning of independence, the *municipios* continued their general governmental structure — an *ayuntamiento* and an *alcalde* (mayor) or *prefecto* or *jefe político* (political chief or governor of province or district). The 1824 Constitution did not devote an article to the *municipios,* but the 1836 document had several articles on the subject. It provided that the municipal authorities should be popularly elected. One article designated the public services to be provided, including sanitation, police, hospitals, jails, primary schools, etc.

The 1857 Constitution gave only incidental attention to *municipios,* not making them obligatory. Residents were obligated to support existing *municipios* through taxes and otherwise. During the life of this Constitution, some states were divided into districts and others into cantons. The district was usually divided into *municipios,* which were divided into municipal agencies. The Díaz regime centralized political power, placing the districts in charge of *jefes políticos* — local leaders of great power who were named by the governors. The evils perpetrated by the *jefes políticos* contributed to the coming of the 1910 Revolution. However, the capital and other large cities enjoyed a considerable measure of material progress in the last two decades of the Díaz era.

No Mexican constitution before that of 1917 had sought, apparently, to give such full provision and autonomy to the "free municipality"; but, as later discussion will show, the autonomy is largely illusory. The Constitutional Convention's committee on the subject favored giving the municipalities more power than they finally were accorded; and the provisions adopted have unduly subordinated them to the governors and legislatures, especially in financial matters.[7]

*Federal requirements*.[8] Article 115 of the federal Constitution was intended to be a charter of municipal freedom, with the states ordered to maintain "the free municipality as the basis of the territorial division of their political and administrative organization."

Each municipality is administered by a council, selected by direct popular vote, in contrast with the indirect voting system used before 1910. The former system had voters choose electors, who in turn selected council members. That procedure gave state authorities great influence in determining the winners. Another provision forbids any "intermediate authority between this body and the government of the state." Women since 1946 have been able to vote and be voted for in municipal elections. 1953

Municipal presidents, aldermen, and syndics of the municipal councils may not be elected or appointed to an immediately succeeding term of office, though their substitutes may be chosen if they have not held the office during their terms as substitutes.

The federal Constitution (Art. 115) sets forth the municipal fiscal powers: "The municipalities shall freely administer their finances, which shall be composed of the taxes imposed by the legislatures of the state, and which, in all cases, shall be sufficient to cover their municipal necessities."

*State control.* The Mexican theory often regards the municipal-state relationship as similar to the state-federal relationship. This is a rather strained interpretation. While the federal government possesses and has often exercised powers of intervention in the affairs of the states, numerous powers and functions are given to the states. The municipalities, however, are creations of the state; and they are supposed to have local administrative powers but no true legislative powers. But even the administrative powers and functions are subject to various restrictions.

The legal dispositions that affect the *municipio* include the federal Constitution (Art. 115); the state constitution; the state's municipal organic law; the law on municipal finance; *reglamentos* of various kinds issued by the state government; and lesser rules issued by the municipality itself.[9]

The states create the original *municipios*, and under certain restrictions the legislature may create new ones out of existing units. But new *municipios* are added slowly.

Types of state control are varied. One way of classifying the states is into those whose constitutions and municipal organic laws empower the legislature to pass on the validity of municipal elections and those leaving such matters to the local municipal council. Also, the states can be grouped into those that require legislative approval for both municipal income and expenditure budgets and those requiring only approval of income programs. The federal Constitution requires only state legislative approval of taxes. Some of the states have charged their regular state accounting or auditing agency with auditing municipal accounts.

Various states have additional legal requirements for municipalities to meet. Aguascalientes and Durango state clearly in their constitutions that the governor is the hierarchical superior of the *ayuntamientos*. The Coahuila governor can declare that the powers of a council have disappeared, and he can then name a provisional body. In Colima, the municipality must get legislative approval for its plans. Some others have additional requirements. One study lists thirteen constitutions which (possibly contrary to the federal Constitution) empower their governors to depose members of the *ayuntamientos*.[10]

An able study by Mecham finds that occasionally the federal Supreme Court comes to the support of the municipality, yet often municipal liberties continue being violated by state authorities.[11] In view of these legal powers in the hands of the state, one student of municipal affairs feels that there is no matter of real municipal importance in which the state does not intervene.[12]

Often, however, state compulsion has been unnecessary in municipal matters, because the effectiveness of the Party machinery and control have made it unnecessary. The Party is organized in most of the larger municipalities, and its organization has substantial local influence (as discussed in Chapter 4, (see pages 51–52). The mayor is the titular leader, and often the actual leader, of the Party locally. His relations with the chairmen of the Party's municipal committee and of the regional (state) executive committee are usually effective. In that way political liaison often obviates higher governmental intervention and secures compliance with state and Party programs. Often the mayor's influence locally is such that candidates for other local offices seek his blessing before the intra-Party election is held.

In addition to these legal and political powers in the hands of the state, there are certain other matters of policy or political convenience on the state's side of the ledger. The first is of convenience to the state and no disadvantage to the municipality: Often states group municipalities into districts for tax-collection or judicial purposes. Of a similar noncoercive nature is the establishment in one state of a Municipal Coordination Office for administering aid funds to the *municipios*. Obviously, this arrangement has potentialities for much important study, planning, and directed development in the municipal field.[13]

*Municipal officials: the council.* The *municipio* is governed by a council of elected members (*ayuntamiento*) and headed by a municipal president, elected for a term of two or three years. The secretary, treasurer, judges, and other officials are appointed by the council.

Elections in a *municipio* are held at two- or three-year intervals, depending on the laws of the state. An electoral council, composed of a representative of each registered political party, sets up the electoral machinery. When the official party has been the only party represented, what competition there is has been among the sectors within the Party. A month before an election, the electoral committee posts publicly a preliminary list of eligible voters. Those persons whose names have been improperly omitted may have them added, and voting credentials are given the voters before election day. On arriving at the polls, the voter exchanges his credential for a numbered ballot for each party having candidates plus a blank ballot for a write-in vote if he prefers such. He votes the ballot he wishes and destroys the others. The polling booth officials represent the different parties. At the end of the day, unused ballots are destroyed; the votes are tabulated and recorded in the presence of watchers from the parties; and ballots and records are sent to the *ayuntamiento*, which announces the results.[14]

The council is an administrative-sublegislative body which directs the affairs of the *municipio* within the limits specified by federal and state laws. Its decisions are taken by majority vote at official meetings. The number of members depends on state law and the size of the municipality, but it is usually not less than five. The term of office is usually two years. In some places the membership is renewed entirely at one time, and in other localities the terms are staggered. In some localities election is at large, and in others members are chosen by districts.[15]

Eligibility for election to the council calls for citizenship; residence in the municipality (but not necessarily within the electoral district — where election is by areas); being literate and twenty-one years of age; and being of good character. In practice, the literacy requirement is not always observed. The elected substitutes for the councilmen gain experience because of the frequent absences of members in many councils — probably due to the low compensation for the work involved.[16] The council meets in the municipal building (*palacio municipal*); it is required by the law of some states to meet as often as weekly, but the actual practice may fall far short of this. The sessions are public unless they are made secret by an extraordinary vote.[17]

Upon assuming office, the new councilmen hear the report of the outgoing municipal president and by majority vote choose the various officers (discussed below). Most of the state constitutions do not specify the other duties and the functioning of the council except for the most general reference. This is left to the municipal organic law of the state, which treats the field in some detail. These varied listings include public security; administration of justice; elementary education; maintenance of the civil registry; construction and conservation of streets and roads; conservation of natural resources; provision of light, water, and sanitary facilities; public health work; cemeteries; concern for agriculture, industry, and commerce; maintenance of markets, jails, parks, and other public works; collection of taxes and other incomes; expenditures of moneys; preparation of budgets and accounts for state approval; initiation of state legislative bills; ordinance-making; and general administration of municipal affairs.[18]

The headquarters are located in the *municipio's* largest *pueblo*, where nearly all business is transacted; but for convenience of administration and control, the council maintains an officer in each of the other villages in the municipality. He serves as a local deputy to enforce the council's rulings in his community.[19]

*The president.* The *regidor* (councilman) chosen to serve as municipal president plays a role approximating that of the American mayor in some cities. His duties are fixed by state law, and they are among the most important in the local government. He is the chief executive officer, and the way in which he functions may largely determine the tone of the municipal administration. A weak incumbent may become a figurehead for some other official who is the real head. In some states the president is popularly elected, while in others he is chosen by the council. He is the council's presiding officer and executive officer, and as such he usually has considerable powers of independent action. He receives a nominal salary.[20]

The functions of the municipal president are numerous. He publishes the laws and rules issued by the state legislature and the municipal council; sees that the laws and rules are enforced; appoints personnel; sees that property is appraised for tax purposes; sees to the public peace and security; sees that the judges' decisions are enforced; ensures freedom of elections; and promotes the development of roads, agriculture, education, welfare, and public health measures.[21]

As the executive officer of the council, the president is the *municipio*'s official representative in dealing with the outside world. He signs most correspondence and official acts; grants many kinds of permits; and, as an official with minor judicial power, he settles many cases involving theft, drunkenness, assault, debt, fraud, etc. On occasion, he levies small fines. Often family quarrels and private difficulties are brought to him for settlement. One study finds that he alone among all the officials must be on the job each day with municipal business.[22]

On a specified date each year, the president renders his annual report to the council, dealing with the record of his achievements. In some states, the report is also published in the state's official periodical or journal.

In the absence of the president, the council usually designates a substitute. If the vacancy is permanent, the council fills the vacancy. If this occurs in the last part of the term, the replacement fills out the unexpired term; if in the first part of the term, elections are called to choose a permanent replacement.[23]

*General administration.* The state law charges the municipality with maintaining certain offices and functions; but often the actual activity of a regime depends to quite an extent on the interests of the mayor and councilmen or strongly organized opinion within the municipality.[24]

I have said that one of the functions of the municipal president is that of issuing permits for various types of activities. In some *municipios*, this comprises much of the routine business of local government. Permits frequently requested are those for holding *fiestas*, for the slaughter of animals, and for the use of municipal resources — cutting wood, pasturing animals, etc.[25]

In many *municipios*, each *regidor* supervises one or more municipal functions, which are often under the supervision or advice of special committees. The committees or councilmen deal with such functions as administering justice, finance, welfare, education, public works, agriculture, industry and commerce, and police. The municipality supplies all its public services except, in many localities, education and public health services, which are often provided by the federal government. The membership of the committees is composed in various ways, ranging from those with members chosen entirely from the council to those composed entirely of nonmembers.[26]

An important type of public service is being performed under the direction of a new kind of board. There are two types of boards: the locally sponsored board (Board of Moral, Civic, and Material Improvement), promoted by the federal Ministry of Gobernación, and the Federal Boards for Material Improvement.[27]

The Federal Boards represent a significant attempt at federal aid to localities through decentralized action. The boards are located at places where customs duties are collected, where a small percentage of the collections goes for their support. Public works constructed under board sponsorship include water works, drainage, other health measures, hospitals, light and power supplies, paving, soil and forest conservation, schools, other public buildings, etc. Each Federal Board includes representatives of the Ministries of National Properties, Hydraulic Resources, and Health and Welfare, as well as the municipal president, a local chamber of commerce representative, and a representative of the taxpayers. The principal sponsor is the Ministry of National Properties.[28]

The other type — the local Board of Moral, Civic, and Material Improvement — has been established in most of the country's municipalities and in many of the subdivisions of the *municipios*. General promotion is done by the Ministry of Gobernación, and many of the states have a coordinating group working with the various local boards. A main purpose of the local board is to obtain and guide the cooperative effort of private persons in promoting a variety of activities useful to the community.[29]

The principal old-line municipal officials are appointive. These include the *síndico* (trustee), secretary, treasurer, chief of police, and the judge and his secretary. All receive extremely low salaries, which probably accounts for much of the graft that exists.[30] At least three different methods are used for naming such officials. One is appointment by the municipal president. A second is appointment by the council on proposal of the president. A third method is sometimes used in appointing financial officers: the council, through the president, requests the local chamber of commerce to make such nominations. The judge is appointed in some places and elected in others.[31]

Obviously, many old appointments terminate with the installation of a new administration. The State of Mexico is an exception to the general rule, in having a statute which seeks to give some job tenure and protection to municipal employees.[32] Virtually all states have laws of "official responsibilities" which seek to prevent malfeasance in office. These are often not too effective.

The organic law of municipalities of the state is the basic guide for municipal operations. The council makes other rules for its own local conduct. There has been little systematizing of municipal administrative law and practices. The State of Chihuahua was the first to adopt an administrative code (in 1950) for the operation of its municipalities.[33]

Often the municipal secretary and the treasurer are the most important administrative officers, carrying on the major part of the municipal business. The secretary is the chief administrative officer. In a typical village he opens and closes the offices each day; signs correspondence; maintains municipal records; advises other officers about the state law; hears complaints; and attends public functions. He also maintains the archives, keeping records of births, deaths, and marriages, as well as official records.[34] The treasurer collects and administers the town funds derived from taxes, assessments, fines, fees, and federal and state aids.

The chief of police is in general charge of criminal law enforcement. He organizes the "voluntary" night watch (*ronda*), a patrol by a small group of citizens.[35]

The federal education law requires municipalities to maintain elementary schools; but, as mentioned above, the educational and health services are often maintained by state or federal employees.

The office of *síndico* (trustee) is an amorphous post, in which the duties partake in varying degrees of the work of a lawyer and a business agent for the *municipio*. Some states' laws say that he must have some knowledge of law, since he represents the municipality in legal matters, checks on municipal contracts, and serves as an agent of the state attorney general. He is responsible for protecting the communal resources — lands, forests, and waters. He investigates violations of state law and has authority to use the local police to apprehend violators. The *síndico* supervises public works, initiates minor works himself, and is in charge of street and bridge repairs and upkeep.[36]

*Courts.* Justice in the *municipio* is administered largely through one or more municipal judges. In some states they are elected, in others appointed by the council. In the State of Michoacán, the supreme court approves the names submitted by the council. Only minor civil and criminal cases come within the jurisdiction of these municipal courts; and appeals, as well as more important cases, go to the state's court of first instance. As mentioned above, many minor cases are settled by the municipal president without reaching a court. No legal training or experience is required of the judges; and in isolated communities the decisions are as likely to conform to custom and tradition as to legal principles and texts.[37]

*Finance.* As in the case of the states, we find great variations in municipal expenditures and incomes per capita. The nationwide average of per-capita municipal expenditures showed the following variations by regional groups of states: North Pacific, 3.49 pesos; Gulf, 3.42 pesos; North, 3.30 pesos; Central, 1.53 pesos; South Pacific, 1.06 pesos; national average, 2.17 pesos. The 1940 range for states was from 6.48 to .75 pesos; and in 1949 it was from 10.04 to 1.41 pesos. From 1945 to 1948, the regional groups kept their relative positions except for a decline in the Gulf area and a rise in the Central area.[38] These budgets are, of course, very small compared with municipal budgets in more advanced countries.

Average expenditures for the period 1939–48, analyzed by services, show public works ranking first with 19.6 per cent of the average budget and *gobernación* (including law enforcement) ranking second with 13.9 per cent. Next came financial administration with 7 per cent and education with 6.4 per cent. Listed for 2.5 per cent of the budget or less were administration of justice, health, welfare, and civil registry and cemeteries.[39] All other public services took 29.9 per cent. Debt service took only 1.6 per cent. The municipalities have learned to expect periodic cancellation of the debts they owe to the federal government.

The largest proportional increase in recent years has been for public works. Considerable variation from these averages is found for individual *municipios*. One municipality of 30,000 people showed these variants: public safety 20 per cent, public works and improvements 7 per cent, and welfare 6 per cent.

An important reason for the increasing influence of the state and federal governments over the municipalities is the insignificant locally raised income of the latter; and in recent years the proportion of the taxes received by the federal government has been increasing, with the states faring somewhat better than the municipalities. In the period 1939–50, the states received 23.4 per cent as much as the federal government and the municipalities 4.9 per cent as much. The local percentage declined from 8.9 per cent in 1939 to 3.5 per cent.[40]

The breakdown by sources for the municipal income for 1939–48 shows contributed services ranking first with 35 per cent of the income, with participations (state and federal aids) producing 14 per cent. Surtaxes on federal tax rates produced 11 per cent, exploitation taxes 10.1 per cent, commerce 9.7 per cent, industries 8 per cent, real property 4.8 per cent, and agriculture 3.2 per cent. During the period covered, the greatest increases were in taxes on industries and the greatest decreases in contributed services. To quite an extent, state and local taxes have fallen on the same things.[41] With incomes as with expenditures, there are wide variations among *municipios*. A study of the state of Veracruz for 1947 showed a per-capita income range of municipalities from 3.07 pesos to .03 peso.

The municipal organic laws of the states usually specify the specific taxes that the legislatures levy for municipal purposes. Among the taxes not mentioned above are Michoacán municipal levies on slaughtering of livestock, space in public markets, use of water, the civil registry (births and marriages), cemeteries, registry of livestock brands, licenses, entertainment admissions, sales, and notarial instruments.[42] The real property tax – still an important levy in some states – is usually levied at a uniform rate but is sometimes varied with the size and needs of the municipality. For example, in Monterrey the rate in 1950 was twelve mills, while in the other municipalities of Nuevo León it was eight mills.

The state law, as mentioned above, provides for municipal financial administration. The treasurer is usually appointed by the council. Revenue and expenditures must adhere to their respective authorizations.

Payments from the treasury are made by written authorization of the council; and treasurer and council are jointly responsible for any financial irregularities. The state auditing office audits the municipal books.[43]

It is obvious from the foregoing that municipal taxes are quite regressive and that the lack of adequate municipal finance is a factor limiting the functioning of local democratic institutions of self-government. Dependence on federal and state aids is heavy. The small size of many *municipios* would provide an inadequate tax base for local finance, even if other factors were favorable. One authority considers that a population of less than 20,000 has great difficulty in supporting adequate services, and about half the *municipios* have fewer than 5,000 people.[44] Finally, there is not adequate financial reporting of municipal financial affairs.

*City planning*.[45] The discussion thus far has been concerned mainly with the small and medium-sized communities; but the problems of conducting municipal government with inadequate resources have been at least as pressing in the larger cities. In these cities an interest in city planning has slowly developed. Preliminary planning studies were made by Monterrey in the mid-twenties. In the next few years a planning committee was established, which stimulated street improvements. Similar efforts were under way in Mexico City, where rather full planning and zoning regulations were adopted for the Federal District in 1936. Interest was further stimulated by an international housing and town planning congress held in the capital in 1938.

In 1943, the National Chamber of Commerce stimulated interest by establishing a committee to promote urban planning; and a master plan was developed for the city of Tampico. During the next few years, Monterrey began work on a master plan for the city, and several other large cities established planning committees. The work of these groups shows a real awareness of the nature of well-rounded planning and of the needs of their respective communities.

Planning has borne fruit in Guadalajara's recent physical reconstruction of city-center areas, where there has been an extensive program of street widening and modernization. Severe city-center deterioration has been inhibited by this program, which included opening new streets; building a new municipal center; providing new market facilities; promoting low-rent housing projects; installation of a new water and sewage system; encouragement of factories to move from the central zone to peripheral areas; and provision of better support for city schools and for cultural activities.[46]

*Municipal improvement.* As in the United States, there has been much written and spoken in eulogy of the "free municipality" as the seedbed of democracy and the foundation of all national welfare; but there has been little done in a fundamental way to achieve the aim.[47] As in the United States, also, there is less interest in local than in national government; and Mexico's high rate of illiteracy adds to the problem. Most of the considerable literature on local government is commentary on Article 115, history, criticism of state controls, or speculation. But a few able works have appeared, which show real familiarity with foreign theory and practice and significant insight into Mexican needs.[48]

The aims of the Constitutional fathers of 1917 were good, but the final compromise text gave the municipalities much less actual power in local matters — and the states much more — than was desirable. This has been an important factor in producing the widespread inefficiency and corruption discussed by both Mexican and foreign commentators. Lewis, for example, finds in Tepoztlán much administrative control by the governor; the absence of effective local parties; lack of harmony and responsibility among officials; lack of civic morale; and general apathy.[49] This may not be a typical picture, but it seems to be widespread. While conditions are often far from good, progress seems to have been made since the Revolution; and it is slowly coming to be recognized that municipal democracy is closely related to national democracy.[50] This is especially true under the present national administration.

Numerous suggestions have been made for municipal government improvement. On the structural side, many call for amending the federal Article 115 to strengthen the *municipio* in such ways as the following: a council elected at large for four-year staggered terms, to provide continuity of programs; permitting re-election; prohibition of state suspension or removal of councilmen; a larger minimum size for municipalities; provision for the council-manager form of government; all intergovernmental disagreements to be settled by the higher courts; provision of the initiative, referendum, and recall; and greater home-rule powers. Capable critics see the need for better administrative practices — in general administrative control and procedure, personnel administration, financial administration, and planning. Improved efficiency of municipal personnel is recognized as an important need, and greatly increased salaries are obviously necessary to hold good people. The need for state-wide civil service laws and retirement systems is recognized.

There has been much discussion of the need to delimit tax fields among the three levels of government, providing the local units more nearly adequate tax resources conforming to the classic criteria of simplicity, equity, adequacy, etc. But there is less agreement on how far the municipalities should go in relinquishing federal aids in return for getting a presumably adequate "local" tax system. As a minimum, there is general agreement on the need for substantial freedom from state government control in both revenue and budgetary matters. In any case, there is need to modernize budget and revenue administration practices.

Municipal government in Mexico has a long history and a *tradition* of autonomy, but the approach toward its goals has been very slow.

*Indian community "government."*[51] No discussion of local government in Mexico could be ended realistically without mention of self-governing institutions in the isolated native communities. This self-government has no constitutional basis, since the *municipio* (often containing several communities) is the only legally recognized local governmental unit. But native government is important, nevertheless, in several parts of the country.

One of the sizable ethnic groups is that of the Tarahumara in the state of Chihuahua. Most of these people are located in eight *municipios*, comprising about 40 per cent of the population of those units. Each Tarahumara community has its own informal government, constituted along lines reaching back to colonial times. Here, community government is quite autonomous, and relations with the *municipio* officials are reasonably harmonious; but an earlier history of exploitation in some states like Chiapas has left a less friendly tradition of local relationships. In Chiapas, the communities have formed a "regional *ayuntamiento*" — a political-religious organism with functionaries, nominally elected, varying in numbers. Some officials are religious; others secular.

The supreme authority in this community is the assembly of its men and women. Of the various officials elected, the chief one is usually known as the governor. Among the Tarahumara, he is theoretically chosen for life; but practically his tenure is limited by his desires and any strong shift of opinion regarding him. The governor is unquestionably the leader, while the other officials seem to serve in more of an advisory capacity. He is the real spokesman of the people. He is the true judge at a legal trial, which is heard before all the officials. His other duties are varied, ranging from encouragement of church attendance on Sunday to presiding over the assembly and settling inheritance disputes.

As mentioned above, the governor holds his office as long as the people back him. One tabulation shows an average tenure of three or four years. When the governor resigns, the other officials usually resign with him. The people in assembly shout the names of candidates. The governor names the candidates in turn; and the winner is judged by volume of response, not by actual count. Acceptance of office, once a man is elected, is obligatory. The sole remuneration for office-holding is honor and prestige. Every Tarahumara man is a potential official, with election depending on his reputation.

Among the Tarahumara, other officials include the *capitanes*, the *fiscales*, and the *mayores*. The *capitanes* serve as messengers for the *gobernadores* (governors). The governor has assistants who act as his advisers. The *mayor* is an official who handles matchmaking and marriages. His messenger-assistants are the *fiscales*. In one of the Tarahumara *municipios* there are twenty-seven communities, with twenty-seven governors and some two hundred and fifty lesser functionaries. The average population of each is about three hundred. In some areas, some community officials bear the same names as are found among municipal officials, such as *síndico* and *regidor*.

Regular political parties, according to one study, are not functioning regularly among most of the indigenous communities.

Justice is administered among the Tarahumara under the governor. The citizen voices his complaint before this official, who sends a *capitan* to seize the culprit. Trials are conducted before the governor with decorum. The plaintiff presents his charges; the defendant answers; questions are asked by the officials; witnesses are heard. The governor weighs the evidence; receives advice from officials; and announces the verdict. There is no appeal from the decision. Serious cases or disputes between Mexicans and Indians come before the state authorities, but there are not many of these disputes. Tarahumara law is not codified, with fixed punishments for all crimes; but the memory of previous punishments has its influence. Second and third offenses receive heavier punishments than first offenses.

Thus, isolated Indian communities carry out many actual governmental functions outside the framework of the constitutional municipality.

### NOTES

[1] Whetten, *op. cit.*, p. 41.
[2] *Ibid.*, pp. 44 *et seq.*; Sría. de Economía, *México en Cifras.*
[3] Germán Georgge Hernández, *El Municipio Libre en México* (UNAM thesis, 1946), pp. 68 *et seq.*
[4] Whetten, *op. cit.*, pp. 40 *et seq.*
[5] *Ibid.*, pp. 526–30. Julio Durán Ochoa, *Población* (1955), pp. 10–21, gives somewhat higher figures for 1950 – roughly comparable to the country's population increase.
[6] Moisés Ochoa Campos, *La Reforma Municipal; Historia Municipal de México* (1955) is the most detailed source. Other useful titles (listed in the bibliography) are by Aguilar Aguilar; Barrera Fuentes; Carballo G.; Castorena; Cerezo; Colín; D'Acosta y Esquivel; Garza; Georgge Hernández; Gómez M.; González Lobo; González Luna; Rodríguez R.; Rolland.
[7] Ochoa Campos, *op. cit.*, Pt. 5; Flores Zavala, *Elementos* . . ., pp. 218–20.
[8] Ochoa Campos, *op. cit.*, pp. 355–89; Fraga, *op. cit.*, pp. 357–65; Tena Ramírez, *op. cit.*, pp. 131–37; Medina and Ortiz, *op. cit.*, pp. 149–56.
[9] Mario Colín, "Notas sobre el Municipio en México" (UNAM thesis, 1949), p. 74.
[10] *Ibid.*, Ch. 4; Georgge Herández, *op. cit.*, pp. 65 *et seq.*; Ochoa Campos, *op. cit.*, pp. 423–25; Ernesto Flores Mellardo, *Anticonstitucionalidad* . . . (1937), pp. 147–48.
[11] Mecham, "Mexican Federalism – Fact or Fiction?" *op. cit.*, p. 31.
[12] Juan M. Cerezo L., *Servicios Públicos Municipales* (UNAM thesis, 1943), pp. 10–11.
[13] Colín, *op. cit.*, p. 60.
[14] D. D. Brand, *Quiroga; A Mexican Municipio* (1951), pp. 103–5.
[15] Whetten, *op. cit.*, pp. 530 *et seq.*; Georgge Hernández, *op. cit.*, pp. 73–77.
[16] See note 15; Farrera, *op. cit.*, p. 50; Brand, *op. cit.*, pp. 102–3.
[17] See note 16.
[18] See notes 14 and 15.
[19] See notes 14 and 15.
[20] Whetten, *op. cit.*, p. 530; Georgge Hernández, *op. cit.*, p. 74; R. L. Beals, *Cheran* . . . (1946); Oscar Lewis, *Life in a Mexican Village* . . . (1951), p. 222.
[21] Medina and Ortiz, *op. cit.*, pp. 153–54.
[22] Lewis, *op. cit.*, p. 222; *Mexican Life*, April 1952, pp. 25–27.
[23] Farrera, *op. cit.*, p. 49.
[24] Brand, *op. cit.*, pp. 106–7.
[25] Lewis, *op. cit.*, pp. 225–26.
[26] Brand, *op. cit.*, pp. 116–17; Georgge Hernández, *op. cit.*, pp. 76–77; Medina and Ortiz, *op. cit.*, p. 155.
[27] *Ordenamientos* . . . (Sría. de Bienes Nacionales, (1951), pp. 131–44; Luis de la Llata, "Las Juntas Federales de Mejoras Materiales" (UNAM thesis, 1952).
[28] Ochoa Campos, *op. cit.*, Pt. 5, Ch. 8.
[29] *Ibid.*, Pt. 5, Ch. 10; Sría. de Gobernación, *Juntas de Mejoramiento* . . . (1953).
[30] Lewis, *op. cit.*, p. 223.
[31] Georgge Hernández, *op. cit.*, p. 73.
[32] *Ibid.*, p. 74.

[33] Chihuahua, *Código Administrativo* . . . (1950).

[34] Medina and Ortiz, *op. cit.*, p. 155; Lewis, *op. cit.*, pp. 222-23; Brand, *op. cit.*, pp. 109-10; *Mexican Life*, April 1952, pp. 25-27.

[35] See note 34.

[36] See note 34.

[37] Whetten, *op. cit.*, pp. 532-34; Brand, *op. cit.*, p. 117; *Mexican Life*, April 1952, pp. 25-27.

[38] Sría. de Economía, *México en Cifras; Anuario Estadístico* (1953), p. 559.

[39] Sría. de Economía, *México en Cifras*.

[40] *Ibid.*

[41] *Ibid.*

[42] Brand, *op. cit.*, pp. 111-15.

[43] Farrera, *op. cit.*, pp. 81 *et seq.*

[44] Gilberto Loyo, *La Política Demográfica de México* (1935), pp. 291 *et seq.*; Whetten, *op. cit.*, p. 529.

[45] Monterrey, Instituto de Estudios Sociales, *Apuntes para el Plano Regulador . . . de Monterrey* (1950); Francis Violich, *Cities of Latin America* . . . (1944), pp. 90-91, 101, 113-14; Carlos Lazo, "Planificación de Tampico," *Espacios*, October 1952, pp. 87-110; Manuel Gandara Mendieta, *De la Administración Municipal* . . . (1953), Chs. 5-6.

[46] *Foreign Service Journal*, June 1952, pp. 20-21, 54-55; *Social Forces*, May 1954, pp. 367-74; *HA*, May 21, 1956, pp. 25-76.

[47] Georgge Hernández, *op. cit.*, pp. 56 *et seq.*

[48] Works (cited in the bibliography) by Cerezo L.; Colín; Garza; Georgge Hernández; Rolland.

[49] Lewis, *op. cit.*, pp. 221-25, 250 *et seq.*

[50] Tena Ramírez, *op. cit.*, p. 136; Colín, *op. cit.*, pp. 68, 73; Padgett, *op. cit.*, pp. 172-80; Brandenburg, *op. cit.*, Ch. 8.

[51] Gonzalo Aguirre Beltrán, *Formas de Gobierno Indígena* (1953), pp. 77-78, 81-84, 107-18, 126 *et seq.*, 179, 206; W. G. Bennett and R. M. Zingg, *The Tarahumara* . . . (1935), pp. 201-18.

# 27

## The Federal District and the Territories

In Mexico, all roads lead to the capital of the country; for the Federal District is the political and governmental center of the nation. Moreover, it is the economic, industrial, educational, social, and cultural center of Mexico. In these ways it resembles the capital cities of many other Latin American countries. Its influence is all-pervasive. Other areas are satellites of greater or lesser magnitude, held in their orbits by the central sun.

The Constitution provided (Art. 44) that the Federal District would have the area existing in 1917 (some 573 square miles); and "in case the federal powers should be removed to another location, it shall be converted into the State of the Valley of Mexico."

The Congress is empowered to change the seat of the government and to "legislate in all matters" relating to the District. The government is under the jurisdiction of the President of the republic. (Art. 73.)

*History.* The origin of the Federal District as the country's capital is found in the Constitution of 1824, which empowered the Congress to choose the location for the capital. In that year, the boundaries of the District were set at a radius of two leagues from the central square of Mexico City; and in 1854 the area was considerably expanded. There was much argument in the 1856 Constitutional Convention over whether or not to move the seat of government to Querétaro of Aguascalientes. Political, economic, and moral arguments were used. The 1857 Constitution (Art. 46) provided that the area covered by the existing Federal District should comprise the State of the Valley of Mexico, but statehood should not be effective "until after the Supreme Federal Powers move to some other place." The same idea is expressed in the 1917 Constitution (Art. 44).[1]

For some time under the 1857 Constitution, Mexico City had its own municipal government like other cities; but the Díaz regime brought a considerable centralization of control over the local government. Income and expenditures rose considerably during this period, which saw the opening of new *colonias* (suburbs or neighborhoods) and the construction of many public buildings, streets, plazas, etc. Sanitary services, markets, etc. were established. Many of these works were carried out by special commissions.[2]

The basic laws of 1867, 1886, and 1897 recognized the financial autonomy of the municipal government of the Federal District; but this was changed by the law of 1903. The District was divided for administration into thirteen municipalities; and financial affairs were directed by the Ministry of Finance. The general administration of District affairs was subordinate to the Ministry of Gobernación. The principal functionaries were the governor, the president of the Superior Council, and the director general of Public Works, all freely appointed and removed by the President.[3]

In 1917, the new Constitution made possible the granting of considerable powers of local self-government to the municipalities of the District, restoring in large part the legal situation existing before 1903. Despite some controversy over exact powers, the general arrangement was as follows. The government of the District (under a governor appointed by the President) was charged with law enforcement for the whole area; overseeing of charitable and penal institutions; education; the higher courts; and public works of a general character. The municipalities were charged with provision of primary education; the lower courts; maintenance of local order; and general authority in strictly local matters.[4] The Constitution provided (Art. 73) that each municipality would be governed by an elective council. The President appointed the District's attorney general. The Congress named the superior judges and the judges of first instance.

Various difficulties were encountered in the process of trying to have a central government and municipal governments function in the same area; and local municipal government was abolished at the end of 1928. Since then, the single Federal District government has functioned as a dependency of the President, maintaining its own fiscal administrative autonomy until the end of 1946. At that time, the latter functions came under the supervision of the Ministry of Finance. The present basic law dates from the end of 1941.[5]

*Organization.*[6] There are several ways in which the Mexican Federal District's government differs from that of our District of Columbia. Important provisions regarding the Federal District's government are set forth in the Constitution. The Constitution provides for its area and for a possible change of location of the seat of government. In both capitals, the Congress legislates for the District as a state does for its area; and the top administrative officers are appointed by the President. One significant difference is in the matter of the political rights of citizens. The residents of the Federal District elect their own deputies and senators to the Congress.[7]

The organic law dealing with the Federal District has eight chapters dealing with the organs of government; functions; territorial basis; organization of the Department (Federal District); districts; the Advisory Council; the Treasury; and the property of the District.[8]

The executive head of the District, the chief, is named and removed by the President. With the president's approval, the chief names and removes the secretary general, the *oficial mayor*, the chief of police, and the heads of divisions. Other personnel are named by the chief, under a measure of civil service protection. The Consultative Council is a purely advisory body, named by the chief for two-year terms on proposal of the principal civic organizations in the District. The groups represented include chambers of commerce, industrial chambers, small business groups, chambers of small industry, property owners, renters, farmers, professional people, public employees, and laborers.[9] Since the abolition of elected municipal councils in the District, this is the only institutionalized way of directly representing the public in the government.

Functions of the Federal District government are of several broad types. The first group includes functions of aid to the federal government. These include election administration, juries, regulation of cults, labor relations, and regulation of monopolies. Functions of local interest are publication and execution of legal matters, issuance of rules, regulation of transit, police service, licenses and permits, health, welfare, safety, etc. Financial functions include presentation of budgetary and tax proposals to the Ministry of Finance, execution of the budget, levying and collecting of taxes and assessments. Miscellaneous functions include cultural diffusion, promotion of tourism, expropriations for reason of public utility, and in general providing for administration of public affairs.[10]

Since the federal government is deeply interested in the affairs of the Federal District, it is often difficult to make a demarcation of functions between what the District should perform and what the central government should provide directly. Education, for example, is financed by the Ministry of Education.

For administrative convenience, the area of the District is divided into a dozen *delegaciones*. These correspond more or less to the former municipalities and are headed by *delegados* appointed by the chief of the District.

*Agencies.*[11] The work of the Federal District government is administered through more than a dozen principal bureaus and other agencies.

The Bureau of Gobernación sees to the correct observance of the laws and regulations; supervises the *delegaciones*; is the channel for relations with the Consultative Council; handles publicity; has control of the penal and correctional establishments; issues licenses; and has other miscellaneous duties.

The Bureau of Public Works has two divisions. The Sub-bureau of Construction and Conservation has offices dealing with construction, paving, parks, public buildings and monuments, public lighting, and inspection of materials. The Sub-bureau of Planning and Program has offices of the master plan, planning, public ways, and the mixed planning commission.

The Bureau of Waters and Sanitation has been faced with tremendous problems of water supply and drainage for a fast-growing population in an area with drainage problems caused by floods and sinking of the area on which the city is built. The construction and servicing of the city's main source of water supply (the River Lerma) is under a separate bureau.[12]

Education, as mentioned above, is provided by the central government. The same is true of the public health service, which is provided by the Health Ministry's Bureau of Health in the Federal District and other subdivisions of that Ministry.

The Bureau of Transit and Transportation has its hands full with managing the traffic and transportation problems of a rapidly growing metropolis, where the mere number of vehicles is a poor index of the problems involved.

The Bureau of Labor and Welfare enforces the factory and labor laws in the District and supervises the work of the Central Board of Conciliation and Arbitration.

The police department includes a criminal identification laboratory, a secret service, and motorized forces, as well as other police personnel. Police schools for the training of personnel have been functioning in recent years. The fire protection service is a unit under the same agency.

The Bureau of Social Action has offices of medical services, public libraries, and popular orientation. A school of nursing was established in 1947; and social workers have been trained for the work of the agency. Museums have been developed in the fields of agriculture, archaeology, anthropology, biology, botany, ceramics, geology, etc.

Athletic activities are promoted by the Bureau of Sports.

The Bureau of Legal Services includes the offices of civil registry, public registry, law, and the public defender.

Three housekeeping agencies are the Bureau of General Services, the Bureau of Administrative Services, and the Controller's Office. The first has charge of street cleaning and shop services; the second, of purchases, payments, warehousing, and personnel; the third is an agency of vigilance for the Ministry of Finance.

The Treasury of the Federal District is one of the most important of the agencies, with numerous departments grouped under three divisions — taxation, collections, and general services.

*Justice.* The Superior Tribunal of Justice for the District and the Federal Territories heads the court system for the Federal District. Eight of its three-judge *salas* handle the work of the District. The judges are named by the President with the approval of the Chamber of Deputies. The Superior Tribunal of Justice appoints the judges of the lower courts. The attorney general for the District and the Federal Territories has the functions common to such offices. (Constitution, Art. 73.) He also is appointed by the President.

*Planning.*[13] Planning is one of the most important problems facing the capital city. As one of the fastest growing major cities of the world, all the problems of urban government face the District — many in an acute form. Population growth outruns housing; children exceed school facilities; street construction and maintenance lags behind needs; traffic control is acute; water supply has long been a pressing problem; and physical stabilization of the soil (originally a spongy lake-bed) is even more pressing and extremely costly. Efforts of varying magnitude have been made to cope with these and other pressing metropolitan government problems, with varying degrees of success; but efforts at true planning came late. There has been limited success to date.

In general, it can be said that planning has thus far been largely uncomprehensive and generally uncoordinated. First steps were taken in the city planning field in the nineteen-twenties. By 1936, rather full planning and zoning regulations were in effect in the capital; but planning machinery was unable to cope with the rapid growth of the central city and its suburbs. A few years ago, official thinking agreed that the Valley of Mexico should be treated as a unit. Therefore, the planning agencies were reorganized and the Regional Planning Commission of the Valley of Mexico was created. This technical advisory group is authorized to investigate and to elaborate plans for the entire Valley. Planning commissions for the Federal District and affected parts of the adjoining states are coordinated with the Regional Planning Commission. The economic importance of the District and its centralized control combine to make coordinated planning both essential and theoretically easy. The government has adequate power, but coordinating of separate agency plans and programs has been slow in coming. For long, broad goals took the place of specific plans aimed toward concrete goals.[14] *Proyectismo*, or "verbal" planning, is slowly giving way to solid factual analysis, followed by sound programming.

Mexico City is the third largest city in North America and second only to Buenos Aires in the Spanish-speaking world. At the beginning of the nineteenth century, it was the largest city in the Western Hemisphere. Its 541,516 people in 1900 had increased to 1,757,530 in 1940 and 2,942,594 in 1950, and its rapid growth continues. There is little likelihood that the capital's central power relationship to the rest of the country will decrease in the foreseeable future.

## The Territories

The territory is the status of an area prior to statehood.[15] The power of the Congress to admit territories, transform them into states, and legislate for the territories (Art. 73) has been discussed in Chapter 25. Until 1953, the three territories, with their populations and areas were as follows: Baja California Norte 227,731 (population) and 27,648 (square miles); Baja California Sur, 60,499 and 27,971; and Quintana Roo, 27,027 and 19,625. The large population increase of Baja California Norte since 1940 brought it statehood in 1953.

The federal Congress is the legislative body for the territories; they have no local legislatures. The area of the territory, as with the state, is divided into *municipios*, which have their locally elected councils. The territory is represented in the Chamber of Deputies of the federal Congress as the states are, with representation based on population.

The governor of the territory is named and removed by the President; and the governor names the other officials. He is advised by a Consultative Council of seven members. The governor is represented in each area by a *delegado*, who in turn has an advisory council. The governor exercises full control within his area, issuing and enforcing the necessary administrative orders.

### NOTES

[1] Tena Ramírez, *op. cit.*, pp. 160–64; Ochoa Campos, *op. cit.*, pp. 293–97.

[2] Ochoa Campos, *op. cit.*, pp. 310–12, 318–21; Georgge Hernández, *op. cit.*, pp. 40–41.

[3] Fernando Fuentes Galindo, *Organización Constitucional del Distrito Federal* (1948), pp. 149–50; Comisión de Reorganización Administrativa y Financiera, *Finances of the Federal District of Mexico* (1918), pp. 7–8.

[4] Comisión de Reorganización Administrativa, *op. cit.*, p. 12; Ochoa Campos, *op. cit.*, pp. 391–95.

[5] Ochoa Campos, *op. cit.*, pp. 395–402; Fraga, *op. cit.*, pp. 345–46; Flores Zavala, *Elementos . . .*, pp. 218–19.

[6] Fuentes Galindo, *op. cit.*, *passim*.

[7] *Ibid.*, pp. 72 *et seq.*

[8] *Ley Orgánica del Departamento del Distrito Federal* (D.O., December 31, 1941); Mendieta y Núñez, *op. cit.*, Ch. 4; Ochoa Campos, *op. cit.*, pp. 395–422.

[9] *Ley Orgánica . . .* ; Fraga, *op. cit.*, pp. 346–49; Dept. del D. F., *Resumen de Actividades* (1948).

[10] Fraga, *op. cit.*, pp. 349 *et seq.*

[11] Dept. del D. F., *Resumen . . .*, *Realizaciones del Gobierno de . . . Alemán* (1952); *Directorio . . .* (1), pp. 479–522; Mendieta y Núñez, *op. cit.*, Ch. 4; Raúl Noriega, *La Obra del Gobierno del Distrito Federal* (1946), *passim*. HA, April 9, 1956, pp. 11–53, gives an extended illustrated account of recent construction and material progress in the city.

[12] *HA*, July 20, pp. 3–9, September 14, 1951, pp. 6–18.

[13] R. W. Holman, "Planning in the Mexican Federal District . . ." (M.A. thesis, Mexico City College, 1950); Francis Violich, *Cities of Latin America . . .* (1944), pp. 59, 90, 91, 97; *HA*, October 13, 1950, pp. 10–14.

[14] Holman, *op. cit.*, pp. 15–29.

[15] Tena Ramírez, *op. cit.*, pp. 168 *et seq.*, 267 *et seq.*; Mendieta y Núñez, *op. cit.*, pp. 145 *et seq.*; Guillermo Caballero Sosa, *Los Territorios en Nuestro Régimen Federal* (UNAM thesis, 1939); Sría. de Gobernación, *Informe* (annual).

# PART VIII

# Conclusions

# 28

A Developing Democracy

Mexico can be regarded as a developing democracy because of its representative governmental structure and its recent progress in the direction of responsibility to the people. The Mexican democratic ideals have been well known since the Revolution — ideals of freedom, justice, human dignity, social welfare, representative government, well-known goals of American and European liberalism and social democracy. The achievements along these lines have varied greatly.

First should be mentioned personal freedom. As Whetten has said, this "is probably the greatest achievement of the Mexican Revolution. In the long run, this may prove important enough to counterbalance whatever mistakes may have been made."[1] Freedom of speech is a fact, as well as a constitutional provision. Even in the still unsettled days of the twenties, Gruening found that "the United States could learn much from Mexico in regard to freedom of expression and tolerance. And a saving grace about Mexico's worst abuses is that those who practice them are generally ready, humorously, to admit the worst." With notable exceptions, he found "an atmosphere of personal independence unknown in most parts of the United States. In Mexico a man may live as he pleases, think what he pleases, says what he pleases — that is considered his own business. He is not ostracized for it."[2]

A high degree of freedom of expression is found in the higher educational institutions; and libraries do not censor materials expressing heterodox views. There are no legal barriers to freedom of the press; and the Mexican press probably leads Latin America in the exercise of this freedom. But press criticism seldom extends to the President. In the past, low journalistic salaries have often been a factor involved in the "purchase" of reporters by some government officials. The government controls communications, transport, and newsprint imports. Thus, an antigovernment journal could be punished, but this has not been done for many years. The exercise of press freedom regarding government is not yet nearly so great as in the United States.[3]

On the other hand, many factors have worked against the development of democratic institutions in Mexico. These include geographic and social and cultural isolation, a heritage of social stratification, lack of educational facilities, the one-party system, personalized leadership and centralized control, nepotism, corruption, and the power of the military. Social and cultural isolation still affect considerable areas of the country, though communications facilities are being pushed with energy. The rapid population increases challenge the government's efforts to expand educational facilities; but slow progress is being made.

Widespread illiteracy has made difficult the functioning of true representative government; but here also progress is being made. Woman suffrage was achieved in local elections in 1946 and in national elections in 1954. Probably both illiteracy and the one-party system are factors in the still modest rate of voting participation. In 1952, about 14 per cent of the total population voted for President; in the United States in 1952 the rate (male) was nearly 20 per cent.

As one able observer, Cline, has pointed out, the predominance of the one official political party gives Mexico the appearance of an undemocratic country; for the same party always wins the presidency and the bulk of the legislative posts.[4] The result was long undemocratic in both appearance and reality. But an important fact is the democratizing process that has been at work within the Party. There has been a definite trend toward the broadening of representation within the ranks of the Party. Since the Party controls the government, that means, in effect, that government is coming to represent more and more people as the structure of the Party has been changed. Ávila Camacho dropped the army officers as a group from Party representation and gave more representation to the lower middle class. Bossism was reduced by increasingly changing membership from a group basis (unions, etc.) to an individual basis. Increasingly, there has been give and take within each of the Party sectors, as well as between sectors. Also, sector groups maintain a considerable measure of independence with reference to the Party committees, subject only to support of the candidates after their nomination. Thus, in recent years the Party has increasingly seen the necessity of putting forth strong legislative candidates. Thus far, the official party is a party of the most numerous groups in the country, and the Party has prospered because it has satisfied these groups and kept them loyal to its candidates. How long can it retain its dominance? The slowly increasing vote of the chief opposition parties raises this question.

Despite improved electoral laws and their administration and despite the present administration's strong drive to moralize the public service, much progress remains to be made. Conditions have changed much — but not completely — since 1944 when Silva Herzog, a foremost government economist and Finance Ministry official, declared that the Revolution faced a crisis largely because of the monopoly of government positions by the official party and because of widespread political and economic immorality on the part of public servants.[5]

Unquestionably, the official party has held power so long by becoming increasingly more responsive to public opinion. One of the latest expressions of this responsiveness is the present administration's strong drive to bring honesty into the public service. It is making substantial progress against great odds. The historic picture is presented by Tannenbaum who said in 1950 that "the decline in the personal integrity so essential to the new responsibilities thrown upon both government and private enterprise . . . is the greatest single moral failure of the Mexican Revolution."[6] In the same year, Mosk also found graft at new highs and governmental efficiency at new lows.[7] The age-old evil of graft and corruption was considered sufficiently serious by President Cárdenas that he secured passage of a law of responsibilities of public officials, requiring officials to file financial statements which could lead to court action against financial malefactors. But this comprehensive statute remained largely a dead letter due to loopholes and lack of effective enforcement in subsequent administrations. Widespread charges of corruption during the Alemán administration were largely unheeded; and amendment of the law and its enforcement awaited the coming of the present administration.[8]

While the Mexican *government* is still largely the *presidency*, the representativeness of the government is increasing through such developments as the increasing representativeness within the official party; the growth of substantial opposition parties; a decreasing dependence on the army as a political instrument; less frequent federal intervention in the affairs of state governments; a tendency toward improvement in the quality of officials and congressmen; and probably some decrease in personalism as the means of governmental leadership, as representative political institutions develop.

While a single term for the president has both its advantages and disadvantages, the application of the rule of no immediate re-election for congressmen, governors, state legislators, and even municipal officials has seemed to produce only disadvantages. The advantages of continuity of experience are eliminated, making more difficult the development of government that is both more representative and more efficient. The Permanent Committee of the Congress seems to serve no useful purpose.

Citizen participation in government through the use of nonpartisan advisory committees has been seldom used by the Congress; and the executive branch made little use of such devices before 1953.[9] The present administration, however, is making some use of such committees and is consulting with civic interests prior to taking certain important administrative or legislative steps.

How the growth of central government power with reference to the states relates to developing democratic institutions is difficult to assess. Such a trend has great potentialities for both good and evil. Given Mexico's governmental traditions and pressing economic problems, her development in this direction was probably inevitable. Both constitutionally and in practice, the central government has always had strong powers with reference to the states. In recent years, as the economic predominance of the center has grown, it has made increasing use of persuasion and decreasing use of naked power in its relations with the states.

Free enterprise, nationalism, and administrative improvement are in vogue in Mexico today. Since governmental policy continues favorable to free enterprise in the economic realm, there is no great fear of "socialism" when the government is able to provide a certain service better than private business can. The need for extensive improvement in administrative organization and functioning is becoming more widely recognized,[10] and some important progress is being made in this direction. Despite its weaknesses, nationalism has been a strong force in promoting the development of Mexico. It is one of the important contributions of the Revolution.

A prominent historian of Latin America makes the following mid-century evaluation of Mexico:

> By the mid-1950's, Mexico had . . . traveled a long, rough road. She had suffered under scoundrels who had betrayed her and well-meaning men incapable of saving her; she had smarted under vexing clashes over the Church, the right of men to land, and the determination of foreigners to exploit her wealth as they saw fit; she had been humiliated by the United States and France. Only occasionally had leaders of sound head and pure heart given her grounds for hope. But there was now healthy optimism among intelligent Mexicans as they reviewed the momentous changes of recent years. There were now schools, as good schools as any in Latin America. The national soil, not long before the monopoly of a few, was now widely distributed. That soil was yielding a little more each year, as irrigation ditches multiplied, more fertilizer was used, and better seeds were sown. And an expanding industry was gradually rescuing Mexico from her ancient colonial economy. Political control of the nation, although still far short of the democratic ideal, was slowly passing into the hands of more people. Mexico was still a poor land . . . but the progress of fifty years gave promise of better things to come.[11]

If the trend toward honesty and integrity in government continues, Mexico can go a long way, even with her limited natural resources, toward becoming an important modern country.

### NOTES

[1] Whetten, *op. cit.*, pp. 571–72.
[2] Gruening, *op. cit.*, pp. 641–42.
[3] Call, *op. cit.*, pp. 191–200.
[4] Cline, *op. cit.*, pp. 324–25.
[5] Silva Herzog, *La Revolución Mexicana en Crisis*, pp. 33–34.
[6] Tannenbaum, *Mexico . . .*, p. 80.
[7] Mosk, *op. cit.*, p. 283.
[8] *Mexican American Review*, August, 1948, p. 17; *Time*, July 27, 1953, p. 24, September 14, 1953, p. 40; García Treviño, *op. cit., passim.*
[9] Goodspeed, "The Development and Use of *Facultades Extraordinarias* . . .," p. 33.
[10] Luis Encinas, *Progreso y Problemas de México* (1954), pp. 112–24.
[11] Herring, *A History of Latin America* (1955), p. 393.

# Bibliography and Index

# Bibliography

## Abbreviations

| | |
|---|---|
| *Am. Soc. R.* ..................... | *American Sociological Review* |
| *Annals* ........................ | *Annals of the American Academy of Political and Social Science* |
| *BEP* .......................... | *Biblioteca Enciclopédica Popular* |
| *BPAU* ........................ | *Bulletin,* Pan American Union |
| *Cur. Hist.* ...................... | *Current History* |
| *D.O.* .......................... | *Diario Oficial* |
| *Ed.* ........................... | Ediciones or Editorial |
| *Fondo* ........................ | *Fondo de Cultura Económica* |
| *Inv. Ec.* ....................... | *Investigación Económica* |
| *MCC* .......................... | M.A. thesis, Mexico City College |
| *Mex. Am. R.* ................... | *Mexican American Review* |
| *MV* ........................... | *El Mercado de Valores* |
| *PIAC* ......................... | *Proceedings,* Inter-American Conference on Conservation of Renewable Natural Resources, 1948. Washington, D.C.: Dept. of State, 1949 |
| *Prob. Agr.* ..................... | *Problemas Agrícolas e Industriales* |
| *Rev. Ec.* ....................... | *Revista de Economía* |
| *Rev. Mex. Soc.* ................. | *Revista Mexicana de Sociología* |
| *SWSSQ* ....................... | *Southwestern Social Science Quarterly* |
| UNAM ........................ | Universidad Nacional Autónoma de México |

## I. Land, History, People

Agnew, James F. "From Encomienda to Ejido (San Pedro de la Labor)." MCC, 1952.

Alanís Patiño, Emilio. "Zonas y Regiones Económicas de México," *Problemas Económico-Agrícolas de México,* July–September 1946, pp. 90–104.

Alemán, Miguel. *Program of Government* . . . San Antonio, Texas, 1946.

Alessio Robles, Miguel. *Historia Política de la Revolución.* Mexico City: Ed. Botas, 1946.

Attolini, José. *Problemas Económico-Sociales de Veracruz.* Mexico City, 1947.

Ávila Camacho, Manuel. *La Ruta de México.* Mexico City: BEP No. 135, Sría. de Educación, 1946.

---

NOTE: For uniformity of appearance, English rules of capitalization have been used in titles throughout.

Bancroft, Hubert H. *History of Mexico*. 6 vols. San Francisco, Calif., 1883–88.

Beals, Carleton. *Porfirio Díaz, Dictator of Mexico*. Philadelphia: Lippincott, 1932.

Beltrán, Enrique. *La Protección de la Naturaleza* . . . Mexico City: BEP No. 206, Sría. de Educación, 1949.

———. *Los Recursos Naturales de México y su Conservación*. Mexico City: BEP No. 106, Sría. de Educación, 1946.

Bennett, Wendell C., and Robert M. Zingg. *The Tarahumara, an Indian Tribe of Northern Mexico*. Chicago: University of Chicago Press, 1935.

Benson, Nettie Lee. "The Preconstitutional Regime of Venustiano Carranza, 1913–1917." M.A. thesis, University of Texas, 1936.

Beteta, Ramón. *The Mexican Revolution, a Defense*. Mexico City: D.A.P.P., 1937.

———. *Pensamiento y Dinámica de la Revolución Mexicana*. Mexico City: Ed. México Nuevo, 1950.

———. "Social Forces in Mexican Life," in H. C. Herring and Katharine Terrill, eds., *The Genius of Mexico*. New York: Committee on Cultural Relations with Latin America, 1931. Pp. 33–45.

———, ed. *Programa Económico y Social de México* . . . (In Spanish and English.) Mexico City, 1935.

Blanco, Gonzalo. "The Water Supply of Mexico City . . ." *PIAC*, 1948, pp. 361–69.

Bravo Ugarte, José. *Historia de México*. 4 vols. Mexico City: Ed. Jus, 1941–44.

Brown, William. "Monterrey, City of Progress," *Mex. Am. R.*, December 1952, pp. 25–26.

Cabrera, Luis (Blas Urrea). *Veinte Años Después*. Mexico City: Ed. Botas, 1937.

Call, Tomme Clark. *The Mexican Venture, from Political to Industrial Revolution in Mexico*. New York: Oxford, 1953.

———. "The Program for Progress," *Mex. Life*, October 1953, pp. 15f.

Callahan, James M. *American Foreign Policy in Mexican Relations*. New York: Macmillan, 1932.

Callcott, W. H. "Economic Conditions in Mexico," in A. C. Wilgus, ed., *The Caribbean Area*. 2 vols. Washington, D.C.: George Washington University Press, 1934. II:375–91.

———. *Liberalism in Mexico, 1857–1929*. Palo Alto, Calif.: Stanford University Press, 1931.

Calles, Plutarco Elías. *Mexico before the World, Public Documents and Addresses* . . . New York: Academy Press, 1927.

Cárdenas, Lázaro. *Cárdenas Habla*. Mexico City: Partido Revolucionario Mexicano, 1940.

Carlson, Fred A. *Geography of Latin America*. New York: Prentice-Hall, 1952.

Carreño, Alberto. "Las Clases Sociales en México," *Rev. Mex. Soc.*, September 1950, pp. 333–50.

Caso, Alfonso. "El Problema Indígena en México," in *México, Realización y Esperanza*. Mexico City: Ed. Superación, 1952. Pp. 485–91.

Cerwin, Herbert. *These Are the Mexicans*. New York: Reynal, 1947.

Chávez Orozco, Luis. *Historia Económica y Social de México*. Mexico City: Ed. Botas, 1938.

Christensen, Asher N. *Evolution of Latin American Government, A Book of Readings*. New York: Holt, 1951.

Cline, Howard F. "Mexico, a Maturing Democracy," *Cur. Hist.*, March 1953, pp. 136–42.

———. *The United States and Mexico*. Cambridge, Mass.: Harvard University Press, 1953.

# BIBLIOGRAPHY

Congreso Nacional de Sociología. *Estudios Sociológicos*. Mexico City, 1952 to present. (Annual proceedings; No. 3 is on crime.)

Cook, Sherburne F. *Soil Erosion and Population in Central Mexico*. Berkeley: University of California Press, 1949.

Correa, Eduardo J. *El Balance de Ávila Camacho*. Mexico City, 1947.

————. *El Balance del Cardenismo*. Mexico City: Acción, 1941.

Correa, Rafael. *Alemán, un Documento Humano*. Mexico City, 1949.

Cosío Villegas, Daniel. "The Press and Responsible Freedom in Mexico," in Ángel del Río, ed., *Responsible Freedom in the Americas*. New York: Doubleday, 1955. Pp. 272–80.

Council on Foreign Relations. *Survey of American Foreign Relations, 1931*. New Haven, Conn.: Yale University Press, 1931. Pp. 1–317.

Crawford, William R. *A Century of Latin American Thought*. Cambridge, Mass.: Harvard University Press, 1944.

Cumberland, Charles C. *Mexican Revolution, Genesis under Madero*. Austin: University of Texas Press, 1952.

————. "Mexican Revolutionary Movements from Texas, 1906–1912," *Southwestern Historical Quarterly*, January 1949, pp. 301–24.

————. "Precursors of the Mexican Revolution of 1910," *Hispanic American Historical Review*, May 1942, pp. 344–56.

D'Acosta, Helia. *Alemanismo, Teoría y Práctica del Progreso de México*. Mexico City: Libros de México, 1952.

Daniels, Josephus. *Shirt-Sleeve Diplomat*. Chapel Hill: University of North Carolina Press, 1947.

Davis, Harold E. *Social Science Trends in Latin America*. Washington, D.C.: American University Press, 1950.

Departamento del Trabajo. *Policies of the Present Administration of Mexico*. Mexico City, 1936.

Dillon, Richard H. "The Rise of Álvaro Obregón." M.A. thesis, University of California at Berkeley, 1949.

Dotson, Floyd. "A Note on Participation in Voluntary Associations in a Mexican City," *Am. Soc. R.*, August 1953, pp. 380–86.

Dupré Ceniceros, Enrique. "The Forest Problem of Mexico," *PIAC*, 1948, pp. 418–25.

Durán Ochoa, Julio. *Población*. Mexico City: Fondo, 1955.

Encinas, Luis. *Progreso y Problemas de México*. Mexico City, 1954.

Federal Reserve Bank of New York. "Mexico's Economic Progress," *Monthly Review*, May 1953, pp. 72–75.

Fergusson, Erna. *Mexico Revisited*. New York: Knopf, 1955.

Gaither, Roscoe B. "Government and Jurisprudence of the Mexicans before the Spanish Conquest," *Virginia Law Review*, March 1920, pp. 422–40.

Gamio, Manuel. *Hacia un México Nuevo, Problemas Sociales*. Mexico City, 1935.

Gill, Tom. *Land Hunger in Mexico*. Washington, D.C.: C. L. Pack Forestry Foundation, 1951.

González Roa, Fernando. "El Aspecto Agrario de la Revolución Mexicana," *Prob. Agr.*, July–September 1953, pp. 7–120.

Gorrow, Bernard J. "The Mexican Social Upheaval of 1910, a Comparative Study of Theories of Revolution." Ph.D. thesis, University of Nebraska, 1951.

Gruening, Ernest. *Mexico and Its Heritage*. New York: Century, 1928.

Gunther, John. "Ávila Camacho of Mexico," *Harpers*, October 1941, pp. 480–89.

Halperin, Maurice. "Mexico Shifts Her Foreign Policy," *Foreign Affairs*, October 1940, pp. 207–21.

Hanson, Simon G. *Economic Development in Latin American*. Washington, D.C.: Inter-American Affairs Press, 1951.

Herring, Hubert C. "In Mexico," *Yale Review*, September 1942, pp. 35-49.

———, and Katharine Terrill, eds. *The Genius of Mexico*. New York: Committee on Cultural Cooperation with Latin America, 1931.

Herring, Hubert C., and Herbert Weinstock, eds. *Renascent Mexico*. New York: Covici, 1935.

Hewes, Gordon W., "Mexicans in Search of the 'Mexican': Notes on Mexican National Character Studies," *American Journal of Economics and Sociology*, January 1954, pp. 209-23.

Hollenback, Audrey. "The Carranza Regime." M.A. thesis, University of California at Berkeley, 1924.

International Bank. See United Nations, International Bank.

Iturriaga, José E. *La Estructura Social y Cultural de México*. Mexico City: Fondo, 1951.

Ives, Ronald L. "The Sonoyta Oasis," *Journal of Geography*, January 1950, pp. 1-14.

James, Preston E. *Latin America*. New York: Odyssey Press, 1950.

Jiménez Rueda, Julio. *Historia de la Cultura, el Virreinato*. Mexico City: Ed. Cultura, 1950.

Johnson, Donald D. "Álvaro Obregón and the Mexican Revolution." Ph.D. thesis, University of Southern California, 1946.

Kemmerer, Edwin W. *Inflation and Revolution, Mexico's Experience of 1912-1917*. Princeton, N.J.: Princeton University Press, 1940.

Kirk, Betty. *Covering the Mexican Front*. Norman, Okla.: University of Oklahoma Press, 1942.

Kluckhohn, Frank L. *The Mexican Challenge*. New York: Doubleday, Doran, 1939.

Link, Arthur S. *Woodrow Wilson and the Progressive Era, 1910-17*. New York: Harper, 1954.

López Rosado, Diego. "Recursos Naturales de México," *Rev. Ec.*, March 1952, pp. 88-91.

Loyo, Gilberto. *La Política Demográfica de México*. Mexico City, 1935.

McCleary, John P. "The Behavior Pattern of the Mexican." MCC, 1948.

Madero, Francisco I. *La Sucesión Presidencial en 1910*. San Pedro, Coahuila, 1908.

Magaña, Gildardo. *Emiliano Zapata y el Agrarismo en México*. 2 vols. Mexico City: Ed. Ruta, 1951.

Marrin, R. L. "Mexican Prospects," *Yale Review*, March 1936, pp. 511-36.

Martin, Percy A., ed. *Who's Who in Latin America*. Palo Alto, Calif.: Stanford University Press, 1935.

May, A. Wilfred. "Boomland Mexico," *United Nations World*, February 1953, pp. 48-50.

Mecham, J. Lloyd. "An appraisal of the Revolution in Mexico," in A. C. Wilgus, ed., *The Caribbean at Mid-Century*. Gainesville: University of Florida Press, 1951. Pp. 170-201.

———. *Church and State in Latin America*. Chapel Hill: University of North Carolina Press, 1934.

———. "The Jefe Político in Mexico," *SWSSQ*, March 1933, pp. 333-52.

Mendieta y Núñez, Lucio. *Las Clases Sociales*. Mexico City: UNAM, 1947.

———. "Racial and Cultural Tensions in Latin America," *International Social Science Bulletin*, No. 3 (1952), pp. 442-51.

*México en el Mundo de Hoy*. Mexico City: Ed. Guarania, 1952.

*México, Realización y Esperanza*. Mexico City: Ed. Superación, 1952.

# BIBLIOGRAPHY

Millán, Verna Carleton. *Mexico Reborn*. Boston: Houghton, 1939.
Molina Enríquez, Andrés. *Los Grandes Problemas Nacionales*. Mexico City, 1909. Also in *Prob. Agr.*, January 1953, pp. 9–197.
Morales, Felipe. *200 Personajes Mexicanos*. Mexico City: Ed. Ateneo, 1952.
Morales Jiménez, Alberto. *Historia de la Revolución Mexicana*. Mexico City: Partido Revolucionario Institucional, 1951.
Mosk, Sanford A. *Industrial Revolution in Mexico*. Berkeley: University of California Press, 1950.
Nathan, Paul. "Mexico under Cárdenas." Ph.D. thesis, University of Chicago, 1953.
Northrop, F. S. C. *The Meeting of East and West*. New York: Macmillan, 1946.
O'Gorman, Edmundo. *Breve Historia de las Divisiones Territoriales*. Mexico City: Ed. Polis, 1937.
Osorio Tafall, B. F. "Los Recursos Naturales Renovables de México . . ." *Inv. Ec.*, No. 2 (1949), pp. 209ff.
Palavicini, Félix F., *et al. México, Historia de su Evolución Constructiva*. 4 vols. Mexico City: Distribuidora Editorial Libro, 1945.
Palerm, A. "Notas sobre la Clase Media en México," *Ciencias Sociales*, December 1952, pp. 129–35.
Pan American Union. *México*. Washington, D.C., 1952.
Pani, Alberto. *Una Encuesta sobre la Cuestión Democrática de México*. Mexico City: Ed. Cultura, 1948.
Parkes, Henry B. *A History of Mexico*. Boston: Houghton, 1950.
Patiño, Lorenzo R. *La Conservación del Suelo y Agua*. Mexico City: Ed. Ruta, 1950.
Patterson, John C. "José María Morelos." Ph.D. thesis, Duke University, 1930.
Peña, Moisés de la. "A New Mexico, Some Observations on General Problems . . ." *Social Sciences in Mexico*, Winter 1947–48, pp. 7–28.
———. "Problemas Demográficos y Agrarios," *Prob. Agr.*, Nos. 3–4 (1950).
Peral, Miguel Ángel, ed. *Diccionario Biográfico Mexicano*. Mexico City: Ed. P.A.C., 1944.
Plank, Marion S. "Venustiano Carranza's Place in the Mexican Revolution." M.A. thesis, University of Arizona, 1949.
Plenn, J. H. *Mexico Marches*. Indianapolis: Bobbs, 1939.
Porrúa Hermanos. *Catálogo de Obras de Derecho*. Mexico City: Ed. Porrúa, 1951.
Portes Gil, Emilio. *The Conflict between the Civil Power and the Clergy, Historical and Legal Essay*. Mexico City: Ministry of Foreign Affairs, 1935.
———. *Quince Años de Política Mexicana*. Mexico City: Ed. Botas, 1941.
Prewett, Virginia. *Reportage on Mexico*. New York: Dutton, 1941.
Priestley, Herbert I. *The Mexican Nation, a History*. New York: Macmillan, 1926.
Quirk, Robert E. "The Mexican Revolution and the Catholic Church, 1910–1929, an Ideological Study." Ph.D. thesis, Harvard University, 1951.
Rabasa, Emilio. *La Evolución Histórica de México*. Mexico City: La Viuda de C. Bouret, 1920.
Rippy, J. Fred. *The United States and Mexico*. New York: Crofts, 1931.
Rittenhouse, Floyd O. "Emiliano Zapata and the Suriano Rebellion." Ph.D. thesis, Ohio State University, 1948.
Riva Palacio, Vicente, ed. *México a Través de los Siglos*. 5 vols. Mexico City, 1887–89.
Roeder, Ralph. *Juárez and His Mexico*. 2 vols. New York: Viking, 1947.
Ross, Edward A. *The Social Revolution in Mexico*. New York: Century, 1923.
Ross, Stanley R. *Francisco I. Madero, Apostle of Mexican Democracy*. New York: Columbia University Press, 1955.
Ruiz Cortines, Adolfo. *Discursos de Ruiz Cortines*. Mexico City: Ed. Ruta, 1952.

Sáenz, Moisés. "The Genius of Mexican Life," in Hubert C. Herring and Katharine Terrill, eds., *The Genius of Mexico.* New York: Committee on Cultural Cooperation with Latin America, 1931. Pp. 3–30.

——, and Herbert Priestley. *Some Mexican Problems.* Chicago: University of Chicago Press, 1926.

Salas, Joseph. "The Foreign Trade of Mexico for the Period 1939–50 . . ." MCC, 1952.

Schlarman, J. H. L. *Mexico.* Milwaukee, Wis.: Bruce Pub., 1950.

Scholes, Walter V. "Cárdenas of Mexico," *Cur. Hist.,* March 1954, pp. 166–70.

Secretaría de Economía, Dirección General de Estadística. *Anuario Estadístico.* Mexico City, 1953.

——. *Compendio Estadístico.* Mexico City, 1953.

——. *México en Cifras.* Mexico City, 1952.

——. *Séptimo Censo General de Población . . . 1950, Resumen General.* Mexico City, 1953.

Secretaría de Gobernación. *Seis Años de Gobierno al Servicio de México, 1934–40.* Mexico City, 1940.

——. *Seis Años de Gobierno . . . 1940–46.* Mexico City, 1946.

Septién, Alfonso. *La Industrialización de México.* Mexico City: La Academia Mexicana de Jurisprudencia, 1952.

Serrano Plaja, Arturo. *Ávila Camacho.* Buenos Aires: Ed. Americalee, 1942.

Silva Herzog, Jesús. *El Pensamiento Económico en México.* Mexico City: Fondo, 1947.

——. *La Revolución Mexicana en Crisis.* Mexico City: Cuadernos Americanos, 1944.

——. "The Rise and Fall of Mexico's Revolution," *Mex. Am. R.,* December 1949, pp. 35, 112.

Simpson, Eyler N. *The Ejido, Mexico's Way Out.* Chapel Hill: University of North Carolina Press, 1937. Also in *Prob. Agr.,* October–December 1952, pp. 15–350.

Simpson, Lesley Byrd. *The Encomienda in New Spain.* Berkeley: University of California Press, 1950.

——. *Many Mexicos.* Berkeley: University of California Press, 1952.

Smith, Lola B. "Policies and Achievements of President Obregón in Mexico, 1920–1924." M.A. thesis, University of California at Berkeley, 1925.

Snow, Edgar. "The Cities of America, Mexico City," *Saturday Evening Post,* May 12, 1951, pp. 26, 166–72.

Sociedad Mexicana de Geografía y Estadística. *Estudio sobre los Recursos Naturales de México.* Boletín de la Sociedad, July–October 1949.

*Statesman's Yearbook, 1953.* New York: St. Martin's Press, 1953.

Steffens, Lincoln. *Autobiography of Lincoln Steffens.* New York: Harcourt, 1931.

Stone, R. G. *Economic and Commercial Conditions in Mexico, 1952.* London: Her Majesty's Stationery Office, 1953.

Strode, Hudson. *Timeless Mexico.* New York: Harcourt, 1944.

Tamayo, Jorge L. *Geografía General de México.* 2 vols. Mexico City, 1949.

Tannenbaum, Frank. *Mexico, the Struggle for Peace and Bread.* New York: Knopf, 1950. Also in *Prob. Agr.,* October–December 1951, pp. 9–154.

——. *The Mexican Agrarian Revolution.* Washington, D.C.: Brookings Institution, 1929.

——. *Peace by Revolution, an Interpretation of Mexico.* New York: Columbia University Press, 1933.

Teja Zabre, Alfonso. *Guide to the History of Mexico.* Mexico City, Ministry of Foreign Affairs, 1935.

# BIBLIOGRAPHY

Thomson, Charles A. "Mexico's Challenge to Foreign Capital," *Foreign Policy Reports*, August 15, 1937, pp. 126-36.

———. "Mexico's Social Revolution," *Foreign Policy Reports*, August 1, 1937, pp. 114-24.

Townsend, William C. *Lázaro Cárdenas, Mexican Democrat*. Ann Arbor, Mich.: George Wahr Publishing Co., 1952.

United Nations, Department of Economic Affairs. *Economic Development in Selected Countries*, Vol I. New York, 1947.

———. *Economic Survey of Latin America, 1949*. New York, 1951.

———. *Economic Survey of Latin America, 1951-1952*. New York, 1954.

United Nations, Economic and Social Council. *Economic Survey of Latin America: Mexico*. New York, 1951.

United Nations, Economic Commission for Latin America. *Economic Survey of Latin America*. New York, 1949.

———. *Economic Survey of Latin America 1950: Recent Developments and Trends in the Mexican Economy*. Mexico City, 1951.

United Nations, International Bank. *The Economic Development of Mexico*. Baltimore: Johns Hopkins Press, 1953.

United Nations, International Monetary Fund. *Mexico's Financial Institutions and the Capital Market*. Washington, D.C., 1949.

United States, Bureau of Foreign Commerce. *Investment in Mexico; Conditions and Outlook for United States Investors*. Washington, D.C., 1956.

United States, Tariff Commission. *Agricultural, Pastoral, and Forest Industries of Mexico*. Washington, D.C., 1948.

Vasconcelos, José. *Breve Historia de México*. Madrid: Ed. Cultura Hispánica, 1952.

Vivó, Jorge A. *Geografía de México*. Mexico City: Fondo, 1948.

Vogt, William. *Road to Survival*. New York: William Sloane, 1948.

Wagner, Helmuth O. *El Bosque y la Conservación del Suelo*. Mexico City: Sría. de Educación (BEP), 1949.

Werlin, Joseph S. "Mexico's Unity," *Yale Rev.*, December 1943, pp. 268-81.

Weyl, Nathaniel and Sylvia. *The Reconquest of Mexico, the Years of Lázaro Cárdenas*. New York: Oxford, 1939.

Whatley, W. A. "The Formation of the Mexican Constitution of 1824." M.A. thesis, University of Texas, 1921.

Whetten, Nathan L. "The Rise of a Middle Class in Mexico," in *La Clase Media en México y Cuba*, Vol. 2, Washington, D.C.: Pan American Union, 1950. Pp. 1-29.

———. *Rural Mexico*. Chicago: University of Chicago Press, 1948.

Whitehouse, Gilbert. "Some Observations on the Industrialization of Mexico." MCC, 1948.

Winton, George B. *Mexico Past and Present*. Nashville, Tenn.: Cokesbury Press, 1928.

Wise, George S. *El México de Alemán*. Mexico City: Ed. Atlante, 1952.

## II. Constitutions, Laws, and Commentaries

### CONSTITUTIONS

*Leyes Constitucionales de México durante el Siglo XIX*, ed. by José M. Gamboa. Mexico City: Sría. de Fomento, 1901.

"The Mexican Constitution of 1917 Compared with the Constitution of 1857," *Annals* supplement, May 1917.

Constitution, 1824. *Constitución Federal de los Estados Unidos Mexicanos San-*

433

*cionada por el Congreso General Constituyente . . . 1824.* Mexico City: Imp. del Supremo Gobierno, 1824.

Constitution, 1917. *Constitución Política de los Estados Unidos Mexicanos . . .* Mexico City: Imprenta de la Cámara de Diputados, 1953.

——. *Anotadas y Concordadas por el Lic. Manuel Andrade.* Mexico City: Información Aduanera de México, 1953.

——. *Diario de los Debates del Congreso Constituyente de 1917.* 2 vols. Mexico City: Edición Oficial, 1917.

——. "Political Constitution of the Mexican United States," in R. H. Fitzgibbon, ed., *The Constitutions of the Americas.* Chicago: University of Chicago Press, 1948. Pp. 496–553.

### LAWS, STATUTES, ETC.

*The Civil Code for the Federal District and Territories of Mexico, and the Mexican Laws on Alien Land Ownership,* tr. by Otto Schoenrich. New York: Baker, Voorhis & Co., 1950.

*Codificación Agraria y Leyes sobre Tierras . . .* Mexico City: Información Aduanera, 1951.

*Codificación de las Disposiciones Administrativas del Distrito Federal.* Mexico City: Edición Oficial, 1943. 2 vols.

*Código Agrario; Texto al Día, Notas, Jurisprudencia, Legislación Complementaria,* Rafael de Pina, ed. Mexico City: Ed. Cicerón, 1953.

*Código Civil para el Distrito y Territorios Federales y Ley del Notariado . . . con Prontuarios Analíticos y Sistemáticos.* Mexico City: Ed. Cicerón, 1952.

*Código de Seguridad Social, sus Reglamentos y Acuerdos del Consejo Técnico del Instituto Mexicano del Seguro Social.* Monterrey, 1953.

*Código Federal de Procedimientos Civiles.* D.O., February 24, 1943.

*Código Fiscal de la Federación,* Antolín Jiménez, ed. Mexico City, 1949.

*Código Penal para el Distrito y Territorios Federales y Ley Orgánica y Normas de Procedimiento de los Tribunales para Menores.* Mexico City: Ed. Porrúa, 1953.

*Código Sanitario Federal.* D.O., January 25, 1950.

*Decreto que Faculta al Ejecutivo Federal para Acordar la Cancelación de los Adeudos Municipales.* D.O., December 26, 1953.

*Decreto que Reforma Diversos Artículos de la Ley Electoral . . .* D.O., January 7, 1954.

*Decretos [re.] Artículos . . .* [of the Civil Code]. D.O., January 9, 1954.

*Estatuto de los Trabajadores al Servicio de los Poderes de la Unión* (in *Ley Federal del Trabajo Reformada,* below).

*Estatuto de los Trabajadores al Servicio de los Poderes de la Unión.* Mexico City: Sindicato Nacional de Trabajadores de Hacienda, 1953.

*El Juicio de Amparo; Ley de Amparo con Exposición de Motivos, Explicaciones, y Formularios.* Mexico City: Publicaciones Farrera, 1949.

*Ley de Amparo Reformada; Doctrina, Legislación y Jurisprudencia.* Mexico City: Ed. Porrúa, 1950.

*Ley de Expropiación* (in *Constitución . . . Anotadas . . .* [by] Manuel Andrade, (pp. 417–22).

*Ley de Monopolios (ibid.,* pp. 187–91).

*Ley de Nacionalidad y Naturalización (ibid.,* pp. 199–212).

*Ley de Pensiones Civiles.* Mexico City: Publicaciones Farrera, 1948.

*Ley de Prevenciones Generales Relativas a la Suspensión de Garantías Individuales* (in *Constitución . . . Anotadas,* pp. 156 *et seq.*).

# BIBLIOGRAPHY

*Ley de Responsabilidades de los Funcionarios y Empleados* . . . Texto al Día y Notas por Rafael de Pina. Mexico City: Ed. Cicerón, 1953.

*Ley del Seguro Social.* Instituto Mexicano del Seguro Social, 1952. (In *Ley Federal del Trabajo Reformada,* below.)

*Ley Electoral de Poderes Federales. D.O.,* December 31, 1945.

*Ley Electoral Federal.* Mexico City: Sría. de Gobernación, 1951.

*Ley Federal del Trabajo Reformada,* con Bibliografía, Comentarios y Jurisprudencia, Alberto Trueba Urbina, ed. Mexico City: Ed. Porrúa, 1953.

*Ley Federal de Turismo [Reglamento,* etc.] (in *Constitución* . . . Anotadas, pp. 476 *et seq.*).

*Ley General de Población* (in *Constitución* . . . Anotadas, pp. 423–36).

*Ley Orgánica del Artículo 28 Constitucional en Materia de Monopolios* [and *Reglamentos*] (*ibid.,* pp. 192 *et seq.*).

*Ley Orgánica de la Universidad Autónoma de México* (in *Constitución* . . . Anotadas, pp. 172 *et seq.*).

*Ley Orgánica del Departamento del Distrito Federal. D.O.,* December 31, 1941.

*Ley Orgánica del Ministerio Público Federal. D.O.,* January 13, 1942.

*Ley Orgánica de los Artículos 103 y 107 Constitucional. D.O.,* January 10, 1936.

*Ley Orgánica de los Tribunales del Fuero Común.* Mexico City: "La Legislación Mexicana," 1933.

*Ley Orgánica del Poder Judicial* . . . (in *Constitución* . . . Anotadas, p. 362 *bis* 9a–30a).

*Ley Orgánica del Presupuesto* . . . *y su Reglamento.* Mexico City: Dirección General de Egresos, 1948.

*Ley Orgánica y Normas de Procedimiento de los Tribunales para Menores.* Mexico City: Porrúa, 1953.

*Ley para el Control de los Organismos Decentralizados* . . . Mexico City, 1948.

*Ley Reglamentaria del Artículo 119 de la Constitución. D.O.,* January 9, 1954.

*Ley Reglamentaria del Artículo 130 Constitucional. D.O.,* January 18, 1927.

*Ley Reglamentaria de las Fr. I y IV del Art. 27 Constitucional* (in *Constitución* . . . Anotadas, pp. 247 *et seq.*).

*Ley Reglamentaria de los Artículos 4 y 5 Constitucionales, Relativos al Ejercicio de las Profesiones* . . . (in *Constitución* . . . Anotadas, pp. 172–45 *et seq.*).

*Ley sobre Atribuciones del Ejecutivo Federal en Materia Económica. D.O.,* December 30, 1950.

*Ley y Reglamento sobre Petróleo* (in *Constitución* . . . Anotadas, pp. 263–67).

*Nueva Ley de Amparo* (*ibid.,* pp. 315 *et seq.*).

*Nueva Ley de Secretarías y Departamentos de Estado* [and *reglamentos,* etc.], (*ibid.,* pp. 363 *et seq.*).

*Nueva Ley General de Bienes Nacionales* (*ibid.,* pp. 213 *et seq.*).

*Nueva Ley Orgánica de la Educación Pública* (*ibid.,* pp. 157 *et seq.*).

*Nueva Ley Reglamentaria del Art. 27 Constitucional en el Ramo de Petróleo* [and *reglamento,* etc.] (*ibid.,* pp. 312.1 *et seq.*).

*Ordenamientos Principales y Disposiciones Conexas de la Sría. de Bienes Nacionales* . . . Mexico City: Sría. de Bienes Nacionales . . . 1951.

*Reglamento de la Ley del Seguro Social* . . . [and related *reglamentos*]. Mexico City: Instituto Mexicano del Seguro Social, 1950.

*Reglamento Interior de la Secretaría del Trabajo* . . . (in *Ley Federal del Trabajo* . . . pp. 335–62).

*Translation of the Agrarian Code* . . . Mexico City: Asociación de Empresas Industriales y Comerciales, 1943.

COMMENTARIES

Aguilar Maya, José. *La Suspensión de Garantías, Estudio Doctrinario y de Derecho Comparado de los Artículos 29 y 49 de la Constitución de 1917.* Mexico City, 1945.

Aguilar Rojas, Mario A. "Libertad de Conciencia y Personalidad Jurídica de la Iglesia en México." UNAM thesis, 1946.

Alarcón García, Celia. "Estudio y Crítica del Artículo Tercero Constitucional." UNAM thesis, 1947.

Alba Hermosillo, Carlos H. *Estudio Comparado entre el Derecho Azteca y el Derecho Positivo Mexicano.* Mexico City, 1949.

Alegría Rasgado, Roberto. "Inaplicabilidad del Sistema Federal en México." UNAM thesis, 1934.

Allewelt, Sue M. "The Mexican Constitution of 1824 and the United States Constitution." M.A. thesis, University of California, 1929.

Almaraz, José. "Law and Justice," *Annals*, March 1940, pp. 39–47.

Álvarez Andrés, Edgar. "Breve Ensayo sobre la Evolución y Trayectoria del Movimiento Constitucional Mexicano." UNAM thesis, 1946.

Atwood, Roberto. *Diccionario Jurídico.* Mexico City: El Nacional, 1946.

Azuela, Mariano. "Lagunas, Errores, y Anacronismos de la Legislación de Amparo," *Foro de México*, November 1953, pp. 3–19.

Baggett, Sam G. "The Delegation of Legislative Power to the Executive under the Constitution of Mexico," *Southern California Law Review*, January 1935, pp. 114–21.

Baltierra Rivera, Leonardo. "Breve Análisis de Evolución Constitucional de México." UNAM thesis, 1945.

Bassols, Narciso. *La Nueva Ley Agraria.* Mexico City, 1927.

Bellón Echevarría, Eduardo. "La Desaparición de los Poderes de los Estados en Nuestro Régimen Constitucional." UNAM thesis, 1942.

Bernal Molina, Julián. *A Statement of the Laws of Mexico in Matters Affecting Business* . . . Washington, D.C.: Inter-American Development Commission, 1948.

Brizio Ponce de León, Arturo. "La No-Reelección en el Derecho Público Mexicano." UNAM thesis, 1952.

Burges, William H. "A Comparative Study of the Constitutions of the United States of Mexico and the United States of America," *American Law Review*, September 1905, pp. 711–26.

Burgoa, Ignacio, "Algunas Consideraciones sobre el Artículo 28 Constitucional," *Problemas Jurídicos de México.* Mexico City: Ed. Jus, 1953, pp. 167–87.

———. *Las Garantías Individuales,* Mexico City: Ed. Botas, 1944.

———. *El Juicio de Amparo.* Mexico City: Ed. Jurídica, 1946.

———. "La Supremacía Jurídica del Poder Judicial de la Federación en México," *Anales de Jurisprudencia*, February 15, 1941, pp. 469–547.

Caballero Sosa, Guillermo. "Los Territorios en Nuestro Régimen Federal." UNAM thesis, 1939.

Cabrera Cosío, Ramón. *Conflictos de Leyes en el Estado Federal Mexicano.* Mexico City, 1947.

Calderón, Guillermo. *Justicia Administrativa.* Mexico City: Imp. "El Libro Diario," 1942.

Calzada y González, Oswald. "El Sistema Federal en México." UNAM thesis, 1935.

Campillo, Aurelio. *Tratado Elemental de Derecho Constitucional Mexicano.* 2 vols. Jalapa, Ver.: La Económica, 1928.

Cantoral Hernández, Mariano. *La Suspensión de Garantías en el Derecho Constitucional Mexicano.* Mexico City, 1942.

# BIBLIOGRAPHY

Carranca y Trujillo, Raúl. *Derecho Penal Mexicano*. 2 vols. Mexico City: Antigua Librería Robredo, 1950.

Carrillo Flores, Antonio. "La Constitución y la Acción Económica del Estado," *Inv. Ec.*, No. 3, 1941, pp. 292ff.

————. *La Defensa Jurídica de los Particulares Frente a la Administración en México*. Mexico City: Porrúa, 1939.

————. *La Economía y los Derechos del Hombre en la Constitución Mexicana*. Mexico City: Ed. Cultura, 1952.

Caso, Ángel. *Derecho Agrario*. Mexico City: Ed. Porrúa, 1950.

Castañeda, Carlos E. "Social Developments and Movements in Latin America," in J. N. Moody, ed., *Church and Society*. New York: Arts, Inc., 1953. Pp. 753–73.

Castellanos Tena, Fernando. "Nuestras Constituciones." UNAM thesis. 1944.

Castorena, José Jesús. *Manual de Derecho Obrero*. Mexico City, 1949.

————. *Tratado de Derecho Obrero*. Mexico City, Ed. Jaris, 1942.

Clagett, Helen L. *A Guide to the Law and Legal Literature of the Mexican States*. Washington, D.C.: Library of Congress, 1947.

————. "The Mexican Suit of Amparo," *Georgetown Law Journal*, May 1945, pp. 418–37.

Cleven, N. Andrew N. "Some Social Aspects of the Mexican Constitution of 1917," *Hispanic American Historical Review*, August 1921, pp. 474–85.

Comstock, Paul B. "Federal and State Jurisdiction in Mexico." M.A. thesis, Columbia University, 1950.

Córdoba Ladrón de Guevara, Darío. *Breves Consideraciones sobre el Estado Federal Mexicano*. Mexico City, 1948.

Cormack, Joseph M. "Operation of the Mexican Labor Law," *Southwestern Law Journal*, Summer 1953, pp. 301–26, and Fall 1953, pp. 464–95.

————, and F. M. Barker. "The Mexican Labor Law," *Southern California Law Review*, March 1934, pp. 251–94.

Coronado, Mariano. *Elementos de Derecho Constitucional Mexicano*. Guadalajara, 1899.

Corzo Macías, Emilio. "La Desaparición de Poderes Locales en la Legislación Mexicana." UNAM thesis, 1948.

Covarrubias González, Baldomero. *Autonomía de los Estados de la Federación*. Mexico City, 1938.

Cristiani C., Á. "El Federalismo Mexicano y las Facultades Constitucionales de los Estados." UNAM thesis, 1939.

Cruz, Manuel Humberto. "La Anticonstitucionalidad de las Facultades Extraordinarias Concedidas al Poder Ejecutivo para Legislar." UNAM thesis, 1937.

Cueva, Mario de la. "El Derecho del Trabajo," in Sría. de Educación Pública, *México y la Cultura*, 1946. Pp. 853–88.

————. *Derecho Mexicano de Trabajo*. Mexico City, 1949.

D'Acosta y Esquivel, Julio. *Breves Consideraciones sobre el Artículo 115 Constitucional*. Mexico City, 1948.

Dealey, James Q. "The Spanish Source of the Mexican Constitution of 1824," *Texas State Historical Association Quarterly*, January 1900, pp. 161–69.

Dekelbaum, E. "The Constitution of the United States Compared with the Constitutions of Mexico, Germany, and Russia," *Notre Dame Lawyer*, December 1928, pp. 178–91.

Domínguez Rodríguez, Ricardo. "El Artículo 97 Constitucional y el Voto Público." UNAM thesis, Ed. Claridad, 1946.

Echánove Trujillo, Carlos A. "El Juicio de Amparo Mexicano," *Rev. Fac. Der.*, January–June 1951, pp. 91–116.

Esquivel Obregón, Toribio. *Apuntes para la Historia del Derecho en México.* 3 vols. Mexico City: Ed. Polis, 1938–44.

Fábila, Manuel. *Cinco Siglos de Legislación Agraria, 1493–1940.* Mexico City, 1941.

Farrera, Augustín. *El Juicio de Amparo.* Mexico City: Publicaciones Farrera, 1942.

Fernández, Narciso J. *De Apatzingán a Querétaro, Congresos y Leyes Constitucionales de México.* Mexico City: El Nacional, 1942.

Fernández Estrada, Alfonso. "Breve Estudio del Estatuto de los Trabajadores al Servicio del Estado." Thesis, Escuela Libre de Derecho, 1945.

Fitzgibbon, Russell H. "Constitutional Development in Latin America, a Synthesis," in A. N. Christensen, *Evolution of Latin American Government.* New York: Holt, 1951. Pp. 210–24.

———. *The Constitutions of the Americas.* Chicago: University of Chicago Press, 1948.

Flores Zavala, Ernesto. "Teoría del Poder Ejecutivo Mexicano," *Justicia,* April 1952, pp. 11340–47.

Fraga, Gabino. *Derecho Administrativo.* (5th ed.) Mexico City: Ed. Porrúa, 1952. (The sixth edition became available too late for use in this work, but it does not differ in pertinent details from the fifth edition.)

Gaither, Roscoe B. *Handbook of Mexican Mercantile Law.* Oberlin: Academy Press, 1948.

Gallant, Bernard. "Making Laws for Mexico," *Survey,* January 20, 1917, pp. 449–51.

Galván González Roa, Gumersindo. "El Federalismo en México." UNAM thesis, 1940.

Gándara Salas, Casimiro Alberto. "La Irresponsabilidad de los Funcionarios y Empleados Públicos . . ." UNAM thesis, 1948.

García Peña Guzmán, Gabriel. "El Régimen Federal en México." UNAM thesis, 1939.

Gavaldón Salamanca, Ignacio. "The Mexican Writ of Amparo." M.A. thesis, University of Texas, 1937.

Gaxiola, F. Jorge. *Algunos Problemas del Estado Federal.* Mexico City: Ed. Cultura, 1941.

Gómez Monroy, Juan. "Comentarios a la Ley Orgánica de Educación Pública en Relación con el Párrafo VI del Artículo 3 Constitucional." UNAM thesis, 1951.

González, Franklin S. "Church-State Controversy in Mexico since 1929." M.A. thesis, University of California at Los Angeles, 1948.

González Reyes, Mario F. "El Órgano Legislativo y su Función en el Derecho Mexicano." UNAM thesis, 1950.

Goodspeed, Stephen S. "The Development and Use of *Facultades Extraordinarias* in Mexico," *SWSSQ,* December 1953, pp. 17–33.

———. "Mexico: President and Constitution," *Mid-America,* April 1954, pp. 96–115.

Gracidas, Carlos L. "Esencia Imperativa del Artículo 123 Constitucional, los Debates en Querétaro . . ." UNAM thesis, 1948.

Hernández, Octavio A. *La Constitución Política de los Estados Unidos Mexicanos: Génesis, Exégesis, Hermeneútica, Crítica . . .* 2 vols. Mexico City, 1946–52.

Herrera Alarcón, José. *Diccionario Mexicano de Legislación y Jurisprudencia.* 2 vols. Mexico City, 1942.

Herrera Guerrero, Héctor Vicente. "La División de Poderes en la Constitución de 1917"; "¿Existe un Cuarto Poder . . .?" UNAM thesis, 1946.

Herrera Lasso, Manuel. "Los Constructores del Amparo," *Revista Mexicana de Derecho Público,* April–June 1947, pp. 369–84.

———. *Estudios de Derecho Constitucional.* Mexico City: Ed. Polis, 1940.

# BIBLIOGRAPHY

Herrero, Vicente. *La Organización Constitucional en Iberoamérica*. Mexico City: Colegio de México, 1944.

Ibarra Partida, Felipe. "La Desaparición de Poderes y la Constitución de Nayarit." UNAM thesis, 1948.

James, Earle K. "Church and State in Mexico," *Annals*, March 1940, pp. 112–20.

———. "Church and State in Mexico," *Foreign Policy Reports*, July 3, 1935, pp. 105–16.

Junco, María Elena. "Irreformabilidad de las Decisiones Políticas Fundamentales de la Constitución." UNAM thesis, 1942.

Knapp, Frank A., Jr. "Parliamentary Government and the Mexican Constitution of 1857," *Hispanic American Historical Review*, February 1953, pp. 65–87.

Laguna Arcos, Enriqueta. "El Ejecutivo y la Promulgación de las Leyes." UNAM thesis, 1950.

Lanz Duret, Miguel. *Derecho Constitucional Mexicano y Consideraciones sobre la Realidad Política de Nuestro Régimen*. Mexico City: Imprenta L. D., 1947.

León Gutiérrez, Hugo. *Las Decisiones Políticas Fundamentales en la Constitución Mexicana*. UNAM thesis, 1944.

López Moreno, Miguel. "Reformas a la Constitución; la Interpretación del Art. 135." UNAM thesis, 1949.

Loredo Castañeda, Emma. *El Senado en la Teoría Jurídica del Estado Federal*. UNAM thesis, 1950.

Lugan, Alphonse. "Church and State in Mexico," *Cur. Hist.*, February 1931, pp. 672–76.

Macfarland, Charles S. *Chaos in Mexico; the Conflict of Church and State*. New York: Harper, 1935.

Mack, Raymond D. "Constitutional Centralism in Mexico, a Study of the Constitutions of 1836 and 1843." M.A. thesis, University of Texas, 1949.

McSorley, Joseph. *An Outline History of the Church by Centuries*. St. Louis: Herder, 1954.

Márquez Montiel, Joaquín. *La Iglesia y el Estado en México* . . . Chihuahua, 1950.

Martínez Báez, Antonio. "El Derecho Constitucional," in *México y la Cultura*. Mexico City: Sría. de Educación Pública, 1946. Pp. 773–91.

Martínez Palafox, Luis. "La Adopción del Federalismo en México." UNAM thesis, 1945.

Matos Escobedo, Rafael. *La Crisis Política y Jurídica del Federalismo*. Jalapa, 1944.

Matulewicz, Anthony C. "The Mexican Constitution of 1824." MCC, 1952.

Mecham, J. Lloyd. "Church vs. State in Mexico," *Southwest Review*, April 1938, pp. 274–96.

———. "Federal Intervention in Mexico," in A. C. Wilgus, ed., *Hispanic American Essays*. Chapel Hill: University of North Carolina Press, 1942. Pp. 256–79.

———. "Mexican Federalism — Fact or Fiction?" *Annals*, March 1940, pp. 23–38.

———. "Origins of Federalism in Mexico," in Conyers Read, ed., *The Constitution Reconsidered*. New York: Columbia University Press, 1938. Pp. 349–65.

———. "The Religious Question in Mexico," in *Mexico and the United States*. Dallas, Texas: Southern Methodist University, 1938. Pp. 118–37.

Melgarejo Randolf, Luis. *El Congreso Constituyente de 1916 y 1917, Reseña Histórica de los Debates* . . . Mexico City: Sría. de Fomento, 1917.

Méndez Gómez, Gelacio. *El Régimen Representativo en México*. Mexico City, 1949.

Mendieta y Núñez, Lucio. *El Sistema Agrario Constitucional* . . . Mexico City: Ed. Porrúa, 1940.

439

Molina Enríquez, Andrés. "El Artículo 27 de la Constitución Federal," *Boletín de la Secretaría de Gobernación*, September 1922, pp. 2–32.
Montiel y Duarte, Isidro. *Derecho Público Mexicano*. Mexico City: Ed. del Gobierno Federal, 1882.
Morales Elizondo, Óscar. "El Principio de la División de Poderes." UNAM thesis, 1945.
Morton, Ward M. "The Mexican Constitutional Congress of 1916–1917," *SWSSQ*, June 1952, pp. 7–27.
Muñoz, Luis. *Comentarios a la Constitución Política* . . . Mexico City: Ed. Lex, 1947.
———. *Comentarios a la Ley Federal del Trabajo: Antecedentes, Concordancias* . . . Mexico City, 1948.
Murillo, Guilebaldo. *Inconstitucionalidad del Actual Artículo 3 de la Constitución Federal*. Mexico City: Ed. Jus, 1941.
Niemeyer, E. V., Jr. "Anticlericalism in the Mexican Constitutional Convention of 1916–1917," *Américas*, July 1954, pp. 31–49.
Ortega Deciga, Ernestina. "Interpretación del Artículo 13 Constitucional." UNAM thesis, 1941.
Ortiz Motta, Arturo. *¿Protege el Artículo 14 Constitucional los Derechos Políticos?* Mexico City: Imp. Aztecas, 1941. (Thesis.)
Ortiz Valencia, Héctor. "Algunas Observaciones acerca del Poder Público desde el Punto de Vista Democrático." UNAM thesis, 1949.
Palavicini, Félix F. *Historia de la Constitución de 1917* . . . 2 vols. Mexico City, 1938.
Pallares, Eduardo. *Diccionario de Derecho Procesal Civil*. Mexico City: Ed. Porrúa, 1952.
Palomares Navarro, Noé. "Nuestro Sistema Federal y la Desaparición de Poderes Locales." UNAM thesis, 1939?.
Parsons, Wilfrid. *Mexican Martyrdom*. New York: Macmillan, 1936.
Pasquel, Leonardo. "Teoría de la División de Poderes y la Realidad Mexicana." UNAM thesis, 1940.
Pattee, Richard. *The Catholic Revival in Mexico; a Report of the Inter-American Committee*. Washington, D.C.: Catholic Association for International Peace, 1944.
Peniche López, Luis Fernando. "El Derecho de Reunión, Firme Baluarte de la Libertad y la Democracia: Historia, Doctrina, Legislación y Jurisprudencia." UNAM thesis, 1949.
Pérez Peñafiel, Juventino. "Facultad Revisora de la Constitución." UNAM thesis, 1951.
Priestley, Herbert I. "Constitutional Interpretation in Mexico," *SWSSQ*, September 1923, pp. 138–62.
Procuraduría General. *Breve Reseña de la Legislación de Emergencia Expedida en los Estados Unidos Mexicanos*. Mexico City, 1944.
Quirk, Robert E., Jr. "The Mexican Revolution and the Catholic Church, 1910–1929: An Ideological Study." Ph.D. thesis, Harvard University, 1951.
Rabasa, Emilio. *El Artículo 14, Estudio Constitucional*. Mexico City: El Progreso Latino, 1906.
———. *La Constitución y la Dictadura, Estudio sobre la Organización Política de México*. Mexico City: Tip. de Revista de Revistas, 1912.
———. *El Juicio Constitucional: Orígenes, Teoría y Extensión*. Paris: Bouret, 1919.
Rabasa, Óscar. "Diferencias entre el Juicio de Amparo y los Recursos Constitucionales Norteamericanos," *El Foro*, September 1947, pp. 253–74.
———. *El Derecho Angloamericano*. Mexico City: Fondo, 1944.

# BIBLIOGRAPHY

Ramírez Pelayo, Odilón. *Necesidad de Reglamentar la Fracción V del Artículo 76 Constitucional en Materia de Desaparición de Poderes de las Entidades . . .* Mexico City, 1944.

Rangel y Vázquez, Manuel. "El Control de la Constitucionalidad de las Leyes y el Juicio de Amparo . . ." UNAM thesis, Ed. Cultura, 1952.

Rebolledo Vergara, Rogelio. "Salubridad General de la República: Interpretación de la Fracción XVI del Artículo 73 Constitucional." UNAM thesis, 1944.

Reyes Hernández, Aurelio. "La División de Poderes en el Derecho Constitucional Mexicano." UNAM thesis, 1942.

Reyes Morales, Marino. *El Senado y la Facultad que se Arroga para Desconocer los Gobiernos Locales.* Veracruz, 1939.

Robles Gil, Guillermo. "Nueva Responsabilidad del Estado en México." UNAM thesis, 1942.

Rodríguez y Rodríguez, Rosendo. "El Artículo Trece." UNAM thesis, 1949.

Rouaix, Pastor. *Génesis de los Artículos 27 y 123 de la Constitución Política de 1917.* Puebla, 1945.

Rubio Valderrama, Armando. "El Artículo 104 Constitucional . . ." UNAM thesis, 1950.

Ruiz, Eduardo. *Derecho Constitucional.* Mexico City, 1902.

Sánchez Mejorada, Carlos. "The Evolution of Federal Institutions in Mexico," *Journal of District of Columbia Bar Association,* April 1944, pp. 169–74.

———. "The Legal System of Mexico," *Law Notes* (Brooklyn), May 1945, pp. 5–23.

Santillán Ortiz, Lamberto. "El Sistema de Control Constitucional en México y en los Estados Unidos del Norte." UNAM thesis, 1944.

Scott, Robert E. "Some Aspects of Mexican Federalism, 1917–1948." Ph.D. thesis, University of Wisconsin, 1949.

Sría. de Hacienda y Crédito Público. *Presupuestos de Egresos de Erario Federal* (annual).

Senties G., Octavio. "Federalismo Constitucional y Centralismo Económico." UNAM thesis, 1942.

Shiels, W. E. "Church and State in the First Decade of Mexican Independence," *Catholic Historical Review,* July 1942, pp. 206–28.

Silva Herzog, Jesús. "Economic Ideas in Mexico in the Constitutional Congress of 1857," *Social Sciences in Mexico,* May 1947, pp. 34–45.

Soto Reyes, Ernesto. *Organización Jurídica y Contenida Social del Estado Mexicano.* Asunción, 1942.

Spain, August O. "Mexican Federalism Revisited," *Western Political Quarterly,* September 1956, pp. 620–32.

Stern, David S. "Full Faith and Credit, the Mexican Experience," *New York University Law Review,* October 1951, pp. 663–76.

Stokes, William S. "Catholicism and Democracy in Latin America," in Ángel del Río, ed., *Responsible Freedom in the Americas.* New York: Doubleday, 1955. Pp. 361–80.

Suinaga Luján, Pedro R. *Veinte Años de Legislación Mexicana, 1931–50.* 3 vols. Mexico City: Ed. Stylo, 1951.

Suprema Corte de Justicia. *El Artículo 97 Constitucional y la Democracia; una Discusión Histórica en el Pleno de la Suprema Corte . . .* Mexico City: Ed. Jus, 1947.

Tena Ramírez, Felipe. *Derecho Constitucional Mexicano.* Mexico City: Ed. Porrúa, 2nd ed., 1949.
(The third edition (1955) became available too late for use in this work, but it does not differ in pertinent details from the second edition.)

————. *México y sus Constituciones*. Mexico City: Ed. Polis, 1937.

Toro, Alfonso. *La Iglesia y el Estado en México*. Mexico City: Sría. de Gobernación, 1927.

Torres de la Garza, Óscar. "La Intervención de los Poderes Federales en los Estados Miembros según Nuestra Constitución." UNAM thesis, 1951.

Tribunal Fiscal. *Jurisprudencia del Tribunal Fiscal de la Federación* . . . Mexico City: Ed. Ley, 1944.

Trigueros S., Eduardo. "El Artículo 121 de la Constitución," *Revista Mexicana de Derecho Público*, October–December 1946, pp. 157–82.

Trueba Urbina, Alberto. *El Artículo 123*. Mexico City: Talleres Gráficos Laguna, 1943.

————. *Derecho Procesal del Trabajo*. 4 vols. Mexico City, 1943–44.

————. *Diccionario de Derecho Obrero*. Mexico City, 1941.

————. *¿Qué es una Constitución Político-Social?* Mexico City: Ed. Ruta, 1951.

Valero Silva, José. *Ambiente Histórico de la Constitución de 1824*. 1952. (Also in *Anales de Jurisprudencia*, July–September 1952, pp. 383–529.)

Vallejo Arizmendi, Jorge. *Estudios de Derecho Constitucional Mexicano*. Mexico City, 1947.

————, and Paul Medina Mora. *Ensayo Bibliográfico de Derecho Constitucional Mexicano y de Garantías y Amparos*. Mexico City: Imp. Universitaria, 1947.

Vance, John T., and Helen L. Clagett. *A Guide to the Law and Legal Literature of Mexico*. Washington, D.C.: Library of Congress, 1945.

Vázquez Hernández, Federico J. *El Artículo 120 Constitucional y el Régimen Federal*. Mexico City, 1946.

Vélez Jiménez, Jorge M. "La Inexacta Interpretación de la Fracción V del Artículo 76 de la Constitución, Viola el Pacto Federal." UNAM, thesis, 1947.

Vera Español, Jorge. *Al Margen de la Constitución de 1917*. Los Angeles: Wayside Press, 1920.

Vera Guillén, Guillermo. *Situación Jurídico-Política de los Estados Miembros; Alcance de la Fracción V del Artículo 76 Constitucional*. Mexico City, 1942.

Villa González, León. *El Principio de la División de Poderes en Nuestras Constituciones*. Mexico City: Mijares y Hermano, 1942.

Villarreal Carrillo, Mario. "La Garantía de Audiencia en Materia Administrativa." UNAM thesis, 1948.

Vite Flores, Edmundo. "Sociología del Juicio de Amparo." UNAM thesis, 1951.

Westrup Puentes, Horacio. "La Separación entre la Iglesia y el Estado." UNAM thesis, 1951.

Whatley, W. A. "The Formation of the Mexican Constitution of 1824." M.A. thesis. University of Texas, 1921.

Zapata Espinosa, Fernando. "La Supremacía Constitucional y sus Problemas, a Luz del Derecho Mexicano." UNAM thesis, Ocampo Hermanos, 1943.

Zarco, Francisco. *Historia del Congreso Constituyente de 1857* . . . Mexico City: Escalante, 1916.

### BASIC LAW IN THE STATES

#### Collections

*Constituciones de los Estados de la República Mexicana Concordadas*, por el Lic. Agustín Farrera. Mexico City: Publicaciones Farrera, 1949. Tomo Primero.

Constitutions of the states. *Boletín de la Secretaría de Gobernación*. April 1924.

#### Individual States

Baja California. "Constitución," in *Periódico Oficial*, August 16, 1953.

# BIBLIOGRAPHY

Chihuahua. *Código Administrativo* . . . Mexico, D.F.: La Impresora, 1950.
————. *Constitución Política del Estado de Chihuahua*. Chihuahua, 1950.
Mexico (State). *Constituciones del Estado de México*; Recopilación y Notas de Mario Colín. Toluca: Instituto Científico y Literario, 1952.
Sonora. *Ley que Reglamenta los Artículos 143 y 144 de la Constitución* . . . *Local sobre Responsabilidad de Altos Funcionarios y Empleados* . . . Hermosillo, 1949.

## III. Legislative, Executive, Judicial

Acosta Romero, Miguel. "Las Comisiones Autónomas en el Derecho Mexicano." UNAM thesis, 1953.
Aguilar, Gustavo F. "La Academia de Capacitación Técnica para Empleados de la Sría. de Hacienda," *Revista de Hacienda y Finanzas*, April 1946, pp. 9f.
Aguilar Aguilar, Jorge. "El Municipio Libre." UNAM thesis, 1946.
Aguilar y Maya, José. *El Ministerio Público Federal en el Nuevo Régimen*. Mexico City: Ed. Polis, 1942.
Aguirre Beltrán, Gonzalo. *Formas de Gobierno Indígena*. Mexico City: Imp. Universitaria, 1953.
Arias Águila, Rubén. "El Procedimiento Administrativo." UNAM thesis, 1946.
Armas Arias, Guillermo. "Planificación Económica Regional, su Proyección a Países no Industrializados." UNAM thesis, 1950.
Barrera Fuentes, Florencio. "Historia y Destino del Municipio en México." UNAM thesis, 1950.
Beals, Ralph L. *Cherán: a Sierra Tarascan Village*. Washington, D.C.: Smithsonian Institution, 1946.
————. "Cherán: a Village of Mexico," *Mex. Life*, April 1952, pp. 25–27.
————. *The Contemporary Culture of the Cáhita Indians*. Washington, D.C.: Bureau of American Ethnology, 1945.
Berlanga Berumen, Marco Antonio. "La Decentralización por Servicio . . ." UNAM thesis, 1945.
Bezares, Abel. "Breve Disertación sobre el Refrendo Ministerial." UNAM thesis, 1949.
Bogardus, Emory S. "Social Planning in Mexico," *Sociology and Social Research*, November 1934, pp. 173–79.
Bosch García, Pedro. "El Liberalismo, la Planeación, y las Empresas del Estado," *Rev. Ec.*, No. 2, 1946, pp. 33–34.
Bosques, Gilberto. *The National Revolutionary Party of Mexico and the Six Year Plan*. Mexico City: The Party, 1937.
Braderman, E. M. "A Study of Political Parties and Politics in Mexico since 1890." Ph.D. thesis, University of Illinois, 1938.
Brand, Donald D. *Quiroga: A Mexican Municipio*. Washington, D. C.: Smithsonian Institution, 1951.
Brandenburg, Frank R. "Mexico, An Experiment in One-Party Democracy." Ph.D. thesis, University of Pennsylvania, 1955.
Bustamante, Eduardo. "Facultades Judiciales de los Órganos Administrativos . . ." *El Foro*, September 1945, pp. 270–93.
————. "Los Sistemas Tributarios de los Estados," *Rev. Ec.*, April 1950, pp. 124–27, and May 1950, pp. 151–53.
Cannon, John P. *A Regional Study of the Municipio of Chalco*. MCC, 1953.
Carballo G., Armando. *El Sistema Municipal en México desde su Implantación hasta la Constitución de 1917*. Mexico City: Imp. Virginia, 1936.
Carrillo Ramírez, Jorge A. "El Control Administrativo de las Instituciones de Crédito." UNAM thesis, 1952.

443

Casas Hernández, Roberto. "Control de los Organismos Decentralizados por Servicios." UNAM thesis, 1949.

Caso, Ángel. *Principios de Organización.* Mexico City: Ed. Porrúa, 1948.

Castorena, J. Jesús. *Municipio Libre.* Mexico City, 1948.

————. *El Problema Municipal Mexicano.* Mexico City: Ed. Cultura, 1926.

Celorio Celorio, Felipe. *Los Partidos Políticos y el Sufragio en México, Inglaterra y Estados Unidos.* Mexico City, 1949.

Cerezo L., Juan Manuel. "Servicios Públicos Municipales." UNAM thesis, 1943.

Chávez, Ezequiel A. *La Organización del Servicio Civil por Medio del Mérito.* Mexico City: Talleres Gráficos de la Nación, 1920.

Chávez Chávez, Rafael. "La Intervención de la Corte en Materia Política." UNAM thesis, 1946.

Clagett, Helen L. *The Administration of Justice in Latin America.* New York: Oceana Publications, 1952.

Cloner, Alexander. "The Cultural Setting of Mexican Public Administration." Manuscript, 1952.

Colín, Mario. "Notas sobre el Municipio en México." UNAM thesis, 1949.

Congreso. *Reglamento para el Gobierno Interior del Congreso* . . . Mexico City, 1953.

Cuarón, J. M. "¿Qué es la Administración Científica de Personal?" *Rev. Ec.,* July 1950.

D'Acosta y Esquivel, Julio. *El Fuero del Municipio: Breve Consideraciones sobre el Artículo 115 Constitucional.* Mexico City, 1948.

Delint López, Luis. *El Ministerio Público en México.* Mexico City, 1949.

Departamento del Distrito Federal. *Realizaciones del Gobierno del* . . . *Alemán.* Mexico City, 1952.

————. *Resumen de Actividades.* Mexico City, 1948.

Dios Sierra, Ofelia de. "Limitaciones Constitucionales al Poder Ejecutivo." UNAM thesis, 1950.

"The Domino Player," *Time* (Latin American ed.), September 14, 1953, pp. 28–31.

Dotson, Floyd, and L. O. Dotson. "Ecological Trends in the City of Guadalajara, Mexico," *Social Forces,* May 1954, pp. 367–74.

Ducker Calo, Guillermo. "La Comisión Permanente." UNAM thesis, 1947.

Durán, Marco Antonio. "Problemas de Administración Pública," *Inv. Ec.,* No. 1, 1947.

Ebenstein, William. "Public Administration in Mexico," *Public Administration Review,* Spring 1945, pp. 102–12.

Eisenberg, Ralph. "Presidential Election in Mexico: 1952." M.A. thesis, University of Illinois, 1953.

Fábila, Alfonso, and Gilberto Fábila. *México: Ensayo Socioeconómico del Estado.* 2 vols. Mexico City, 1951.

Flores Mellardo, Ernesto. *Anticonstitucionalidad de la Facultad que Varias Constituciones Locales Conceden a los Gobernadores de los Estados para Disponer a los Miembros de los Ayuntamientos.* Mexico City: Ed. de Izquierda de la Cámara de Diputados, 1937.

Foster, George M. *A Primitive Mexican Economy.* New York: Augustin, 1942.

Fuente, Julio de la. *Yalalag: una Villa Zapoteca Serrana.* Mexico City: Museo Nacional de Antropología, 1949.

Fuentes Galindo, Fernando. *Organización Constitucional del Distrito Federal.* Mexico City, 1948.

Garza, Sergio de la. *El Municipio: Historia, Naturaleza y Gobierno.* Mexico City, 1947.

# BIBLIOGRAPHY

Georgge Hernández, Germán. "El Municipio Libre en México." UNAM thesis, 1946.

Gómez Montoya, Máximo. "El Municipio Sinaloense dentro del Sistema Municipal Nacional." UNAM thesis, 1941.

Gómez Yañez, Miguel Ángel. "La Organización Administrativa y las Comisiones Autónomas," *Revista de la Escuela Nacional de Jurisprudencia*, April–June 1949, pp. 95–113.

González Lobo, Salvador. "El Municipio Mexicano." UNAM thesis, 1940.

González Luna, Efraín. *Naturaleza y Funciones del Municipio*. Mexico City, n.d.

Goodspeed, Stephen S. "The Role of the Chief Executive in Mexico: Policies, Powers, and Administration." Ph.D. thesis, University of California, 1947. (Also in *Prob. Agr.*, January–March 1955, pp. 13–208).

Guiteras Holmes, C. *Sayula* [a Mexican village]. Mexico City: Sociedad Mexicana de Geografía y Estadística, 1952.

Gutiérrez Cirlos, Ernesto. *Consideraciones sobre el Sufragio y Medidas para una Reforma de Nuestro Sistema Electoral*. Mexico City: Imp. Virginia, 1945.

Harrsch Núñez, Teodoro. "Breve Estudio sobre Algunos Aspectos de la Decentralización por Servicios." UNAM thesis, 1949.

Hayner, Norman S. "Mexico City: Its Growth and Configuration," *American Journal of Sociology*, January 1945, pp. 295–304.

Hernández Reyes, Rogelio. "Puntos Básicos para una Reorganización Constitucional del Sufragio." UNAM thesis, 1947.

Hernández Rodríguez, Felipe. "El Refrendo en el Derecho Mexicano." UNAM thesis, 1944.

Holman, Robert W. "Planning in the Mexican Federal District and its Relation to the National Industrialization Program under President Alemán." MCC, 1950.

Huitren Huitren, Antonio. *Los Partidos Políticos en el Régimen Constitucional*. Mexico City: Imp. Virginia, 1947.

Ives, Ronald L. "Puerto Peñasco, Sonora," *Journal of Geography*, December 1950, pp. 349–61.

Johnson, John J. "The Latin American Municipality Deteriorates," *Inter-American Economic Affairs*, Summer 1951, pp. 24–35.

Johnson, Richard A. "Municipal Reconstruction: the New Guadalajara," *Foreign Service Journal*, June 1952, pp. 20–21, 54–55.

Jorrín, Miguel. *Governments of Latin America*. New York: Van Nostrand, 1953.

Laguna Arcos, Enriqueta. "El Ejecutivo y la Promulgación de las Leyes." UNAM thesis, 1950.

Lewis, Oscar. *Life in a Mexican Village: Tepoztlán Restudied*. Urbana: University of Illinois, 1951.

Llata, Luis de la. "Las Juntas Federales de Mejoras Materiales." UNAM thesis, 1952.

Lobato, Ernesto. "La Burocracia Mexicana," *Rev. Ec.*, October 1951, pp. 307–12.

———. "Situación Económica de la Burocracia Mexicana," *Rev. Ec.*, December 1952, pp. 380–88.

Lomeli Cerezo, Aurelio. "Breve Estudio del Departamento del Distrito Federal." UNAM thesis, 1952.

Loredo Castañeda, Emma. *El Senado en la Teoría Jurídica del Estado Federal*. Mexico City, 1950.

Luna Morales, Clara. "El Sufragio Femenino en México." UNAM thesis, 1947.

Macdonald, Austin F. *Latin American Politics and Government*. New York: Crowell, 1954.

Mancera Ortiz, Rafael. *La Administración Pública en los Planes de Desarrollo Económico*. Mexico City, 1953.

——. *Mexico's Attitude towards Development Programs* (address at IX International Congress of Administrative Sciences). Mexico City, 1953.

Manzanera Del Campo, María Elena. "La Igualidad de Derecho Políticos." UNAM thesis, 1953.

Martínez, Jesús. "Como Mejorar la Administración Pública en México," *Rev. Ec.*, January 31, 1947, pp. 34–40.

Martínez Báez, Antonio. "El Ejecutivo y su Gabinete," *Revista de la Facultad de Derecho*, April–June 1952, pp. 53–70.

Martínez Cabañas, Gustavo. "Los Fundamentos de la Administración Pública," *Rev. Ec.*, No. 1, 1947, pp. 26–29.

Maza, Ignacio Muriel de la. "El Municipio en México, Naturaleza e Historia." UNAM thesis, 1948.

Mecham, J. Lloyd. "The *Jefe Político* in Mexico," *SWSSQ*, May 1933, pp. 133–42.

——. "The Ministry of State in Latin America," *SWSSQ*, September 1927, pp. 143–68.

Medina, Hernán, and Manuel Ortiz C. *Las Instituciones Jurídico-Políticas de México*. Mexico City: Ed. Cicerón, 1953.

Méndez Barraza, Alfonso. *Los Partidos Políticos en México*. Mexico City, 1949.

Méndez Cervantes, Óscar. "La Restauración Municipal en México." UNAM thesis, 1942.

Mendieta y Núñez, Lucio. *La Administración Pública en México*. Mexico City: Imp. Universitaria, 1942.

——. *Los Partidos Políticos*. Mexico City, 1947.

Menez, Joseph. "Presidents and Constitutions in the Americas," *Mid-America*, January 1954, pp. 3–38, and April 1954, pp. 75–95.

"A Mexican Federal Commission on Economic Planning," *International Labour Review*, September 1942, pp. 314–15.

"A Mexican National Economic Council," *BPAU*, October 1941, pp. 607–8.

Mijares Palencia, José. *El Gobierno Mexicano, su Organización y Funcionamiento*. Mexico City: Sociedad Mexicana de Publicaciones, 1936.

Mijares Palencia, José and Charles E. De Haven. *The Mexican Government: Its Organization*. Mexico City: Sociedad Mexicana de Publicaciones, 1937. (An abbreviated English version of the preceding work).

Monterrey, Instituto de Estudios Sociales. *Apuntes para el Plano Regulador de la Ciudad de Monterrey*. Monterrey, 1950.

Moreno, Daniel A. "El Distrito Federal." UNAM thesis, 1944.

Ney Morales, Filiberto. *Los Monopolios en México*. UNAM thesis, 1949.

Noriega, Raúl. *La Obra del Gobierno del Distrito Federal*. Mexico City, 1946.

Oaxaca (Estado), Poder Ejecutivo. *Informe del C. Eduardo Vasconcelos, Gobernador del Estado . . . 1948*. Oaxaca, 1948.

Oceguera Ochoa, José María. "La Presidencia de la Cámara." UNAM thesis, 1945.

Ochoa Campos, Moisés. *La Reforma Municipal; Historia Municipal de México*. UNAM thesis, 1955.

Ogarrio R. España, Julio. "El Problema de la Ciudadanía de la Mujer y de los Ministros de Culto . . ." Thesis, Escuela Libre de Derecho, 1951.

Ornelas Kuchle, Luis F. "Génesis y Evolución del Municipio en México." UNAM thesis, 1951.

Orozco Ávila, Palmira. "Procedimiento ante los Tribunales para Menores." UNAM thesis, 1952.

Ortiz Cabrera, Jorge Antonio. "El Veto en Materia Constitucional." UNAM thesis, 1949.

Ortiz Múgica, Federico. "Comentario al Funcionamiento y Resoluciones de la Suprema Corte de la Justicia de la Nación." UNAM thesis, 1941.

# BIBLIOGRAPHY

Padgett, Leon V. "Popular Participation in the Mexican 'One-Party' System." Ph.D. thesis, Northwestern University, 1955.

Padilla, Juan I. *Sinarquismo: Contra-Revolución*. Mexico City: Ed. Polis, 1948.

Parkes, Henry B. "Political Leadership in Mexico," *Annals*, March 1940, pp. 12–22.

Partido de la Revolución Mexicana. *The Second Six-Year Plan, 1941–1946* . . . Mexico City, 1939?.

Partido Nacional Revolucionario. *Plan Sexenal del Gobierno Mexicano*. Mexico City, 1934.

Partido Revolucionario Institucional. *Asamblea Nacional Informe*. Mexico City, 1950.

Peralta Peralta, Isaias I. "Aspiración a una Nueva Organización de los Juzgados de Paz." UNAM thesis, 1953.

Pérez y Pérez, María. "Los Tribunales para Menores." UNAM thesis, 1947.

Presidente (Alemán). *VI Informe del Presidente Alemán* . . . Mexico City: Ed. Ruta, 1952.

Presidente (Ruiz Cortines). *Jamás Defraudaré la Fe que la Ciudadanía Ha Depositado en Mí*. Mexico City, 1952.

Quiñones López, Ernesto. *Función de la Contaduría Mayor de Hacienda en el Control Legislativo de las Finanzas*. Mexico City, 1950.

Rabasa, Emilio. "El Senado y la Comisión Permanente," *Revista Mexicana de Derecho Público*, July–September 1946, pp. 67–84.

Radvanyi, Laszlo. "Planeación del Desarrollo Económico," in *El Desarrollo Económico de México*. Mexico City: Escuela Nacional de Economía, 1952. Pp. 125–39.

Ramírez Castro, Wenceslao. "El Ministerio Público . . ." UNAM thesis, 1944.

Raynal Escobedo, Humberto. "El Fideicomiso y los Servicios Públicos Municipales." UNAM thesis, 1943.

Reyes Morales, Marino. "El Senado Mexicano y la Facultad que se Arroga para Desconocer los Gobiernos Locales." UNAM thesis, 1939.

Reyes Tayabas, Jorge. "El Poder Ejecutivo Frente a las Leyes Inconstitucionales." UNAM thesis, 1944.

Rivera Arnais, Fernando. "Relaciones entre el Público y la Administración," *Rev. Ec.*, December 1946, pp. 32–36.

Rodríguez Reyes, Álvaro. "La Economía y la Administración," *Rev. Ec.*, November 1951, pp. 335–39.

Rodríguez Rodríguez, Jesús. "Historia y Política del Municipio en México." UNAM thesis, 1942.

Rodríguez Valderrama, Jaime. "La Jurisprudencia de la Corte y el Precedente Norte-Americano." UNAM thesis, 1950.

Rolland, M. C. *El Desastre Municipal en la República Mexicana*. Mexico City, 1952.

Ruiz Esparza y Yarza, Flavio. "La Reglamentación de las Leyes por el Ejecutivo." UNAM thesis, 1942.

Salazar Viniegra, Guillermo. *El Problema del Tránsito en el Distrito Federal*. Mexico City: Banco de México, 1950.

Salceda, Alberto G. "La Elección del Presidente de la República," *Revista de la Facultad de Derecho*, April–June 1952, pp. 35–52.

Salinas, Raúl. "Organización y Dirección Administrativa." *Rev. Ec.*, January 1947, pp. 30–33.

Sánchez Pérez, Erasmo S. "El Municipio Libre y su Realidad en Nuestra Administración." UNAM thesis, 1940.

Schaeffer, Wendell K. G. "National Administration in Mexico: Its Development and Present Status." Ph.D. thesis, University of California, Berkeley, 1950. Also in *Prob. Agr.*, January–March 1955, pp. 209–314.

Schurz, William L. "Government," in Asher N. Christensen, ed., *The Evolution of Latin American Government*. New York: Holt, 1951. Pp. 12–52.

Scully, Michael. "President Ruiz Cortines: Mexico's Lonely Graft-Buster," *World*, June 1954, pp. 18–21.

Secretaría de Bienes Nacionales e Inspección Administrativa. *Directorio del Gobierno Federal: Poderes Legislativo, Ejecutivo, y Judicial.* Mexico City, 1951. (Cited as *Directorio* . . .(1).) (Revised edition, late 1956.)

——. *Directorio del Gobierno Federal: Organismos Decentralizados y Empresas de Participación Estatal.* Mexico City, 1951. (Cited as *Directorio* . . . (2).)

Secretaría de Hacienda y Crédito Público, Comisión Reorganizadora, 1927–1928. *Informe de sus Labores.* Mexico City, 1928.

Servin, Armando. "La Tesorería del Distrito Federal . . .", *Rev. Ec.*, August and September 1951, pp. 229–31, 266–68.

Shedd, Margaret. "Thunder on the Right in Mexico: the *Sinarquistas* in Action," *Harpers*, April 1945, pp. 414–25.

Siller Rodríguez, Rodolfo. *La Crisis del Partido Revolucionario Institucional.* Mexico City: Talleres Galeza, 1956 (UNAM thesis).

Stone, Shirley. "The Mexican Presidential Election of 1940, as Seen Through the Press of the Capital." M.A. thesis, Columbia University, 1949.

Suárez Téllez, José María. *¿Quiere Usted ser Diputado?* Mexico City: Colección de Estudios Políticos y Sociales, 1946.

Suprema Corte de Justicia de la Nación. *Informe Rendido a la Suprema Corte . . . por su Presidente . . .* Mexico City: Antigua Imprenta de Murguia, 1953.

——. *Jurisprudencia Definida . . . (1917–1948)*, in *Semanario Judicial de la Federación*, Apéndice al Tomo 97. 1949. 3 vols.

——. *Semanario Judicial de la Federación.*

Tena Ramírez, Felipe. "La Facultad de la Suprema Corte en Materia Electoral," *Revista Mexicana de Derecho Público*, July–September 1946, pp. 37–63.

United Nations, Economic Commission for Latin America. *Relaciones del Estado con los Sectores Decentralizados y Paraestatales en México* (Reunión Técnica sobre Administración Presupuestaria). Mexico City, 1953.

Urbina, Salvador. "Organización Ejecutiva," *Revista de la Escuela Nacional de Jurisprudencia*, April–June 1940, pp. 139–46.

Vela, Alberto R. "El Senado de la República," *Repr. Campechano*, May 1949, pp. 159–93.

Velásquez Carrasco, Luis. "Breve Estudio sobre la Democracia y el Estudio del Sufragio en México." UNAM thesis, 1943.

Violante, Carlos. "Obra de la Dirección de Pensiones," in *México, Realización y Esperanza*. Mexico City: Ed. Superación, 1952. Pp. 461–73.

Zevada, Ricardo L. "El Departamento del Distrito Federal," *Revista de la Facultad de Derecho*, March 1929, pp. 8 et seq.

## IV. Agencies and Operations

Abraham, Willard. "A City School in Mexico," *Clearing House*, December 1949, pp. 205–8.

Aguilar, Gustavo F. *Los Presupuestos Mexicanos, desde los Tiempos de la Colonia hasta Nuestros Días.* Mexico City, 1947.

Aguilar Uranga, Manuel. "Eficiencia en la Operación de los Ferrocarriles Nacionales," *Rev. Ec.*, March 1952, pp. 85–87.

# BIBLIOGRAPHY

——. "Los Ferrocarriles como Organismo del Servicio Público . . . ," *Rev. Ec.*, January 1952, pp. 33–36.

——. "Los Ferrocarriles Nacionales de México." UNAM thesis, 1950.

Aguinaco Alemán, Vicente. "Un Tribunal Federal de Justicia Administrativa." UNAM thesis, 1949.

Alanís Patiño, Emilio. "Las Tierras de Riego," *Prob. Agr.*, April 1950, pp. 49–168.

Alba, Victor. "Significado del Movimiento Obrero Latinoamericano," *Humanismo*, October 1952 to December 1953 (8 installments).

Albarelli, Francis J. "The Importance of Irrigation in the Economic Development of Mexico." MCC, 1953.

"Alcabalas," *Revista Fiscal y Financiera*, December 1948, pp. 60–71.

Alcázar Arias, José. "El Sistema Bancario Mexicano," in *México, Realización y Esperanza*. Mexico City: Ed. Superación, 1952. Pp. 503–10.

Alisky, Marvin. "Radio's Role in Mexico . . . ," *Journalism Quarterly*, Winter 1954, pp. 66–72.

Almaraz, José. "New Penal Legislation in Mexico," in H. C. Herring and Katharine Terrill, eds., *The Genius of Mexico*. New York: Committee on Cultural Relations with Latin America, 1931.

Alpuche, Fernando. "Afianzamiento del Seguro Social," in *México, Realización y Esperanza*. Mexico City: Ed. Superación, 1952. Pp. 453–60.

Alvarado, David. "En Lucha Contra el Dolor," in *México, Realización y Esperanza*. Mexico City: Ed. Superación, 1952. Pp. 475–83.

Amorós G., Roberto. *La Comisión Nacional del Café*. Mexico City: Ed. Ruta, 1950.

Andrade Alcocer, Gonzalo. "Conservation of Mexico's Renewable Resources as Fundamental Bases for its Agricultural Development," in *PIAC*, pp. 623–26.

*Anuario Financiero de México*. Mexico City: Asociación de Banqueros de México, 1953.

Arce Cano, Gustavo. *Alemán y el Seguro Social*. Mexico City: Ed. Ruta, 1951.

Arco Ibarra, Roxana. "Los Ferrocarriles en la Economía de México," *Inv. Ec.*, No. 4, 1950, pp. 427–55.

Argil, Gustavo. *Asistencia Hospitalaria en México*. Mexico City, 1951.

Arkos Melo, Guizzella de. "Comentario a los Impuestos Personales en México." UNAM thesis, 1951.

Attolini, José. *Economía de la Cuenca del Papaloapán: Agricultura*. Mexico City: Instituto de Investigaciones Económicas, 1949.

Aubrey, Henry G. "Structure and Balance in Rapid Economic Growth: the Example of Mexico," *Political Science Quarterly*, December 1954, pp. 517–40.

Bahamonde, Antonio. *México es Así*. Mexico City: México Nuevo, 1940.

Bailey, Bernadine. "Mexico: Laboratory of the Future," *United Nations World*, December 1952, pp. 47–50.

"Banco de México," *Bankers Magazine*, May 1928, pp. 790–96.

Banco de México. [Informe] *Asamblea General Ordinaria de Accionistas*. Mexico City, 1954.

——. *Proyecto de Inversiones del Gobierno Federal y Dependencias Decentralizadas . . . 1947–1952*. Mexico City, 1948.

Banco Nacional de Crédito Agrícola. *Informe* (1951 and earlier years).

Banco Nacional de Crédito Ejidal. *Informe* (1951 and earlier years).

Banks, Mary Jo. "A Study of the Federal Labor Code of Mexico." M.A. thesis, Columbia University, 1948.

Barbour, Philip L. "Commercial and Cultural Broadcasting in Mexico," *Annals*, March 1940, pp. 94–102.

449

Barriga Vázquez, Benjamín. "The Rural Cultural Missions of Mexico," *Social Sciences in Mexico*, Fall 1947, pp. 30–38.

"Basic Education in Mexico; the Nayarit Project," *London Times Educational Supplement*, March 14, 1952, p. 220.

Bassols, Narciso. "¿Qué Son, por Fin, las Juntas de Conciliación y Arbitraje?" *Revista General de Derecho y Jurisprudencia*, 1930, pp. 185–211.

Beck, Donald W. "The Railroad and its Economic Significance in Mexico." MCC, 1952.

Beltrán, Enrique. "Conservation Education in Mexico," in *PIAC*, pp. 626–30.

Benjamin, Harold. "Education in Mexico's Six-Year Plan," *School and Society*, November 17, 1934, pp. 66–68.

———. "Revolutionary Education in Mexico," *Annals*, November 1935, pp. 181–89.

Bernal Molina, María de los Ángeles. "Análisis Sociológico y Valoativo de la Campaña Alfabetizadora." UNAM thesis, 1948.

Berzunza, Carlos R. "National Defense," in *Encyclopedia Americana*, 1954, V. 18. Pp. 779–80.

———, and Manuel Sánchez Sarto. "Transportation and Communication," in *Encyclopedia Americana*, 1954, V. 18. Pp. 771–73.

Beteta, Ramón. "Mexico's Foreign Relations," *Annals*, March 1940, pp. 170–80.

———. "Some Economic Aspects of Mexico's Six-Year Plan," in Hubert C. Herring and Herbert Weinstock, eds., *Renascent Mexico*. New York: Covici-Friede, 1935. Pp. 88–109.

Blanco, Gonzalo. "El Abastecimiento de Agua a la Ciudad de México," *Rev. Ec.*, February 1950, pp. 63–65.

———. *Agriculture in Mexico*. Washington, D.C.: Pan American Union, 1950.

Bonilla Marín, Gabriel. *Teoría del Seguro Social*. Mexico City, 1945.

Bonilla y Segura, Guillermo. *Report on the Cultural Missions of Mexico*. Washington, D.C.: U.S. Office of Education (Bulletin 1945, No. 11), 1945.

Booth, George C. *Mexico's School-Made Society*. Palo Alto: Stanford University Press, 1941.

Brand, Donald D. "United States–Mexican Scientific and Cultural Relations," *Annals*, January 1948, pp. 67–76.

Bremauntz, Alberto. *La Educación Socialista en México, Antecedentes y Fundamentos de la Reforma de 1934*. Mexico City, 1943.

Buckwald, William. "The Employment of United States Citizens in Latin America," MCC, 1950.

Bustamante, Miguel. "Local Public Health Work in Mexico," *American Journal of Public Health*, July 1931, pp. 725–36.

———. "Public Health and Medical Care," *Annals*, March 1940, pp. 153–61.

Caldwell, Roy. "Our Recent Relations with Mexico." M.A. thesis, Southern Methodist University, 1941.

Call, Tomme C. "Governmental Finance," *Mex. Life*, November 1953, pp. 23–24.

"Cambios Ocurridos en la Estructura Agraria Mexicana Comparación entre los Datos del Censo Agrícola y Ejidal de 1940 y el de 1950," *Prob. Agr.*, October–December 1953, pp. 161–67.

Camiro, Max. "Los Seguros Sociales . . . ," *Revista de la Escuela Nacional de Jurisprudencia*, January–June 1944, pp. 43–77.

Carbajal y González, Manuel. "Petróleos Mexicanos y la Constitución Política de los Estados Unidos Mexicanos." UNAM thesis, 1945.

"Cárdenas, Autor de la Política Ferroviaria del México Moderno," *Revista Fiscal y Financiera*, June 1952, pp. 19–24.

Carranca y Trujillo, Raúl. "Penal Legislation in Mexico," *Social Sciences in Mexico*, Fall 1947, pp. 6–16, and Winter 1947–48, pp. 89–106.

# BIBLIOGRAPHY

Carreño, Alberto María. *La Diplomacia Extraordinaria entre México y Estados Unidos, 1789–1947.* 2 vols. Mexico City: Ed. Jus, 1951.

Carrillo Flores, Antonio. "Financiamiento del Desarrollo Económico de México," *Prob. Agr.*, January–March 1950, pp. 9–47.

———. "Un Programa Integral de Acción Económica," *MV*, May 3, 1954, pp. 145–49.

———. "El Sistema Monetario Mexicano," *MV*, September 2, 1946, pp. 5–10.

Carrión Simbrelo, Joaquín. "Concepto y Naturaleza Jurídica del Contrato Colectivo de Trabajo," *Anales de Jurisprudencia*, April–June 1951, pp. 293–487.

Castro, Juventino V. "Revisión Penológica y Penitenciaria de la Legislación Mexicana," in Asociación Nacional de Funcionarios Jurídicos de México, *Problemas Jurídicos de México.* Mexico City: Ed. Jus, 1953. Pp. 235–45.

Cave, Marion S. *Forest Legislation in Mexico.* Washington, D.C.: Coordinator of Inter-American Affairs, 1945.

Ceniceros, José Ángel. *La Delincuencia Infantil en México.* Mexico City: Ed. Botas, 1948.

———. *Trayectoria del Derecho Penal Contemporaneo, la Reforma Penal en México.* Mexico City: Ed. Botas, 1943.

Chapela, Gonzalo. *La Cláusula de Exclusión.* Mexico City: Academia Mexicana de Jurisprudencia . . . , 1946.

Chase, Stuart, *Mexico, a Study of Two Americas.* New York: Macmillan, 1931.

Chavero, Alfredo. "Social Insurance Reform in Mexico," *Bulletin of the International Social Security Association*, July 1949, pp. 11–18.

Clark, Marjorie Ruth. *Organized Labor in Mexico.* Chapel Hill: University of North Carolina Press, 1934.

Colegio de Estudios Penales. *Problemas Penales de México.* Mexico City, 1952.

Comas, Juan. "Making Mexico One," *Américas*, March 1954, pp. 19–20, 44–46.

Comisión de Reorganización Administrativa y Financiera. *Finances of the Federal District of Mexico*, by Arthur N. Young. Mexico City, 1918.

Comisión Federal de Electricidad. *Electric Projects of the Republic of Mexico, 1947–1952, Report to the International Bank . . .* Mexico City, 1948.

———. *Obras de Electrificación . . .* Mexico City, 1948.

Comisión Nacional de Irrigación. *Irrigation in Mexico.* Mexico City, 1936.

———. *La Obra de la Comisión Nacional de Irrigación Durante el Régimen del . . . Cárdenas, 1934–1940.* Mexico City, 1940.

Confederación de Cámaras Industriales. "El Seguro Social Debe Ajustarse a la Realidad Mexicana," *Rev. Ec.*, March 1950, pp. 98–100.

Confederación de Trabajadores de México. *Panorama de la Obra Progresista.* Mexico City, 1950?.

Cook, Katherine M. *The House of the People.* Washington, D.C.: U.S. Office of Education, 1932.

Córdova Ramírez, César D. "La Conciliación en Nuestra Legislación Laboral," *Revista de Hacienda y Finanzas*, June 1951, pp. 60–67.

Cortina, Alfonso. "Problems of Mexico's Economic Development," *Social Science*, October 1951, pp. 238–42.

Cosío Villegas, Daniel. *La Cuestión Arancelaria en México: Historia de la Política Aduanal.* Mexico City, 1932.

———. "México y Estados Unidos," *Cuadernos Americanos*, November–December 1947, pp. 8–27.

Crawford, H. P. "Bank of Mexico," *University of Cincinnati Law Review*, Summer 1954, pp. 281–96.

Dalton, Jess N. "Mexican Taxes," *Journal of Bar Association of State of Kansas*, February 1948, pp. 302–14.

Davis, Horace B. "Numerical Strength of Mexican Unions," *SWSSQ*, June 1954, pp. 48–55.

Deaver, John V. "The Mexican Income Tax and Some Related Problems." *MCC*, 1949.

Delmez, Albert J. "The History of the Cultural Missions in Mexican Education." Ph.D. thesis, University of Missouri, 1949.

De Luna, Frank. "The Reciprocal Trade Agreements Act of the United States and the Trade Agreement with Mexico." *MCC*, 1951.

Departamento Agrario. *Memoria*. Mexico City, 1950 and earlier years.

Departamento del Distrito Federal. *Realizaciones . . . , 1946–1952*. Mexico City, 1952.

———. *Resumen de Actividades*. Mexico City, 1948.

———, Dirección General de Tesorería. *Informe sobre la Reorganización de la Tesorería del Distrito Federal*. Mexico City, 1949.

Dirección General de Pensiones Civiles de Retiro. *Dirección de Pensiones Civiles*. Mexico City, 1950. [A report 1925–50.]

"Draft Social Insurance Bill in Mexico," *International Labour Review*, March 1942, pp. 345–48.

Durán, Marco Antonio. "Crédito Agrícola y Tenencia de la Tierra," *Prob. Agr.*, July–September 1952, pp. 303–16.

———. "Del Agrarismo a la Revolución Agrícola," *Prob. Agr.*, October 1946, pp. 3–84.

Engle, Mary Margaret. "The History of Public Welfare in Mexico, 1920–1940." M.A. thesis, Duke University, 1940.

Escobeda Tarango, Belina. "Observaciones sobre la Ley Mexicana del Seguro Social." UNAM thesis, 1952.

Fábila, Alfonso. "El Ensayo Piloto de Nayarit," *El Nacional (Suplemento Dominical)* March 12, 1954.

Fernández de Castro, Carlos. "Azúcar, el Monopolio," *Revista Fiscal y Financiera*, September 1951, pp. 40–44.

Fernández y Fernández, Ramón. "Esbozo de una Política Agrícola," *Rev. Ec.*, July 1953, pp. 210–15.

———. "La Secretaría de Agricultura y Ganadería," *Rev. Ec.*, October 1951, pp. 297 *et seq.*

Fisher, Glen H. "Directed Culture Change in Latin America: . . . the Mexican Pilot Project in Basic Education in Santiago, Nayarit . . ." Ph.D. thesis, University of North Carolina, 1953.

Flores de la Peña, Horacio. "Algunos Problemas de la Reforma Agraria," *Rev. Ec.*, October 1945, pp. 8–14.

Flores Fernández, Edmundo. "Comparative Analysis of the Agrarian Problems of Peru and Mexico." Ph.D. thesis, University of Wisconsin, 1948.

Flores Mellado, Ernesto. "Anticonstitucionalidad de la Facultad que Varias Constituciones Locales Conceden a los Gobernadores de los Estados para Deponer a los Miembros de los Ayuntamientos." UNAM thesis, 1937.

Flores Vilchis, Othón. "El Problema Agrario en el Estado de Morelos." UNAM thesis, 1950.

Flores Zavala, Ernesto. *Elementos de Finanzas Públicas Mexicanas*. Mexico City: Ed. Stylo, 1951. (The 1955 edition was not available in time for use in this work. It does not differ in pertinent details from the 1951 edition.)

———. *Panorama de la Tributación en México y la Tercera Convención Nacional Fiscal*. Mexico City: Ed. Jus, 1948.

Foreman, W. James. "Changing Land Tenure Patterns in Mexico," *Land Economics*, February 1950, pp. 65–77.

# BIBLIOGRAPHY

Fosdick, Raymond B. *The Story of the Rockefeller Foundation*. New York: Harper, 1952.

Foster, George, ed. *A Cross-Cultural Anthropological Analysis of a Technical Aid Program*. Washington, D.C.: Smithsonian Institution, 1951.

Fuentes Díaz, Vicente. *El Problema Ferrocarrilero de México*. Mexico City, 1951.

Gaither, Roscoe B. "The Mexican Expropriation of Oil Properties," *United States Law Review*, June 1938, pp. 322–36.

Galán Balboa, Carmen. "Subsidios en México." UNAM thesis, 1945.

Gálvez, Enrique. "El Seguro Social en México," *Rev. Ec.*, September 1950, pp. 316–21.

Gándara Mendieta, Manuel. *De la Administración Municipal: Urbanismo*. Mexico City, 1953.

Gaona, Josefina. *Introducción al Estudio del Trabajo Social*. Mexico City: Ed. Cultura, 1951.

García Cruz, Miguel. *La Seguridad Social*. Mexico City, 1951.

García Souza, Jesús. "Aspecto del Impuesto sobre la Renta en México," *Rev. Ec.*, January 1947, pp. 17–21.

García Treviño, Rodrigo. *Precios, Salarios y Mordidas*. Mexico City: Ed. América, 1953.

Gardiner, Clinton H. "Mexico's Campaign against Illiteracy," *Social Education*, October 1949, pp. 277–78.

Garrison, Dorotha J. "Reclamation Project of the Papaloapán River Basin in Mexico," *Economic Geography*, January 1950, pp. 59–64.

Garza, Servando J. *Las Garantías Constitucionales en el Derecho Tributario Mexicano*. Mexico City: Ed. Cultura, 1949.

Genel Manzo, Rafael. "La Agricultura Nacional y su Irrigación," *Rev. Ec.*, December 1951, pp. 379–82.

——. "La Política de Irrigación y el Desarrollo Agrícola de México," *Rev. Ec.*, September 1951, pp. 276–79.

Georgi, A. A. "Education in Mexico," *Education*, March 1948, pp. 402–6.

Gil, Federico G. "Responsible Parties in Latin America," *Journal of Politics*, August 1953, pp. 333–48.

Glade, William P. "The Role of Government Enterprise in the Economic Development of Underdeveloped Regions: Mexico, a Case Study." Ph.D. thesis, University of Texas, 1955. (Unavailable in time for perusal for this study.)

Gleason, William E. "An Analysis-Study of the Financial Condition of *Petróleos Mexicanos*." MCC, 1949.

Goldsberry, John W. "The Airlines of Mexico and their Contribution to the Economic Development of the Country." MCC, 1951.

Gómez, Ana M. "The Mexican Agrarian Program since 1940." M.A. thesis, Columbia University, 1948.

——. "Mexican Agrarian Policy — Postwar Developments," *Foreign Agriculture*, October 1948, pp. 221–24.

Gómez Granillo, Moisés. *La Agricultura y el Crédito Ejidal*. Mexico City, 1952.

Gómez Morín, Manuel. *Diez Años de México: Informe del Jefe de Acción Nacional*. Mexico City: Ed. Jus, 1950.

González, Joaquín R. *Diccionario Manual del Seguro Social*. Monterrey, 1947.

González Aparicio, Luis. "The Papaloapán Basin," in *PIAC*, pp. 736–42.

González Bustamante, Juan José. *La Reforma Penitenciaría en México*. Mexico City, 1946.

González Casales, Ramiro. "Nuestra Organización Tributaria Constitucional y el Centralismo Económico (La Doble Tributación y el Sistema de Participaciones)". UNAM thesis, 1952.

453

González García, Federico. *El Problema Fundamental de México.* Mexico City: Sría. de Educación, 1943.

González Mesa, Carmen. "Papel y Funciones del Tribunal Fiscal . . ." UNAM thesis, 1949.

González Roa, Fernando. *Chapters on the Agrarian Question in Mexico* (in *Las Cuestiones Fundamentales de Actualidad en México,* 1927). New York: State Department of Social Welfare, 1937.

Goodman, Roland. "It's Oil that Keeps Mexico Running," *New Republic,* August 8, 1949, pp. 12–15.

Gordon, Wendell C. *The Economy of Latin America.* New York: Columbia University Press, 1950.

Graham, David L. "The United States and Mexico: a Reluctant Merger," *Yale Review,* Winter 1954, pp. 235–45.

Gray, George W. "Blueprint for Hungry Nations," *New York Times Magazine,* January 1, 1950, pp. 8 *et seq.*

Guajardo Davis, Guillermo. "The Problem of Protective Tariffs: An Answer to Henry Hazlitt," *Social Sciences in Mexico,* Spring 1948, pp. 16–20.

Gurza, Jaime. *Las Funciones del Banco de México.* Mexico City, 1941.

Guzmán y Raz Guzmán, Jesús, ed. *Las Relaciones Diplomáticas de México con Sud-América; Colección de Documentos . . .* Mexico City: Sría. de Relaciones Exteriores, 1925.

Hambleton, Hugh G. "The Petroleum Industry in Latin America." MCC, 1949.

Hayner, Norman S. "Criminogenic Zones in Mexico City," *American Sociological Review,* August 1946, pp. 428–38.

Hernández A., María Isabel, and Ofelia Sánchez Vázquez. "Better Health for Mexico City's Mothers and Children," *The Child,* October 1950, pp. 42–43.

Hernández Arreola, J. Augusto. "Notas sobre Justicia Contributiva." UNAM thesis, 1950.

Hernández Chazaro, Francisco. "La Comisión del Papaloapán." UNAM thesis, 1953.

Hill, Rachel N. "A Sketch of the Mexican Labor Movement with Special Emphasis on the C.T.M." M.A. thesis, Columbia University, 1946.

Holms, Henry A. *How Mexico is Governed.* New York: Foreign Policy Association, 1952. (Headline Series.)

Howerth, I. W. "The Federal System of Education in Mexico," *School and Society,* September 11, 1937, pp. 325–31.

Hughes, Lloyd H. *The Mexican Cultural Mission Programme.* Paris: UNESCO, 1951.

Ibáñez Villegas, Raúl. "Las Carreteras Nacionales," *Rev. Ec.,* May 1952, pp 163–65.

"Imperialismo y Buena Vecindad: Mesa Rodante," *Cuadernos Americanos,* September 1947.

"Industrial and Labor Conditions," *Monthly Labor Review,* October 1934, pp. 883–98.

Infield, Henrik F., and Koka Freier. *People in Ejidos: A Visit to the Cooperative Farms of Mexico.* New York: Praeger, 1954.

"El Instituto Mexicano del Seguro Social," *Inv. Ec.,* No. 2, 1943, pp. 195–211.

Instituto Mexicano del Seguro Social. *La Extensión del Seguro Social al Campo.* Mexico City, 1952.

——. *Memorias de Labores, 1951–52.* Mexico City, 1953.

——. *México y la Seguridad Social.* 3 vols. Mexico City, 1952.

——. *El Seguro Social Mexicano: Síntesis Informativa.* Mexico City, 1952.

"Las Inversiones en la Agricultura de 1939 a 1952," *MV,* April 5, 1954, pp. 109–10.

# BIBLIOGRAPHY

Iverson, Kenneth R. "The 'Servicio' in Theory and Practice," *Public Administration Review*, Autumn 1951, pp. 223–28.

Jones, Chester Lloyd. "Production of Wealth in Mexico," *Annals*, March 1940, pp. 55–69.

Keenan, Lawrence Paul. "A Survey of Existing Highway Transportation Facilities in Latin America." MCC, 1949.

Kibele, Robert C. "Reserve Requirements of Commercial Banks in Mexico and the Effects on the National Economy." MCC, 1951.

Kneller, George F. *The Education of the Mexican Nation*. New York: Columbia University Press, 1951.

Kunz, Josef L. *The Mexican Expropriations*. New York: New York University School of Law, 1940.

Lara Beautell, Cristóbal. *La Industria de Energía Eléctrica*. Mexico City: Fondo, 1953.

Larroyo, Francisco. "Breve Historia de la Educación en México," in *Anuario de Estadística Educativa*. Mexico City: Sría. de Educación Pública, 1947, pp. 13–70.

———. "La Educación," in *México y la Cultura*. Mexico City: Sría. de Educación Pública, 1946, pp. 583–626.

———. *Historia Comparada de la Educación en México*. Mexico City: Ed Porrúa, 1952.

Laufenberger, Henry. *Finanzas Comparadas*. Mexico City: Fondo, 1951.

Lavalle Urbina, María. *La Delincuencia Infantil*. Mexico City: Ed. Jurídico Sociales, 1948.

Lavín, José Domingo. *Petróleo: Pasado, Presente y Futuro de una Industria Mexicana*. Mexico City: E.D.I.A.P.S.A., 1950.

"La Legislación del Crédito Agrícola en México," *Revista de Hacienda y Finanzas*, February 1948, pp. 13–19.

Lemus García, Raúl. *El Crédito Agrícola y su Evolución en México*. Mexico City, 1949.

Lewis, Flora. "Why There is Anti-Americanism in Mexico," *New York Times Magazine*, July 6, 1952, pp. 10 *et seq.*

Llata, Luis de la. "Las Juntas Federales de Mejoras Materiales." UNAM thesis, 1952.

Logan, Virgil G. "Mexico's Unified School System," *Journal of Educational Research*, October 1953, pp. 117–26.

———. "Speech Education in Mexico." Ph.D. thesis, University of Wisconsin, 1951.

Lombardo Toledano, Vicente. "The Labor Movement," *Annals*, March 1940, pp. 48–54.

López, Roberto. "El Banco Nacional de Comercio Exterior," *Rev. Ec.*, February 1942, pp. 26–34.

López Aparicio, Alfonso. *El Movimiento Obrero en México: Antecedentes, Desarrollo, y Tendencias*. Mexico City: Ed. Jus, 1952.

López González, Julieta. "El Turismo y el Desarrollo Económico de México," *Rev. Ec.*, January 1951, pp. 453–55.

López Rosado, Diego. "La Política de Obras Públicas y la Economía Nacional," *Inv. Ec.*, No. 1, 1947.

———. "La Política de Obras Públicas en México." UNAM thesis, 1948.

López Rosado, Felipe. *Economía Política*. Mexico City, 1953.

Lowry, Philip H. "The Mexican Policy of Woodrow Wilson." Ph.D. thesis, Yale University, 1949.

Luna Peralta, Vidal. "Comentarios Demo-Económicos en Torno de la Ley del Seguro Social y el Instituto Asegurador." UNAM thesis, 1943.

455

McBride, George M. *The Land Systems of Mexico*. New York: American Geographical Society, 1923.

McCaleb, Walter F. *The Public Finances of Mexico*. New York: Harper, 1921.

McCormick, Archie T. E. "Some Observations on the Mexican Educational System." MCC, 1951.

McKeever, Justin A. "A History of the Tourist Trade in Mexico and its Economic Implications." MCC, 1951.

McLaughlin, Kathleen. *New Life in Old Lands*. New York: Dodd, 1954.

Macmahon, Arthur W. "The Mexican Railways under Workers' Administration," *Public Administration Review*, Autumn 1941, pp. 458–71.

———, and W. R. Dittmar. "The Mexican Oil Industry since Expropriation," *Political Science Quarterly*, March and June 1942, pp. 28–50, 161–88.

Macmahon, W. E. "Case of the American Oil Companies," in *Mexico and the United States*. Dallas: Southern Methodist University, 1938. Pp. 78–88.

McMurry, Ruth, and Muna Lee: *The Cultural Approach*. Chapel Hill: University of North Carolina Press, 1947.

Malagón, Javier. "Four Centuries of the Faculty of Law in Mexico," *Hispanic Amer. Hist. Rev.*, August 1952, pp. 442–51.

Mancera Ortiz, Rafael. *The Budget as Stabilizer of Economic Growth*. Mexico City, 1953. (Address to IX International Congress of Administrative Sciences.)

Manero, Antonio. "Public Works in Mexico," *Social Sciences in Mexico*, May 1947, pp. 51–55.

Margain, Hugo B. *Evolución de la Hacienda Pública*. Mexico City: Sría. de Hacienda, 1952.

———. "Organización Fiscal de la Federación," in *México, Realización y Esperanza*. Mexico City: Ed. Superación, 1952. Pp. 511–24.

Martínez y Martínez, Jorge. "Nacionalización de la Industria Eléctrica." UNAM thesis, 1949.

Martínez Sobral, Enrique. *Elementos de Hacienda Pública*. Mexico City: Ed. Botas, 1939.

Mata Velázquez, Guillermo. *La Organización y el Funcionamiento de la Dirección del Impuesto sobre la Renta en México*. Mexico City, 1950.

Méndez Berman, León. *Los Sindicatos Obreros en México*. Mexico City: Ed. Acción Obrero, 1950.

Mendieta y Núñez, Lucio. "The Balance of Agrarian Reform," *Annals*, March 1940, pp. 121–31.

———. *El Crédito Agrario en México*. Mexico City, 1933.

———. *El Problema Agrario de México*. Mexico City: Porrúa Hermanos, 1946.

———. "The Sociology of Politics," *International Social Science Bulletin*, Spring 1950, pp. 14–16.

Mendoza, Salvador. "Mexico's Bold Experiment in New Criminal Code," *Cur. Hist.*, October 1929, pp. 107–11.

———. "The New Mexican System of Criminology," *Journal of Criminal Law and Criminology*, May 1930, pp. 15–25.

———. "El Nuevo Código Penal de México," *Hispanic American Historical Review*, August 1930, pp. 299–312.

———. "Recent Tendencies in Mexican Criminal Procedure," *BPAU*, May 1930, pp. 433–39.

Mendoza Franco, Roberto. *Política Portuaria*. Mexico City, 1946.

Mesa Andraca, Manuel, and Emilio Alanís Patiño. "La Agricultura en México," *Prob. Agr.*, January–March, 1951, pp. 23–183.

Mesa Andraca, Manuel. "Los Problemas Económico-Agrícolas de México," *Prob. Agr.*, July 1946, pp. 3–48.

# BIBLIOGRAPHY

"Mexico Today," *Bankers Magazine*, January 1936, pp. 39–83.
Mijares y Dávalos, Juan G. "Breves Reflexiones acerca de la Exención de Impuestos." UNAM thesis, 1952.
Miller, Edward G. "Rewards of U.S.-Mexican Cooperation," *Department of State Bulletin*, March 31, 1952, pp. 498–500.
Miranda, F. P. "The Public Health Department in Mexico City," *American Journal of Public Health*, October 1930, pp. 1125–28.
Modelski, Joseph B. "*The Production of Steel in Mexico.*" MCC, 1951.
Molina Enríquez, Andrés. "Mexico's Defense.' *Atlantic Monthly*, March 1939, pp. 378–84.
Molins Fábrega, Narciso. "Labor Movement," *Encyclopedia Americana*, 1954, V. 18. Pp. 770–71.
Monzón A., Leopoldo. "El Control de Presupuestos en Materia de Egresos," *Rev. Ec.*, June 1947, pp. 28–31.
Moore, Clarence A. "Agricultural Development in Mexico," *Journal of Farm Economics*, February 1955, pp. 72–80.
Mora, Raymond S. "The Capital Market in Mexico and its Future." MCC, 1952.
Mora Ortiz, Gonzalo. *El Banco Nacional del Comercio Exterior.* Mexico City: Ed. Ruta, 1950.
Morales Alcocer, Pascual. "La Función del Ministerio Público." UNAM thesis, 1951.
Morales Cabañas, Óscar. "Finanzas Públicas del Estado de Veracruz," *Revista de Hacienda y Finanzas*, May 1948, pp. 53–58.
Moreno, Antonio. "Los Grupos Sociales en la Delincuencia," *Anales de Jurisprudencia*, July–September 1952, pp. 273–370.
Moreno Verdín, Luis. "Mexico's New Six-Year Plan," *Mex. Am. R.*, December 1952, pp. 20–22, 80–86.
Morton, Stewart. "A Billion Pesos for Communications," *Mex. Life*, April 1954, pp. 15–16.
Morton, Ward McK. "Government Regulation of Labor in Mexico under the Constitution of 1917," Ph.D. thesis, University of Texas, 1941.
Mosk, Sanford A. "The Pathology of Democracy in Latin America: An Economist's Point of View," in Asher N. Christensen, *Evolution of Latin American Government, A Book of Readings.* New York: Holt, 1951. Pp. 162–81.
Mosley, Ramón. "Some Observations on Mexican Secondary Education." MCC, 1949.
Moyo Porrás, Edmundo. "Reorganización Financiera de los F.F.C.C.N.N." *Rev. Ec.*, July 1953, pp. 219–21.
Mulvey, Ruth Watt. "A New Day in Butterfly Basin," *Reader's Digest*, August 1951, pp. 129–32.
Munguía, Enrique. *The Agrarian Problem in Mexico.* Geneva: ILO, 1937. (Reprint from *International Labour Review*, July–August 1937.)
Murklund, Harry B. "Toward More Democracy in Mexico," *Foreign Policy Bulletin*, June 15, 1952.
Nacional Financiera. *Informe* (annual). Mexico City.
———. *Quince Años de Vida.* Mexico City, 1949.
National Planning Association. *Technical Cooperation in Latin America.* Washington, D.C.: National Planning Association, 1956.
Ney Morales, Filiberto. "Los Monopolios en México." UNAM thesis, 1944.
Noble, Gontrán. *Crédito Agrícola en México.* Mexico City, 1949.
———. *La Reforma Agraria en México.* Mexico City, 1949.
Northrup, Richard S. "Survey of the Development of the Labor Movement in Mexico." MCC, 1951.

Novoa, Carlos. *Planeación Económica de México*. Mexico City: Revista de Economía, 1952.

"Nueva Paridad del Peso Mexicano," *MV*, April 26, 1954, pp. 137–38.

Olea y Leyva, Teófilo. "Vieja y Nueva Política Criminal," in Asociación Nacional de Funcionarios Judiciales, *Problemas Jurídicos de México*. Mexico City: Ed. Jus, 1953. Pp. 261–68.

Orive Alba, Adolfo. *Política de Irrigación en México*. Mexico City, 1945.

———. "Los Sistemas de Riegos . . . ," in Sría. de Educación Pública. *Problemas Vitales de México*. Mexico City, 1946, pp. 5–34.

Orozco, Alfonso. "La Industria Petrolera Mexicana como Empresa de Propiedad Pública," *Inv. Ec.*, No. 4, 1949, pp. 449–77.

Ortiz Mena, Raúl. "El Sistema Monetario de México," in *Sistemas Monetarios Latino-Americanos*. Córdoba, Argentina: Universidad de Córdoba, 1943. Pp. 263–305.

Osorio Tafall, B. F. "Planning the Utilization of Renewable Natural Resources in Relation to the Industrialization of Mexico," *PIAC*, pp. 510–13.

———. "Los Problemas de los Suelos y del Agua en México," *Rev. Ec.*, July 1948, pp. 18–23.

Patch, Don Ivan, Jr. "The International Bank for Reconstruction and Development: Its Establishment and its Use of the Developmental Loan in Latin America." MCC, 1950.

Patiño, Lorenzo R. "Organization of the Mexican Soil and Water Conservation Service," *PIAC*, pp. 759–71.

Pavón Flores, Mario. *La Cláusula de Exclusión*. Mexico City: Ed. Fidel, 1945.

Pelayo Alvarado, Juan. "Tribunal Fiscal . . . , su Integración y Funcionamiento." UNAM thesis, 1947.

Peña, Moisés de la. "El Fracaso del Crédito Agrícola en México," *Rev. Ec.*, November 1943, pp. 29–31.

———. "Problemas Demográficos y Agrarios," *Prob. Agr.*, July 1950, pp. 9–335.

Peraza E., Gaudencio. *Una Interpretación Revolucionaria de la Educación*. Mexico City, 1946.

Phipps, Helen. "The Agrarian Phase of the Mexican Revolution of 1910–1920," *Political Science Quarterly*, March 1924, pp. 1–18.

———. *Some Aspects of the Agrarian Question in Mexico: A Historical Study*. Austin: University of Texas Press, 1925.

Porte Petit, Celestino. *El Instituto de la Juventud Mexicana*. Mexico City: Ed. Ruta, 1950.

Portes Gil, Emilio. *Historical Evolution of the Territorial Property of Mexico*. Mexico City: Ateneo Nacional de Ciencias y Artes de México, 1945.

Powell, J. Richard. "Some Financial Aspects of the Mexican Petroleum Industry," *Inter-American Economic Affairs*, Winter 1952, pp. 14–31.

———. *The Mexican Petroleum Industry, 1938–1950*. Berkeley: University of California Press, 1956.

Presidente. *La Educación Pública en México a través de los Mensajes Presidenciales desde la Consumación de la Independencia hasta Nuestros Días*. Mexico City: Talleres Gráficos de la Nación, 1926.

———. *La Hacienda Pública de México a través de los Informes Presidenciales a Partir de la Independencia hasta 1950* . . . Mexico City: Talleres Gráficos de la Nación, 1951.

———. *México Coopera con las Naciones Aliadas, Nuestra Bandera en los Campos de la Lucha*. Mexico City: Sría. de Gobernación, 1944.

———. *Un Siglo de Relaciones Internacionales de México a través de los Mensajes Presidenciales* . . . Mexico City: Sría. de Relaciones Exteriores, 1935.

# BIBLIOGRAPHY

Prewett, Virginia. "The Mexican Army," *Foreign Affairs*, April 1941, pp. 609–20.
Priestley, Samuel E. G. "The Agrarian Problem in Mexico." Ph.D. thesis, New York University, 1950.
"Quince Años de Vida de la Nacional Financiera, S.A.," *Revista Fiscal y Financiera*, February 1950, pp. 30–45.
Quiñones, Mario. "Public Health Organization in Mexico," *American Journal of Public Health*, April 1943, pp. 353–56.
Realme Rodríguez, Óscar. "Los Ferrocarriles y su Influencia en la Integración Social y Económica de México," *Inv. Ec.*, No. 4, 1951, pp. 451–68.
Real Mier y Concha, Eugenio. "Las Facultades Concurrentes en Materia Tributaria." UNAM thesis, 1948.
Redfield, Robert. "The Indian in Mexico," *Annals*, March 1940, pp. 132–43.
Reese, James R. "The Effects of Foreign Tourist Trade on Mexico's Balance of Payments." MCC, 1952.
Reina Hermosillo, Praxedes. "The Role of Nacional Financiera in the Development of Industry in Northern Mexico," in *Basic Industries in Texas and Northern Mexico*. Austin: University of Texas Press, 1950. Pp. 7–10.
Reyes Valenzuela, Carlos. "Carácter Jurídico de la Comisión Federal de Electricidad." UNAM thesis, 1950.
Rippy, Merrill. "The Economic Repercussions of Expropriation . . . ," *Inter-American Economic Affairs*, Summer 1951, pp. 52–70.
————. "Oil and the Mexican Revolution." Ph.D. thesis. University of Texas, 1950.
————. "Who's Revolutionary in Mexico?" *Nation*, July 19, 1952, pp. 52–53.
Rivas Andrade, Aristeo. *Funcionamiento de las Juntas de Mejoramiento Moral, Cívico y Material en el Estado de Veracruz*. Jalapa, 1953.
Rivera Marín, Guadalupe. *El Mercado de Trabajo: Relaciones Obrero-Patronales*. Mexico City: Fondo, 1955.
Rockefeller Foundation. *Programa Agrícola Mexicano*. New York: Rockefeller Foundation, 1950.
————. *Annual Report, 1952*. New York: Rockefeller Foundation, 1952.
Rodríguez Adame, Julián. "Antecedentes y Realizaciones de la Reforma Agraria Mexicana," *Prob. Agr.*, October–December 1953, pp. 67–82.
Rodríguez Langone, Antonio. "Human Aspects of Mexican Irrigation," *American Society of Civil Engineers Proceedings*, December 1950, pp. 1–12. (Separate No. 46.)
————. "Recent Developments in Irrigation in Mexico," *Proc. of U.N. Scientific Conference on Conservation . . . of Resources*. New York: United Nations, 1951, pp. 388–91.
Rodríguez Aragón, Ismael. "Education," in *Encyclopedia Americana*. 1954. V. 18. Pp. 780–83.
Rojas Coria, Rosendo. *Tratado de Cooperativismo Mexicano*. Mexico City: Fondo, 1952.
Romero Kolbeck, Gustavo, and Victor Urquidi. *La Exención Fiscal en el Distrito Federal como Instrumento de Atracción de Industrias*. Mexico City, 1952.
Romero Macías, Hugo. "Coordinación de Transportes Terrestres," *Rev. Ec.*, September 1948, pp. 11–14.
Ruiz Equihua, Arturo. "La Cuenca del Río Tepalcatepec," *Rev. Ec.*, August, 1947, pp. 13–18.
————. "La Industria Nacional del Turismo," *Rev. Ec.*, June 1947, pp. 12–17.
Ruiz Galindo, Antonio. "The Necessity of Industrial Standards," *Social Sciences in Mexico*, Spring 1948, pp. 21–24.
Rulfo B., Juan M. "Panorama Agrícola de la Nación," in *México, Realización y Esperanza*. Mexico City: Ed. Superación, 1952. Pp. 533–50.

THE MEXICAN GOVERNMENT TODAY

Salas Villagómez, Manuel. "La Deuda Pública . . ., Examen del Caso de México." UNAM thesis, 1950.
Sánchez, George I. *The Development of Higher Education in Mexico.* New York: King's Crown Press, 1944.
———. "Education," *Annals*, March 1940, pp. 144–52.
———. "Education in Mexico," in A. H. Moehlman and J. S. Roucek, eds., *Comparative Education.* New York: Dryden Press, 1952. Pp. 85–108.
———. "Mexico's Cultural Missions," *Mex. Life*, September 1938, pp. 21–25.
———. *A Revolution by Education.* New York: Viking Press, 1936.
Sánchez Esquivel C., Florencio. "El Empréstito en México." UNAM thesis, 1951.
Sánchez Mejorada, Carlos. "The Writ of Amparo," *Annals*, January 1946, pp. 107–11.
Sánchez Mejorada, Javier. "Communications and Transportation," *Annals*, March 1940, pp. 78–93.
Sánchez Pontón, Luis. *Hacia la Escuela Socialista, la Reforma Educacional en México.* Mexico City: Ed. Patria, 1935.
Sánchez Sarto, Manuel. "Economic, Industrial, Agricultural, and Financial Factors," in *Encyclopedia Americana*, 1954, V. 18. Pp. 752–67.
Santamarina Vázquez, Agustín. "Las Exenciones Fiscales como Medio de Fomento y Protección a la Industria." Thesis, Escuela Libre de Derecho, 1949.
Sarames, George N. "Third System in Latin America: Mexico," *Inter-American Economic Affairs*, Spring 1952, pp. 61–69.
Scully, Michael. "President Ruiz Cortines: Mexico's Lonely Graft-Buster," *World*, June 1954, pp. 18–21.
Secretaría de Agrícola y Fomento. *Plan de Movilización Agrícola de la República Mexicana.* Mexico City, 1945.
———. *Regiones Económicas de la República Mexicana.* Mexico City, 1936.
Secretaría de Agricultura y Ganadería, *Resumen del Informe de Labores . . . 1951–52.* Mexico City, 1952.
Secretaría de Bienes Nacionales e Inspección Administrativa. *Informe . . .* Mexico City, 1952.
Secretaría de Comunicaciones y Obras Públicas. *Program for the Extension and Modernization of the National System of Telecommunication.* Mexico City, 1952.
———. *Memoria, 1952–53.* Mexico City, 1953.
Secretaría de Economía. *Memoria, 1951–52.* Mexico City, 1952.
———. *Planificación Económica.* Mexico City, 1944.
———. *Resumen de Labores, 1947–1952.* Mexico City, 1952.
Secretaría de Educación Pública. *La Educación Pública en México, 1934 a . . . 1940.* Mexico City, 1941.
———. *Memoria, 1951–52.* Mexico City, 1952.
———. *México y la Cultura.* Mexico City, 1946.
Secretaría de Gobernación. *Informe.* Mexico City, (annual).
———. *Juntas de Mejoramiento Moral, Cívico y Material.* Mexico City, 1953.
Secretaría de Hacienda y Crédito Público. *Tres Años (1947–49) de Política Hacendaria: Perspectiva y Acción . . .* Mexico City, 1951.
———. *The True Facts about the Expropriation of the Oil Companies' Properties in Mexico.* Mexico City: Talleres Gráficos de la Nación, 1940.
Secretaría de Recursos Hidráulicos. *Informe de Labores . . . 1951–1952.* Mexico City, 1952.
———. *Labores Realizadas.* Mexico City, 1953.
———. *Puntos Salientes de la Labor Realizada.* Mexico City, 1953.
Secretaría de Relaciones Exteriores. *La Secretaría . . . y su Labor.* Mexico City, 1949 and earlier years.

# BIBLIOGRAPHY

Secretaría de Salubridad y Asistencia. *Memoria, 1947–1950.* Mexico City, 1951.

———. *Memoria de la Primera Reunión Nacional de Asistencia Social . . .* Mexico City, 1952.

Secretaría del Trabajo y Previsión Social. *Memoria de las Labores . . . 1952–1953.* Mexico City, 1953.

Saunders, Lyle, and Olen E. Leonard. "Las Espaldas Mojadas en el Bajo Valle del Río Grande de Texas," *Prob. Agr.,* January–March 1952, pp. 10–56.

Seligman, Daniel. "The Maddening, Promising Mexican Market," *Fortune,* January 1956, pp. 103–12, 173–76.

Servín, Armando. "La Concepción Técnica del Ingreso Gravable y Nuestra Ley del Impuesto sobre la Renta," *El Trimestre Económico,* April–June 1946, pp. 34–71.

———. "La Estructuración Moderna del Presupuesto Público y sus Propósitos Fundamentales," *Inv. Ec.,* No. 4, 1950, pp. 456–66.

———. "La Ocupación Plena, la Política Fiscal y las Inversiones Públicas," *El Trimestre Económico,* January–March 1946, pp. 644–71.

Sherwood, W. T. "Tax Administration in Mexico," *National Tax Journal,* March 1949, pp. 63–70.

Silva, José. "Concurrent Fiscal Jurisdiction in Mexico," *Taxes: The Tax Magazine,* November 1942, pp. 658–63.

Silva Herzog, Jesús. "La Epopeya del Petróleo en México," *Cuadernos Americanos,* January–February 1953, pp. 7–63.

———. "Liberalismo o Intervención," *Rev. Ec.,* November–December 1946, pp. 24–26.

———. "Mexico's Case in the Oil Controversy," *International Conciliation,* December 1938, pp. 511–20.

———. *Petróleo Mexicano, Historia de un Problema.* Mexico City: Fondo, 1941.

Simpson, John W. "The International Economic Position of Mexico, 1900–1949." Ph.D. thesis, Ohio State University, 1950.

Solis Ogarrio, Jorge. "Ensayo Nacional con el Maíz," *Rev. Ec.,* June 1950, pp. 184–87.

Soto y Gama, Antonio Díaz. "The Agrarian Movement in Mexico," in Hubert C. Herring and Katharine Terrill, eds. *The Genius of Mexico.* New York: Committee on Cultural Cooperation with Latin America, 1931. Pp. 177–84.

Soule, George, *et al. Latin America in the Future World.* New York: Farrar & Rinehart, 1945.

Stanley, Joseph W. "La Casa del Pueblo: Mexico's Experiment in Rural Education." Ph.D. thesis, Stanford Universtiy, 1948.

Stanley, Ruth H. "A Mexican Pueblo in Transition," *Journal of Geography,* October 1950, pp. 269–78.

Sterling, Henry S. "The Emergence of the Medium-Size Private Farm as the Most Successful Product of Mexico's Agrarian Reform," *Annals of the Association of American Geographers,* March 1949, pp. 58–59.

Stevens, Virgil H. "United States–Mexican Relations during World War II," M.A. thesis, University of Southern California, 1948.

Stocking, George W. "The Mexican Oil Problem," in *Mexico and the United States.* Dallas: Southern Methodist University, 1938. Pp. 45–66.

Stullken, Virginia P. "Keystone of Mexican Government: Secretaría de Gobernación." M.A. thesis, University of Texas, 1955.

Tamayo, Jorge L. "México y su Política Rural," *Cuadernos Americanos,* May 1947, pp. 38–51.

Tannenbaum, Frank. "Land Reform in Mexico," *Annals,* July 1930, pp. 238–47.

——. "Personal Government in Mexico," *Foreign Affairs*, October 1948, pp. 44–57.

Teeters, Negley K. *World Penal Systems, A Survey*. Philadelphia, 1944.

Tercero, Dorothy M. "Electric Power for Mexico," *BPAU*, December 1944, pp. 695–97.

——. "Mexican Irrigation Commission," *BPAU*, May 1946, pp. 265–66.

Thomson, Charles A. "Agrarian Reform in Mexico," in *Mexico and the United States*. Dallas: Southern Methodist University, 1938. Pp. 29–44.

——. "Land for Peons: Agrarian Reform in Mexico," in Asher N. Christensen, *Evolution of Latin American Government*. New York: Holt, 1951. Pp. 558–72.

——. "Mexico's Challenge to Foreign Capital," *Foreign Policy Reports*, August 15, 1937.

Torres Gaitán, Ricardo. *Política Monetaria Mexicana*. Mexico City: Librería Ariel, 1944.

Treviño, Norberto. *Estudio sobre los Problemas de Salubridad y Asistencia en Tamaulipas*. Mexico City: Talleres Gráficos de la Nación, 1952.

Treviño Siller, José. "Algunos Aspectos de la Irrigación en México," *Revista de Hacienda y Finanzas*, April 1951, pp. 18–22.

——. "Algunas Notas sobre la Tercera Convención Fiscal," *Revista de Hacienda y Finanzas*, March 1948, pp. 5–10.

——. "Algunas Notas sobre la Tercera Convención Fiscal: Plan Nacional de Arbitrios," *Revista de Hacienda y Finanzas*, June 1948, pp. 6–12.

——. "Algunos Problemas de la Industria Turista en México," *Revista de Hacienda y Finanzas*, January 1951, pp. 52–55.

——. "La Educación en México," *Revista de Hacienda y Finanzas*, June 1951, pp. 54–59.

——. "Problemas Económicos: Nuestra Industria Petrolera," *Revista de Hacienda y Finanzas*, May 1950, pp. 3–7; July 1950, pp. 3–7; October 1950, pp. 21–27.

Triffin, Robert. "Central Banking and Monetary Management in Latin America," in Seymour Harris, ed., *Economic Problems of Latin America*. New York: McGraw, 1944. Pp. 93–116.

Trueba Rodríguez, Salvador. "Regulación Jurídica y Financiera de la Deuda Pública en el Estado Mexicano." UNAM thesis, 1948.

Trueba Urbina, Alberto. *Diccionario de Derecho Obrero*. Mexico City: Ed. Botas, 1941.

——. *Evolución de la Huelga*. Mexico City: Ed. Botas, 1950.

United Nations, Economic and Social Council. *Industrial Development in Mexico*. New York, 1950.

——. *Land Reform: Defects in Agrarian Structure as Obstacles to Economic Development*. Lake Success, 1951.

United Nations, Economic Commission for Latin America. *Legal and Economic Status of Foreign Investments in Selected Countries of Latin America: Foreign Investments in Mexico*. Montevideo, 1950.

——. *Clasificación de los Ingresos y Egresos del Sector Gubernamental de México . . . (Documento . . . no. 8 . . . , Reunión Técnica sobre Administración Presupuestaria)*. Mexico City, 1953.

——. *Gastos de Capital del Gobierno Federal*, por Ifigenia M. de Navarrete *(Documento . . . no. 13 . . . , Reunión Técnica sobre Administración Presupuestaria)*. Mexico City, 1953.

——. *Recent Events and Trends in the Economy of Mexico*. Mexico City, 1951.

United Nations Educational, Scientific, and Cultural Organization. *Estudio acerca de la Educación Fundamental en México*. Mexico City: Sría. de Educación Pública (BEP 183), 1947.

# BIBLIOGRAPHY

——. *Instituciones Científicas de México.* Montevideo: UNESCO, 1950.

——. *International Yearbook of Education.* Paris: UNESCO, 1952 (and earlier years).

——. *World Handbook of Educational Organization and Statistics.* Paris: UNESCO, 1952.

United Nations, Food and Agricultural Organization. *Prospects for Agricultural Development in Latin America.* Rome: FAO, 1953.

United Nations, International Bank . . . , Combined Mexican Working Party. *The Economic Development of Mexico.* Baltimore: Johns Hopkins Press, 1953.

United Nations, International Labour Organization. *Labour Courts in Latin America* . . . Geneva: ILO, 1949.

United Nations, International Monetary Fund. *Mexico's Financial Institutions and the Capital Market.* Washington, D.C., 1949.

United States Office of Education. *Education in Mexico.* Bulletin 1956, No. 1. Washington, D.C., 1956.

Universidad Nacional, Escuela Nacional de Economía. *El Desarrollo Económico de México.* Mexico City, 1952.

——. *La Intervención del Estado en la Economía.* Mexico City, 1955.

Vázquez Alfaro, Guillermo. *La Reforma Agraria de la Revolución Mexicana.* Mexico City, 1953.

Vega Hernández, Jaime. "La Sucesión Presidencial en México." UNAM thesis, 1949.

Velasco Terres, Raúl. "El Auge Petrolero de México," *Rev. Ec.,* February 1950, pp. 57–62.

Villa Rojas, Alfonso. "The Role of Anthropology in the Papaloapán Project," *PIAC,* pp. 289–96.

Violich, Francis. *Cities of Latin America; Housing and Planning to the South.* New York: Reinhold, 1944.

Von Kahler, Anita. "Kilowatts for Prosperity," *Américas,* January 1953, pp. 3–5.

Watson, Goodwin. *Education and Social Welfare in Mexico.* New York: Council for Pan-American Democracy, 1940.

Watson, Henry A. "Electrification in the Industrialization of Mexico . . ." MCC, 1952.

Wilson, Charles M. *Ambassadors in White: the Story of American Tropical Medicine.* New York: Holt, 1942.

Wilson, John M. "The Relations between the United States and Mexico, 1917–1935." M.A. thesis, University of Southern California, 1936.

Wooster, Julia L. "The Mexican Agricultural Credit System," *Foreign Agriculture,* February 1943, pp. 27–38.

Wylie, Kathryn H. "Land, Credit, and Irrigation Policy in Mexico," *Foreign Agriculture,* October 1946, pp. 136–46.

——. "Production and Marketing Policies in Mexico," *Foreign Agriculture,* November 1947, pp. 160–68.

Wythe, George. *Industry in Latin America.* New York: Columbia University Press, 1949.

Yañez Maya, Jesús. "Convención Nacional Fiscal: Resumen General de sus Trabajos," *Revista Fiscal y Financiera,* January 1948, pp. 9–19.

Zamora, Fernando. *Industrialización y Planeación Regional de México.* Mexico City: Sría. de Economía, 1950.

## V. Periodicals

American City
Americas

*Américas*
*Asistencia Social* (Dirección de Asistencia Social)
*Aviation Week*
*Bangrícola* (Banco Nacional de Crédito Agrícola)
*Boletín* (Dirección de Economía Rural)
*Boletín del Instituto de Derecho Comparado de México*
*Boletín de Minas y Petróleos* (Dir. General de Industrias Extractivas)
*Boletín de la Sociedad Mexicana de Geografía y Estadística*
*Boletín Estadístico* (Comisión Nacional Bancaria)
*Boletín Mensual de Economía Rural*
*Boletín: The Municipal Digest of the Americas* (Comisión Panamericana de Co-
    operación Intermunicipal, Havana)
*Bulletin of the Pan American Union*
*Business Week*
*Carta Semanal* (Confederación de Cámaras Nacionales de Comercio)
*Civil Engineering*
*Comercio Mexicano*
*Cuadernos Americanos*
*Diario Oficial* (Sría. de Gobernación)
*18 de Marzo: la Vida Petrolera Mexicana* (Petróleos Mexicanos)
*Engineering News Record*
*Examen de la Situación Económica de México* (Banco Nacional de México)
*Foreign Commerce Weekly*
*El Foro* (organ of the bar association)
*Hispanic American Historical Review*
*Hispanoamericano*
*Ingeniería Hidráulica en México* (Sría. de Recursos Hidráulicos)
*Investigación Económica* (Escuela Nacional de Economía)
*Jus: Revista de Derecho y Ciencias Sociales*
*Justicia*
*Latinoamérica* (Catholic Church organ)
*El Mercado de Valores*
*Mexican American Review*
*Mexican Life*
*Modern Mexico*
*La República* (organ of PRI)
*Problemas Agrícolas e Industriales*
*Review of the Economic Situation of Mexico* (Banco Nacional de México)
*Revista de Administración Pública* (organ of the new Instituto de Administración
    Pública de México)
*Revista del Comercio Exterior*
*Revista de Economía*
*Revista de la Escuela de Contabilidad, Economía y Administración* (Monterrey)
*Revista de Estadística* (Dir. General de Estadística)
*Revista de la Facultad de Derecho de México*
*Revista de Hacienda y Finanzas*
*Revista del Ateneo Nacional de Ciencias y Artes*
*Revista del Instituto de Salubridad y Enfermedades Tropicales*
*Revista Fiscal y Financiera*
*Revista Mexicana de Sociología*
*Revista Mexicana del Trabajo* (Sría. del Trabajo y Previsión)
*Tiempo*
*Tierra* (Sría. de Agricultura y Ganadería)

# BIBLIOGRAPHY

*Time*
*Trimestre de Barómetros* (Dir. de Estudios Económicos, Sría. de Economía)
*El Trimestre Económico*
*United Nations Bulletin*
*Visión*
Official journals of the states

## VI. Newspapers

*Christian Science Monitor*
*Excelsior*
Houston (Texas) *Chronicle*
*Nacional*
*News* (Mexico City)
New York *Times*
*Novedades*
*Universal*
World News Service, McGraw-Hill Company, Mexico City (An important file of this news bureau's published and unpublished dispatches)

# Index

buildings nationalized, 37; Alemán and Church, 37; governmental regulatory machinery, 37; Protestants allege discrimination, 37; number of Church properties, 38

Cinema Bank, National, 208

Cinematographic Art, National Council of, 180

Cinematography, Bureau of, 180

Circle of Free Workers, 309

Circuit courts, 115

Citizenship: acquisition by birth, 87; acquisition by naturalization, 87, 177; and nationality, 88; rights and duties of, 88; loss of, 88; rights and duties of aliens, 88

*Ciudad*, 391

Civil Code, 84

Civil rights: suspension of, 80–81; slavery forbidden, 83; occupation, 83; compulsory labor, 83; speech, press, petition, assembly, 83–84; education, 83, 86–87; equality before law and due process of law, 84; security of person, 84–85; in criminal suits, 85; marriage, 85; property restrictions, 85–86; social-economic rights, 85–86; and religion, 85–87; suspension of, 86; actual freedom, 87; protection of, 175

Civil servants, and the Patry, 43

Civil service: Mendieta y Núñez on bureaucracy and public administration, 127; as field of study, 127–28; Silva Herzog and training in United States, 128; history of, 128; Rodríguez and civil service law, 128; Cárdenas and civil service law, 128–29; laws of *1938* and *1941*, 128–29; courses in administration, 128, 136n19; types of employees, 129; Ávila Camacho and the law, 129; salaries, 129–30; and social services, 130

Personnel: unions and strikes, 55, 133–34; unions and the Party, 57–58; numbers, selection, and tenure, 130–31; promotions, leaves, and vacancies, 131; tests and training, 131; retirement, 131–32; punishable offenses, 132–33; Tribunal of Arbitration, 133; personnel office, 155

Progress and shortcomings: Mendieta y Núñez on, 135; Ebenstein on, 135–36; low salaries and overstaffing, 157

Climate, 4–5

Cline, Howard F., on the Party, 420

Cloner, Alexander, on Ministry of National Properties, 144

Closed shop, 327

Code system of law, 73

Colonial agriculture, 269–70

Colonial life and government, 10

Colonization, law on, 84

Commerce, Bureau of, 220

Commerce, foreign, 184

Commerce, regulation of, 77. *See also* Government and the economy

Committees, coordinating, 139

Communications, 227–44. *See also* Aviation, civil; Cinematography; Highways; Postal service; Radio broadcasting; Railroads; Telegraph and telephone services; Television broadcasting; Transportation

Communications, isolation and, 378

Communications, Ministry of. *See* Ministry of Communications and Public Works

Communications (state government), 385

Communist Federation of the Mexican Proletariat, 61

Communist Party, strength of, 61

Communists in agrarian groups, 53

Communities, types and sizes, 391–92

Community government, 404–5

Conciliation and arbitration boards. *See* Boards of conciliation and arbitration; Federal Board of Conciliation and Arbitration

Conciliation boards, federal. *See* Federal boards of conciliation

Confederation of Mexican Workers. *See* Mexican Confederation of Labor

*Congregación*, 392

Congress: early years, 11, 12; and states, 78; and constitutional amendments, 78; powers, 80; suspension of civil rights, 80–81; and President, 80–82; and courts, 82; impeachments, 82; comparison with U.S. Congress, 91; under earlier constitutions, 91; composition and membership, 91–92; Chamber of Deputies, 91, 92, 95, 97–98, 104; substitutes, 92; no re-election, 92; nature of legislative powers, 96; Senate, 97–98, 104, 105, 106; Permanent Committee, 98–99, 104–5; investigations, 99; shortcomings, 99–100; and President, Party, and interest groups, 100; role and occupations of individual members, 100–1; and Minis-